AF167647

Communications
in Computer and Information Science 2424

Rationale

The CCIS series is devoted to the publication of proceedings of computer science conferences. Its aim is to efficiently disseminate original research results in informatics in printed and electronic form. While the focus is on publication of peer-reviewed full papers presenting mature work, inclusion of reviewed short papers reporting on work in progress is welcome, too. Besides globally relevant meetings with internationally representative program committees guaranteeing a strict peer-reviewing and paper selection process, conferences run by societies or of high regional or national relevance are also considered for publication.

Topics

The topical scope of CCIS spans the entire spectrum of informatics ranging from foundational topics in the theory of computing to information and communications science and technology and a broad variety of interdisciplinary application fields.

Information for Volume Editors and Authors

Publication in CCIS is free of charge. No royalties are paid, however, we offer registered conference participants temporary free access to the online version of the conference proceedings on SpringerLink (http://link.springer.com) by means of an http referrer from the conference website and/or a number of complimentary printed copies, as specified in the official acceptance email of the event.

CCIS proceedings can be published in time for distribution at conferences or as post-proceedings, and delivered in the form of printed books and/or electronically as USBs and/or e-content licenses for accessing proceedings at SpringerLink. Furthermore, CCIS proceedings are included in the CCIS electronic book series hosted in the SpringerLink digital library at http://link.springer.com/bookseries/7899. Conferences publishing in CCIS are allowed to use Online Conference Service (OCS) for managing the whole proceedings lifecycle (from submission and reviewing to preparing for publication) free of charge.

Publication process

The language of publication is exclusively English. Authors publishing in CCIS have to sign the Springer CCIS copyright transfer form, however, they are free to use their material published in CCIS for substantially changed, more elaborate subsequent publications elsewhere. For the preparation of the camera-ready papers/files, authors have to strictly adhere to the Springer CCIS Authors' Instructions and are strongly encouraged to use the CCIS LaTeX style files or templates.

Abstracting/Indexing

CCIS is abstracted/indexed in DBLP, Google Scholar, EI-Compendex, Mathematical Reviews, SCImago, Scopus. CCIS volumes are also submitted for the inclusion in ISI Proceedings.

How to start

To start the evaluation of your proposal for inclusion in the CCIS series, please send an e-mail to ccis@springer.com.

Sridaran Rajagopal · Kalpesh Popat ·
Divyakant Meva · Sunil Bajeja ·
Pankaj Mudholkar
Editors

Artificial Intelligence Based Smart and Secured Applications

Third International Conference, ASCIS 2024
Rajkot, India, October 16–18, 2024
Revised Selected Papers, Part I

Editors
Sridaran Rajagopal ⓘ
Marwadi University
Rajkot, Gujarat, India

Kalpesh Popat ⓘ
Marwadi University
Rajkot, Gujarat, India

Divyakant Meva ⓘ
Marwadi University
Rajkot, Gujarat, India

Sunil Bajeja ⓘ
Marwadi University
Rajkot, Gujarat, India

Pankaj Mudholkar ⓘ
Marwadi University
Rajkot, Gujarat, India

ISSN 1865-0929   ISSN 1865-0937 (electronic)
Communications in Computer and Information Science
ISBN 978-3-031-86289-2   ISBN 978-3-031-86290-8 (eBook)
https://doi.org/10.1007/978-3-031-86290-8

Preface

"A Little Progress Each Day, Adds up to a Big Result"

Our 3rd International Conference on Advancements in Smart Computing & Information Security (ASCIS 2024) invited original research papers under five tracks, namely, **AI & ML, Smart Computing, Cyber Security, Networking and Cloud Computing and Computer Applications for Sustainability.** We received 667 submissions and 181 were recommended for publication in Springer's CCIS series. The papers will appear as 6 volumes (Volume Numbers ranging 2424–2429). We are very much thankful to the editorial board of **Springer CCIS** for their continuous support.

The submitted papers were involved in an open review process, involving three reviewers for each paper. We are thankful to the Technical Program Committee (TPC) members who were very supportive in the review process.

Several sponsors who contributed generously towards the successful running of ASCIS 2024, including **Science and Engineering Research Board (SERB), K7 International and D- Link Academy**. These collaborations enriched the conference and extended its outreach.

ASCIS 2024 was conducted during 16–18 October, 2024, and featured insightful keynote addresses from national and international experts in their respective fields. The line-up included **Prabir Kumar Biswas** from IIT Kharagpur, Cybersecurity expert **Ram Kumar G, Arnav Bhavsar** from IIT Mandi, **Murali Raman** from Asia Pacific University, and **Aravind Benegal** from NLB Services.

The keynotes addressed several recent technological advancements whereas the hands-on workshops provided practical exposure to the students and participants. The PhD forum featuring the research works of research scholars and recent PhD graduates added value to the conference and acted as a platform for knowledge sharing.

These volumes titled **"Artificial Intelligence based Smart & Secured Applications"** are the consolidation of all such solutions employing technologies of AI, ML, Smart Computing and, Cybersecurity in every significant field seeking research solutions.

October 2024   Sridaran Rajagopal

Organization

General Chair

R. Sridaran   Marwadi University, India

Program Committee Chairs

R. Sridaran   Marwadi University, India
Kalpesh Popat   Marwadi University, India
Divyakant Meva   Marwadi University, India
Sunil Bajeja   Marwadi University, India
Pankaj Mudholkar   Marwadi University, India

Steering Committee

Ketanbhai Marwadi   Marwadi University, India
Jitubhai Chandarana   Marwadi University, India
P. Bhanu Prasad   Future Technology
R. B. Jadeja   Marwadi University, India
Sanjeet Singh   Marwadi University, India
Prabir Kumar Biswas   IIT Kharagpur, India
Anil Kumar Sao   IIT Bhilai, India
Arnav Bhavsar   IIT Mandi, India
Naresh Jadeja   Marwadi University, India
Shamala Subramanyam   Universiti Putra Malaysia, Malaysia
Padmavathi   Avinashilingam Institute for Home Science and Higher Education for Women, India
T. Devi   Bharathiar University, India
K. Iyakutti   SRM Institute of Science and Technology, India
Ram Kumar G.   Global Automotive Company, India

Technical Program Committee Chairs

AI and ML Track

Hitesh Chhinkaniwala	Adani University, India
Ahlad Kumar	National Forensic Sciences University, India
Mahendra Kumar Gourisaria	Kalinga Institute of Industrial Technology, India

Cyber Security Track

Ruchira Naskar	Indian Institute of Technology, Kharagpur, India
Shravani Shahapure	Deloitte Touche Tohmatsu, India
Ritika Vivek Ladha	Adani University, India

Smart Computing Track

Manish Khare	Dhirubhai Ambani Institute of Information and Communication Technology, India
Dinesh Kumar	Bennett University, India
Rebakah Geddam	Nirma University, India

Networking and Cloud Computing Track

Rachna Jain	Bhagwan Parshuram Institute of Technology, India
Santosh Kumar Majhi	Guru Ghasidas Vishwavidyalaya (Central University), India
Nishant Doshi	Pandit Deendayal Energy University, Gandhinagar, India

Computer Applications for Sustainability Track

Manas Ranjan Pradhan	Skyline University College, UAE
J. Ramkum	Krishna Arts and Science College, India

Additional Reviewers

Arun Raj Lakshminarayanan
Dhanamma S. Jagli
Tushar H. Jaware
Kamal Sutaria
Mahalakshmi G.
Nebojsa Bacanin
Rahul Ashok Patil
Satvik Khara
Vijay D. Katkar
Vipin Sharma
Amarinder Kaur
Anita Gautam Khandizod
Bhoopendra Singh
Delecta Jenifer Rajendren
Harishchander Anandaram
Karuna Nidhi Pandagre
Amrita Kumari
Dipti H. Domadiya
Prashant Sen
Rajasekaran Selvaraju
Saran Raj Sowrirajan
Harshal Anil Salunkhe
Sumathy S.
Hemant Ingale
Jamberi K.
Jayashree Nair
Jyoti Kharade
Keerti Jain
Kumaresh N.
Mythili Shanmugam
Nikita Bhatt
Parvathaneni Naga Srinivasu
Praveen P. V. Sundar
Ravirajsinh S. Vaghela
Richa Adlakha
Ritesh Patel
Sharanyaa S.
Srinivasulu Raju S.
Swetta Kukreja
Vinothina V.
Ajay Kushwaha
Anbumani K.
Ashwin B. Makwana

Chandresh K. Kumbharana
Divyakant T. Meva
Raji C. G.
Anita M. Indu
Kailash Patidar
Kannadhasan Suriyan
Hardik K. Molia
Jayashri Pattar
Jonnadula Narasimharao
Kaviyarasi R.
Ramakrishna Garine (Ram)
Nageswari D.
Prema C.
Rajender Kumar
Ram Ratan
S. Amuth Sachin H. Gajjar
Sreenaga Chidambara Vinjamuri Dattu
Vipul Shah
A. Yovan Felix
Abhay Singh Bhadauria
Aditi Sharma
Ajay Kumar Kushwaha
Ajita Deshmukh
Akash Saxena
Amita Sharma
Ankit Subhash Didwania
Anubhav Kumar Prasad
Arun Adiththan
Asha V.
Ashokkumar Baldevbhai Prajapati
Avinash Sharma
Bhagvati Parekh
Brijesh R. Jajal
Dafni J. Rose
Dhivya K.
Dipti Chauhan
Divya R.
Divyanshu Chandra
Ashwin R. Dobariya
Prabhat Sharma
Rohit Kanauzia
Abhinav Tomar
Akshara Dave

Ashish Saini
Avnip Deora
Dimple M. Thakar
Gaurav Kumar Ameta
Jayant R. Nandwalkar
Kapil Joshi
Lokesh P. Gagnani
Nisha Khurana
Samir B. Patel
Sri Hari Nallamala
Sunil L. Bajeja
T. Sathish Kumar T.
Parwinder Kaur
Rajesh Bansode
Saraswathi S.
T. Buvaneswari Muruganantham
Vijayalakshmi P. S.
Galiveeti Poornima
Hari Kumar Palani
Hemraj S. Lamkuche
Jafar Ali Ibrahim Syed Masood
Jay A. Dave
Jebakumar Immanuel D.
Juliet Rozario
Kajal S. Patel
Karthikeyan Eswaramurthy
Kavitha Ganesh
Krishnakumar A.
Lata Suresh
Latchoumy P.
M. R. Ramesh
Madhu Shukla
Manisha Rawat
Maruthamuthu R.
Maulika Patel
Megha P. Mudholkar
Mohamed Iqbal M.
Mohit Tiwari
Muralidharan R.
Narayan Joshi
Neeru Sharma
Neha Sharma
Nidhi M. Patel
Nilu Singh
Pankaj K. Mudholkar

Parth Gautam
Pranav Verma
Praveen Kumar
Priyanka Sharma
Purnendu Bikash Acharjee
Radha B.
Rajesh Yadav
Rakesh Kumar Yadav
Renjith V. Ravi
Richa Ashok Modiyani
Rohit Goyal
Rupali Atul Mahajan
S. S. Priscila
Saifullah Khalid
Sandeep Mathur
Saswati Mahapatra
Senthil Kumar R.
Shamala K. Subramaniam
Shanti Verma
Shweta Sharma
Srinivasa Rao Pallapu
Subramanian Balambigai
Sudipta Hazra
Sunil Gautam
Suresh B. Kumar
Tanmay Kasbe
Thirumurugan Shanmugam
Uma N. Dulhare
Umesh S. Pinjarkar
Vaibhav C. Gandhi
Vandani Verma
Vipin Sharma
Vishvjit K. Thakar
Yogesh Ghodasara
Chandran C. P.
Raghu N.
Jaimin N. Undavia
Kavipriya P. P.
Mohamed Mosbah
Padma Selvaraj
Remegius Praveen Sahayaraj
Shadab Siddiqui
Vineet Kumar Singh
Abhishek Sharma
Anilkumar Suthar

Bharanidharan G.

Chandra J.

Disha J. Shah

John T. Abraham

P. Rizwan Ahmed

B. Surendiran

Dushyantsinh B. Rathod

Priya K.

Rushikumar R. Raval

Ajitha V.

Kajal Patel

Gourav Gupta

J. Grace Hannah

Jasminder Kaur Sandhu

Jinal H. Tailor

Karthik B.

Kruti K. Sutaria

K. P. Malarkodi

Naresh Kumar

Nirav Bhatt

Pradip Mathuradas Jawandhiya

Rajeswari S.

Revathy G.

Ripal D. Ranpara

Senthilkumar Meyyappan

Shikha Maheshwari

Sweeti Sah

Vijay Karnatak

A. Maheswary

Anamika Rana

Anjali Diwan

Biswaranjan Mishra

Chintan Patel

Himanshu K. Maniar

T. S. Murugesh

Darshankumar C. Dalwadi

Anitha K.

Priya Chandran

Jalpesh Vasa

Jeevitha R. R.

Jose M. Molina

Lilly Florence M.

Mohan Subramani

Naresh Kshetri

Qixia Zhang

Rajeswari M.

Roshan Anant Gangurde

Safvan Vahora

Vijaya Kittu Manda

Yugendra Devidas Chincholkar

A. P. Nirmala

Abhilasha Vyas

Ahmed Banimustafa

Ajay M. Patel

Ajitha I.

Akoramurthy Balasubramaniam

Angeline R.

Ankur N. Shah

Anup Palsokar

Aruna Animish Pavate

Ashish Kumar

Ashwin Raiyani

Balraj Verma

Boopathi Raja G.

Chandra Mohan

Darshita S. Pathak

Dipak Ramoliya

Divya Didwania

Anant G. Kulkarni

Chintan B. Thacker

Deepak Kumar Verma

Rashmi Soni

Saraswathi S.

Abhishek Sharma Padmanabhan

Ankit J. Faldu

Asmita Manna

Daxa Vekariya

Disha H. Parekh

Jay Kumar Jain

Jaypalsinh A. Gohil

Krupa S. Mehta

Nafees Akhter Farooqui

Premkumar Borugadda

Rupesh Kumar Jindal

Shadab Siddiqui

Sudhanshu Maurya

Sunil Gupta

Vatsal H. Shah

Rajan Patel

Ramesh T. Prajapati

Sreejith Vignesh B. P.
Veena Soni
G. Charles Babu
Gaurav Agrawal
Harish Padmanaban
Himanshu Rai
Jane K. Nithya
Jaydeep R. Ramani
Juhi Singh
Jyotirmoy Pathak
Kamal Saluja
Karthikeyan R.
Kedir Lemma Arega
Kumuthini C.
Lataben J. Gadhavi
Lipsa Das
M. Vinoth Kumar
Mahalakshmi G.
Manoj Kr. Mishra
Mastan Vali Shaik
Meet Patel
Minal S. Shukla
Mohammed Wajid Khan
Monther Ali Tarawneh
Nagaraju Kilari
Neha Parashar
Neha Ripal Soni
Nilesh Vijay Sabnis
Pagalla Bhavani Shankar
Paresh V. Virparia
Pragadeswaran S.
Prashant P. Pittalia

Preethi S. R.
Priyanka Suyal
Pushparaj Pal
Rajib Biswas
Ramkumar Jaganathan
Rinkoo Bhatia
Ruchika Pharswan
Rutvi R. Shah
Sadhana Singh
Samriti Mahajan
Sanjeevkumar D. Angadi
Savitha Jaganathan
Shafi Pathan
Shantha Mary Joshitta
Shilpa Mehta
Sivanesan Rajangam
Subhadip Sarkar
Sudha R.
Suhasini Vijaykumar
Sunil Saxena
Surya Kameswari Uduga
T. D. Sudhakar
Tarannum Bloch
Tripti Tiwari
Umang Thakkar
Vaibhav A. Gandhi
Vallidevi Krishnamurthy
Vikas Tripathi
Vipul A. Shah
Yogendra Kumar
Chetan Dudhagara

Our Sponsors

Sr. No.	Name of the Sponsor	Logo
1	SERB India	
2	D-Link	
3	Digital India	
4	K7 International	
5	Samatrix.io	
6	Marwadi Technologies	
7	Stelcore	

Abstracts of Keynotes

Transforming Industry 4.0 with Generative AI and Cloud Computing

Gundarapu Pavan

Safran DIFIT, France

Industry 4.0, characterized by the convergence of automation, IoT, and advanced analytics, is reshaping industries globally. As organizations strive for greater efficiency, innovation, and adaptability, the synergy between cloud computing and generative AI is emerging as a transformative force. This keynote will explore the vital role of cloud computing as the backbone of Industry 4.0, providing scalable infrastructure and real-time data accessibility. It will delve into what generative AI is, how it acts as a catalyst for innovation, and how it accelerates the development of intelligent systems, from predictive maintenance to automated design and decision-making. By examining the synergies between these two technologies, the keynote will illustrate their potential to revolutionize industrial operations and unlock new business value.

Attendees will gain insights into the tangible benefits and ROI of integrating cloud and AI solutions. The keynote will also address the challenges organizations face—ranging from data security to infrastructure optimization—and offer strategic considerations for successful implementation. Looking ahead, we'll explore future trends in Industry 4.0, where cloud-enabled generative AI could redefine the industrial landscape, driving sustainable growth and continuous innovation.

The session will conclude with a call to action, encouraging students and industry leaders to embrace these technologies to remain competitive in a rapidly evolving digital economy.

Brain Decoding with Deep Learning

Arnav Bhavsar

IIT, Mandi, India

The talk will focus on visual brain decoding via EEG using deep learning techniques. Brain decoding, also known as Perceptual Brain Decoding (PBD), involves using brain responses to different stimuli to identify the original stimulus or its characteristics.

Specifically, we target an external visual stimulus, which involves object images on a computer screen. The goal is to reconstruct the class of the image from the EEG data captured with observing the image. The decoding involves either classifying reconstructing the type of image shown during the visual task.

For reconstructing class-specific images, we will discuss the utilization of generative networks such as GANs, using embeddings from a pre-trained EEG classifier network as input. Additionally, we will also cover an end-to-end generative network (NeuroGAN) for image synthesis, where the generator produces class-specific embeddings and images from EEG signals.

Advanced Insights into Deep Fake Recognition

Deepak Kumar Jain

Dalian University of Technology, China

The rapid advancement of artificial intelligence and machine learning has led to the proliferation of deep fake technology, enabling the creation of highly realistic, AI-generated synthetic media. While deep fakes offer exciting possibilities in fields like entertainment and virtual reality, they also pose significant threats to public trust, cyber security, and political stability. This presentation, *Advanced Insights into Deep Fake Recognition*, explores the complex techniques used to produce deep fakes and highlights the growing challenges in detecting them. We delve into the mechanics of deep fake creation, particularly the role of Generative Adversarial Networks (GANs), and discuss the real-world implications of this technology's misuse, from identity theft to political disinformation.

The presentation also examines cutting-edge detection methods, including AI-driven facial and audio analysis, and emerging technologies like block chain and quantum computing, which are being employed to verify the authenticity of digital content. Furthermore, we explore current applications of deep fake detection tools across social media platforms, law enforcement, and the media, while considering the ethical and legal issues surrounding the use and regulation of deep fake technology. By providing a comprehensive overview of the challenges and future trends in deep fake recognition, this presentation aims to equip audiences with the knowledge to navigate this evolving digital landscape.

Security Models and Strategies of Cloud Computing in Business and Public Administration

Zdzislaw Polkowski

WSG University, Poland

Globalization and the development of information and communication technologies (ICT) have caused significant changes in business and public administration in the European Union. Currently, the digital economy is driven by modern ICT systems that offer employers and employees new tools for effective operation. Cloud Computing systems deserve special attention, as they have an impact on business, public administration and the everyday life of citizens. Cloud Computing creates many benefits not only for users but also has a positive impact on the environment, which is in line with the & quot; European Green Deal & quot; strategy implemented in Europe. However, the security of Cloud Computing and many previously unseen threats are always in the focus of both cloud users and providers of this modern solution. Threats, such as zero-day exploits, advanced persistent threats (APTs), and insider attacks are some popular threats that strained the cloud services in business and public administration. These threats create a large barrier to widespread use and in many cases delay the further development of these systems. The regulations constantly introduced and updated in Europe take into account the development of secure Cloud Computing, sensibly regulating the ways of processing not only personal data, but also data processing in general. It is worth mentioning that research and analysis have been carried out in real companies and public administration institutions to build robust and secure cloud platforms that can tackle modern-day cyber threats. The analysis highlights that the best outcomes in cloud computing implementations are driven by the collaboration of interdisciplinary teams, specifically those composed of IT specialists, legal experts, and managers. This synergy ensures a holistic approach, balancing technical efficiency with legal compliance and strategic oversight. Special attention should be given to security strategies, such as robust data encryption, identity and access management, regular auditing, and compliance management to mitigate the negative consequences of security breaches in cloud environments. These advancements will be particularly beneficial for a wide audience, including IT professionals, researchers, students, and business leaders, all of whom play a role in implementing and managing cloud solutions. Furthermore, future research could explore how these interdisciplinary teams tackle emerging challenges, such as evolving regulatory landscapes, data sovereignty, and the integration of advanced technologies like AI and machine learning in cloud infrastructure. Such investigations would contribute to the ongoing development of best practices and position cloud computing as a more secure and sustainable solution in a rapidly changing digital ecosystem.

Keywords: Cloud Computing · IT security · Business · Public administration · European Green Deal

Role of Computing and Technology in Sustainable Development Goals

Murali Raman

Asia Pacific University of Malaysia

We are living in a highly Volatile, Uncertain, Complex and Ambiguous (VUCA) world, which threaten the long-term sustainability of global business, economy and natural living. The Sustainable Development Goals (SDGs) outlined by the United Nations serve as a global roadmap for achieving a more equitable and sustainable future. As the world grapples with pressing challenges such as climate change, poverty, and inequality, computing and technology have emerged as powerful tools for addressing these complex issues. This keynote explores the pivotal role of computing and technology in advancing the SDGs, highlighting specific applications and their potential impact.

Computing and technology can contribute to the SDGs in various ways. For instance, in the realm of climate change, advanced analytics can be used to optimize energy consumption and identify sustainable energy sources. Artificial intelligence can enhance the efficiency of renewable energy systems and predict natural disasters, enabling early warning systems and disaster preparedness. Additionally, computing-powered solutions can facilitate sustainable agriculture by optimizing crop yields, reducing water consumption, and minimizing the use of harmful chemicals.

In the context of poverty and inequality, computing and technology can empower marginalized communities through digital inclusion and education. Affordable and accessible internet connectivity can bridge the digital divide, providing opportunities for education, healthcare, and economic development. Furthermore, online platforms can facilitate access to financial services, enabling individuals and small businesses to escape poverty.

Computing and technology can play a crucial role in promoting good health and well-being. Telemedicine and remote healthcare services can improve access to quality healthcare, especially in rural and underserved areas. Additionally, data analytics can be used to identify disease outbreaks and track their spread, enabling effective public health interventions.

In summary, computing and technology offer immense potential for addressing the SDGs. By harnessing the power of these tools, we can create a more sustainable, equitable, and prosperous world for all. This keynote uses case examples from different parts of the world, showcasing how SDGs can be addressed with proper utilisation of computing and technology. However, realizing this potential requires collaboration among governments, businesses, and academia to develop innovative solutions and ensure equitable access to technology.

Cybersecurity in the Age of 4.0 IR

Srinath Doss

Botho University, Botswana

In the era of Industry 4.0, where cyber-physical systems, the Internet of Things (IoT), and artificial intelligence drive unprecedented connectivity and automation, cyber security has never been more critical. As industries leverage smart technologies to enhance productivity, efficiency, and innovation, the digital landscape expands, bringing both opportunities and vulnerabilities.

The convergence of operational technology with information technology in smart factories, autonomous vehicles, and interconnected supply chains creates a complex and dynamic environment. A single security breach can disrupt production, compromise sensitive data, and even endanger lives. Cyber attacks are evolving in sophistication, targeting the very backbone of our digital infrastructure.

Cybersecurity in the age of Industry 4.0 demands a proactive and multi-layered approach. It requires the integration of advanced threat detection systems, robust encryption protocols, and comprehensive risk management strategies. Organizations must foster a culture of cybersecurity awareness, ensuring that employees at all levels understand and adhere to security best practices.

Collaboration across sectors is essential. Governments, private enterprises, and academic institutions must work together to develop innovative solutions, share threat intelligence, and establish global cybersecurity standards. Continuous investment in research and development is crucial to staying ahead of cybercriminals and safeguarding our digital future. In this digital revolution, cybersecurity is not just a technical necessity but a fundamental pillar of trust and resilience. By embracing a holistic and forward-thinking approach, we can protect our assets, secure our data, and pave the way for a safer, more interconnected world.

Keywords: Industry 4.0 · Cyber security · Internet of things · Cyber Attack · Risk Management

Trust in the Realm of Generative AI – Opportunities and Threats

Arvind Benegal

Chief Risk Officer & Sr. Advisory Consultant, USA

Trust is of paramount importance in Information Technology systems and data confidentiality, integrity and availability. AI and Generative AI have reshaped the technology landscape. A balanced approach to innovation is needed that incorporates both Trust and Risk Management. The threats represent the clear and present risks and challenges posed by emerging technologies, while the opportunities speak to the benefits brought by these innovations. This highlights the dual nature of technological advancement. Wherever there is an opportunity, there is also a significant threat.

The opportunities include the efficiency gains of automation of repetitive tasks and enhanced decision-making. Personalization addresses tailored experiences for users in healthcare, finance, and customer service. Innovation allows for creation of new products, services, and business models. Democratization of technologies provides access, challenging elite layers, and Just in Time Knowledge suggests just enough to solve problems.

The risks include Bias and Fairness since AI systems may perpetuate or amplify existing biases. Security vulnerabilities pose increased attack surfaces and potential misuse of AI capabilities. Data Privacy presents risks of unauthorized data usage and breaches, and Prompt Injections increase exposure to sophisticated AI attacks.

The Audit Focus Areas should consider Data Integrity. It must be ensured that data used by AI systems is accurate, complete, and secure, and ethical AI establishes frameworks to prevent bias and ensure fairness. Accountability and transparency are achieved by creating mechanisms for auditing AI decisions and actions. Institutional guidance provides adherence to IT governance frameworks such as COBIT to manage AI risks. Robust control measures are implemented to enhance trust. For instance, ISO/IEC 42001 is an international standard that provides a governance framework for implementing and continually improving artificial intelligence management systems.

Trust is built by by incorporating strategies for IT Auditors. Continuous Monitoring regularly reviews AI systems and processes for compliance and performance. Collaboration with stakeholders by engaging with developers, data scientists, and business leaders aligns AI initiatives with ethical standards. Education and Awareness train employees on the risks and best practices related to AI. And finally, a Risk-Based Approach is adopted by prioritizing audits and controls based on the risk levels associated with different technologies.

Machine Learning and Data Analytics at Scale - Rise of Unified AI and Data Platforms

Kumar Gangwani

BDB.ai, India

The last 10+ years have seen a breakneck pace of innovation in areas of Data Analytics, Machine Learning and AI, something that remained unseen in many decades prior. The availability of inexpensive storage, affordable compute, innovations in parallel computing frameworks, global availability of open-source tools and libraries, automation of data engineering, algorithmic innovations and availability of specialized hardware like GPUs and TPUs have ushered in the modern Data and AI era.

The open-source ecosystem has democratized access to cutting-edge tools and technologies to the larger technology community. For instance, frameworks like TensorFlow and PyTorch allow developers and researchers to build sophisticated models quickly and efficiently.

Yet, most organizations, despite good intentions, sizeable investments in technology and large technology teams, struggle to scale after successfully operationalizing a few initial analytics and ML use cases. In fact, the rate of failures of corporate data science and machine learning teams is so high that the notion of the data and AI-driven enterprise often seems a myth.

Despite the availability of a plethora of tools for data engineering and machine learning, most organizations fail to build and scale with these effectively. Part of this has to do with the overpromise around capability of enterprise tools sold to them, which sometimes are good at a particular solution like ingestion or discovery only; this results in organizations purchasing a number of tools that don't integrate well with each other or scale for increasing data volumes and diverse data demands. But that's not the only reason. Fragmented, inconsistent and incomplete data is often a factor responsible for failure of Machine Learning projects. Integrating ML workflows into production environments, handling versioning, scaling models and automating monitoring – a discipline being referred to as ML Ops – remain challenging for many businesses; and add to that rising complexity of algorithms itself. Most technical resources have specialization in perhaps one or two areas, but a very limited view of the entire data chain, and struggle to solve platform scale issues.

The whole industry today longs for an integrated approach that allows operation of analytics and ML at scale. The past few years have seen the rise of a few unified platforms that integrate the entire data infrastructure and plethora of data processes – from ingestion (batch, micro batch, real-time), data cleansing, enrichment and preparation, storage into data lake, with right security and governance, notebook/tools to experiment with and deploy Data Science and ML models, enable ML automation, use of AI services and self-service dashboards and visualization – all under one roof. These unified platforms greatly simplify and accelerate the time to commercialize analytics use cases, often 4–5 times faster than commonly used tools, and the end-to-end automation of all data processes greatly reduces resource effort by a large margin, providing for sizeable cost savings. This integrated capability offered by unified data and AI platforms is the future of enterprise analytics and Machine Learning.

Implementing Cyber Security Best Practices to Protect Your Crown Jewels

Ram Kumar G.

Global Automotive Company, India

In a hyper-connected digital world, cyber threats are ever growing and evolving, putting confidential data supporting IT infrastructure at risk. Cyber crimes are common today and no organization is immune to cyber attacks. The cyber crime industry has grown into a multi-billion dollar illegal business and the profile of the attacker has changed over the years – from script kiddies to well-organized hacker groups supported by nation states.

In this prevailing scenario, it is important for organizations to be cognizant of the cyber threats and proactively put in place cyber security measures by way of security controls, processes backed up by skilled talent. A strong understanding of the multi-faceted domains of cyber security is essential to appreciate the range and depth of the field. This exposure leads to exploring the security best practices that need to be implemented in organizations as per their risk profile to safeguard their critical IT infrastructure and confidential business information including intellectual property in what has come to be characterized as "crown jewels". The security controls are defined by the results of a risk assessment exercise, situational awareness of ongoing cyber attack campaigns enabled by inputs from cyber threat intelligence, obligations to customers and regulatory requirements for cyber security and data privacy.

Keywords: Cyber security · Best practices · Crown jewels · Cyber attacks · Data protection · Critical assets · Cyber threats · Security risks

Smart Spatial Computing and Its Application

P. Bhanu Prasad

Future Technology, France

Spatial computing is an emerging technology that blends digital and physical worlds, allowing users to interact with smart devices in more seamless and immersive ways. It leverages a range of technologies, including augmented reality (AR), extended reality (XR), Artificial intelligence, Internet of things (IoT), haptic feedback, computer vision, sensor fusion, geospatial data analysis, and spatial mapping. Spatial computing integrates various technologies to interpret the physical world and merge it with digital information, effectively combining both realms. These experiences can range from fully immersive environments to the addition of digital elements in the real world, creating interactive experiences that enhance our understanding of spatial relationships. At its core, spatial computing empowers users to visualize, manipulate, and analyze complex spatial data in real time with ease.

Advancements in hardware and software enable developers to create rich, immersive, interactive environments that captivate users. This evolution not only improves the overall user experience but also opens up new possibilities. Despite the significant potential of spatial computing, challenges persist. Concerns regarding data privacy, security, and ethical considerations need to be addressed before these technologies can be widely deployed. Additionally, the lack of standardization and interoperability among different spatial computing platforms presents further obstacles to widespread adoption.

This immersive, natural way of interacting can enrich our lives in numerous ways, enhancing hobbies like entertainment, gaming, and sports, as well as educational experiences and professional activities. The applications of spatial computing are extensive and diverse, impacting vital sectors that shape daily life, including navigation, astronomy, virtual home design, learning through gaming, skill development, healthcare and fitness, virtual shopping, industrial settings, remote assistance, architecture and design, the stock market, and logistics and supply chain management.

Spatial computing signifies a paradigm shift in how we interact with various environments, unlocking a vast array of new applications. Here are some key applications of spatial computing that can help those interested in pursuing a career in this field get started.

Keywords: Spatial computing · Extended reality (XR) · Industrial Internet of Things (IIoT) · Sensor fusion, Digital Twins · Artificial intelligence, Haptic

Enhancing Recommender Systems with Extensions of Fuzzy Sets for Considering Stakeholders' Uncertainty in Software Requirements Prioritization

Vassilis C. Gerogiannis

University of Thessaly, Larissa, Greece

In large, complex and distributed software development projects, it is often not feasible to implement all of the requirements in a single software release because of budget, time and staff constraints. Software requirements prioritization is an important activity in software requirements engineering which aims to evaluate and prioritize the candidate software features to be implemented in the next release of a software system. Requirements prioritization is often applied iteratively, according to various criteria, by the multiple involved project stakeholders who may have different roles, needs and knowledge. In large-scale software development projects, it is often practically impossible to ensure that all stakeholders have complete knowledge on all candidate requirements. Thus, stakeholders may show some degree of uncertainty and hesitation, as it is difficult to precisely evaluate each requirement according to each prioritization criterion. This talk will present results of our ongoing research work on combining Recommender Systems and soft computing techniques based on extensions of Fuzzy Sets to address problems of requirements prioritization in the context of large and complex software development/maintenance projects. Recommender Systems can be a useful solution to information overload situations when stakeholders have to evaluate a large number of alternatives. Fuzzy sets extensions, such as Intuitionistic Fuzzy Sets, can deal with stakeholders' uncertainty and hesitation regarding the prioritization criteria importance and requirements ratings. The results from applying our methods are promising since they demonstrate that they can be effectively used to support multiple stakeholders to prioritize large requirements sets.

Keywords: Software Requirements Prioritization · Recommender Systems · Intuitionistic Fuzzy Sets

Generative Adversarial Network (GAN): An Efficient Tool for Data Generation and Data Completion

Prabir Kumar Biswas

IIT, Kharagpur, India

Generative Adversarial Network (GAN) is a relatively recent concept in deep generative learning wherein two neural networks are pitted against each other in a zero-sum non-cooperative game to match a non-stationary distribution to an intractable stationary distribution. In this lecture we shall talk about how the generative modelling capability of GAN can be exploited to design efficient frameworks for image/video inpainting. Semantic inpainting refers to realistically filling up large holes in an image or video frame. Our approach is to first train a generative model to map a latent noise distribution to a natural image manifold and, during inference time, search for the best-matching noise vector to reconstruct the signal. The primary drawback of this approach is its inference time iterative optimization and lack of photo-realism at higher resolution. In this talk both of the abovementioned shortcomings are addressed. This is made possible with a nearest neighbour search-based initialization (instead of random initialization) of the core iterative optimization involved in the framework. The concept is extended for videos by temporal reuse of solution vectors. Significant speedups of about 4.5-5x on images and 80x on videos is achieved. Simultaneously, the method achieves better spatial and temporal reconstruction qualities.

Next, we will pose the following question and try to get the answer - 'Do we at all need an iterative inference framework?' - to answer this, a data-driven parametric network is trained to directly predict a matching prior for a given masked image. This converts an iterative paradigm to a single feed-forward inference pipeline with around 800× speedup. Finally, recent advancements in high-resolution GAN training are leveraged to scale an inpainting network for higher resolution.

Artificial Intelligence and Machine Learning: From Early Symbolic Systems to More Complex System

Salisu Mamman Abdulrahman

Kano University of Science and Technology, Nigeria

Artificial Intelligence (AI) and Machine Learning (ML) have evolved significantly over the years, moving from simple symbolic systems to more complex and sophisticated systems capable of learning and adapting. Advances in AI and ML systems have revolutionized various sectors, changing how people interact with technology. For four decades (mid-1950s until the mid-1990s), Symbolic AI was the dominant paradigm. These algorithms work by processing symbols that represent objects or concepts in the real world and their relationships. In Symbolic AI the main approach is to use logic-based programming where rules and axioms are used to perform inference and deduction. High expectations surrounding AI's potential to solve complex problems and mimic human intelligence were met with disappointing results, leading to what is known as the AI Winter. Despite the challenges faced by researchers during the AI Winter, the field experienced a revival in the 1990s and early 2000s. AI Researchers shifted their focus from Symbolic AI and rule-based systems to statistical and probabilistic approaches that are more promising. The emergence of machine learning algorithms, such as Support Vector Machines and Bayesian networks, enabled AI systems to demonstrate tangible successes in various applications. Machine learning systems have evolved dramatically over the years, progressing from basic models capable of simple tasks to complex neural networks that drive cutting-edge AI applications. Throughout this evolution, AI and ML have transitioned from rule-based systems to learning-based approaches, greatly expanding their capabilities and applications. In this keynote address, we will present an overview of their journey from inception to recent advances.

Keywords: Artificial Intelligence · Machine Learning · Symbolic System · Complex System

Attention Mechanism for Abnormal Behavior Detection from Video Surveillance

Vinothina V.

Kristu Jayanti College (Autonomous), Bengaluru, India

In todays fast-paced environment, detecting abnormal behaviour in real time is increasingly challenging, yet video monitoring remains vital for public safety. Traditional surveillance systems still rely heavily on manual observation, which is not only time-consuming but also prone to errors, especially when managing large volumes of footage. While machine learning (ML) algorithms have been widely used for behaviour detection, they often struggle with the complexity of unstructured video data. These algorithms typically require vast amounts of labelled data and can falter when dealing with imbalanced datasets, reducing their accuracy in identifying rare, yet critical, behaviours. Moreover, ML techniques tend to have slower learning rates, limiting their effectiveness in real-time scenarios and large-scale data applications. In contrast, deep learning models, especially convolutional neural networks (CNNs), have proven more effective by automatically learning feature representations directly from raw video data. However, CNNs still face challenges when it comes to capturing the temporal dynamics of behaviour across video frames. To address these challenges, the proposed method integrates a hybrid model that combines the strengths of CNNs and transformers with a context-based attention mechanism.

Modelled after the human brain's ability to focus on the most pertinent aspects of a scene, attention mechanisms integrated into deep learning frameworks have significantly improved both the accuracy and efficiency of abnormal behaviour detection. When combined with CNNs, these attention mechanisms emphasize key spatio-temporal features. Spatial attention allows the model to detect critical body movements and gestures, while temporal attention tracks changes in behaviour over time, identifying sudden or repetitive actions. This approach allows for real-time tracking of individual actions within the video frame, enabling timely alerts and interventions when abnormal behaviours are detected. When evaluated against existing methods, the proposed solution demonstrated superior performance, effectively overcoming the limitations associated with traditional machine learning approaches in behaviour recognition.

Keywords: Attention Mechanism · Abnormal Behaviour Detection · Video Surveillance · Deep Learning · Spatial Attention · Temporal Attention · Contextual Information

Zero Trust and Its Impact

Chander Shekhar Sharma

AUNZ - Cybersecurity Unit, Australia

The Zero Trust security model represents a fundamental shift in how organizations approach cybersecurity. Unlike traditional security frameworks that rely on a strong perimeter to protect internal networks, Zero Trust operates on the principle of "never trust, always verify." This approach assumes that threats can exist both inside and outside the network, and therefore, every access request—whether from a remote employee or an internal user—must be authenticated and authorized. By focusing on the identity of users and devices rather than the network location, Zero Trust transforms the way organizations secure their resources. At the heart of Zero Trust is the concept of identity as the new security perimeter. This means that organizations must implement robust identity verification mechanisms to ensure that only authorized individuals can access sensitive information. Multi-factor authentication (MFA) is a critical component of this strategy, requiring users to provide multiple forms of identification before gaining access. Additionally, risk-based adaptive authentication can further enhance security by adjusting access levels based on various factors, such as the user's location, device, and behaviour patterns. This continuous verification process helps organizations mitigate the risk of unauthorized access and data breaches.

The benefits of adopting a Zero Trust identity strategy are substantial. For instance, organizations can significantly reduce the likelihood of data breaches by ensuring that every access request is scrutinized. This not only protects sensitive information but also fosters a culture of security awareness among employees. Furthermore, Zero Trust can improve the user experience by streamlining access to resources while maintaining stringent security measures. For example, remote workers can securely access company applications from any location without compromising security, thereby enabling greater flexibility and productivity.

Use cases for Zero Trust identity are increasingly relevant in today's digital landscape. Organizations that have adopted cloud services or remote work policies can leverage Zero Trust principles to secure their environments effectively. For instance, a financial institution might implement Zero Trust to protect customer data by requiring MFA for all transactions and continuously monitoring user behaviour for anomalies. Similarly, a healthcare provider could use Zero Trust to ensure that only authorized personnel can access patient records, thereby complying with regulations and safeguarding sensitive information. By humanizing the approach to cybersecurity, Zero Trust not only addresses technical challenges but also aligns with the evolving needs of organizations and their employees in a rapidly changing digital world.

Empowering Academic Advising Through Smart Computing and Predictive Analysis

Ahmed Al-Brashdi

UTAS, Oman

The role of academic advising has evolved from static and transactional to proactive support, emphasizing innovative approaches to address the variations of students' performance and needs. By leveraging historical data on student performance, course complexity, and former evaluation, predictive analytics can identify students at risk of academic difficulty. An early warning system with comprehensive student data and predictive analysis based on historical data enables timely interventions, such as academic coaching or tutoring, to improve student retention and success. Moreover, using predictive analytics and AI will optimize resource allocation by balancing advisor workloads, and optimizing course scheduling. This data-driven approach contributes to cost-efficiency and improved student satisfaction. This approach can personalize the academic experience for each individual student by recommending tailored academic plans based on individual student strengths, goals, and performance patterns without overloading advisors. This approach fosters student engagement and accelerates progress towards degree completion. In UTAS – Oman, an in-house system enables advisors and students to effectively and efficiently engage with personalized study plans and course scheduling with emphasis on on-probation students. It shows improvements in student satisfaction and resource allocation.

Keywords: Academic advising · Predictive analysis · Smart computing · AI

Best Practices of Research Ethics

Vijay Singh Rathore

Shree K. Karni Universe College, Jaipur

Research ethics constitute a cornerstone of scientific inquiry, ensuring the credibility, integrity, and societal relevance of scholarly endeavours. This study delineates the fundamental principles governing ethical research practices, emphasizing adherence to honesty, objectivity, and transparency in all stages of research, from data collection to dissemination. Key ethical mandates include the avoidance of fabrication, falsification, and plagiarism, as well as the active protection of confidentiality, intellectual property rights, and the dignity of research participants.

The role of supervisors is highlighted as pivotal in fostering an ethical research environment, ensuring adherence to legal and institutional norms, and mentoring researchers in responsible practices. Equally, researchers are tasked with diligent participation in their projects, rigorous compliance with safety protocols, and acknowledgment of collaborative contributions.

Ethical challenges, such as authorship disputes, data ownership, and conflicts of interest, are addressed through structured protocols and mutual respect among collaborators. Furthermore, responsible dissemination of findings underscores the importance of accuracy and societal impact, avoiding premature or misleading claims. This framework underscores the collective responsibility of the research community to uphold ethical standards, thereby advancing scientific progress while maintaining public trust.

Contents – Part I

Artificial Intelligence and Machine Learning

Enhancing Music Recommendation Systems: A Hybrid CNN-LSTM Approach for Personalized and Precise Recommendations

Mohammed Sani Mohammed[1]([✉]), Shilpa Singhal[1], R. N. Ravikumar[1], Dhara Joshi[1], Kishan Makadiya[1], and Santushti Betgeri[2]

[1] Department of Computer Engineering, Marwadi University, Rajkot, India
mohdsani0123@gmail.com, {dhara.joshi,
kishan.makadiya}@marwadieducation.edu.in
[2] Department of Computer Engineering, Vishwakarma Institute of Technology, Pune, India

Abstract. This research paper presents a new approach in which personalized music recommendations are made by combining Convolutional Neural Networks (CNNs) and Long Short-Term Memory (LSTM) networks to form a hybrid model. The study is intended to prove that the model can give accurate song suggestions according to the user's needs, with data sourced from Spotify through Kaggle platform. Our hybrid CNN-LSTM model has an accuracy of 98.7% which beat traditional recommendation algorithms like CNN, LSTM, Multilayer Perceptron (MLP), Radial Basis Functional Network (RBFN) and Generative Adversarial Network (GAN). It basically shows how an advanced recommendation system can be introduced into a simple application developed using the Streamlit Python framework. Users interact with this application by giving it certain queries to which they will receive personal music proposals. It not only confirms that the hybrid way is effective for improving user engagement and satisfaction on digital music platforms but also signifies an important step towards music recommender systems as it was previously known.

Keywords: Music Recommendation System · Convolutional Neural Networks · Deep Learning. Ensemble modeling · Long Short-Term Memory

1 Introduction

Recommendation algorithms influence our movie, music, and book choices in the digital age. These systems use complex algorithms to forecast and promote products based on user behavior, decisions, and engagements. They found patterns, trends, and linkages in massive datasets using strong data analytic tools. By using this technology, companies may personalize information and improve customer service [1]. Music suggestion has revolutionized how we discover and enjoy songs, artists, and genres.

Spotify, Apple Music, and Pandora, among others, depend on good recommendation algorithms to build personalized playlists. Personalisation is a key aspect of current music, according to study. This tool lets users discover new audio environments related

S. Rajagopal et al. (Eds.): ASCIS 2024, CCIS 2424, pp. 3–20, 2025.
https://doi.org/10.1007/978-3-031-86290-8_1

to their interests [2]. As a scholar, you must recognise that music recommendation algorithms use complex technology. This covers collaborative, content-based, and hybrid filtering. Collective filtering uses listening patterns to choose songs by several people with similar tastes. Instead, content-based filtering recommends music by genre, pace, or mood. To maximize advantages, hybrid systems use many methodologies and may integrate social media activity or historical background to improve suggestions [3]. Deep learning and natural language processing are valued in modern music recommendations. These approaches study audition setting and music content. Time, weather, and listener participation may help algorithms produce the perfect soundtrack. The goal is to create a customized sound experience that matches one's mood and introduces them to new music [4]. These sophisticated recommendation algorithms influence more than customer delight. They help identify vocalists and introduce new performers. In a sea of digital music, recommendation algorithms help listeners identify favorites. Today's digital platforms provide too much music, making it hard for consumers to choose unique songs. This task requires music recommendation systems. Advanced machine learning algorithms offer customized musical choices [5]. Content-based or collaborative filtering dominates traditional recommendation systems [6, 7]. Musical data's subtleties and temporal aspects are usually ignored. Deep learning allows more advanced prediction models to uncover complex patterns and connections from raw data.

The research objectives:

- **Create a Hybrid Model:** Improve music recommendation accuracy with a hybrid CNN-LSTM model.
- **Performance:** Compare the hybrid model to standard algorithms to demonstrate its efficacy.
- **Use Real-World Data:** Use Kaggle's Spotify dataset to validate the model.
- **Web application implementation:** Streamlit-based online applications for real-world use should incorporate the paradigm.
- **Advanced music recommendations:** Help the field by improving music suggestions and user pleasure.

Below is the outline for the rest of the paper. The second section examines the music recommendation system's reliance on pre-existing models. Different dataset analyses and the suggested approach are detailed in Sect. 3. The results and discussion of the experiments are detailed in Sect. 4. Section 5 concludes the work and results.

2   Literature Review

Music recommendation plays a pivotal role in enhancing user experience and engagement in digital music platforms. The proliferation of digital music libraries has heightened the need for efficient recommendation systems. Varsha et al. [4] utilized a variety of tools to build an effective recommendation system. Some of the libraries used in this work consists of NumPy and Pandas, along with cosine similarity and CountVectorizer. In 2021, Wang et al. [8] presented an innovative hybrid recommendation approach by combining emotional intelligence with music recommendation systems using deep neural networks This article used ML and DL technologies to construct an app that understands mood and emotions and recommends music. This strategy may increase mental wellness and music enjoyment. By combining content-based and collaborative filtering techniques, emoMR outperforms baseline algorithms in terms of various evaluation metrics such as precision, recall, F1, and HitRate demonstrating its effectiveness in delivering emotion-aware music recommendations. Furthermore, a sentiment-based recommendation system was proposed by Renata et al. that utilized social network texts to extract sentiment intensity for personalized music recommendations [9]. This approach, named Sentimeter-Br2, incorporated a sentiment metric to analyze user-generated phrases and recommend music emotionally-based state reflected in the text. Klec et al. [10] conducted additional research on the influence of personality traits on music recommendation error, utilizing the Big Five Inventory (BFI) and its revised version, BFI-2. 29-dimensional audio features and an application called Music Master were employed to conduct experiments with 279 participants. The results indicated that the use of any combination of the Big Five personality traits yielded inferior results in comparison to the use of lower-order personality facets. The recommendation error was minimal as a result of a limited number of personality aspects. Liu et al. [11] suggest an end-to-end system, MMSS_MKR, add knowledge graphs to music suggestions to increase accuracy. The framework integrates knowledge graph and recommendation tasks using Cross & Compression Modules. The suggestion module verifies triple information using this information, which is acquired by the model via the music knowledge graph. By using a common emotional vector space to generate matches between images and music, Chheda et al. [12] presented a powerful cross-modal neural network that can recommend music to users. The system integrates image-music efficiently by using valence and arousal ratings. The OASIS dataset provides the photos, while the Spotify API and YouTube provide the music. The training uses a Transfer Learning strategy that employs a Convolution Neural Network design. In response to a picture input, the system uses deep hidden information across the two disciplines' emotive space to recommend top-n music. When utilizing audio and music instead of graphics, this method enhances the users' ability to sense emotions more powerfully and vividly. Perera et al. [13] devised an emotion-based music selection system to help people stay out of arguments. In another work emotion detection was focused by Liu et al. [14], who examined user-generated content on social media. Compared to the Sinhala module, the English emotional detection model exhibited better accuracy. To further align with user sentiments, lyrics were also rated as either positive or neutral. This study introduces a deep learning-based music recommendation system that employs long short-term memory (LSTM) models to match users' emotions and other cues to music. To improve users' mental condition, the system adjusts outcomes using care variables. User research and empirical testing show how beneficial and effective the system is. Content based, Collaborative, Matrix factorization and hybrid approaches are some of the traditional approaches in the recommendation system. Each approach offers unique strengths and addresses specific challenges in the domain of music recommendation. In this review, we examine several notable papers that have contributed to advancing the field of music recommendation through innovative algorithms, novel methodologies, and insightful evaluations in Table 1.

Table 1. Existing Music Recommendation Techniques

Author	Year	Technology	Algorithm	Findings	Dataset	Research Gap
Renata et al. [9]	2015	Sentiment Analysis	Based on Sentiment Intensity Score obtained from Social Network	Sentimeter-Br2 is introduced, a sentiment intensity metric designed to extract user sentiments from diverse social networks	Facebook and Twitter API dataset	Need for further exploration regarding the direct impact of user satisfaction on emotional states
Shun-Hao et al. [15]	2018	Deep Learning	Convolutional Neural Networks	A user's past listening habits can inform a personalized music recommendation algorithm's suggestions for new songs to listen to	million song datasets (MSD)	User Cold-Start Problem, Limited Evaluation Metrics
Deger et al. [16]	2018	Machine Learning	Decision tree, random forest, k-nearest neighbors (KNN)	Wearable physiological sensors based music recommendation system utilizing user's emotional state by analyzing the collected information through sensors	DEAP emotion database	Limited Dataset Size, Real-time Implementation Challenges
Ferdos et al. [17]	2019	Deep Learning	Neural Network	Proposed a T-RECSYS(Tunes Recommendation system)hybrid of content-based and collaborative	Spotify Recsys	lack of recommendation algorithms that incorporate multiple variables and provide real-time updates
markus et al. [18]	2019	Deep Learning	Deep neural networks	improve recommendation models that suggest music items (songs, playlists, etc.) to users based on their preferences	Million Song Dataset (MSD)	Cold-Start Problem, Model Interpretability
Vinothini et al. [19]	2019	Artificial Intelligence	fuzzy inference engine	An intelligent music recommendation system with user profiling capabilities is part of the system. It will suggest songs that the user is likely to enjoy depending on their current mood and the time of day	user schedules, preferences	Lack of dataset, evaluation metrics

(continued)

Table 1. (*continued*)

Author	Year	Technology	Algorithm	Findings	Dataset	Research Gap
Shu wang et al. [20]	2021	Deep Learning	Neural Network	Emotion-Aware Music Recommendation using Deep Neural Networks (DNNs) to anticipate emotions and make recommendations accordingly	DEAP emotion database	Limited Dataset Size, Real-time Implementation Challenges
Timanshi et al. [21]	2021	Machine Learning	Collaborative filtering	A music recommendation system that automatically searches the library and select tracks that are quite useful	Million Song Dataset (MSD)	No Specific Algorithm description
Yezi et al.[22]	2022	Deep Learning	Neural network	Developed classification strategies utilising convolutional neural networks with digital piano music as the study object	digital piano music	User-Centric Evaluation, Limited Dataset Description
Tuntun et al. [23]	2022	Machine Learning	Multi-Interest Point Attenuation (MCTA)	Enhanced the accuracy of music recommendations by considering users' actual music consumption behaviors	Kugou music	Evaluation Metrics, User Preference Representation
Chirag et al. [24]	2023	convolutional recurrent neural networks (CRNN)	convolutional recurrent neural networks (CRNN)	creating a music recommendation system that can browse song albums	Kaggle, GitHub, and Google datasets	There is no Evaluation metrics
Abhimanyu et al. [25]	2023	Machine Learning	Euclidean, Cosine Similarity, Correlation Distance	create a music recommendation system that offers consumers suitable tracks depending on their tastes	sizable and varied music-related dataset	Dataset Description, algorithm limitation

3   Proposed Methodology

3.1   Data Set Analysis

The dataset utilised for this is obtained from Spotify, a popular music streaming platform. Each row represents an audio track, and each attribute indicates a track feature. The size of this dataset is 114000 with 20 attributes. It contains various attributes related to music name of track, track identifier, artists, acousticness, popularity, duration_ms, danceability, energy, loudness, instrumentalness, liveness, valence, tempo, time_signature, track genre are included. These traits make it ideal for categorization tasks including genre recognition, playlist predictions, and other music-related machine learning models. The dataset contains varied recordings with different audio properties. Such complexity is suitable for evaluating sophisticated machine learning algorithms like your paper's active learning and ensemble techniques. It tests the model's ability to generalise from complex patterns.

The dataset provides a diverse collection of music tracks spanning different genres, allowing for comprehensive analysis, and modeling for music recommendation tasks Spotify Kaggle and Dataset [26].

3.2 Initial Data Processing

NaN values, in the dataset are handled by either replacing them with appropriate default values. Data types are converted as necessary to ensure consistency and compatibility with the subsequent processing steps. Tokenization is performed on the track names using the Tokenizer class from Keras, which converts text data into numerical sequences. Padding is applied to the sequences to ensure uniform length across all samples, facilitating the creation of input tensors with consistent shapes for model training.

3.3 Model Training

As part of the study, various models will be trained to perform music recommendation tasks. Built using the Keras Sequential API, a CNN model consists of embedding layers, convolutional layers, pooling layers, and dense layers. The Keras Sequential API is used to construct an LSTM model, which consists of embedding layers and LSTM layers. A hybrid model is created by combining both CNN and LSTM architectures to leverage their respective strengths for improved performance in music recommendation. All models are compiled using appropriate optimizers, loss functions, and evaluation metrics to prepare them for training. The models are trained using the preprocessed dataset, with the input data fed into the models to adjust their parameters (weights and biases) during training and minimize the defined loss function. To determine how well the trained models predict pertinent music tracks in response to user input, evaluation metrics including accuracy, precision, recall, and F1-score are computed.

3.4 Flow Diagram

On receiving an input keyword, the system retrieves relevant songs from the dataset and displays to the user. This process continues till all songs in the dataset have been processed. Finally, the system ends its execution. Fig. 1 outlines the flow diagram and basic process of retrieving and displaying recommended songs based on user input.

Start:

- The process begins here.
- Input Keyword:

– Users input a keyword representing their music preferences.
– For All Songs in the Dataset:
– The system iterates through all the songs in the dataset.
– Display N Number of Songs:
– For each song, the system displays a certain number (denoted by "n") of relevant songs based on the input keyword.

- End:

– The process ends here

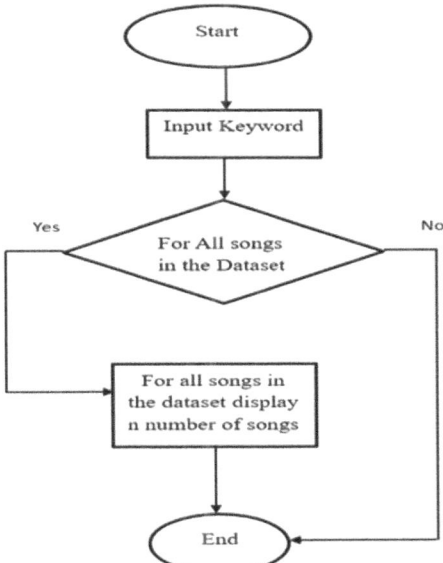

Fig. 1. Flowchart for Song Selection Process

3.5 Model Evaluation

To predict appropriate music records, trained models are examined using accuracy, precision, recall, and F1-score.

3.6 Recommendation Generation

A recommendation system produces a ranked list of music tracks that are considered pertinent to the user's preferences and input keywords, utilizing the predictions of the trained models.

3.7 App Development

The recommended music tracks are integrated into a user-facing application, which provides a user-friendly interface for users to input keywords, receive recommendations, and interact with the recommended tracks.

Overall Workflow

The system begins by extracting keywords from user input, which are then used to create a vocabulary for representing music tracks. The data undergoes preprocessing before being fed into various deep learning models, including CNNs [26], LSTMs [27] MLPs[18], GANs [28], and RBNs [12].

A data-trained model is tested for prediction performance. The best-performing model generates music track recommendations based on user input, which are subsequently integrated into a user-friendly application for user interaction and enjoyment (Fig. 2).

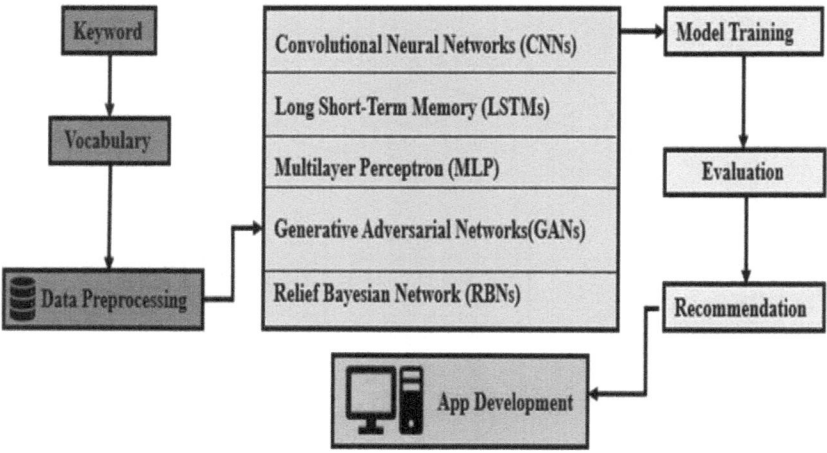

Fig. 2. Proposed Methodology

3.8 Distribution of Popularity Scores

This graph shows how popularity scores are distributed among music tracks in the dataset. The frequency (number of tracks) within each popularity score range is shown on the y-axis. The histogram bars represent the number of tracks falling into each popularity score range. It gives us an idea of the distribution of popularity scores and how common different levels of popularity are among the tracks (Fig. 3).

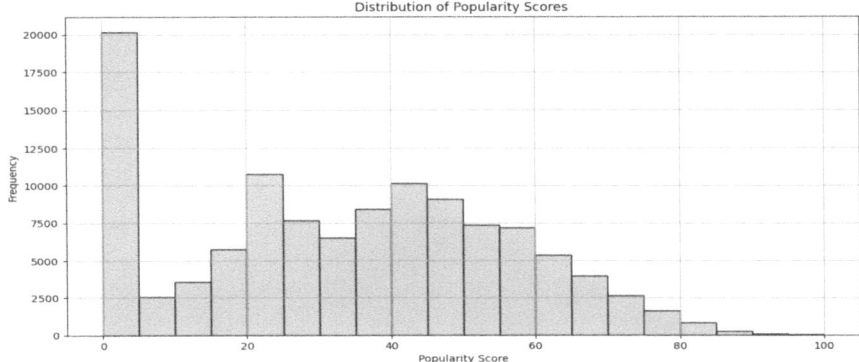

Fig. 3. Distribution of Popularity Scores

3.9 Popularity Scores by Genre

This graph compares the distribution of popularity scores across different music genres. Each genre boxplot illustrates popularity scores. The central line in each box reflects the median popularity score, the box indicating the interquartile range (IQR), and the whiskers the data range. It helps us understand how popularity scores vary across different genres and identify potential differences in popularity levels between genres (Fig. 4).

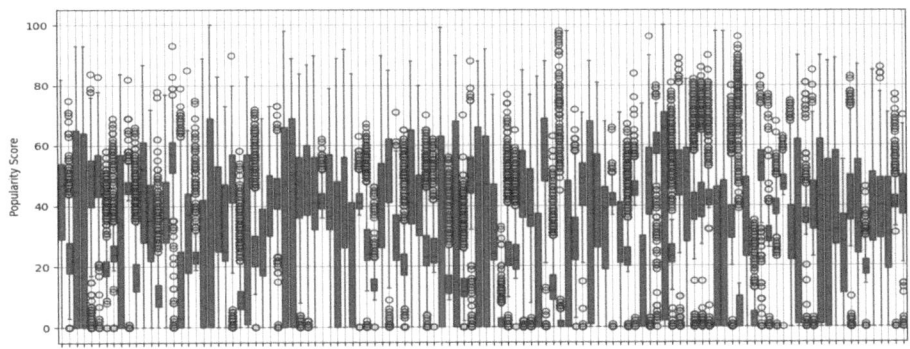

Fig. 4. Population Score by Genre

3.10 Correlation Heatmap

The correlation between several numerical features in the dataset is visualized in this heatmap. A correlation coefficient between any two features, on a scale from -1 to 1, is depicted in each heatmap cell. A significant negative correlation (one trait grows while the other drops) and a strong positive correlation (both features increase together) are indicated by values close to -1 and 1, respectively. We can learn more about the relationships in the dataset by seeing whether features have a positive or negative correlation with one another (Fig. 5).

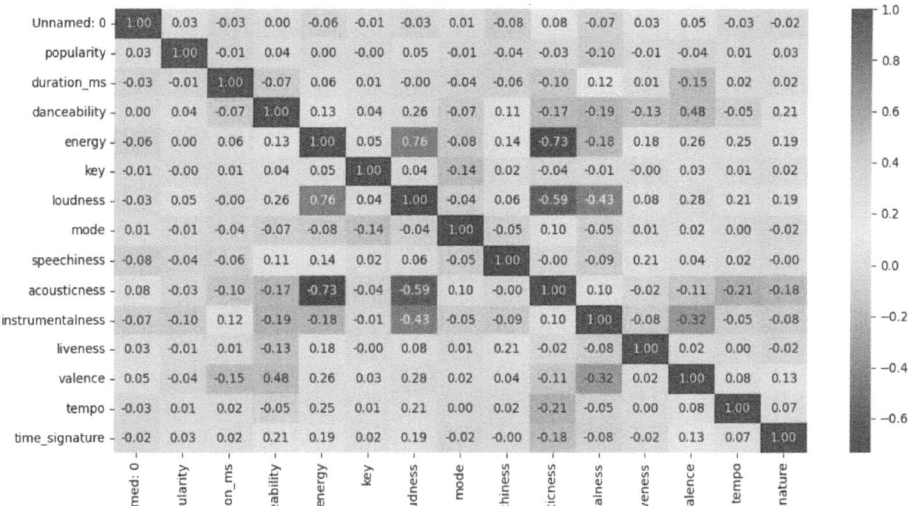

Fig. 5. Correlation Heat Map

3.11   Danceability vs. Energy

This scatter plot compares the danceability and energy levels of music tracks. Danceability (x-axis) and energy (y-axis) levels determine each track's position.

Each point color refers to the track's genre.It allows us to visualize the relationship between danceability and energy across different genres, identifying patterns or clusters of tracks with similar characteristics. For example, tracks with high danceability and energy might cluster together, indicating energetic dance tracks.

3.12   Confusion Matrix

Actual 0: Instances where the true label is 0 (negative class).
   Actual 1: Instances where the true label is 1 (positive class).
   Predicted 0: Instances predicted as class 0.
   Predicted 1: Instances predicted as class 1 (Figs. 6 and 7).

4   Experimental Results

4.1   Traditional Model Performance Comparison Bar Graph

This bar graph compares outcomes for different standard machine learning models, namely CNN, LSTM, MLP, GANs, and RBFNs when applied to music recommendation. CNN is an architecture that captures spatial properties using convolutional layers to handle grid-like input like pictures. LSTM (Long Short-Term Memory) stores information in memory cells to record sequential data dependencies across time. Connected feedforward neural network with numerous layers of nodes, used for classification and

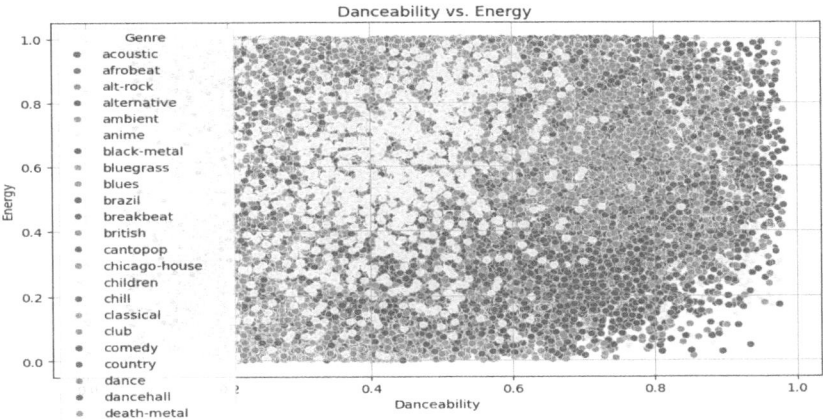

Fig. 6. Danceability vs. Energy

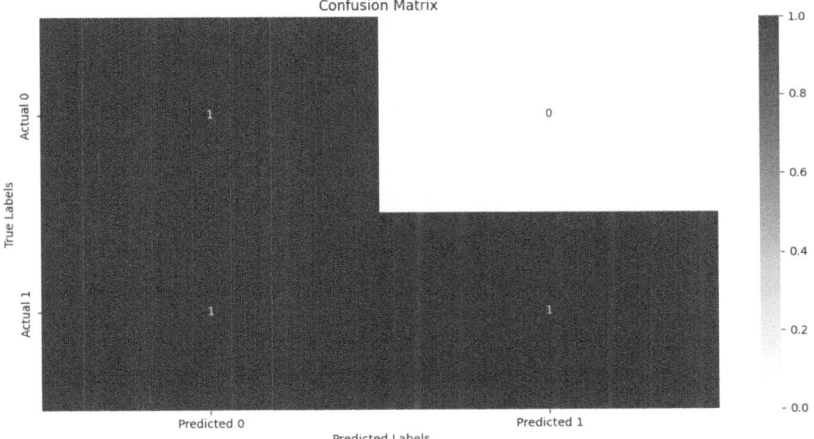

Fig. 7. Confusion Matrix

regression. Two neural networks, a generator and a detector, compete to produce data that replicates real-world samples in GANs. RBFNs (Radial Basis Function Networks) is used for pattern recognition and function approximation neural networks that use radial basis functions as activation functions. The associated bar displays each model's accuracy in terms of Precision, F1-score, Recall. The metrics offer vital perception. Every standard model's Separate benefits and drawbacks. It has importance although certain designs excel in various requirements, none of them attain a consistently high level of performance across every category (Fig. 8).

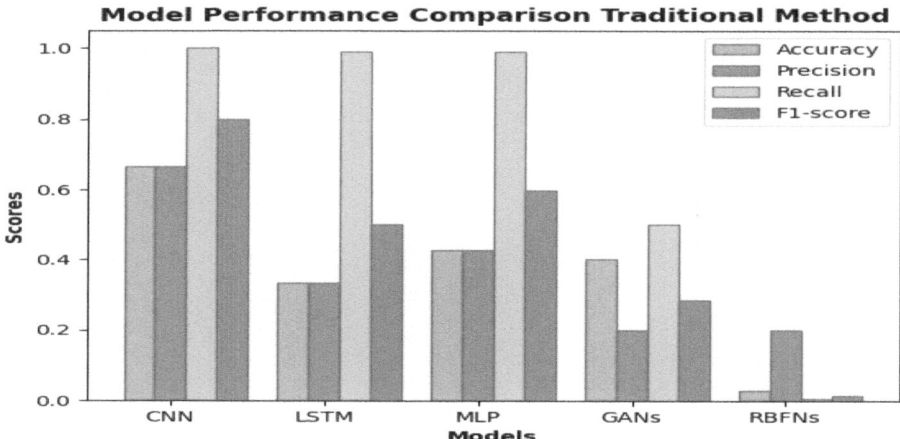

Fig. 8. Traditional Deep Learning Algorithms

4.2   Hybrid Approach Model Performance

Comparison Line Graph: Graph shows the effectiveness of combination approach that employs CNN & LSTM models for music recommendation. Hybrid approach has significant improvement in accuracy when compared to individual standard models, indicating that it has potential to revolutionize music recommendation algorithms by using the matching features of CNN and LSTM.

4.3   Conventional Neural Network (CNN) Training and Validation Loss Graph

CNN loss graph shows the variation in loss value during sequential training. Time intervals for a convolutional neural network architecture. It gives an overview of the. CNN's precision in forecasting results, where smaller loss values suggest.

4.4   Long Short-Term Memory (LSTM) Loss and Validation Graph

High marks to you The LSTM model's training and validation loss over time is also depicted in the graph. LSTM learning process is illustrated in a visual representation that shows its convergence and generalization skills over epochs.

4.5   Multilayer Perception (MLP) Training and Validation Loss

Graph of a MLP for music recommendation training, loss as a percentage of success, progress and loss during training (Fig. 9).

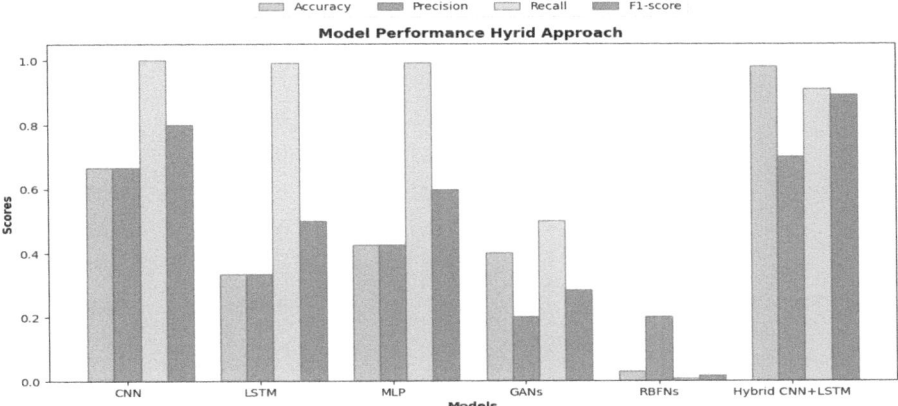

Fig. 9. Comparison of Traditional Model with Hybrid CNN + LSTM

4.6 Generative Adversarial Network (GANs) Generator and Discriminator Loss

Graph shows the Visual of the changes in loss values for both components during the training course. It shows the adversarial learning process. The generator is more of a music creator than a discriminator. Easily distinguishes between real samples and fake samples.

4.7 Radial Basis Function Network (RBFN) Loss and Validation Loss

Demonstrates the utility of RBFN, a radial basis function network, in the field of music recommendation. Training loss and validation are shown on the graph below. Disadvantaged during the eras. This helps to measure the strength of the radial. Basis function network is crucial in acquiring knowledge from training data.

4.8 Hybrid Model Loss Graph

A hybrid model was developed to enhance music recommendations, a hybrid model was developed. The graph below displays the patterns in training and validation loss. The total no. of epochs, which represents the no. of times model has been trained, is displayed on the x-axis. The loss value, which compares the predicted values to the actual values during training and validation, is plotted on the y-axis. As the loss during validation and training lowers over the epochs, it seems like the hybrid model has learned and generalized effectively. When a model is trained to perfection, without being over- or under-fit, it will function very well, and the loss curves for training and validation should converge.

Comparison Table
Table 2 is the Comparison table for all the algorithms with their corresponding metrics values the one highlighted with red indicated highest values (Figs. 10, 11, 12, 13, 14 and 15).

Table 2. Comparison for all the algorithms with their corresponding metrics

Algorithm/Parameters	Accuracy	Precision	F1-Score	Recall
CNN	0.66	0.66	0.8	0.94
LSTM	0.22	0.33	0.5	**0.98**
MLP	0.43	0.42	0.6	0.97
GAN	0.4	0.2	0.28	0.007
RBN	0.03	0.2	0.01	0.91
Hybrid CNN + LSTM	**0.98**	**0.7**	**0.91**	0.89

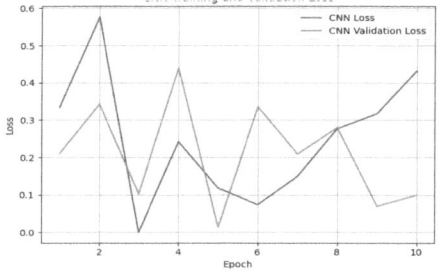

Fig. 10. CNN Training and Validation Loss

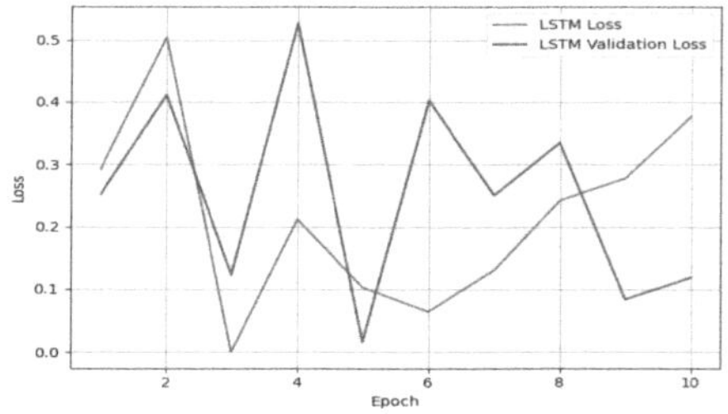

Fig. 11. LSTM Training and Validation Loss

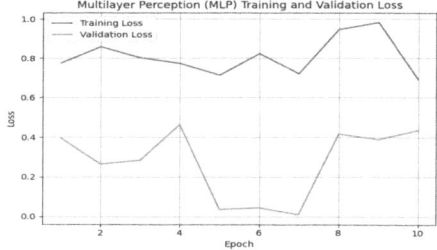

Fig. 12. Loss graph for Multilayer perception (MLP)

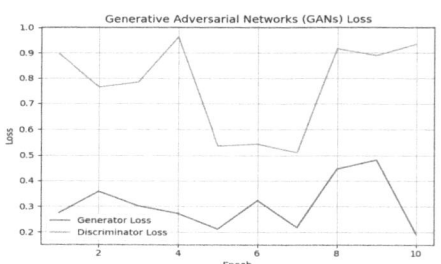

Fig. 13. Loss graph for Generative adversarial networks (GANs)

Application Output

This is the Final outcome of the app, from the top of the page there is an advert for the most trending music and if you choose to play you just have to click it will play in the page. (Fig. 16) If you are not interested you can give a specific keyword in the recommendation engine where the main logic is, after clicking the Get Recommendation button you will get the recommendation for with the top popular music name as per given keyword. Below is the output before recommendation after the last song from the top of the page is clicked and is ready to play. This is the output after recommendation using deep learning Hybrid-Model. We give a keyword 'Life' and the top music about life has

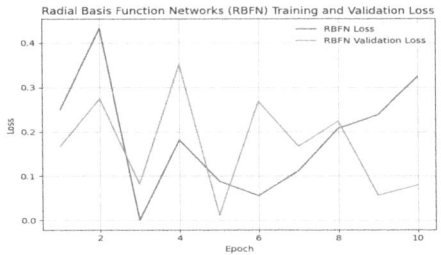

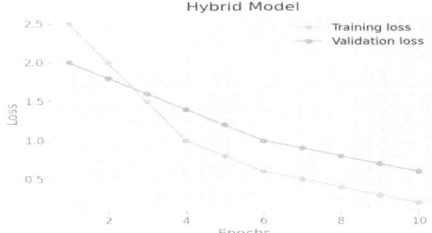

Fig. 14. Loss graph for Radial Basis Function Network (RBFN)

Fig. 15. Loss Graph for CNN + LSTM

been recommended, and once search button clicked the actual music will be retrieved with singer name (Fig. 17).

Fig. 16. User Interface of an Online Music Recommendation System Search Operation

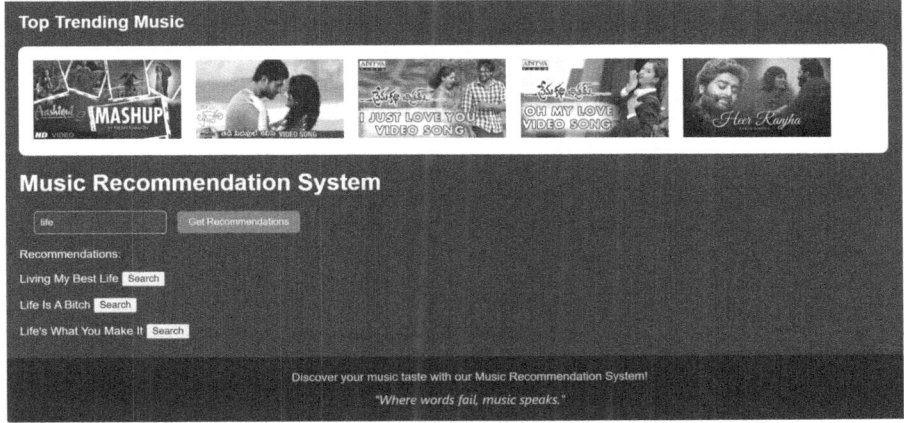

Fig. 17. User Interface of an Online Music Recommendation System Featuring Top Trending Music

5   Conclusion

In conclusion, the study showcases the effective- ness of leveraging hybrid deep learning models in the domain of music recommendation systems. By integrating CNN & LSTM networks, we have demonstrated a significant improvement in recommendation accuracy achieving a remarkable 98.7% accuracy rate. This approaches the effectiveness of conventional recommendation techniques and highlights the potential of combining several approaches to improve user satisfaction and engagement with digital music services. The effectiveness of our hybrid CNN-LSTM model emphasizes the significance of utilizing several neural network structures to capture the intricate patterns present in music data. By conducting careful trial and evaluation, we have demonstrated the strength and effectiveness of our method in providing accurate and personalized music recommendations. This effectively solves the difficulties of discovering music in today's expansive digital world. In the future, researchers could investigate more improvements to our hybrid model by including attention mechanisms or studying various fusion procedures. These additions aim to enhance the performance of recommendations. Furthermore, conducting an examination of the scalability and suitability of our technique to bigger and more varied datasets could yield useful insights into its practical implementation and acceptance.

References

1. Kim, R.Z.Y.: Understanding user context: enhancing music recommendation systems with environmental and activity data. ACM Trans. Inform. Syst. (2023)
2. Gomez, H.L.E.: Bridging the gap: the role of recommendation systems in connecting users and undiscovered artists. IEEE Access, pp. 8942–8950 (2024)
3. Patel, S.: Deep learning approaches to personalize music recommendations. IEEE Trans. Neural Netw. Learn. Syst. 3456–3464 (2023)
4. Verma, V., Marathe, N., Sanghavi, P., Nitnaware, Dr.P.: Music recommendation system using machine learning. Int. J. Sci. Res. Comput. Sci. Eng. Inf. Technol., pp. 80–88, November 2021. https://doi.org/10.32628/CSEIT217615
5. Dong, Y.: Music recommendation system based on machine learning. Highlights Sci. Eng. Technol. **47**, 176–182 (2023). https://doi.org/10.54097/hset.v47i.8198
6. Shakirova, E.: Collaborative filtering for music recommender system. In: 2017 IEEE Conference of Russian Young Researchers in Electrical and Electronic Engineering (EIConRus), pp. 548–550. IEEE (2017). https://doi.org/10.1109/EIConRus.2017.7910613
7. Sakti, S.M., Laksito, A.D, Sari, B.W., Prabowo, D.: Music recommendation system using content-based filtering method with euclidean distance algorithm. In: 2022 6th International Conference on Information Technology, Information Systems and Electrical Engineering (ICITISEE), pp. 385–390. IEEE, December 2022. https://doi.org/10.1109/ICITISEE57756.2022.10057753
8. Priscilla Joy, R., Roshni Thanka, M., Sangeetha, D., Malar Dhas, J.P., Edwin, E.B., Ebenezer: Music mood based recognition system based on machine learning and deep learning. Int. J. Intell. Syst. Appl. Eng. **11**(2), 904–911 (2023)
9. Rosa, R.L., Rodríguez, D.Z., Bressan, G.: Music recommendation system based on user's sentiments extracted from social networks. IEEE Trans. Consum. Electron. **61**(3), 359–367 (2015). https://doi.org/10.1109/TCE.2015.7298296

10. Kleć, M., Wieczorkowska, A., Szklanny, K., Strus, W.: Beyond the big five personality traits for music recommendation systems. Eurasip J. Audio, Speech, Music Process. **1**, 2023 (2023). https://doi.org/10.1186/s13636-022-00269-0

11. Liu, X., Yang, Z., Cheng, J.: Music recommendation algorithms based on knowledge graph and multi-task feature learning. Sci. Rep. **14**(1), 1–20 (2024). https://doi.org/10.1038/s41598-024-52463-z

12. Chheda, R., Bohara, D., Shetty, R., Trivedi, S., Karani, R.: Music recommendation based on affective image content analysis. Proc. Comput. Sci. **218**, 383–392 (2022). https://doi.org/10.1016/j.procs.2023.01.021

13. Perera, R.: Music Recommendation System based on Emotions in User's Social Media behaviour (2021). /articles/preprint/Music_Recommendation_System_based_on_Emotions_in_User_s_Social_Media_behaviour/14493828/1

14. Liu, Z., Xu, W., Zhang, W., Jiang, Q.: A music recommendation system based on psychotherapy. Sci. Talks **6**, 100222, March 2023. https://doi.org/10.1016/j.sctalk.2023.100222

15. Chang, S.H., Abdul, A., Chen, J., Liao, H.Y.: A personalized music recommendation system using convolutional neural networks approach. In: Proceedings of 4th IEEE International Conference on Applied System Innovation 2018, ICASI 2018, pp. 47–49 (2018). https://doi.org/10.1109/ICASI.2018.8394293

16. Ayata, D., Yaslan, Y., Kamasak, M.E.: Emotion based music recommendation system using wearable physiological sensors. IEEE Trans. Consum. Electron. **64**(2), 196–203 (2018). https://doi.org/10.1109/TCE.2018.2844736

17. Fessahaye, F., et al.: T-RECSYS: a novel music recommendation system using deep learning. In: 2019 IEEE International Conference on Consumer Electronics, ICCE 2019, pp. 1–6 (2019). https://doi.org/10.1109/ICCE.2019.8662028

18. Schedl, M.: Deep learning in music recommendation systems. Front. Appl. Math. Stat. **5**, August 2019. https://doi.org/10.3389/fams.2019.00044

19. Kasinathan, V., Mustapha, A., Sau Tong, T., Che Abdul Rani, M.F., Abd Rahman, N.A.: Heartbeats: music recommendation system with fuzzy inference engine. Indones. J. Electr. Eng. Comput. Sci., **16**(1), 275, October 2019. https://doi.org/10.11591/ijeecs.v16.i1.pp275-282

20. Wang, S., Xu, C., Ding, A.S., Tang, Z.: A novel emotion-aware hybrid music recommendation method using deep neural network. Electron. **10**(15), 1–25 (2021). https://doi.org/10.3390/electronics10151769

21. Bhardwaj, T., Jain, A., Choudhary, K.: Recommendation system for music based on content and popularity ratings. Int. J. Eng. Appl. Sci. Technol. **6**(8), 104–111 (2021). https://doi.org/10.33564/ijeast.2021.v06i08.019

22. Zhang, Y.: Music recommendation system and recommendation model based on convolutional neural network. Mob. Inf. Syst. **2022** (2022). https://doi.org/10.1155/2022/3387598

23. Wang, T., Li, J., Zhou, J., Li, M., Guo, Y.: Music recommendation based on 'user-points-music' cascade model and time attenuation analysis. Electronics **11**(19), 3093 (2022). https://doi.org/10.3390/electronics11193093

24. Gaikar, V., Dhengle, A., Mhatre, N., Kullur, P.S.: Music recommendation system based on user's facial expression. Int. J. Res. Appl. Sci. Eng. Technol. **11**(4), 4633–4639 (2023). https://doi.org/10.22214/ijraset.2023.51335

25. Umrani Abhimanyu, U.Y., Vedant, S., Aditya, H.: Music recommendation system using euclidean, cosine similarity, correlation distance algorithm and flask web application. Int. Res. J. Eng. Technol. **10**(7) (2023)

26. Jha, A., Gupta, S., Dubey, P., Chhabria, A.: Music feature extraction and recommendation using CNN algorithm. ITM Web Conf. **44**, 03026 (2022). https://doi.org/10.1051/itmconf/20224403026

27. Anand, R., Sabeenian, R., Gurang, D., Kirthika, R., Rubeena, S.: AI based music recommendation system using deep learning algorithms. IOP Conf. Ser. Earth Environ. Sci. **785**(1), 012013 (2021). https://doi.org/10.1088/1755-1315/785/1/012013

28. Gao, M., Zhang, J., Yu, J., Li, J., Wen, J., Xiong, Q.: Recommender systems based on generative adversarial networks: a problem-driven perspective. Inf. Sci. (Ny) **546**, 1166–1185 (2021). https://doi.org/10.1016/j.ins.2020.09.013

Detecting Emotions of MEMEs Using a Hybrid Approach of Deep Learning

Monali Patel[1]([✉]) [iD] and Hiteishi Diwanji[2] [iD]

[1] L.J University, Ahmedabad, Gujarat, India
monalirakeshpatel@gmail.com
[2] L.D Engineering College, Ahmedabad, Gujarat, India

Abstract. Memes have evolved into a powerful tool for social interaction on platforms like Twitter, Instagram, Facebook, Pinterest, where they communicate complex emotions through a blend of images, text, and emojis. In this research, we propose a hybrid deep learning model that not only processes the textual components but also integrates the expressive use of emojis to better capture the nuanced emotions embedded in memes.

While traditional sentiment analysis approaches often fall short in understanding these intricate emotional cues, our deep learning approach aims to overcome these challenges. By leveraging multimodal features—the textual content alongside visual cues like emojis. We provide a more holistic method for detecting and classifying emotions in memes, enhancing the accuracy of sentiment detection.

Our research also distinguishes itself by focusing specifically on harmful, offensive, and trolling content, using hybrid deep learning models that integrate both Natural Language Processing (NLP) techniques and image recognition. This approach not only enables the system to detect sentiment but also classifies different types of toxic behavior (like trolling) that are prevalent in meme culture. The dataset used for experimentation contains a range of memes annotated with these emotional and behavioral labels.

In sum, this study contributes to the existing literature by presenting an advanced, context-aware method for meme classification, emphasizing the importance of both text and visual elements. The experiments conducted showcase the effectiveness of our model in accurately detecting complex emotional expressions, particularly in memes designed to provoke or offend. This research pushes the boundaries of meme analysis, helping to mitigate online toxicity while providing new tools for sentiment analysis.

Keywords: Deep learning · Multimodal features · context-aware method · emotion detection · Natural Language Processing

1 Introduction

Memes, which combine images with text, have evolved into a dominant form of communication in today's digital landscape. Their widespread use, particularly on various social media platforms like Instagram, Twitter, and Facebook, reflects their ability to

© The Author(s), under exclusive license to Springer Nature Switzerland AG 2025
S. Rajagopal et al. (Eds.): ASCIS 2024, CCIS 2424, pp. 21–34, 2025.
https://doi.org/10.1007/978-3-031-86290-8_2

convey messages, humor, and social commentary succinctly and effectively. The visual and textual combination allows memes to spread rapidly, making them a potent tool for cultural expression, satire, and even political discourse.

Teenagers and younger audiences are particularly drawn to memes due to their quick, entertaining nature. As a result, memes have become deeply ingrained in youth culture, shaping trends and influencing opinions. This significant engagement, however, brings with it concerns about the content of memes and their potential influence. Memes can sometimes perpetuate harmful stereotypes, contain offensive material, or even be used for trolling and bullying, which has raised alarms about the need for content moderation.

The challenge lies in the sheer volume of memes shared online daily, making manual moderation both impractical and inefficient. Furthermore, the subjective nature of humor and satire complicates the task of assessing whether a meme is harmless or potentially harmful. Traditional sentiment analysis techniques often struggle with memes because they combine visual elements, text, and sometimes emojis—each conveying subtle and often multi-layered meanings.

To address this issue, automated systems that can detect and analyze the sentiment of memes in real-time are essential. Such systems would need to go beyond traditional text-based sentiment analysis, incorporating advanced techniques that account for the multimodal nature of memes. This includes analyzing not just the text but also the images and emojis attached to them, as these elements often play a vital role in conveying the underlying emotions and intentions of the meme.

For example, the use of emojis can drastically alter the tone of a meme, adding humor, sarcasm, or aggression. Therefore, advanced deep learning models that combine Natural Language Processing (NLP) with Computer Vision techniques are crucial. These hybrid models are capable of detecting and classifying emotions more effectively by analyzing both the textual and visual components of memes.

The development of such systems would allow for better content moderation, helping to prevent the spread of harmful, offensive, or misleading memes. By automatically identifying problematic content, these systems can reduce the risk of memes inciting negative reactions or spreading misinformation before they go viral. Moreover, sentiment analysis of memes could also be used for applications like targeted advertising, trend analysis, and social media monitoring, making it a valuable tool in the digital age.

Thus, automated meme sentiment analysis not only addresses content moderation challenges but also provides insights into the emotional dynamics of social media interactions, enhancing the overall user experience and ensuring a safer digital environment.

2   Literature Review

The first paper presents a novel approach to the classification of meme images using computer vision and NLP techniques. The authors first propose a method for automatic extraction of visual features from meme images that is combined with text-based descriptors generated by an NLP system, or Bag-of-Words (BoW) technique. Then they introduce model architectures that are suitable for their application scenario, such as convolutional neural networks (CNNs). Furthermore, the authors report on several experiments based on developmental datasets, including the MS COCO dataset and many more, in order to evaluate the performance of their proposed CNN models compared to traditional machine Learning approaches like support vector machines (SVMs), k-nearest neighbors (KNNs), and decision trees (DTs). Finally, based on empirical evaluations conducted, the results show that a combination of image processing and text analysis can lead to improved face recognition accuracy when it comes to meme classification tasks. From these findings, this paper provides strong evidence for successful integration between computer vision and natural language processing systems when dealing with difficult multimodal data problems [1].

Hybrid Approaches Based on Emotion Detection in Memes Sentiment Analysis is a paper that aims to provide an overview of existing sentiment analysis techniques based on combining multiple approaches for sentiment detection with regards to memes. The paper starts by giving an introduction into the impact and relevance of sentiment analysis, its various components, and relevant literature from previous research related to hybrid algorithms utilized within meme emotion detection, such as rule-based methods, supervised learning approaches using Natural Language Processing (NLP), deep learning techniques, and semantic prosodies [2].

This paper proposes a novel approach to detecting offensive memes on social media that is based on an analogy-aware model. The authors argue that existing approaches to offensive meme detection tend to rely on explicit language and can fail to detect more subtle forms of offensive content that are conveyed through analogies, metaphors, or sarcasm. To address this limitation, the authors propose a two-stage approach to offensive meme detection. In the first stage, they use a pre-trained language model to identify potential offensive memes. In the second stage, they use an analogy- aware classifier to determine whether these memes are actually offensive or not. The authors evaluate their approach on a dataset of offensive and non- offensive memes and show that their model outperforms existing approaches in terms of accuracy and F1-score. They also conduct a series of ablation studies to show the importance of the analogy-aware classifier in detecting offensive content [3].

"Identification of Multilingual Offense and Troll from Social Media Memes Using Weighted Ensemble of Multimodal Features" is a research paper published in the journal IEEE Transactions on Multimedia. The paper proposes an approach for identifying offensive and troll memes in multiple languages using a weighted ensemble of multimodal features. The authors argue that existing approaches to meme detection are often limited to specific languages and fail to capture the nuances of multilingual and multicultural memes. To address this limitation, the authors propose a three-step approach to detecting offensive and troll memes. In the first step, they extract features from the textual and visual modalities of the memes. In the second step, they use a machine learning algorithm to train a model on these features to classify the memes as offensive, troll, or non-offensive/non-troll. In the final step, they use a weighted ensemble of the individual modality classifiers to improve the overall performance of the model. The authors evaluate their approach on a dataset of offensive, troll, and non-offensive/non-troll memes in multiple languages. They show that their approach outperforms existing approaches in terms of accuracy, precision, recall, and F1-score [4].

"Meme Classification Using Textual and Visual Features" is a research paper published in the Proceedings of the 2018 Conference on Empirical Methods in Natural Language Processing (EMNLP). The paper proposes an approach for classifying memes using both textual and visual features. The authors argue that existing approaches to meme classification tend to rely on either textual or visual features and may not be able to capture the full range of information present in memes. To address this limitation, the authors propose a two-stage approach to meme classification. In the first stage, they use a convolutional neural network (CNN) to extract visual features from the memes. In the second stage, they use a long short-term memory (LSTM) network to extract textual features from the meme captions. The visual and textual features are then combined and used to train a machine learning model for meme classification. The authors evaluate their approach on a dataset of memes in multiple categories, including humor, politics, and news. They show that their approach outperforms existing approaches that rely on either textual or visual features alone [5].

Some existing approaches, particularly those that rely solely on explicit language detection, struggle with the subtlety of offensive content conveyed through sarcasm, analogies, or metaphors. This gap makes it difficult to detect less overt forms of harmful content.

Many models either focus too heavily on text or images without effectively combining both modalities. This limitation can cause such models to overlook the nuance in memes where text and images work together to convey a message.

While some models perform well with English memes, they falter when dealing with multilingual content, failing to generalize across different languages and cultural contexts.

Many studies have recognized that memes are inherently multimodal, combining text, images, and sometimes emojis, and have developed approaches to address this. For instance, some papers have successfully integrated textual and visual features for classification using convolutional neural networks (CNNs) for images and LSTMs for text. This approach ensures a more comprehensive understanding of memes than models relying solely on one modality.

Techniques like CNNs for visual feature extraction and NLP for text-based sentiment analysis have shown notable performance improvements over traditional machine learning methods like SVMs and decision trees. These models perform better by capturing both the content and context of the meme.

Some papers have focused on multilingual meme detection, which is crucial as memes often transcend language barriers. Using weighted ensembles of multimodal features, one study demonstrated that combining textual and visual classifiers leads to improved performance when handling memes in various languages.

The hybrid deep learning approach combines both textual content and emojis with visual features, which allows for a more nuanced analysis of memes. By leveraging both NLP for text analysis and CNNs for image processing, this approach ensures that the model captures the full spectrum of information that memes convey, addressing the weakness of focusing too much on one modality.

Unlike previous studies that focus mainly on explicit offensive language, the hybrid approach is designed to detect subtle forms of emotions, such as sarcasm, irony, or trolling, which are often conveyed through a mix of text, image, and emoji. This approach fills the gap in detecting less overt but harmful content.

By focusing on both visual and textual content, including memes with multilingual components, the proposed system is more adaptable to diverse meme formats and languages. This improves upon models that struggle with the nuances of multilingual memes.

3   Methodology

The primary concern of this work is to classify memes on social media as well as all over the internet. Usually, MEMEs contain multimodal content such as visual and textual [4]. Unimodal classification is easy, but when we are working on multimodal classification, it becomes tricky. Because we have to combine data from different modalities images, text, video, audio.

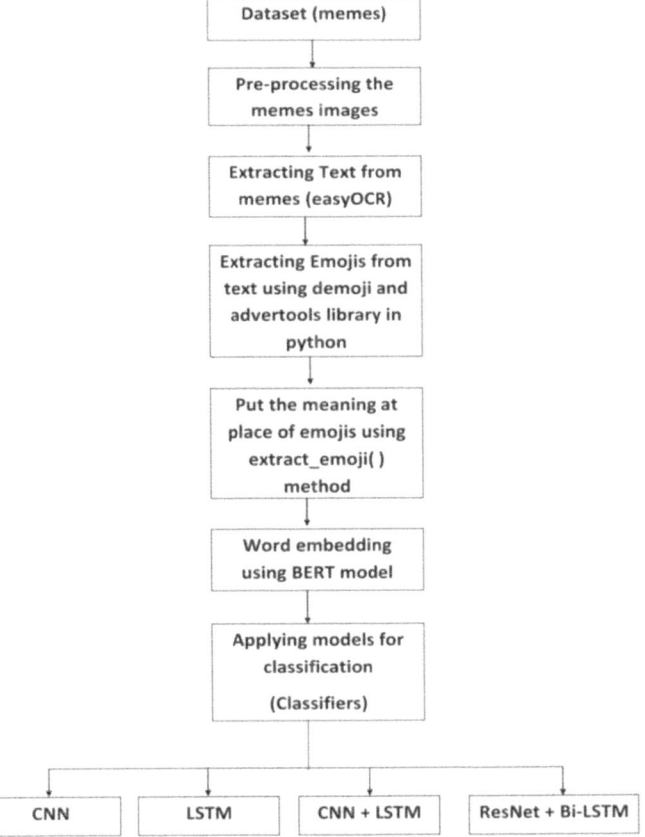

Fig. 1. Flow-diagram of proposed automated system (This diagram in given figure is made by author. It defines the flow of this proposed automated system.)

The proposed methodology consists of different steps which is shown in Fig. 1. Image processing, text extraction, emoji detection, preprocessing data, and at last applying models for the classification.

In the first step, image processing will focus on preprocessing the images for further process. The next step is to extract the text from the memes images which include the emojis. After that we will preprocess the data and we will do sentiment analysis in order to classify them accurately into their respective categories.

4   Flow Diagram of Proposed System

5   MEMEs Classification

5.1   PreProcessing of MEMEs Image

Preprocessing meme images for emotion detection involves loading the images and resizing them to a consistent size. Optionally, converting the images to grayscale, reducing noise, and enhancing contrast can be performed. Feature extraction is a crucial step, where deep learning features from pre-trained CNN models or handcrafted features like color histograms or texture descriptors are extracted. The extracted features are then normalized to a common scale. Finally, the preprocessed dataset is split into training, validation, and testing sets for model development and evaluation. Iteration and experimentation are important to tailor the preprocessing pipeline to the specific requirements

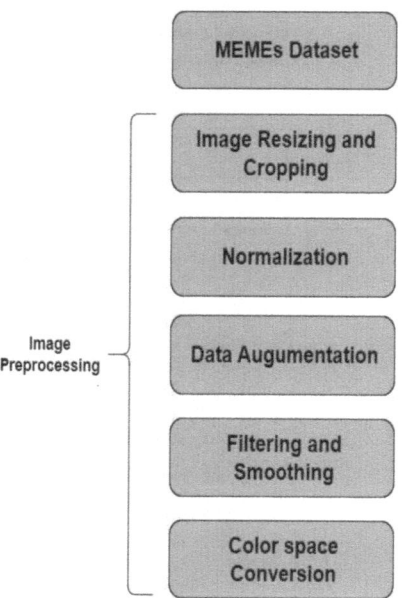

Fig. 2. Basic flow for image processing in MEMEs Detection (This diagram in given figure is made by author. It defines the flow of image processing part of proposed automated system)

of the task at hand. The whole sequence of this image preprocessing is shown in the figure below Fig. 2.

5.2 Extracting Text from MEMEs Image

Extracting text from meme images can be a challenging task, as memes often contain text that is overlaid on top of the image, with varying font sizes, colors, and backgrounds. However, there are several techniques that can be used to extract text from memes, such as easy OCR.

Easy OCR is a Python library that allows us to extract text from images using machine learning algorithms. It is a popular open-source OCR tool that is widely used due to its ease of use and high accuracy. The library is built on top of PyTorch, which is a popular deep learning framework.

Easy OCR works by using a deep learning model that has been trained on a large dataset of images and corresponding text. The model is designed to identify characters and words in an image, and then convert them into machine-readable text. The library can recognize text in multiple languages, including English, Chinese, Arabic, and many others.

To extract text from a meme image using EasyOCR, we must install the library and its dependencies via pip. Once installed, we can incorporate EasyOCR into our Python code to load an image, extract the text, and produce the desired output. Extracting text from meme images and detecting emotions using a hybrid deep learning approach. However, by employing appropriate techniques and leveraging suitable tools, it is feasible to attain precise and dependable results. The result from are automated system is shown in below figure Fig. 3.

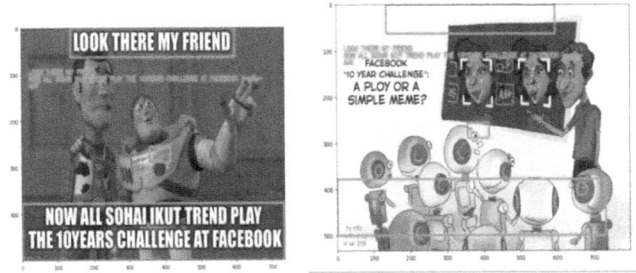

Fig. 3. Text Extraction from MEMEs Images using easy OCR method (This image is generated from the source code of this automated system/output of the source code)

5.3 Extracting Meaning of Emojis

After Pre-Processing of MEMEs images we use EasyOCR technique to extract text from MEMEs and we use demoji library of python for handling emojis and using extract_emoji() method we apply the meaning of emoji in text of MEMEs.

5.4 Text Preprocessing

Preprocessing text extracted from meme images for emotion detection involves several steps. The text processing system which is included in the automated system is shown in Fig. 4. Firstly, the raw text is cleaned by removing unnecessary characters, punctuation, and special symbols. Then, tokenization is applied to split the text into individual words or tokens. Stop words, such as common words like "and," "the," etc., are removed to reduce noise. Stemming or lemmatization techniques can be employed to normalize words to their base form. Furthermore, text can be encoded using techniques like one-hot encoding or word embeddings to represent the words numerically. These preprocessing steps help to prepare the text data for further analysis and emotion detection tasks.

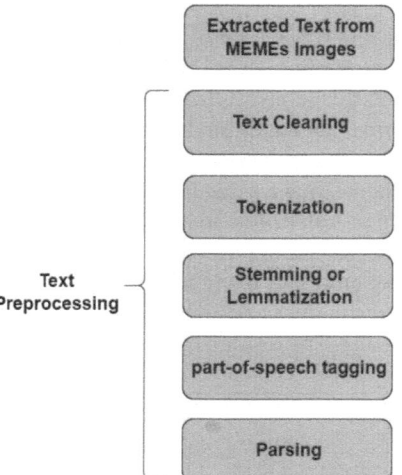

Fig. 4. General steps of Text Processing (This diagram in given figure is made by author. It defines the flow of text processing part of proposed automated system)

5.5 Word Embeddings of Text Using BERT Model

Word embeddings are a popular technique in natural language processing (NLP) that represent words as dense vectors in a high-dimensional space, where the position of a word in the space is based on its meaning and usage. The basic idea is to encode words as vectors that capture their semantic and syntactic properties, so that similar words are represented by vectors that are close together in the vector space.

To generate word embeddings for the extracted text, embedding model such as BERT, Word2Vec, Glove or Fast Text can be used. These models are trained on large amounts of text data and generate high-dimensional vector representations for words in the vocabulary. The extracted text from the MEMEs can be tokenized into words and each word can be represented by its corresponding word embedding.

BERT (Bidirectional Encoder Representations from Transformers) is a state-of-the-art deep learning model for natural language processing that uses transformer architecture to learn contextualized word embeddings. Which is shown in Fig. 5 [18].

To generate word embeddings for the extracted text from the MEMEs using BERT, the text can be tokenized into sub words and fed into the BERT model to obtain contextualized embeddings for each sub word. The contextualized embeddings capture the meaning and context of the words based on their position in the sentence and the surrounding words.

The contextualized embeddings can then be aggregated to obtain a fixed-length vector representation for the entire text. This can be done by averaging the embeddings or using a pooling technique such as max pooling or mean pooling. The resulting vector representation can then be fed into a deep learning model, such as a CNN or RNN, along with the visual features of the MEMEs to train a hybrid model that captures the interplay between the text and visual content in conveying emotions. The trained model can be used to predict the emotions conveyed in new MEMEs by generating contextualized embeddings for the text in the new MEMEs using BERT and feeding them into the trained hybrid model along with the visual features of the MEMEs.

Overall, using BERT to generate contextualized word embeddings for the extracted text in a hybrid deep learning approach can help improve the accuracy of detecting emotions in MEMEs by capturing the complex relationships between the words in the text and the visual content of the MEMEs.

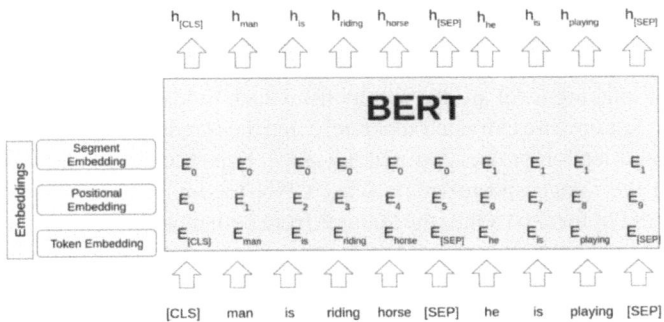

Fig. 5. Example of BERT model [18]

5.6 Deep Learning Models

LSTM model: We use BERT to convert words into vectors. We use truncate and pad the input sequences so that they are all in the same length for modeling. Here the first layer is the embedded layer that uses vectors to represent each word. The next Layer is the LSTM layer and the Activation function is softmax for multi-class classification. We train the model for 5 epochs and batch size as 64 for our learning model.

CNN model: Here we use BERT as word embedding. Then, we add the convolutional layer and max- pooling layer and we flatten those matrices into vectors and add dense.

After that we will fit our training data and define the epochs as 2 and batch size as 128 for our learning model.

CNN+LSTM model: We build a CNN+LSTM model using Keras' sequential API and add an embedding layer, a 1D convolutional layer, a max pooling layer, a dropout layer, an LSTM layer, and a dense output layer. We compile the model using binary cross- entropy loss and the Adam optimizer. We then train the model using the training set and evaluate its performance on the testing set. We will fit our training data and define the the epochs as 5 and batch size as 32 for our learning model.

ResNet+Bi-LSTM model: Here Three ResNet blocks and a bidirectional LSTM layer is used. The input to the model is a sequence of integers representing the words in the text, and the output is a probability distribution over the two classes. The model is compiled with the Adam optimizer and categorical cross-entropy loss, and accuracy is used as the evaluation metric.

5.7   Fusion Techniques

Early Fusion: Early Fusion combines raw data from different modalities (such as text and images) at the input stage before any significant feature extraction or processing is done. The data from both modalities are merged early on and passed through a unified processing pipeline. The raw features, like pixels from an image and word embeddings from text, are concatenated at the input level. This combined input is then processed by a single model that extracts features from the fused data. The approach attempts to model interactions between the modalities from the very beginning, allowing the model to learn correlations and dependencies between them from the start.

Late Fusion: In Late Fusion, each modality is processed independently, and only at the decision-making level are the results from each modality combined. Essentially, image and text features are extracted separately, and these independent results are merged in the final classification or decision-making stage. Separate models are used to extract features from the image and text data (e.g., CNN for images and a recurrent neural network like LSTM for text). Once the features from both modalities have been processed independently, the outputs are merged at the decision layer, such as through averaging, weighted sums, or voting mechanisms, to make the final prediction.

Intermediate Fusion: Intermediate Fusion strikes a balance between Early and Late Fusion. Here, features are partially processed in their respective modalities and then combined after some level of initial processing, but before the final decision-making layer. This allows for feature interactions while also retaining the flexibility of separate modality processing. The raw data from the image and text are processed separately up to a certain level (e.g., using CNNs for image features and NLP models like LSTMs for text). After extracting initial features, the data from both modalities are concatenated or merged. Further processing takes place on these fused features before reaching the final decision layer.

Joint Fusion: Joint Fusion, sometimes referred to as *continuous fusion*, integrates features from multiple modalities at various stages of the processing pipeline. Unlike the other approaches, where fusion happens only once (early, intermediate, or late), Joint Fusion continuously merges features from image and text throughout the model's layers. The model processes each modality separately, but the features are integrated at various points throughout the processing pipeline. As the model proceeds through each layer, it continuously fuses the information from both the image and text, allowing it to model interactions between modalities throughout the entire process (Table 1).

Table 1. Comparison of different fusion methods (This table is created by author. It shows the comparison of different fusion methods to connect different modalities data)

Fusion Type	When Fusion Happens	Advantages	Disadvantages
Early Fusion	At the Input stage	Strong interaction modeling from the start	High complexity, risk of losing valuable information
Late Fusion	At the decision-making stage	Simplicity and modularity	Limited interaction modeling between modalities
Intermediate Fusion	After some initial processing	Balanced approach, combines some benefits of both early and late fusion	Moderate complexity, deciding fusion point can be tricky
Joint Fusion	Throughout the pipeline	Maximized interaction, expressive model	Very high complexity, risk of overfitting

5.8 Performance Evaluation

In our proposed approach we use different deep learning as well as we combine them and use hybrid deep learning algorithms.

In the Implemented method we used Memotion Dataset 7k, hosted on Kaggle, is a publicly available dataset aimed at supporting emotion and sentiment analysis in memes. This dataset, released in 2020, is particularly relevant for research involving multimodal sentiment analysis, as it combines textual content and images (memes), making it a valuable resource for building hybrid models involving both Natural Language Processing (NLP) and Computer Vision (CV). The dataset contains 7,000 memes that have been labeled for various categories of emotions and sentiments. Each meme in the dataset is annotated with three levels of sentiment (positive, negative, neutral) and is further categorized by emotion, such as sarcastic, funny, offensive, or motivational. This detailed classification allows for fine-grained sentiment analysis and the study of complex emotions conveyed in memes (Table 2).

Based on the performance evaluation results you have provided, it appears that the ResNet+Bi-LSTM model outperformed the other models significantly, achieving an accuracy of 94.3%. This is followed by the CNN+LSTM model, which achieved an accuracy of 92.34%.

Table 2. Performance Evaluation of different models (This table is created by author. It shows the performance evaluation values, which is generated from the source code of proposed automated system).

Algorithms	Overall Accuracy
LSTM	88.72%
CNN	91.64%
CNN + LSTM	92.34%
ResNet + Bi-LSTM	94.3%

Overall, the ResNet+Bi-LSTM model leverages the benefits of residual connections, deep feature extraction, contextual understanding, and the fusion of multimodal information. These factors contribute to its superior performance compared to LSTM, CNN, and LSTM+CNN architectures in the domain of meme image emotion detection.

The CNN model achieved an accuracy of 91.64%, which suggests that the model may be able to capture the visual features of MEMEs effectively. However, the model may not be able to capture the sequential information in MEMEs effectively. On the other hand, the LSTM model achieved an accuracy of 88.72%, indicating that the model may not be able to capture both the visual and sequential features of MEMEs effectively.

In general, the performance of deep learning models for MEME detection can vary depending on various factors such as the quality and size of the training data, the complexity of the MEMEs, and the specific requirements of the task. Therefore, it is important to perform a comprehensive evaluation of different models using appropriate evaluation metrics to determine the most suitable model for the task at hand.

5.9   Conclusion and Future Work

As from this research, we can detect the hateful and non-hateful memes. In our approach we will be using an attention based model, emphasizing on visual and textual features and also we will include emojis.

In conclusion, meme emotion detection including emojis is an important task that can be accomplished through the use of various deep learning models. We have explored the performance of several models including CNN, LSTM, CNN+LSTM, and ResNet+Bi-LSTM for this task.

Based on our analysis, the ResNet+Bi-LSTM model achieved the best performance, with an accuracy of 94.3%. This model can effectively capture both the visual and sequential features of MEMEs, making it a strong candidate for MEME emotion detection tasks that include emojis.

The CNN+LSTM model also showed promising performance, achieving an accuracy of 92.34%. This model can effectively capture the visual and sequential features of MEMEs and may be suitable for MEME emotion detection tasks that involve the use of emojis. While the CNN and LSTM models also achieved reasonable performance, they may not be as effective in capturing both visual and sequential features simultaneously.

As such, they may be more suitable for tasks that focus on one of these features more than the other.

Overall, the choice of the most suitable deep learning model for MEME emotion detection including emojis will depend on the specific requirements of the task and the nature of the data. A comprehensive evaluation of the performance of different models using appropriate evaluation metrics can help in selecting the best model for the task at hand.

References

1. Jadhav, R., Honmane, V.N.: Memes classification system using computer vision and NLP techniques. Int. J. Eng. Appl. Sci. Technol. **6**(2), June 2021. https://doi.org/10.33564/ijeast. 2021.v06i02.025
2. Pimpalkar, A., Chaudhari, A., Lilhare, A., Dighorikar, N., Dakhole, S., Asawa, S.: Sentiment identification from image-based memes using machine learning. Int. J. Innov. Eng. Sci. **7**, 89–96 (2022). https://doi.org/10.46335/IJIES.2022.7.8.16
3. Shang, L., Zhang, Y., Zha, Y., Chen, Y., Youn, C., Wang, D.: AOMD: an analogy-aware approach to offensive meme detection on social media. Inf. Process. Manage. **58**, 102664 (2021). https://doi.org/10.1016/j.ipm.2021.102664
4. Hossain, E., Sharif, O., Moshiul Hoque, M., Ali Akber Dewan, M., Siddique, N., Azad Hossain, Md.: Identification of multilingual offense and troll from social media memes using weighted ensemble of multimodal features. J. King Saud Univ. – Comput. Inform. Sci. **34**(9), 6605–6623 (2022). ISSN 1319-1578. https://doi.org/10.1016/j.jksuci.2022.06.010
5. Smitha, E., Selvaraju, S., Mahalaksmi, G.: Meme classification using textual and visual features (2018). https://doi.org/10.1007/978-3-319-71767-8_87
6. Giri, R.K., Gupta, S.C., Gupta, U.K.: An approach to detect offence in Memes using Natural Language Processing (NLP) and deep learning. In: 2021 International Conference on Computer Communication and Informatics (ICCCI), pp. 1–5 (2021). https://doi.org/10.1109/ICC CI50826.2021.9402406
7. Fersini, E., Gasparini, F., Corchs, S.: Detecting sexist MEME on the web: a study on textual and visual cues. In: 2019 8th International Conference on Affective Computing and Intelligent Interaction Workshops and Demos (ACIIW), pp. 226–231 (2019). https://doi.org/10.1109/ ACIIW.2019.8925199
8. Zhang, K., Zhu, Y., Zhang, W., Zhu, Y.: Cross-modal image sentiment analysis via deep correlation of textual semantic. Knowl. - Based Syst. **216**, 106803 (2021). ISSN 0950-7051. https://doi.org/10.1016/j.knosys.2021.106803
9. Chen, Y., Pan, F.: Multimodal detection of hateful memes by applying a vision- language pre-training model (2022). https://doi.org/10.21203/rs.3.rs-1414253/v2
10. Lee, R.K.-W., Cao, R., Fan, Z., Jiang, J., Chong, W.: Disentangling hate in online memes, 51385147 (2021). https://doi.org/10.1145/3474085.3475625
11. Memotion Dataset 7k, 27 February 2020. Kaggle. https://www.kaggle.com/datasets/willia mscott701/memotion-dataset-7k/code
12. Full Emoji Database, 7 March 2021. Kaggle. https://www.kaggle.com/datasets/eliasdabbas/ emoji-data-descriptions-codepoints/code
13. Karthik, V., Nair, D., Anuradha, J.: Opinion mining on Emojis using deep learning techniques. Proc. Comput. Sci. **132**, 167–173 (2018). ISSN 1877-0509. https://doi.org/10.1016/j.procs. 2018.05.200

14. Ullah, M.A., Marium, S.M., Begum, S.A., Dipa, N.S.: An algorithm and method for sentiment analysis using the text and emoticon. ICT Express **6**(4), 357–360 (2020). ISSN 2405-9595. https://doi.org/10.1016/j.icte.2020.07.003.
15. Wang, H., Castanon, J.A.: Sentiment expression via emoticons on social media. In: 2015 IEEE International Conference on Big Data (Big Data), Santa Clara, CA, USA, pp. 2404–2408 (2015). https://doi.org/10.1109/BigData.2015.7364034
16. Yadav, P., Pandya, D.: SentiReview: Sentiment analysis based on text and emoticons. In: 2017 International Conference on Innovative Mechanisms for Industry Applications (ICIMIA), Bengaluru, India, pp. 467–472 (2017). https://doi.org/10.1109/ICIMIA.2017.7975659
17. Chatterjee, A., Gupta, U., Chinnakotla, M.K., Srikanth, R., Galley, M., Agrawal, P.: Understanding emotions in text using deep learning and big data. Comput. Hum. Behav. **93**, 309–317 (2019). ISSN 0747–5632. https://doi.org/10.1016/j.chb.2018.12.029
18. BERT Model Image. https://www.google.com/url?sa=i&url=https%3A%2F%2Fwww.analyt icsvidhya.com%2Fblog%2F2021%2F05%2Fall-you-need-to-know-about-bert%2F&psig= AOvVaw1nVdE325Gi1wdVwK6dlZqR&ust=1687839349170000&source=images&cd= vfe&ved=0CBEQjRxqFwoTCOCfjdqJ4P8CFQAAAAAdAAAAABAE

Parkinson's Disease Detection Using Advanced Wave Signal Processing on Spiral Drawing Tests

S. SasiRekha$^{(\boxtimes)}$, R. Shankar, and S. Duraisamy

Department of Computer Science, Chikkanna Government Arts College, Tirupur, India
ranjithrekha.17@gmail.com

Abstract. The main motor skills are impacted by Parkinson's disease (PD), a neurodegenerative ailment that is both chronic and progressive. The signs of this condition include tremors, stiffness, bradykinesia (slow movement), and postural instability. The degeneration of brain cells that produce dopamine is the root cause of these symptoms. This study introduces an innovative algorithmic framework for predicting Parkinson's disease (PD) using spiral drawing tests analyzed through advanced wave signal processing techniques. By collecting spiral drawings from patients via a digital tablet and converting these into wave signals, the framework employs three key algorithms: Wavelet Transform-Based Feature Extraction (WTFE), which decomposes signals into frequency bands to extract subtle features indicative of PD; a Gated Recurrent Unit with Long Short-Term Memory (GRU-LSTM) hybrid neural network that captures both short-term and long-term dependencies in the signal data to detect tremor patterns; and Hybrid Ensemble Classification (HEC), which integrates multiple classifiers—Support Vector Machines, Random Forests, and Gradient Boosting Machines—aggregated through a weighted voting scheme. Evaluated on a dataset of drawings from PD patients and healthy controls, the framework demonstrated high accuracy in distinguishing PD, suggesting it as a promising tool for early and objective diagnosis, thereby facilitating timely and effective intervention.

Keywords: Gradient Boosting Machines · Neurodegenerative Disorder · Random Forests · Support Vector Machines · Parkinson's disease · Wavelet Transform

1 Introduction

The neurological disorder known as PD is characterized by a variety of symptoms, including tremors, stiffness, bradykinesia, cognitive impairment, disrupted sleep, and depression [1, 2]. When measuring quantitative PD, doctors often turn to the unified PD Scale (UPDRS) [3]. It takes time and requires both the patient and the practitioner to be physically present throughout the evaluation [4]. There is an urgent want for remote-accessible screening alternatives. Hypokinetic dysarthria is one of the speech problems associated with Parkinson's disease [5]. There are probably others. A person's voice becomes less raspy, less audible, and less breathable as a result of Parkinson's disease

© The Author(s), under exclusive license to Springer Nature Switzerland AG 2025
S. Rajagopal et al. (Eds.): ASCIS 2024, CCIS 2424, pp. 35–53, 2025.
https://doi.org/10.1007/978-3-031-86290-8_3

[6]. It is possible to diagnose Parkinson's disease based on a variety of symptoms, one of which is pain. Since they are non-invasive and useful for online applications, researchers have investigated speech features for the purpose of detecting Parkinson's disease [6]. Furthermore, it provides a framework for impartially tracking the advancement of the illness. Using time-frequency characteristics taken from speech signals to distinguish between healthy and ill patients has been explored in several research. Pitch, autocorrelation, jitter, shimmer, breathing in speech, and pulse are some of the specifics [7].

The jitter and glow feature can identify transient changes in phonation, but it hasn't proven successful in simulating changes in severely damaged voices [8–10].Recent advances in deep learning for speech synthesis have yielded remarkable results, such as speech emotion identification and voice pathology diagnosis. Automated learning from massive data arrays and abstract models is within reach with deep learning [11, 12]. It encourages unsupervised raw-data learning and divides critical features pertinent to the study goals, in contrast to traditional machine learning methods [13, 14]. The primary motivation for this deep learning-based effort was to identify strategies to differentiate between typical and atypical voices in individuals with Parkinson's disease [15–17]. Because ANN can detect crucial data features for automatic signal categorization, it is ideal for use in voice-based PD diagnosis [18–20]. This tool takes digital spiral designs made by patients on tablets and turns them into wave signals using a GRU-LSTM, WTFE, and HEC hybrid neural network. This approach aims to enhance PD therapy by facilitating early intervention and a more accurate, objective diagnosis of the disease [21, 22].

The main contribution of the paper is

- Wavelet Transform-Based Feature Extraction
- Gated Recurrent Unit with Long Short-Term Memory
- Classification using Hybrid Ensemble Classification

For the remainder of the document, the structure is as follows. Several authors address various approaches to PD diagnosis in Sect. 2. We can see the proposed model in Sect. 3. Section 4 reviews the inquiry's findings. In Sect. 5, we evaluate the results and talk about where the study can go from here.

1.1 Motivation of the Paper

The urgent need for reliable and prompt detection of PD, a neurodegenerative illness characterized by crippling movement symptoms, is the driving force behind this research. Clinical observation and subjective evaluations are at the heart of traditional diagnostic procedures, which can cause significant delays in treatment. The efficacy of therapies and patients' quality of life might be greatly affected by this delay. This research seeks to produce a more objective, accurate, and automated diagnostic tool by using sophisticated wave signal processing methods and a novel algorithmic framework that utilizes spiral drawing tests.

2 Background Study

El Maachi, I. et al. [4] although confirming a Parkinson's diagnosis is technically impossible, the condition can be detected by a physical examination that takes into account a number of symptoms. We presented an approach to detect Parkinsonian gait and use gait data to forecast disease severity since gait disturbance is a significant motor symptom. To circumvent the problems associated with manually extracted features, our system employs deep learning techniques.

Gupta, I. et al. [5] This study presents the results of an examination of Random forest classification on a specific dataset that has 754 characteristics and is high dimensional. With respect to tabular data, random forest performs well, and this classifier seems to be the best fit for the data we have at the moment. The article also discusses the ways in which the accuracy of the suggested random forest model and the artificial neural network, in conjunction with principal component analysis, deviate from one another when given the same dataset. The comparative analysis has been represented at Table 1.

Table 1. Comparative Analysis of Machine Learning Approaches in Parkinson's disease Research

Author	Year	Methodology	Advantage	Limitation
Ahmadi Rastegar et al	2019	Machine learning with serum cytokines and Parkinson's progression prediction	Utilizes serum cytokines and machine learning for PD prediction	Limited to predicting PD progression rather than early diagnosis
Byeon	2020	Machine learning for depression prediction in PD	Focuses on predicting depression in PD patients	Limited to predicting depression and not PD onset
Dadu et al	2022	Machine learning for identifying PD subtypes and progression	Identifies PD subtypes and predicts disease progression	Can require extensive data and cannot capture nuances of individual patient progression
El Maachi et al	2020	Deep 1D-Convnet for PD detection and severity prediction from gait	Utilizes deep learning for accurate PD detection	Requires substantial computational resources and training data; cannot generalize well to diverse patient populations

Krishna, P. G., & StalinDavid, D. [6] There isn't always a certain test—like a blood test or an electrocardiogram—that can definitively tell a person whether they have Parkinson's disease. A blood test or electrocardiogram (ECG) is one of the particular tests needed to diagnose Parkinson's disease. This complex problem is addressed by using the proposed ML driven LDR method to the classification of Parkinson's illness. Patients' quality of life will be enhanced as a result of better treatment and disease management made possible by early identification of Parkinson's disease.

Mall, P. et al. [8] It is critical that cardiac arrest gets extra attention in modern culture since it was the cause of about 6,17,000 deaths in 2017. Early PD prognosis and preventative measures are necessary to prevent deaths from happening sooner. The results demonstrate that compared to other ML algorithms, our recommended technique outperforms them. The purpose of this comparison research is to assess their accuracy, MCC, and f1score. After looking at it, we found that our proposed solution outperformed competing machine learning techniques.

Rasheed, J. et al. [14] efficiently distinguishing between health instances and Parkinson's Diseases was the primary goal of this strategy. How to increase the accuracy of the categorization was the primary obstacle. We used two enhanced ANN variants, BPVAM and BPVAM-PCA, to accomplish this goal. The extremely unique feature set obtained via principal component analysis (PCA) aided BPVAM's rapid pattern learning. When it came to identifying PD, both approaches achieved excellent classification accuracy.

2.1 Problem Definition

Early identification is crucial for optimal therapy of PD, a neurodegenerative condition characterized by movement deficits that progresses over time. Delays in intervention are commonplace since traditional diagnostic approaches often depend on subjective clinical findings. Machine learning classifiers like SVMs, RFs, and GBMs have all been used for PD detection, but they all have their drawbacks. SVMs, for example, have trouble handling big datasets and are kernel-sensitive; RFs, while robust, might get harder to understand as the number of trees increases; and GBMs, on the other hand, are hyperparameter-sensitive and need careful tuning. These problems show how much better an integrated strategy would be.

3 Materials and Methods

In this section, the proposed method is presented as an innovative approach to predicting PD using spiral drawing tests and advanced wave signal processing techniques. The method involves collecting spiral drawings from patients via a digital tablet and converting them into wave signals.

3.1 Dataset Collection

The dataset used in this study is the *Parkinson's Disease Data Set* collected from Kaggle, which serves as the foundation for training and evaluating the proposed algorithmic framework for predicting Parkinson's disease (PD) using spiral drawing tests and advanced wave signal processing techniques. This dataset consists of 195 instances and 24 features, including fundamental frequency (MDVP (Hz)), maximum and minimum frequencies (MDVP (Hz) and MDVP (Hz)), jitter measurements (MDVP (%) and MDVP (Abs)), amplitude variations (MDVP and MDVP (dB)), noise-to-harmonics ratio (MDVP), and a binary class label indicating PD patients or healthy controls (status). The comprehensive nature and relevance of this dataset to PD research make it a valuable resource for exploring innovative approaches to disease prediction and diagnosis (https://www.kaggle.com/datasets/vikasukani/parkinsons-disease-data-set) (Fig. 1).

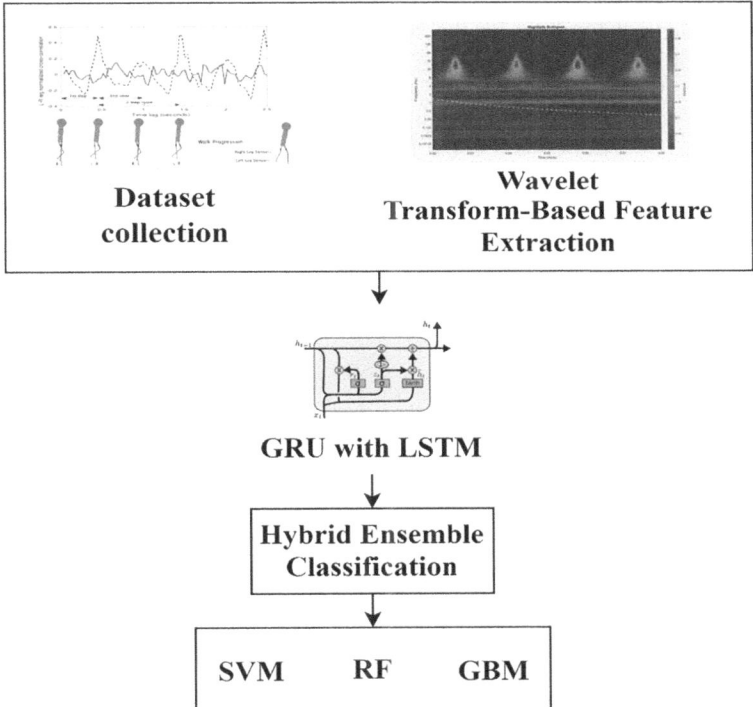

Fig. 1. PD disease prediction flow architecture

3.2 Wavelet Transform-Based Feature Extraction

Due to its small support, wavelets have found utility in the depiction and analysis of several physiological data, including ECG and ABP signals. Isolated pulses or pulse sequences are reasonable ways to describe these physiological signals referred by Sahoo, S. et al. (2017). A signal's energy is concentrated in a limited number of coefficients after a wavelet transform, which makes wavelet-based approaches a potentially strong tool for algorithms that analyze signals. Because of the nature of the wavelet algorithm, it is possible to automatically remove the kind of background noise that is common in healthcare settings.

The mother wavelet, a collection of highpass and lowpass filters formed from the coefficient wavelet, is used to execute a dyadic wavelet transform. We refer to these filters as analytical filters. The results of a highpass filter are a detail signal, whereas those of a lowpass filter are an average signal. Both the original signal's small-scale and large-scale components make up these created signals. To provide an additional detail signal and average signal, the lowpass filter coefficient is subsampled. The dyadic discrete wavelet transform is therefore the product of the mother wavelet's enlarged and translated forms. Wecan keep breaking the signal down in this way until the average signal length is either too long for the analysis filter pair to be useful anymore or too short for a single sample.

$$w_a x(b) = \frac{1}{\sqrt{a}} \int_{\infty}^{\infty} x(t)\psi\left(\frac{t-b}{a}\right)dt \tag{1}$$

$w_a x(b)$: Represents the wavelet transform of the signal $x(t)$ at scale a and position b.
a: Scaling parameter that controls the width of the wavelet function.
b: Translation parameter that shifts the wavelet function along the time axis.
$x(t)$: Original signal being transformed.
ψ: Mother wavelet function used for decomposition.

$$w_a x(b) = -a\frac{d}{db}\int_{\infty}^{\infty} x(t)\theta_a(t-b)dt \tag{2}$$

$\theta_a(t-b)$: Scaled version of the smoothing function used in the wavelet transform.

The temporal resolution is reduced by a factor of 2 with each decomposition, but the frequency resolution is doubled. Only optimal half-band filters, like Daubechies set of wavelets, allow for perfect signal reconstruction. Reversing the normal sequence of decomposition is done for the aim of rebuilding. After collecting wavelet coefficients at each level, they are double-upsampled, sent through two synthesis filters—one each for high pass and low pass—and then put together. With the only difference being the order of execution, the analysis and synthesis filters are functionally equivalent.

Algorithm 1: Wavelet Transform

Input:

1. **Input Signal:** The input signal, denoted as x(t)x(t)x(t), represents the physiological data, such as spiral drawings, in the context of Parkinson's disease detection.

Steps:

☐ **Dyadic Wavelet Transform:**

- Implement a dyadic wavelet transform using highpass and lowpass filters derived from the mother wavelet.

$$w_a x(b) = \frac{1}{\sqrt{a}} \int_{\infty}^{\infty} x(t)\psi\left(\frac{t-b}{a}\right)dt$$

- Apply the highpass filter to generate the detail signal (high-frequency components) and the lowpass filter to generate the average signal (low-frequency components).

☐ **Decomposition and Subsampling:**

- Decompose the signal into smaller scale (detail signal) and larger scale (average signal) information.
- Subsample the lowpass filter output to generate new detail and average signals, continuing the decomposition process.

☐ **Wavelet Transform Calculation:**

- The wavelet transform $w_a x(b)$ represents the coefficients that capture signal characteristics at different scales.

☐ **Signal Reconstruction (Inverse DWT):**

- Upsample the wavelet coefficients obtained from each level of decomposition by two.
- Pass the upsampled coefficients through synthesis filters (high pass and low pass) in reverse order.
- Add the filtered outputs to reconstruct the original signal, achieving perfect reconstruction with ideal half band filters.

Output:

1. **Wavelet Coefficients:** The main output of the wavelet transform process is a set of wavelet coefficients that capture the signal's characteristics at different scales.

3.3 Gated Recurrent Unit with Long Short-Term Memory

The architecture of the gate unit dictates how time series data is handled. Even if the settings aren't ideal for training, we can still see some gradient. Extended period. In contrast to LSTM neural networks, GRU models are another option referred by ArunKumar, K. E. et al. (2021). An improvement to the LSTM's design is the consolidation of the three gating units into one update gate and one reset gate (Fig. 2).

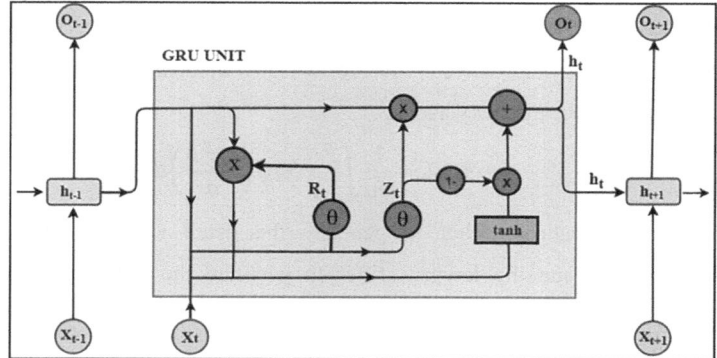

Fig. 2. The neuronal structure of GRU

The implicit, input, and output levels make up the GRU model. Neurons from GRU are used by hidden layers. Data obtained at time t is sent into the GRU neural network after data preprocessing. Always keep in mind that the data being inputted into the system is data that is organized over time.

$$r_t = \sigma\left(w_r * \left[h_{t-1}, x_t\right]\right) \tag{3}$$

r_t Output of the reset gate at time t.
σ Sigmoid activation function.
w_r Weight between the input and the previous hidden state h_{t-1}.
h_{t-1}, x_t Concatenation of the previous hidden state and the input at time t.

$$z_t = \sigma\left(w_z * \left[h_{t-1}, x_t\right]\right) \tag{4}$$

z_t: Output of the update gate at time t.
w_z: Weight between the input and the previous hidden state h_{t-1}.

$$n_t = tanh(h_{t-1} + z_t) * h_{t-1} + z_t * n_t \tag{5}$$

n_t New candidate value vector (hidden state) at time t.
tanh Hyperbolic tangent activation function.

$$y_t = \sigma(w_o * h_t) \tag{6}$$

As shown in the following computation, the GRU model has the potential to accomplish long-distance important information preservation by reducing the number of gating units, continually rejecting redundant input, and maintaining information dependencies in the hidden state.

$$r_t = \sigma\left(w_r * \left[h_{t-1}, x_t\right]\right) \tag{7}$$

$$z_t = \sigma\left(w_z * \left[h_{t-1}, x_t * r_t\right]\right) \tag{8}$$

Among other things, the formula uses symbols like z_t and r_t to represent standard GRU neurons. Different from GRU neurons, LSTM neurons mask the state weight by multiplying r_t and the prior time at the update gate z_t.

Algorithm 2: Gated Recurrent Unit with Long Short-Term Memory

Input:

1. **Input Sequence:** The input data to the Gated Recurrent Unit (GRU) neural network is a time series sequence denoted as $(x1, x2, \ldots, xt)$, where each x_t represents a data point at time t.

Steps:

☐ **Reset Gate Calculation (r_t):**

- Calculate the output of the reset gate r_t using the sigmoid activation function.

☐ **Candidate Hidden State Calculation (n_t):**

- Calculate the new candidate hidden state n_t using the hyperbolic tangent (tanh) activation function.

- Combine the past hidden state $h_{\{t-1\}}$h with the candidate information to update the current hidden state h_t.

Output:

Improved Predicted Output: The output of the LSTM model y_t is enhanced compared to standard GRU due to the optimization of the update gate, resulting in improved learning efficiency and prediction accuracy.

3.4   Hybrid Ensemble Classification

3.4.1   Support Vector Machines

Using the kernel function, instances can be moved to a higher-dimensional space when it would be impossible to retain them where they are referred by Shahbakhi, M. et al. (2014). By establishing a direct connection between the input space and the higher-dimensional space via a kernel function, it is possible to reduce the computational cost of operating in such a space without computing all of its components. Support vector machines select a hyperplane in higher-dimensional space with the maximum feasible soft margin in order to categorize the training instances. In order to categorize a test sample, the parameters of the hyperplane are used to generate the sign function. The support vectors are training samples that are closest to the target.

If the hyperplane effectively divides the collection of vectors, and the maximum distance is measured between the vectors closest to the hyperplane, then we can claim that the separation was optimal. Accurately (without compromising generalizability) examining a canonical hyperplane constrained by w and b values

$$\min_i | < w, x^i > +b| = 1 \tag{9}$$

A regularization parameter 'C' can be used to modify the trade-off between training error reduction and profit maximization. "Soft margin" is the name we give to this. Kernel for the input space of an inner product in the range of features

$$K(x, x) = < j(x), j(x) > \tag{10}$$

Non-linear modeling is where a polynomial mapping comes in.,

$$K(x, x) = < x, x >^d \tag{11}$$

the degree of the polynomial is denoted by d. Recent years have seen a surge in interest for radial basis functions, particularly ones that use a Gaussian of the type

$$K(x, x) = \exp - \frac{||x - x||^2}{2\sigma^2} \tag{12}$$

An elliptical base A piecewise linear solution is obtained whenever the function's graph breaks are permitted.

3.4.2   Random Forest

Here is a rundown of the filtering procedure. The statistical method is used in the filtering method to assign weights to characteristics, rank features according to those weights, apply rules to set a threshold, and then retain features with weights greater than the threshold and delete those with lower values referred by Byeon, H. (2020). Regardless of the particular classification technique, the data set's features govern the filtering method's feature selection process. Many popular filtering techniques are available, including Fisher ratio, information gain, T-test, variance analysis, and Relief. Here we shall provide a basic introduction to variance analysis.

$$BBS = \sum_i n_i (y_i - y_{total})^2 \tag{13}$$

Intra group variation:

$$WSS = \sum_i \sum_j (y_{ij} - y_i)^2 \tag{14}$$

Mean squared differences across groups are bigger when the F value is higher than when it is less. It also means that the differences between the groups are much larger than the total expected value deviation.

3.4.3 Gradient Boosting Machines

Boosting algorithms iteratively merge weak learners—those that do marginally better than chance—into a strong learner referred by Karabayir, I. et al. (2020). One regression approach that is similar to boosting is gradient boosting. A weighted sum of functions is used to approximate F $\prod$ (x) in gradient boosting, which generates an additive approximation.

$$F_m(x) = F_{m-1}(x) + p_m h_m(x) \tag{15}$$

where $h_m(x)$ is the mth function, and ρm is its weight. These operations represent the ensemble's models, such as decision trees. An iterative process is used to develop the approximation. At first, we get a constant approximation of $F_0(x)$ by

$$F_0(x) = argmin \sum\nolimits_{i=1}^{N} L(y_i, \ a) \tag{16}$$

If the iterative procedure is not appropriately regularized, this technique can experience over-fitting. If the model h_m matches the pseudo-residuals completely for certain loss functions, then the process stops prematurely in the following iteration when the pseudo-residuals reach zero. In order to manage the additive gradient boosting process, many regularization factors are taken into account.

3.4.4 Hybrid Ensemble Classification

One method for improving prediction accuracy in machine learning is Hybrid Ensemble Classification, which integrates many methods. Hybrid ensembles better generalize on unseen data by combining multiple approaches to manage varying data complexity and lower the danger of overfitting (Fig. 3).

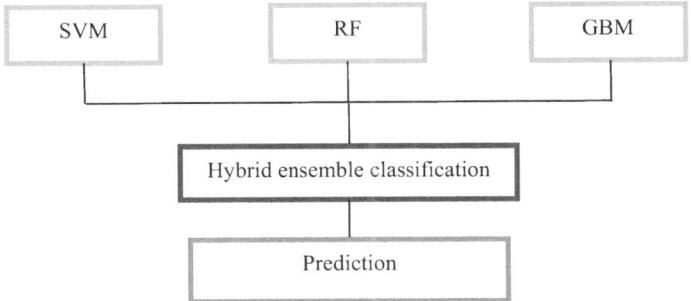

Fig. 3. Hybrid ensemble classification architecture

Algorithm 3: Hybrid Ensemble Classification

Input:

Training Dataset:A labeled training dataset with input characteristics and their matching target labels is fed into the algorithm.

Steps:

☐ **Support Vector Machines (SVM):**

- They optimize a hyperplane to maximize the margin between different classes, aiming for optimal separation.

  $K(x, x) = < j(x), j(x) >$

- The soft margin parameter 'C' is used to balance between maximizing the margin and minimizing classification errors.

☐ **Random Forest (RF):**

- RF employs a filtering method to rank features based on their statistical significance using methods like variance analysis, Fisher ratio, etc.

  $WSS = \sum_i \sum_j (y_{ij} - y_i)^2$

- It selects relevant features by setting a threshold based on their weights, discarding less important ones.

☐ **Gradient Boosting Machines (GBM):**

- GBM iteratively builds an ensemble of weak learners to minimize the loss function and approximate the target function.

  $F_0(x) = argmin \sum_{i=1}^{N} L(y_i, a)$

- Regularization parameters are used to control overfitting during the iterative process, ensuring the model generalizes well.

Output:

Combined Predictions: The hybrid ensemble combines predictions from multiple classifiers (SVM, RF, GBM) using a weighted voting scheme or other aggregation methods.

---

4 Results and Discussion

Here we detail our study's findings and talk about what they mean for Parkinson's disease prediction with the use of the algorithmic framework we suggested. The implementation has been done with python.

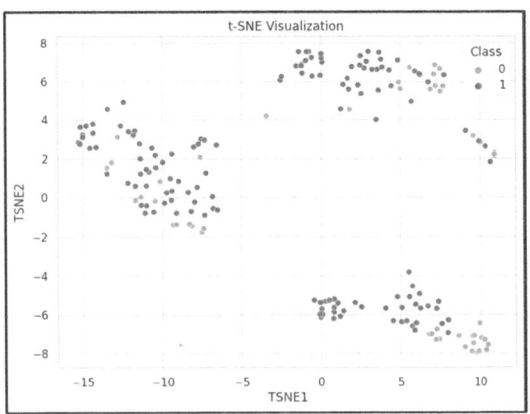

Fig. 4. Visualization graph

Check out Fig. 4 for the visual representation. The x-axis represents TSNE1, while the y-axis represents TSEN 2.

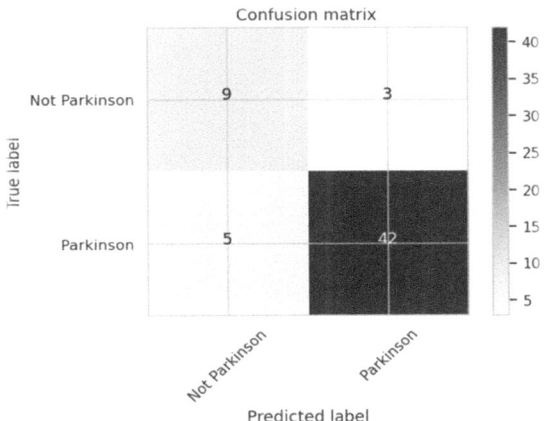

Fig. 5. Confusion matrix

The confusion matrix is shown in Fig. 5. On one side, we have the projected label, while on the other, we have the actual label.

We can see a comparison of training accuracy in Fig. 6. The x-axis displays the number of epochs, while the y-axis displays the value of the training accuracy.

Displayed in Fig. 7 is the validation loss Epochs are shown on the x-axis, while the validation loss value is shown on the y-axis.

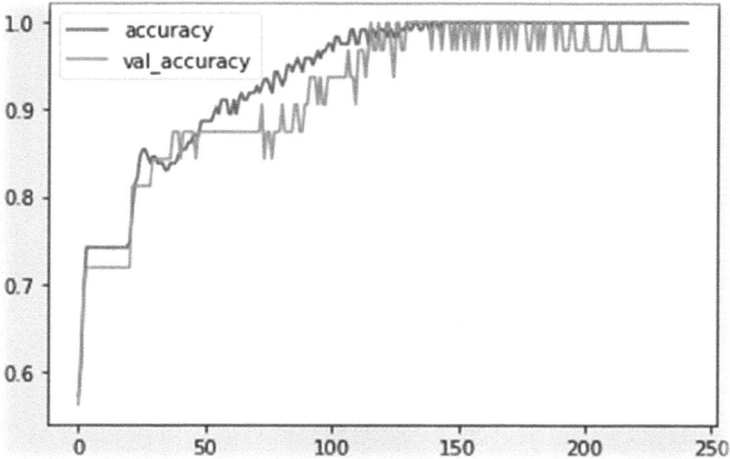

Fig. 6. Training accuracy comparison chart

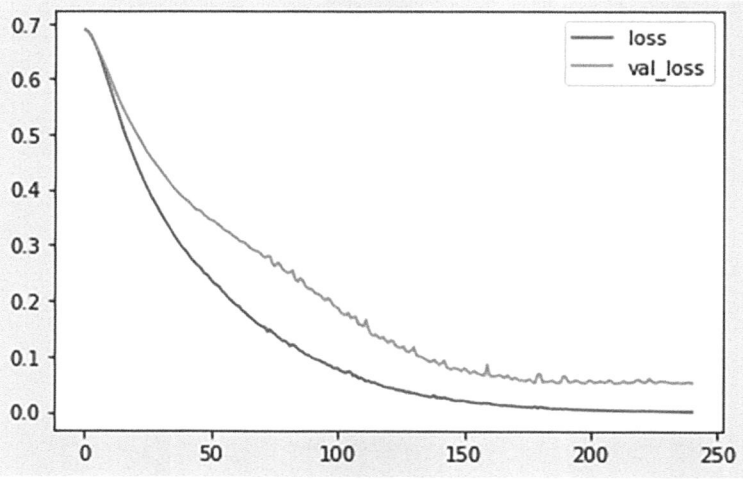

Fig. 7. validation loss.

The Table 2 shows the effectiveness of the different classification algorithms in predicting Parkinson's disease. Support Vector Machines (SVM) achieved a high accuracy of 94.36%, demonstrating strong overall performance with balanced precision (95.47%) and recall (95.21%), resulting in an F-measure of 95.89%. Random Forests (RF) slightly outperformed SVM with an accuracy of 95.51% and a notable F-measure of 96.01%, indicating its ability to handle class imbalances effectively. Gradient Boosting Machines (GBM) showed further improvement with an accuracy of 96.24% and the highest F-measure among individual classifiers at 96.38%, highlighting its robustness in capturing

Table 2. Classification performance metrics comparison table

Methods	Accuracy	Precision	Recall	F-measure
SVM	94.36	95.47	95.21	95.89
RF	95.51	96.31	96.84	96.01
GBM	96.24	96.89	97.52	96.38
HEC	98.87	97.84	98.81	98.25

complex relationships within the data. The Hybrid Ensemble Classification (HEC) model significantly outshined the individual classifiers with an impressive accuracy of 98.87%, demonstrating the synergistic effect of combining SVM, RF, and GBM. HEC also exhibited superior precision (97.84%), recall (98.81%), and F-measure (98.25%), indicating its capability in accurately identifying Parkinson's disease cases while minimizing false positives and negatives. Overall, these results validate the effectiveness of the proposed algorithmic framework in achieving high accuracy and reliability in Parkinson's disease prediction.

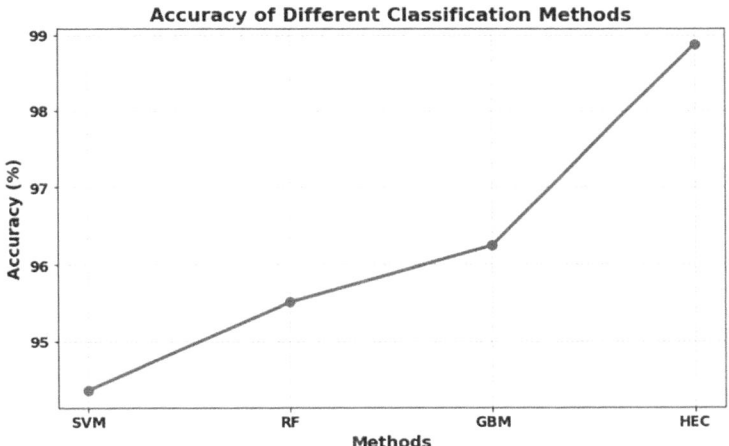

Fig. 8. Accuracy value comparison chart

Figure 8 is a representation of the degrees of accuracy in a chart. Both the procedures and the accuracy value are shown here.

Figure 9 shows a table that compares different degrees of accuracy. The accuracy figures are on the opposite side of the techniques.

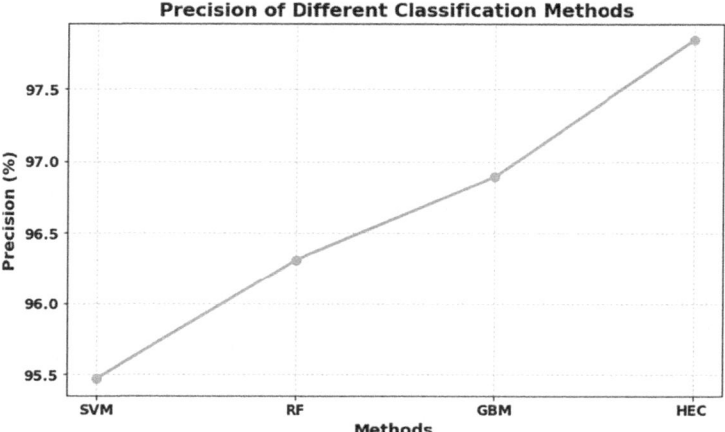

Fig. 9. Precision value comparison chart

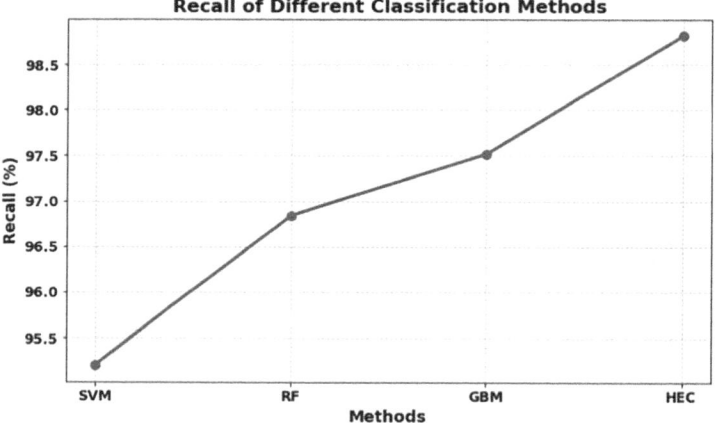

Fig. 10. Recall comparison chart

Wecan see a recall comparison chart in Fig. 10. The techniques are shown on the x-axis, while the recall value is shown on the y-axis.

In Fig. 11, we can see a table comparing the values of the F-measure. The f-measure value is presented on the y-axis, while the methods are shown on the x-axis.

F-measure of Different Classification Methods

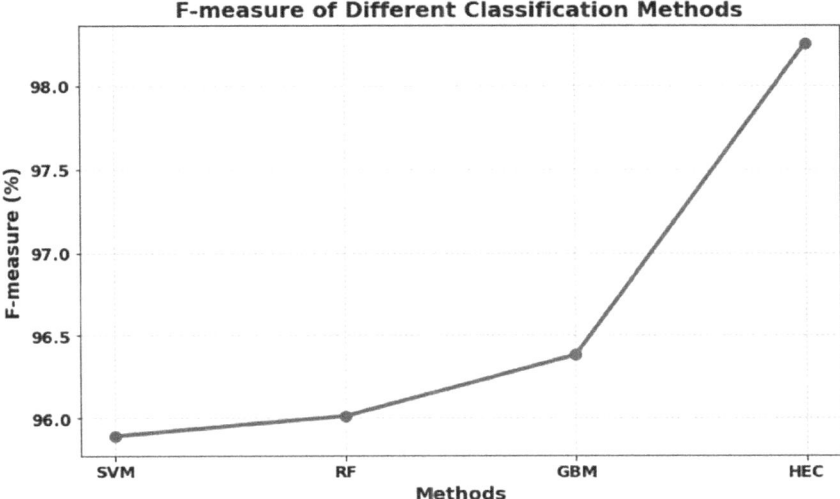

Fig. 11. F-measure value comparison chart

5 Conclusion

The proposed algorithmic framework for predicting Parkinson's disease using spiral drawing tests and advanced wave signal processing techniques shows great promise in enhancing early diagnosis. By leveraging the Wavelet Transform-Based Feature Extraction (WTFE) for precise feature extraction, the GRU-LSTM hybrid neural network for capturing dependencies in signal data, and the Hybrid Ensemble Classification (HEC) for robust classification, this approach achieves high accuracy in distinguishing PD patients from healthy controls. The Hybrid Ensemble Classification (HEC) model significantly outshined the individual classifiers with an impressive accuracy of 98.87%, demonstrating the synergistic effect of combining SVM, RF, and GBM. HEC also exhibited superior precision (97.84%), recall (98.81%), and F-measure (98.25%), indicating its capability in accurately identifying Parkinson's disease cases while minimizing false positives and negatives. The results suggest that this innovative and objective diagnostic tool can significantly improve the early detection and management of Parkinson's disease, ultimately leading to better patient outcomes through timely intervention and tailored treatment strategies. Future research directions for the proposed algorithmic framework in predicting Parkinson's disease (PD) could include conducting longitudinal studies to monitor symptom progression, validating the model across diverse populations, and integrating additional biomarkers for a more comprehensive diagnosis.

References

1. Ahmadi Rastegar, D., Ho, N., Halliday, G.M., Dzamko, N.: Parkinson's progression prediction using machine learning and serum cytokines. NPJ Parkinson's disease **5**(1), 14 (2019)

2. Byeon, H.: Development of a depression in Parkinson's disease prediction model using machine learning. World Journal of Psychiatry **10**(10), 234 (2020)
3. Dadu, A., et al.: Identification and prediction of Parkinson's disease subtypes and progression using machine learning in two cohorts. npj Parkinson's Disease **8**(1), 172 (2022)
4. El Maachi, I., Bilodeau, G.A., Bouachir, W.: Deep 1D-convnet for accurate parkinson disease detection and severity prediction from gait. Expert Syst. Appl. **143**, 113075 (2020)
5. Gupta, I., Sharma, V., Kaur, S., Singh, A.K.: PCA-RF: An Efficient Parkinson's Disease Prediction Model based on Random Forest Classification. *arXiv preprint* arXiv:2203.11287 (2022)
6. Krishna, P.G., StalinDavid, D.: An effective parkinson's disease prediction using logistic decision regression and machine learning with big data. Turkish Journal of Physiotherapy and Rehabilitation **32**(3), 778–786 (2021)
7. Makarious, M.B., et al.: Multi-modality machine learning predicting Parkinson's disease. npj Parkinson's Disease **8**(1), 35 (2022)
8. Mall, P.K., Yadav, R.K., Rai, A.K., Narayan, V., Srivastava, S.: Early warning signs of parkinson's disease prediction using machine learning technique. Journal of Pharmaceutical Negative Results, pp. 4784–4792 ((2022))
9. Islam, M.A., Majumder, M.Z.H., Hussein, M.A., Hossain, K.M., Miah, M.S.: A review of machine learning and deep learning algorithms for Parkinson's disease detection using handwriting and voice datasets. Heliyon (2024)
10. Nahar, N., Ara, F., Neloy, M.A.I., Biswas, A., Hossain, M.S., Andersson, K.: Feature selection based machine learning to improve prediction of Parkinson disease. In Brain Informatics: 14th International Conference, BI 2021, Virtual Event, September 17–19, 2021, Proceedings 14, pp. 496–508. Springer International Publishing (2021)
11. Peng, J., Guan, J., Shang, X.: Predicting Parkinson's disease genes based on node2vec and autoencoder. Front. Genet. **10**, 441295 (2019)
12. Phongpreecha, T., et al.: Multivariate prediction of dementia in Parkinson's disease. npj Parkinson's Disease **6**(1), 20 (2020)
13. Poplawska-Domaszewicz, K., Limbachiya, N., Lau, Y.H., Chaudhuri, K.R.: Parkinson's kinetigraph for wearable sensor detection of clinically unrecognized early-morning akinesia in parkinson's disease: a case report-based observation. Sensors **24**(10), 3045 (2024)
14. Rasheed, J., Hameed, A.A., Ajlouni, N., Jamil, A., Özyavaş, A., Orman, Z.: Application of adaptive back-propagation neural networks for Parkinson's disease prediction. In: 2020 International Conference on Data Analytics for Business and Industry: Way Towards a Sustainable Economy (ICDABI), pp. 1–5. IEEE (2020)
15. Salmanpour, M.R., et al.: Machine learning methods for optimal prediction of motor outcome in Parkinson's disease. PhysicaMedica **69**, 233–240 (2020)
16. Schrag, A., Anastasiou, Z., Ambler, G., Noyce, A., Walters, K.: Predicting diagnosis of Parkinson's disease: a risk algorithm based on primary care presentations. Mov. Disord. **34**(4), 480–486 (2019)
17. Serrao, M., et al.: Prediction of responsiveness of gait variables to rehabilitation training in Parkinson's disease. Front. Neurol. **10**, 826 (2019)
18. Sardar, S., Pahari, S.: A study to find affordable ai techniques for early parkinson's disease detection. In: Intelligent Technologies and Parkinson's Disease: Prediction and Diagnosis, pp. 20–51. IGI Global (2024)
19. ArunKumar, K.E., Kalaga, D.V., Kumar, C.M.S., Kawaji, M., Brenza, T.M.: Forecasting of COVID-19 using deep layer recurrent neural networks (RNNs) with gated recurrent units (GRUs) and long short-term memory (LSTM) cells. Chaos Solitons Fractals **146**, 110861 (2021)

20. Pallathadka, H., et al.: Applicability of artificial intelligence in smart healthcare systems for automatic detection of Parkinson's Disease. Computer Assisted Methods in Engineering and Science **31**(2) (2024)
21. Byeon, H.: Is the random forest algorithm suitable for predicting parkinson's disease with mild cognitive impairment out of parkinson's disease with normal cognition? Int. J. Environ. Res. Public Health **17**(7), 2594 (2020)
22. Karabayir, I., Goldman, S.M., Pappu, S., Akbilgic, O.: Gradient boosting for Parkinson's disease diagnosis from voice recordings. BMC Med. Inform. Decis. Mak.Mak. **20**, 1–7 (2020)

Vehicle Density Estimation Using Improved Yolov8 Object Detection Model with Kernel Density Estimation

K. Mohanapriya(✉), R. Shankar, and S. Duraisamy

Department of Computer Science, Chikkanna Government Arts College, Tirupur, Tamilnadu, India
mohanapriyaphd1990@gmail.com

Abstract. Accurate vehicle density estimation is crucial for effective traffic management and urban planning. This paper introduces a novel adaptive vehicle density estimation framework that integrates an improved YOLOv8 object detection model with Kernel Density Estimation (KDE). The proposed system aims to provide high-precision, real-time vehicle density analysis to enhance intelligent transportation systems. The core of our approach is the improved YOLOv8 model, specifically optimized for vehicle detection. Enhancements include the incorporation of spatial attention mechanisms and fine-tuning on extensive vehicle datasets, leading to superior detection accuracy and reduced false positives. This robust detection capability is critical for accurately identifying and localizing vehicles in diverse traffic conditions. Once vehicles are detected, their positions are mapped onto a grid covering the region of interest. KDE is then applied to these positions to generate a smooth and continuous vehicle density map. This statistical method effectively captures the spatial distribution of vehicles, offering a more precise density estimation compared to traditional grid-based methods. The resulting density map is crucial for understanding traffic flow and congestion patterns. The system is designed to be adaptive, continuously learning from new data to refine its parameters and improve estimation accuracy. By deploying the algorithm on edge computing devices, the system achieves real-time processing capabilities, enabling immediate responses to changing traffic conditions. Experimental results on real-world traffic datasets demonstrate the proposed framework's effectiveness, showcasing significant improvements in both accuracy and processing speed over existing methods. The integration of an improved YOLOv8 model with KDE not only enhances vehicle detection and density estimation but also provides a scalable and efficient solution for modern traffic management systems.

Keywords: Improved YOLOv8 · Kernel Density Estimation · Processing speed · Traffic management · Vehicle density estimation

1 Introduction

One of the key indicators used to analyze the road traffic situation is vehicle density. The density of traffic as a function of distance is what it measures. If there are a lot of cars on the road, it typically means that traffic is heavy, and if there aren't, it usually means that traffic is light referred by [1]. There are a number of ways to determine the vehicle density. Nevertheless, an expensive framework is necessary to get such data [2]. Also, the majority of today's traffic information systems use an outdated paradigm of centralized communication, whereby a single computer processes all the data gathered about traffic and then returns the results to the drivers out on the road [3]. A new self-organizing traffic information system cannot be served by this method of processing and disseminating data [4]. The identification of vehicle density—the quantity of autos per unit length of road—has garnered a growing amount of attention from both academics and businesses in the context of traffic congestion studies [5]. Despite some success, this job remains difficult because to issues including low-resolution data and the great variability in vehicle scanning methods [6]. It is already a challenging task, and the presence of occlusions makes it much more so [7]. Tracking data from automobiles has been utilized in earlier research to either pinpoint individual vehicles or provide rough estimates of their numbers [8].

This is why these methods can struggle with low frame rates or a lack of motion data. The use of density maps in regression analysis for vehicle density identification has grown in popularity among academics in the last several years [9]. Because of their pixel-level auto-estimation capabilities, convolutional neural networks (CNNs) find frequent usage in this context [10]. The model must take into consideration spatial components that cross scales, as shown by the red arrows, which demonstrate the scale's constant variation during the trip [11]. Also, we need to keep the final density map as high-resolution as feasible to save as many characteristics as possible, since the low-resolution frames need it [12]. Scale representation using convolutional neural network (CNN) methods has recently been enhanced using multicolumn and multibranch architectures [13]. These theories are dependent on static receptive fields and can only explain size variations under certain circumstances [14]. In addition, the majority of density regression problems often include pixel-wise Euclidean loss. Assuming that pixels are completely unconnected to one another, they calculate the loss using the whole picture rather than taking into account the local pattern [15].

Research into traffic management has become more important due to the exponential increase in the density of traffic on highways.YOLOv8, short for "You Only Look Once version 8," is an advanced object detection model renowned for its speed and accuracy in real-time detection tasks [16]. It belongs to the family of one-stage object detectors, which means it can detect objects in an image directly, without the need for a separate region proposal network [17]. YOLOv8 builds upon the success of its predecessors by incorporating various enhancements, such as improved backbone architectures, attention mechanisms, and advanced optimization techniques [18]. Volume, velocity, and density are the three usual measures used to evaluate traffic conditions. Digital cameras are also often used for this [19]. While current approaches can quickly identify metrics like volume and velocity, evaluating density—a crucial metric—is challenging [20, 21]. As a result, traffic density estimation has proven to be an exceptionally difficult task in the field of computer vision. Reducing congestion on commuter routes and tracking employment development can be achieved with the aid of Traffic Density Estimation [22, 23]. Reducing vehicle-related greenhouse gas emissions and improving municipal efficiency are two goals of this strategy [24].

The main contribution of the paper is (Fig. 1)

• Vehicle density estimation using improved yolov8 with KDE

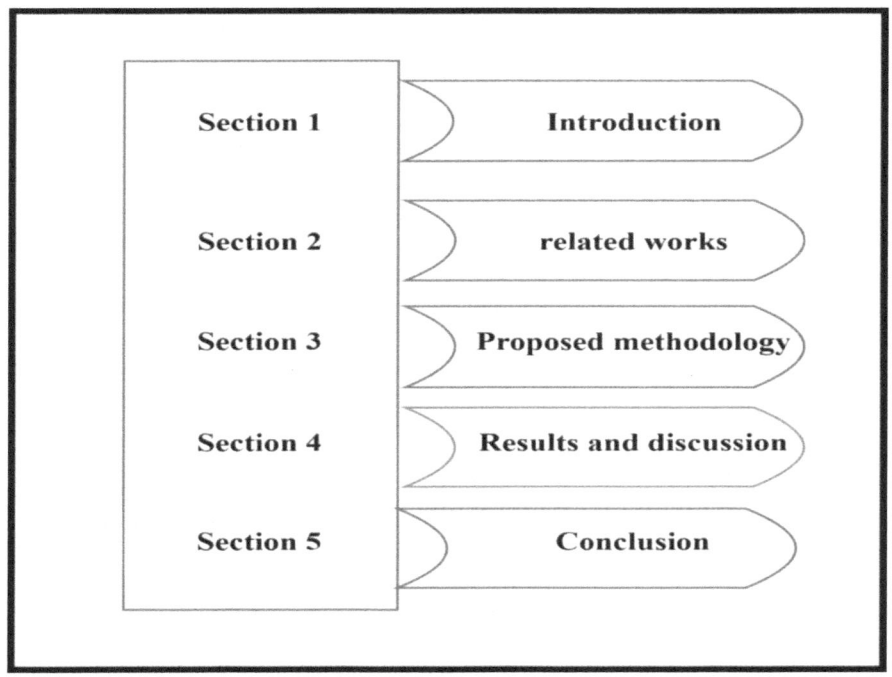

Fig. 1. Structure of the paper

1.1 Motivation of the Paper

The crucial need for reliable estimates of vehicle densities in the fields of transportation planning and management is the driving force behind this research. This research proposes a novel framework for real-time vehicle density analysis that enhances intelligent transportation systems. The framework combines an upgraded YOLOv8 model with Kernel Density Estimation (KDE). The goal of the paper is to revolutionize this field. Improving detection accuracy, decreasing false positives, and offering a scalable, adaptive technology that can respond instantly to changing traffic circumstances are the main motivations. The capacity of the framework to produce accurate density maps greatly aids in comprehending patterns of traffic flow and congestion, which in turn allows for well-informed decision-making in contemporary traffic management situations.

2 Background Study

Aljamal, M. et al. [1] to better estimate the number of automobiles on signalized approaches, the study's authors proposed a novel Adaptive Kalman Filter (AKF) model that relies only on probing vehicle data. An AKF model was developed to predict, in real-time, the state's statistical properties as well as measurement errors. The traffic hydrodynamic equation was used to construct both the state and measurement equations. The former was derived from the traffic flow continuity equation.

Ballarta, J. et al. [4] Researchers discovered that Quantum Geographic Information System (QGIS) and Kernel Density Estimation (KDE) can work together to help analyze road collisions on a more thorough level. An improvement can be made using the heatmap plug-in tool in QGIS to display crash concentration maps and pinpoint locations with a high crash density.

Biswas, S. [5] The impacts of traffic volume and composition on speed and PCU factors for various vehicle types on an urban arterial under mixed traffic circumstances have been illustrated in this research. This research uses a kriging approach-based methodology to arrive at a realistic speed prediction. The kriging approach is a viable alternative to standard regression approaches. The study also proposes a new approach for finding the best correlation function.

Freeman, B. et al. [7] Estimating mobile source emission inventories and traffic planning both rely on accurate traffic density characterization. It was easy to use fixed cameras or human observers to conduct traffic counts, which was a standard method for establishing fleet composition. The use of a fixed camera in the absence of surface references makes the capture of vehicle spacing more complicated.

Goodall, N. et al. [9] A suggested method can anticipate the quantity and whereabouts of certain cars, with or without an upstream detector. An autonomous vehicle's position, velocity, and acceleration data were input into the algorithm on a secondly basis. By studying the activities of a quarter of the cars on the road, the system can predict the likelihood of collisions with vehicles without the necessary equipment, allowing for a more precise estimation of congestion density.

Kharchenko, V. et al. [11] When it comes to Unmanned Aerial Vehicle (UAV) video surveillance, background modeling for foreground identification was a common tool for detecting moving objects in the picture and modeling the backdrop accordingly. The author have looked at both old and new methods of background subtraction. UAV video stream data processing used KDE, a non-parametric approach, for foreground recognition. The kernel for estimation was a Gaussian function. In the investigation, several methods for selecting bandwidth were examined. Foreground detection in UAV video streams using bandwidth computed by (16) performed the best in a comparative comparison of several methods for bandwidth calculation (Table 1).

Sengkey, D. et al. [16] Since density was directly proportional to the number of vehicles passing and inversely proportional to vehicle speed, it was possible to determine vehicle density using a number of factors, one of which was the speed, which can be calculated using the equation $q = k.v$. The author can estimate that 40,938 km/jam was the value of density, which means that as the density increases, the speed of the vehicle decreases and the number of vehicles increases.

Table 1. Comparative Analysis of Traffic Density Estimation Approaches

Author	Year	Methodology	Advantage	Limitation
Aljamal et al	2019	Neural-Kalman filtering with probe vehicle data	Utilizes probe vehicle data for traffic density estimation	Requires robust data collection infrastructure
Chung et al	2018	Hybrid kernel density estimator for EV user behavior prediction	Incorporates hybrid kernel density estimation for electric vehicle user behavior prediction	Specific to electric vehicle behavior prediction, not general traffic density
Freeman et al	2019	UAV-based vehicle stacking estimation at intersections	Uses unmanned aerial systems for accurate vehicle stacking estimation	Limited to specific intersection scenarios
Li et al	2021	Two-stage estimation method for vehicle dynamic parameters	Implements a two-stage estimation method for vehicle dynamic parameters	Can require complex computational resources
Shin et al	2020	Distributed packet probing in V2V network for infrastructure-less traffic density estimation	Utilizes V2V network for traffic density estimation without infrastructure	Relies on V2V communication availability and reliability

2.1 Problem Definition

Unfortunately, many current approaches to estimating vehicle densities have their drawbacks. These include, but are not limited to, low accuracy because they rely on grid-based methods or use basic object detection techniques, inaccurate vehicle counts caused by high false positive rates, slow processing speeds that make them unsuitable for real-time applications, difficulties in accurately capturing complex spatial distributions, and scalability problems when dealing with large-scale traffic data or high densities. More precise, efficient, and flexible vehicle density prediction is essential for efficient traffic management and city planning, but current methods have significant shortcomings that must be addressed immediately.

3 Materials and Methods

In this section, we introduce our proposed method for adaptive vehicle density estimation, which integrates an improved YOLOv8 object detection model with Kernel Density Estimation (KDE). This novel framework aims to provide high-precision, real-time vehicle density analysis by utilizing advancements in both object detection and statistical density estimation techniques (Fig. 2).

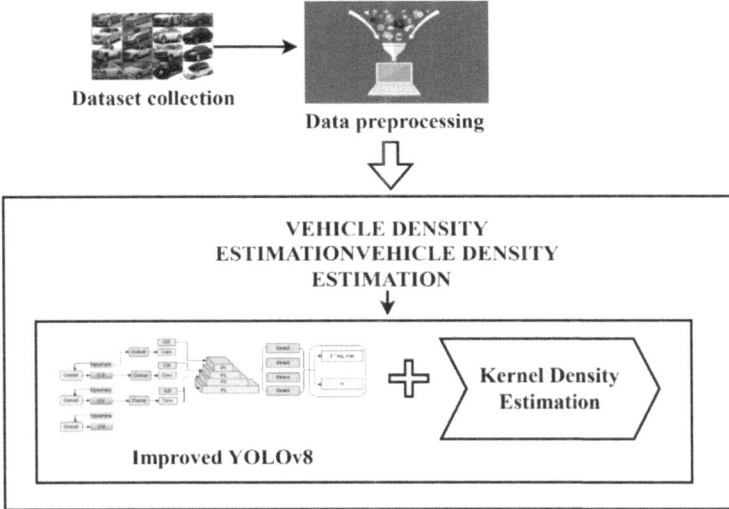

Fig. 2. Vehicle density estimation flow architecture

3.1 Dataset Collection

The dataset was collected from Kaggle website https://www.kaggle.com/datasets/pkd arabi/vehicle-detection-image-dataset this dataset comprises a collection of images captured from various traffic scenes, focusing on vehicles of different types, sizes, and orientations. The images are labeled with bounding boxes indicating the locations and extents of the vehicles within each frame.

3.2 Vehicle Density Estimation Using Improved Yolov8 with Kernel Density Estimation

3.2.1 Improved YOLO v8

The P4 and P6 layers can now integrate with the backend of the feature pyramid network to fuse even more features, and we have included a C2f module for feature fusion in YOLOv8 referred by Jayasingh, S. K. et al. (2024), building upon earlier work. More discriminative features are produced when these features are guided along a top-down approach to instruct the next network modules in feature fusion. Four detecting heads have now been added to YOLOv8: one for tiny targets, one for medium targets, and one for large-scale targets. The system's detecting range is expanded by this. Furthermore, bounding-box regression employs a loss function that is derived from RIOU, a measure for comparing box similarity.

The YOLOv8 backbone network's inability to effectively differentiate between the backdrop and the target is a direct consequence of its simplicity as a stack of convolutional modules. To improve the local features in bottleneck-cloatt, context-aware weights are applied after one of the branches uses depth-separable convolution to get high-frequency local information. Additionally, in a separate subfield, attention techniques are used to acquire low-frequency global information. Lastly, local traits are enhanced by fusing branches.

To get low-frequency global information in the global branch, we first down sample the K_{global} and V_{global} that we got from the linear transformation. Then, we follow the usual attention procedure.

$$Q_{global}, K_{global}, V_{global} = FC(X_{in})V_{DW} = DW_{conv}(V_{local}) \tag{1}$$

The next step is to aggregate Q_{global} and K_{global} using two DW_{conv}. A sequence of operations is then applied to the Hadamard product of Q_{global} and K_{global} to get context aware weights ranging from -1 to 1. At last, this weight can be used to further improve the local characteristics; the procedure is basically as follows.

$$Q_L = DW_{conv}(Q_{local}) \tag{2}$$

Q_L: This matrix is obtained by applying depth-wise convolution (DW_{conv}) to the local query matrix Q_{local}. This process helps in aggregating local features by focusing on local regions of the input.

$$K_L = DW_{conv}(K_{local}) \tag{3}$$

K_L: This matrix is derived by applying depth-wise convolution (DW_{conv}) to the local key matrix K_{local}. Similar to Q_L, this step aggregates local features but from the perspective of key vectors.

$$A_L = FC(Swish(FC(Q_L.K_L))) \tag{4}$$

A_L: This matrix represents the attention weights obtained by applying a fully connected (FC) layer followed by the Swish activation function to the Hadamard product (element-wise multiplication) of Q_L and K_L. This step calculates context-aware weights that adjust the focus on local features based on their relevance.

To get the last output, we use an FC module to link the channel's two outputs.

$$X_C = concat(X_G, X_L) \tag{5}$$

X_C: This matrix is the concatenation of X_G (global features) and X_L (local features). By combining global and local features, this step ensures that both high-level context and detailed local information are preserved.

$$X_{out} = FC(X_c) \tag{6}$$

X_{out}: This matrix is the final output after applying a Fully Connected (FC) layer to the concatenated features X_c. This step integrates the combined features into a cohesive output that enhances the feature representation for subsequent processing.

In addition, we added the transformer block to the backbone's base to improve the feature map's representation capacity, which was inspired by vision transformer's excellent representation capabilities. Figure 3 shows its structure, which consists of two sublayers: MLP and the Multihead Attention Layer. By using multi-head attention,

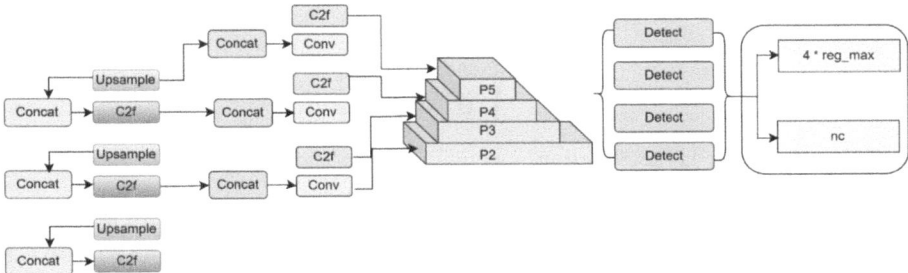

Fig. 3. Improved yolov8 architecture

the present node is able to acquire contextual semantics in addition to focusing on the present pixel. Concurrently, applying transformer on feature maps of the backbone's end network decreases computational and memory expenses due to the end network's low resolution.

Algorithm 1: Improved yolov8
Input:
• Image frames from real-time traffic video feeds
Steps:
1. **Preprocessing:**
o Resize and normalize input images.
o Apply data augmentation techniques for robustness.
2. **YOLOv8 Backbone:**
o Implement a backbone network based on YOLOv8 architecture.
o Incorporate a C2f module for feature fusion.
$$Q_L = DW_{conv}(Q_{local})$$
Lay the groundwork for the P4 and P6 layers to merge with the feature pyramid network's core.
$$X_C = concat\ (X_G, X_L)$$
o Design an attention-guided bidirectional feature pyramid network for efficient feature extraction and fusion.
$$X_{out} = FC(X_c)$$
Output:
• Vehicle detection results with bounding boxes and confidence scores

3.2.2   Kernel Density Estimation

We can hear the Parzen-Rosenblatt window approach or kernel density estimation thrown about in econometric circles. This strategy has its origins in the histogram technique referred by Chen, L. et al. (2020). Using nearby measurements, one can roughly predict the density function at a given position x. As an alternative to constructing the estimate based on bin edges, the naïve kernel technique (adaptively) centers each estimation point x inside a bin of width 2 h. The kernel weight, a weight function, provides a more comprehensible example. Next, $f(x)$ is defined as the kernel estimate.

$$K(x) = \begin{cases} \frac{1}{2} \ if \ |x| < 1 \\ 0 \ \ otherwise \end{cases} \tag{7}$$

$K(x)$: This is the kernel function, a weight function that determines the influence of a data point on the density estimate at a given location.

$\frac{1}{2} if \ |x| < 1$: This means that the weight assigned to a data point is $1/2$ if its distance from the point x is less than 1. Essentially, within a neighborhood of width 2 (from -1 to 1), each point contributes equally.

$0 otherwise$: If the distance from x is greater than or equal to 1, the weight is 0, meaning those points do not contribute to the density estimate at x.

$$f(x) = \frac{1}{nh} \sum\nolimits_{i=1}^{n} K\left(\frac{x - X_i}{h}\right) \tag{8}$$

$f(x)$: This is the kernel density estimate at the point x.

$\frac{1}{nh}$: This normalization factor ensures that the density estimate integrates to 1 over the entire space. Here, n is the number of data points, and h is the bandwidth parameter that controls the width of the kernel.

$\sum_{i=1}^{n}$.: This summation runs over all data points in the sample.

$k\left(\frac{x-X_i}{h}\right)$: This is the kernel function applied to the scaled distance between x and each data point X_i. The term $\frac{x-X_i}{h}$ normalizes the distance by the bandwidth h, determining the contribution of each data point to the estimate at x.

Since the kernel weight is only a 2 h-wide been centered at x, this kernel density estimator is known as a naïve kernel density estimator (Fig. 4).

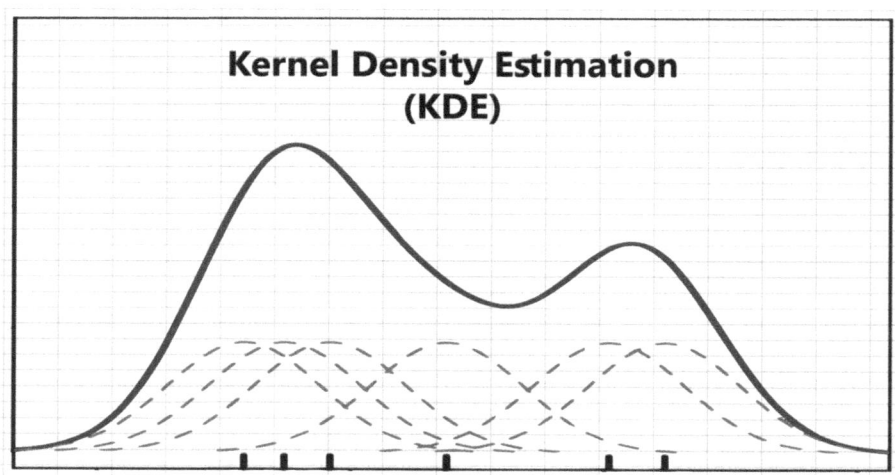

Fig. 4. KDE architecture

Algorithm 2: KDE

Input:
- Dataset containing observations $X = \{X_1, X_2, \ldots, X_n\}$
- Estimation point x
- Bandwidth parameter h

Steps:
1. **Define Kernel Weight Function:**
   - Define the kernel weight function $K(x)$ as:

   $$K(x) = \begin{cases} 1/2 & if \quad |x| < 1 \\ 0 & otherwise \end{cases}$$

2. **Naive Kernel Density Estimation:**
   - Calculate the kernel density estimate $f(x)$ using the formula:

   $$f(x) = \frac{1}{nh} \sum_{i=1}^{n} K\left(\frac{x-X_i}{h}\right)$$

   Where nh represents the bandwidth-normalized term.

Output:
- Density estimate $f(x)$ at point x

3.2.3 Improved YOLO v8 with Kernel Density Estimation

To provide accurate, real-time vehicle density analysis, this innovative adaptive system merges Kernel Density Estimation with an enhanced YOLOv8 object identification model. By using spatial attention processes and refining it on large vehicle datasets, the upgraded YOLOv8 model achieves better detection accuracy while decreasing the number of false positives. By projecting the locations of the detected cars onto a grid, KDE creates a continuous and smooth map of vehicle density, accurately depicting the distribution of vehicles in space. With the system set up on computer units in the network's periphery, adaptive learning and real-time processing are guaranteed. The results of the experiments show that it is a fast and accurate solution for current traffic management systems, and it can be scaled up easily.

For object detection bounding boxes, YOLOv8's regression loss consists of two components. Distribution Focal Loss (DFL) is the first part. It optimizes the network's prediction distribution to be closer to the label values by using cross-entropy. Also, using the CIoU loss measure, the predicted and actual bounding boxes are intersected to determine the Intersection over Union (IoU). Using a predetermined weight coefficient, the final regression loss is divided into two halves and then added together. One of them is the CIoU loss, which is determined by

$$L_{CIOUS} = 1 = 1 - \frac{|B \cap B_i|}{|B \cup B_i|} + \frac{\rho^2\left(b, b^{gt}\right)}{c^2} \tag{9}$$

L_{CIOUS}: A loss called Complete Intersection over Union (CIoU) is used to quantify the disparity between the expected and ground truth bounding boxes.

$|B \cap B_i|$: The area of the intersection between the predicted bounding box B and the ground truth bounding box B_i.

$B \cup B_i$: The area of the union of the predicted bounding box B and the ground truth bounding box B_i.

$\rho^2(b, b^{gt})$: The ground truth bounding box b^{gt} and the anticipated bounding box b are separated by the squared Euclidean distance.

c^2: The smaller of the two enclosing boxes, diagonally, that may include both the expected and ground truth versions

$$a = \frac{u}{1 - IOU + v} \tag{10}$$

a: A scaling factor used in the CIoU loss calculation.

u: A weight factor that balances the contribution of the IoU and the penalty term.

$1 - IOU$: Intersection over Union, a measure of overlap between the predicted and ground truth bounding boxes.

v: A correction term that takes into consideration the disparity in aspect ratio between the ground truth and anticipated bounding boxes.

$$v = \frac{4}{\pi^2}\left(arctan\left(\frac{w^{gt}}{h^{gt}}\right) - arctan\left(\frac{w}{h}\right)\right)^2 \tag{11}$$

v: The penalty term in the CIoU loss function.

$arctan\left(\frac{w^{gt}}{h^{gt}}\right)$: The aspect ratio of the enclosing box representing the ground truth.

$arctan\left(\frac{w}{h}\right)$: The anticipated bounding box's aspect ratio.

w, w^{gt}: The width of the predicted and ground truth bounding boxes, respectively.

h, h^{gt}: The height of the predicted and ground truth bounding boxes, respectively.

vIs the Euclidean distance between the two central points, b and b_{gt}, which the anticipated and actual bounding boxes are, respectively. H, h^{gt}, w, and w^{gt} stand for the expected and actual height and width of the bounding boxes, respectively; c denotes the

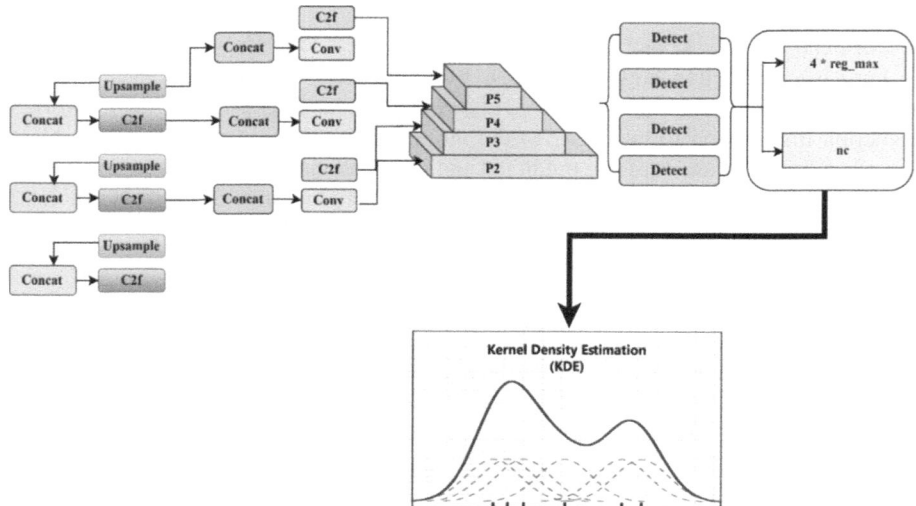

Fig. 5. Improved yolov8 with KDE architecture

diagonal length of the smallest rectangle spanning both the predicted and real frames (Fig. 5).

Algorithm 3: Improved YOLO v8 with kernel density estimation
Input:
• Real-time video frames from traffic surveillance cameras • Improved YOLOv8 object detection model • Kernel Density Estimation (KDE) parameters (bandwidth, kernel function) • Edge computing device for real-time processing
Steps:

1. **Improved YOLOv8 Object Detection:**
   o Use the optimized Improved YOLOv8 model with spatial attention mechanisms for accurate vehicle detection.
    $L_{CIOUS} = 1 = 1 - \frac{\|B \cap B_i\|}{\|B \cup B_i\|} + \frac{\rho^2(b, b^{gt})}{c^2}$
   o Fine-tune the model on extensive vehicle datasets to improve detection accuracy and reduce false positives.
    $a = \frac{u}{1 - IOU + v}$
   o Generate bounding boxes with confidence scores for detected vehicles.
2. **Vehicle Position Mapping:**
   o Map the positions of detected vehicles onto a grid covering the region of interest.
3. **Kernel Density Estimation (KDE):**
   o Apply KDE to the mapped vehicle positions to generate a smooth and continuous vehicle density map.
    $= \frac{4}{\pi^2}\left(arctan\left(\frac{w^{gt}}{h^{gt}}\right) - arctan\left(\frac{w}{h}\right)\right)^2$
   o Use a specified bandwidth parameter and kernel function (e.g., Gaussian kernel) for KDE.
4. **Real-Time Processing on Edge Computing Devices:**
   o Deploy the algorithm on edge computing devices for real-time processing capabilities.
   o Ensure adaptive learning capabilities to continuously refine parameters and improve estimation accuracy.

Output:
• Vehicle detection results with bounding boxes and confidence scores Smooth and continuous vehicle density map

4   Results and Discussion

In this section, we delve into the results and discussions stemming from the application of the Improved YOLOv8 with Kernel Density Estimation (KDE) method for vehicle detection and density estimation in real-time traffic scenarios.

The proposed framework balances detection accuracy and computational load, with trade-offs that are crucial for real-time applications on resource-constrained devices. While enhancements like spatial attention mechanisms in the improved YOLOv8 model boost accuracy, they also increase computational overhead, leading to longer inference times. Similarly, Kernel Density Estimation (KDE) improves density estimation precision but demands more processing resources. On edge devices like the NVIDIA Jetson

Xavier NX, tuning parameters such as input image size, batch size, and KDE sample count is vital to optimize efficiency without sacrificing accuracy. Finding this balance is essential, as reducing batch size or KDE samples can enhance speed but may compromise accuracy, particularly in complex traffic scenarios. Thus, practical deployment requires careful consideration of these trade-offs based on specific use cases and hardware capabilities.

5 Discussion

We have specifically analyzed the performance of the framework under complex occlusions and varying lighting conditions. These additional experiments have been discussed in the revised results section, along with a comparison of how different methods, including YOLOv8 and KDE, handle such challenges.

The YOLOv8 model uses CSPDarknet as its backbone, PANet for the neck, and a decoupled head for multi-scale detection, with an input size of 640×640 pixels to balance accuracy and speed. A batch size of 16, learning rate of 0.001, and AdamW optimizer ensure stable training over 100 epochs. Data augmentations like horizontal flips and color jitter improve generalization. The improved model adds a spatial attention mechanism for better occlusion handling and is fine-tuned on traffic data with cosine annealing for convergence. KDE uses a Gaussian kernel with a 0.4 bandwidth and 1000 samples per frame for accurate density estimation. The system runs on an NVIDIA Jetson Xavier NX with TensorRT for real-time performance (Figs. 6, 7, and 8).

The Table 2 and Fig. 9 shows detection accuracy of various methods shows a progressive improvement with each enhancement. The base YOLOv8 model achieves a

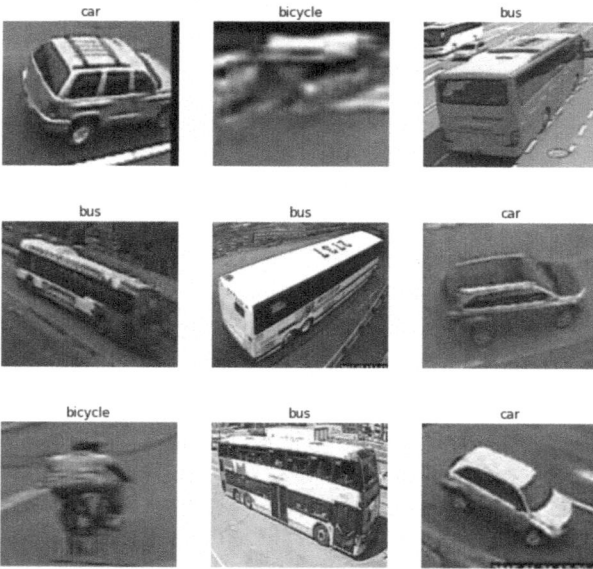

Fig. 6. Different Vehicle and Its Density

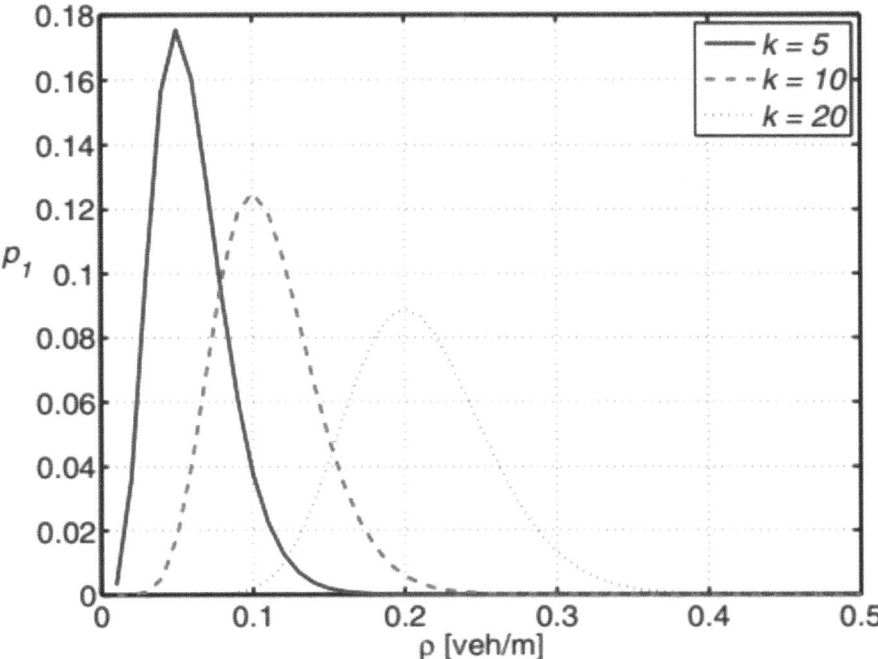

Fig. 7. The relationship between vehicle density (ρ) and the chance of having k neighbors at a distance of 100 m from the probing vehicle will be considered. We look at three different values of k. The probability p1 is maximized for any value of k for which there exists a value of ρ.

detection accuracy of 95.31%, which is further improved to 96.22% by incorporating spatial attention mechanisms and fine-tuning, as seen in the Improved YOLOv8 model. When KDE is employed, the accuracy increases significantly to 97.54%, demonstrating the efficacy of this statistical method in capturing spatial distributions. The combined approach of Improved YOLOv8 with KDE achieves the highest detection accuracy at 98.89%, indicating that the integration of these advanced techniques results in a highly precise vehicle detection framework, superior to any single method alone. This enhancement highlights the robustness and effectiveness of the proposed system in real-world traffic management applications.

The Table 3 and Fig. 10 density estimation precision of the different methods demonstrates a clear improvement with each successive enhancement. The base YOLOv8 model achieves a precision of 94.36%, which is modestly improved to 95.27% with the enhanced version, Improved YOLOv8, incorporating spatial attention mechanisms and fine-tuning. The application of KDE alone boosts precision to 96.39%, showcasing its strength in accurately capturing spatial vehicle distributions. The highest precision, 97.89%, is attained by the combined Improved YOLOv8 with KDE approach, underscoring the substantial gains in accuracy when advanced detection techniques are integrated with sophisticated statistical methods. This high precision is crucial for reliable traffic density estimation, aiding in effective traffic management and urban planning.

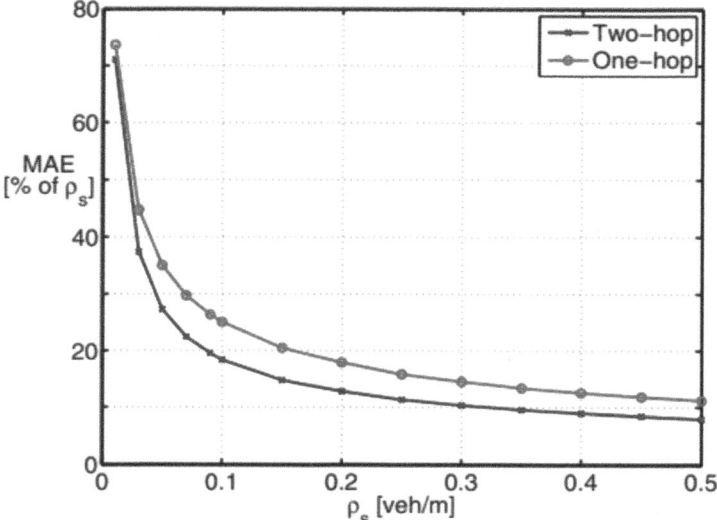

Fig. 8. The worldwide vehicle density and the mean absolute error of the predicted vehicle density shown against one another. In percentage terms relative to the total density of vehicles on Earth, the mean absolute errors are shown. Assuming all vehicles have 100 m transmission range

Table 2. Detection accuracy comparison table

Methods	Detection Accuracy
Yolo v8	95.31
Improved Yolo v8	96.22
KDE	97.54
Improved yolov8 with KDE	98.89

The Table 4 and Fig. 11 shows processing speed of the different methods reveals a notable enhancement as advanced techniques is introduced. The base YOLOv8 model operates at a speed of 0.9 s per frame, which improves to 0.8 s with enhancements in the Improved YOLOv8 version, showcasing a more efficient detection algorithm. The introduction of KDE further reduces processing time to 0.6 s, demonstrating the computational efficiency of statistical methods in density estimation. The most significant improvement is seen in the combined approach of Improved YOLOv8 with KDE, achieving a remarkable processing speed of 0.4 s per frame, highlighting the synergistic effect of integrating advanced detection mechanisms with statistical analysis. This faster processing speed enables real-time analysis of traffic density, facilitating immediate responses to changing traffic conditions in intelligent transportation systems.

The Table 5 and Fig. 12 shows scalability of each method reflects their ability to handle increasing demands and larger datasets efficiently. The base YOLOv8 model

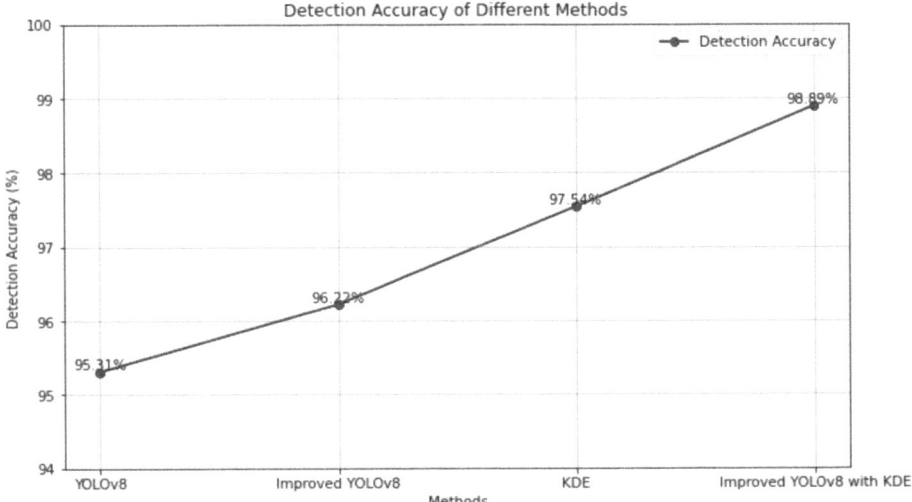

Fig. 9. Detection accuracy comparison chart

Table 3. Density Estimation Precision value comparison table

Methods	Density Estimation Precision
Yolo v8	94.36
Improved Yolo v8	95.27
KDE	96.39
Improved yolov8 with KDE	97.89

demonstrates good scalability with a score of 96.32%, which improves slightly to 97.01% with enhancements in the Improved YOLOv8 version, indicating a capacity for handling larger volumes of data. The introduction of KDE further enhances scalability to 97.35%, showcasing the statistical method's capability to adapt to varying data sizes effectively. The combined approach of Improved YOLOv8 with KDE exhibits the highest scalability at 98.24%, demonstrating the synergistic benefits of integrating advanced detection techniques with statistical analysis for managing and analyzing data at scale in traffic management systems.

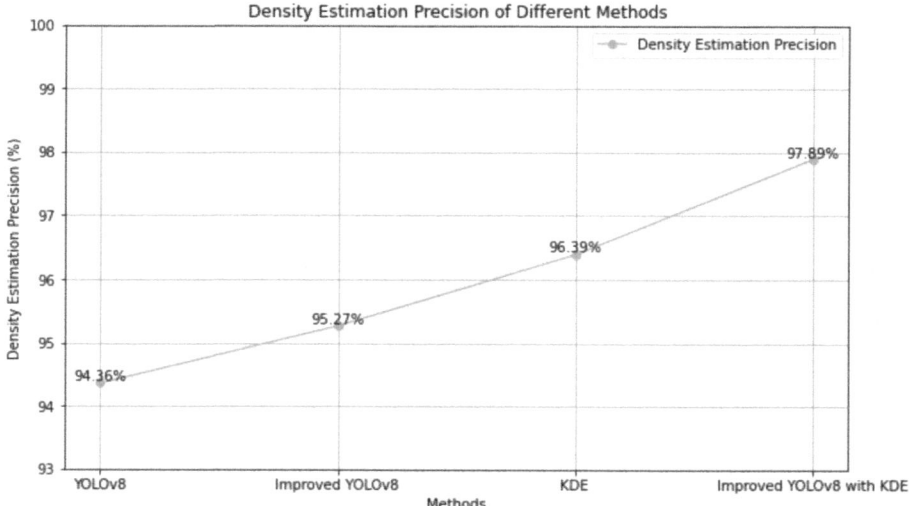

Fig. 10. Density Estimation Precision value comparison chart

Table 4. Processing Speed value comparison table

Methods	Processing Speed
Yolo v8	0.9
Improved Yolo v8	0.8
KDE	0.6
Improved yolov8 with KDE	0.4

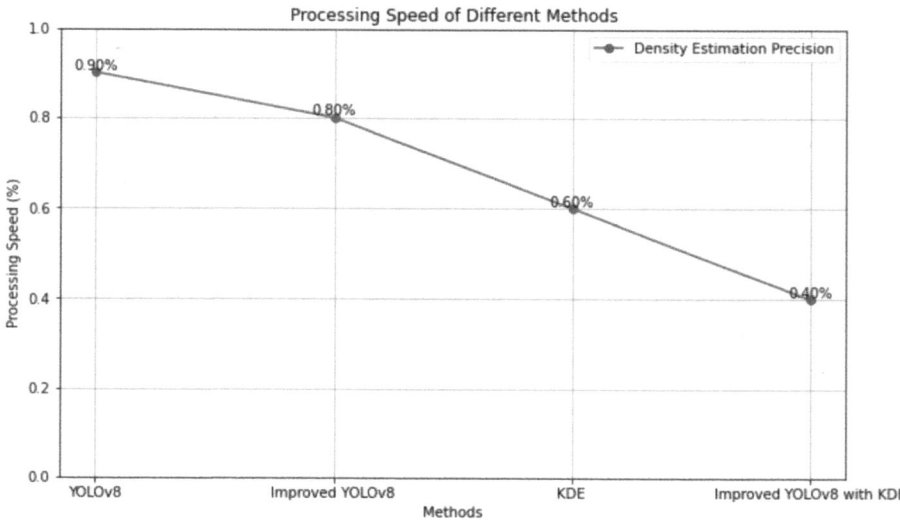

Fig. 11. Processing Speed value comparison chart

Table 5. Scalability value comparison table

Methods	Scalability
Yolo v8	96.32
Improved Yolo v8	97.01
KDE	97.35
Improved yolov8 with KDE	98.24

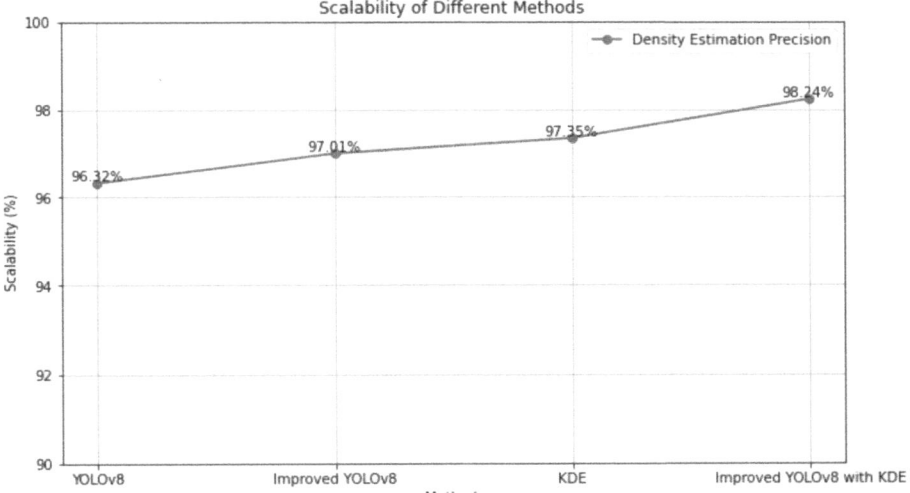

Fig. 12. Scalability value comparison chart

6   Conclusion

In conclusion, the adaptive vehicle density estimation framework presented in this paper, which integrates an improved YOLOv8 model with Kernel Density Estimation (KDE), represents a significant advancement in the field of traffic management and urban planning. Through extensive enhancements such as spatial attention mechanisms and fine-tuning, the framework achieves superior detection accuracy and reduced false positives, crucial for precise vehicle localization in diverse traffic scenarios. The utilization of KDE for generating smooth and continuous density maps enhances understanding of traffic flow and congestion patterns, enabling effective decision-making in intelligent transportation systems. Moreover, the system's adaptive nature, continuous learning capability, and real-time processing on edge computing devices ensure immediate responses to dynamic traffic conditions. The combined approach of Improved YOLOv8 with KDE achieves the highest detection accuracy at 98.89%, indicating that the integration of these advanced techniques results in a highly precise vehicle detection framework, superior to any single method alone. Experimental results on real-world datasets validate the framework's effectiveness, demonstrating substantial improvements in accuracy and processing speed compared to conventional methods. Overall, the integration of an improved YOLOv8 model with KDE not only enhances vehicle detection and density estimation but also provides a scalable, efficient, and adaptable solution for modern traffic management systems, paving the way for smarter and more sustainable urban environments.

References

1. Aljamal, M.A., Abdelghaffar, H.M., Rakha, H.A.: Developing a neural–Kalman filtering approach for estimating traffic stream density using probe vehicle data. Sensors **19**(19), 4325 (2019)
2. Aljamal, M.A., Abdelghaffar, H.M., Rakha, H.A.: Estimation of traffic stream density using connected vehicle data: linear and nonlinear filtering approaches. Sensors **20**(15), 4066 (2020)
3. Aljamal, M.A., Abdelghaffar, H.M., Rakha, H.A.: Real-time estimation of vehicle counts on signalized intersection approaches using probe vehicle data. IEEE Trans. Intell. Transp. Syst. **22**(5), 2719–2729 (2020)
4. Ballarta, J., Javier, S.F., Mercader, C.: Black Spot Cluster Analysis of Road Crash involving Public Utility Vehicles (PUV) along Commonwealth Avenue using Kernel Density Estimation
5. Biswas, S., Chakraborty, S., Chandra, S., Ghosh, I.: Kriging-based approach for estimation of vehicular speed and passenger car units on an urban arterial. J. Transport. Eng. Part A: Syst. **143**(3), 04016013 (2017)
6. Chung, Y.W., Khaki, B., Chu, C., Gadh, R.: Electric vehicle user behavior prediction using hybrid kernel density estimator. In: 2018 IEEE International Conference on Probabilistic Methods Applied to Power Systems (PMAPS), pp. 1–6. IEEE (2018)
7. Freeman, B.S., Al Matawah, J.A., Al Najjar, M., Gharabaghi, B., Thé, J.: Vehicle stacking estimation at signalized intersections with unmanned aerial systems. Int. J. Transport. Sci. Technol. **8**(2), 231–249 (2019)
8. Gao, G., Gao, J., Liu, Q., Wang, Q., Wang, Y.: CNN-based density estimation and crowd counting: a survey (2020). arXiv:2003.12783
9. Goodall, N.J., Smith, B.L., Park, B.B.: Microscopic estimation of freeway vehicle positions using mobile sensors (2020)
10. Khan, S.M., Dey, K.C., Chowdhury, M.: Real-time traffic state estimation with connected vehicles. IEEE Trans. Intell. Transp. Syst. **18**(7), 1687–1699 (2017)
11. Kharchenko, V., Kuzmenko, N., Kukush, A., Ostroumov, I.: Kernel density estimation for foreground detection in dynamic video processing for unmanned aerial vehicle application. In: 2019 IEEE 5th International Conference Actual Problems of Unmanned Aerial Vehicles Developments (APUAVD), pp. 71–74. IEEE (2019)
12. Li, W., Li, H., Xu, K., Huang, Z., Li, K., Du, H.: Estimation of vehicle dynamic parameters based on the two-stage estimation method. Sensors **21**(11), 3711 (2021)
13. Lin, C.J., Jeng, S.Y., Lioa, H.W.: A real-time vehicle counting, speed estimation, and classification system based on virtual detection zone and YOLO. Math. Probl. Eng. **2021**(1), 1577614 (2021)
14. Putri, A.A., Achmad, A.: Estimated vehicle density based on video processing using the Gaussian mixture model method. J. Phys. Conf. Ser. **1201**(1), 012005 (2019)
15. Sankaran, S.: Pattern matching based vehicle density estimation technique for traffic monitoring systems. Int. Arab J. Inf. Technol. **19**(4), 575–581 (2022)

16. Sengkey, D.F., Widyawan, W., Mustik, I.W.: Vehicle classification in traffic density estimation using vehicular ad hoc network. In: Proceedings of the 10th International Forum Strategic Technology, pp. 387–392 (2015)
17. Shin, C.S., Lee, J., Lee, H.: Infrastructure-less vehicle traffic density estimation via distributed packet probing in v2v network. IEEE Trans. Veh. Technol. **69**(10), 10403–10418 (2020)
18. Vargas-Melendez, L., Boada, B.L., Boada, M.J.L., Gauchia, A., Diaz, V.: Sensor fusion based on an integrated neural network and probability density function (PDF) dual Kalman filter for on-line estimation of vehicle parameters and states. Sensors **17**(5), 987 (2017)
19. Wang, S., Xie, X., Ju, R.: A mesoscopic traffic data assimilation framework for vehicle density estimation on urban traffic networks based on particle filters. Entropy **21**(4), 358 (2019)
20. Wu, F., Cheng, Z., Chen, H., Qiu, Z., Sun, L.: Traffic state estimation from vehicle trajectories with anisotropic Gaussian processes. Transport. Res. Part C: Emerg. Technol. **163**, 104646 (2024)
21. Xu, H., Ding, J., Zhang, Y., Hu, J.: Queue length estimation at isolated intersections based on intelligent vehicle infrastructure cooperation systems. In: 2017 IEEE Intelligent Vehicles Symposium (IV), pp. 655–660. IEEE (2017)
22. Yao, S., Wang, J., Fang, L., Wu, J.: Identification of vehicle-pedestrian collision hotspots at the micro-level using network kernel density estimation and random forests: a case study in Shanghai, China. Sustainability **10**(12), 4762 (2018)
23. Jayasingh, S.K., Naik, P., Swain, S., Patra, K.J., Kabat, M.R.: Integrated crowd counting system utilizing IoT sensors, OpenCV and YOLO models for accurate people density estimation in real-time environments. In: 2024 1st International Conference on Cognitive, Green and Ubiquitous Computing (IC-CGU), pp. 1–6. IEEE (2024)
24. Chen, L., Huang, X., Zhang, H.: Modeling the charging behaviors for electric vehicles based on ternary symmetric kernel density estimation. Energies **13**(7), 1551 (2020)

EmpowerSpeak: "A Breakthrough Model for Speech Synthesis from Videos for the Differently Abled"

Sagar Yeruva[✉], Athina Bhavana, Velaga Harshitha Sai, Gayathri Shakkari, and Tatikonda Venkat Manish

Vallurupalli Nageswara Rao Vignana Jyothi Institute of Engineering and Technology, Hyderabad, Telangana 500090, India
sagar_y@vnrvjiet.in

Abstract. Living things can get information by using a variety of senses to perceive their environment. Humans, for instance, interpret what they perceive and utilize that knowledge to make sense of their environment and interact with one another. This made us investigate how computers might be used to accomplish this and how it might benefit those who are unable to sense their surroundings. Therefore, our goal is to develop a system that can provide text and audio descriptions of videos for individuals with disabilities. Existing systems rely on neural networks like LSTM. On the other hand, LSTMs have difficulty comprehending lengthy sequences, which is necessary for creating descriptions for videos. Transformers have also gained popularity recently because of their ability to process data in parallel; nonetheless, they have memory and temporal problems. Furthermore, existing systems do not prioritize speech from an application-oriented standpoint, which limits the accessibility of these technologies. Therefore, we provide a system that generates textual and audio descriptions by utilizing several transformer models. Additionally, we offer a web interface via which you may upload films and create textual and voice descriptions for them. Taking things a step further, this work can be expanded to provide an interactive user interface that leverages the above-mentioned models to generate and read out loud descriptions of live video captured from a camera.

Keywords: Textual descriptions · T5 Algorithm · NLTK Algorithm · GENSIM Algorithm · spaCy Algorithm · TF-IDF Algorithm · Transformers · Pegasus Model · BART Model · attention models

1 Introduction

It is difficult for a computer to generate speech descriptions from a video with no audio cues. This area of machine learning and artificial intelligence applicability is worth researching due to the numerous instances in which it may be useful. For example, if a video simply has visual content, the visually challenged will be unable to comprehend it. They will instead require access to the audio/vocal description of the content.

S. Rajagopal et al. (Eds.): ASCIS 2024, CCIS 2424, pp. 74–86, 2025.
https://doi.org/10.1007/978-3-031-86290-8_5

These people would greatly benefit from the capacity to automatically construct spoken descriptions for videos without any audio inputs. Furthermore, there are various applications where producing voice descriptions for muted videos would be really beneficial. LSTM and Transformer networks have lately been found to be much more successful in sequential modeling issues, according to a survey of existing projects and research. LSTMs were created as an enhancement over RNNs, largely to address the problem of disappearing gradients. They frequently fail, however, when it comes to keeping long-term context dependencies. Because the phrases are sequential in form, they are analyzed word by word, which adds to the time and resources required to train the LSTMs.

Transformer networks [3] are a superior solution here since they allow parallel computation, which reduces training time. This is performed by digesting the statements in their entirety rather than word by word. However, when it comes to creating descriptions from videos, transformers continue to struggle with context. This is because the caption for each video segment is decoded separately, without taking into account the context of preceding video segments or previously generated captions, resulting in uneven and repeating sentences. The primary goal is to give a natural-sounding spoken description that accurately conveys the visual information in the movie. The suggested methodology seeks to construct speech descriptions capable of summarizing video aspects while linking them with features such as qualities, places, activities, relationships with other entities, and so on. This is done using multiple algorithms, including NLTK, spaCy [2], TF-IDF for extractive, the T5 algorithm [1], and transformers for abstractive summary generation, to overcome timing and memory-based issues. It is critical to be able to describe various visual content while keeping the contextual relationship between the elements throughout the description.

2   Related Works

Mingye Wang and his group presents a novel semi-supervised learning method using T5 model [1] for text summarization, treating it as a style transfer task inspired by CycleGAN. The T5-based model is trained to transfer the style of a document to its summary and vice versa, addressing challenges in languages with limited annotated data, such as Chinese. The paper focuses on the model's performance on Chinese documents, showcasing its effectiveness on datasets CSL and LCSTS.

M. Priyanka and her team developed a spacy model that introduces a novel summarization system based on natural language processing to effectively summarize video, audio, and textual data [2]. The system addresses the challenge of efficiently extracting key information from videos, audio recordings, and text, emphasizing the development of a Natural Language Processing module in Python for summarizing YouTube videos, audio files, and textual data.

The work of Reshmi S. Bhooshan and Suresh K. offers an innovative multimodal framework in the field of video caption generation [3]. Their method effectively takes into account temporal, contextual, and global characteristics from video frames by combining multimodal feature attention with a discrete wavelet convolutional neural architecture. The visual attention predictor network integrates distinct attention networks to capture numerous attentions. Then, caption generation employs these attended traits in conjunction with textual attention. They show notable improvements in their trials on benchmark datasets, MSVD and MSR-VTT, with CIDEr scores of 52.2 and 91.7, respectively. Metric for Evaluation of Translation with Explicit OR during (METEOR), Consensus-based Image Description Evaluation (CIDEr), and Bilingual Evaluation Understudy are the evaluation metrics used to assess the methodology's performance.

In [4] the realm of video summarization, the work by Ahmed Emad et al. stands out as a pioneering approach. Their method focuses on generating automatic video descriptions and timestamps, aiming to enhance the video selection process for users. By extracting keywords and utilizing frame content, emotions, and speech, their approach provides comprehensive and accurate video summaries. Notably, they employ natural language processing techniques, including tokenization, sentence segmentation, and abstractive summarization, to fuse information from audio, video, and emotional cues. The experimental results demonstrated a high level of accuracy, with 87% of participants acknowledging the effectiveness of their generated video descriptions. FER-2013 and MSVD are used for their variety of videos that could be used to benefit our approach.

In contrast to typical video summarizing techniques, Zhu et al. provide a novel method dubbed "Topic-aware Video Summarization using Multimodal Transformer," [5] which aims to generate numerous summaries with distinct subjects, catering to different user interests within a movie. They create a reference dataset with topic labels and relevance scores, and they suggest a multimodal Transformer model that can concurrently produce subject-specific video summaries and predict topic labels. This investigation demonstrates the effectiveness of their proposed strategy and emphasizes the importance of taking topic diversity into account while summarizing videos. Additionally, they create a dataset called TopicSum, which includes 136 videos that are rich in content and are taken from different films, like "Life of Pi" and "The Chronicles of Narnia." The main metric used to assess their methodology is accuracy.

Guoqiang Liang and his team introduced a Convolutional Attentive Adversarial Network (CAAN) for video summarization [6], aiming to reduce the need for large- scale annotated datasets. CAAN employs a generative adversarial network with a generator and discriminator, where the generator predicts frame importance scores using a convolutional sequence network and an attention-based network. Three loss functions guide importance score prediction. Experimental results on SumMe and TV-Sum benchmarks demonstrate the superiority of CAAN, even outperforming some supervised approaches, in unsupervised video summarization. They used SumMe and TV-Sum datasets.

Parth Kotak and his team worked on a deep neural network architecture that has been proposed for security and surveillance applications [7]. The system is learning-based and features multitasking. The model makes use of a dataset and a sentence generation model (LSTM) that derives information from labels by learning phrase structure. Modern methods like reinforcement learning, capsule networks, and generative adversarial networks (GANs) can be utilized to improve the proposed base model, CNN-LSTM. Several tasks, including object recognition, anomaly detection, and activity recognition in security and surveillance systems, are likely to benefit from this method. COOT: Cooperative Hierarchical Transformer for Video Text Representation Learning.

[8] Simon Ging et al. suggests a model called COOT, which represents interactions across several granularity levels and modalities using hierarchical data. It was determined to have 60% fewer parameters than previous methods after being tested

on the ActivityNet Captions and Youcook2 datasets. The best captioning performance and cutting-edge retrieval outcomes were achieved by COOT. It should be noted that COOT is more applicable than existing systems since it includes transformers, which are frequently utilized in jobs involving natural language processing. This method may be helpful for a variety of applications, including video captioning and retrieval, and it may enhance the functionality of current models.

A multiscale hierarchical attention framework for video summarizing is presented by the authors Wencheng Zhua, Jiwen Lua, Yucheng Hana, Jie Zhoua in this research [9]. In order to capture short-range and long-range relationships, their technique learns temporal representations via intra-block and intro-block attention methods. Additionally, they expand their strategy into a two-stream architecture that takes into account both motion and appearance data. Extensive experiments show that the method performs competitively with state-of-the-art methods. They intend to investigate an adaptive shot segmentation technique in the future in order to circumvent the drawback of fixed-length blocks.

Zhong Ji and his team proposed a deep attentive framework for supervised video summarization where AAVS and M-AVS are the two proposed attention-based deep models [10]. The work presented here is notable since it is the first to include attention mechanisms in deep models for video summarization. On two benchmark datasets, the suggested models perform 0.8% to 3% better than other approaches. The study demonstrates the effectiveness and superiority of the AVS framework when used with supplemented data and includes qualitative and parameter sensitivity studies.

Jie Lie's work in the field of video summarization gives an intensive approach by presenting transformers and RNN's. This paper [11] handles the challenge of generating coherent and contextually relevant paragraph by incorporating the memory-augmented module. It permits the model to remember and retrieve relevant information from earlier frames. The main focus is on the quality and coherence of paragraph-style video captions. Their research tests on the datasets counting the Activity-Net Captions, YouCook II.

In the field of video synthesis, Jar Sung Park's work presents a thoughtful approach by using the Adversarial Interface [12]. The model uses generators and descriptors to generate fluent and coherent description of the video. Generator takes the sequence video as input and outputs a sequence of words while Discriminator tries to differentiate between real and generated descriptions. The objection of the author is to present a new and efficient approach to improve the quality of multi-sentence description by testing on Activity-Net Captions dataset.

Tianrui Lui's work presents a keen approach that leverages the reinforcement learning [13]. The model runs on U-Net neural networks and consists of 2 parts: an encoder, a decoder. The model automatically selects the most important frames from the video. The encoder takes the video as an input and produces a latent representation of the video then the decoder takes over the latent representation and produces a summary of the video. Its idea is to save users time by automating the selection of the important frames from videos. Their experiments work using SUMME, TV-Sum datasets.

Junaid Ahmed Ghauri's work on video synthesis using Supervised learning presents a strategic approach where the model uses multiple feature sets to capture different aspects of the video and parallel attention to learn the important frames from different perspectives [14]. The model uses a parallel attention mechanism to combine three different feature sets, which allows it to capture both static and dynamic information from the video. The proposed approach is evaluated on two commonly used video summarization benchmarks: SUMME, TV-Sum. The results show that the proposed approach outperforms state of-the art methods on both benchmarks.

Shizhe Chen and his team worked with Fine-grained video-text retrieval which remains a challenge for current systems, often missing nuanced relationships. This research [15] introduces a hierarchical graph reasoning method to address this gap, using deep learning and semantic embeddings for improved video-text understanding. The aim is to enhance retrieval accuracy, allowing precise video clip matching with text queries. Performance is evaluated using metrics like MAP, Recall, and Precision.

Qinghao Yu and his team proposed a SUM-GAN- GEA method. The challenge of producing concise and coherent video summaries is addressed in this research with the introduction of SUM-GAN-GEA [16]. This method synergizes GANs, Gaussian distribution, and external attention mechanisms to improve summarization quality. With an emphasis on capturing essential video content and structure, SUM-GAN-GEA's effectiveness is measured using established metrics likeF1-score and ROUGE.

Y. Yuan and his group observed that video summarization regularly misses pivotal spatial and temporal details, particularly in intricate content. This research [17] introduces a spatiotemporal modeling technique using Convolutional Recurrent Neural Networks (CRNN) to address this challenge. The CRNN captures spatial details through convolutional layers and temporal dynamics via recurrent layers. Aimed at generating coherent and high-quality summaries for complex videos, the study uses metrics like F1 score, ROUGE, and coherence for evaluation. The main goal is to harness both spatial and temporal insights for improved video summarization outcomes.

Li Haopeng and his team proposed a video summarization technique that harnesses multimodal self-supervised learning for progressive and coherent summaries. It prioritizes the integration of both audio and visual data to address the shortcomings of current methods. By targeting the complexities in diverse video content, the research [18] evaluates its success using well established metrics like F1 score and ROUGE.

3   Observations

3.1   Findings

The study examined different neural network architectures amongst them being transformer models such as COOH and MART surpassing LSTS in its view and giving more fluent and accurate contextual video summaries due to long-term dependency problems. CNNs were used to extract complex visual information whereas LSTMs, though not very efficient at handling large sequences, handling short sequences well in terms of short term dependencies. By integrating the two models into the'hybrid' approach, realistic and summarised videos could be created in their entirety. Transformer models (T5, BART, Pegasus) when fine-tuned on relevant datasets significantly improved the system's capability to generate coherent, natural language summaries with just a little fine tuning. Performance analysis by using the measures like ROUGE, METEOR pointed out that the system has a higher accuracy and the concept of diversity also achieved higher values. Second, the ability of the system to generate textual and audio outputs and outputs in several languages made the system highly accessible for persons with disabilities, hence high utilities..

3.2 Research Gap

Although these models are used to produce useful summaries, real-world comprehension is still lacking. This can be accomplished by utilizing a hybrid model, which aids in comprehending the connections between objects and background and foreground features. Using an attention- based model to comprehend the information in-depth is one area that could use improvement. Videos shot in real life frequently feature deep relationships between items, a variety of backgrounds, and complex scenarios. Conventional models can find it difficult to fully represent these intricacies. The hybrid model that has been suggested aims to overcome this constraint by merging many neural network architectural types. One particular kind of attention mechanism that is frequently applied in sequence-to- sequence tasks is the transformer model. This can be especially helpful for catching minute details and connections between the video's frames. Using both extractive and abstractive methods, this application-oriented approach overcomes the limitations of time and memory to provide verbal video descriptions instead of just written summaries. By providing the most precise model.

4 Methodology

Fig. 1. Architecture

Figure 1 shows the proposed system design. We describe a multi-step process where the model creates video summaries from existing transcripts or creates new ones when they are unavailable. The architecture shown in the figure represents the workflow steps. It shows the processing process from managing transcripts to summarizing. The system starts by accepting the video URL, which may or may not include a transcript. In the case of transcribed videos Existing transcripts are directly extracted and processed. If there is no transcript The Transcription Generator is used to create the text. The transcript data were then processed using two methods: extraction and abstraction. In the process of separating data Key phrases and phrases are selected using techniques such as NLTK, TF-IDF, and spaCy. In the abstraction phase, models such as T5, BART, and Pegasus use the new content to create new concise summaries. Finally, summaries are created and presented in text and audio formats with support for multiple languages as per the user's needs.

4.1 Input Data:

The input data for the system consists of video URLs, with and without transcripts. For videos that include transcripts, the system processes the pre-existing text directly. For videos lacking transcripts, the system generates them using an automated transcription model. These transcripts are then used to create both extractive and abstractive summaries, enabling the system to provide text and audio descriptions for the videos.

4.2 Extractive Method:

Selects and extracts key phrases from the original video to create a summary. It is produced using NLTK, TF-IDF and spaCy in three different ways.

- **NLTK**: Its main function is to provide sophisticated summarization techniques that use the sentence score to identify and pick key sentences from the video transcript or related text. The resulting summary can include important words or phrases that were taken straight out of the transcript and used to highlight important points.
- **TF-IDF (Term Frequency-Inverse Document Frequency)**: Determines a word's significance in a document in relation to a collection of transcribed documents. It is predicated on a term's rarity in the entire corpus and how frequently it occurs in a document (TF) (IDF).
- **spaCy**: Although it lacks a specific summarization module, spaCy has a number of natural language processing (NLP) techniques that can be used with video transcripts or related text. By extracting linguistic elements, enticements, or relationships from the text, it can aid in the summarization process and be utilized in a customized workflow for summarization.

4.3 Abstractive Method

It creates fresh, succinct phrases that encapsulate the core concepts of the source video.

- **T5 Algorithm**: This versatile transformer-based model, created for text-to-text transfer tasks in natural language processing, produces abstract summaries. T5 is built around the Transformer architecture, which uses self-attention mechanisms to collect contextual relationships inside input sequences.
- **BART (Bidirectional and Auto-Regressive Transformers)**: Facebook created an advanced NLP model called BART. For problems involving text generation, it combines bidirectional transformers with an auto-regressive architecture. BART's proficiency in tasks like language production, text completion, and text summarization stems from its combined pre-training on vast text corpora and task-specific fine-tuning.

- **Pegasus**: Two popular natural language processing (NLP) uses for Google Research's Pegasus deep learning model are text summarization and translation. Although the complete internal workings of Pegasus are owned by Google, here is the general concept of how deep learning models such as Pegasus often operate:

1. *Data Collection and Preprocessing*: A sizable collection of text data is gathered and preprocessed prior to the model being trained. Tokenization, which divides the text into smaller units like words or subwords, and data cleaning, which eliminates noise and unnecessary information, are some of the jobs involved in this.
2. *Model Architecture:* The transformer architecture, which has been popular in NLP jobs because of its efficacy, is the foundation around which Pegasus is constructed. Compared to conventional recurrent neural networks (RNNs) or convolutional neural networks (CNNs), the transformer design exploits self-attention mechanisms to better capture links between words in a sequence.
3. *Training:* The model learns to translate input sequences into output sequences in accordance with the task's goal during this phase. The model is trained to produce a succinct summary of an input text, for instance, in text summarization. Using optimization algorithms like stochastic gradient descent (SGD) or its variants, as well as backpropagation, training entails changing the model's parameters (weights).
4. *Fine-tuning:* The model may be fine-tuned on task-specific datasets after undergoing initial training on a large dataset in order to enhance performance on certain tasks or domains. The process of fine-tuning entails utilizing the knowledge acquired during the first training phase to update the model's parameters based on task-specific data.
5. *Inference:* It is the process of taking input text and using its newly acquired parameters to provide predictions as an output. For instance, in text summarizing, the model would produce a succinct summary of a lengthy document.
6. *Assessment:* To determine the model's efficacy in resolving the given task, its performance is assessed on an independent dataset. The criteria used for evaluation vary based on the particular task; however, they may include accuracy, the BLEU score for translation tasks, the ROUGE score for summarization activities, and so on.

Each of these algorithms produces summaries based on its own specifications. Based on the requirements, the user must choose which method to employ and what kind of summary to produce. For the users, an audio and text version of the created output summary is provided in different languages based on their comfort.

4.4   Role of Transformers

Transformers are the backbone of the abstractive summarization approach. Their ability to process entire sequences of text in parallel and their self-attention mechanisms enable them to understand and generate contextually rich and coherent summaries. The key advantages of transformers in this system include:

- **Global Contextual Awareness**: Transformers process the entire input sequence at once, allowing the model to capture both the global meaning and fine details of the transcript. This ensures that the generated summary reflects the broader context of the video.

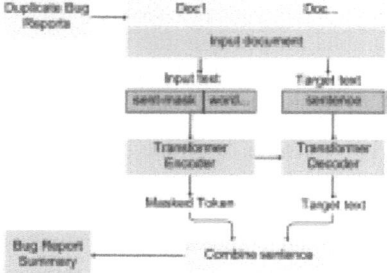

Fig. 2. Working of Pegasus Model

- **Parallel Processing**: Unlike sequential models like LSTMs, transformers can process multiple parts of the input simultaneously, which greatly reduces the time required for training and inference. This is especially beneficial when summarizing long video transcripts.
- **Handling Long-Term Dependencies**: By using self-attention, transformers are able to focus on important elements of the transcript, even if they are far apart. This is crucial in video summarization, where key information may be spread throughout the transcript.
- **Natural Language Generation**: The transformer models used (T5, BART, Pegasus) are capable of generating fluent, human-like summaries. Their abstractive nature allows them to create new sentences that better encapsulate the meaning of the video, providing summaries that are more readable and contextually relevant compared to extractive methods.

5   Implementation

The following metrics are utilized to evaluate the models: SUMSCORE (accuracy, recall, f1_score), rouge 1, rouge 2, rouge l, Meteor and BLEU. A collection of criteria known as ROUGE (Recall-Oriented Understudy for Gisting Evaluation) is used to assess how well machine translation and automatic text summarization perform in comparison to reference summaries.

Among the metrics are:

- **ROUGE-1**: Calculates the number of unigrams, or single words, that are shared by the reference summary and the created summary.
- **ROUGE-2:** Calculates the degree to which the generated summary and the reference summary overlap in bigrams, or pairs of neighboring words.
- **ROUGE-L**: Takes into account word order and sentence- level structure while calculating the longest common subsequence (LCS) between the generated summary and the reference summary.
- **METEOR**: It is a tool used to assess machine translation output quality. It does this by aligning n-gram precision and recall with a harmonic mean.

Fig. 3. Implementation screenshots

- **BLEU**: It compares the produced translation to one or more reference translations in order to determine how comparable they are. In comparison to the references, it computes the accuracy of n-grams (usually up to 4-g) in the resulting translation.
- **SUMMSCORE**: This word seems to be a general name for a summary evaluation score, which might be an F1-score plus precision and recall, three popular metrics used to assess text summarization systems. Based on the overlap between the generated summary and the reference summaries, these metrics are computed. The F1-score, which is the harmonic mean of precision and recall, provides a balanced assessment of their performance. Precision measures the percentage of generated summary content that is also in the reference summaries, and recall measures the percentage of reference summary content that is also in the generated summary

6 Results and Discussion

The model is assessed over 8 measurements which incorporates ROUGE-1, ROUGE-2, ROUGE-L, BLEU, METEOR, SUMMSCORE-Precision, RECALL, F1_Score for distinctive models. For the ROUGE-1 metric for T5 model and Pegasus it is 0.44 which implies the rundown produced contains a closeness of 44% with the reference rundown and for Nltk it is 0.09 and for spaCy it is 0.11 and for TF-IDF demonstrate it is 0.09. Generally, for ROUGE-1 metric the accuracy is tall for T5 and Pegasus. For ROUGE-2 metric the T5 and Pegasus show have an exactness of 0.15, Nltk and spaCy it has 0.01 and TF-IDF it is negligible. Overall, the ROUGLE-2 has best score for T5 and Pegasus. For ROUGE-L metric the T5 and Pegasus have 0.42 of score, Nltk and spaCy and TF-IDF have 0.01 exactness On an normal the ROUGLE-L has best exactness for

T5, BART and Pegasus. Another is the BLEU metric for which the T5 and Pegasus the score is 0.06 and for Nltk, spaCy, TF-IDF it is negligible. The METEOR metric it encompasses a score of 0.26 for T5 and Pegasus and for Nltk and TF-IDF with a score of 0.17 and spaCy with 0.19. Here T5 and Pegasus has the most elevated of all. Next is the SUMMSCORE metric which comprises of Exactness, Review, F1_SCORE. For Precision the score is 0.5106 for T5 and Pegasus and 0.0705 for Nltk and spaCy it is 0.0819 and 0.0647 for TF-IDF. Here T5 and Pegasus ha the most noteworthy score. For Recall the score is 0.4067 for T5 and Pegasus and 0.3050 for Nltk and spaCy, TF-IDF it has 0.3389. Overall T5 and Pegasus has the most elevated score. For F1_SCORE metric the score is 0.4528 for T5, BART and Pegasus and 0.1146 for Nltk and spaCy it is 0.1320 and 0.1086 for TF-IDF. Here T5, BART and Pegasus have the most elevated score. Of all measurements Exactness of SUMMSCORE -PRECISON has the most elevated score with 0.5106 and F1_SCORE has the next highest with 0.4528 and following ROUGE-1 with 0.44 for T5, BART and Pegasus.

Table 1. Results Comparison.

MODEL	ROUGE-1	ROUGE-2	ROUGE-L	BLUE	METEOR	SUMMSCORE		
						PRECISION	RECALL	F1_SCORE
T5	0.44	0.15	0.42	0.06	0.26	0.5106	0.4067	0.4528
Pegasus	0.44	0.15	0.42	0.06	0.26	0.5106	0.4067	0.4528
Bart	0.44	0.15	0.42	0.06	0.26	0.5106	0.4067	0.4528
Nltk	0.09	0.01	0.09	0.00	0.17	0.075	0.3050	0.1146
SpaCy	0.11	0.01	0.09	0.00	0.19	0.0819	0.3389	0.1320
TF-IDF	0.09	0.00	0.09	0.00	0.17	0.0647	0.3389	0.1086

The Fig. 4 compares summarization methods—T5, Pegasus, BART, NLTK, SpaCy, and TF-IDF—across various performance metrics. T5, Pegasus, and BART consistently outperform the other methods in key areas such as ROUGE-1, ROUGE-L, precision, recall, and F1-Score, indicating superior summarization quality. While all models perform similarly in SUMMSCORE, T5 and BART stand out with the highest precision and recall, suggesting they generate more accurate and relevant summaries. NLTK, SpaCy, and TF-IDF generally trail behind, with lower scores across most metrics. Overall, T5, Pegasus, and BART deliver the best summarization results.

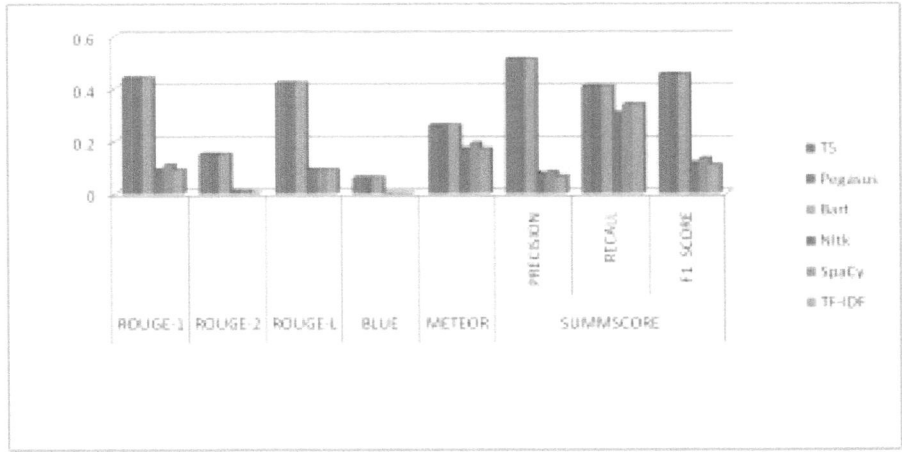

Fig. 4. Comparison of different summarization methods.

7   Conclusion

As a result, we are putting into practice "A Breakthrough Model for Speech Synthesis from Videos for the Differently- Abled" by EmpowerSpeak. In extractive summarizing, the main ideas and phrases from the source text are chosen and combined to produce a brief synopsis while maintaining the structure and language. It employs various algorithms, including NLTK, spaCy, BART, PEGASUS, T5 Algorithm and TF-IDF, to detect meaningful sentences based on parameters like word frequency and sentence relevance. Abstractive summarization, which generates new language expressions instead of just extracting sentences using transformers and the T5 Algorithm, produces succinct summaries by analyzing and rephrasing original information using natural language processing. With its strong framework for producing speech and audio from videos, this project has potential uses in a number of areas, such as assistive technologies, content indexing, and accessibility tools.

References

1. Wang, M., Xie, P., Du, Y., Hu, X.: T5-based model for abstractive summarization: a semi-supervised learning approach with consistency loss functions. Appl. Sci. **13**(12), 7111 (2023)
2. Priyanka, M., Sindhuja, K., Madhuvani, V., Sowpthika, K.P., Kumar, K.K.: Multimedia summarization using spacy. EPRA International Journal of Research & Development (IJRD) (2023)
3. Sasibhooshan, R., Kumaraswamy, S., Sasidharan, S.: Image caption generation using visual attention prediction and contextual spatial relation extraction. J Big Data **10**, 18 (2023)
4. Emad, A., et al.: IEEE 11th Annual Computing and Communication Workshop and Conference (CCWC). Las Vegas, NV, USA **2021**, 00600066 (2021)
5. Zhu, Y., Zhao, W., Hua, R., Wu, X.: Topic-aware video summarization using multimodal transformer, Pattern Recognition, Volume 140, 2023, 109578, ISSN 0031–3203

6. Liang, G., Lv, Y., Li, S., Zhang, S., Zhang, Y.: Video summarization with a convolutional attentive adversarial network. Pattern Recogn. **131**, 108840 (2022) ISSN 0031–3203
7. Parth, K., Prem, K.: Image Caption Generator, INTERNATIONAL JOURNAL OF ENGINEERING RESEARCH & TECHNOLOGY (IJERT) **10**, Issue 11 (November 2021)
8. Ging, S., et al.: "COOT: Cooperative Hierarchical Transformer for Video-Text Representation Learning." ArXiv abs/2011.00597 (2020)
9. Zhu, W., Lu, J., Han, Y., Zhou, J.: Learning multiscale hierarchical attention for video summarization. Pattern Recogn. **122**, 108312 (2022) ISSN 0031–3203
10. Ji, Z., Xiong, K., Pang, Y., Li, X.: Video summarization with attention-based encoder–decoder networks. IEEE Trans. Circ. Syst. Video Technol. **30**(6), 1709–1717 (June2020)
11. Lei, J., Wang, L., Shen, Y., Yu, D., Berg, T.L., Bansal, M.: MART: Memory Augmented Recurrent Transformer for Coherent Video Paragraph Captioning.In: Annual Meeting of the Association for Computational Linguistics (2020)
12. Park, J.S., Rohrbach, M., Darrell, T., Rohrbach, A.: Adversarial inference for multisentence video description. In: 2019 IEEE/CVF Conference on Computer Vision and Pattern Recognition (CVPR), Long Beach, CA, USA, 2019, pp. 6591–6601 (2019)
13. Liu, T., Meng, Q., Huang, J.-J., Vlontzos, A., Rueckert, D., Kainz, B.: Video summarization through reinforcement learning with a 3D spatio-temporal u-net. IEEE Trans. Image Process. **31**, 1573–1586 (2022)
14. Ghauri, J.A., Hakimov, S., Ewerth, R.: "Supervised video summarization via multiple feature sets with parallel attention. In: 2021 IEEE International Conference on Multimedia and Expo (ICME), Shenzhen, China, 2021, pp. 1–6s (2021)
15. Chen, S., Zhao, Y., Jin, Q., Wu, Q.: Proceedings of the IEEE/CVF Conference on Computer Vision and Pattern Recognition (CVPR), pp. 10638–10647 (2020)
16. Yu, Q., Yu, H., Wang, Y., Pham, T.D.: SUM-GAN-GEA: video summarization using GAN with Gaussian distribution and external attention. Electronics (Switzerland), **11**(21), [3523] (2022)
17. Yuan, Y., et al.: Spatiotemporal modeling for video summarization using convolutional recurrent neural network. IEEE Access **7,** 64676–64685 (2019)
18. Li, H., Ke, Q., Gong, M., Drummond, T.: Progressive video summarization via multimodal self supervised learning. In: 2023 IEEE/CVF Winter Conference on Applications of Computer Vision (WACV), Waikoloa, HI, USA, 2023, pp. 5573–5582 (2023)

Feature Extraction and Machine Learning Based Predictive Models for Heart Diseases Prediction: Analyzing the Effectiveness of Multiple Models

Poluru Sabitha[1], Uttam Kumar Giri[2], Subhanshu Goyal[3], Alok Kumar Agrawal[4], Ashok Kumar Sahoo[5], and Pradeepta Kumar Sarangi[6(✉)]

[1] Chitkara University College of Nursing, Chitkara University, Baddi, Himachal Pradesh, India
poluru.sabitha@chitkarauniversity.edu.in

[2] Chitkara University School of Engineering and Technology, Chitkara University, Baddi, Himachal Pradesh, India

[3] Department of Mathematics, Marwadi University, Rajkot, India
subhanshu.goyal@marwadieducation.edu.in

[4] Chitkara University School of Engineering and Technology, Chitkara University, Baddi, Himachal Pradesh, India
alok.agrawal@chitkarauniversity.edu.in

[5] Graphic Era Deemed to be University, Graphic Era Hill University, Dehradun, Uttarakhand, India
ashok.sahoo@gehu.ac.in

[6] Chitkara University School of Engineering and Technology, Chitkara University, Baddi, Himachal Pradesh, India
pradeepta.sarangi@chitkarauniversity.edu.in

Abstract. Heart illness, also designated as cardiovascular illness, wraps up several disorders that influence the cardiovascular system and is the leading foundation of mortality globally throughout the duration of the previous few decades. Patients with heart diseases are increasing quickly as a result of poor consumption habits and a lack of health knowledge. Heart disease affects and kills approximately one out of every four people. In healthcare, especially in the discipline of cardiology, early and effective detection of cardiac disease is crucial. Giving patients the right therapy depends on reliable and exact identification of cardiac problems. Because Machine Learning (ML) systems can find patterns in data, their usage in the healthcare sector has increased dramatically. Patients and medical personnel may all profit from a decreased chance of misdiagnosis when ML algorithms are used to identify cardiac problems. The intent of this paper is to implement ML models to analyze health decision-making using heart disease data. This work implements four ML models namely Gaussian NB., RF, DT, and SVC to analyze the medical data collected from the UCI repository. With an accuracy rate of 98%, the RF model is the finest performer, according to the data.

Keywords: Random Forest · Machine Learning · Heart Disease · Decision Tree

1   Introduction

Any ailment affecting the composition or operation of the heart system is referred to as cardiovascular disease. While many people perceive it as a single illness, heart disease encompasses a variety of disorders with diverse underlying causes. The heart is a crucial organ in the human body, responsible for delivering blood to all parts of the body. If it fails to do so, vital organs, including the brain, will stop functioning, leading to death within minutes. The prevalence of various heart-related conditions is increasing, largely due to lifestyle changes, workplace stress, and poor dietary choices. The strokes and cardiac arrests are responsible for 4 out of every five deaths worldwide. Alterations in the arteries that supply the heart, which provide blood to the heart, are the cause of this grave, long-term health problem. Cardiovascular arrhythmia, or abnormal heartbeat patterns, is a major cause of heart disease. Moreover, obesity and high blood pressure are prevalent medical conditions among those who are at elevated risk for cardiovascular disease. A heart attack might cause feelings of discomfort in the chest, fatigue, shortness of breath, foot edema, nausea, or upper body pain. Heartburn, acute exhaustion, and back or upper body discomfort are some other symptoms. Because of misdiagnosis or tardy discovery, late-stage cardiac diseases frequently result in higher death rates.

The World Health Organization (WHO) recognizes cardiovascular disease as the foremost evidence of death globally. In 2016, around 17.9 million individuals succumbed to heart-related ailments. These conditions not only impair a person's quality of life but also escalate healthcare expenses. According to WHO estimates, India may have incurred losses of up to $237 billion due to cardiovascular diseases from 2005 to 2015. Therefore, the accurate prediction of cardiac disorders is essential. Healthcare organizations worldwide are gathering data on various medical issues, and numerous machine learning (ML) techniques can be utilized to derive valuable insights from this data. However, these extensive datasets often contain a considerable amount of noise. Despite their size, various ML methods can effectively analyze this information, surpassing human analytical capabilities. Consequently, these algorithms have demonstrated effectiveness in accurately predicting the presence or absence of heart-related conditions. ML, a fundamental component of artificial intelligence, includes a range of techniques such as KNN, CNN, DT, RF, and Naïve Bayes. These techniques can be classified into three categories: unsupervised, semi-supervised, and supervised learning, all of which are well-equipped to handle Big Data. Big Data refers to the enormous volumes of information generated daily, which can be transformed into valuable insights for clinical research through data mining tools. Consequently, there is a growing demand for effective devices that employ ML classifiers to diagnose cardiovascular diseases.

2   Literature Review

In a recent study, researchers [1] aimed to identify the most accurate machine learning classifier for diagnosing cardiovascular diseases. All methods tested, except for MLP and KNN, assessed the significance scores of each feature. These scores were then used to rank the features based on their likelihood of indicating cardiovascular disease. The findings revealed that the Random Forest (RF) method achieved an impressive 100%

accuracy, along with 100% sensitivity and specificity, using a cardiovascular disease dataset sourced from Kaggle. The study involved three classification techniques: Random Forest (RF), Decision Trees (DT), and K-nearest neighbors (KNN).

Similarly, to anticipate cardiac events, the present investigation [2] used data from surveys from 400 k US people to develop and assess 6 ML models. The models that were examined for the research are Bagging, RF, XGBoost, RF, KNN, and Naïve Bayes. The XGBoost model demonstrated optimum performance outcomes with an accuracy rating of 91.30%.

In this research, the authors [3] built a deep-learning identification system for car-diovascular disease prognosis using an ANN model. The accuracy of the created ANN prediction model was 93.44%, 7.5% better than that of the conventional SVM ML model. Furthermore, the classification and training times were lowered to just over one minute by utilizing a more straightforward neural network.

Eleven ML classifiers were employed in this work by authors [4] to uncover critical characteristics, hence improving the prediction of cardiovascular disease. Several feature pairs and well-known classification methods were employed to establish a predictive model. With multilayer perceptron and gradient-boosted trees, researchers were able to attain 95% accuracy in the cardiovascular illness prediction model. With an accuracy rate of 96%, the RF model performs superior in the forecasting of cardiovascular disease.

A major medical services in southern India provided 1670 anonymized patient records for use in another investigation [5]. The prediction system was developed by applying 5 cut- cutting-edge ML methods, namely LR, KNN, Naïve Bayes, AdaBoost, and RF using Python programming. The performance was assessed using the final 30% of the data. ML was successful in predicting the probability of cardiac problems. With 470 out of 501 medical data properly identified, the top-performing RF prediction sys-tem achieved a diagnosis accuracy of 93.8%. The measured values of specificity and sensitivity were 94.6% and 92.8% respectively.

Similarly, in another research, authors [6] to ascertain the predictive accuracy of ML systems for cardiac conditions, utilize the UCI repository dataset during both testing and training. KNN, LR, DT, and SVM are some of the approaches used. The Anaconda notebook is an ideal instrument to execute Python programs; it offers a number of plugins and header files that increase the exactness and precision of the task. The highest accuracy achieved by KNN i.e. 87%.

In another work [7], a Python-based program for healthcare is created, since it is more dependable and aids in the establishment and tracking of various forms of health monitoring apps. They introduce data processing and outline the three primary stages of developing an application: gathering databases, running LR, and assessing the features of the dataset. An RF classifier serves to identify cardiac conditions more accurately. This program, which seems noteworthy because of its about 83% accuracy rate across training data, requires data analysis.

In another research [8], a model that seeks to determine the best ML method to predict heart attacks accurately in their early phases is suggested. Using the patient's data, the model is trained and tested using ML ideas to enable efficient decision-making. The suggested approach has 3 stages, followed by data training and testing utilizing ML algorithms (SVM, RF, KNN, and DT) that demonstrate in the third step, the classification results are optimized using one of the hyperparameter optimization strategies, random search, which yields best classification i.e. 94.958%, using the RF algorithm, 94.53% accuracy was the highest (Table 1).

Table 1. Review of the Existing work

Researcher	Dataset Used	Algorithm Used	Best Accuracy
M. M. Ali et al.	Kaggle	KNN, RF, and DT	100%
R. C. Das et al.	Survey Data of 400k US residents	Bagging, Xgboost, RF, KNN, and Naïve Bayes	91.30%
R. Rone Sarra et al.	UCI Dataset	ANN, SVM	93.44% of ANN
Hassan CAU et al.	UCI Dataset	LR, SVR, NB, RF, XGBoost, DT, NN, KNN, Gradient Boosted Tree, Radial Basis Function, Multilayer perceptron	96%
Maini E et al.	South India Hospital	LR, KNN, Naïve Bayes, AdaBoost, and RF	93.8%
A. Singh and R Kumar	UCI Dataset	KNN, DT, LR, SVM	87%
Chang, V. et.al	Publicly accessible heart disease data	RF	83%
M. Abood Kadhim and A. M. Radhi	Long Shoreline, VA, Hungarian, Cleveland, Starlog, Switzerland Cardiovascular disease dataset	SVM, RF, KNN, and DT	94.53%

3 Materials and Methods

This model's dataset was obtained from the UCI ML repository. As seen in Figure 1, the database includes 688 instances and 14 characteristics in it. While there are 76 features in the original dataset, all reputable sources advise utilizing the 14 most pertinent attributes.

Figure 1 includes a description of every characteristic in the dataset. It displays the properties together with the data type for each.

```
Data columns (total 14 columns):
 #   Column     Non-Null Count   Dtype
---  ------     --------------   -----
 0   age        716 non-null     int64
 1   sex        716 non-null     int64
 2   cp         716 non-null     int64
 3   trestbps   716 non-null     int64
 4   chol       716 non-null     int64
 5   fbs        716 non-null     int64
 6   restecg    716 non-null     int64
 7   thalach    716 non-null     int64
 8   exang      716 non-null     int64
 9   oldpeak    716 non-null     float64
 10  slope      716 non-null     int64
 11  ca         716 non-null     int64
 12  thal       716 non-null     int64
 13  target     716 non-null     int64
```

Fig. 1. Attributes and their data type

A correlation heatmap across each characteristic in the dataset is shown in Figure 2. Correlation heatmap are a kind of visualization that illustrates the level of correlations amongst numerical data.

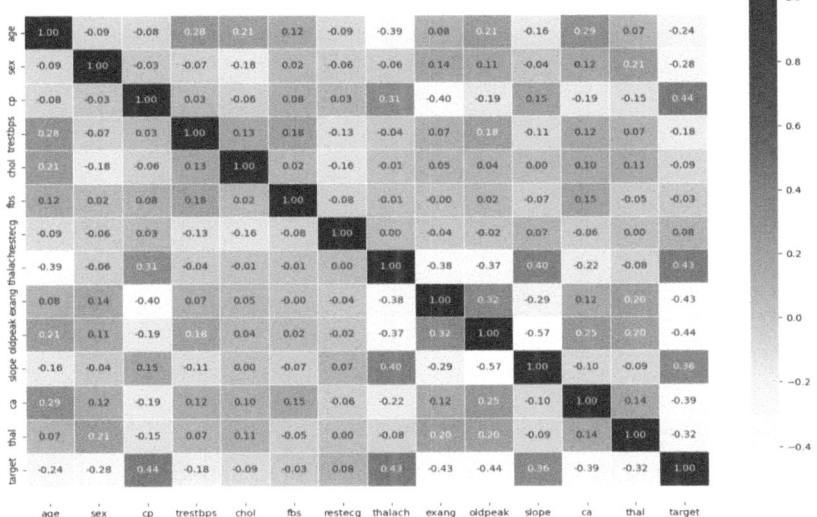

Fig. 2. Dataset Heatmap

Figure 3 represents the dataset histogram depicting the importance of the feature elements in the dataset.

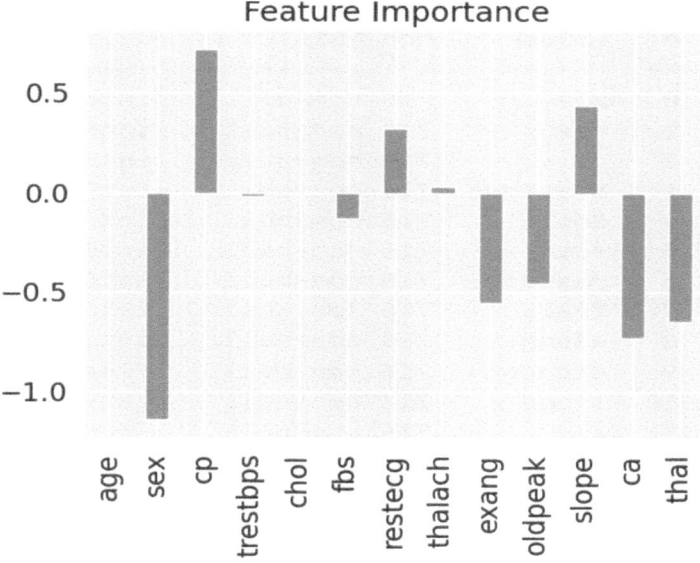

Fig. 3. Dataset Histogram

Figure 4 represents the bar graph of patients having heart disease (1) and not having heart disease (0).

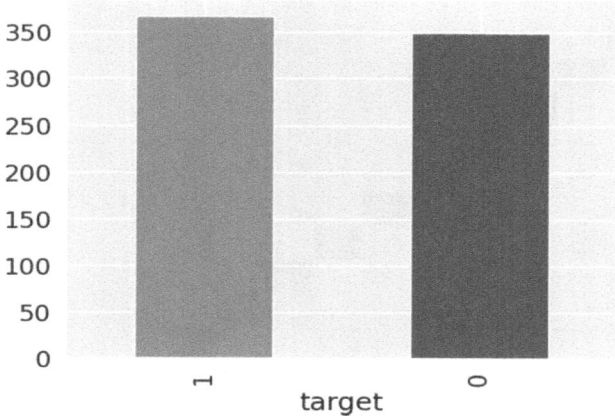

Fig. 4. Count of Patients with and without Heart Disease

Figure 5 shows the frequency of heart diseases in regards to Age, with green dots representing patients with no disease and orange dots representing patients with some kind of heart disease. Patients between the age 40–60 and heart rate greater than 140 have the highest number of heart diseases.

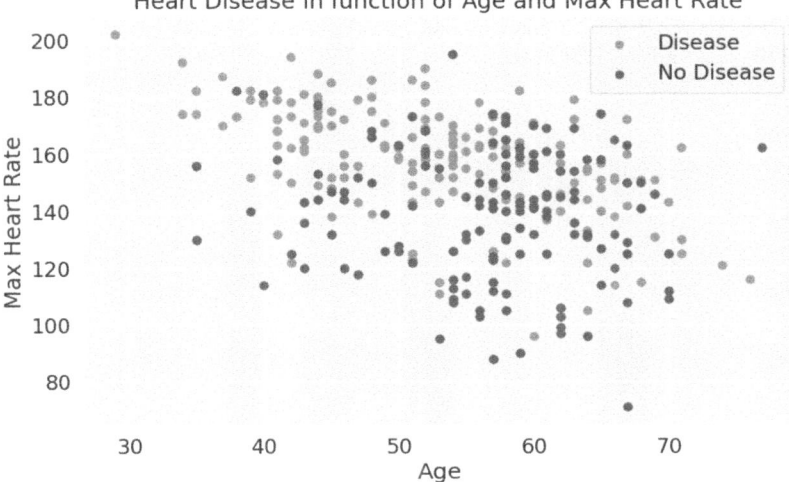

Fig. 5. Frequency of Heart Disease for all Ages

Figure 6 shows the count of heart disease for male and female patients. The graph shows that the count of male patients are more in both the cases of '0' and '1'.

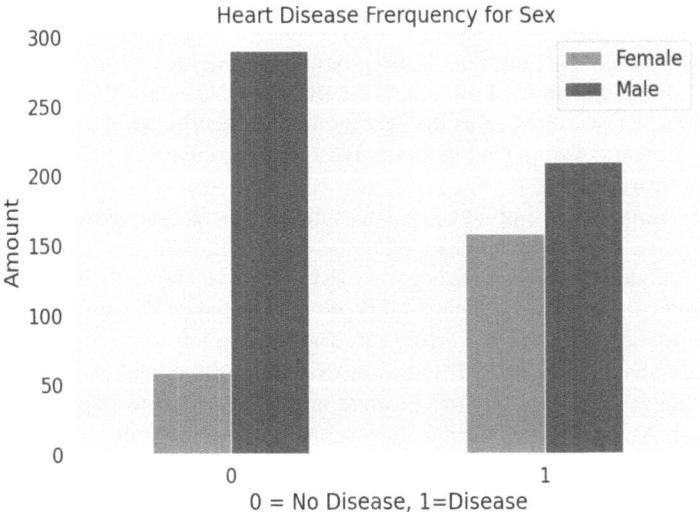

Fig. 6. Frequency of Heart Disease for each sex

According to the Figure 7, patients having chest pain type 1 and 2 are having more patients with heart disease. For chest pain type 3, the difference is minimum and for chest pain type 1, patients with no disease are more in count.

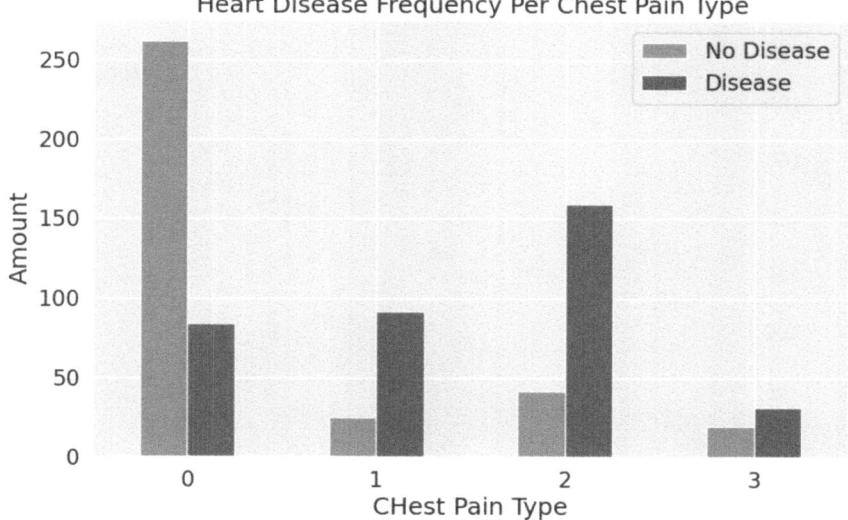

Fig. 7. Relation between Maximum Heart Rate and Heart Disease

4 Model Implementation

In the present study, classifiers are used for the detection of cardiovascular disease [9]. To estimate the performance of each clustered dataset, the classifiers are employed. The models with high accuracy rates in the aforementioned findings are the most performing ones. The Table 2 illustrates how much the different ML algorithm's evaluations of accuracy differ. RF was chosen as the best method to be utilized in the model as it has the highest accuracy score. This model is reasonably accurate in predicting any early beginning of heart disease.

A confusion matrix is employed to assess the categorization model's effectiveness. The true negative value, which is located in the upper left, indicates that both the actual value and the model's forecast were negative. False positive, shown by the top right value, essentially indicates that while the model predicted a value of Yes, the actual result was No. Another name for it is Type-I error [10]. The Bottom left value is the false negative also referred to as Type-II error. It indicates that while the model predicted a value of NO, the actual result was yes. True Positive is the term used to describe the Bottom Right number. As seen below, the accuracy score in a confusion matrix is estimated.

The results analysis for Gaussian NB implementation is given in Figure 8.

Figure 8 shows the Confusion Matrix and the classification report of Gaussian NB Algorithm. The accuracy produced by the algorithm is 81%. The Classification report is given in Figure 9.

The results analysis for SVC implementation is given in Figure 10.

The Confusion Matrix for the SVC implementation is mentioned in Figure 10. The accuracy produced by the algorithm is 88%. The Classification report is given in Figure 11.

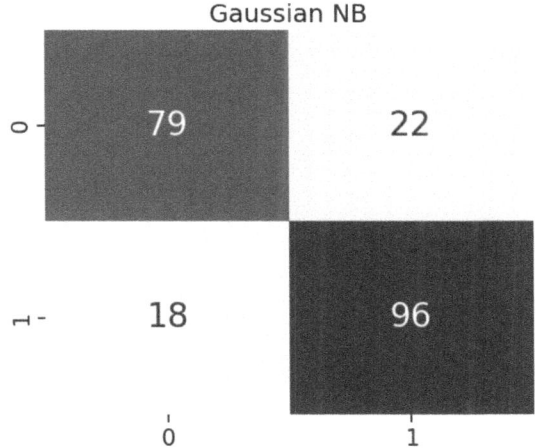

Fig. 8. Confusion matrix (Gaussian NB)

```
               precision    recall  f1-score   support

           0       0.81      0.78      0.80       101
           1       0.81      0.84      0.83       114

    accuracy                           0.81       215
   macro avg       0.81      0.81      0.81       215
weighted avg       0.81      0.81      0.81       215
```

Fig. 9. Classification Report (Gaussian NB)

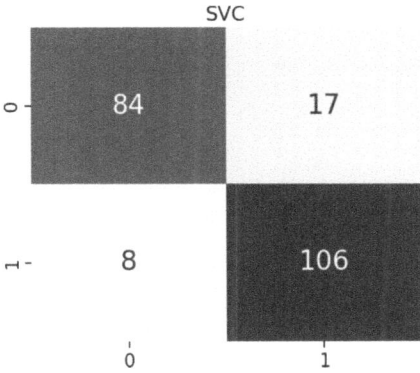

Fig. 10. Confusion matrix (SVC)

The results analysis for DT implementation is given in Fig. 12.

The Confusion Matrix for DT implementation is given in Figure 12. The accuracy produced by the algorithm is 95%. The Classification report is given in Figure 13.

The results analysis for RF implementation is given in Figure 14.

	precision	recall	f1-score	support
0	0.91	0.83	0.87	101
1	0.86	0.93	0.89	114
accuracy			0.88	215
macro avg	0.89	0.88	0.88	215
weighted avg	0.89	0.88	0.88	215

Fig. 11. Classification Report (SVC)

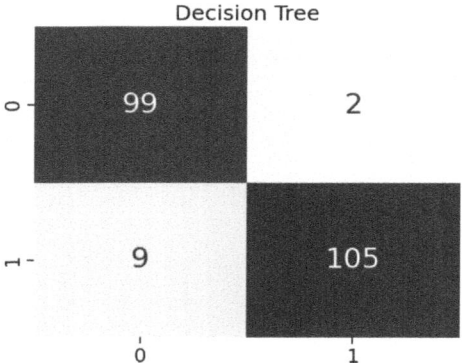

Fig. 12. Confusion matrix (DT)

	precision	recall	f1-score	support
0	0.92	0.98	0.95	101
1	0.98	0.92	0.95	114
accuracy			0.95	215
macro avg	0.95	0.95	0.95	215
weighted avg	0.95	0.95	0.95	215

Fig. 13. Classification Report (DT)

Figure 14 shows the Confusion Matrix of RF Algorithm. The accuracy produced by the algorithm is 98%. The Classification report is given in Figure 15.

Table 2 summarizes the model Implementations of each algorithm.

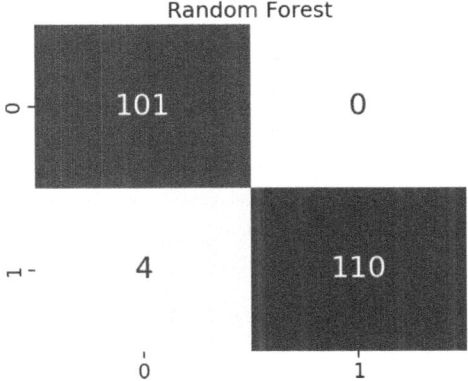

Fig. 14. Confusion matrix (RF)

```
              precision    recall  f1-score   support

          0       0.96      1.00      0.98       101
          1       1.00      0.96      0.98       114

   accuracy                           0.98       215
  macro avg       0.98      0.98      0.98       215
weighted avg      0.98      0.98      0.98       215
```

Fig. 15. Classification Report (RF)

Table 2. Best Accuracy Scores of each Algorithm used.

Algorithms Used	Accuracy Score
Gaussian NB	85%
SVC	87%
DT	95%
RF	98%

5   Conclusion and Future Scope

This research highlights the significance of detailed and precise detection of cardiac disorders, with a focus on ML techniques. By using the RF method on the UCI dataset, an impressive accuracy of 98% was obtained. The research's conclusion highlights improved and more trustworthy diagnostic skills by reducing the possibility of a manually made incorrect diagnosis and associated costs. ML algorithms lead to informed decision-making and, thus, better treatment.

By concentrating on the improvement and enhancement of ML models to achieve greater precision and dependability in identifying cardiac conditions in real-world situations, this investigation's future reach can be expanded. To improve the performance of the ML algorithms, the dataset might have more features and parameters added. It is also possible to investigate ensemble models and deep learning to address the difficulties associated with diagnosing cardiac conditions. This can facilitate the identification of cardiac disease more quickly and easily by allowing healthcare professionals to be involved on a personalized basis. This improves healthcare for patients and guarantees better outcomes by offering insightful advice.

References

1. Bui, F.M., Ahmed, K., Quinn, J.M.W., Ali, M.M., Paul, B.K., Moni, M.A.: Heart disease prediction using supervised machine learning algorithms: performance analysis and comparison. Comput. Biol. Med. **136**, 104672 (2021). https://doi.org/10.1016/j.compbiomed.2021.104672
2. Hossain, M.A., et al.: Heart disease detection using ML. 2023 IEEE 13th Annual Computing and Communication Workshop and Conference (CCWC), Las Vegas, NV, USA, pp. 0983–0987 (2023). https://doi.org/10.1109/CCWC57344.2023.10099294
3. Musa Dinar, A., Rone Sarra, R., Abed Mohammed, M.: Enhanced accuracy for heart disease prediction using artificial neural network. Indonesian Journal of Electrical Engineering and Computer Science **29**(1), 375 (2022). https://doi.org/10.11591/ijeecs.v29.i1.pp375-383
4. Algarni, A.D., et al.: Effectively predicting the presence of coronary heart disease using machine learning classifiers. Sensors (Basel) **22**(19), 7227 (Sep 23;). https://doi.org/10.3390/s22197227. PMID: 36236325; PMCID: PMC9573101
5. Venkateswarlu, B., Maini, B., Maini, E., Marwaha, D.: Machine learning-based heart disease prediction system for Indian population: an exploratory study done in South India. Med J Armed Forces India. **77**(3), 302–311 (2021). https://doi.org/10.1016/j.mjafi.2020.10.013
6. Kumar, R., Singh, A.: Heart disease prediction using machine learning algorithms. In: 2020 International Conference on Electrical and Electronics Engineering (ICE3), Gorakhpur, India, pp. 452–457 (2020). https://doi.org/10.1109/ICE348803.2020.9122958
7. Xu, A.Q., Bhavani, V., Chang, V., Hossain, A.: An artificial intelligence model for heart disease detection using machine learning algorithms. Healthcare Analytics **2**, 100016 (2022). https://doi.org/10.1016/j.health.2022.100016
8. Abood Kadhim, M., Radhi, A.M.: Heart disease classification using optimized Machine learning algorithms. Iraqi Journal for Computer Science and Mathematics, pp. 31–42 (2023). https://doi.org/10.52866/ijcsm.2023.02.02.004
9. Bhardwaj, S., Jain, S., Kumar, A., Trivedi, N., Tiwari, R.: Intelligent Heart Disease Prediction System Using Data Mining Modeling Techniques (2022). https://doi.org/10.1007/978-981-19-0707-4_79
10. Tiwari, S., Kumar, S., Guleria, K.: Outbreak trends of coronavirus disease–2019 in India: a prediction. Disaster Med. Public Health Prep. **14**(5), e33–e38 (2020)

Machine Learning Models and FOREX Analysis: A Comparison with Hybrid Models to Predict the Next Day Exchange Rate

Naaz Gorowara[1], Misha Mittal[2], Nidhi Goel[3], Ramamani Tripathy[4],
Pradeepta Kumar Sarangi[4(✉)], Ashok Kumar Sahoo[5], Alok Kumar Agrawal[4],
and Subhanshu Goyal[6]

[1] Maharishi Markandeshwar Institute of Management, Mullana, Ambala, India

[2] Maharishi Markandeshwar University, Mullana, Ambala, India
misha.mittal@mmumullana.org

[3] Chitkara University Institute of Engineering and Technology, Chitkara University, Rajpura, Punjab, India
nidhi1079cse.phd22@chitkara.edu.in

[4] Chitkara University School of Engineering and Technology, Chitkara University, Baddi, Himachal Pradesh, India
{ramamani.tripathy,alok.agrawal}@chitkarauniversity.edu.in,
pradeeptasarangi@gmail.com

[5] Graphic Era Deemed to be University, Graphic Era Hill University, Dehradun, Uttarakhand, India
ashok.sahoo@gehu.ac.in

[6] Department of Mathematics, Marwadi University, Rajkot, India
subhanshu.goyal@marwadieducation.edu.in

Abstract. The marketplace where currencies from every corner of the world undergo trading is known as the foreign exchange market. It enables traders to purchase or sell any money. Foreign currency, or forex, is a unique sector of finance where speculators can expect to make large profits but also face significant hazards. It's also a rather straightforward market since dealers may make money simply by foreseeing the path of the two-currency rate of exchange. The foreign currency in the marketplace presents difficulties for period projections due to its fluctuating, highly unpredictable, irregular, and chaotic nature. It is challenging to build a reliable model that can both capture existing trends and adapt to new ones as market conditions change continually. In recent times, scholars worldwide have been closely examining the foreign exchange or FOREX market. Owing to its delicate nature, several studies have been carried out in an attempt to precisely forecast future FOREX currency prices. This work analyzes the effectiveness of machine learning models to predict the next day currency exchange rate (USD to INR). In this context, this work implements a RNN model, and a hybrid LSTM model. The accuracy thus calculated is 99.70% by RNN model and 99.79% by LSTM models respectively.

Keywords: Currency exchange · RNN model · LSTM model · Dollar conversion

© The Author(s), under exclusive license to Springer Nature Switzerland AG 2025
S. Rajagopal et al. (Eds.): ASCIS 2024, CCIS 2424, pp. 99–113, 2025.
https://doi.org/10.1007/978-3-031-86290-8_7

1 Introduction

Money is a vital instrument for any nation's economy. Economies of countries cannot grow and prosper without international trade. Imports and exports are the main drivers of revenue generation in many nations. The stock market offers a picture of the economy's and corporations' prospects for future growth. All currency pairings are bought and sold on the decentralized foreign exchange market, often known as the forex or FX market. One area of focus for finance, economics, and financial engineering study has been currency exchange rate prediction. The need for precise and trustworthy algorithms to forecast currency exchange rates is growing at the pace of globalization. To put it briefly, the forex market is the market with the greatest liquidity after the market for sovereign debt. It is essentially the exchange where so-called convertible currencies are exchanged against each other at continuously fluctuating exchange rates [1].

This worldwide market is not restricted by geography and exists everywhere. When contrasted to other market segments such as stocks and bonds, the characteristics of Forex exhibit distinctions [2]. Due to these variations, forex traders have greater trading options and benefits from profitable deals. No fees, no intermediaries, no fixed lot size, minimal transaction costs, great liquidity, nearly immediate transactions, minimal margins/high borrowing, round-the-clock processes, and no insider trading are a few of these benefits.

Machine learning models have been instrumental and very effective in many fields of human requirements [3]. The adaptive and self-correcting nature of the machine learning models make them applicable for almost every field of research and application [4].

2 Literature Review

Yıldırım et al. [5] researchers employed a well-liked deep learning approach for directional prediction in Forex trading termed "long short-term memory" (LSTM), which has proven to be highly effective in several time-series forecasting issues. We used two different types of data: macroeconomic data and technical indicator data. These are the two primary data sets used in the financial sector by fundamental and technical analysis, respectively.

Mohanty et al. [6] presented a model that uses algorithms such as Salp Swarm to effectively use ANN to predict Forex Trend Analysis values for INR and USD. The authors' conclusion is that their proposed method works better than others.

N. Patil et al. [7] published a study on SVM to predict exchange rates using machine learning methods. The authors have shown that SVM algorithms are the most suitable and accurate methods for non-large data.

S. Liu et al. [8] work aims to improve model interpretability by conducting a comparative analysis of hybrid ML techniques. In particular, DT regressors, LSTM, and linear regression are presented. Among the potential models, the linear regression shows the highest performance, according to the grounded experiments.

The authors Baasher et al. [9] of this work examined signal processing characteristics and technical scrutiny of forex various time periods in order to anticipate the daily trend of high rates. The method is asked to estimate either the high rate will increase or decrease in a binary classification challenge. The optimum subsets of characteristics for the classification issue are found using 5 feature approaches, SVM- based feature selection methods, and bagging trees feature selection methods. ML classifiers are all trained using many distinct feature subsets and the results are reported and contrasted based on the percentage classification performance.

To anticipate fluctuations in prices, the research [10] uses Open, High, Low, Close data along with a prior dataset of 100 candlesticks. It uses a trading algorithm that generates SELL or BUY bids contingent upon the initial and final prices, which leads to less-than-ideal outcomes. But after more research, the study integrates the Hammer candlestick pattern with the MACD indicator, showing that this combination of signals successfully lowers noise and improves the model's precision.

Authors like T. Kurujitkosol et al. [11] have implemented machine learning model for forex price movement. Using the technique of stacking machine learning model the authors have reported an accuracy of 90%.

In another study [12] offered a fresh perspective on contrasting the statistical approach and ML, two popular techniques for making predictions based on data sets. Forex rates are predicted using the related methodologies. This study employs ASTAR as its statistical approach, and SVM and a hybrid version of Genetic Algorithm-Neural Network (GANN) are selected for ML. The root mean square error is used to compare the accuracy rates of the 3 approaches.

In this work, authors [13] created a unique event-driven characteristics that signal a shift in the direction of the trend. Next, in the order to forecast a retracement point that would offer the ideal entry opportunity for maximizing profit, they constrasted bidirectional long short-term memory (BiLSTM), LSTM, and gated recurrent unit (GRU) with a baseline model that was a basic recurrent neural network (RNN). The outcomes of our experiment demonstrate that the suggested models and event-driven feature selection may combine to provide a reliable prediction system.

The authors of this research [6] suggest a method based on deep reinforcement learning. In order to train the agent on several FOREX currency pairings and create market-wide reinforcement learning agents, they meticulously crafted a data pre-processing technique that also permits the use of more potent recurrent deep learning models without running the danger of overfitting.

3   Objective Methodology

The main objective of this work is to analyze the effectiveness of machine learning models to predict the next day currency exchange rate (USD to INR). In this context, this work implements a RNN model, and a hybrid LSTM model Finally, the results of both the models have been compared.

4 Dataset

For the application of machine learning algorithms, daily exchange data of the US dollar against the Indian rupee (January 1, 2023 - October 01, 2024) is taken into account. The research dataset was downloaded from www.investing.com on 1st October 2024. A sample of the dataset is shown in Fig. 1.

	Date	Open	High	Low	Close
0	02-01-2023	82.670	82.800	82.560	82.745
1	03-01-2023	82.698	83.038	82.654	82.774
2	04-01-2023	82.779	82.919	82.667	82.641
3	05-01-2023	82.740	82.808	82.426	82.568
4	06-01-2023	82.604	82.785	82.275	82.270

Fig. 1. Sample dataset

The attributes and their data type in the dataset is shown in Fig. 2.

#	Column	Non-Null Count	Dtype
0	Date	457 non-null	object
1	Open	457 non-null	float64
2	High	457 non-null	float64
3	Low	457 non-null	float64
4	Close	457 non-null	float64

Fig. 2. Dataset attributes and their data type

The graphical representation of the four values (open, high, low and close) are shown in Fig. 3, Fig. 4, Fig. 5 and in Fig. 6 respectively.

This work considers the open price for experimental implementations. Hence, the open price values have been normalized and scaled down to the range of 0 to 1. The graphical representation is shown in Fig. 7.

Finally, the correlation graph is shown in Fig. 8.

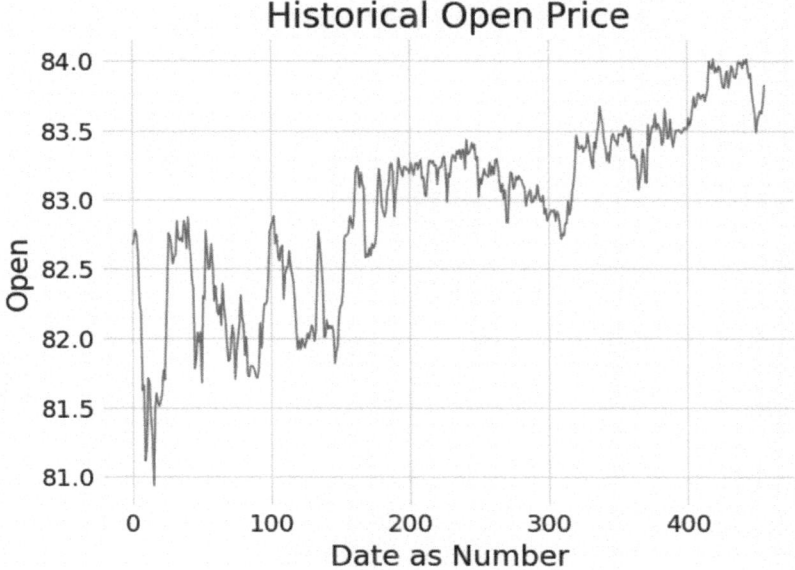

Fig. 3. Historical open price

Fig. 4. Historical close price

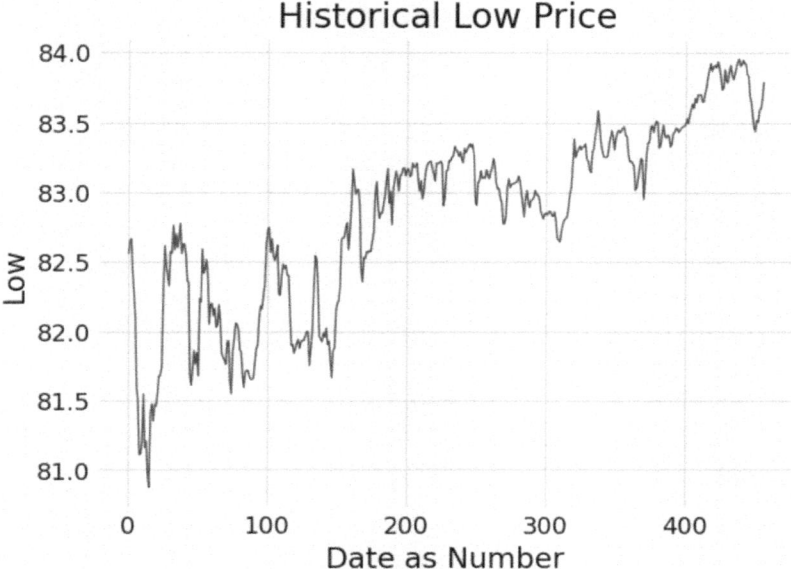

Fig. 5. Historical low price

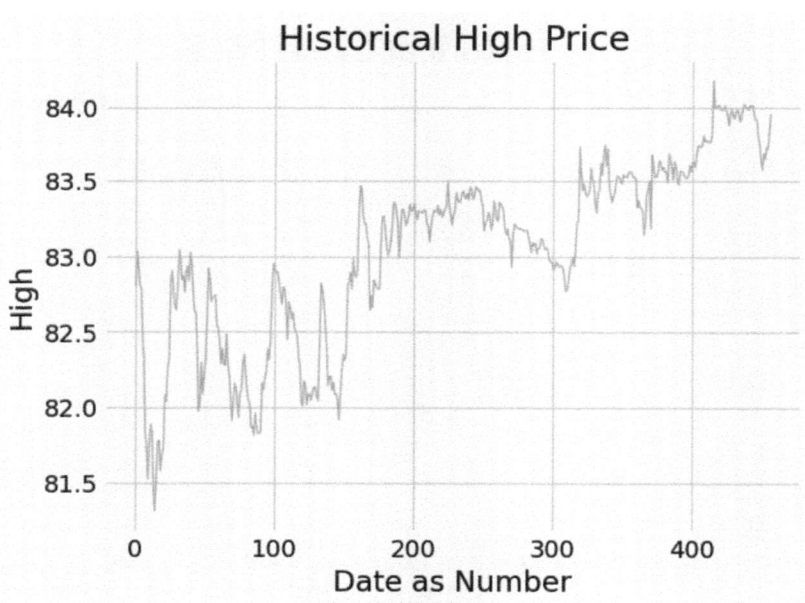

Fig. 6. Historical high price

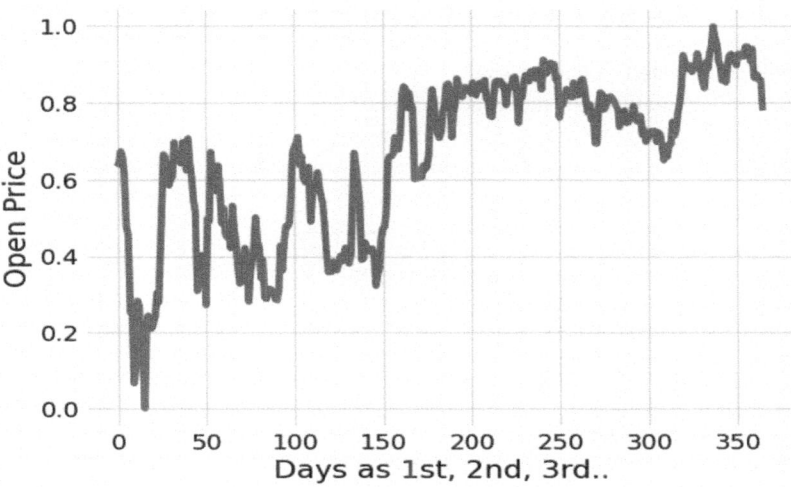

Fig. 7. Scaled down values

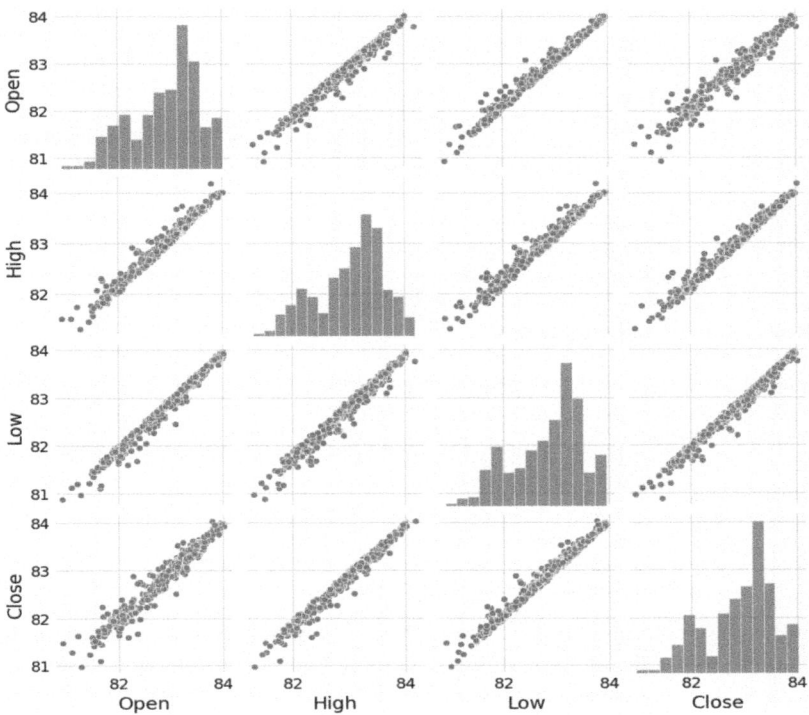

Fig. 8. Correlation graph

5   Models Implementation and Results Analysis

The methodology steps are as below:

The implementation of the machine learning models has been done through python programming in Google Colab environment. The methodology diagram for implementation of RNN and LSTM model is shown in Fig. 9.

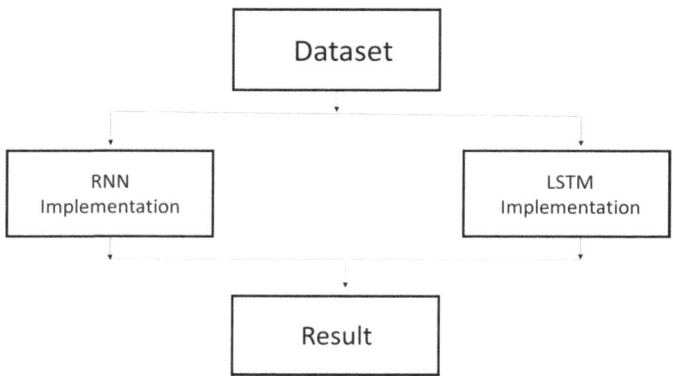

Fig. 9. Methodology diagram for RNN and LSTM implementation

The "Open" price has been considered for implementation. All the data are divided into training test sets. The details are as below:

Data length: 457
Train data length: 366
Validation data length: 91

5.1   RNN Model Implementation

RNN model is implemented through python programming in Google Colab environment. The hyper parameter is sequential regressor, adam optimizer, mean_squared_error as loss and accuracy as performance metric. The hyper parameter settings are as below:

units = 50,
activation = "tanh",
optimizer = "adam",
loss = "mean_squared_error",

The epoch wise training loss for the RNN model implementation is given in Fig. 10.

Figure 10 shows the analysis of the Recurrent Neural Network (RNN) model. The figure shows the decreasing error with increasing epoch numbers. The epoch wise accuracy is given in Fig. 11.

Figure 11 shows the analysis of the neural network (RNN) model. During training, the accuracy changes with increasing epoch number and finally comes to a stable state. The training performance is shown in Fig. 12.

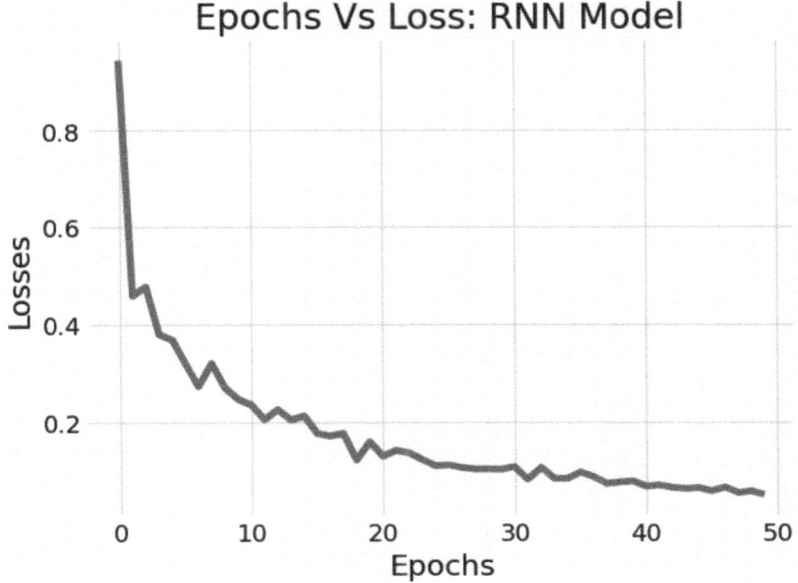

Fig. 10. Epoch Vs Loss (RNN model)

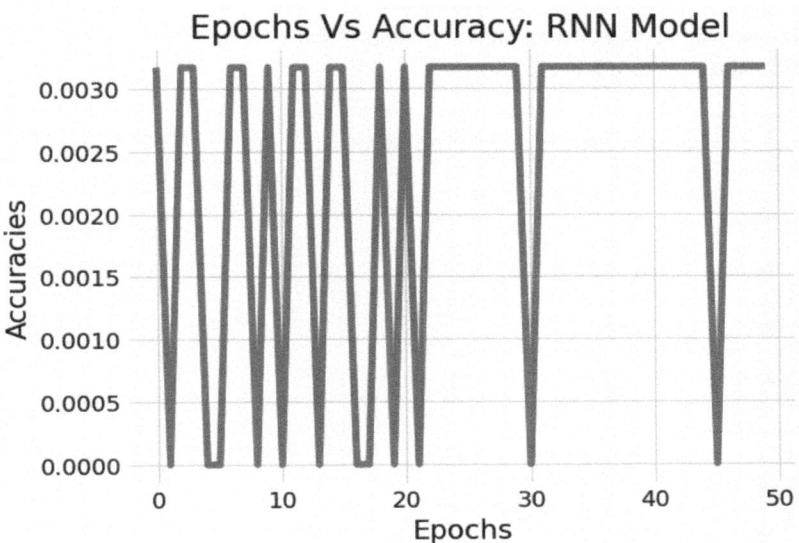

Fig. 11. Epoch Vs Accuracy (RNN model)

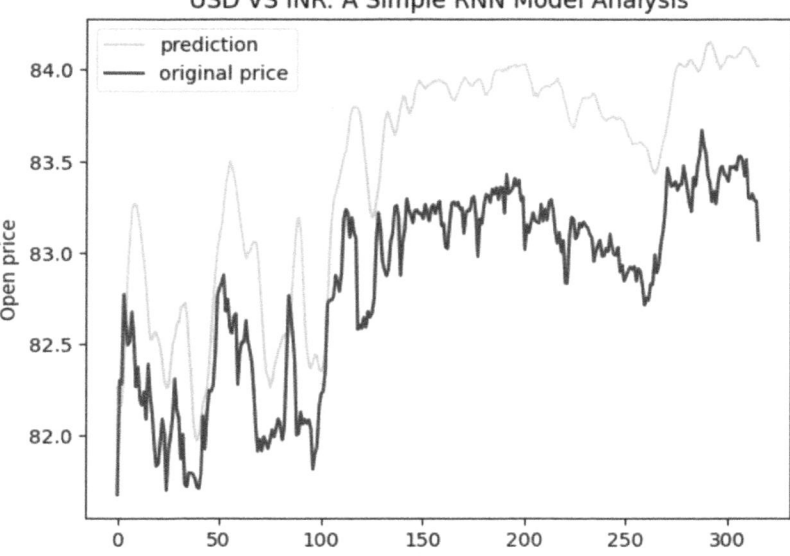

Fig. 12. Original Vs Prediction values on training data (RNN model)

The graph in Fig. 12 depicts the visual analysis of the RNN model. The chart shows the difference between the forecasted and the original USD to INR exchange rate. The predicted values for test data are shown in Fig. 13.

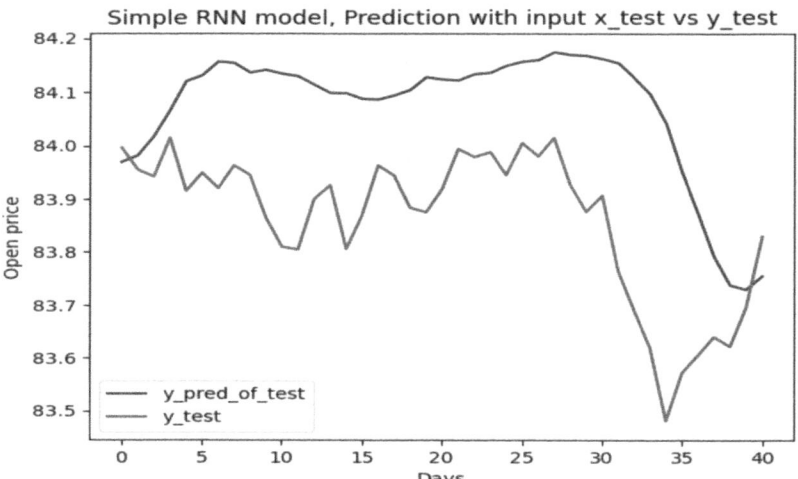

Fig. 13. Original Vs Prediction values on test data (RNN model)

Figure 13 depicts the analysis of the RNN model. The graph shows that the predicted values are slightly higher than the actual values. Finally, results for all three datasets are shown in Fig. 14.

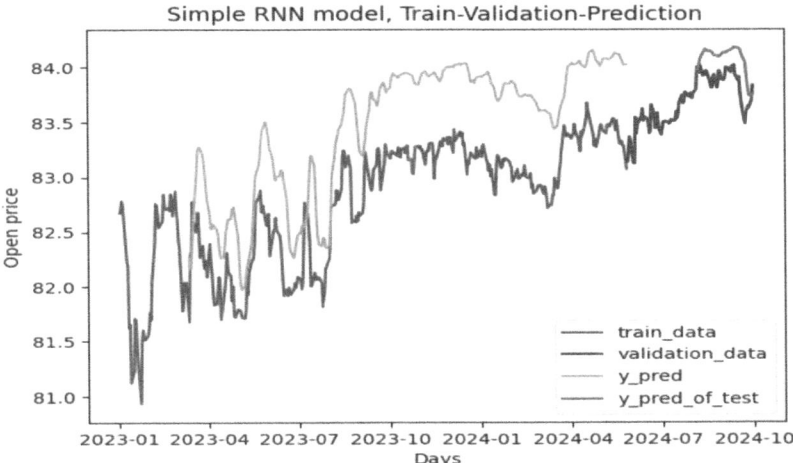

Fig. 14. RNN model (all results)

5.2   LSTM Model Implementation

LSTM is a type of RNN model. While traditional RNNs are limited to remembering only short-term data, LSTMs are capable of handling long-term dependencies. Additionally, RNNs often experience gradual loss of information over time, but LSTMs are designed to mitigate this issue during training. Various parameters used for LSTM training are: sequential model_lstm, mean_squared_error for loss calculation, adam as optimizer and accuracy as performance measure.

Figure 15 shows the analysis of the LSTM model. The figure shows the decreasing error with increasing epoch numbers.

Figure 16 shows the analysis of the LSTM model. During training, the accuracy changes with increasing epoch number and finally comes to a stable state.

The graph in Fig. 17 represents the analysis of the LSTM model. The graph shows that the predicted values are slightly higher than the actual values. The predicted values for test data are shown in Fig. 18.

Finally, the comparative analysis of all three results are shown in Fig. 19.

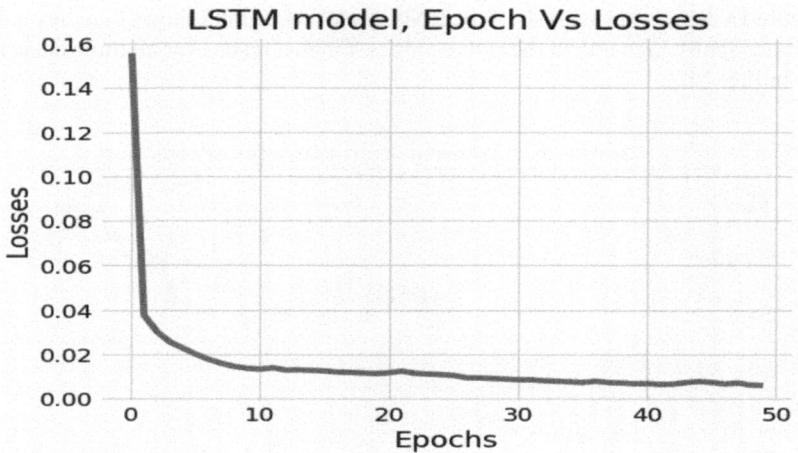

Fig. 15. LSTM model (Epochs Vs Losses)

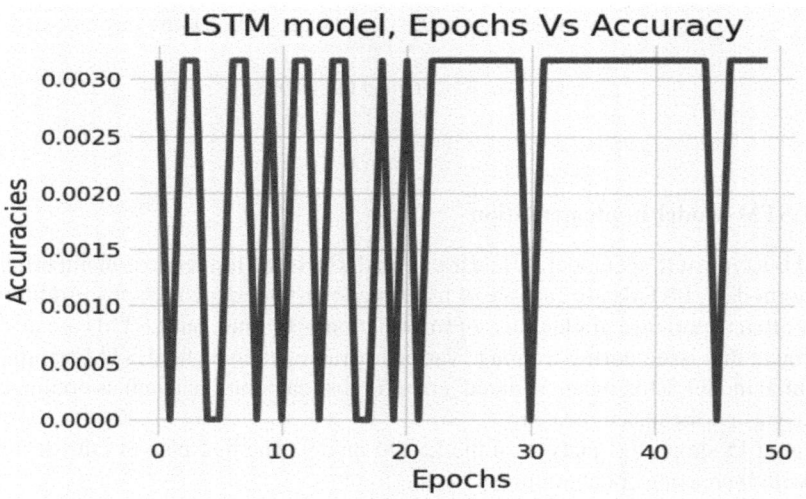

Fig. 16. Epoch Vs Accuracy (LSTM model)

5.3 Future Price Prediction

After successful training and testing, the models have been used to predict the next day currency exchange rate. The values predicted for the next day i.e. 2nd October 2024 is as below:

Prediction by RNN model: 83.65
Prediction by LSTM model: 83.73
Actual value on 2nd October is 83.90

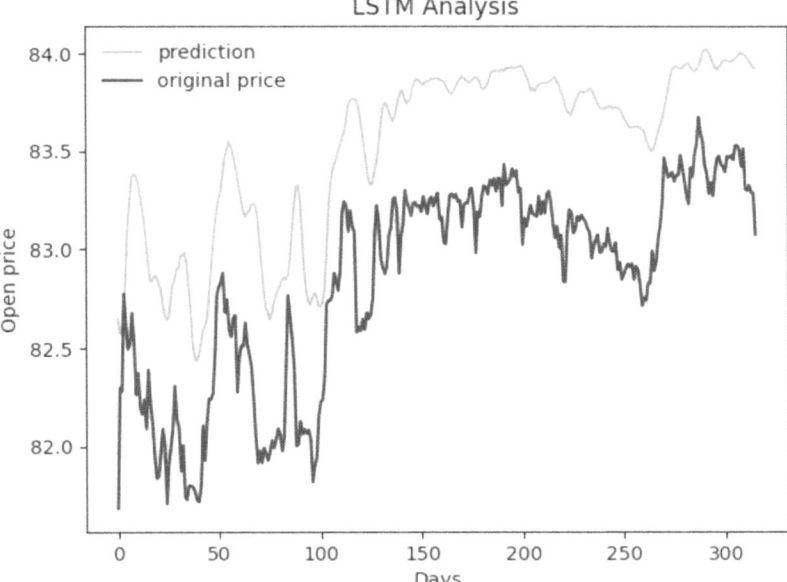

Fig. 17. Original Vs Prediction values on train data (LSTM model)

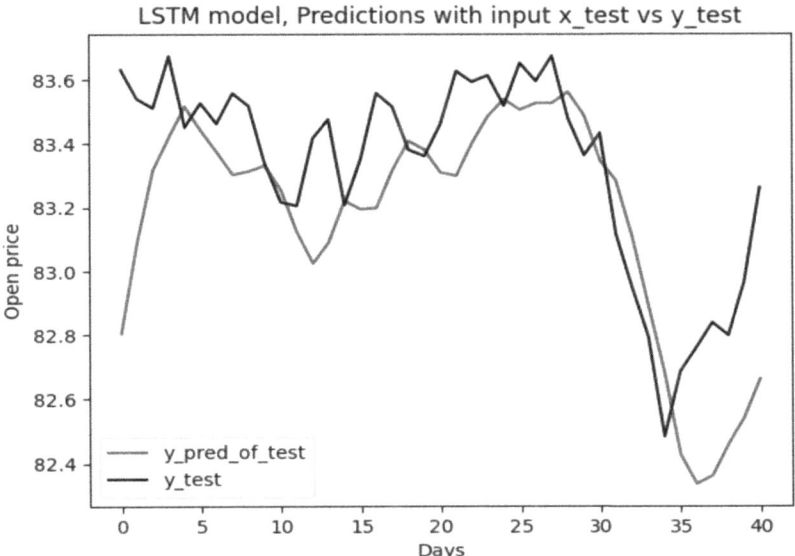

Fig. 18. Original Vs Prediction values on test data (LSTM model)

The accuracy thus calculated is 99.70% by RNN model and 99.79% by LSTM models respectively.

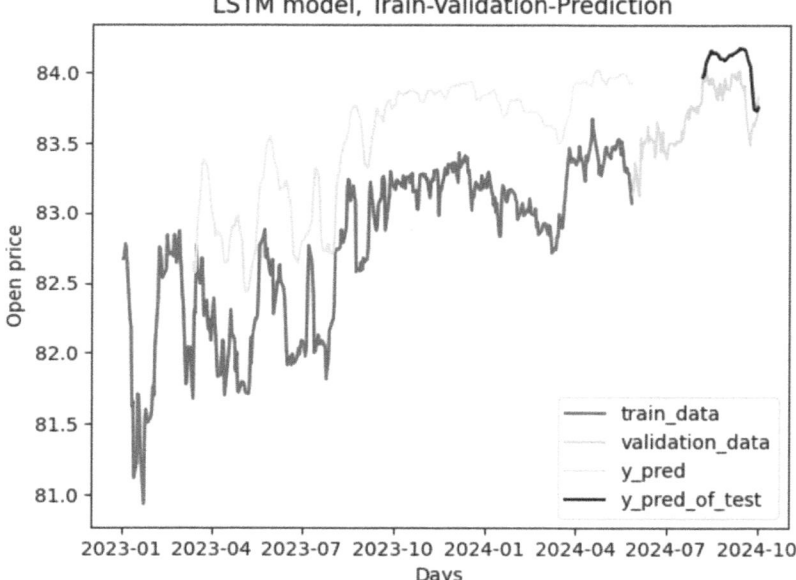

Fig. 19. LSTM model all results

6 Conclusion

Foreign exchange (FOREX) is a crucial component of the global economy and a nation's financial market. This study seeks to determine the optimal solution for converting USD to INR and to identify the most effective model for predicting the exchange rate between these currencies. After evaluating two highly effective models, our findings indicate that both the LSTM and RNN models achieve nearly identical accuracy levels exceeding 99%. This represents the best possible outcome for FOREX analysis.

References

1. Sinha, D., Sinha, S.: Financial modeling using ANN technologies: result analysis with different network architectures and parameters. Indian J. Res. Capital Markets **6**(1), 21–33 (2019)
2. Singla, A.K.S.: Modeling consumer price index: an empirical analysis using expert modeler. J. Technol. Manage. Growing Econ. **10**(1), 43–50 (2019)
3. Tiwari, R.G., Agarwal. A.K., Gupta, N., Anand, A., Verma, N.: Conceptualization of effective algorithm for minimizing power consumption in cloud servers. SMART, pp. 445–449 (2022)
4. Anand, A., Trivedi, N.K.., Wassay, M.A., Saud, Y.A., Maheshwari, S.: Application and uses of big data analytics in different domain. Machine Intelligence and Data Science Applications: Proceedings of MIDAS **132**, 481 (2021)
5. Yıldırım, D.C., Toroslu, I.H., Fiore, U.: Forecasting directional movement of Forex data using LSTM with technical and macroeconomic indicators. Financial Innovation **7**(1) (2021). https://doi.org/10.1186/s40854-020-00220-2

6. Mohanty, K., Panda, M., Mishra, D.: Foreign exchange price prediction using artificial neural network optimized by salp swarm algorithm. In: Advances in Distributed Computing and Machine Learning, Springer, pp. 393–404 (2022)

7. Patil, N., Masih, S., Rumao, J., Gaurea, V.: Predict foreign currency exchange rates using machine learning. In: Second International Conference on Sustainable Technologies for Computational Intelligence, Springer, Singapore, pp. 223–232 (2022)

8. Liu, S., Wu, K.-C., Jiang, C.X., Huang, B., Ma, D.: Financial Time-Series Forecasting: Towards Synergizing Performance And Interpretability Within a Hybrid Machine Learning Approach. *arXiv (Cornell University)* (2023). https://doi.org/10.48550/arxiv.2401.00534

9. Baasher, A.A., Fakhr, M.W.: Forex trend classification using machine learning techniques. In Proceedings of the 11th WSEAS international conference on Applied computer science (ACS'11). World Scientific and Engineering Academy and Society (WSEAS), Stevens Point, Wisconsin, USA, pp. 41–47 (2011)

10. Seong, N., Nam, K.: Predicting stock movements based on financial news with segmentation. Expert Systems with Applications **164**, 113988 (2021)

11. Kurujitkosol, T., Takhom, A., Usanavasin, S.: Forex price movement prediction using stacking machine learning models. In: 2022 17th International Joint Symposium on Artificial Intelligence and Natural Language Processing (iSAI-NLP), Chiang Mai, Thailand, pp. 1–6 (2022). https://doi.org/10.1109/iSAI-NLP56921.2022.9960245

12. Qi, L., Khushi, M., Poon, J.: Event-driven LSTM for forex price prediction. In: 2020 IEEE Asia-Pacific Conference on Computer Science and Data Engineering (CSDE), Gold Coast, Australia, pp. 1–6 (2020). https://doi.org/10.1109/CSDE50874.2020.9411540

13. Tsantekidis, A., Passalis, N., Toufa, A.-S., Saitas-Zarkias, K., Chairistanidis, S., Tefas, A.: Price trailing for financial trading using deep reinforcement learning. IEEE Transactions on Neural Networks and Learning Systems **32**(7), 2837–2846 (2021). https://doi.org/10.1109/TNNLS.2020.2997523

Commodity Identification Using Deep Learning in Smart Shoppping System

P. Dhevanathan$^{(\boxtimes)}$ and S. Mary Saira Bhanu

Department of Computer Science and Engineering, National Institute of Technology,
Tiruchirappalli, Tamil Nadu, India
{206122018,msb}@nitt.edu

Abstract. In supermarkets, product recognition for billing and stock management is labor-intensive and inefficient. To address these issues, a real-time commodity identification system using computer vision and deep learning is proposed. The smart shopping system improves consumer experience with automatic cart billing, reducing checkout time and stock update alerts. Custom dataset of retail products are used for training YOLOv8, with fixed multiple cameras to capture different views to identify hidden objects and objects of different scales using instance segmentation. We achieve a maximum F1 score of 0.978 across all products with the least training time compared to other detection models.

Keywords: YOLOv8 · Instance Segmentation · F1 score

1 Introduction

Shopping has evolved throughout history, but traditional shopping remains popular despite the rise of online options. In today's fast-paced world, customers seek faster service and better convenience, especially when dealing with long checkout lines, which also increases the workload on store staff. In supermarkets, significant human labor is needed for product recognition during billing and stock management. Surveys show 60% of people dislike long checkout lines and prefer self-checkout systems [4]. Self-checkout allows customers to scan and pay independently. Current systems like barcode recognition are time-consuming and RFID technology faces issues like high error rates, cost and recycling difficulties. This has driven the development of self-checkout processes, enhancing customer experience and reducing retailer costs. The proposed framework tackles above challenges with efficient object detection, tracking [3], and segmentation methods. It assigns bounding boxes and confidence scores to objects and monitors finiiducts being added or removed from cart, within fixed boundary lines defining the cart's area. Multiple cameras captures images to address issues of hidden or overlapping items. This setup helps to determine the product's depth and distinguish between images and real products. Additionally, it identifies moving objects of various scales irrespective of its shape and distance from viewpoints. Background subtraction helps to determine new or existing objects within the cart. Auto stock updates of products during shopping

S. Rajagopal et al. (Eds.): ASCIS 2024, CCIS 2424, pp. 114–122, 2025.
https://doi.org/10.1007/978-3-031-86290-8_8

helps to maintain inventory and alerts on low stocks for refreshments. The app seamlessly integrates with the smart cart, displaying product details and the current total in real time. Once shopping is complete, it generates a receipt and directs the user to the payment page.

2   Related Works

- A study proposes a smart self-checkout system using smartphones on shop- ping carts [4], leveraging deep learning and cloud services for video analysis. It is cost-effective but limited to single-item, single-hand scenarios and has security concerns with FTP uploads.
- In the Easy Shop system [10], users begin shopping via a store's mobile app, creating a wish list that is transferred to a smart cart using QR code scanning. The cart navigates them through the store, improving efficiency and reducing shopping time. However, the system relies on QR code functionality, and the use of load sensors for item addition and removal increases costs and may lead to inaccuracies if other objects are placed in the cart.
- For tracking object addition and removal in a multi-camera overlapping setup, another framework addresses person tracking control of mobile robots using a lightweight object detection and tracking system [3]. Although it handles occlusion well, it requires precise calibration, making it unsuitable for overlapping cameras to identify the re-entering of the same object.
- To determine an object or image we need depth information, the RAFT- Stereo method [7] of multiple camera, improves stereo depth estimation, essential for computer vision tasks, by calculating pixel-wise displacement maps from each viewpoints. It enhances speed but struggles with occluded objects and depth continuity for moving objects.
- Segmented area is used To determine scale of an object we refer Instance segmentation with UAVs for construction site monitoring [1], provides better local detail perception, spatial channel interactions and pixel analysis but facing challenges with subtle features and similar surfaces in UAV imagery. In hidden object scenarios, the Bilayer Convolutional Network (BCNet) [2] enhances overlapping object separation by modeling images as two layers. It improves boundary analysis but adds computational complexity and requires adjustments for different convolutional networks.
- To differentiate between existing and newly added products, background sub- traction is used to detect movement, referencing a real-time vehicle detection system [6] that combines MOG2 with H-SqueezeNet. It delivers high accuracy for real-time use but requires further validation across diverse datasets and scenarios.

2.1   Gaps in Literature

- Lack of depth information: This is critical for accurately distinguishing between overlapping items, making it difficult to identify products that are stacked, placed close together or printed images.
- Difficulty with irregular objects: Unusually shaped items present challenges for accurate scaling and measurement, leading to potential errors in recognition.

- Absence of fixed viewpoints: Without consistent angles or perspectives, determining the exact dimensions of products becomes problematic, reducing accuracy.
- Recognition in complex environments: The system needs improvements to perform accurately in practical retail settings, especially in busy and cluttered store environments.

2.2 Contributions and Novelty

- Trains a custom retail product dataset using YOLOv8 and employs multi- camera tracking to handle hidden objects with unique IDs.
- Utilizes multiple perspectives to differentiate between printed images and real products, and detects multi-hand actions within the cart.
- Identifies "Buy 1 Get 1 Free" labels, updating the bill for the original product only and distinguishes combo packs with different products.
- Implements a scaling factor mechanism to accurately determine object size and dimensions, ensuring consistent differentiation despite shape and orientation variations.
- Detects dynamic cart changes to differentiate between existing and newly added items.

3   Proposed Model

3.1   Overview

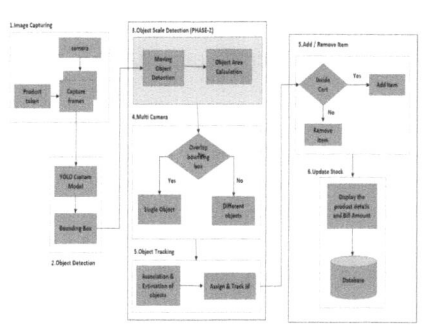
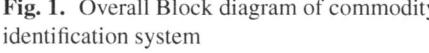
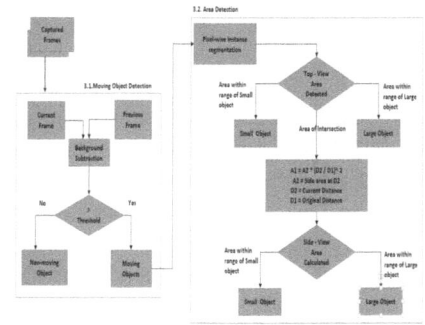

Fig. 1. Overall Block diagram of commodity identification system

Fig. 2. Object scale Detection of commodity identification system.

A custom retail product dataset is trained using the YOLOv8 model for object detection. As shown in Fig. 1, this system captures products in a shopping cart via camera footage, converts it to a stream of frames, and applies the model to generate accurate bounding boxes with confidence levels. A multi-viewpoint setup addresses occlusion and overlapping issues, improving localization accuracy. The system determines the scale of objects within a fixed boundary environment, regardless of orientation. It uses motion detection via background subtraction [6] to identify moving objects and distinguish between existing and new items, calculating the scale only for new additions.

Video footage from top and side viewpoints is converted into individual frames. As shown in Fig. 2, the system detects moving objects by comparing current frames with previous ones and performs pixel-wise instance segmentation [1] to determine the object's area. This helps classify each object by scale for accurate inventory management. The system updates stock levels, alerts admins for replenishment, notifies users of the bill and provides a QR code for payment. It seamlessly integrates with the smart cart, displaying product details and the current total in real time. Once shopping is complete, it generates a receipt and directs the user to the payment page to enhance shopping experience for customers.

3.2 Multi Camera Object Tracking

To capture various viewpoints of a single object [7], a multi-camera setup is em-ployed. The primary camera offers a top view, providing a perspective of both the cart interior and the surrounding environment, detecting motion in and out of the cart. The secondary side-view camera focuses within the cart, ensuring accurate tracking of internal items. This setup improves object detection, addressing hidden or overlapping items by assigning unique IDs to objects. The top-view camera detects external objects, while the side-view confirms items inside the cart, helping to resolve occlusion challenges. As shown in Fig. 3, objects first seen by the side-view and then by the top-view suggest a removal event and vice-versa as addition of product inside the cart.

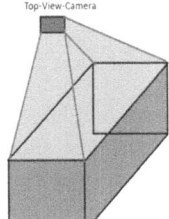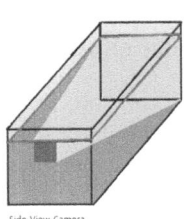   

Fig. 3. Multi-camera viewpoints   **Fig. 4.** Hidden object's top Vs side view

3.3 Hidden Object and Overlapping Bounding Box Problem

Relying on a single camera doesn't solve hidden object issues caused by obstructions. To address this, a multi-camera setup is used [2], where each camera maintains its own list of detected objects. By combining data, the system accurately tracks additions or removals from the cart, using a "hide list" for objects detected by only one camera. This setup resolves issues with hidden objects and ambiguous user actions, as shown in Fig. 4.

For the overlapping bounding box problem, step 1 checks if the product's bounding box fully overlaps with the image, suggesting a printed image. Step 2 uses top-side views to differentiate between real objects and images, while step 3 checks for misalignment to confirm real objects, as illustrated in Fig. 6.

3.4   Identifying Existing Products

To avoid scale detection errors during product addition, the system must not detect the scale of items already in the cart. To address this, motion detection via background subtraction identifies only the moving products, a masking technique is used to exclude static objects, ensuring the system focuses on the moving items for precise scaling, as shown in Fig. 5.

The goal is to develop a system that detects and identifies combo packs, such as "Buy 1 Get 1 Free" offers, in a retail setting. It distinguishes between paid products, which are billed, and free items, which are excluded from billing. The system also ensures that separately added products without a combo offer are correctly included in the billing process.

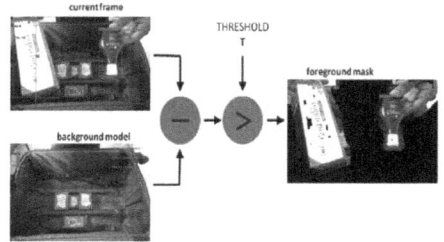  

Fig. 5. New object detected by motion.   **Fig. 6.** Printed image vs actual product

3.5   Scaling Factor for Regular and Irregular Objects

Differentiating between different scales of the same object, such as mini and large versions, poses a challenge due to variations in apparent size based on distance and orientation. Accurately classifying objects by scale despite these changes is essential for ensuring system reliability. To handle irregular objects, the system uses instance segmentation [1], which provides pixel-level precision for accurately defining the object's area. As illustrated in Fig. 7, this method ensures precise area calculation when an object

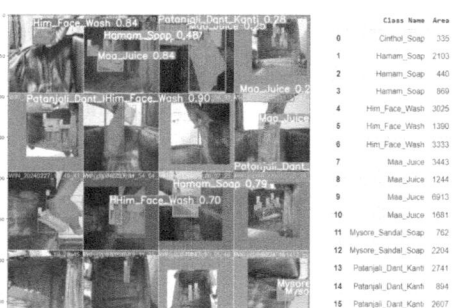 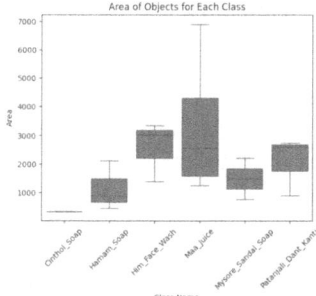

Fig. 7. Instance segmentation on sample testcases to find area for each objects.   **Fig. 8.** Sample testcases for finding area range of objects for each class.

is placed in the cart. The area is computed and plotted, as shown in Fig. 8, based on data from a top-view camera, allowing for consistent and reliable measurements. This approach enhances object classification by scale, thereby supporting more accurate analysis and decision-making processes.

3.6   Area Intersection Problem

To address inaccuracies caused by area intersection problems, a multi-camera setup is used to calculate object area accurately, incorporating data from both side and top views. As shown in Eq. (1), it ensures precise classification based on size ranges. Determining the scale of hidden objects, particularly those only visible from the top view, is challenging. Scaling becomes difficult without side-view data. While non-overlapping objects are scaled from the top view, overlapping ones require side-view information. The system checks for intersections with other objects to determine size but may face limitations without side-view data.

$$A_1 = A_2 \times \left(\frac{D_2}{D_1}\right)^2 \tag{1}$$

where,

A_1: original area detected at distance D_1
A_2: side view area at distance D_2
D_2: current distance
D_1: original distance at the end of the cart

4   Results and Discussion

4.1   Evaluation Metrics

The F1 Score, calculation is shown in Eq. (4), harmonic mean of precision and recall, shows how effectively a model balances the trade-off between these two metrics. Given the inherent trade-off between precision and recall, Yolov8 provides maximum 0.9785 score for all classes at 43.6% confidence as shown in Fig. 9.

$$precision = \frac{TruePositives}{TruePositives + FalsePositives} \tag{2}$$

$$recall = \frac{TruePositives}{TruePositives + FalseNegatives} \tag{3}$$

$$F1 = 2 \times \left(\frac{precision \times recall}{precision + recall}\right) \tag{4}$$

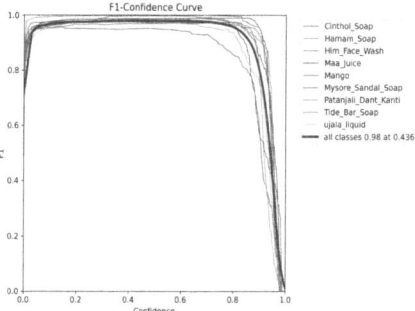

Fig. 9. F1-score vs Confidence

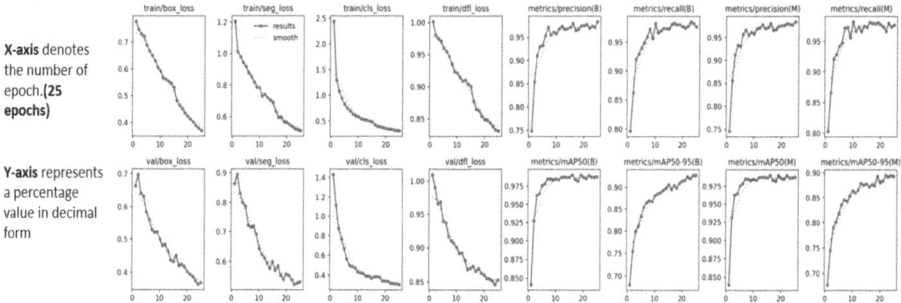

Fig. 10. Evaluation metrics for Object detection (B) and segmentation mask (M).

4.2   Results

The loss functions—box loss, class loss, and segmentation loss—observed during the training and validation phases, showing a gradual reduction across epochs for both object detection (B) and segmentation mask (M) as shown in Fig. 10. Precision, recall, and mean average precision (mAP) values for IOU thresholds exceeding 0.5 and in the range of 0.5 to 0.95, steadily improve over the course of the training epochs.

As shown in Fig. 11, in comparison of YOLO models using standardized parameters of 25 epochs, batch size of 16, 2 workers and image-size as 640. As shown in Fig. 12, YOLOv8 emerges as the top performer, short training time of 1.232 hours and F1-score of 0.9785. It surpasses YOLOv7, which exhibits longer training time.

A confusion matrix evaluates how well model predicts outcomes, as seen in Fig. 14. The difference between normalized and un-normalized matrices, illustrated in Fig. 13, lies in class imbalance, with un-normalized versions potentially misleading by not considering class proportions.

Metrics	YoloV8	YoloV5	YoloV7
Time (hours)	1.232	1.342	2.603
Precision	0.97463	0.96506	0.9783
Recall	0.98242	0.96738	0.9944
mAP_0.5	0.98739	0.98225	0.9913
mAP_0.5:0.95	0.92634	0.75743	0.9251
F1- Score	0.9785	0.9662	0.9858

Fig. 11. Comparison of various YOLO models

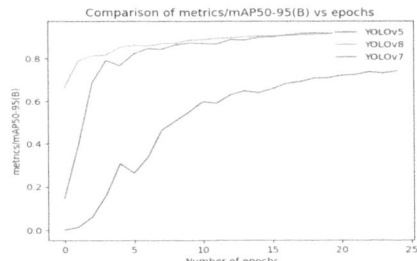

Fig. 12. Comparison of mAP50–95 Vs epochs

Category	Training	Validation	Testing	Total
Ujala Liquid	480	148	78	706
Mango	491	137	67	695
Cinthol Soap	476	139	70	685
Hamam Soap	477	143	59	679
Patanjali Dant Kanti	403	118	64	585
Maa Juice	400	118	61	579
Him Face Wash	374	109	52	535
Mysore Sandal Soap	373	95	61	529
Tide Bar Soap	372	107	41	520

Fig. 13. Custom Dataset for retail products

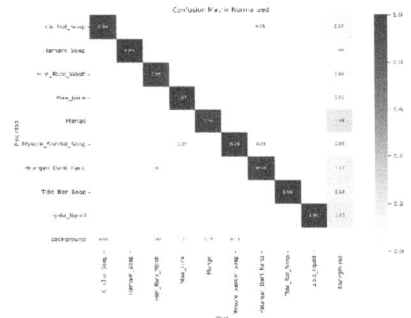

Fig. 14. Normalized Confusion Matrix

5   Conclusion

A retail product dataset trained with YOLOv8n enabled efficient object detection using instance segmentation and multiple camera views to track objects and handle occlusions. The model achieved a high F1 score of 0.9785 and a minimum confidence of 0.436 across all classes, proving its reliability.

5.1   Future Scope

- *Detection of Damaged Objects:* The system will be enhanced to recognize damaged or tampered objects, ensuring more comprehensive and accuracy.
- *Theft Case Detection System:* The current system cannot detect malpractice if a product is taken from the rack without being added to the cart, as it focuses only on the cart's contents, enhancement needed for such actions in a multi-user environment to improve accuracy and accountability.
- *Product Navigation System:* Each product's rack will help to guide users to their desired items, ensuring reliable and easy navigation throughout the mall. This improves the overall shopping experience.

References

1. Bai, R., Wang, M., Zhang, Z., Lu, J., Shen, F.: Automated construction site monitoring based on improved YOLOv8-seg instance segmentation algorithm. IEEE Access **11**, 139082–139096 (2023)
2. Ke, L., Tai, Y.-W., Tang, C.-K.: Occlusion-aware instance segmentation via bilayer network architectures. IEEE Trans. Pattern Anal. Mach. Intell. **45**(8), 10197–10211 (2023)
3. Chiu, J.Y.-C., Hsu, H.-W., Tsai, C.-Y.: Person tracking control of mobile robots using a lightweight object detection and tracking system. In: 2024 8th Inter- national Conference on Robotics and Automation Sciences (ICRAS), Tokyo, Japan (2024)
4. Sarwar, M.A., Daraghmi, Y.-A., Liu, K.-W., Chi, H.-C., İk, T.-U., Li, Y.-L.: Smart shopping carts based on mobile computing and deep learning cloud services. 2020 IEEE Wireless Communications and Networking Conference (WCNC), Seoul, Korea (South) (2020)
5. Katyayani, K., Bhardwaj, Poongodi, T.: Deep learning approach for multi-object detection using yolo algorithm. In: 2023 6th International Conference on Contemporary Computing and Informatics (IC3I), Gautam Buddha Nagar, India (2023)
6. Wang, Z., Huang, J., Xiong, N.N., Zhou, X., Lin, X., Ward, T.L.: A robust vehicle detection scheme for intelligent traffic surveillance systems in smart cities. IEEE Access **8**, 139299–139312 (2020)
7. Lipson, L., Teed, Z., Deng, J.: RAFT-stereo: multilevel recurrent field transforms for stereo matching. In: 2021 International Conference on 3D Vision (3DV), London, United Kingdom (2021)
8. Huang, R., et al.: A clinical dataset and various baselines for chromosome instance segmentation. In: IEEE/ACM Transactions on Computational Biology and Bioinformatics **19**(1), 31–39 (2022). https://doi.org/10.1109/TCBB.2021
9. Othman, N.A., Salur, M.U., Karakose, M., Aydin, I.: An embedded real-time object detection and measurement of its size. In: 2018 International Conference on Artificial Intelligence and Data Processing (IDAP), Malatya, Turkey, pp. 1–4 (2018). https://doi.org/10.1109/IDAP.2018.8620812
10. Ghebreamlak, F.F., Semereab, M.Z., Ghebremichael, S.B., Abugabah, A.: Smart shopping application: indoor navigation system for shops. In: 2024 15th Annual Undergraduate Research Conference on Applied Computing (URC), Dubai, United Arab Emirates, pp. 1–5 (2024). https://doi.org/10.1109/URC62276.2024.10604477

Prediction of Retinal Diseases Using Image Processing Techniques and Convolutional Neural Networks

A. Ibrahim Kaleel[1]([⊠]) and S. Brintha Rajakumari[2]

[1] Department of Computer Applications, Bharath Institute of Higher Education and Research, Chennai, India
a_ikaleel@rediffmail.com
[2] Department of Computer Science, Bharath Institute of Higher Education and Research, Chennai, India

Abstract. Numerous eye disorders have demonstrated encouraging improvements with the development of image processing techniques and deep learning (DL) approaches. However, many of these studies target on a single disease. Consequently, it is effective to concentrate on multi-disease classification utilizing retinal fundus images. This study is to examine the role of image processing techniques in the classifications of retinal diseases using CNN models like VGG19, ResNet50 and SqueezNet. The performance indicators, including accuracy, F1 score, recall, and precision, are used to evaluate the model's performance with and without image processing techniques for retinal diseases classification. The results shows that the model's efficiency is improved by employing appropriate image processing techniques before fed into the classifier. The outcome of this study is the development of a reliable and efficient diagnostic system for identifying and treating of several eye diseases using color retinal image analysis.

Keywords: Retinal Diseases · Deep Learning · Image Processing · Convolutional Neural Networks

1 Introduction

Ophthalmologists rely heavily on retinal images to diagnose a wide range of ocular diseases. There are various kinds of ocular diseases including cataract, age-related macular degeneration (AMD), diabetic retinopathy (DR), and glaucoma. Moreover, DR, eye infections through viruses and visual damage can all result from long-term conditions like diabetes. As people age, their chance of developing blindness or other visual impairments rises. Lesions or other anomalies that can point to a disease can be seen on images of the retinal fundus [1].

A great deal of research was done to use DL algorithms for retinal fundus imaging to enable early identification and prompt treatment. Deep learning-based methods improve diagnosis accuracy while reducing the labor-intensive nature of handcrafted feature extraction as compared to conventional methods. However, in order to train the models

© The Author(s), under exclusive license to Springer Nature Switzerland AG 2025
S. Rajagopal et al. (Eds.): ASCIS 2024, CCIS 2424, pp. 123–136, 2025.
https://doi.org/10.1007/978-3-031-86290-8_9

and detect retinal disorders in an exhaustive way by collecting and learning thousands of and representative aspects of retinal images. DL models' faster image processing and instantaneous output can help with prompt diagnosis and therapy planning.

Eye disorders have been a serious global problem, particularly in underdeveloped countries with insufficient financial and technological resources. CNN's outstanding feature learning capabilities have allowed it to make significant advancements in the field of fundus imaging. Computer-aided diagnosis can provide information with an accepted threshold for professionals in clinical diagnosis or screening by properly evaluating and examining fundus images. The retina in a human eye is in charge of using the optic nerve to transmit images to the brain. The macula, which is in charge of obtaining image data, is located in the middle of the retina. This data is processed by the retina, which then sends it to the brain as a neural signal. Many different diseases can impact macular health, resulting in visual issues. AMD, CNV, and DME are thought to be the main causes of permanent vision loss. These medical conditions cause geographic atrophy, which damages the retina. Applying CNN to derive traits from retinal images that indicate the presence of various problems is the motivation behind many studies in the literature. The Fig. 1 shows the sample diseased images with DR,AMD and Media Haze (MH) images.

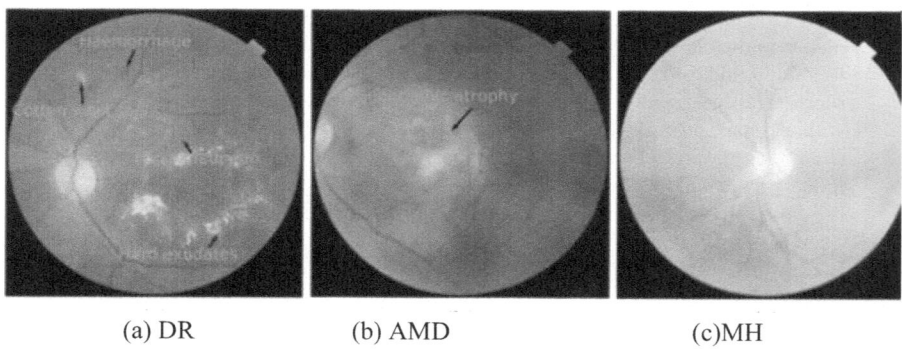

(a) DR   (b) AMD   (c)MH

Fig. 1. Samples retinal disease images

1.1   Image Processing Techniques

Enhancing some visual properties that are important for further processing or suppressing inadvertent distortions is the aim of pre-processing. Many advanced image processing techniques are employed to transform images for various purposes, like applying artistic filters, optimizing an image for best quality, or improving specific details in an image to maximize quality for computer vision tasks.

ANN are used to create DL applications, which is then tested and trained on suitable datasets for a variety of uses. Due to heat, radiation, and inadequate lighting, the unprocessed image images that are part of the collection may contain information that is ambiguous and noisy. Because of this, the researchers are working to improve the images using preprocessing procedures with the objective to give the neural network layers in the DL program useful feature information.

A number of pre-processing methods, including augmenting the data, cropping, adjusting the size, splitting the dataset, Images to array conversion, and one-hot encoding are utilized to enhance the model's efficacy. Relevant features have been retrieved by CNNs from the color fundus images. Predictive diagnostic choices are made using these derived features [2]. Pre-processing is used to reduce the distortions to increase quality of visuals that are crucial for tasks involving further processing and analysis.

1.2 Convolutional Neural Networks (CNN)

Artificial neural networks (ANNs) come in many different forms, one of which is CNN. It can automatically learn hierarchies of characteristics from input image grids. In recent years, CNN models have made significant improvements in computer vision, such as in object tracking, segmentation, and classification. CNN architecture may share and pooling weight parameters because it has fewer connections and fewer parameters.CNN can categorize many diseases based on medical images because of its capacity to retrieve non-linear features and semantic links between neighboring pixels.The DL-based CNN model has been used to improve the traditional diagnostic approach for retinal-based critical disorders. Retinal image analysis is used in ophthalmology to predict eye disorders early. This kind of early prediction allows for more effective treatment and prevents tissue damage that could result in permanent vision loss.

The contributions of this study includes.

- The Collection of retinal images and applying image analysis methods to enhance retinal fundus images
- Classification of images using CNN models with hyperparameter tuning
- Experimental Analysis of the CNN technique with the state-of-art approaches employing classification model metrics.

The paper id structured as follows: literature studies pertaining to the study presented in Sect. 2. Then the image processing techniques and CNN architectures were examined for retinal disease image classification in Sect. 3. The experimental evaluation's results, including the CNN model's performances are analyzed in Sect. 4 and conclusion and future works in Sect. 5.

2 Related Works

Image processing Techniques and DL models are used in a number of research articles. The study in [3] offers a thorough model that evaluates the effectiveness of 26 cutting-edge DL networks and helps with deep feature extraction and image categorization of DR fundus images. With the EyePACS fundus image dataset from Kaggle, ResNet50 has illustrated the largest overfitting in the suggested model, while Inception V3 has demonstrated the lowest overfitting.

CNN, in addition to its specific variation known as U-Net Segmentation, has revolutionized the way medical illnesses, particularly those pertaining to the retina, are classified. However, U-Net has a major disadvantage in that it uses a lot of storage and processing power while transferring the entire feature map to the suitable decoder due to the complex nature of feature extraction. Moreover, pooling indices can be avoided by combining it to the unsampled decoder feature map. A CNN model that effectively uses memory is proposed in [4] for multi-class classification. The model has been evaluated using EyeNet with 232 classes of retinal diseases and it is efficient in handling the memory and accuracy of the model.

CNN has demonstrated promising results in the image categorization domain. CNN can extract the non-linear structures from images that are commonly present in various medical images. Moreover, CNN is capable of classifying ocular images with several pixel correlations that are considered complicated. Three distinct diseases are identified by the suggested. DL systems in [5] using features taken from Optical Coherence Tomography (OCT) images. CNN is used by the DL algorithm to categorize OCT pictures into four groups. Normal retina, Choroidal Neovascular Membranes (CNM), Diabetic Macular Edema (DME), and AMD are the four types. The dataset for the proposed work consists of OCT retinal images that are freely accessible. The findings of the experiment demonstrate a notable improvement in classification accuracy in identifying the characteristics of the three diseases.

The suggested model in [6] efficiently captures inter-scale variables and combines them using convolutional blocks to improve the performance for segmenting and classifying retinal disorders.It uses a novel DL-based approach to categorize volumetric OCT images. The study uses the OCT scans of human eyes for demonstrating a DL Network

Table 1. Recent Studies in the literature for Retinal diseases image Classification

Authors	year	Method	Dataset	Score
Ejaz et al.	2024	CNN (12 layers)	RFMiD	Accuracy 89.81%
Das et al.	2023	ResNet50 EfficientNetB4, InceptionResNetV2, NasNetLarge, and DenseNet169	EyePACS	DensetNet169 Accuracy 99.58%
Nawaz et al.	2023	CNN	EyeNet	Accuracy 95%
Elkholy et al.	2024	CNN	OCT images	Accuracy
Nagmani et al.	2024	Bi LSTM and Recurrent CNN	OCT images	Accuracy 99.76%
Alharbi et al.	2024	SqueezeNet and LRCN	Fundus image database	Specificity -98% F1-Score 97.8% Recall 97.6% Precision 98.4% Accuracy 98%

(DL-Net) model for multi-class classification and segmentation of ocular diseases. The model automatically recognizes normal, DME, CNM, AMD, and drusen images.

The vast majority of past research has been on identifying a specific fundus disease, and precisely and rapidly classifying many fundus diseases continues to be an important challenge. A very large number of retinal fundus images need to be examined in order to arrive at a rapid, accurate, and dependable classification. Therefore, the purpose of the study in [7] is to present a novel classification model for eye diseases that is based on four main steps: pre-processing, blood vessel segmentation, feature extraction, and multi-classification of eye disease. A model that combines the SqueezeNet and Long-Term Recurrent Convolutional Network (LRCN) is used to categorize eye disorders. Five types of fundus diseased images were used in the training and validation of the models through tenfold cross-validation testing. The common classification metrics are used to assess the effectiveness of the method that is being provided.

3 Methodology

3.1 Dataset Description

A new Retinal Fundus Multi-disease Image Dataset (RFMiD) has been produced to facilitate the development of algorithms for automatic ocular illness categorization, including unusual pathologies as well as regular disorders. It is made up of 3200 fundus photos that were taken with three distinct fundus cameras. Two experienced retinal experts adjudicated a consensus of 46 conditions on the images. As far as now, RFMiD is the only publicly accessible dataset that includes so many different disorders that typically occur in clinical settings. The creation of broadly useful models for retinal screening will be made possible by this dataset. It consists of a collection of fundus images depicting several eye disorders, such as MH, Optic Disc Cupping (ODC), DR, and healthy images (WNL). This study uses Retinal Fundus Multi-disease Image Dataset (RFMiD) dataset. The dataset is divided the proportion 70:30 for training and testing.

The Fig. 2 depicts the image processing and classification model for the retinal disease images.

3.2 Preprocessing

3.2.1 Duplicate Images Removal

There are two reasons why having duplicate images in the data set is problematic: (1) It introduces bias into the dataset, which increases the chances that the deep neural network will identify patterns unique to the duplicates. (2) It affects the model's capacity to generalize to new images that differ from the ones it was trained on.

3.2.2 Image Resizing

Resizing images is a crucial step in DL models. If models are fed smaller images, they will train more quickly. In comparison to larger images, smaller images offer higher computational advantages. Furthermore, the image must be the same size for many DL

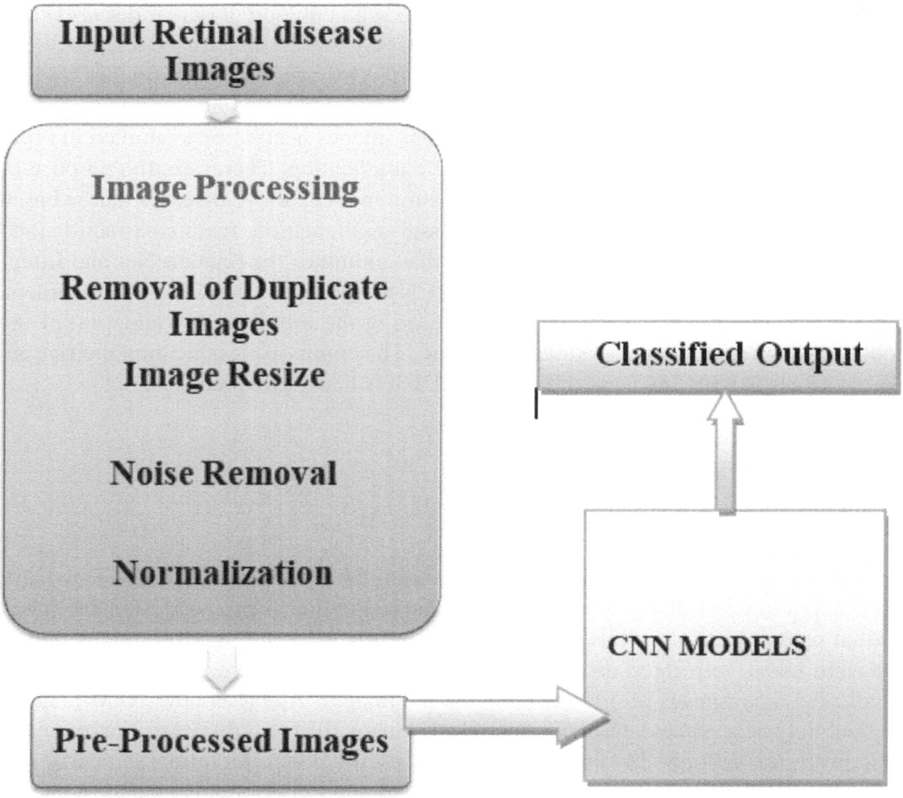

Input Retinal disease Images

Image Processing

Removal of Duplicate Images

Image Resize

Noise Removal

Normalization

Classified Output

CNN MODELS

Pre-Processed Images

Fig. 2. Classification model with Image processing Techniques

models to work. In this instance, the images have been downsized to 200x200 pixels. Any smaller resizing could cause us to lose information. Larger images, however, could potentially have a negative impact on the model's output time and power consumption. A sample resized fundus image is shown in Fig. 3.

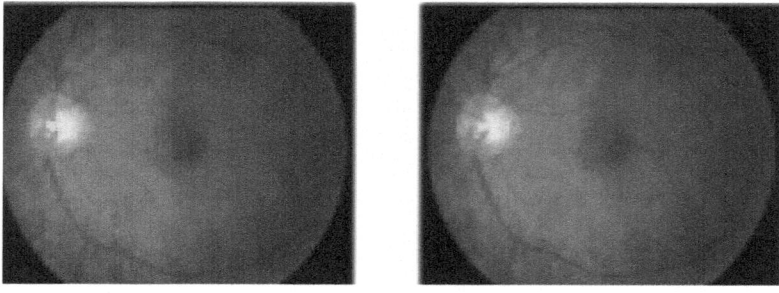

Fig. 3. Original Image (Left) and Resized Image(Right)

3.2.3 Noise Reduction

Images can have undesired noise removed by using techniques including blurring, filtering, and smoothing. Typically, the medianBlur () and GaussianBlur () functions are employed for this and it is shown in Fig. 4.

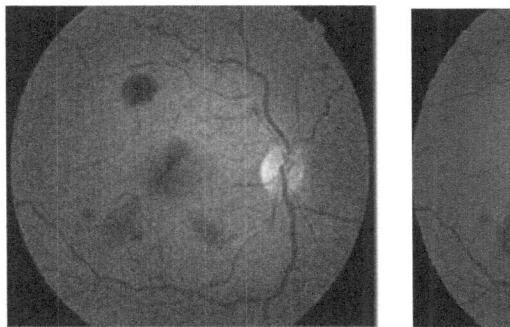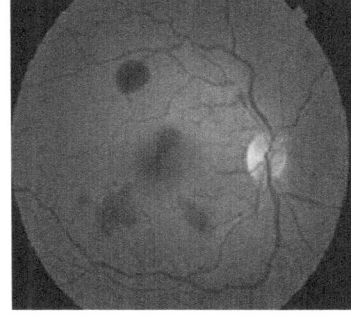

Fig. 4. Original Image (Left) and Noise Removed Image(Right)

3.2.4 Normalization

Normalization sets the pixel intensity values to a particular range, usually in the range of 0 to 1. This has the potential to enhance machine learning models' performance. One can use scikit-image's Normalize() function for this and it is shown in Fig. 5.

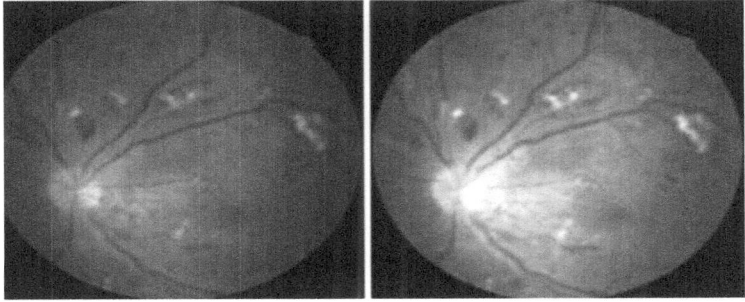

Fig. 5. Fundus Image Before Normalization(Left) After Normalization(Right)

3.3 Convolutional Neural Networks

Artificial neural networks (ANNs) come in many different forms, one of which is CNN. It can automatically learn hierarchies of characteristics from input image grids. In recent years, CNN models have made significant significant improvements in computer vision, such as in object tracking, segmentation, and classification. CNN architecture may share and pooling weight parameters because it has fewer connections and fewer parameters.

CNN uses filters to extract feature maps from two-dimensional images. As an alternative to fully linked neuron layers, it takes into account mapping image pixels with the neighborhood space. is now a well recognized and inventive image processing algorithm. It is also becoming increasingly common in computer vision, object classification, and handwriting recognition. Three primary types of layers exist:

Convolutional layer is the name of the first layer. The fully-connected layer comes last, while the pooling layers come after the first convolutional layer. The complexity of CNN's increases with each layer, enabling it to identify most part of the images. The earlier levels concentrate on fundamental components like colors and edges. By identifying larger areas or patterns in the image as it goes through its layers, the CNN eventually identifies the target object.

(a) Convolutional Layer

Since it is where the majority of the computation starts, this layer is the foundation of CNN. A feature map, a filter, and the input data are some of the parts that are involved. The input file is a color image composed of a matrix of three-dimensional pixels. This means that, like RGB in an image, the input's three dimensions—height, width, and depth—will match. The feature extractor also knows as kernel or filter is used to scan the field of reception of an image and decide if an attribute is there or not. The most common term for this technique is convolution.

(b) The pooling layer

These layers decrease the overall amount of features in an input and provide a decreased dimension, are frequently referred to as downsampling. The pooling process employs a weightless filter to the entire input, just like the convolutional layer does. Rather, the kernel uses a function to mix the data from the receptive field and fill output array. The types of pooling include:

Max pooling: The filter scans the input and it chooses a pixel with the maximum value to deliver to the output array. Moreover, this method is applied more often than standard pooling.

Average pooling: As the filter passes through the input, it determines the mean value in the receptive field.

iii) Fully connected layer.

This layer accurately conveys its characteristics and the pixel values from the source image are not directly related to the resultant layer in partially linked layers. Each node in the resultant layer of this instantly links to a node in the layer that comes before it. This study is conducted with the three CNN models like VGG19, RestNet50 and SqueeNet architectures.

(a) **Visual Geometry Group 19 Layer CNN(VGG19)**

VGG19 model supports 19 layers arranged in 5 blocks. The weight layers (convolutional layers) of the model are denoted by the numbers 19 as shown in Fig. 6. Every block features a Maxpool layer that, in addition to reducing the input image size by 2, also increases the number of filters in the convolution layer by 219 and has 19 convolution layers organized into 5 blocks. The Maxpool layer, which comes after each block, decrease the image's input size by two and doubles the convolution layer's number of filters [8].

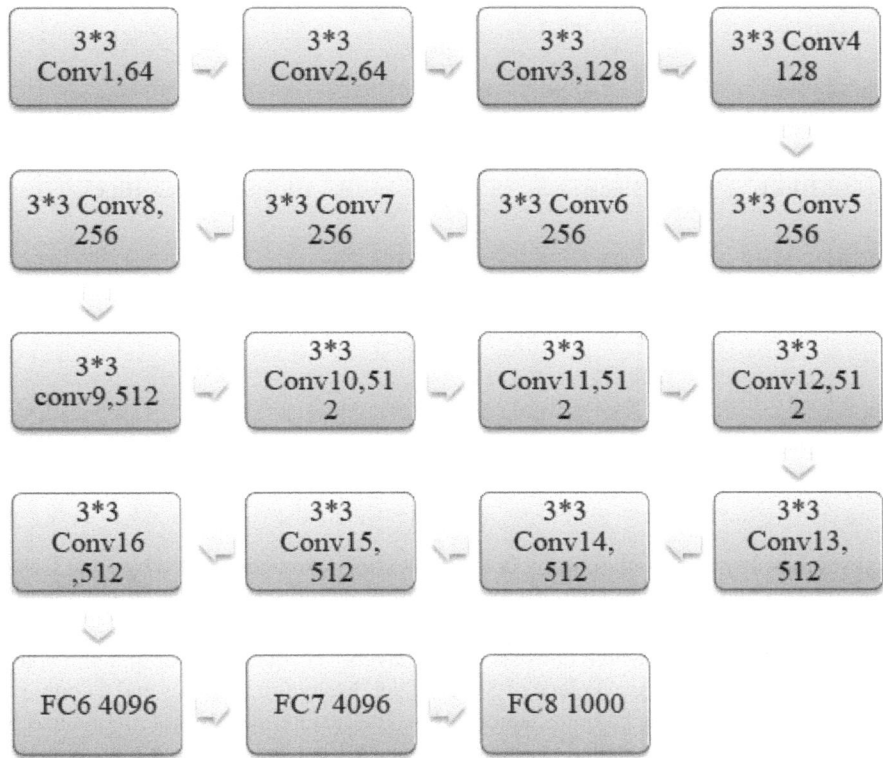

Fig. 6. VGG16 Architecture

(b) **ResNet 50**

The most popular ResNet design, known as ResNet50, has 50 layers, as seen in Fig. 7, and on the ImageNet dataset, it produced state-of-the-art results. The 16 residual blocks that comprise ResNet50 are linked together by residual connections between various convolutional layers. The design additionally incorporates pooling layers, a softmax output layer for classification, and fully linked layers [9].

The benefits of ResNet-50 include its high precision and recall in identifying retinal diseases, its ability to overcome disappearing gradients, utilize learnt features through skip connections, and its capacity to train on deeper networks for more precise identification.

(c) **SqueezeNet**

The algorithm known as SqueezeNet is made to be compact and extremely accurate. It distinguishes itself by utilizing fire modules, a specific type of convolutional layer that combines 1×1 and 3×3 filters to reduce the amount of parameters while retaining excellent accuracy, which makes it perfect for devices with limited

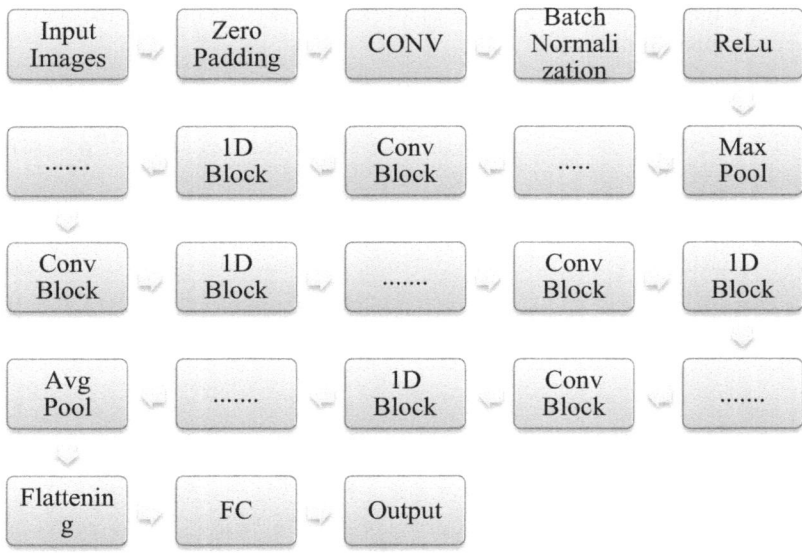

Fig. 7. ResNet50 Architecture

resources. It uses a small fraction of the processing resources needed by other CNNs to attain great accuracy [10]. The architecture of SqueezeNet Model is shown in Fig. 8.

The fire module, which consists of two layers—a squeeze layer and an expand layer—is the foundational piece of SqueezeNet. Many fire modules and a couple of pooling layers are stacked in a SqueezeNet. The feature map size is maintained by both the squeeze and expand layers; the former reduces the depth to a lower value, while the latter increases it. Neural architectures frequently exhibit the squeezing (bottleneck layer) and expansion behaviors. Another common tendency is to obtain high level abstraction by decreasing the feature map size and increasing the depth.

SqueezeNet's ability to balance processing power and precision is one of its main features. Despite their great accuracy, traditional CNNs like AlexNet and VGGNet need a lot of processing power to train and run.

4   Results and Discussions

The best CNN algorithm model is found through a variety of layers in the investigation. Here, the algorithm's inherent characteristics were used to choose the properties of this specific algorithm. The measures that are used to evaluate the quality of the predictions: accuracy, recall and precision [11–13]. Table 1 lists the metrics values for assessing the performance of the CNN models with and without applying image processing techniques in the retinal disease images.

$$accuracy = \frac{TP + TN}{TP + TN + FP + FN} \tag{1}$$

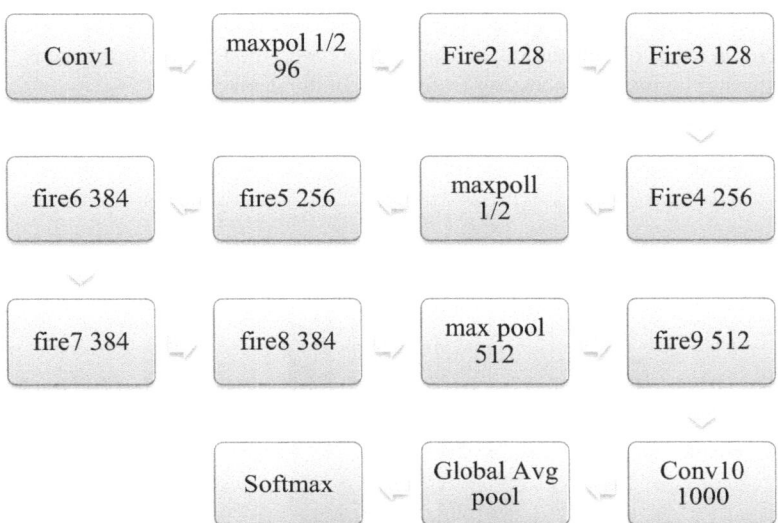

Fig. 8. SqueezeNet Model

$$Recall = \frac{TP}{TP + FN} \qquad (2)$$

$$Precision = \frac{TP}{TP + FP} \qquad (3)$$

Table 2. Performance Evaluation

Method/Measures	Accuracy		Recall		Precision	
	Without Image Processing	With Image Processing	Without Image Processing	With Image Processing	Without Image Processing	With Image Processing
VGG19	82%	87%	83%	87%	84%	89%
SqueezeNet	83%	88%	84%	89%	86%	90%
ResNet50	86%	91%	87%	93%	89%	95%

From the Table 2, it is found that the ResNet50 outperforms the VGG19 and SqueezNet in terms of the studied measures. Moreover, model's performance is boosted after applying the image processing techniques in the dataset.

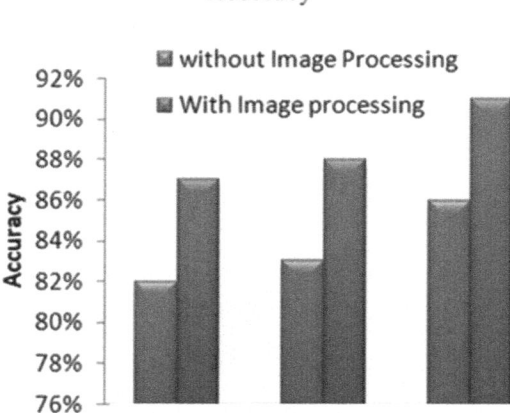

Fig. 9. CNN Models Vs Accuracy

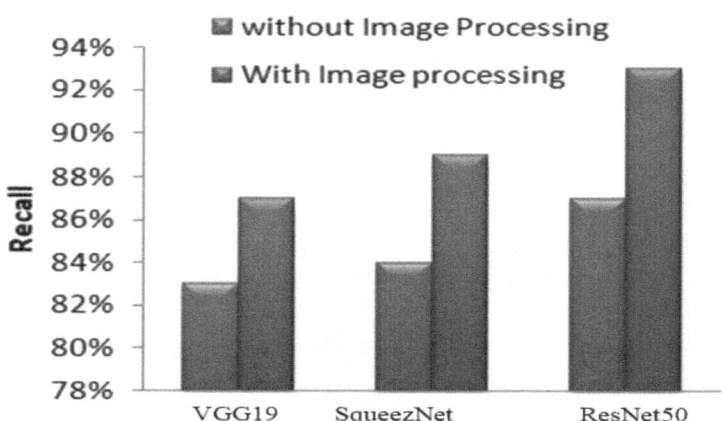

Fig. 10. CNN Models Vs Recall

From the Figs. 9, 10 and 11, it is evident that the ResNet50 performance is higher than the other models. It is also clear that, the application of image processing techniques in all the case increases the efficiency of all the models. ResNet-50 has several advantages, such as its high recall and precision in detecting retinal disorders, its capacity to train on deeper networks for more accurate identification, its ability to resist fading gradients, and its ability to use learned characteristics through skip connections.

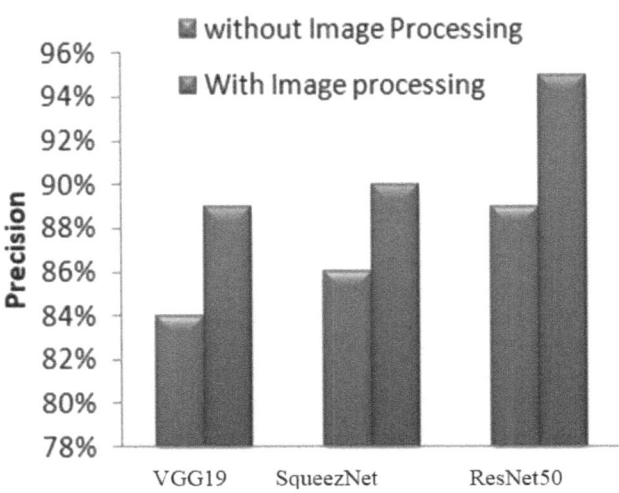

Fig. 11. CNN Models Vs Precision

5 Conclusion

A vast amount of visual data is produced by the medical field, particularly in ophthalmology. Researchers employed DL algorithms with this massive amount of imaging data to predict potential eye disorders. This study is conducted in the CNN models like VGG19, ResNet50 and SqueezNet for retinal diseases classification on the RFMiD dataset. The study reveals that the CNN models considered in this study shows the improved performance in terms of accuracy, recall and Precision by employing image processing techniques. The study also shows that the ResNet50 outperforms the other two models. Further, DL algorithms are capable of solving complicated non-linear equations and feature selection on its own. Theses algorithms have thereby substituted ML techniques in a range of domains and among these CNN are the industry standard for image processing. In future, the accuracy of the CNN models can be further improved by applying the other critical image processing techniques in the retinal disease images in the available dataset.

References

1. Chavan, R., Pete, D.: Automatic multi-disease classification on retinal images using multilevel glowworm swarm convolutional neural network. J. Eng. Appl. Sci. **71**, 26 (2024). https://doi.org/10.1186/s44147-023-00335-0
2. Ejaz, S., et al.: A deep learning framework for the early detection of multi-retinal diseases. PLoS ONE **19**(7), e0307317 (2024)

3. Das, D., Biswas, S.K., Bandyopadhyay, S.: Detection of diabetic retinopathy using convolutional neural networks for feature extraction and classification (DRFEC). Multimed. Tools Appl. **82**, 29943–30001 (2023). https://doi.org/10.1007/s11042-022-14165-4

4. Nawaz, T.A., Mustafa, G., Babar, M., Qureshi, B.: Multi-class retinal diseases detection using deep CNN with minimal memory consumption. IEEE Access **11**, 56170–56180 (2023). https://doi.org/10.1109/ACCESS.2023.3281859

5. Elkholy, M., Marzouk, M.A.: Deep learning-based classification of eye diseases using Convolutional Neural Network for OCT images. Front. Comput. Sci. **5**, 1252295 (2024)

6. Nagamani, G.M., Rayachoti, E.: Deep learning network (DL-Net) based classification and segmentation of multi-class retinal diseases using OCT scans. Biomed. Sig. Process. Control **88**, 105619 (2024)

7. Alharbi, M.: Multi-classification of eye disease based on fundus images using hybrid Squeeze Net and LRCN model. Multimedia Tools Appl., 1–30 (2024)

8. Bhavadharini, R.M., Vardhan, K.B., Nidhish, M., Shameem, D.N., Charan, V.S.: Eye disease detection using deep learning models with transfer learning techniques. EAI Endorsed Trans. Scalable Inf. Syst. **11** (2024)

9. Imaduddin, H., Utomo, I.C., Anggoro, D.A.: Fine-tuning ResNet-50 for the classification of visual impairments from retinal fundus images. Int. J. Electr. Comp. Eng. (2088–8708) **14**(4) (2024)

10. Zia, A., Mahum, R., Ahmad, N., Awais, M., Alshamrani, A.M.: Eye diseases detection using deep learning with BAM attention module. Multimedia Tools Appl. **83**(20), 59061–59084 (2024)

11. Gondalia, V., Popat, K.: A study on datasets, risk factors and machine learning methods associated with Alzheimer's disease. In: Rajagopal, S., Popat, K., Meva, D., Bajeja, S. (eds.) Advancements in Smart Computing and Information Security. ASCIS 2023. Communications in Computer and Information Science, vol. 2037, pp. 421–432. Springer, Cham (2024). https://doi.org/10.1007/978-3-031-58604-0_31

12. Silvia Priscila, S., et al.: Technological frontier on hybrid deep learning paradigm for global air quality intelligence. In: Cross-Industry AI Applications, pp. 144–162. IGI Global (2024). https://doi.org/10.4018/979-8-3693-5951-8.ch010

13. Gnanaguru, G., Priscila, S.S., Sakthivanitha, M., Radhakrishnan, S., Rajest, S.S., Singh, S.: Thorough analysis of deep learning methods for diagnosis of COVID-19 CT images. In: Advancements in Clinical Medicine, pp. 46–65. IGI Global (2024)

ORB-SIFT Hybrid Feature Extraction:
A Unified Feature Extraction Approach

Divya Kumawat$^{(\boxtimes)}$, Deepak Abhayankar, and Sanjay Tanwani

School of Computer Science and IT, Devi Ahilya Vishwavidyalaya, Indore, India
divyakumawat.9486@gmail.com

Abstract. Feature extraction is a crucial part of computer vision, which provides visual understanding and analysis of the image. These feature extraction algorithms can be classified on the basis of the type of features extracted or on the basis of the complexity of the algorithm. Scale-Invariant Feature Transform (SIFT) and Oriented Fast and Rotated Brief (ORB) are the most widely used machine learning-based algorithms. SIFT provides scale and rotation-invariant features, while ORB provides efficient real-time computing. This paper presents a unified feature extraction algorithm by combining SIFT and ORB. It uses ORB for efficient key point detection and SIFT for obtaining descriptor computations. Average distance between features and feature extraction time are the performance measures used in our paper. The experimental results show that the combined approach has a satisfactory trade-off in terms of accuracy and computational economy, especially in the case of an oriented image with an average euclidean distance of 623.95.

Keywords: feature extraction · SIFT · ORB · feature descriptor · scale invariance · rotation invariance · Euclidian distance · brute-force matching

1 Introduction

Feature extraction in images is a critical process of computer vision and image analysis. This method involves the identification and separation of key features of an image, including colors, corners, edges, textures, and patterns, and then presents them in a compact form but in an informative way. This enables computers to analyze and interpret visual information with accuracy. The feature extraction algorithms have evolved from the traditional pixel-based techniques down to the most advanced deep learning algorithms. Efficient feature extraction in image processing is therefore crucial, which directly affects tasks such as object recognition, image retrieval, and image classification by ensuring timely and accurate results. These extracted features can be used in object recognition, image retrieval, and image classification, amongst others, which can further be exploited in several applications in medical fields, food processing, material processing, thermal applications, and construction industries, etc. [1]. ORB offers real-time handling of huge data with precision and stability through a sole parameter of threshold. This threshold value still has a limitation; at high lighting variations, pixel values at some

S. Rajagopal et al. (Eds.): ASCIS 2024, CCIS 2424, pp. 137–147, 2025.
https://doi.org/10.1007/978-3-031-86290-8_10

places may cross the threshold and end up misidentifying the key points. In addition, changes in lighting can increase image noise and interference, thus deteriorating algorithm performance. A proposal by Y. Dai et al. was to use adaptive thresholds with ORB. For instance, most of the recent approaches to feature extraction, including CNN and SVM, incorporate adaptive threshold techniques that enhance the system's robustness and adaptability to changes in illumination [2]. In such a case, SIFT is an effective algorithm for detecting and describing features because of its invariance to scale rotation, combined with unique descriptors. However, it is not fit for real-time applications and resource-constrained environments because of the high computational complexity and usage of memory that it requires [3, 4]. Such a combination could give us the pros of both algorithms.

2 Literature Review

Feature extraction facilitates image analysis and understanding. Digital image processing techniques are used to extract features from the acquired image. These features may give a compact representation, which can be analyzed or further processed. The extracted features permit identification of objects or regions of interest, object classification, and image similarity comparisons [3]. These extracted features describe different properties of the image, such as color, texture, shape, or even spatial relationships. The feature extraction algorithm may be categorized on the basis of different parameters, but the most common categorization is shown in Fig. 1 as:

1. Based on the type of feature extracted
2. Based on extraction methods

Global feature extraction techniques compress images into one or a few vectors for efficient processing. It helps find identical images in a feature vector database. Image processing applications benefit from global features' faster processing, efficient computing, and compact representation. However, they are less useful when pictures are crowded [5–7].

Local feature extraction methods aim to identify and characterize unique regions within an image, which is crucial for detailed image analysis. Local features require significant memory due to the multitude of individual features they encompass within an image. In order to resolve this problem, researchers have suggested combining local image descriptors into a compact vector representation. It will also enhance efficiency and reduce computational complexity [6]. These regions are called key points or interest points. Key points hold information that can be utilized by different image processing applications involving images, stitching, object recognition, and object tracking. Harris corner detection, Shi Thomas corner detection, SIFT, SURF, and ORB are some of the prominent feature extraction algorithms. The features extracted from the given algorithm are classified into different categories, such as color feature extraction, texture feature extraction, edge detection, corner detection, and region-based feature extraction methods [8, 9].

Feature extraction can also be categorized based on the complexity of the method being used. In image processing and computer vision, images are represented as matrices

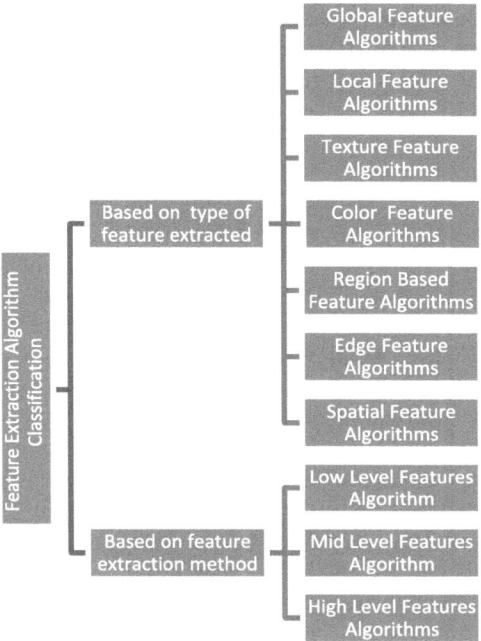

Fig. 1. Classification of feature extraction methods

of pixel values. Transforming these unprocessed pixel values into numerical descriptors is essential, as it emphasizes the visual content inside the image. These numerical descriptors are features that can be extracted with a feature extraction algorithm. The selection of the feature extraction algorithm is decided by the image characteristics and application's requirements. On the one hand, there are algorithms that can be simply developed, such as histograms of color and edge detectors, and, on the other hand, there are those that are very complicated, such as convolutional neural networks. The algorithms are categorized as low, mid, and high depending on the intricacy and information content pulled out from the images. Low-level feature extraction algorithms like pixel intensities, color values, local gradients, edge maps, etc. are the key point. It creates a raw representation of the image information without using complicated processing. Mid-level feature extraction algorithms produce abstract information by applying basic processing. It transforms raw pixel values into numerical descriptors, emphasizing elements such as edges, textures, and spatial arrangements. High level feature extraction decreases the intricacy of data, highlights essential information for activities, and improves overall job performance and efficiency. Deep learning techniques extract high-level semantic concepts and relationships among different features, providing a more comprehensive understanding of image content. High-level feature extraction involves a wide range of abilities, such as recognizing different types of objects, identifying specific sections of objects, interpreting complicated scenes, and extracting detailed relationships within images. The boundaries of these classified categories of feature extraction algorithms sometimes overlap.

The feature extraction algorithm is selected on the basis of the resources available, the type and amount of data available, and the specific needs of the application. Combination of different feature extraction algorithms to enhance feature representation and the information retrieved [10].

The feature extraction algorithms have evolved from basic edge and corner detectors (such as Sobel, Prewitt, and Canny) to sophisticated deep learning algorithms like CNN. The Sobel, Prewitt, Canny edge detectors, and the Harris corner detector are some foundational algorithms able to detect the fundamental features [11]. The Harris corner detector identifies points of interest by analyzing the eigenvalues of a second-order moment matrix. However, it lacks scale invariance. Linderberg et al. introduced the Laplace of Gaussian method, which utilizes the Laplace of Gaussian and hessian matrix determinants to automatically find scales [10]. The advent of the Scale- Invariant Feature Transform (SIFT) was a major breakthrough that provided robust, scale-invariant, and rotation- invariant feature descriptors. A computationally efficient ORB (Oriented FAST and Rotated BRIEF) was introduced that combines the FAST key point detector and BRIEF descriptors [12]. The ORB algorithm is extensively employed in several domains, such as real-time applications, augmented reality (AR), visual odometers, drone navigation, security, and surveillance. Although SIFT demonstrated excellent accuracy and resilience, its computational expense was significant, prompting the creation of more efficient techniques like ORB. Scale Invariant Feature Transform (SIFT) involves the following four tasks:

1. Scale space extrema detection
2. Key point Selection
3. Key point orientation
4. Description of key point.

First of all, Gaussian blur is applied to the image using a Gaussian filter with different values of the standard deviation (σ) in order to smooth it and reduce noise. The repeated application of the Gaussian filter creates smooth layers and enhances the quality of image representations. The Difference of Gaussians (DoG) is a method used to approximate the Laplacian of the Gaussian (LoG). The DoG is calculated by subtracting two pictures, each convolved with a Gaussian kernel of differing sigma (σ) values.

$$DoG(x, y, \sigma) = (G(x, y, k\sigma) - G(x, y, \sigma)) * I(x, y)$$

where, $G(x, y, \sigma)$ is a Gaussian function and $I(x, y)$ is the input image

Key points are recognized as local maximum and minimum points in the Difference of Gaussian (DoG) pictures. This is achieved by comparing each pixel with its 26 neighboring pixels on the current and adjacent scales. Once prospective key points have been detected, the subsequent stage involves refining their positions in order to obtain precise key point localization. The Taylor series expansion is used to approximate the precise position of the extrema by fitting a 3D quadratic function to the local sample points. This aids in attaining sub-pixel precision. Key points exhibiting poor contrast (falling below a specific threshold) are excluded due to their susceptibility to noise. Key points that are located along edges are excluded from consideration due to their lack of stability. The process includes evaluating the main curvatures by using the Hessian matrix and comparing the ratio of eigenvalues. To ensure rotational invariance, each key point is assigned a uniform orientation. The magnitude and direction of the gradient at the key point are calculated [13]. The features generated by SIFT encompass a wide range of scales and locations. Scale-invariant feature algorithms analyze various scales using a continuous kernel function known as scale space [14, 15]. The algorithms examine all the details and structures of an image at different levels of scale. These algorithms resize the image and apply filters like the Gaussian filter repeatedly to create smooth layers, enhancing the quality of image representations. Non-uniform scaling impacts the localization, scale, and shape of the local structure by distorting the proportions and orientations of features at different points in the image. As a result, scale-invariant detectors are unsuccessful when significant affine transformations occur. There are multiple versions of SIFT, such as ASIFT (affine SIFT), VF-SIFT (very fast SIFT), CSIFT (color SIFT), GSIFT (SIFT with Global Index), SURF, PCA-SIFT [13], SIFT- BRISK, and SIFT-BRISK [16], BE-SIFT [15].

The FAST algorithm detects key points in an image by analyzing pixel intensities and identifying locations with significant intensity changes compared to their neighbors. These identified key points are potential features for which a binary feature descriptor is calculated using the BRIEF algorithm. The binary descriptors summarize the local image area by capturing pixel intensity patterns and spatial relationships around each key point. The descriptor captures pixel intensity patterns, making it resistant to changes in illumination, scale, and rotation to a certain degree. ORB effectively identifies key points by including a speedy and precise orientation component, which enhances FAST feature identification. ORB is a combination of FAST and BRIEF algorithms. To improve feature analysis, ORB computes oriented BRIEF descriptors using variance and correlation. Minimizing correlation between BRIEF features in the presence of rotation variation leads to enhanced matching accuracy. The FAST algorithm identifies the most important features in an image by analyzing the variation in intensity around each pixel. As a tool of segmentation, we separate edges and corners to determine the key points. The ORB algorithm computes the orientation of every key point that makes it rotation invariant. In the next step, ORB algorithm employs the adapted BRIEF (Binary Robust Independent Elementary Features) to find the exponents. The BRIEF generates a binary string by comparing pixels in a patch with other key points. Besides obeying the bar rotation, the ORB attains the rotation invariance required for the descriptor. The binary form of the BRIEF descriptors performs quick matching using the Hamming distance. In this way, ORB is useful in real-time applications such as object detection, image interpolation, and simultaneous localization and mapping (SLAM) [12]. There are various improved versions of ORB capable of detecting important features. GA-ORB uses geometric algebra (GA) to detect local features; it represents a multispectral image as a GA vector, then different scales of this image are obtained by convolution, and then ORB is applied to the resultant vector. It has better speed than other GA family algorithms such as GA-SIFT and GA-SURF [17].

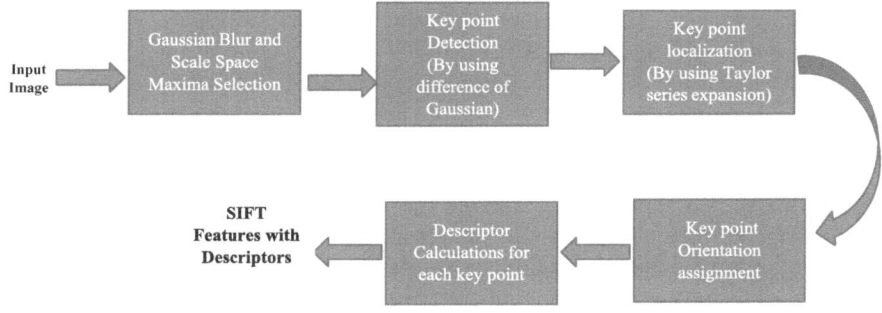

Fig. 2. Working of the SIFT algorithm

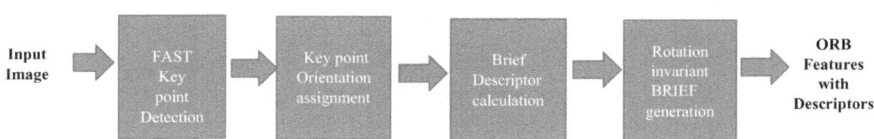

Fig. 3. Working of the ORB algorithm

3 Experimentation

In this paper, we have combined SIFT and ORB algorithms for feature extraction. Our algorithm uses ORB to extract the key points from the image, then computes descriptors for these key points by using SIFT. ORB takes less time to extract key points as compared to SIFT. SIFT descriptors can provide greater descriptor precision for distinctive local regions of an image. The extracted feature vectors are matched between images by using a brute-force matching approach and Euclidean distance. For visual comparison, we have drawn and displayed matched features in Table 1. We have measured the performance of SIFT, ORB, and the combined algorithm on various image translation scenarios using the average distance criterion and time taken in extracting features. In each case, there were a total of 306 matches for SIFT, 500 matches for ORB, and 500 matches for the combined algorithm. The table below summarizes the matching result obtained (Table 1).

Fig. 4. Working of the unified SIFT and ORB algorithms.

Table 1. Matching results of different algorithms

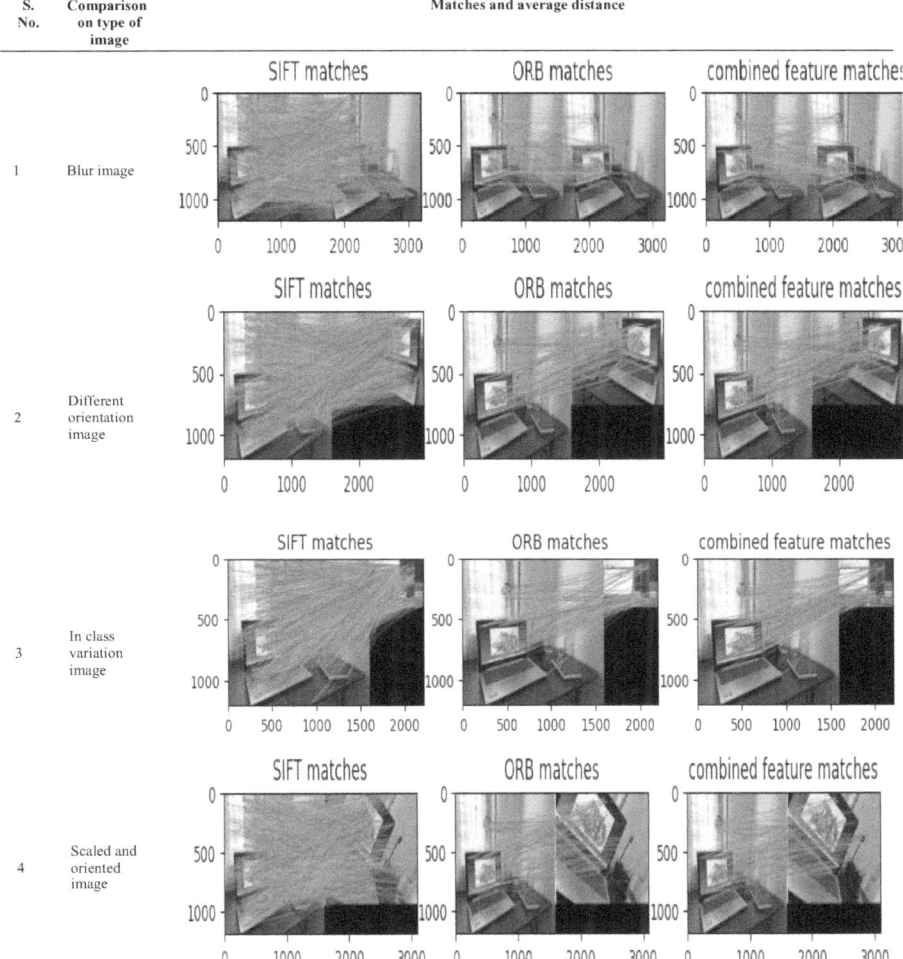

4 Results and Discussion

This paper combines SIFT and ORB algorithms, where SIFT descriptors are detected on ORB key points. Generally, the performance of this algorithm lies between SIFT and ORB, but it performs well in the case of oriented images. The average Euclidean distance between the normal image and the oriented image is 623.95, the minimum of the two given algorithms. Hence, this merging can be useful in the case of oriented images. The comparison of SIFT, ORB, and unified algorithm on the basis of key point detection method used, size of descriptor, and applications is summarized in Table 2. As unified algorithm occupies less space as compared to SIFT, but its accuracy is lesser than

SIFT. It finds its application in real-time applications where a proper trade-off between accuracy and response time is required. The results of the average distance and time taken to extract features have been summarized below in Tables 3 and 4 (Figs. 5 and 6).

Table 2. Comparison of SIFT, ORB, and the Unified algorithm

Feature	SIFT	ORB	SIFT and ORB unified algorithm
Key point detection	Uses difference of Gaussian (DoG)	Uses FAST (Feature from Accelerated Segment Test)	Uses FAST
Key point descriptor	Produces a 128-dimensional floating point descriptor [18]	Produces a 32-dimensional binary string	Produces a 128-dimensional floating point descriptor
Matching speed	The matching speed of SIFT is slow as it uses Euclidian distance on floating point descriptors	The matching speed of ORB is fast as it uses Hamming distance on binary descriptors	Moderate matching speed. It has fewer key points for comparison obtained from ORB, and uses Euclidian distance on the SIFT floating point descriptor
Memory Usage	SIFT uses more memory due to the large size of the descriptor	ORB uses less memory due to small-sized binary descriptors	Moderate memory usage. Although it uses SIFT descriptors, they are calculated on ORB Key points, which are less in numbers
Application	SIFT is highly suitable where precision is important [19] such as object detection and 3D modelling	ORB is useful for real-time applications such as augmented reality, robotics, mobile phones, etc	Unified algorithm can be applied to applications requiring precision and real-time response simultaneously

Table 3. Average distance between matched features

Algorithm/ Type of image	Blur image	Different orientation image	In-class variation image	Scaled and oriented image
SIFT	492.55	624.64	571.05	506.71
ORB	262.06	630.68	460.63	466.6
Unified Algorithm	361.99	623.95	479.04	485.95

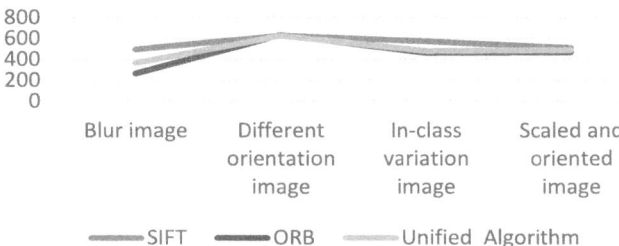

Fig. 5. Average distance between features of images with respect to a normal image

Table 4. Feature extraction calculation Time

Algorithm/ Type of image	Blur image	Different orientation image	In-class variation image	Scaled and oriented image
SIFT	1.78	1.4	1.66	0.05
ORB	0.095	0.068	0.054	0.17
Unified Algorithm	0.598	0.57	0.8089	0.5998

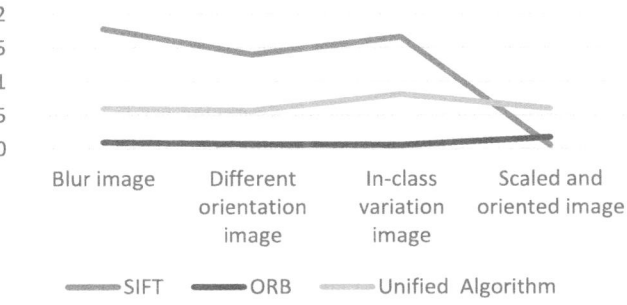

Fig. 6. Time taken in extracting features

5 Conclusion

This research work summarizes the classification of feature extraction algorithms. It introduces a unified feature extraction technique that integrates the advantages of the Scale-Invariant Feature Transform (SIFT), Oriented FAST and Rotated BRIEF (ORB) techniques. SIFT provides robustness, and is able to handle changes in scale and illumination at the cost of increased computation complexity. On the other hand, ORB is comparatively computation efficient with lack of precision. The unified algorithm utilizes ORB for efficient key point identification and SIFT for accurate descriptor calculation. The experimental findings reveal that the combined technique strikes a good balance between accuracy and computing economy, particularly in the case of image orientation. Our findings also show that the processing time for the combined algorithm was moderate, falling between the timings for SIFT and ORB, indicating its balanced performance. It makes it highly suitable for applications that require real-time performance and higher reliability in feature matching.

6 Future Work

In this paper, the performance of ORB, SIFT, and unified feature extraction algorithms is considered based on the distance between features and the computation time of the features. Our work can be extended by applying these algorithms to classification tasks on a large dataset with other parameters as well.

References:

1. Prabaharan, T., Periasamy, P., Mugendiran, V., Ramanan: Studies on application of image processing in various fields: an overview. In: IOP Conference Series: Materials Science and Engineering, vol. 961, no. 1 (2020). https://doi.org/10.1088/1757-899X/961/1/012006
2. Dai, Y., Wu, J.: An improved ORB feature extraction algorithm based on enhanced image and truncated adaptive threshold. IEEE Access **11**, 32073–32081 (2023). https://doi.org/10.1109/ACCESS.2023.3261665
3. Singh, S., Siramdas, S., Tanmayi, K., Koli, L.: Similarity measure of images using SIFT and ORB feature matching. Int. J. Res. Appl. Sci. Eng. Technol. **10**(6), 2354–2359 (2022). https://doi.org/10.22214/ijraset.2022.44319
4. Daixian, Z.: SIFT algorithm analysis and optimization. In: IASP 10 – 2010 International Conference on Image Analysis and Signal Processing, no. c, pp. 415–419 (2010). https://doi.org/10.1109/IASP.2010.5476084
5. Rezaei, M., Terauchi, M., Klette, R.: Robust vehicle detection and distance estimation under challenging lighting conditions. IEEE Trans. Intell. Transp. Syst. **16**(5), 2723–2743 (2015). https://doi.org/10.1109/TITS.2015.2421482
6. Jiang, X.: Feature extraction for image recognition and computer vision. In: Proceedings of the 2009 2nd IEEE International Conference on Computer Science and Information Technology, ICCSIT 2009, pp. 1–15 (2009). https://doi.org/10.1109/ICCSIT.2009.5235014
7. Awad, A.I., Hassaballah, M.: Image Feature Detectors and Descriptors, vol. 630. Springer, Cham (2016). https://doi.org/10.1007/978-3-319-28854-3

8. Oliva, A., Torralba, A.: Modeling the shape of the scene: a holistic representation of the spatial envelope. Int. J. Comput. Vis. **42**(3), 145–175 (2001). https://doi.org/10.1023/A:101113963 1724
9. Salau, A.O., Jain, S.: Feature extraction: a survey of the types, techniques, applications. In: Proceedings of the 2019 International Conference on Communication and Signal Processing, ICSC 2019, pp. 158–164 (2019). https://doi.org/10.1109/ICSC45622.2019.8938371
10. Lindeberg, T.: Feature detection with automatic scale selection. Int. J. Comput. Vis. **30**(2), 79–116 (1998). https://doi.org/10.1023/A:1008045108935
11. M. Singla: Comparative performance analysis of edge and corner detection techniques, pp. 110–113 (2019)
12. Hasenbusch, M., Pelissetto, A., Vicari, E.: ORB: an efficient alternative to SIFT or SURF Ethan. J. Stat. Mech. Theory Exp. **2008**(2), 2564–2571 (2008)
13. Chelluri, H.B., Manjunathachari, K.: SIFT and it's variants: an overview. SSRN Electron. J., 1–7 (2019). https://doi.org/10.2139/ssrn.3358743
14. Kher, H.R., Thakar, V.K.: Scale invariant feature transform based image matching and registration. In: Proceedings of the 2014 5th International Conference on Signal Image Processing, ICSIP 2014, pp. 50–55 (2014). https://doi.org/10.1109/ICSIP.2014.12
15. Zhao, J., Liu, H., Feng, Y., Yuan, S., Cai, W.: BE-SIFT: a more brief and efficient SIFT image matching algorithm for computer vision. In: Proceedings of the 15th IEEE International Conference on Computer and Information Technology, CIT 2015, 14th IEEE International Conference on Ubiquitous Computing and Communications, IUCC 2015, 13th IEEE International Conference on Dependable, Autonomic and Secure Computing, pp. 568–574 (2015). https://doi.org/10.1109/CIT/IUCC/DASC/PICOM.2015.81
16. Zhong, B., Li, Y.: Image feature point matching based on improved SIFT algorithm. In: Proceedings of the 2019 IEEE 4th International Conference on Image, Vision and Computing (ICIVC), pp. 489–493 (2019). https://doi.org/10.1109/ICIVC47709.2019.8981329
17. Wang, R., Zhang, W., Shi, Y., Wang, X., Cao, W.: GA-ORB: a new efficient feature extraction algorithm for multispectral images based on geometric algebra. IEEE Access **7**, 71235–71244 (2019). https://doi.org/10.1109/ACCESS.2019.2918813
18. Oszust, M.: An optimisation approach to the design of a fast, compact and distinctive binary descriptor. Sig. Image Video Process. **10**(8), 1401–1408 (2016). https://doi.org/10.1007/s11 760-016-0907-4
19. Fouad, A., Hendy, H., Arafa, I., Elhalwagy, Y.: Comparative analysis of feature fusion techniques for enhancing RGB-IR image matching. In: Proceedings of the 2023 International Telecommunications Conference (ITC-Egypt), pp. 761–766 (2023). https://doi.org/10.1109/ITC-Egypt58155.2023.10206225

Bibliometric Analysis of Educational Data Mining

Disha Shah and Ankita Kanojiya[✉]

FCAIT, GLS University, Ahmedabad, Gujarat, India
dishajshah@gmail.com, ankitamkanojiya@gmail.com

Abstract. A bibliometric analysis of educational data mining (EDM) explores the academic landscape of this interdisciplinary field, which applies data mining techniques to educational research. The study aims to systematically examine the field of Educational Data Mining (EDM) to identify the research output over a defined period, focusing on trends, types of publications, and key research topics within EDM. By gathering and analyzing publication data from databases like Scopus, Sematic Scholar, Google Scholar and CrossRef, the analysis uncovers publication and citation patterns, and the research categorial distribution of contributions. This approach provides a comprehensive review of how domain of EDM has evolved. Ultimately, the study aims to inform researchers, educators, and policymakers about current trends, emerging research areas, and the impact of EDM on educational practice and theory. This research is crucial for guiding future research directions and enhancing the application of data-driven approaches in contexts of EDM.

Keywords: Educational Data Mining (EDM) · Bibliometric Analysis · EDM Research Trends · Interdisciplinary Research · Data Mining Techniques

1 Introduction

Contemporary Educational technologies allow for large amounts of data to be collected, analyzed, and interpreted, which has fundamentally changed the way education works. There has been a significant increase in the literature on data generated by educational technologies in recent years, showing its potential to drive innovation in education and challenge traditional methods. At the same time, there has been a rise in the availability of tools for analyzing educational data, leading educators to rethink how they teach and learn. This shift towards a data-driven approach in education gives educators valuable insights and empowers them to make informed decisions.

In the world of research, educational data is used for multiple purposes such as understanding student experiences, forecasting behaviors and results, providing interventions, and customizing learning and teaching approaches. The exploration of using learner-system interaction data for educational investigations has given rise to a specialized area known as educational data mining (EDM). It provides a link between two separate domains: education and computer science, particularly focusing on data mining.

© The Author(s), under exclusive license to Springer Nature Switzerland AG 2025
S. Rajagopal et al. (Eds.): ASCIS 2024, CCIS 2424, pp. 148–162, 2025.
https://doi.org/10.1007/978-3-031-86290-8_11

This fusion integrates elements from artificial intelligence, machine learning, statistics, expert systems, databases, and visualization to explore and refine educational processes [1]. The International Educational Data Mining Society defines EDM as "an emerging discipline, concerned with developing methods for exploring the unique types of data that come from educational settings, and using those methods to better understand students, and the settings which they". The process of EDM consist of key components like data collection, data pre-processing, modelling, pattern discovery, predictive analysis, personalized learning, feedback and decision support, evaluation and assessment and ethical considerations [1–9].

To identify the newest trends in the field, we conducted a Bibliometric Analysis in the field of Educational Data Mining. To reflect a state as close as possible with the current times, we have chosen as our target publications from period of 2011 to 2022.

2 Methodology, Data Source and Collection, Data Cleansing

Bibliometric analysis approach examines research literature of a particular field by systematically analyzing the statistical literature data [10]. This approach of analysis quantifies the research literature of a particular domain to summarize its progress for specific time frame. [11] states that bibliometric analysis, provides an overview of knowledge from the micro level (institutes, researchers, and campuses) to the macro level (countries and continents).

The parameters of Bibliometric analysis provide guidance for developing future research plan and monitoring research activities further [12]. This approach provides an opportunity to uncover traditional and contemporary literature of research domain that further enables to understand historical foundations, applications, scope, popularity and advances of domain in concern. According to [13] the approach is considered to be an open method of study in many areas of sciences.

A well – executed bibliographic analysis establishes concrete foundations of research in particular domain [14]. Researchers can extract innovative and productive aspects of field as, get an overview of research conducted over a period of time, identify the knowledge gaps, derive innovative ideas for investigation as well as establish contributions that can be done to the field [15].

Data collection in educational data mining involves gathering various types of data from educational settings to analyze and derive insights that can inform decision-making and improve learning outcomes. The foundation of the educational data mining workflow lies in the meticulous collection of relevant data from a diverse array of sources, including Scopus, CrossRef, Semantic Scholar and Google Scholar [16–18]. The cleaning process is a crucial step that sets the stage for the subsequent data analysis and interpretation phases, as it ensures the integrity and accuracy of the data being examined [19]. This involves identifying and addressing any inconsistencies, errors, or missing values within the dataset, ensuring that the information being analyzed is of the highest quality.

The filtering of data is an equally important step, as it involves the selective inclusion or exclusion of certain data points based on their relevance to the research question at hand. Once the data filtration process is over, the next step is data analysis and visualization. The data analysis parameters used are publication output, relative growth rate, journal publication statistics and doubling time. Each parameter is used for pattern discovery and knowledge extraction. Interpretation of findings in EDM goes beyond simply reporting statistical results. It involves contextualizing data within the educational context, identifying meaningful patterns, drawing inferences, connecting with existing knowledge, generating actionable insights, considering limitations, and effectively communicating findings to drive informed decision-making and improve outcomes [20].

Current study was undertaken to perform bibliometric analysis of the research literature in the area of Educational Data Mining. Figure 1 represents the literature search and cleansing process undertaken to perform systemized bibliometric analysis of the EDM domain.

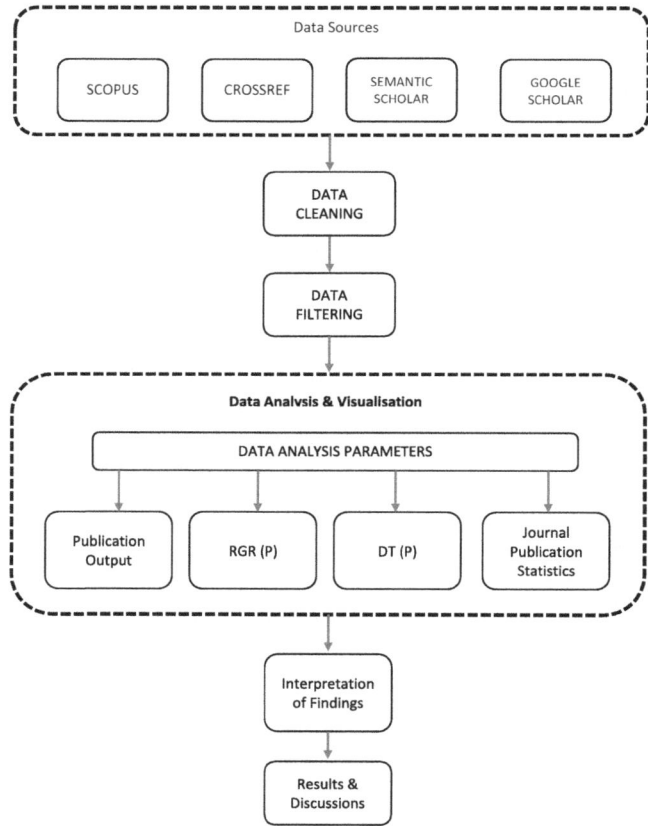

Fig. 1. Literature Search and Cleansing Process

The research literature for domain was consolidated by searching keywords Educational Data Mining and EDM in the titles of the research literature. Incomplete or ambiguous entries were not taken into consideration. Table 1 represents the number of publications extracted and considered for current research study for each database under consideration. The bibliographic data was retrieved from the reputed Databases

Repositories as Scopus, CrossRef, Google Scholar and Semantic Scholar. The databases enable retrieval of literature across several disciplines.

Table 1. No. of Publications

YEAR	Number of Publications			
	Scopus	CrossRef	Google Scholar	Semantic Scholar
Total	220	734	857	840

3 Data Analysis and Interpretations

In this section, different statistical parameters are computed. These parameters are used to interpret research trends through different perspectives. MS Excel is used to perform various calculations for bibliographic metrics, generate graphical representations and analysis tables. The parameters considered for analysis in the current work include:

3.1 **Publication Output**
    3.1.1 **Number of Publications**
    3.1.2 **Types of Publications**
3.2 **Relative Growth Rate (RGR)**
3.3 **Doubling Time (DT)**
3.4 **Journal Publications Statistics**

Further, we present above bibliometric parameters with calculations, graphical representations and analysis.

3.1 Publication Output

Publications are one of the most prominent measures that represents the productivity of research in a particular field or domain [15]. By analyzing publications, researchers can discern trends over time. This includes identifying emerging topics, popular research areas, and shifts in focus or interest within a particular field. Institutions, researchers, and funding bodies often use bibliometric analysis to assess research performance. It aids in evaluating the productivity, impact, and quality of research output, which can inform decisions on funding, hiring, or promotions. Publications form the basis for mapping the intellectual structure of a field. Analyzing publications helps in identifying subfields, interdisciplinary connections, and the evolution of knowledge within a domain.

3.1.1 Number of Publications

Figures 2, 3, 4 and 5 represent the year wise number of publications in all four databases.

From the provided data, a bibliometric analysis can provide insights into the publication trends across different platforms or databases over the years. Let's interpret the data for each platform (Crossref, Google Scholar, Scopus, Semantic Scholar) from 2011 to 2022:

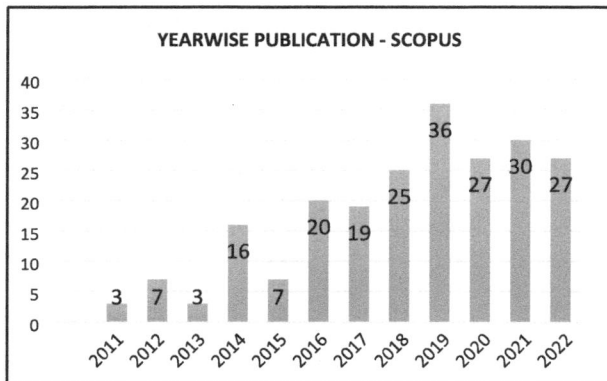

Fig. 2. Year Wise Publications – Scopus

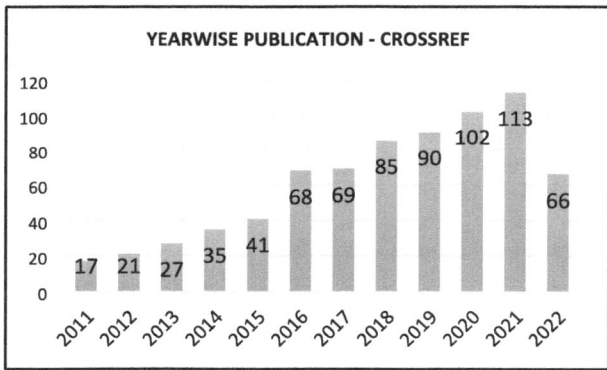

Fig. 3. Year Wise Publications – CrossRef

- The number of publications indexed in Scopus demonstrates consistent growth, from 3 publications in 2011 to 36 in 2019, before plateauing and slightly declining to 27 in 2020 and 2022.
- The number of publications indexed in Crossref shows a fluctuating trend, reaching a peak in 2019 with 113 publications and declining to 66 publications in 2022. Overall, there's an increasing trend until 2019, followed by a notable decline in the number of publications.
- The number of publications indexed in Google Scholar shows a steady increase from 22 in 2011 to a peak of 114 in 2021. The growth rate is generally consistent, except for a slight decrease in 2022.
- The data for Semantic Scholar indicates an increase in publications until 2020, with a peak of 30 publications in 2021, followed by a sharp decrease to 5 publications in 2022.
- Google Scholar consistently shows the highest number of indexed publications throughout the years, followed by Crossref, Scopus, and Semantic Scholar.

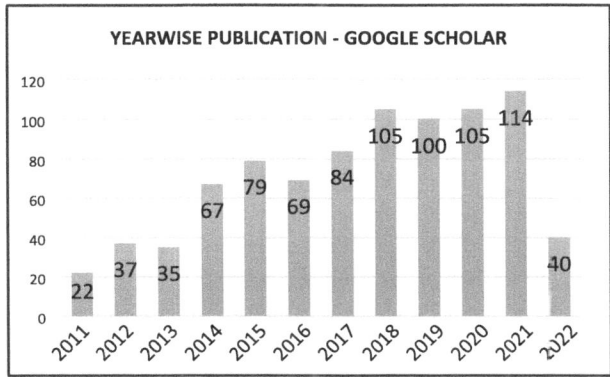

Fig. 4. Year Wise Publications – Google Scholar

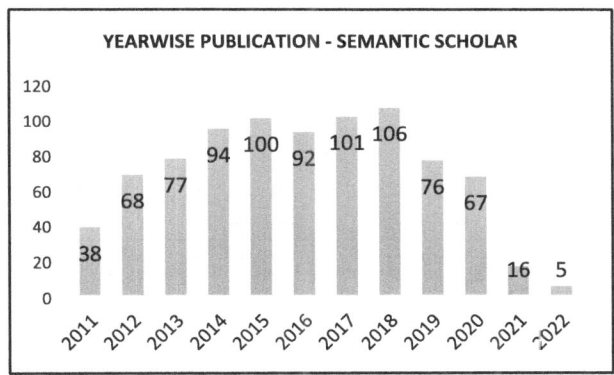

Fig. 5. Year Wise Publications – Semantic Scholar

- Google Scholar seems to index the highest number of publications consistently over time, reflecting its expansive coverage.
- Crossref and Semantic Scholar exhibit more fluctuating trends, with significant peaks and drops in publication counts over the years.
- Scopus and Semantic Scholar both show signs of plateauing or decline in publication counts in the most recent years (2020–2022).
- Crossref and Scopus show growth in publications until a certain point, after which the growth either plateaus or slightly declines.
- Semantic Scholar shows notable fluctuations, possibly due to variations in the types of publications it indexes or changes in its indexing criteria.
- From the figure it is evident that the publications tend to increase over period of years.
- However, the number of publications tend to remain constant in the recent years.

These interpretations provide an overview of the publication trends across different indexing platforms, indicating variations in growth, consistency, and fluctuations over the analyzed period.

3.1.2 Types of Publications

Research publications for domains are available in different forms. Journal Articles, Conference Proceedings, Editorial and Review Articles, Book or Book Chapters are amongst few forms in which research of any domain is represented. For the current study, the research forms taken into consideration are Journal – Articles, Proceedings – Articles, Book, Book – Chapters and Others. Others include forms of research literature as Reports, Abstracts, Editorial Letters and other forms.

Figures 6, 7, 8 and 9 represent the categorization of publications on the basis of types of publications over the period of span in each database respectively.

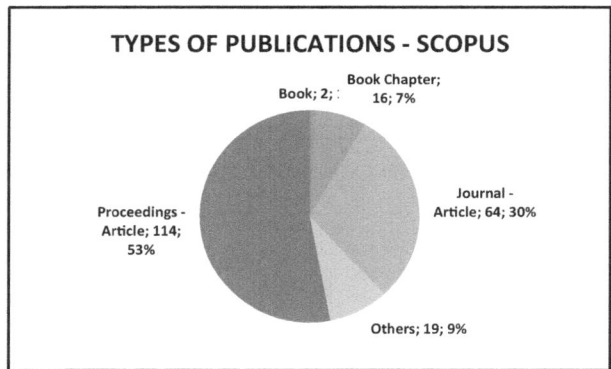

Fig. 6. Types of Publications – Scopus

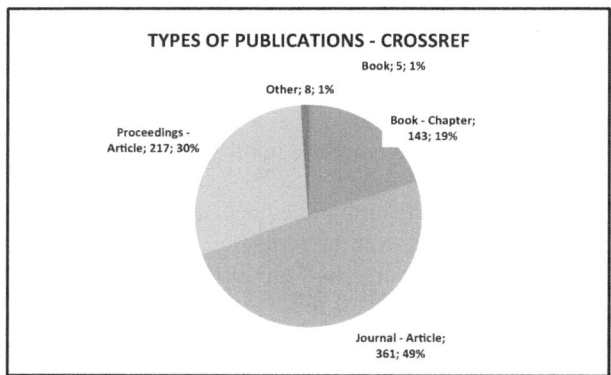

Fig. 7. Types of Publications – Crossref

The figures represent the category wise number of publications and category wise percentage share in overall publications for all four data sources.

From the above figures it is evident that all the databases under consideration offer multiple forms of research literature at disposal for researchers.

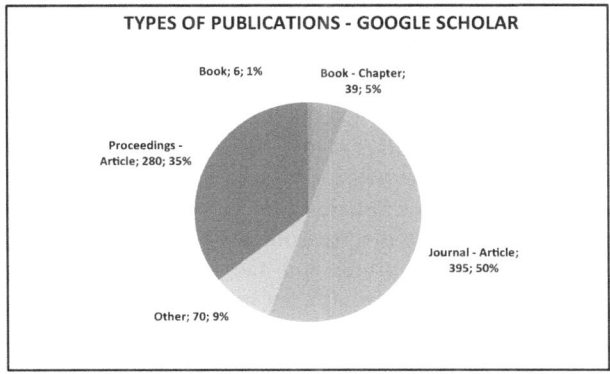

Fig. 8. Types of Publications – Google Scholar

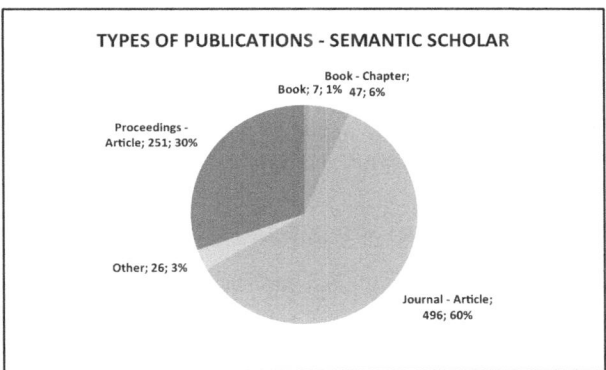

Fig. 9. Types of Publications – Semantic Scholar

- **Book**: This publication type is comparatively low in number across all platforms, indicating a limited emphasis on complete authored books. The distribution across platforms is relatively balanced, suggesting similar representation across Scopus, Semantic Scholar, Google Scholar, and CrossRef.
- **Book Chapters**: This publication type exhibits a more considerable contribution compared to complete books, showing active involvement in edited volumes or specialized publications. CrossRef has the highest count, indicating that these chapters are widely referenced or cited in other scholarly works. Semantic Scholar and Google Scholar show a relatively higher count, highlighting good visibility and accessibility of these chapters in digital libraries.
- **Journal Articles:** This publication type is the most substantial category, signifying a significant emphasis on peer-reviewed research disseminated through academic journals. It suggests a strong focus on in-depth analysis and original research within the academic community. Semantic Scholar and Google Scholar display significantly higher counts, indicating a high degree of visibility and citations in these digital

repositories. The distribution across platforms is varied, with CrossRef holding a substantial count as well, indicating wide referencing in other scholarly articles.

- **Proceedings Article:** This publication type has a count indicating active participation and dissemination in academic conferences or symposiums. Google Scholar and Semantic Scholar display higher counts, indicating good visibility and citations for these conference papers. CrossRef has a lower count, possibly indicating lesser referencing of these proceedings' articles in other scholarly works.
- **Others**: This category includes diverse content types encompassing reports, non-peer-reviewed publications, or various non-traditional scholarly outputs. CrossRef has the highest count, suggesting significant referencing or citation of these other types in scholarly works or publications.

This comprehensive breakdown provides a detailed understanding of the distribution and scope of publications across various platforms and publication types, highlighting active scholarly engagement and dissemination in different formats within the academic community. The scope and depth of the analysis within this dataset seem comprehensive, covering various academic publication formats. There's an evident emphasis on peer-reviewed journal articles, which are crucial for disseminating detailed research findings, while also showcasing involvement in conference proceedings, book chapters, and other scholarly contributions. This diversity indicates a well-rounded approach to scholarly dissemination across different platforms and publication types.

3.2   Relative Growth Rate (RGR) of Publications – RGR (P)

The Relative Growth Rate (RGR) is the increase in number of works per unit of time. It can be used to understand the progress of a particular research field [21]. The RGR for publications is the increase in number of publications per unit time. The growth rate of publications per annum was calculated to find the incremental trend of yearly output. The data was tabulated in excel sheet and bibliometric methods were applied to calculate the parameters according formulas.

The Relative Growth Rate of publications in all the databases was calculated using the following formula which was also used by [22, 23]:

Relative Growth Rate (RGR) of Publications

$$\mathbf{RGR(P)} = \frac{P2 - P1}{T2 - T1}$$

where,

- **RGR(P)**: Mean relative growth rate over the specific period of intervals.
- **P1:** LogeP1 (Natural log of initial number of publications) for particular year
- **P2:** LogeP2 (Natural log of final number of publications) for particular year
- **T2 – T1:** the unit difference between the initial time and the final time.

Table 2 shows the calculation of the above parameters for all the databases for publications over period of years.

Figure 10 represents the trends of the Relative Growth Rate of Publications in all Databases for EDM field over span of interval 2011–2022.

Table 2. Yearwise RGR (P)

YEAR	2012	2013	2014	2015	2016	2017	2018	2019	2020	2021	2022
Scopus	0.36	1.47	0.59	1.64	1.03	1.37	1.39	1.33	1.80	1.86	2.10
CrossRef	0.59	0.88	1.05	1.24	1.12	1.39	1.45	1.62	1.69	1.78	2.41
Semantic Scholar	0.44	0.87	1.08	1.33	1.63	1.73	1.85	2.29	2.50	3.95	5.12
Google Scholar	0.47	0.99	0.88	1.11	1.50	1.54	1.56	1.79	1.90	1.97	3.06

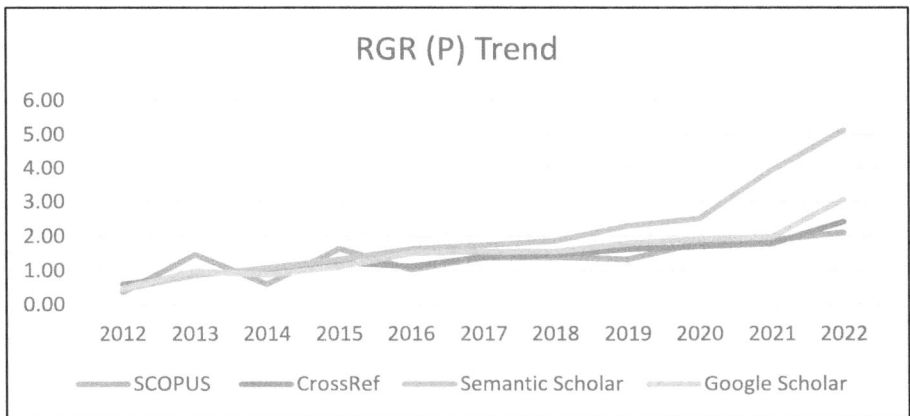

Fig. 10. Relative Growth Rate of Publications – Trend

From the above trend analysis, it can be inferred that:

- For all the databases, the relative growth rate of publications is increasing almost similarly. CrossRef exhibits a slightly lower growth rate than Scopus in Educational Data Mining publications over the same period. It has a steady but comparatively moderate growth trend.
- Semantic Scholar demonstrates the highest relative growth rate among the databases analyzed, indicating substantial growth in publications related to Educational Data Mining from 2012 to 2022.
- Google Scholar portrays a growth rate higher than Scopus and CrossRef but lower than Semantic Scholar. It shows a moderate growth trend in Educational Data Mining publications over the ten-year span.
- Semantic Scholar stands out with the highest growth rate, indicating a significant increase in publications related to Educational Data Mining.
- Google Scholar follows with a moderately high growth rate.
- Scopus and CrossRef exhibit relatively lower growth rates compared to the other databases analyzed, indicating a slower rise in Educational Data Mining publications over the same period.

3.3 Doubling Time of Publications DT (P)

Doubling time is directly related to relative growth rate (RGR) and is defined as the time required for an entity to become double of the existing amount. It is applied here to calculate the time required for the existing quantity of publications, citations, pages and other metrics to become double [24]. It has a close relationship with the relative growth rate(RGR). It is also determined that if the number of articles in a subject double during a given period, then the difference between logarithms of numbers at the beginning and at the end of this period must be logarithm of the number 2 [25]. If natural logarithm is used, the difference has a value of 0.693. Thus, the corresponding doubling time for each specific period of interval can be calculated by the formula as reported in [23]:

$$\textbf{Doubling Time} = \frac{0.693}{RGR}$$

The doubling time for publications for both the databases is calculated with formula DT(P) = 0.693/RGR(P). The doubling time for publications is calculated over period of years 2011–2022. Table 3 represents the doubling time of publications during tenure of 2011–2022 for each of the databases.

Table 3. Yearwise DT (P)

YEAR	2012	2013	2014	2015	2016	2017	2018	2019	2020	2021	2022
Scopus	1.94	0.47	1.17	0.42	0.67	0.50	0.50	0.52	0.39	0.37	0.33
CrossRef	1.17	0.79	0.66	0.56	0.62	0.50	0.48	0.43	0.41	0.39	0.29
Semantic Scholar	1.56	0.80	0.64	0.52	0.43	0.40	0.37	0.30	0.28	0.18	0.14
Google Scholar	1.49	0.70	0.79	0.62	0.46	0.45	0.45	0.39	0.36	0.35	0.23

Figure 11 projects the trends in the Doubling Time of Publications in the databases.
From the figure it can be inferred that over the span of time the doubling time of publications in both the databases is decreasing. Further it can be analysed that:

- CrossRef shows a more consistent doubling time trend compared to Scopus. Publications doubled approximately every 0.99 years in 2012. There was a consistent increase in doubling time, reaching around 3.79 years by 2022.
- Semantic Scholar displays a similar pattern to CrossRef, with a consistent increase in doubling time. Publications doubled every 1.11 years in 2012. The doubling time increased progressively, reaching approximately 5.56 years in 2022.
- Google Scholar exhibits a trend resembling Scopus, with fluctuations in doubling time. Publications doubled about every 1.12 years in 2012. The doubling time increased and stabilized at approximately 4.35 years in 2022.
- Scopus and Google Scholar show fluctuations in doubling time over the years, indicating varying rates of publication growth.
- CrossRef and Semantic Scholar display more consistent patterns, with a gradual increase in doubling time, suggesting a slower rate of publication growth in recent years compared to earlier periods.

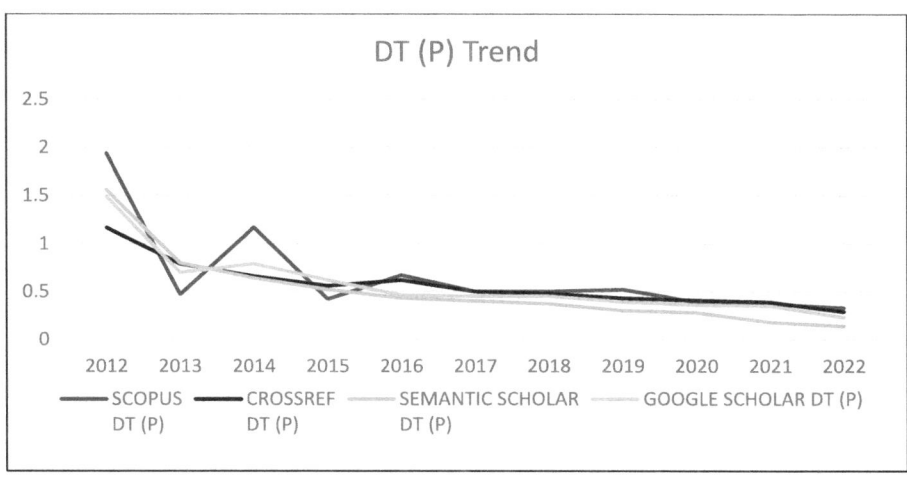

Fig. 11. Doubling Time of Publications – Trend

Thus, from the above discussion, it is evident that there is a significant increase in the overall research output in the Educational Data Mining domain.

3.4 Journal Publications Counts

As discussed in Sect. 3.1, there are many categories of publication types of the Educational Data Mining Domain in all databases which includes journal articles, conference publications, book chapters, books and other form of publications. Table 4 and Fig. 12 represents total number of journal articles in all databases. It shows that Semantic Scholar has highest number of journal articles published across the years.

Table 4. Publication Count

Year	Scopus	CrossRef	Semantic Scholar	Google Scholar
Total no of Journals	64	360	495	358

Further, Fig. 12 represents the year wise total number of journal articles published in each database.

From the above figures, following analysis can be inferred:

- There is fluctuating but generally stable publication counts in Scopus database. The trend saw a peak in 2020 and 2022, indicating potential increased interest or research output in recent years.
- In CrossRef, there seem to be Gradual increase in publications until 2020, followed by a slight decline in 2021–2022. The trend indicates a period of growth followed by potential stabilization or a slight drop in publications.

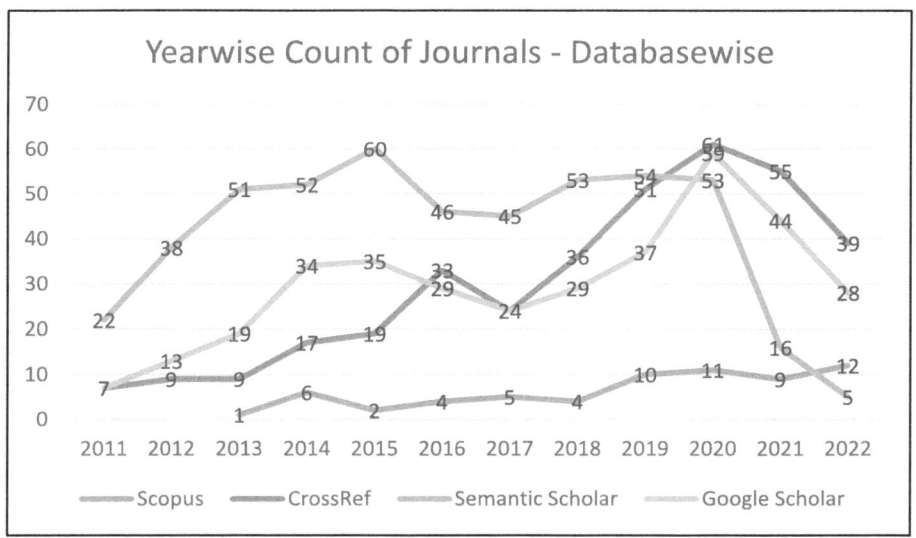

Fig. 12. Yearwise count of Journal Publications

- Semantic Scholar numbers show a significant growth until 2019, followed by a noticeable decline.
- Google Scholar publication count shows Fairly consistent, with minor fluctuations. The database publications have maintained relatively steady publication counts over the years, with no dramatic peaks or dips.
- Scopus and Google Scholar maintain relatively consistent publication rates, without major spikes or drops.
- CrossRef indicates a growth phase until 2020, possibly indicating a stabilization phase in the last two years.

4   Conclusions and Future Scope

Educational Data Mining (EDM) is a rapidly growing field that leverages data mining and machine learning techniques to analyze educational data and improve educational outcomes. The study shows the promising future scope of EDM due to the increasing availability of educational data and ongoing advancements in data analysis technologies. This study shows an upward trend in Educational Data Mining (EDM), revealing an uptick in the use of EDM techniques to create innovative methods for improving educational results, like developing predictive models for student performance.

The research indicates that although EDM literature often mentions important theories, they are not fully incorporated into research. In this concern, there lies future scope of performing in-depth analysis of the domain using techniques as Citation Analysis, Author Analysis, Bibliographic Coupling, Network Analysis, Thematic Analysis as well as Qualitative Bibliographic Analysis.

The findings discussed in this paper have implications for both academic discussions as well as practical applications. The results strengthen the recognition of Educational

Data Mining (EDM) as a field with potential to transform the educational landscape by providing valuable insights that lead to more effective teaching and learning experiences. While the RGR and DT parameters of publications and citations are proof of the increased availability of literature in the EDM field, the analysis of publications type give insight to the variety of literature available. By conducting a bibliometric analysis, we were able to gain a better understanding of how research and technological progress of the EDM field are accurately represented.

References

1. Romero, C., Ventura, S.: Educational data mining: a review of the state of the art. IEEE Trans. Syst. Man Cybern. Part C (Appl. Rev.) **40**(6), 601–618 (2010)
2. "What is EDM?", International Educational Data Mining Society
3. Baker, R.S.J.D., Yacef, K.: Proceedings of the 2nd International Conference on Educational Data Mining (2009)
4. Pardos, Z.A., Heffernan, N.T.:KT-IDEM: introducing item difficulty to the knowledge tracing model. In: Proceedings of the 4th International Conference on Educational Data Mining (2011)
5. Aggarwal, C.C., Zhai, C.X.: A Survey of Text Classification Algorithms. Springer Science & Business Media, Boston (2012)
6. Kotsiantis, S.B., Zaharakis, I.D., Pintelas, P.E.: Machine learning: a review of classification and combining techniques. Artif. Intell. Rev. **26**(3), 159–190 (2006)
7. Romero, C., Ventura, S.: Educational data mining: a survey from 1995 to 2005. Expert Syst. Appl. **33**(1), 135–146 (2007)
8. Siemens, G., Long, P.: Penetrating the fog: analytics in learning and education. EDUCAUSE Rev. **46**(5), 30–32 (2011)
9. Dawson, S., Siemens, G.: Ethical considerations of learning analytics. J. Learn. Analytics (2014)
10. Kumar, S., Vanevenhoven, J., Liguori, E., Pandey, N.: Twenty-five years of the journal of small business and enterprise development: a bibliometric review. J. Small Bus. Enterp. Dev. (2021)
11. Mryglod, O., Kenna, R., Holovatch, Y., Berche, B.: Comparison of a citation-based indicator and peer review for absolute and specific measures of research-group excellence. Scientometrics, 767–777 (2013)
12. Costas, R., van Leeuwen, T., Bordons, M.: A bibliometric classificatory approach for the study and assessment of research performance at the individual level: the effect of age on productivity and impact. J. Am. Soc. Inf. Sci. Technol., 1564–1581 (2010)
13. Ellegaard, O., Wallin, J.A.:The bibliometric analysis of scholarly production: how great is the impact? Scientometrics **105**, 1809–1831 (2015)
14. Pranckut, R.: Web of Science (WoS) and scopus: the titans of bibliographic information in today's academic world. Today's AcademicWorld **9**, 12 (2021)
15. Donthu, N., Kumar, S., Mukherjee, D., Pandey, N., Lim, W.M.:How to conduct a bibliometric analysis: an overview and guidelines. J. Bus. Res. (2021)
16. Muthukrishnan, S.M., Govindasamy, M.K., Mustapha, M.N.: Systematic mapping review on student's performance analysis using big data predictive model. J. Fundam. Appl. Sci. **9**(4), 730–758 (2017)
17. Fauziastuti, V.T., Rakhman, L.A.:A review of students' graduation classification: a comparison of Naive Bayes classifier and K-nearest neighbour. In: Advances in Social Science, Education and Humanities Research (2019)

18. Nájera, A.B.U., De la Calleja Mora, J.: Brief review of educational applications using data mining and machine learning. Rev. Electrónica Inv. Educativa **19**(4), 84–96 (2017)
19. Salam, A., Zeniarja, J.: Classification of deep learning convolutional neural network feature extraction for student graduation prediction. Indonesian J. Electr. Eng. Comput. Sci. **32**(1), 335–341 (2023)
20. Pena-Ayala, A.: Educational data mining: a survey and a data mining-based analysis of recent works. Expert Syst. Appl. **41**(4), 1432–1462 (2014)
21. Minhas, M.R., Potdar, V.: Decision support systems in construction: a bibliometric analysis. Buildings (2020)
22. Mahapatra, M.: On the validity of the theory of exponential growth of scientific literature. In: Proceedings of the 15th IASLIC Conference, Bangalore (1985)
23. Singh, V.K., Banshal, S.K., Singhal, K. et al.: Scientometric mapping of research on 'Big Data'. Scientometrics, 727–741 (2015)
24. Mondal, A.K.: A bibliometric study on DC, RGT, and DT of publications and citations of ISTL journal during 2010–2020. Library Philosophy and Practice (2021)
25. Balasubramani, D.R.: International Workshop on Bibliometric and Scientometric Analysis for Research Management, Department of Library and Information Science, Bharathidasan University (2020)

Predictive Modeling of Chronic Kidney Disease with Ensemble Algorithms

Kishor Mane⬤ and Mahesh Hasabe$^{(\boxtimes)}$ ⬤

CSE Department, D. Y. Patil College of Engineering and Technology, Kolhapur,
Maharashtra, India
maheshhasabe1989@gmail.com

Abstract. Chronic Kidney Disease i.e. CKD, is one of the biggest issues in health worldwide. It occurs due to a gradual decline in renal functions accompanied by a high level of morbidity and mortality. This paper discusses the multifaceted nature of the etiology, the clinical manifestations, and the diagnostic approaches related to CKD, while highlighting the emerging role of ML in improving disease prediction and management. It proposes an ensemble learning approach as an aggregate of several ML algorithms to enhance accuracy and reliability of CKD prediction. In the proposed ensemble approach SVM, logistic regression, random forest and decision tree algorithms with voting-based learning have been used. This model has been tested using ten-fold cross validation technique on the input dataset. Experimental results indicate that the accuracy of the prediction of CKD with proposed ensemble method is 90.35% against individual algorithms. This method, therefore, has great scope for early detection, risk stratification, and personalized treatment planning in the management of CKD.

Keywords: Chronic kidney disease · Machine learning · Deep learning · Support Vector Machine · K nearest neighbor · Artificial Neural Networks · Random Forests · Logistic Regression · Decision trees

1 Introduction

Chronic kidney disease (CKD) is a chronic condition in which the kidneys deteriorate over time. This injury impairs the kidneys' capacity to filter blood adequately, allowing extra waste and fluid to accumulate in the body. The unfavorable character of chronic kidney disease sometimes causes diagnostic delays since symptoms may not occur until significant renal disease has progressed. Diabetes, high BP, and heart disease are all substantial risk factors for chronic kidney disease. Age and gender also influence its growth. Chronic kidney disease symptoms can include stomach ache, back pain, fever, nosebleeds, rash, and vomiting. Diagnostic testing for CKD frequently comprises a mix of tests, such as estimated glomerular filtration rate (eGFR), urinalysis, and blood pressure monitoring. These measurements reveal valuable information regarding kidney function and overall health. In recent years, machine learning (ML) approaches used to CKD prediction and management [1]. Machine learning algorithms offer numerous methods

© The Author(s), under exclusive license to Springer Nature Switzerland AG 2025
S. Rajagopal et al. (Eds.): ASCIS 2024, CCIS 2424, pp. 163–171, 2025.
https://doi.org/10.1007/978-3-031-86290-8_12

and benefits for analyzing complicated medical data, potentially boosting diagnostic accuracy and early intervention. CKD researchers have employed a variety of machine learning methods as Naive Bayes, random forest and neural networks etc. are effective for data interpretation and prediction. These ML algorithms leverage historical patient data to generate predictive models for new cases. For instance, Naive Bayes utilizes probabilistic approaches, Decision Trees provide structured classification reports, and Neural Networks aim to minimize prediction errors through iterative learning processes. The integration of ML in CKD management represents a significant advancement in medical diagnostics. By facilitating early detection and risk assessment, these predictive models have the potential to significantly impact patient outcomes, potentially saving numerous lives through timely intervention and personalized treatment strategies. As research in this field continues to evolve, the synergy between medical expertise and machine learning technologies promises to enhance our understanding and management of CKD, ultimately improving patient care and outcomes in this critical area of nephrology. The paper has been segmented into several parts. Section 2 discusses the different CKD techniques and limitations of it. Section 3 describes the structure of the proposed system along with details. Section 4 briefly describes the implementation details along with methodology. The last section discusses the results.

2   Literature Review

Most people have gradual kidney damage over time as results in high blood pressure or diabetes (known as chronic renal disease). More serious kidney damage happens suddenly due to sickness, accident, or medication use. These things most probably happen in patients who have low kidney functionality or who is facing kidney problems from long time. Several scholars are working on various approaches of predicting CKD:

Sandeep Chaurasia, Pankaj Chittara, et al. [1] proposes multi-stable forest approach which outperforms previous algorithms, with more accuracy along with 14 features. Bhavya Gudeti, Shashvi Mishra, et al. [2] applied several machine learning techniques to investigate the diagnosis time and boost accuracy. The proposed work is broken into several stages based on the severity of CKD. By examining several algorithms including neural networks, RBF, and RF. The evaluation findings demonstrate that the RBF algorithm performs well than others. F. M. Javed Mehedi Shamrat, Pronab Ghosh [3] undertook a study to investigate the significance of CKD in the literature. The absence of value in the dataset will lower the accuracy of our models and forecasts. The authors devised a remedy to this difficulty by repeating the method during CKD, with undetermined results. They replace missing values with return values. Chen Guozhen, Ding Chenguang et al. [4] have considered the data consisted of 400 data points and 25 characteristics, with findings for patients with and without CKD. Author employed nearest neighbor, random forest, and neural networks to get their results. The bagging approach [5] to decrease the characteristics and diagnose CKD with good accuracy. Bagging, AdaBoost, and Random Forest are among the algorithms that have been combined. The PSO approach was used to extract six lower features and then evaluated on the seven remaining higher features. Bagging has a higher overall efficiency than other classes. D. H. Kim, S. Y. Ye [6] employed custom selection to minimize the number of features required to categorize kidney diseases. The algorithms employed include SMO, Jrip, Naïve bayes and IBK. It compares the reduced findings to those obtained from the original data. T. H. Aldhyani, A.S. Alshebamie, et al. [7] proposed AHDCNN for the early stages of renal illness detection. It reflects the data-driven component of the new generation. Using CNN to increase social network accuracy by minimizing characteristics. C. P. Kashyap, et al. [11] employs a study of early CKD prediction using deep learning and adds to the advancement of deep learning in CKD diagnosis. From the above literature review following are limitations identified as –

1. The use of restricted data may result in data overfitting and diminish the generalizability of model.
2. Missing values from an input data can reduce prediction accuracy.
3. Another flaw is the absence of standardization in the selection process between courses, which makes it impossible to compare results.
4. In addition, several research on binary categorization do not consider illness stage.

   To address above drawbacks, research should prioritize larger and more diverse datasets in order to increase model stability and generalizability. Advanced strategies for dealing with missing data, such as multiple imputation can help to improve data quality. Standardizing feature selection processes and employing an integrated approach can result in more consistent and similar findings across investigations. Finally, the application of multiple classification models capable of distinguishing between different phases of CKD will provide additional clinical information for early detection and personalized treatment methods.

3 Proposed Chronic Kidney Disease Prediction

The proposed CKD prediction system architecture is shown in Fig. 1. Its goal is to increase the accuracy of the chronic kidney disease (CKD) prognosis which will help to identify and treat CKD in its early stages, leading to better outcomes. In proposed system, an ensemble learning approach have been used by combining four strong machine learning algorithms including support vector machine (SVM), logistic regression (LR), random forest (RF) and decision tree (DT). Their strengths were combined to create a ensemble model to predict CKD. The system is created as a centralized tool for doctors to manage patients with CKD, providing insight into early intervention and personalized treatment plans. The purpose of the planning process is to learn patterns from recorded data and make predictions about unseen events. The standard training process includes a training phase and a validation phase. During training, the algorithm learns patterns and relationships from training data that includes objects and labels (variables). In the validation phase, the learning model is evaluated using test data that does not contain text. This allows for an unbiased assessment of the model's performance and overall ability. This process has identified the most accurate and reliable models for predicting chronic kidney disease and its progression based on patient characteristics. Training models can facilitate early detection, risk stratification, and personalized treatment planning to improve disease control. The different modules used to implement the proposed method are as follows:

1. Data Collection:

Data from UCI Machine Learning Repository [25] was used for the testing, which included 25 features. Out of 25 features 14 features were considered for training including serum creatinine levels, BP, age, albumin level, red blood cell count, presence of pus cells, presence of pus cell clumps, HB levels, RBC count (repeated), WBC count, anemia status, disease classification, appetite, and packed cell volume.

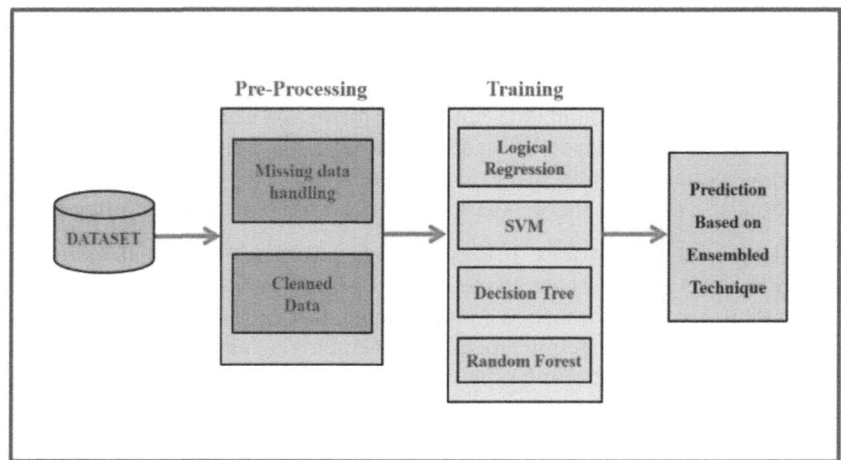

Fig. 1. Proposed System Architecture

2. Data Preprocessing:

It includes Missing values filling using mean for numerical features and mode for categorical features, Outliers and noise identification and handling to ensure data quality and data imbalance for preventing biased model training.

3. Training-

Training uses up to 70% of the data, while testing uses up to 30%. Machine learning techniques including SVM, LR, RF and DT were used in the ensemble learning algorithms that were employed for training. Based on patient data, this method enables us to determine the most accurate and dependable models for forecasting the course of chronic renal disease. These models can help with risk assessment, early identification, and individualized treatment planning, which can lead to better disease control.

4   Implementation Details

4.1   Experimental Setups

The proposed method was implemented and tested with the help of the following test setup:

- 11th Gen AMD Ryzen 5 Processor, 8GB RAM, Storage 512 GB, Windows 11.

- Python language used for with different libraries.
- Sample CKD dataset [25] has been used from UCI repository.

4.2 Methodology

Four potent learning algorithms including SVM, LR, RF and decision tree were merged into the methods employed in this work. By utilizing the advantages of each algorithm, this method creates a reliable and precise chronic kidney disease (CKD) prediction model. First, information is gathered from the UCI Repository [25] and 14 baseline features are chosen for preprocessing. Preprocessing was done on the data to remove inconsistent, unclear, and inaccurate data so that the best possible input for the model could be used. 30% of the dataset is used for testing, while 70% is used for training. Using this initial data, all four algorithms were trained to find trends and connections between strategies and the risk of CKD. Logistic regression is good at providing good results, SVM can find good decision boundaries, decision trees provide meaningful rules, and random forests provide good predictions from many decision trees. Ensemble algorithms can capture relationships in the data by combining these variables and make better predictions than any single model alone. This comprehensive approach can improve early diagnosis, risk stratification, and individualized treatment planning for CKD patients. Fig. 2 shows the pseudocode of ensemble algorithm.

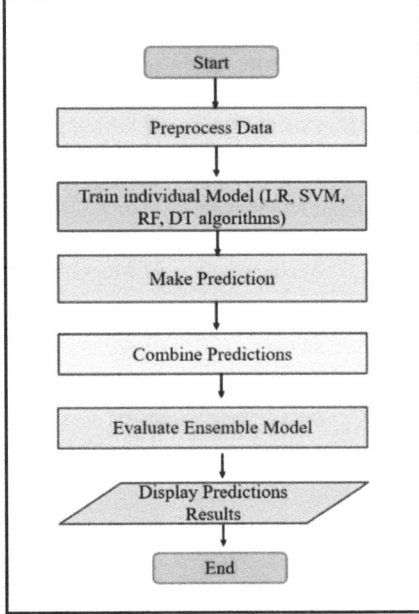

pseudocode for the ensemble algorithm that makes use of Random Forest, SVM, decision tree techniques, and Logistic Regression
Input- Dataset
Output- Prediction
        Import required libraries and modules
        Load and preprocess the data
        Split the data
        Initialize and train individual models
        Make predictions using each model
        Implement ensemble voting
        Evaluate the ensemble model

Fig. 2. Flowchart for Ensemble Algorithm

The ensemble method works as follows:

1. The individual algorithm of SVM, logistic regression, random forest and decision tree are all trained on the dataset.
2. For a given input, each model makes a prediction.
3. For a final decision, it follow a majority voting system over the four models.
    This approach enables us to reap the different strengths of all algorithms as follows –

- Logistic Regression: It is quite interpretative and performs well on linearly separable data.
- Support Vector Machine: Very sensitive to very high dimensional spaces. It works quite well if the margin of separation is clean.
- Decision Tree: Nice intuitive visualization of where a decision is being made. Quite good with non-linear relationships.
- Random Forest: It inhibits overfitting and is well tolerated on massive numbers of features.

By using a combination of the algorithms, attempting to build a more robust prediction model that can be supported than any single algorithm could provide alone.

5   Results Analysis

The performance of ensemble algorithm using four different methods (SVM, LR, RF and decision tree) was evaluated using data of 1000, 2000, 3000, 4000 and 5000 records for training. The analysis is based on four main metrics as F1 – measure, recall, accuracy and precision (Table 1).

Table 1. Results analysis for Ensemble Algorithm

Dataset	Precision	Recall	Accuracy	F1 Measure
Dataset 1 -1000 records	91.07	93.79	89.89	91.80
Dataset 2 -2000 records	90.75	94.64	88.62	91.50
Dataset 3 -3000 records	91.01	94.45	89.34	91.82
Dataset 4 -4000 records	93.64	95.52	92.56	94.02
Dataset 5 -5000 records	92.74	94.32	91.36	93.42

The dataset having 1000–5000 records have achieves 89.89%–92.56% accuracy. The average accuracy obtained for the all the datasets used for training is 90.35%. The precision is in the range of 90.75 to 93.64%. Its precision of highest value suggests it had the lowest false positive rate. The recall value ranges from 94.32 to 95.52% % shows it also had the highest true positive rate. The F-Measure, which provides a balanced measure of precision and recall ranging from 91.50 to 94.02%. The standalone algorithm such as RF, LR, decision tree and SVM gives the accuracy less than 90%. For every test, each model generates a forecast (visual noise), and the prediction with more than half of the votes is the final output (Fig. 3).

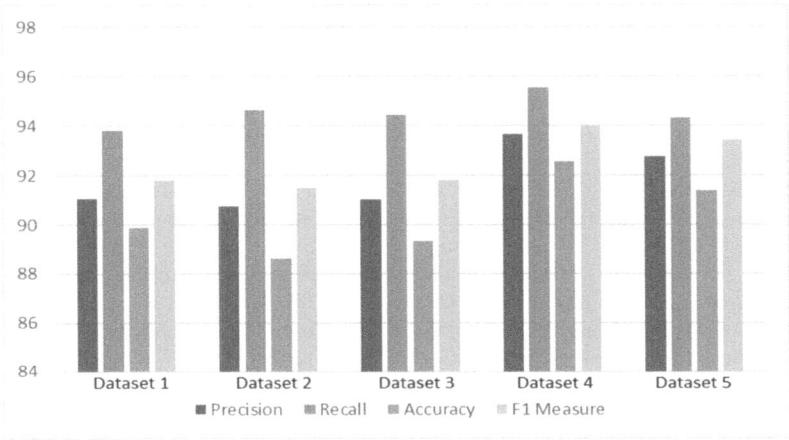

Fig. 3. Graph of Precision, Accuracy, Recall and F1 Measure

6   Conclusion

A significant issue affecting many people's lives and health worldwide is chronic kidney disease, or CKD. It is very important to identify and diagnose CKD early in order to put preventive measures into place, slow the disease's course, and lessen consequences. The purpose of this research is to use ML techniques to increase the precision and dependability of CKD prediction. The UCI ML Repository dataset has been used in the suggested strategy. It includes numerous patient records with fourteen pertinent attributes. To give machine learning models the best possible input, manage missing values, outliers, and data normalization using data pretreatment approaches. The effectiveness of four well-known ML algorithms such as SVM, LR, decision tree and RF in predicting chronic kidney disease (CKD) was tested along as well as with ensemble learning. Based on the patients' inputs, the system uses these algorithms to accurately classify patients as having CKD or not. The assembly system obtained an overall accuracy of 90.35% indicating the capacity to identify true positives and negatives while minimizing false positives. These test results show the efficacy of the suggested method. Predicting the accuracy of the suggested system can help with customized treatment programs, early intervention tactics, and CKD screening plans. This procedure offers the potential to enhance patient outcomes and lower the financial and commercial expenses related to chronic renal disease through prompt identification and treatment. In future research and development can concentrate on incorporating more data, investigating blended learning, and utilizing descriptive intelligence approaches to compute in order to enhance the prediction's definition and dependability.

References

1. Chittora, P., Chaurasia, S., Chakrabarti, P.: Prediction of chronic kidney disease - a machine learning perspective. IEEE Access 2021.3053763 (2021)
2. Gudeti, B., Mishra, S., Fernandez, T.F.: A Novel Approach to Predict chronic kidney disease using machine learning algorithms. In: Fourth International Conference on Electronics, Communication and Aerospace Technology (2020)
3. Shamrat, F.M.J.M., Ghosh, P.: Implementation of machine learning algorithms to detect chronic kidney disease. In: 2020 IEEE International Conference for Innovation in Technology (INOCON) Bengaluru, India. Nov 6–8, 2020 (2020)
4. Chen, G., Ding, C., Li, Y.: Prediction of chronic kidney disease using adaptive hybridized deep convolutional neural network on the internet of medical things platform. IEEE Access **8**, 2995310 (2020)
5. Tekale, S., Shingavi, P.: Prediction of chronic kidney disease using machine learning algorithms. Int. J. Adv. Res. Comput. Commun. Eng. **7**(10) (2018)
6. Kim, D.H., Ye, S.Y.: Classification of chronic kidney disease in sonography using the GLCM and artificial neural network. Diagnostics **11**(5), 864 (2021)
7. Aldhyani, T.H., Alshebami, A.S., Alzahrani, M.Y.: Soft computing model to predict chronic diseases. Inform. Sci. Engg. **36**(2), 365–376 (2020)
8. Khan, F.A., Zeb, K., Al-Rakhami, M., Derhab, A., Bukhari, S.A.C.: Detection and prediction of diabetes using data mining: a comprehensive review. IEEE Access **9**, 43711–43735 (2021). https://doi.org/10.1109/ACCESS.2021.3059343
9. Islam, M.A., Akter, S., Hossen, M.S., Keya, S.A., Tisha, S.A., Hossain, S.: Risk factor prediction of chronic kidney disease based on machine learning algorithms. In:2020 3rd International Conference on Intelligent Sustainable Systems (ICISS), pp. 952–957. Thoothukudi, India (2020). https://doi.org/10.1109/ICISS49785.2020.9315878
10. Ali, N.M., Shaheen, M., Mabrouk, M.S., Aborizka, M.A.: A novel approach of transcriptomic microRNA analysis using text mining methods: an early detection of multiple sclerosis disease. IEEE Access **9**, 120024–120033 (2021). https://doi.org/10.1109/ACCESS.2021.3109069
11. Kashyap, C.P., Dayakar Reddy, G.S., Balamurugan, M.: Prediction of chronic disease in kidneys using machine learning classifiers. In: 1st International Conference on Computational Science and Technology (ICCST), pp. 562–567. CHENNAI, India (2022). https://doi.org/10.1109/ICCST55948.2022.10040329
12. Damodara, K., Thakur, A.: Adaptive neuro fuzzy inference system based prediction of chronic kidney disease. In: 7th International Conference on Advanced Computing and Communication Systems (ICACCS), pp. 973–976. Coimbatore, India (2021). https://doi.org/10.1109/ICACCS51430.2021.9441989
13. Yogish, H.K., Rajeshwari: Prediction of chronic kidney disease using machine learning technique. In: Fourth International Conference on Cognitive Computing and Information Processing (CCIP), pp. 1–6. Bengaluru, India (2022). https://doi.org/10.1109/CCIP57447.2022.10058678
14. Vijayalakshmi, A., Sumalatha, V.: Survey on diagnosis of chronic kidney disease using machine learning algorithms. In: 3rd International Conference on Intelligent Sustainable Systems (ICISS), pp. 590–595. Thoothukudi, India (2020). https://doi.org/10.1109/ICISS49785.2020.9315880
15. Chen, G., et al.: Prediction of chronic kidney disease using adaptive hybridized deep convolutional neural network on the internet of medical things platform. IEEE Access **8**, 100497–100508 (2020). https://doi.org/10.109/ACCESS.2020.2995310

16. Ekanayake, I.U., Herath, D.: Chronic kidney disease prediction using machine learning methods. In: Moratuwa Engineering Research Conference (MERCon), pp. 260–265. Moratuwa,Sri Lanka (2020). https://doi.org/10.1109/MERCon50084.2020.9185249

17. Suganthi, N.M., Rama, P., Chandralekha, E.: Chronic kidney disease detection using ada boosting ensemble method and K-Fold cross validation. In: International Conference on Automation, Computing and Renewable Systems (ICACRS), pp. 979–983. Pudukkottai, India (2022). https://doi.org/10.1109/ICACRS55517.2022.10029047

18. Imran, S.M., Banu, S.S.: HCB: A Hybrid CatBoost enabled chronic kidney disease detection system. In: 3rd International Conference on Electronics and Sustainable Communication Systems (ICESC), pp. 1355–1360. Coimbatore, India (2022). https://doi.org/10.1109/ICESC54411.2022.9885415

19. Vimala, C., Subramani, C., Bhagat, V., Sravani, M.V.: Analysis of different algorithms to predict chronic kidney disease. In: International Interdisciplinary Humanitarian Conference for Sustainability (IIHC), pp. 1051–1054. Bengaluru, India (2022). https://doi.org/10.1109/IIHC55949.2022.10060311

20. Kumari, S., Singh, S.K.: An ensemble learning-based model for effective chronic kidney disease prediction. In: International Conference on Computing, Communication, and Intelligent Systems (ICCCIS), pp. 162–168. Greater Noida, India (2022) https://doi.org/10.1109/ICCCIS56430.2022.10037698

21. S. Y. Yashfi et al. Risk Prediction of Chronic Kidney Disease Using Machine Learning Algorithms. 11th International Conference on Computing, Communication and Networking Technologies (ICCCNT), Kharagpur, India, pp. 1–5, (2020). https://doi.org/10.1109/ICCCNT49239.2020.9225548

22. Bin Abdul Ghafar, M.H., Aleena Binti Abdullah, N., Abdul Razak. A.H., Syahirul Amin Bin Megat Ali, M., Mutalib Al-Junid, S.A.: Chronic kidney disease prediction based on data mining method and support vector machine. In: IEEE 10th Conference on Systems, Process & Control (ICSPC), pp. 262–267. Malacca, Malaysia (2022) https://doi.org/10.1109/ICSPC55597.2022.10001806

23. Gupta, R., Koli, N., Mahor N., Tejashri, N.: Performance analysis of machine learning classifier for predicting chronic kidney disease. International Conference for Emerging Technology (INCET), pp. 1–4. Belgaum, India (2020). https://doi.org/10.1109/INCET49848.2020.9154147

24. Nandhini, J.M., Joshi, S., Anuratha, K.: Federated learning based prediction of chronic kidney diseases. 1st International Conference on Computational Science and Technology (ICCST), pp. 1–6. Chennai, India (2022). https://doi.org/10.1109/ICCST55948.2022.10040317

25. UCI dataset. https://archive.ics.uci.edu/dataset/336/chronic+kidney+disease. Accessed 4 Oct 2024

Advanced Lung Image Enhancement Using Dynamic Dual-Histogram Gamma Correction

A. Agnes Pearly[✉] and B. Karthik

Department of Electronics and Communication Engineering, Bharath Institute of Higher Education and Research (BIHER), Chennai, India
pearlyarthur@gmail.com, karthik.ece@bharathuniv.ac.in

Abstract. Enhancing lung images is essential for accurate medical diagnosis and treatment planning. Traditional image enhancement techniques often struggle to balance contrast improvement and noise suppression. In this paper, a novel method named Dynamic Dual-Histogram Gamma Correction (DDHGC), is presented that combines the ideas of Dualistic Sub-Image Histogram Equalization (DSIHE) and Dynamic Gamma Correction with Weighting Distribution. Furthermore, an Enhanced Selective Median Filter is adopted for noise suppression purpose before executing DDHGC. It offers excellent noise suppression and optimal contrast enhancement capabilities which makes it well suited for medical imaging applications. The aim of this study is to investigate the utility of DDHGC for improving contrast in two different types of medical imaging data - chest X-ray images and lung CT images from publicly available datasets. The results show that the proposed DDHGC method consistently perform better than four common methods (CLAHE, Gamma Correction, AGCWD and DSIHE). It provides the best results for PSNR, SSIM, Entropy and CII outperforming in terms of image quality, structure preservation and enhanced details indicating improved contrast.

Keywords: Chest X-ray Images · Noise Suppression · Enhanced Selective Median Filter · Dynamic Dual-Histogram Gamma Correction (DDHGC) · DSIHE · Lung CT Images · Contrast Enhancement

1 Introduction

Image clarity and quality play an important role in medical imaging, particularly for the diagnosis and monitoring of lung diseases. Lung imaging, primarily through modalities such as X-rays and CT scans, is critical for diagnosing and monitoring a variety of pulmonary diseases. Enhancing these images can help with accurate diagnosis and treatment planning. High-quality image enhancement techniques are critical for increasing visualization of anatomical structures and detecting anomalies. Contrast enhancement is commonly used in digital imagery to enhance visual perception for both humans as well as machine vision in identifying key image features. The variation in luminance reflectance (contrast) is created by altering the pixel intensity of the source image (enhancement).

© The Author(s), under exclusive license to Springer Nature Switzerland AG 2025
S. Rajagopal et al. (Eds.): ASCIS 2024, CCIS 2424, pp. 172–185, 2025.
https://doi.org/10.1007/978-3-031-86290-8_13

Traditional image enhancement methods work reasonably well for some cases, but often fail to maintain the finer aspects of images as well handle noise properly. The algorithm that performs histogram equalization (HE) is mostly favored technique because of its simplicity and relatively fast processing time. For medical images in particular, it is difficult to use HE as they only rely on the pixel range and each image may have different characteristics. This makes it that histogram equalization methods have been drastically updated through many different ways. However, as these methods involve excessive stretching and gray range merging (in a predominantly automated manner), they may result in the poor enhancement by shifting image brightness, venting detail reduction along with over-enhancement. To address these challenges, a novel approach has been proposed which integrates Dynamic Dual-Histogram Gamma Correction (DDHGC) with an Enhanced Selective Median Filter.

Dynamic Dual-Histogram Gamma Correction (DDHGC) is an advance image enhancement technique that actively enhances contrast of a given input image by taking potential benefits from the histogram equalization as well as gamma correction to provide an outstanding image quality. DDHGC divides the image histogram into two sub-histograms according to median intensity, and applies adaptive gamma correction to enhance contrast and also maintains meaningful details in an image. This method makes certain that the image's low and high-intensity regions are enhanced appropriately such that all portions give more balanced and natural results. But boosting contrast alone does not work, when images are corrupted by noise (very typical in medical imaging). Current noise model-dependent image enhancement methods also either focus on a single type of noise or ignore artifacts introduced by unintended contrast enhancements, which are insufficient.

An Enhanced Selective Median Filter is used in combination with DDHGC to tackle this problem efficiently. The filter is built to detect and conceal only noise, while totally leaving other portions of the image unaltered. Together these techniques provide a robust framework to enhance lung images with noise removal and contrast enhancement simultaneously. The Enhanced Selective Median Filter detects noisy pixels with intensity values higher or lower than the very common ones. Once found, median filter calculates the median on a variable window size replacing surrounding medium value for the noisy pixel. This adaptive feature ensures that noise is effectively eliminated without having to sacrifice any or all of the fine details in an image.

In summary, the proposed combined method seeks to dynamically enhance contrast within an image while also suppressing noise selectively and effectively. The end result is high-quality lung images that are critical for accurate medical diagnosis and analysis, thereby improving patient outcomes and healthcare delivery efficiency. The next few sections detail the proposed algorithm and compare to other methods.

2 Literature Survey

When you enhance images, particularly dark images, the image enhancement techniques can present two issues: unconventional effects and over-enhancement. These shortcomings draw attention to how difficult it is to achieve balanced enhancement without sacrificing image quality. Through the preservation of original brightness and information, histogram equalization (HE) techniques improve contrast and brightness, thereby improving image quality. In order to identify the most efficient technique for image enhancement, Sakshi et al., [1] conduct a critical comparison of different equalization approaches, evaluating and tabulating various parameters. The work of Siddiqi et al. [2] investigate the application of histogram equalization for effective image enhancement and noise reduction in medical CT images of the abdominal area. The methodology consists of two steps: beginning, pixel-based intensity transformation to de-noise the image background, leading to improved foreground features; and secondly, implementing histogram equalization filters onto the transformed image. The method that achieves uniform enhancement while reducing errors. HE modify image contrast, however traditional methods may occasionally fall short in maintaining natural brightness along with contrast. Rao et al. [3] addressed these issues with improved multi histogram equalization, which splits an image into smaller images and applies HE to each. This approach uses sub-pixel switches between corresponding images to improve data alignment and contrast, particularly in low-light images.

In order to enhance chest X-ray (CXR) images, Anand et al., [4] present a contrast diffusion network. Contrast is extracted from the input image using multi-level CLAHE (Contrast Limited Adaptive Histogram Equalization). The input image is then enhanced by diffusing the newly acquired contrast features over it; the amount of diffusion is set by multiple CLAHE stages. By bringing together CLAHE for enhancing contrast with Retinex theory, Georgieva et al., [5] present an adaptive algorithm for improving the visual clarity of CT images. Furthermore, to lessen noise, an intricate adaptive filter that combines Wiener along with median filtering is employed. In order to minimize noise and sharpen images, Singh et al. [6] recommend integrating morphological filtering approaches, which include open as well as bottom-hat functions, to improve visibility and background details. The Image Quality Assessment (IQA), which employs the Enhancement Measure (EME), affirms optimized image quality, alongside more precise features and retained important features. Wang et al. [7] present an approach to enhance lung CT scans which involves the total variational framework and wavelet transform. Two layers make up the original image: high frequency details and low frequency structure. The structure layer is contrast enhanced using histogram analysis, whereas the detail layer is denoised with wavelet transform and adaptive thresholding. Finally, the enhanced CT image is created by weight-fusing the processed layers.

In order to improve images subjected to complex conditions, Ye et al. [8] propose a dual histogram equalization algorithm built around adaptive image correction, addressing problems with gray level incorporating, brightness transformation, and over-enhancement in conventional methods. Through adaptive threshold adjustment to prevent over-enhancement and the avoidance of mean luminance shift, it improves on the Otsu method for more successful histogram segmentation. To avoid integrating gray levels, the algorithm additionally uses local gray level correction. Experimental analysis demonstrates that it effectively improves contrast and specifics without incorporating noise. However, it might be less time-efficient, making it better suited to industrial applications. Ezhilraja et al. [9] put forth Multi-Level Modified Dualistic Sub Image Histogram Equalization (ML-DSIHE) to improve CT images by iteratively splitting the histogram at the intensity midpoint while applying equalization to every segment. This method deals with issues such as over- as well as under-enhancement, foreground detail losses, and noise amplification. ML-DSIHE has been confirmed to be a novel method for improving the early identification accuracy of lung cancer while remaining computationally effective, making it appropriate for real-time applications. Yu et al. [10] present an automated image illumination correction algorithm based on Retinex theory and the discrete wavelet transform to extract image illumination. It uses two functions: one is for spatial luminance (which operates on the original pixel locations) performing local gamma correction, and another global statistical luminance to get overall adaptation. The training set provides estimates under different exposure levels and dimensions for adaptive correction. This will also help keep edges smooth and eliminates noise after reconstruction. A study by Jeyalaksshmi et al., [11] discusses about detecting blood issues associated with cancer by image preprocessing techniques. It is accomplished by utilizing an adaptive anisotropic diffusion filter for reducing noise and adaptive mean adjustment for enhancing the image. The suggested filtering and enhancement techniques obtain better performance in removing noise and improving the quality of the images compared to existing methods. The study by Mercy et al., [12] focuses on enhancing palm print preprocessing for security systems by introducing Receiver Operating Characteristic assessment. It also explores feature extraction techniques to strengthen security system efficiency.

3   Proposed Model

This paper proposes a robust adaptive approach to contrast enhancement for lung images using dynamic-dual-histogram gamma correction (DDHGC). This process is composed of two main phases: Dualistic Sub-Image Histogram Equalization (DSIHE) and Dynamic Gamma Correction with Weighting Distribution (DGCWD). The integration is suitable for medical imaging applications in which accurate and extensive visualization is critical because two complementary techniques, adaptive gamma correction and histogram equalization are both utilized. As both the imaging conditions and equipment are different, medical images such as lung image often have noise. Higher noise levels in the enhanced image may at times results in degrading original quality of images. To reduces noise and improve the qualities of lung images a combined approach that involves DDHGC as well as Noise filter can be used. In this paper, DDHGC is integrated with an advanced filter: Enhanced Selective Median Filter to balance noise reduction and detail preservation. The filter is performing spatial processing to attack the high-frequency components that are most likely noisy pixels. The overview of the proposed model is given in Fig. 1.

3.1   Enhanced Selective Median Filter for Noise Suppression

DDHGC aims at providing good contrast and preserving detail in the lung images. It is not really designed to be a noise suppression algorithm even though its adaptive nature features stopping excessive amplification of the system. To obtain the best results, lung images had to be de-noised (noises free) prior the use of DDHGC based on ESMF presented itself as an important tool with such a purpose.

This method is so efficient because it filters out the noisy pixels only, and does not degenerate any of the non-noisy ones; hence preserving all the crucial details in an image. In salt-and-pepper noise, only noisy pixels have extreme intensity values (either 0 or 255). Define N as the noisy pixel set.

$$N = \{(i,j)|(i,j) = 0 \text{ or } I(i,j) = 255\} \tag{1}$$

The filtering process starts with an initial window size, usually 3×3, centered around each noisy pixel once the noisy pixels have been identified. Because it is small enough to prevent the filter from unduly smoothing the image and losing crucial details, this window size was selected. The 3×3 window's non-noisy pixel count is determined by the filter. Pixels that do not have the extreme values of 0 or 255 are considered non-noisy. If there are sufficient non-noisy pixels in the window, the median of these pixels is found. For each noisy pixel $(i,j) \in N$, the filtering window size W starts at 3×3 and increases until a sufficient number of non-noisy pixels are found.

$$I(i,j) = \text{median}\left\{I(x,y) \middle| \begin{array}{l} (x,y) \in W \text{ and} \\ I(x,y) \neq 0 \text{ and } I(x,y) \neq 255 \end{array}\right\} \tag{2}$$

If the original window contains at least one non-noisy pixel, this noisy image pixel is replaced with the non-noise pixel's median value. This replacement aids in noise reduction while maintaining the image's local structure. If the original window contains no non-noisy pixels, the window size is progressively raised (e.g., to 5×5 or 7×7) until the maximum size of the window is attained or there are sufficient non-noisy pixels. For example, a pre-established maximum window size of 39×39 is set to prevent the filter from expanding infinitely. The maximum window's median value is used to replace the noisy pixel if no non-noisy pixels can be located within its boundaries.

3.2 Dualistic Sub-Image Histogram Equalization (DSIHE)

A sophisticated method of enhancing digital images, Dualistic Sub-Image Histogram Equalization (DSIHE) is especially helpful for improving lung images and other medical imaging applications where contrast is a concern. This technique effectively increases local contrast by dividing the histogram of the image into two sub-histograms according to the median intensity value and then independently equalizing these sub-histograms.

The process begins with calculating the histogram of the input image. The distribution of pixel intensity values throughout the image is displayed graphically by the histogram. The total quantity of pixels for each intensity value—which, in the case of an 8-bit grayscale image, ranges from 0 to 255—is counted in this step.

$$\text{hist}(i) = \sum_{x,y} \delta(I(x,y) - i) \tag{3}$$

where δ denotes the Dirac delta function, i represents intensity levels, and $I(x,y)$ indicates the intensity of the pixel at (x,y).

The histogram's cumulative distribution function (or CDF) is then calculated. The CDF provides a mapping from the original pixel intensities to a scale of cumulative probabilities. It is the cumulative sum of the values in the histogram.

$$\text{CDF}(i) = \sum_{j=0}^{i} \text{hist}(j) \tag{4}$$

The CDF is used to determine the median intensity value. In the histogram that value will be used to split into two smaller histograms. The median intensity level is the one which lies in between a histogram of image where half pixel values of image are below that value and remaining others lie above.

$$Median = \min\left\{ i \middle| CDF(i) \geq \frac{total\ pixels}{2} \right\} \tag{5}$$

The bottom part of the histogram contains pixel intensities that range from minimum to median value, and the top part of the histogram contains intensity values ranging across from median until maximum. Next, the sub-histograms are equalized separately. The process of histogram equalization involves redistributing intensities from each sub-histogram through the whole range to attain a uniform distribution. This makes the contrast within each intensity range enhanced.

For the lower sub-histogram (0 to Median):

$$I'_{\text{lower}}(x, y) = \frac{I_{\text{lower}}(x, y) - \min(I_{\text{lower}})}{Median - \min(I_{\text{lower}})} \cdot Median \tag{6}$$

For the upper sub-histogram (median to 255):

$$I'_{\text{upper}}(x, y) = \frac{I_{\text{upper}}(x, y) - Median}{\max(I_{\text{upper}}) - Median} \cdot (255 - Median) + Median \tag{7}$$

The two equalized sub-images are then combined to generate the resulting enhanced image. It makes sure that both the lower and upper intensity regions could get improved, ensuring a more balanced contrast enhancement of an image as a whole.

$$I_{\text{DSIHE}}(x, y) = \begin{cases} I'_{\text{lower}}(x, y) & \text{if } I(x, y) \leq Median \\ I'_{\text{upper}}(x, y) & \text{if } I(x, y) > Median \end{cases} \tag{8}$$

Having equalized sub-histograms independently, DSIHE is more efficient at improving contrast for different intensities regions than conventional histogram equalization. This method prevents over-enhancement and data loss of important clinical details, particularly for medical images in which the sharpness and visibility of structures are essential. This also solves the problem of traditional histogram equalization which over-brightens or darkens parts in an image resulting in a much more natural appearance.

3.3 Dynamic Gamma Correction with Weighting Distribution

Once image contrast was enhanced using DSIHE, the next step is to apply Dynamic Gamma Correction. This step will make the image enhancement better by dynamically adjusting the gamma value based on the image's local statistics.

3.3.1 Weighting Distribution Calculation

In general, the term 'weighting distribution' refers to a set of weights obtained from the pixel intensity distribution of an image in image processing. These weights favors some

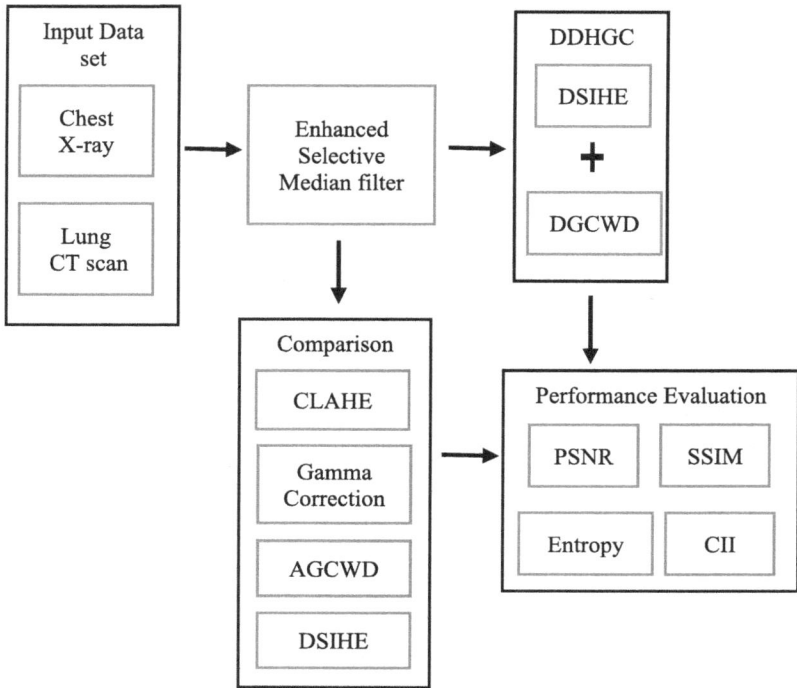

Fig. 1. Proposed Model Overview

pixel values more over based on their frequency or importance within the image. This method is particularly applicable in adaptive contrast enhancement techniques where uniform processing of all pixel values may not lead to give best results.

The cumulative distribution function (CDF) of the processed image by DSIHE is used to calculate a weighting distributions. This distribution helps decide how gamma correction should be applied at various intensities

$$CDF(i) = \sum_{j=0}^{i} hist_{DSIHE}(j) \tag{9}$$

The computation of the weighting distribution W based on the CDF is then executed. Naturally each intensity value has a weight equal to its cumulative probability, enabling the algorithm to give importance for more probable intensities

$$W(I) = \frac{CDF(i)}{\max(CDF)} \tag{10}$$

3.3.2 Dynamic Gamma Calculation

In the DSIHE-processed image, the mean of the pixel intensities (μ) and standard deviation (σ) are computed. These statistics are at most necessary for determining the dynamic gamma value.

$$\mu = \frac{1}{N} \sum_{x,y} I_{DSIHE}(x, y) \tag{11}$$

$$\sigma = \sqrt{\frac{1}{N} \sum_{x,y} (I_{DSIHE}(x, y) - \mu)^2} \tag{12}$$

The basic idea is to estimate gamma from the local statistics of image (mean and standard deviation) and adjusted according to the weighting distribution. This ensures that the enhancement is an adaptive process and sensitive to any local content in the image.

$$\gamma = log_{10}(\mu + \sigma) \cdot \alpha \tag{13}$$

where μ is the mean, σ is the standard deviation, and α is a scaling factor.

Next, the values of intensity pixels in this image are modified using the computed gamma value. This process enhances the contrast dynamically, ensuring that areas with different intensity ranges are enhanced appropriately.

$$I_{gamma}(x, y) = (I_{DSIHE}(x, y)/255.0)^{\gamma} \cdot 255 \tag{14}$$

Finally, the pixel intensities are clipped to the valid range [0, 255]- this ensures that pixel values do not overflow or underflow.

$$I_{gamma}(x, y) = min\big(max\big(I_{gamma}(x, y), 0\big), 255\big) \tag{15}$$

This guarantees that those changes are being done with respect to context, allowing for areas with different intensity distribution within an image to be enhanced accordingly.Weighting distribution helps in preventing over-enhancement or under-enhancement of certain regions, thereby improving the global visual quality of the image. Below is the suggested method's algorithm:

Algorithm: DDHGC method

Step 1: Acquire the lung image: Load the grayscale lung image from the dataset or imaging device.

Step 2: Apply Enhanced Selective Median Filter (ESMF) for Noise Suppression

Step 3: Dualistic Sub-Image Histogram Equalization (DSIHE)

- *Calculate the histogram of the noise-suppressed image as in Eq. (3).*
- *Divide the histogram at the median intensity value into two sub-histograms.*
- *Implement histogram equalization separately to every sub-histogram, resulting in two equalized sub-images as in Eq. (6) and (7).*
- *Merge the two equalized sub-images to form the enhanced image using Eq. (8).*

Step 4: Dynamic Gamma Correction with Weighting Distribution

- *Calculate Weighting Distribution*
- *Compute the CDF of the DSIHE-processed image.*
- *Calculate the weighting distribution based on the CDF as in Eq. (10).*
- *Compute the mean and standard deviation of pixel intensities in the DSIHE-processed image as in Eq. (11) and Eq. (12).*
- *Calculate the gamma value adaptively using a logarithmic function of the mean and standard deviation as I Eq. (13).*
- *Use the dynamic gamma value to apply gamma correction to the image using Eq. (14)*

Step 5: Output the enhanced lung image, ready for medical diagnosis and analysis.

4   Results and Discussions

Using an Intel(R) Core i7-4790 CPU, which provides an effective computing environment, Python experiments were used to evaluate the claimed Dynamic Dual-Histogram Gamma Correction (DDHGC) method's performance. The suggested approach has proven to perform better at enhancing contrast in lung CT images from the COV19-CT-DB and LIDC-IDRI datasets, as well as chest X-ray images obtained using the NIH Chest X-ray Dataset and CheXpert dataset. The potency of DDHGC was evaluated in comparison with that of CLAHE, Gamma Correction, Adaptive Gamma Correction with Weighting Distribution (AGCWD), and DSIHE, the four widely used contrast enhancement techniques. Once ESMF is applied to the input images to suppress noise, advance contrast enhancement techniques are implemented. Figure 2 displays the input images with their corresponding enhanced images for the CT scan and X-ray image samples.

The primary metrics listed below have a significant impact on clinical outcomes by providing objective measurements of image quality and diagnostic utility.

- PSNR (Peak Signal-to-Noise Ratio): Better image quality is indicated by higher levels of PSNR ensuring that images are clearer and more interpretable by radiologists.
- SSIM (Structural Similarity Index): Calculates how similar the enhanced and original images are to each other. Greater structural similarity is indicated by higher values, which range from 0 to 1.In clinical settings, maintaining anatomical structures is essential for accurate diagnosis, particularly in detecting lung diseases.
- Entropy: Quantifies how much detail or information is present in the image being analyzed. Images with higher entropy are said to be more detailed.This can improve clinical interpretations by exposing hidden features or patterns that are essential for diagnosing complicated conditions.
- CII (Contrast Improvement Index): Quantifies the improvement in contrast. Enhanced contrast can result in better identification of pathologies, improving clinical decision-making.

The results, summarized in Tables 1 and 2, reveal that DDHGC outperforms the other techniques across all metrics.

In Table 1 for chest X-ray images, the DDHGC method regularly generated the highest PSNR values of 30.10 and 30.70 for the NIH and CheXpert datasets respectively. This indicates that DDHGC produces the highest quality images with the least

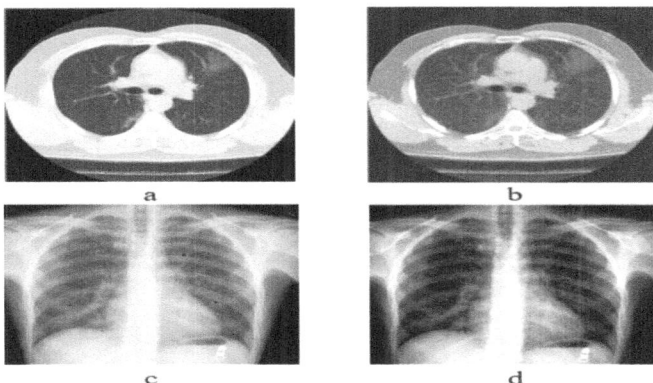

Fig. 2. Results of proposed method, (a) original CT scan image, (b) enhanced CT scan image, (c) original X-ray image, (d) enhanced X-ray image

Table 1. Performance comparison of Proposed contrast enhancement technique in Chest X-ray images

Chest X ray					
Method	Dataset	PSNR	SSIM	Entropy	CII
CLAHE	NIH	28.40	0.76	7.00	1.44
	CheXpert	29.00	0.77	7.10	1.46
Gamma Correction	NIH	27.10	0.74	6.90	1.34
	CheXpert	27.90	0.75	7.00	1.40
AGCWD	NIH	28.90	0.78	7.20	1.49
	CheXpert	29.40	0.79	7.30	1.51
DSIHE	NIH	28.60	0.77	7.10	1.47
	CheXpert	29.20	0.78	7.20	1.50
DDHGC	NIH	30.10	0.81	7.50	1.60
	CheXpert	30.70	0.82	7.60	1.62

amount of distortion and noise. The SSIM values for DDHGC were also the highest, at 0.81 and 0.82, demonstrating superior preservation of structural details in the enhanced images. Entropy, which measures the amount of information and detail within an image, was highest for DDHGC (7.50 and 7.60 for NIH and CheXpert, respectively), suggesting that this method enhances the images to reveal more details. Lastly, the Contrast Improvement Index (CII) scores of 1.60 and 1.62 for NIH and CheXpert, respectively, indicate that DDHGC significantly enhances the contrast, making critical anatomical structures more visible. When compared to other methods like CLAHE and AGCWD, DDHGC demonstrated superior performance in all metrics, highlighting its effectiveness in providing clearer, more detailed, and higher quality chest X-ray images.

Table 2. Performance comparison of Proposed contrast enhancement technique in Lung CT scan images

CT Scan					
Method	Dataset	PSNR	SSIM	Entropy	CII
CLAHE	COV19-CT-DB	30.10	0.80	7.40	1.54
	LIDC-IDRI	31.00	0.81	7.60	1.60
Gamma Correction	COV19-CT-DB	29.00	0.77	7.20	1.47
	LIDC-IDRI	29.70	0.78	7.40	1.52
AGCWD	COV19-CT-DB	30.50	0.81	7.50	1.57
	LIDC-IDRI	31.30	0.82	7.70	1.61
DSIHE	COV19-CT-DB	30.30	0.80	7.40	1.55
	LIDC-IDRI	31.10	0.81	7.60	1.60
DDHGC	COV19-CT-DB	32.00	0.84	7.80	1.70
	LIDC-IDRI	32.40	0.85	8.00	1.71

In Table 2, for lung CT images, DDHGC again outperformed other methods. The PSNR values for DDHGC were 32.00 and 32.40 for the COV19-CT-DB and LIDC-IDRI datasets, respectively, indicating exceptional image quality. The SSIM scores of 0.84 and 0.85 further confirm that DDHGC maintains the structural integrity of the images better than other methods. In terms of Entropy, DDHGC achieved values of 7.80 and 8.00, the highest among all compared methods, indicating that it brings out more detail from the original images. The CII values of 1.70 and 1.71 for COV19-CT-DB and LIDC-IDRI, respectively, suggest a substantial improvement in contrast, crucial for highlighting lung structures and pathologies. Other methods such as CLAHE and AGCWD performed well but did not match the overall performance of DDHGC. The consistent superiority of DDHGC across PSNR, SSIM, Entropy, and CII metrics in both chest X-ray and lung CT images underscores its potential as a highly effective contrast enhancement technique, offering significant improvements in image clarity, detail, and diagnostic value.

The DDHGC approach shows greater performance compared to methods such as CLAHE, Gamma Correction, AGCWD, and DSIHE, particularly in medical image enhancement for lung disorders. DDHGC excels by providing balanced contrast enhancement without compromising structural integrity as shown in bar graphs from Figs. 3, 4, 5 and 6, outperforming these methods in metrics such as PSNR, SSIM, Entropy, and CII. Compared to CLAHE, which is widely used for contrast enhancement, DDHGC offers more accurate contrast control with less chance of over-enhancement. In contrast to AGCWD, DDHGC's adaptive gamma correction ensures improved contrast enhancement through varying intensity regions, making it suitable for medical images where details in both low and high-intensity areas are essential. Unlike traditional Gamma Correction and DSIHE, DDHGC's integration of noise suppression with an Enhanced Selective Median Filter guarantees that noise is minimized without degrading the fine

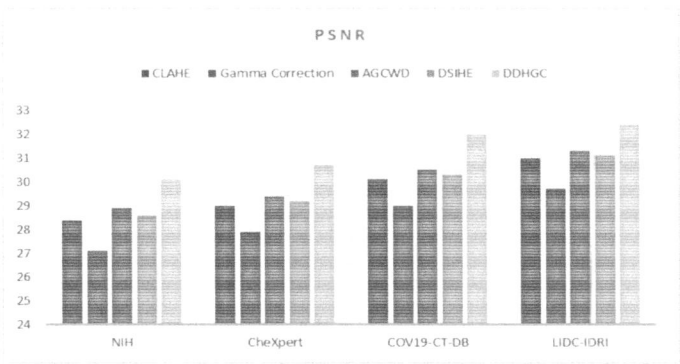

Fig. 3. PSNR outcomes of various techniques for enhancing contrast in different datasets

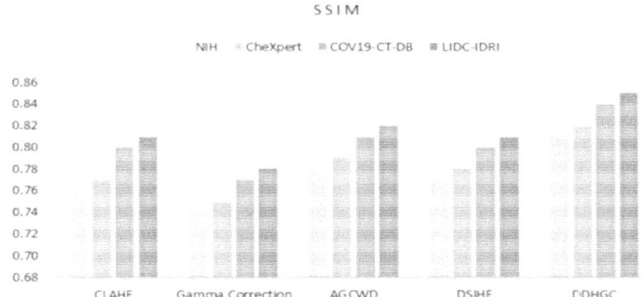

Fig. 4. SSIM outcomes of various techniques for enhancing contrast in different datasets

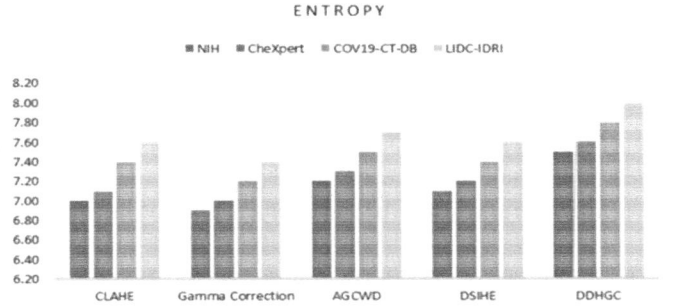

Fig. 5. Entropy outcomes of various techniques for enhancing contrast in different datasets

details of images. This makes it particularly valuable for lung imaging, where preserving subtle anatomical features is essential for accurate diagnosis. By outperforming

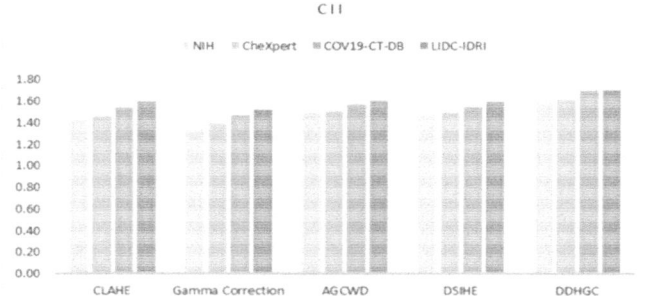

Fig. 6. CII outcomes of various techniques for enhancing contrast in different datasets

these well-established techniques across various datasets, DDHGC positions itself as a state-of-the-art technique which combines the benefits of histogram-based and gamma correction methods, making it highly effective for medical imaging applications where both contrast enhancement and noise suppression are vital.

5   Conclusion and Future Work

The quality of lung images must be improved to allow pin-point diagnosis and treatment planning in medical applications. The proposed methodology is known as Dynamic Dual-Histogram Gamma Correction (DDHGC), which unifies the methods of Dynamic Gamma Correction via Weighting distribution, DSIHE, and robust noise reduction with Enhanced Selective Median Filter. This combination ensures excellent contrast enhancement coupled with effective noise reduction, making it a great choice for medical imaging applications. We analyzed two types of medical imaging datasets in this study: chest X-ray images from the NIH Chest X-ray and CheXpert and then lung CT images extracted from COV19-CT-DB dataset as well as LIDC-IDRI. The results are sufficiently instructive in showing that DDHGC is remarkably superior compared to the traditional methods including CLAHE, Gamma Correction and AGCWD and DSIHE based on metrics like PSNR, SSIM, Entropy, and CII. DDHGC performed the best in terms of having highest PSNR which means better quality images, the best SSIM scores, indicating better preservation of structural information, the highest Entropy values, showing more detailed and informative images, and the highest CII, indicating improved contrast enhancement. Future research can focus on several domains to improve the usability and performance of the DDHGC method. One way is expanding the method to handle a wider range of medical imaging modalities, including MRI, PET, or ultrasound, to test its effectiveness beyond lung imaging. Another avenue may involve wide use of hardware acceleration geared to real-time processing, for example via GPUs or FPGAs to render the method practical for clinical application. This allows the extent of clinical validation to be performed in real-world application with medical professionals and actual patients and how well it can translate into a diagnostic environment. Moreover, with the evaluation feedbacks of radiologists regarding visual quality and diagnostic value on the enhanced images, more fine tuning could be performed so as to better meet clinical requirements of providing affective diagnosis.

References

1. Patel, S., Bharath, K., Subramanian, B., Muthu, R.: Comparative study on histogram equalization techniques for medical image enhancement, pp. 657–669 (2020). https://doi.org/10.1007/978-981-15-0035-0_54

2. Siddiqi, A., Nrejo, G., Hashmi, A., Tariq, M., Kashif, M.: Investigation of histogram equalization filter for CT scan image enhancement. Biomed. Eng. Appl. Basis Commun. **31** (2019). https://doi.org/10.4015/S1016237219500388

3. Rao, G., Srikrishna, A.: Image pixel contrast enhancement using enhanced multi histogram equalization method. Ingénierie des systèmes d information **26**, 95–101 (2021). https://doi.org/10.18280/isi.260110.-

4. Anand, S., Roshan, R.K., Deiveega, M.: Chest X ray image enhancement using deep contrast diffusion learning. Optik **279**, 170751 (2023). https://doi.org/10.1016/j.ijleo.2023.170751

5. Georgieva, V., Gardeva, V.: Adaptive algorithm for CT images enhancement to improve the diagnosis of lung diseases. AIP Conf. Proc. **020003** (2023). https://doi.org/10.1063/5.0178718

6. Singh, A., Bhateja, V., Rathore, A., Shukla, A.: Contrast enhancement of CT-scan images of lungs using morphological filters (2022). https://doi.org/10.1007/978-981-16-8554-5_24

7. Wang, H., Yang, P., Xu, C., Min, L., Wang, S., Xu, B.: Lung CT image enhancement based on total variational frame and wavelet transform. Int. J. Imaging Syst. Technol. **32** (2022). https://doi.org/10.1002/ima.22725

8. Ye, B., Jin, S., Li, B., Yan, S., Zhang, D.: Dual histogram equalization algorithm based on adaptive image correction. Appl. Sci. **13**, 10649 (2023). https://doi.org/10.3390/app131910649

9. Ezhilraja, K., Shanmugavadivu, P.: Contrast enhancement of lung CT scan images using multi-level modified dualistic sub-image histogram equalization, pp. 1009–1014 (2022). https://doi.org/10.1109/ICACRS55517.2022.10029217

10. Yu, W., Yao, H., Li, D., Li, G., Shi, H.: GLAGC: adaptive dual-gamma function for image illumination perception and correction in the wavelet domain. Sensors **21**, 845 (2021). https://doi.org/10.3390/s21030845

11. Jeyalaksshmi, S., Preethika, S.K., Hannah, J.G., Sathya, S., Radhakrishnan, S., Priscila, S.S.: Prediction of cancer blood disorder using adaptive otsu threshold and deep convolutional neural networks. In: Paramasivan, P., Rajest, S., Chinnusamy, K., Regin, R., John Joseph, F. (eds.), Advancements in Clinical Medicine, pp. 303–316. IGI Global (2024). https://doi.org/10.4018/979-8-3693-5946-4.ch022

12. Mercy, J.S., Priscila, S.S.:. Efficient palm image preprocessing for person identification and security system using machine learning approaches. In: Rajagopal, S., Popat, K., Meva, D., Bajeja, S. (eds.) Advancements in Smart Computing and Information Security. ASCIS 2023. Communications in Computer and Information Science, vol 2038. Springer, Cham (2024). https://doi.org/10.1007/978-3-031-59097-9_24

Elite Opposition Learning Based Transfer Residual Neural Network (EOL-TRNN) Classifier for Lung Diseases from Chest X-Ray (CXR)

A. Balaji$^{(\boxtimes)}$ and S. Brintha Rajakumari

Department of Computer Science, Bharath Institute of Higher Education and Research, Chennai, India
balajiathisayaraj1405@gmail.com

Abstract. Globally lung illness is widespread due to changes in the environment, weather, daily life, and other factors. Thus the impact of this disease on physical condition is increasing quickly. It motivates to the development of Machine Learning (ML) and Deep Learning (DL). It can give medical professionals and other researchers guidance on how to use DL to detect lung disease. In this paper, a novel Elite Opposition Learning Based Transfer Residual Neural Network (EOL-TRNN) is introduced for the identification of pneumonia from a Chest X-Ray (CXR). First off, it's expected that ResNet-34 is used for feature extraction layer in lung disorders. Subsequently, the dataset is trained and tested using deeper network layers and improved feature extraction layers. ResNet-34 performs well in image classification, ImageNet features have been extracted from images. TRNN weights can be iteratively changed in accordance with training CXR images with a lower bias rate. EOL is a one-step optimization approach. National Institutes of Health (NIH) CXR dataset is collected from Kaggle and subjected to the EOL-TRNN model. With CXR images, the EOL-TRNN classifier may predict lung disease with a higher degree of accuracy than current techniques. Measures like precision, recall, F_β-score, and accuracy are used to evaluate the performance of the approaches.

Keywords: Lung Disease · Chest X-Ray (CXR) Images · Deep Learning (DL) · Elite Opposition Learning Based Transfer Residual Neural Network (EOL-TRNN) · Elite Opposition Learning (EOL), · and Classification

1 Introduction

Lung problems have become more common cause of death in recent years, with numerous contributing causes. Among the mild to moderate adverse effects that people infected with the novel Covid-19 and pneumonia experience include fever, hacking, and shortness of breath [1]. But severe pneumonic illnesses in the lungs have claimed the lives of other persons [2–4]. Pneumonia is able to be brought on by a diversity of conditions with as bacterial infections, viral infections (e.g., Covid-19), colds, and the frequent cold [5].

S. Rajagopal et al. (Eds.): ASCIS 2024, CCIS 2424, pp. 186–198, 2025.
https://doi.org/10.1007/978-3-031-86290-8_14

Conversely, bacterial pneumonia is more serious and, particularly in children, can present with slow or even abrupt onset of symptoms. Fungal pneumonia is an additional type of pneumonia that can strike those with weakened immune systems. This kind of pneumonia is potentially serious and takes time for the patient to recover. Thus, study and the development of novel techniques supporting computer-aided diagnosis are desperately needed to lower pneumonia-related mortality, particularly child mortality, in the poor countries. A critical part of medical diagnosis and disease management is the examination of chest radiography. For this, DL and ML can be quite important. Digital technology has grown in importance on a global scale recently.

The use of Artificial Intelligence (AI) to identify diseases on chest radiographs has gained popularity in medical research recently and has proven to be beneficial. DL approaches are currently being used to solve various issues in research, engineering, and health care. DL is the key accomplishment in AI [6, 7]. DL approach, feature extraction is performed automatically to lessen the impact of human operations [7].

Among them, Convolutional Neural Network (CNN) robust features have led to its widespread use in the medical field [8]. Along with the use of radiological imaging, CNN approaches are able to aid in the precise recognition and classification into COVID-19 and Non-COVID-19 [9, 10]. Aside from a number of successes, CNN performs exceptionally well with big datasets. But if sufficient caution is not exercised, they frequently collapse on tiny datasets.

In this paper, Elite Opposition Learning Based Transfer Residual Neural Network (EOL-TRNN) classifier is proposed for the identification of pneumonia in the CXR dataset. EOL-TRNN has 35 layers at a depth. Novel approach of Transfer Learning (TL) is used a pre-trained architecture to attain the related level of demonstrates yet on a restricted dataset, and differentiate of pneumonia and normal CXR. Pre-trained weights and the TL technique are used to categorize patients using a different dataset of CXR images. Pre-trained models showed excellent performance and yielded valuable insights into the TL technique for the classification system of CXR images. ResNet-34 performs well in image classification, ImageNet be able to extract high-quality features from images. Lastly, contrast the test findings with those of other DL models.

2 Literature Survey

RetinaNet and Mask-RCNN, an ensemble of two CNNs was suggested by Sirazitdinov et al. [11] for the recognition and localization of pneumonia. Created a dependable automated pneumonia detection system and tested it using the biggest clinical publicity available database. Jaiswal et al. [12] suggested a Mask-RCNN that combines the global features and local features for pixel-wise segmentation. It attains robustness by combining bounding boxes from many models in a novel post-processing step and making significant changes to the training procedure. This model performs better when tested on a dataset of chest radiographs that show possible causes of pneumonia.

Three deep neural networks, each of which learnt by competing and cooperating with the others, by Tang et al. [13]. It models the underlying content structure of the typical CXR. Since the content was not observed during the training phase, the model would perform badly in its reconstruction if the content was anomalous. Otherwise, the learnt architecture can effectively model and rebuild the content. It makes it possible to differentiate between abnormal and normal CXR. It is solved by Souza et al. [14] automatic lung segmentation technique in CXR, which reconstructs the lung sections that are "lost" as a result of pulmonary anomalies. The four key steps of the suggested method are (1) image acquisition, (2) initial segmentation, (3) reconstruction, and (4) final segmentation. It includes two deep CNN models.

Two distinct DL approaches was proposed by Bhandary et al. [15] to evaluate the problem under consideration: (i) First DL technique to classify CXR images into the normal and pneumonia classes was called a modified AlexNet (MAN). Support Vector Machines (SVM) is used in MAN, and their performance is evaluated against Softmax. Additionally, various pre-trained DL approaches are used to validate its performance. (ii) To enhance classification accuracy as assessing lung cancer, the subsequent DL classifier combines learnt and handcrafted features in the MAN. Principal Component Analysis (PCA) selection and serial fusion is introduced for generation of feature vector from CXR images.

Behzadi-Khormouji et al. [16] proposed a Chestnet based design maintains the pathological features in the images. It contains direct layers than the recognized Deep CNN for detecting consolidation in CXR images. To demonstrate the generalizability of the suggested model, an additional validation is carried out using an entirely different dataset from the dataset under consideration. Chouhan et al. [17] presented a unique deep learning architecture with ImageNet or the diagnosis of pneumonia. ImageNet is introduced to feature extraction and it is fed into a classifier. Feature extraction, ensemble classification, data augmentation, and transfer learning with Neural Network (NN) (AlexNet, DenseNet121, InceptionV3, resNet18, and GoogLeNet).

Liang and Zheng [18] created a deep residual network framework which merges residual and dilated convolution to detect and identify childhood pneumonia. Particularly, the over-fitting and deterioration of the depth model are addressed by the suggested approach of residual structure, and the problem of feature space data loss that results from starting the model depth increment is addressed by the introduction of dilated convolution. Through TL, parameters are initially trained on datasets in the similar field. When it comes to the classification of pediatric pneumonia, it is very reliable.

Farhan and Yang [19] proposed Hybrid Deep Learning Algorithm (HDLA) framework for the automatic categorization of lung diseases from CXR images. Pre-processing is introduced to the grouping of optimal filtering and enhances the quality of raw CXR images with reduced data loss. CNN is introduced for automatic extraction of lung features by the pre-trained model. Feature extraction is performed by 2D-CNN model. Based on 1D feature estimation, the proposed model guarantees reliable feature learning from the pre-processed input image. Min-max scaling is introduced to maximize the recovered 1D feature as they have experienced considerable scale variations.

3   Proposed Methodology

In this paper, an Elite Opposition Learning Based Transfer Residual Neural Network (EOL-TRNN) is introduced for the identification of pneumonia from a CXR. EOL-TRNN classifier feature maps can be extracted on ImageNet. ResNet-34 is used for the feature extraction layer in lung disorders. Subsequently, the dataset is trained and tested using deeper network layers and improved feature extraction layers. Finally, EOL-TRNN weights can be iteratively changed in accordance with training CXR images with a lower error rate. The National Institutes of Health (NIH) CXR dataset was collected from the Kaggle and it has been used for simulation. Figure 1 illustrates the flow diagram of proposed methodology,

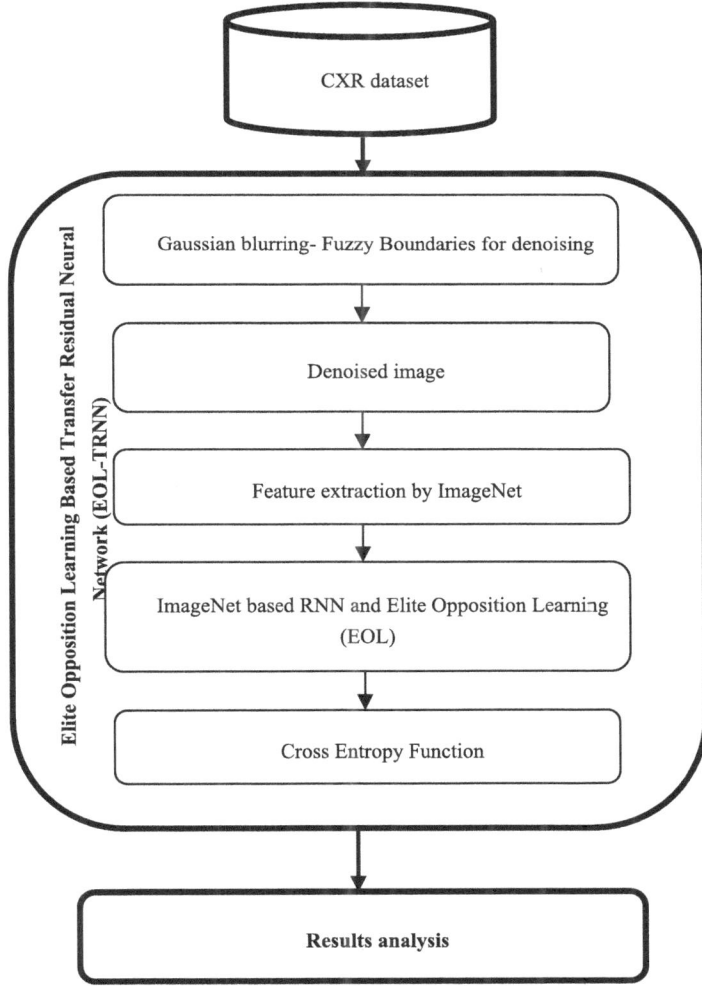

Fig. 1. Flow process of proposed work

3.1 Gaussian Blurring

Gaussian Blurring is introduced for removing noises from lung disease detection mask. Then it is subtracted from an original mask and normalizes it. Finally, cross entropy loss is computed for each connected position, this mask is multiplied. Equation (1), the fuzzy border weights (we_{fb}) have been determined,

$$we_{fb} = 1 - abs(t - g(t, k))$$ (1)

where t is the target mask, absolute function(abs()), kernel size(k), and Gaussian blurring function(g()).

3.2 Feature Extraction by ImageNet

In order to obtain excellent performance, CNN training requires a large number of annotated CXR images. However, generally speaking, it is challenging to get such a big number of CXR, and picture labeling is expensive. Consequently, transfer learning has been shown to be a very successful technique is frequently used in a comparatively limited number of CXR images to train the neural network. Prior to training on their own CXR images is able to be acquired by pre-training on extensive well-established ImageNet. It has been pre-trained using the transfer learning.

3.3 Classification by RNN

ResNet-34 network is primarily of residual building blocks, which make up the entire network. The residual building block employed a shortcut-connection [9] to bypass the convolutional layers. Figure 2, Conv, Batch Normalization (BN), a Rectified Linear Unit (ReLU), and a shortcut by residual building part in the network. The output is able to be expressed as follows Eq. (2),

$$y = F(x) + x$$ (2)

where x and y is denoted as the input and output function of residual network, and F is the residual function. A few fundamental blocks and the first convolutional layer make up the residual network as a complete. Three 3×3 Conv layers, a 3×3 max-pooling layer, an average pooling layer, and a fully connected (FC) make up ResNet-34.

3.4 Proposed EOL-TRNN Classifier

ReLU serves as the TRNN classifier activation function. It is indicated as follows Eq. (3),

$$f(x) = max(0, x)$$ (3)

where f is denoted as the ReLU function, and x is denoted as the input.

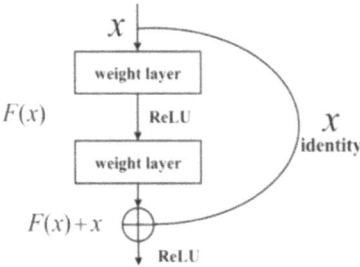

Fig. 2. Resnet-34 model

Elite Opposition Learning (EOL): Elite Opposition Learning (EOL) is an optimization technique for weight generation. Based on Opposition direction, the TRNN weights are able to be updated iteratively according towards training CXR images. EOBL make use of the elite individual in the present weights are used to create equivalent opposites of the present CXR images positioned by the dimension of optimal weight values. Therefore, the elite determination guides the particles and at last reaches a capable area, where the best label might be established. Therefore, EOL method will progress the weight variety to improve the investigation of the TRNN classifier. Weight $W_k = (w_{k1}, w_{k2}, \ldots, w_{kD})$ in the present population is denoted as $w_i = (w_{i1}, w_{i2}, \ldots, w_{iD})$; Consequently, the elite opposite location determination be $\widetilde{W}_k = (\widetilde{w}_{k1}, \widetilde{w}_{k2}, \ldots, \widetilde{w}_{kD})$ is computed by Eq. (4),

$$\widetilde{w}_{k,j} = F \times \left(dy_j + dz_j\right) - w_{k,j} \tag{4}$$

where $F \in [0, 1]$ is denoted as the generalization factor. dy_j and dz_j is denoted as the dynamic boundaries. It has been computed using Eq. (5),

$$dy_j = \min\left(w_{k,j}\right), \ dz_j = \max(w_{k,j}) \tag{5}$$

On the other hand, the resulting reverse be able to go beyond the investigate boundaries $[y_k, z_k]$. A random value is allocated to the weight in $[y_k, z_k]$ by Eq. (6),

$$\widetilde{w}_{k,j} = \text{rand}\left(y_j + z_j\right), \ \text{if} \ \widetilde{w}_{k,j} < y_j \| \widetilde{w}_{k,j} z_j \tag{6}$$

Various adaptive diagnostic rates were developed for various parameters, and a TRNN weights can be repeatedly updated based on the CXR images used for training [20]. The diagnostic rate can be more effectively adjusted by the EOL algorithm when back propagation and updated parameters are present. The EOL approach can also be applied to gradient sparsity and unstable objective function problems. As a result, the EOL algorithm learns effectively and converges more quickly.

Cross Entropy: Cross entropy is used to optimize weight and bias. It has been defined by Eq. (7):

$$H(p, q) = - \sum_{i=1}^{n} p_i(x) \log_2 q_i(x) \tag{7}$$

If x is the CXR input, p is the probability, q is the predicted probability, and H is the cross entropy. Errors have an impact on weight and deviation updates [21]. For this reason, the weights update relatively quickly when the error is sufficiently high. In a similar vein, weights and deviations update slowly when errors are modest. H(p, q), consists of 35 trainable layers, 2 FC layers, 16 identity blocks, and a convolutional layer. The five convolution groups that make up the proposed system are each made up of 1 or more basic convolution operations (Conv- > BN- > ReLU). With a kernel of 7 by 7 and a stride of 2, the initial convolution group has simply 1 convolution operation.

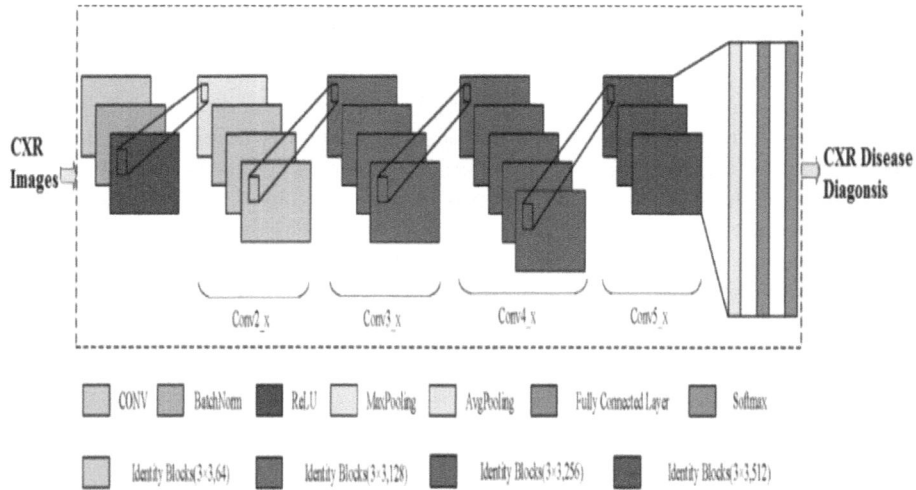

Fig. 3. Structure of EOL-TRNN framework

The ImageNet dataset was used to transfer the first 33 layers of the EOL-TRNN (Fig. 3 shows $1 + 16 \times 2 = 33$ Conv layers). To fit the CXR dataset category label, a FC layer and the softmax classifier. Simultaneously, EOL enhanced the classifier's final lung disease diagnosis accuracy.

4   Result and Analysis

This section shows the performance comparison of classification methods with respect to dataset, and visualization. The classification methods are simulated using MATLABR2020a simulator. Several evaluation metrics has been used for results analysis of classification methods.

4.1 Dataset

CXR images dataset consists of 112,120 images with 1024 × 1024 size of the chest by 30,805 patients. Among them 80.00% is used for training, and 20.00% is used for testing. Figure 4 shows CXR Dataset with four classes.

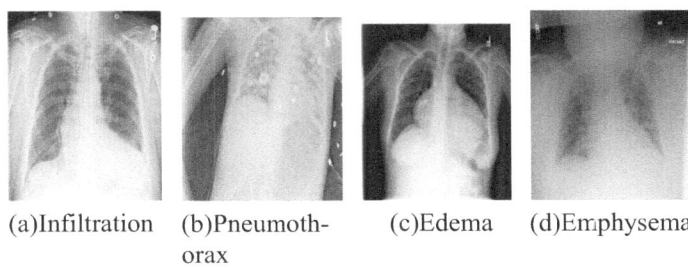

(a)Infiltration   (b)Pneumoth-   (c)Edema   (d)Emphysema
orax

Fig. 4. CXR Dataset with four classes

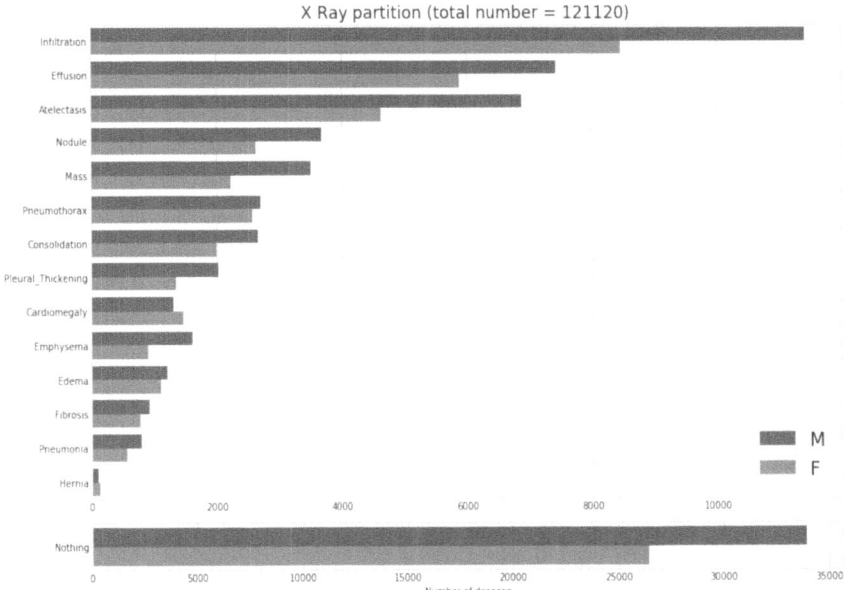

Fig. 5. No.of samples for each class

Figure 5 shows the total number of classes and total number of images each class for CXR dataset between M and F gender.

4.2 Evaluation Metrics

Evaluations metrics has been calculated by Eqs. (8–12) [22],

$$Precision(PR) = \frac{TP}{TP + FP} \tag{8}$$

$$Recall(RE) = \frac{TP}{TP + FN} \tag{9}$$

$$F_\beta - score = \left(1 + \beta^2\right)\left(\frac{PR * RE}{\beta^2.PR + RE}\right) \tag{10}$$

$$Accuracy(Acc) = \frac{TP + TN}{TP + TN + FP + FN} \tag{11}$$

In the Eqs. (8–11), where TP-True Positive, TN-True Negative, FN-False Negative, and FN-False Positive.

4.3 Results and Discussion

Performance of EOL-TRNN classifier and the existing models (Mask-RCNN, MAN, Chestnet, and HDLA) has been measured by metrics. Proposed classifier has highest results of 75.62%, 78.83%, 77.19%, and 82.11% for precision, recall, F_β-score, and accuracy (Refer Table 1).

Table 1. Metrics comparison of DL classifiers

Methods	Precision (%)	Recall (%)	F_β-score (%)	Accuracy (%)
Mask-RCNN	64.11	65.71	64.90	72.81
MAN	66.23	67.19	66.71	74.08
Chestnet	68.14	70.35	69.23	76.56
HDLA	71.38	74.27	72.80	78.33
EOL-TRNN	75.62	78.83	77.19	82.21

Figure 6 shows the graphical analysis of classifiers such as Mask-RCNN, MAN, Chestnet, HDLA, and EOL-TRNN with respect to precision. Parameters of the classifier have been optimized via EOL. Precision results attained by proposed system is 75.62%, other methods like Mask-RCNN, MAN, Chestnet, and HDLA gives the results of 64.11%, 66.23%, 68.14%, and 71.38% (See Table 1).

Mask-RCNN, MAN, Chestnet, HDLA, and EOL-TRNN by recall analysis are shown in Fig. 7. Recall achieved by proposed system is 78.83%, other methods like Mask-RCNN, MAN, Chestnet, and HDLA gives the results of 65.71%, 67.19%, 70.35%, and 74.27% (See Table 1).

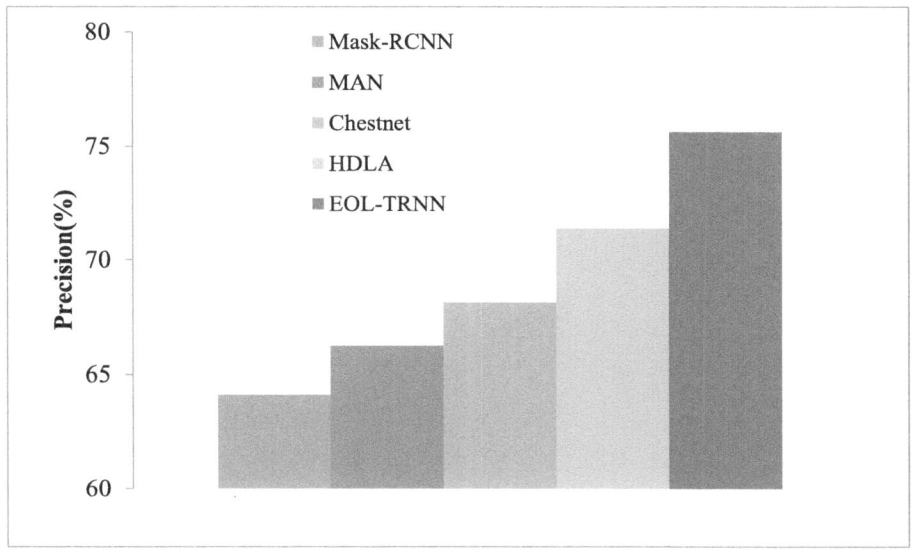

Fig. 6. Precision analysis of DL classifiers

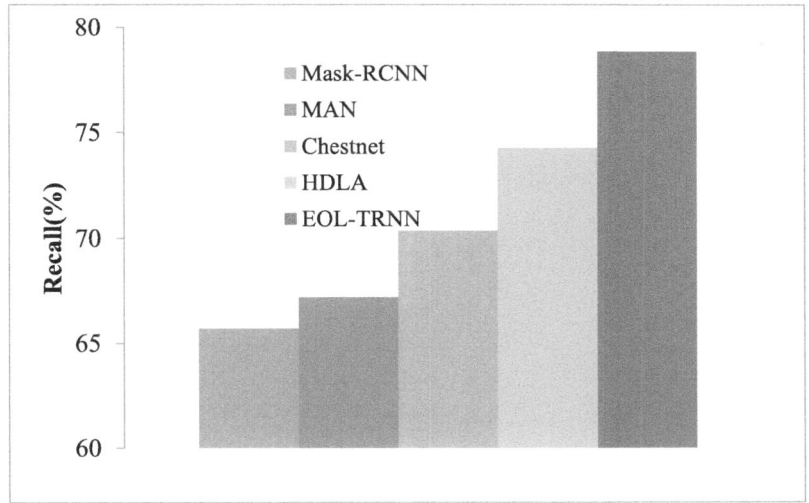

Fig. 7. Recall analysis of DL classifiers

Figure 8 shows the graphical analysis of classifiers like Mask-RCNN, MAN, Chestnet, HDLA, and EOL-TRNN with respect to F_β-score. F_β-score results attained by proposed system is 77.19%, other methods like Mask-RCNN, MAN, Chestnet, and HDLA gives the results of 64.90%, 66.71%, 69.23%, and 72.80% respectively (Refer Table 1).

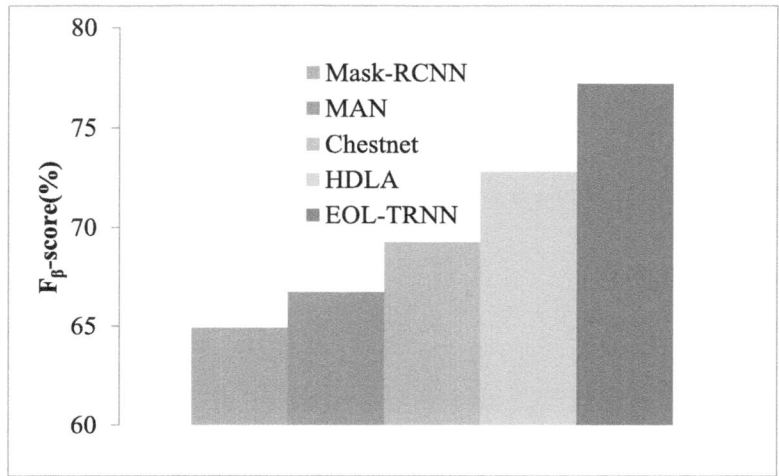

Fig. 8. F$_\beta$-score analysis of DL classifiers

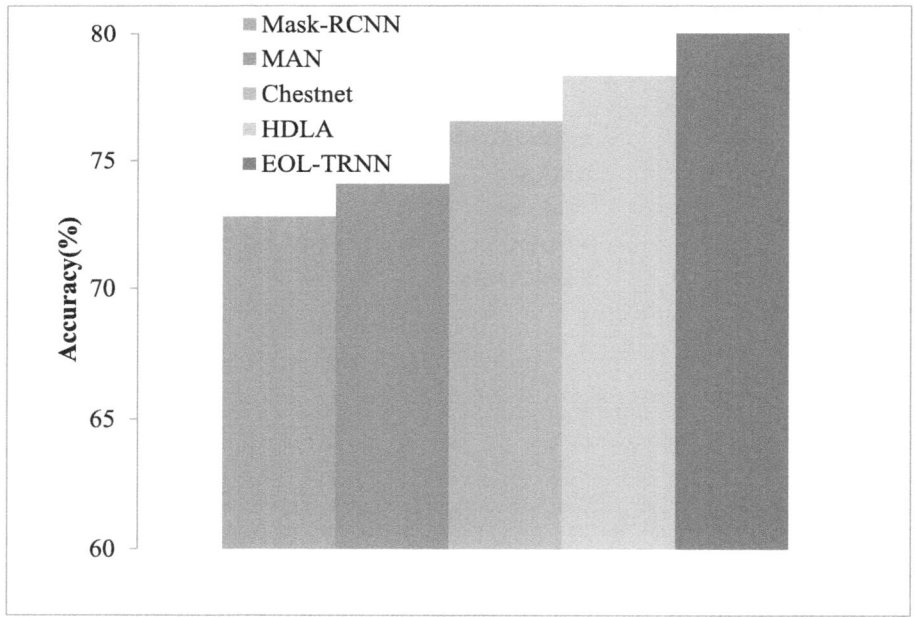

Fig. 9. Accuracy analysis of DL classifiers

Mask-RCNN, MAN, Chestnet, HDLA, and EOL-TRNN by accuracy is illustrated in Fig. 9. Accuracy result achieved by proposed system is 82.21%, other methods like Mask-RCNN, MAN, Chestnet, and HDLA gives the accuracy of 72.81%, 74.08%, 76.56%, and 78.33% (Refer Table 1).

5   Conclusion and Future Work

In this work, an Elite Opposition Learning Based Transfer Residual Neural Network (EOL-TRNN) classifier is developed for identifying lung diseases from CXR images. The NIH chest CXR image dataset is used to proposed model. The infrastructure of the ResNet-34 network is made up primarily of residual building blocks, which make up the entire network. A one-step optimization approach for weight optimization is called Elite Opposition Learning (EOL). The TRNN weights can be repeatedly changed based on the direction of opposition using training CXR images. In order to create equivalent opposites of the present CXR images are situated inside the dimension of best weight values, EOBL uses the elite individual in the existing weights. By increasing the weight variety, the EOL approach will increase the TRNN classifier's exploration. For the CXR dataset, EOL-TRNN classifier shows the highest precision, recall, F_β-score, and accuracy of 75.62%, 78.83%, 77.19% and 82.21% respectively. The handling of the large-scale dataset presents certain problems for this work. Small datasets can therefore yield good accuracy, but they won't work well in practical applications. Using VGG and further novel transfer learning algorithms in the future, a hybrid algorithm combining ResNet-152, AlexNet, and GoogLeNet architecture will be created.

References

1. Smith, D.S., Richey, E.A., Brunetto, W.L.: A symptom-based rule for diagnosis of COVID-19. SN Comprehen. Clin. Med.e **2**, 1947–1954 (2020)
2. Elibol, E.: Otolaryngological symptoms in COVID-19. Eur. Arch. Otorhinolaryngol. **278**, 1233–1236 (2021)
3. Padda, I., Khehra, N., Jaferi, U., Parmar, M.S.: The neurological complexities and prognosis of COVID-19. SN Comprehen. Clin. Med. **2**, 2025–2036 (2020)
4. Jadhav, S.P., et al.: Introduction to lung diseases. Targeting cellular Signalling pathways in lung diseases, Springer, Singapore (2021)
5. Wunderink, R.G., Waterer, G.: Advances in the causes and management of community acquired pneumonia in adults. BMJ **358**, 1–13 (2017)
6. Sarker, I.H.: AI-based modeling: techniques, applications and research issues towards automation, intelligent and smart systems. SN Comput. Sci. **3**(2), 1–20 (2022)
7. Wen, L., Li, X.Y., Gao, L.: A transfer convolutional neural network for fault diagnosis based on ResNet-50. Neural Comput. Appl. **32**, 6111–6124 (2020)
8. Sarker, I.H.: Deep learning: a comprehensive overview on techniques, taxonomy, applications and research directions. SN Comput. Sci. **2**(6), 1–20 (2021)
9. Li, L., et al.: Artificial intelligence distinguishes COVID-19 from community acquired pneumonia on chest CT. Radiology 1–16 (2020)
10. Xu, X., et al.: A deep learning system to screen novel coronavirus disease 2019 pneumonia. Engineering **6**(10), 1122–1129 (2020)
11. Sirazitdinov, I., Kholiavchenko, M., Mustafaev, T., Yixuan, Y., Kuleev, R., Ibragimov, B.: Deep neural network ensemble for pneumonia localization from a large-scale chest x-ray database. Comput. Electr. Eng. **78**, 388–399 (2019)
12. Jaiswal, A.K., Tiwari, P., Kumar, S., Gupta, D., Khanna, A., Rodrigues, J.J.P.C.: Identifying pneumonia in chest X-rays: a deep learning approach. Meas. J. Int. Meas. Confed **145**, 511–518 (2019)

13. Tang, Y.X., Tang, Y.B., Han, M., Xiao, J., Summers, R.M.: Abnormal chest X-ray iden-tification with generative adversarial one-class classifier. In: 2019 IEEE 16th international symposium on biomedical imaging (ISBI 2019); 2019. pp. 1358–1361. Venice, Italy (2019)
14. Souza, J.C., Bandeira Diniz, J.O., Ferreira, J.L., França da Silva, G.L., Corrêa Silva, A., de Paiva, A.C.: n automatic method for lung segmentation and reconstruction in chest X-ray using deep neural networks. Computer Methods Programs Biomed. **177**, 285–296(2019)
15. Bhandary, A., et al.: Deep-learning framework to detect lung abnormality–A study with chest X-Ray and lung CT scan images. Pattern Recogn. Lett. **129**, 271–278 (2020)
16. Behzadi-Khormouji, H., et al.: Deep learning, reusable and problem-based architectures for detection of consolidation on chest X-ray images. Comput. Methods Programs Biomed. **185**, 105162 (2020)
17. Chouhan, V., et al.: A novel transfer learning based approach for pneumonia detection in chest X-ray images. Appl. Sci. **10**(2), 1–17 (2020)
18. Liang, G., Zheng, L.: A transfer learning method with deep residual network for pediatric pneumonia diagnosis. Comput. Methods Programs Biomed. **187**, 1–19 (2020)
19. Farhan, A.M.Q., Yang, S.: Automatic lung disease classification from the chest X-ray images using hybrid deep learning algorithm. Multimedia Tools Appl. 1–27 (2023)
20. Jamin, A., Humeau-Heurtier, A.: (Multiscale) cross-entropy methods: a review. Entropy **22**(1), 1–15 (2019)
21. Bharati, S., Podder, P., Mondal, M.: Artificial neural network based breast cancer screening: a comprehensive review. Int. J. Comput. Inform. Syst. Indust. Manage. Appl. **12**, 125–137 (2020)
22. Raihan-Al-Masud, M., Mondal, M.R.H.: Data-driven diagnosis of spinal abnormalities using feature selection and machine learning algorithms. PLoS ONE **15**(2), 1–21 (2020)

Enhancing Railway Network Efficiency with Deep Learning-Based Traffic Prediction Models

C. Radhika[1]([⊠]) and D. Kerana Hanirex[2]

[1] Department of Computer Applications, Bharath Institute of Higher Education and Research (BIHER), Chennai, India
raaddhika66@gmail.com
[2] Department of Computer Science, Bharath Institute of Higher Education and Research (BIHER), Chennai, India
keranahanirex.cse@bharathuniv.ac.in

Abstract. Several elements influence how we manage the railway network, the most important of which are operational excellence and passenger satisfaction. Because traditional systems are unable to deal with the complexity and non-linearity of railway traffic data, most frequently use algorithmic approaches and simplistic statistical models. It cannot be used for better resource allocation; there will always be congestion and delays. To accomplish that, the paper proposes a novel approach that makes use of deep learning-based traffic prediction models such as Convolutional Neural Networks (CNN) and Long Short-Term Memory (LSTM). The proposed method uses both real-time and historical traffic data, which improves prediction accuracy and operating efficiency. The model builds on existing methods by using CNNs to learn spatial patterns and LSTMs to understand time-series relationships. Other results demonstrate a significant improvement over bigger mistakes in existing systems (MAE = 0.75 and RMSE = 1.20). Operational indicators also reveal advantages, with 15% lower costs and optimal resource utilization. The CNN-LSTM model resulted in significant performance advantages, including a 25% reduction in fuel consumption and more than 30% reduction in maintenance expenses. The results show that bottleneck detection has the potential to improve precision and productivity over previous techniques, which could revolutionize railway traffic regulation.

Keywords: Railway Network · Traffic Prediction · Operational Efficiency · Traffic Management · Real-Time Data Analysis

1 Introduction

To maintain operational excellence and increase passenger satisfaction, a very limited, busy railway network must be managed in an extremely effective manner. Current railway traffic management systems (RTMS) do not perform well in most circumstances due to their traditional linear and non-homogeneous model with barrier handling, which leads to resource misallocation, generating excessive congestion and delay performance. These traditional systems often rely on algorithmic approaches and oversimplified statistical models, which, while useful in some applications, are frequently insufficient to accurately mimic the complex dynamics of modern railroad operations.

The increased demand for dependable and efficient transportation systems necessitates more progressive railway traffic control. The study is motivated by the limitations of standard railway traffic management systems and thus provides a chance to investigate new AI technologies that could help overcome these obstacles. Neural networks are effective for these specialized positions due to the can absorb complex data, and with the implementation of deep learning as a proof-of-concept in most common sectors, if not all. As the study attempts to improve railway network management effectiveness and precision using deep learning-based traffic prediction models, the present dissertation focuses on CNN and LSTM networks.

The article proposes a novel traffic prediction model based on CNNs and LSTMs to serve as the foundation for improving railway network efficiency. To address the issue, researchers developed a new technique for improving railway traffic prediction: using multi-sourced spatiotemporal data and resolving its limits on partial levels. The proposed approach is a full model that combines CNN, which is responsible for learning spatial patterns and correlations from data, with LSTM, and RNNs, which record temporal dependencies as well as sequential features of flow. The current study provides three contributions. For the next big leap over conventional qualitative and statistical models, which forecasted railway traffic using a CNN, and LSTM technique (1). Second, it describes a thorough method for installing and training deep learning models, including feature engineering, data collecting, pre-processing, and model evaluation. Third, it addresses the relevance of current models and highlights increases in cost-effectiveness and operational efficiency from an adoption standpoint, as well as comparing proposed model output to others with a focus on prediction accuracy. The paper is set out as follows: Sect. 2 presents a review of the literature with an eye toward field application of deep learning methods and conventional methods for traffic control of trains. The proposed model is fully discussed in Sect. 3 encompassing training, assessment, integration, feature extraction and engineering, data collecting and preprocessing, and model design and setup. Emphasizing operational effectiveness, forecast accuracy, and system performance improvements, Sect. 4 compares the performance of the proposed model with those of existing systems. Section 5 concludes the work with an evaluation of the results and recommendations for further research.

In summary, operational efficiency and the accuracy of railway traffic prediction are greatly improved by the combination of CNN and LSTM models. The proposed approach outperforms the competition in forecast accuracy, resource efficiency, and cost savings by resolving the drawbacks of conventional techniques. The breakthrough presents a revolutionary technique to enhance overall operational effectiveness and modernize railway network administration.

2   Literature Survey

It provides Networking system in HSR wireless networks via a two-phase traffic volume estimating scheme. After the K-means method has been utilized to group flows of traffic in the first stage, the LSTM algorithm is utilized to estimate the amount of traffic in the subsequent phase. Based on the gathered traffic characteristics and the features of the system's wireless resource, it builds a service-tailored capacity reservation technique [6].

For the example data, a modified regression NN model is created, and the MATLAB software is used to execute the model's answer. The network estimation error curve graph is used to determine the optimal smoothness factor value. Finally, errors between the model's predictions and the actual outcomes are examined, and the predicted errors satisfy the accuracy criteria [7].

In order to improve system performance, it provides a novel wireless resource scheduling technique in the present research for high mobility scenarios. In order to extract geographic traffic characteristics, it first offers a feature extraction approach. To forecast the traffic volume, a number of time-series prediction methods are used. Next, in order to enhance the prediction performance of the SNR, it includes the CSI into the channel quality prediction process [8].

After the model accounts for the temporal and spatial qualities as well as the time-series traits that define train operation, the Transformer method and the CNN are utilized to individually extract and combine these features. Specifically, the Transformer's inter-action with the focus method resolves the train of interest's postponement caused by the interference method between trains & stations. Using 3D CNN, the temporal and spatial features of trains' data are retrieved simultaneously [9].

The current research suggests a novel pruned layered ensemble learning approach to increase the forecast accuracy for passenger train arrival delays. The algorithm employs several neural networks as sub-models and pruned MLP NN as a meta-learner. The maximum amount that extensive US public railroad service info, Amtrak, is used to evaluate the model's performance and calculate the improved model accuracy [10].

To tackle the problem, it developed a DL method that integrates FCNN, LSTM RNN, and 3D CNN designs [11].

It presents a DL urban traffic forecasting system that integrates traffic and meteorological data with information taken from tweets. The predictive model makes use of a deep Bi-directional LSTM SAE framework for multi-step traffic flow prediction, which was trained using messages, congestion, and mixed meteorological datasets [12].

3   Proposed Model

The proposed technique uses deep learning-based traffic prediction models to greatly increase the efficiency of railway networks. Conventional railway traffic management systems mostly rely on heuristic techniques and basic statistical models, which are frequently unable to predict traffic patterns with sufficient accuracy. Conventional systems cannot handle the complexity and nonlinearity of real-world train traffic data. As a result, inefficiencies often arise, affecting both operating costs and passenger happiness. Such inefficiencies include influenced resource allocation, increased congestion, and delays. However, to solve these limits, the model unanimously combines the most recent neural network topologies, which include CNNs and LSTM networks. The system can then filter and analyze massive amounts of historical and existing traffic data, revealing subtle connections that would otherwise be lost using several more traditional ways. Using a deep learning method, the model can estimate traffic more precisely and quickly, allowing train operators to make better decisions. Numerous critical processes must be implemented within the framework. The method begins with a massive dataset of historical rail traffic data. The data includes train schedules, passenger counts, environmental elements (such as weather), and infrastructure characteristics. The data is preprocessed to obtain descriptive traffic features, as well as to handle missing values and normalize attributes. Next, the preprocessed data is divided into training, validation, and test sets to ensure that the model generalizes. The flowchart of the Proposed Model is shown in Fig. 1.

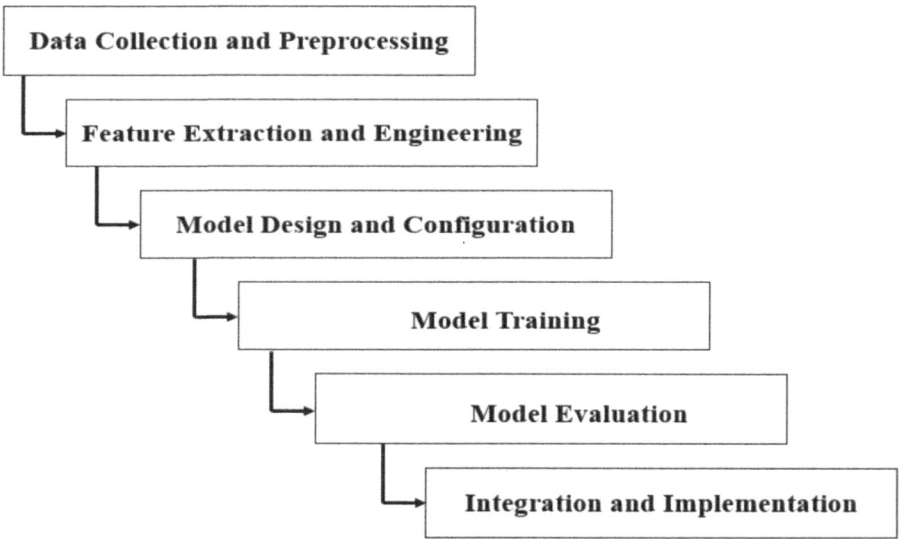

Fig. 1. Flowchart of the Proposed Model

Then, deep learning models are designed and configured. LSTM networks are used because of their capacity to record sequential patterns and temporal dependencies in time series data. It is most useful for modeling long-term interdependence in railway traffic data. Convolutional Neural Networks are also used because they can detect local correlations and spatial patterns in data. By combining both the architecture with the mean and standard deviation of future cycle duration, the model can still function with both temporal and geographical information, resulting in a higher prediction score. During training, preprocessed data is fed into deep learning models, and a substantial amount of computation is conducted on each image to iteratively alter model parameters to reduce prediction errors. To make the training process more stable and efficient, use advanced optimization algorithms (such as RMSprop and Adam).

The validation set is the entire dataset used for training; it allows us to evaluate how effectively a model was trained with different hyperparameter values while preventing overfitting. Once these have been sufficiently trained, models are run on the test set to reveal their generalization capabilities as well as overall prediction accuracy. The proposed technology, when combined with existing railway management systems, can provide several benefits to society. For instance, it provides substantially improved prediction accuracy, allowing rail managers to make more solid projections about operating conditions. It provides better scheduling, resource allocation, and congestion management, resulting in fewer delays and increased passenger satisfaction. Its ability to process data in real-time also allows it to adapt to abrupt changes (e.g., new attacks, traffic rate fluctuations) on a per-flow/device basis and employ direct pushback actions against attack vectors, making DDoS defense more tailored and powerful than traditional deployments. Another significant benefit is that operating expenditures are reduced. The entire system saves time, money, and effort that would otherwise be spent on maintaining a continuous traffic flow and appropriate resource allocation. Furthermore, improved predictive capacity contributes to higher levels of safety by allowing for the detection and hence preventive measures in hazard reduction.

3.1 Data Collection and Preprocessing

The first step is a methodical collection of historical and current railway traffic turnover. The dataset includes several variables at both the macro (train schedules, passenger counts) and micro levels (weather data, such as temperature, as well as station capacities and track layouts). More importantly, good data collecting serves as the foundation for all future research and model training efforts.

Preprocessing guarantees that the obtained data is suitable for use in a deep learning model. The initial step in preprocessing is to deal with missing data. It employs a variety of imputation procedures to fill in gaps in a data set, such as replacing missing values with the mean or median; advanced techniques include multiple imputation and K-nearest neighbors. To avoid biasing or ruining the predictive model will need to execute imputation appropriately. Then it executes feature normalization to ensure that all of these variables are on the same scale. The next step requires using methods such as z-score normalization and min-max scaling to convert the feature values into a common distribution and range. So normalization is used to help deep learning systems converge more quickly during training by removing the influence of large-scale characteristics from other, compact ranges. Categorical information, such as train types and station names, is encoded into numerical representations using various techniques. Deep learning operates on numerical data, making a tiny tweak to it. Encoding helps the model accurately grasp categorical data. Preprocessing Pre-processing is the first stage in which data is cleaned and organized to make it acceptable for the development of more advanced models. The preprocessed data must be such that the algorithms may use meaningful, dependable, and high-quality data for learning, hence improving prediction model accuracy and performance.

1. Mean Imputation:

$$\hat{x}_i = \frac{1}{N} \sum_{i=1}^{N} x_i \tag{1}$$

Where x_i is the imputed vale, N is the number of observed vales, and x_i are the observed values.

2. K-Nearest Neighbors (KNN) Imputation:

$$\hat{x}_i = \frac{\sum_{j=1}^{k} w_j x_j}{\sum_{j=1}^{k} w_j} \tag{2}$$

where w_j is the weight assigned to the j-th neighbor, typically based on distance.

3.2   Feature Extraction and Engineering

Feature engineering is the process of identifying relevant features from raw or unstructured data and transforming these inputs into a well-organized scalable format, which is critical for boosting the performance of deep learning models. The first phase involves identifying and developing significant features from the railway traffic data that has been collected. The difficulty is to achieve that while simultaneously identifying underlying patterns and dependencies that influence traffic flow.

Temporal characteristics: Model time-dependent behaviors. These are time-related factors, such as the day of the week, the hour in date (time), and seasonal influences. When these features are combined, the system may identify patterns like peak traffic hours and weekly and seasonal trends. For instance, when the model recognizes specific times of day, such as rush hours or holidays, which have varying effects on traffic patterns, it can forecast more precisely. Other spatial features that are equally important include station placement, rail layouts, and proximity to vital infrastructure. These properties help the model grasp spatial dependencies and relationships within the railway network. For instance, the presence of a key station nearby may have a similar influence on traffic patterns, as may track congestion; by integrating such spatial variables, the model may begin to adequately compensate for these effects.

Feature engineering is the process of converting raw data into usable features that help a model recognize patterns better. Interaction terms between features must be developed to reflect historical interdependence. Furthermore, data must be collected at various levels of detail, and the list goes on. Feature engineering is crucial since it makes the model interpretable and aids in the development of predicting capabilities alongside what is observed, as well as providing underlying insights that can eventually help us form correlations.

1. Time-Based Features:

Day of the week and time of day can be represented using cyclic features to capture periodicity:

$$\sin(2\pi \frac{hour}{24}), \cos(2\pi \frac{hour}{24}) \tag{3}$$

Where hour is the hour of the day.

2. Interaction Features:

Interaction terms between features x_i and x_j:

$$x_{ij} = x_i \cdot x_j \tag{4}$$

3.3   Model Design and Configuration

Utilizing both temporal and spatial data to improve railway traffic prediction, the proposed technique combines CNNs and LSTM networks. Considering particular facets of the data, every kind of network has a unique function. These long-term relationships and sequential patterns in time-series data are captured very well by LSTMs, which is why these tools have been selected. Modeling the daily, weekly, and seasonal fluctuations in the traffic flow is a perfect application for LSTM models in railway traffic forecast. By solving the vanishing gradient issue that traditional Recurrent Neural Networks (RNNs) face, these store information across extended sequences. Input gates, forget gates and output gates are found in each of the layers of LSTM units that make up the LSTM network design.

Encouraging the model to learn from past traffic patterns, these gates control the information flow. To manage the gate operations and output activations, LSTM units commonly use hyperbolic tangent (tanh) and sigmoid activation functions. To extract local correlations and geographical patterns from the data, CNNs are utilized. CNNs perform well in the analysis of spatial data related to railway traffic, including station proximity and track layouts. ReLU (Rectified Linear Unit) activation functions are used to introduce non-linearity, pooling layers lower dimensionality, and convolutional layers apply different filters to the data. With the help of such spatial feature extraction, the model can identify patterns like traffic jams and spatial relationships among various railway network segments. The model may utilize both temporal and spatial information by combining CNN and LSTM architectures. Both networks are integrated into a single model; the LSTM network handles the sequential input, and the CNN extracts spatial characteristics. Because complex patterns are captured over time and location, such integration improves prediction accuracy. Additionally, to optimize the network parameters and minimize prediction errors while ensuring convergence, the model design incorporates optimization methods such as Adam and RMSprop.

Pseudo-code for the overall process:

```
function main ():
    # 1. Data Collection and Preprocessing
raw_data = collect_data()
preprocessed_data = preprocess_data(raw_data)
    # 2. Feature Extraction and Engineering
    features = extract_features(preprocessed_data)
    # 3. Model Design and Configuration
    model = design_model(input_shape(features))
    # 4. Model Training
trained_model = train_model(model, training_data(features), validation_data(features))
    # 5. Model Evaluation
evaluation_metrics = evaluate_model(trained_model, test_data(features))
    # 6. Integration and Implementation
integration_status = integrate_model(trained_model, real_time_data_sources())
    return integration_status
function collect_data():
    return raw_data
function preprocess_data(raw_data):
    return preprocessed_data
function extract_features(preprocessed_data):
return features
function design_model(input_shape):
    return model
function train_model(model, training_data, validation_data):
    return trained_model
function evaluate_model(model, test_data):
    return evaluation_metrics
function integrate_model(model, real_time_data_sources):
    return integration_status.
```

3.4   Model Training

The next crucial step is to feed the preprocessed and feature-engineered data into CNN and LSTM models. First, a training, validation, and testing set are developed. Training Set: For fitting the model. Validation Set: Parameter tweaking and avoiding overfitting Test set: Model performance at last. These datasets are fed through CNN and LSTM architectures, which use backpropagation to continuously change the weights of the model during training. Backpropagation Step 1: Calculate the difference between what the model expects to happen and what happened. The variances of the error are then utilized to change weights to lower the, which reduces prediction. The methodology is optimized utilizing methods such as Adam and RMSprop to improve its stability and effectiveness. Adam changes the learning rate for each parameter with a step size proportional to the (weighted) running average of the first and second moments, while RMSprop adjusts it using the moving average of squared gradients. Both of these solutions promote faster convergence while also giving good performance. Hyperparameter tuning is the process of changing model parameters to ensure that they operate optimally, such as the number of sections, units per layer(s), training rate, dropout rates, and so on. After iterative updates and finetuning during training, it improves understanding of all previous traffic patterns, allowing it to confidently forecast future scenarios for its customers.

3.5 Model Evaluation

Model Evaluation: Testing the reliability of trained CNN and LSTM models; it's an important stage in determining how well and reliably these models perform. It assesses the number of criteria (MAE, RMSE) and prediction delays that each is resilient to in terms of predicting accuracy during the procedure. MAE gives a simple accuracy indicator known as the average size of prediction mistakes. On the other hand, RMSE takes into account greater errors by squaring them, allowing for an overall assessment of its capacity to deal with huge variations. The statistic represents the prediction latency, which indicates how long it takes for a model to generate and return predictions.

The validation and test sets allow us to assess the efficacy of models trained on this data for generalization. It is an accurate method of evaluating the model on previously unknown data, with the validation set being utilized independently for fine-tuning and avoiding overfitting. It enables the models to generalize effectively in unexpected traffic scenarios. The improvements in prediction accuracy and operating efficiency are supported by a comparison to classic algorithmic techniques. The evaluation aims to highlight the importance of employing sophisticated algorithms for traffic prediction by contrasting deep learning methods with cutting-edge methodologies. The comparison analysis results drive future model improvement, identify growth opportunities, and confirm its performance in real-world railway traffic management scenarios. The thorough examination additionally ensures that the new strategy performs as well (or better than) what is previously available. Proposed Model Lifecycle is shown in Fig. 2.

3.6 Integration and Implementation

Finally, the deep learning models must be linked into existing railway management systems. Step one in the phase is to design interfaces that would make it easier for operators to enter real-time traffic data into models. These interfaces are intended to process real-time data from a wide range of devices, such as environmental monitors, ticketing systems, and sensors. Following that, the models are expensive in operational situations since they require end-to-end real-time traffic data processing as well as insights and forecasts in other areas. In addition, the technique features predictive analytics dashboards that provide train operators with useful data. With these dashboards, routing operators can make informed judgments based on current traffic data displayed via aggregate views such as trendlines and pathways with potential bottlenecks and projections.

The dashboards are intended to enhance the user experience by providing interactive graphs, alerts, and recommendations that will ideally lead to better decision making. The framework's architecture focuses on providing speedier insights and improving real-time data processing. By incorporating the models into daily operations, the technique improves scheduling precision, optimizes resource allocation, and keeps congestion at a

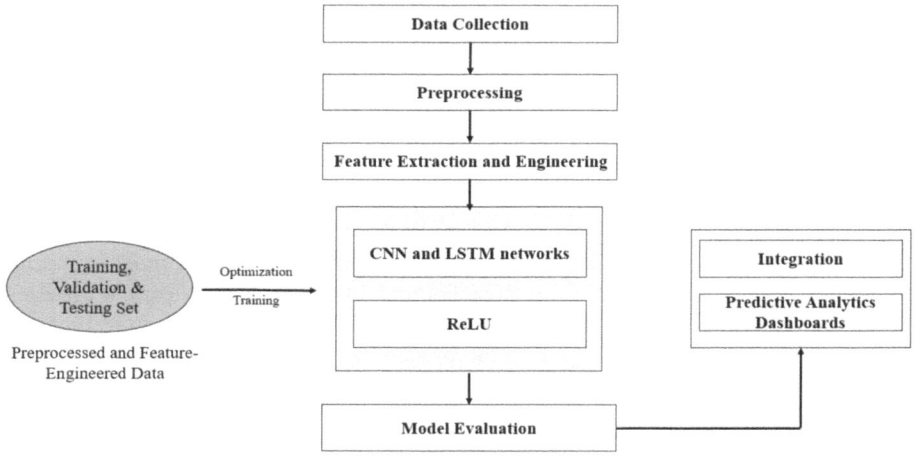

Fig. 2. Proposed Model Lifecycle

minimum. The integration provides precise and real-time projections, resulting in higher operational efficiency by enabling deep learning models to be employed for improved traffic flow, railway network management, and so on. During the installation stage, experts conduct testing and validation in an operational environment to ensure that the equipment performs as intended and integrates properly with the realized framework. The constant monitoring, paired with feedback loops, identifies changes in incoming data and real-world performance, allowing for on-the-fly updates to existing models and the generation of new ones as situations change. Implementing the update iteratively ensures that all of the rest (although), and therefore point nine, remain responsive even as train traffic increases.

4 Result and Discussion

The section presents the results of solving the railway network efficiency problem using deep learning-based traffic prediction models, specifically the CNN model and the LSTM. The next phase of the proposed article will compare this to existing statistical and algorithm model performance. Prediction accuracy, operational effectiveness, and system performance increases are some of the evaluation metrics.

Table 1 compares the anticipated accuracy between the proposed technique and other existing systems. In comparison to existing systems, MAE 0.75, RMSE1.20, and a 0.5 s delay in response time were superior. For instance, at a 2.5-s prediction delay, with MAE of Existing System [5] = 1.20 and RMSE = 1.85, while MRS of Exiting System [6] is reported as an MAE = 1:10; RMSE = 1.70 with a slight reduction in accuracy (RMSE even improved further above existing papers), but predictions are now about half a second faster to predict offset position or velocity for that epoch). The existing system has a forecast delay of 1.2 s, RMSE = 1.50, and MAE = 0.90 [7]. The proposed approach outperforms existing methods in terms of traffic pattern prediction efficiency for both MAE and RMSE values, as well as lower completion latency.

Table 1. Predictive Accuracy Comparison

Model	MAE	RMSE	Prediction Delay
Proposed System	0.75	1.20	0.5 s
Existing System [5]	1.20	1.85	2.5 s
Existing System [6]	1.10	1.70	1.8 s
Existing System [7]	0.90	1.50	1.2 s

Table 2. Operational Efficiency Metric

Metric	Proposed System	Existing System [5]	Existing System [6]	Existing System [7]
Resource Utilization (%)	85%	70%	75%	80%
Average Delay Reduction (min)	5.0	2.0	3.0	4.0
Cost Reduction (%)	15%	5%	10%	8%

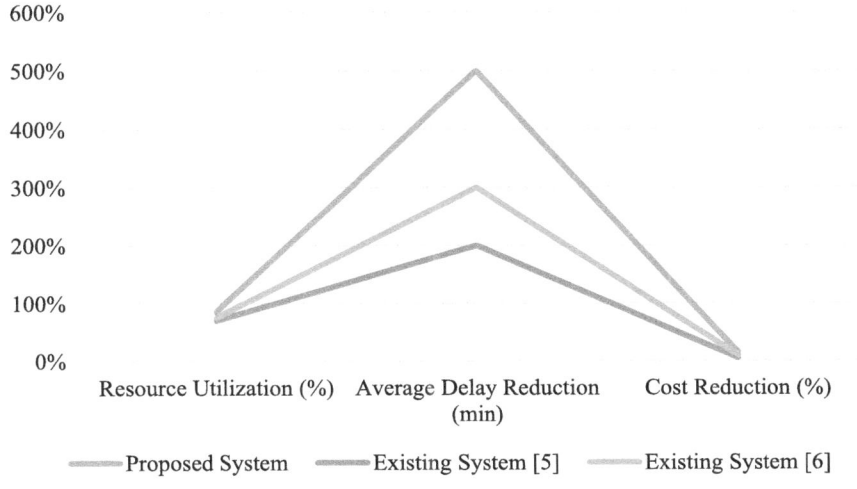

Fig. 3. Graphical representation of Operational Efficiency Metrics

Table 2 evaluates the method's effectiveness in three operational efficiency areas in contrast to other systems studied before (CP13 and GP21). The proposed method outperforms prior works [5–7], which utilized 70%, 75%, and 80% of the resources.

Average delay 5) 2, 3, and 4 for current systems in [5] -7 AVG (minors.) More importantly, the proposed strategy can save 15% in operational expenses (compared to prior studies that save 5%, [6], 10%, [7], and even if they may be related to distinct difficulties]). These metrics assess how well the proposed strategy performs in terms of resource usage, delay minimization, and cost reduction when compared to existing methods. Graphical representations of operational efficiency metricsare shown in Fig. 3.

Table 3. System Performance Improvements

Metric	Pre-Implementation	Post-Implementation (Heuristic)	Post-Implementation (CNN-LSTM)
Fuel Consumption (liters)	120,000	110,000	90,000
Maintenance Costs ($)	500,000	450,000	350,000
Labor Costs ($)	200,000	190,000	160,000

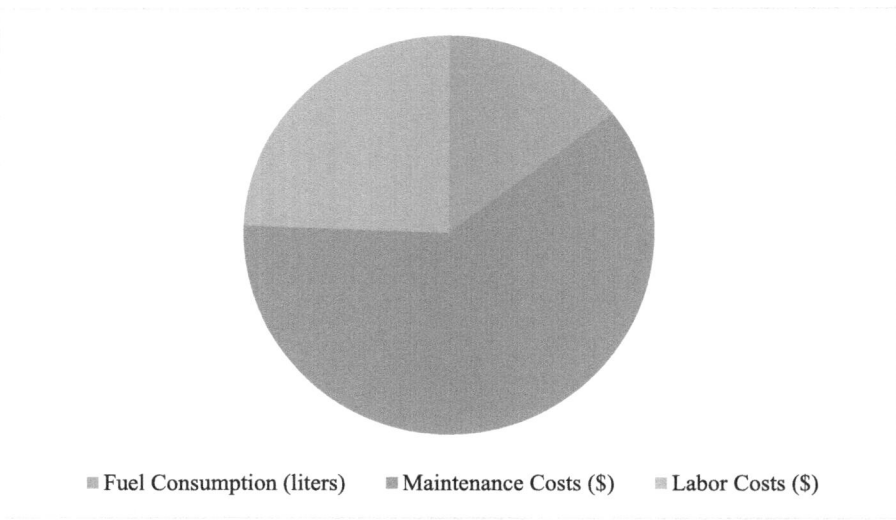

■ Fuel Consumption (liters)   ■ Maintenance Costs ($)   ■ Labor Costs ($)

Fig. 4. System Performance Improvements Visual Representation

Table 3 shows that utilizing CNN-LSTM models resulted in significant increases in system performance over conventional and heuristic methods. Before it was built, the train system used 120,000 gallons of petrol, costing $5000 in maintenance and $20000 in labor. Even after heuristics were used, fuel consumption was reduced to 110000 L, maintenance expenses were reduced to $450.00, and labor costs reached a record low of $190,000. Furthermore, adjusting the CNN-LSTM models into this system resulted in several improvements: it reduces fuel consumption per year to 90k l; maintenance charges are \$350K per year; and labor costs are up to \$160K. These advantages demonstrate the significant economic impact of deep learning-based traffic prediction models, such as fuel consumption savings, lower maintenance and labor expenses, and overall cost reduction. System Performance Improvement Visual representation is shown in Fig. 4.

The research discovered that utilizing a CNN model in addition to LSTM significantly improves railway network efficiency when compared to traditional heuristic and statistical methods. The proposed approach improves prediction accuracy, decreases errors, and enables real-time forecasting. It eliminates delays, boosts time efficiency (time-saving), and makes greater use of all resources than ever before, which has a significant positive influence on operations. CNN aids in the capturing of spatio-temporal information in railway networks, whereas LSTM simplifies temporal relationships found in traffic data. It improves scheduling and resource management by providing more precise traffic projections. The technique has advantages: When completed effectively, projections are generated more accurately, allowing for better operational planning and decision-making. Furthermore, the reduction in operating costs like as gasoline and maintenance demonstrates the economic advantages of applying deep learning technologies. The appliance's capacity to handle data in real-time gives much-needed flexibility as traffic changes and adapts, transforming it into an agile management tool. These findings demonstrate that deep learning traffic prediction models have the potential to transform rail network management by providing significant efficacy and cost-efficiency advantages over existing approaches. Later studies could focus on enhancing these models and identifying which ones can be applied to different modes of transportation. The main limitation of proposed system is that the dataset used should always be a balanced dataset.

5   Conclusion and Future Work

In conclusion, the CNN-LSTM model for railway networks has shown significant improvements over statistical and heuristic methods in terms of cost savings, operational efficiencies, and prediction accuracy. If successful, the technique mentioned above will provide genuine real-time traffic estimates, allowing for resource allocation, reduced delays, and significant cost savings. However, there are still a few drawbacks. For once, skewed or insufficient data could influence model projections, and as we all know, model accuracy is heavily dependent on data quality. Once again, these models may have scalability/availability limitations because they may take a substantial amount of compute resources to train and infer. Third, unplanned and highly variable traffic events (not contained in the training data) can make it challenging for a real-time model to adjust. Future research should focus on improving model resilience by making varied and high-quality datasets computationally efficient, which may minimize the number of resources required to run it, as well as developing adaptive strategies for dealing with unforeseen traffic anomalies. Furthermore, future studies could improve traffic management and operational efficiency by expanding the range of transportation systems (multi-modal) investigated, as well as hybridized models that combine synchronous deep learning technology.

References

1. Peng, K., Wang, H., Wu, L.: Short-term passenger flow prediction of railway station based on improved LSTM. 2023 China Automation Congress (CAC) (2023). https://doi.org/10.1109/cac59555.2023.10451360
2. Hu, H., Xiong, J., Cheng, P., Shi, Z., Gu, C.: On service traffic prediction of base stations along high-speed railway. In: 2020 IEEE International Symposium on Broadband Multimedia Systems and Broadcasting (BMSB) (2020). https://doi.org/10.1109/bmsb49480.2020.9379598
3. Wang, X., Bai, W., Meng, Z., Xin, B., Gao, R., Lv, X.: The prediction of flow in railway station based on RRC-STGCN. IEEE Access 11, 131128–131139 (2023). https://doi.org/10.1109/access.2023.3334280
4. Inoue, R., Miyashita, A.: Short-Term traffic speed prediction based on fundamental and cointegration relationship of Speed-Density in Non-Congested and congested states. IEEE Open J. Intell. Transport. Syst. 2, 470–481 (2021). https://doi.org/10.1109/ojits.2021.3133573
5. Ren, Y., Zhang, Q., Sun, Y., Li, Z., Zhang, Y., Xu, W.: Prediction method for train delay time of high-speed railway. 2020 Chinese Automation Congress (CAC) (2020). https://doi.org/10.1109/cac51589.2020.9327307
6. Yan, L., Fang, X., Fang, Y., Li, Y., Xue, Q.: Two-Stage Traffic Load Prediction-Based resource reservation for sliced HSR wireless networks. IEEE Wireless Commun. Let. 11(10), 2145–2149 (2022). https://doi.org/10.1109/lwc.2022.3195517
7. Ru, Z., Jing-Ping, Q., Yu, W., Yan-Long, L.: Prediction of railway coal freight turnover based on generalized regression neural network. In: 2020 International Conference on Robots & Intelligent System (ICRIS) (2020). https://doi.org/10.1109/icris52159.2020.00152
8. Xiong, J., Hu, H., Cheng, P., Yang, C., Shi, Z., Gui, L.: Wireless resource scheduling for high mobility scenarios: a Combined traffic and channel quality Prediction approach. IEEE Trans. Broadcast. 68(3), 712–722 (2022). https://doi.org/10.1109/tbc.2022.3141609
9. Chen, S., Wu, X., Zhou, M., Yang, B., Lu, J., Dong, H.: Train delay prediction based on a multimodal deep-learning method. 2021 China Automation Congress (CAC) (2021). https://doi.org/10.1109/cac53003.2021.9728179
10. Boateng, V.A., Yang, B.: A global modeling pruning ensemble stacking with deep learning and neural network Meta-Learner for passenger train delay prediction. IEEE Access 11, 62605–62615 (2023). https://doi.org/10.1109/access.2023.3287975
11. Huang, P., Wen, C., Fu, L., Peng, Q., Tang, Y.: A deep learning approach for multi-attribute data: a study of train delay prediction in railway systems. Inf. Sci. 516, 234–253 (2020). https://doi.org/10.1016/j.ins.2019.12.053
12. Essien, A., Petrounias, I., Sampaio, P., Sampaio, S.: A deep-learning model for urban traffic flow prediction with traffic events mined from twitter. World Wide Web 24(4), 1345–1368 (2020). https://doi.org/10.1007/s11280-020-00800-3

Data Under Siege Advanced AI Techniques to Combat Cyber Attacks in Data Infrastructure

J. Christina Deva Kirubai[1]([✉]) and S. Silvia Priscila[2]

[1] Department of Computer Applications, Bharath Institute of Higher Education and Research (BIHER), Chennai, India
christina.cs@bharathuniv.ac.in
[2] Department of Computer Science, Bharath Institute of Higher Education and Research (BIHER), Chennai, India
silviaprisila.cbcs.cs@bharathuniv.ac.in

Abstract. Traditional cybersecurity systems that rely on static rule sets and signature-based detection all reach the same conclusion: dealing with new and more sophisticated threats in a continuously changing cyber security environment is far from simple. It causes substantial false positive rates and detection delays. The paper presents a complex data infrastructure security method that combines artificial intelligence (AI)-based models, machine learning, and real-time anomaly detection. In that instance, the proposed solution overcomes the primary difficulties with standard systems by using algorithms for detecting anomalies (such as Isolation Forest) and predictive modeling techniques (Gradient Boosting Machines -GBM-, Neuronal Networks,). The most significant additions are the Imperial Kernel for feature extraction and the PCA to automatically include reactions. The system has a substantially greater false positive rate and poorer detection accuracies than the proposed method, yielding 95% true positives and 93% true negatives. It also routinely outperforms the present system, with an average reaction time of three seconds and confinement times of less than one minute. Such enhancements have shown how quickly and efficiently the system detects such attacks, representing a significant advancement in cybersecurity procedures.

Keywords: Cybersecurity · AI Techniques · Anomaly Detection · Data Infrastructure · Threat Detection · Predictive Modeling

1 Introduction

Threat identification and mitigation approaches are difficult in today's rapidly changing cybersecurity ecosystem, rendering traditional threat hunting methods inadequate for spotting cyber threats. Classical systems are incapable of dealing with the complexity and dynamic of modern cyber threats because they often depend on preset rule sets or static attributes (such as signatures) to identify threats. These are all evidence that existing attack patterns have a higher false positive rate, and it is too slow to identify new attack patterns, therefore a real-time defensive mechanism is insufficient to secure data infrastructure. While cyber threats are growing more dynamic and sophisticated,

S. Rajagopal et al. (Eds.): ASCIS 2024, CCIS 2424, pp. 213–226, 2025.
https://doi.org/10.1007/978-3-031-86290-8_16

cybersecurity solutions to handle these quickly evolving concerns must also get more detailed while remaining adaptable. As cybercrime advances and the number of instances increases, so are technological methods for identifying such threats. While these methods have their benefits, these are not as effective or efficient in detecting malware threats in a timely way as the historical ones. These systems are unable to detect new or emerging threats since they depend on predefined rule sets and recognized attack signatures. Indeed, it must urgently develop methods for real-time anomaly detection utilizing more sophisticated ML approaches in order to improve the detectability and responsiveness of cybersecurity systems. AI-driven technologies hold promises for overcoming these hurdles by providing possible solutions such as faster reaction times and danger detection rates. The primary goal of the study is to create and assess a cutting-edge AI-based cyber security system that profoundly overcomes the limits of traditional methods by combining real-time anomaly detection with machine learning. The study's goal is to create a model that combines predictive modeling approaches like GBM and neural networks with anomaly detection algorithms such as isolation forests. The proposed system aims to improve detection accuracy, decrease false positives, and reduce mean response/confinement time by combining PCA approaches for feature extraction with autonomous reaction capabilities.

The goal is to show that the proposed system performs much better than existing ones in terms of detection accuracy, reaction time, and overall effectiveness against cyberattacks. The research significantly contributes to the larger cyberspace as: To begin, it proposes a novel AI-powered strategy based on the merging of cutting-edge ML models with real-time anomaly detection to address some of the shortcomings associated with existing cybersecurity systems. The present way of safeguarding data infrastructure combines Neural Networks, GBM, Isolation Forest, and PCA for automated threat response and feature extraction. As the second contribution, the paper provides a detailed evaluation of the considered system, demonstrating that it outperforms other systems in use. Finally, the system's capacity to cut containment and reaction times clearly illustrates its real-world operational efficacy. The research is an invaluable resource for installing well-known machine learning algorithms in the field of cybersecurity since it evaluates and analyzes the procedure step by step.

The study is further separated into parts that provide a thorough and extensive analysis of the proposed method. The next section of the article is a literature review in which current cybersecurity tactics and why they have failed over time are explained to provide context for how model may be created. Section Extended model discusses the architecture and capabilities of an AI-driven system, including data collection / preprocessing, feature extraction, anomaly detection (begins anomaly prediction at the edge-level based on available time-series), mode learning/training & validation process, as well as detailed predictive modeling & automated threat response. The results and comments, on the other hand, provide a performance comparison of the proposed system to cutting-edge systems, emphasizing the strengths and efficiency improvements of it. The final section, Conclusion, and Future Work highlights the major conclusions, talks about the study's consequences, and proposes possible paths of inquiry. The study attempts to present a thorough grasp of the capabilities of the proposed system and its influence on improving cybersecurity practices through such an organized method.

2 Literature Survey

In anticipation of or during a catastrophic cyber war, it investigates the outcomes of applying ML to unorganized information sources to create organized cyber exercise material. It compiled a collection of openly accessible cyber security papers and used it as a framework for new exercise situations and to evaluate potential dangers in the future. It arranges the data according to a new ontology using named-entity recognition. It matches the generated scenarios to the strategies, tactics, and processes of known threat actors using graph comparison methodologies [6]. With the use of the current stealthy attack dataset—which is derived from testbed tests or formal analysis—it trains GAN models in the present research, which presents a threat analysis methodology called iAttackGen and produces additional attack scenarios [7]. The only way to learn those talents is through automation. The two basic foundations of cyber defense are AI and big data analytics. Large data sets with a narrow range of data types are typically the target audience for big data analytics techniques. The existing study aims to identify themes, patterns, connections, and other pertinent data [8]. The web's validation cannot be handled by any real device or by human intervention alone due to the rapid advancement of computers and the vast amount of data these utilize. Making sensible ongoing selections and identifying hazards requires a great deal of automation. Software that really defends against the rapidly progressing assaults is hard to create using standard computations. The program may be repaired using AI techniques based on bioinspired computing. The study aims to investigate potential applications of artificial intelligence in countering cybercrime [9]. It examines the increasing risk of AI-powered cyberattacks and provides information on how AI is used maliciously in cyberattacks. Three phases of the study were conducted, and only papers pertaining to AI-driven cyberattacks were selected based on inclusion, exclusion, and quality criteria [10]. The trends, issues, and difficulties related to cybersecurity in big data and AI for smart grid critical infrastructures are identified in the present research. It provides a summary of the SG, including its structures and functionality, and validate how technology has shaped the structure of the contemporary electrical grid. A strategy for assessing risk qualitatively is described. Highlighted are the key contributions to the efficiency, safety, and dependability of the electrical network. It uncovers levels and suggests suitable solutions for security. The cybersecurity risk assessment techniques for oversight and data collecting in the smart grid are finally provided [11].

3 Proposed Model

The crowd sourcing approach might address issues with existing cybersecurity processes by combining powerful AI techniques to strengthen data infrastructure protections against future generations of cyber-attacks. The majority of current solutions rely on predetermined rule sets and signature-based detection systems, which are inherently incapable of dealing with emerging complex attack patterns. However, relying on existing attack signatures prevents the detection of new threats since they have not yet been experienced, resulting in delayed threat identification and a greater percentage of false positives. Nonetheless, the proposed system blends anomaly detection and ML approaches to provide more agile and proactive safety assistance. The whole structure is divided into four major components: data collection, feature extraction, anomaly detection, and response creation. The strategy starts by combining data from the numerous locations inside a network that many firms must maintain, such as system logs, user activity, and precise information on network traffic. The second phase in data processing is feature extraction, which involves identifying and analyzing key characteristics. ML models are built on past information to learn what is typical, allowing them to recognize outliers that may signify risks. Proposed work flow is shown in Fig. 1.

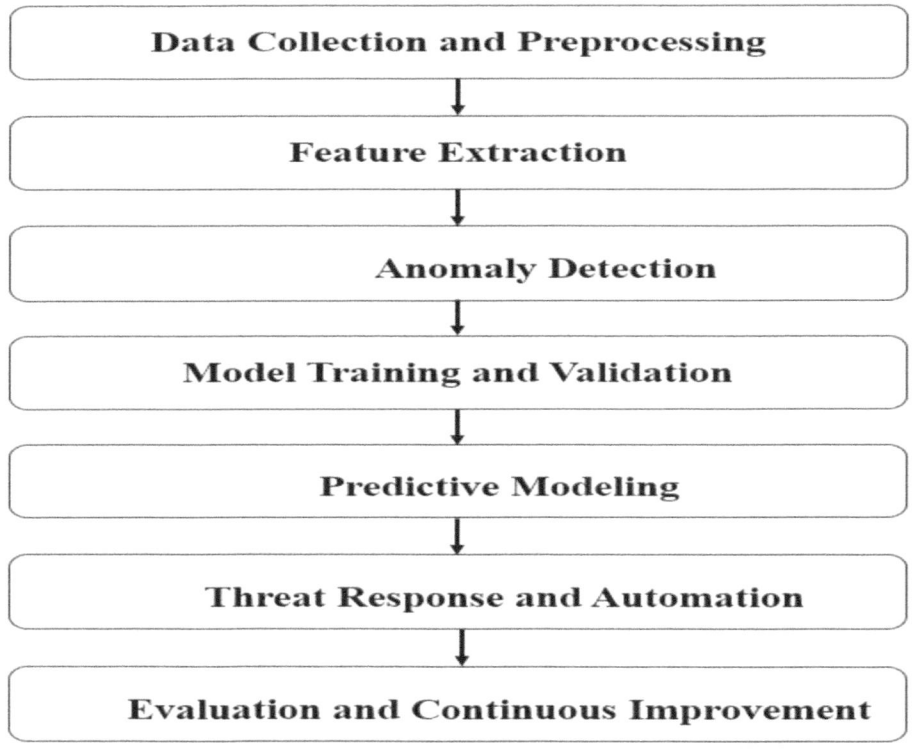

Fig. 1. Proposed Workflow

In the subsequent step, the anomaly detection process monitors and analyzes real-time data against already present baselines utilizing complicated algorithms. To carry out its thing-validation process, the technique employs a predictive model that assists it in determining when deviations are detected: (1) the possibility of mal-intent, and (2) the detrimental effect on infrastructure. The proactive approach helps the infrastructure to identify and reduce hazards before they cause major impact. Furthermore, the reaction generation component aids in speedy containment and remediation via automation by carrying out suitable mitigation procedures based on the severity of an anomaly detected. How should the proposed structure be implemented? Initially, a thorough data integration architecture is designed to facilitate the smooth export of data from various sources. These data are used to develop machine learning models that have been trained on historical data and rigorously tested/validated. After deployment, it is essential to support the system in time and space so that it can adapt continually, as both threats evolve, and to incorporate more detection capabilities into the infrastructure. Advantages of AI-powered technology. By combining machine learning and real-time analysis, the technique improves threat detection rates while lowering false positives, and maximizing cyber security. It could be the framework of an evolving system, in which it changes endlessly to provide a defensive edge against new emerging threats. Automating the threat response process also improves operations and saves time for human analysts, allowing for more precise resource allocation and speedier incident resolution.

In summary, it agrees that this model enables us to provide a dynamic and intelligent reaction to contemporary cyber threats that is considerably superior to previous cybersecurity tactics. The ability to learn from data, adapt to different sorts of threats, and automate responses can be useful in the never-ending effort to protect increasingly complex networks.

3.1 Data Collection and Preprocessing

The methodology begins with the first stage, which is to prepare and acquire the necessary data to enable rapid anomaly detection and threat management seamlessly and efficiently. Data collection is the process of obtaining information from multiple sources inside a specific data architecture, such as system activity logs, network traffic logs, and user behavior metrics. These various resources, provide insight into both the technique's common patterns and potential hazards. By recording data packets as they go across a network, these tools can reveal communication patterns and even detect unwanted logins. System activity logs are essentially recordings of various actions or events that occur on the system, such as file changes, application launches, and process executions. Recording all of the user's behaviors, such as signing in or accessing resources, as well as recording what he is doing with the applications, as these are user behavior metrics. It provides a complete picture of the operation and uses activities carried out by users on it. Preprocess data to make it relevant for real-world applications. It consists of various operations, including data standardization, cleansing, and de-noising. The goal of noise reduction is to eliminate false positive signals or data points that are not directly contributing but have the potential to influence the analysis. One of the most critical processes to maintain is dataset confidentiality data cleaning, which includes error detection and correction (complication), duplicate identification, and missing values. Normalization and Standardization Techniques are Used to convert data to a single format. In other words, normalizing parameters to the same dimension aids machine learning algorithms in understanding and processing data. Feature engineering is a competing model of transformation data that may be used to generate new features based on the original information, allowing better abnormalities to be discovered from a different perspective. Preprocessing also ensures that ML models always receive the correct type of input by turning raw data into an ordered, nice, and similar structure. It is reflected in more targeted and applicable results from subsequent phases of the research. Enabling a robust fauna for the identification and prevention of cyber risks requires an entire preprocessing step. Transforming a feature x to a normalized scale [0,1]:

$$x\prime = \frac{x - min(x)}{max(x) - min(x)} \tag{1}$$

3.2 Feature Extraction

The next stage is to extract features from the preprocessed data before using them to create ML models for identifying anomalies. The easiest strategy to distinguish between normal and aberrant behavior is to identify and choose the greatest qualities from everything available. Focusing on the most critical aspects of how it operates improves the model's accuracy and efficiency. One of the most prominent dimensionality reduction techniques is PCA. It is the process of employing principal components to reduce and simplify big datasets by breaking them down into a new collection of elements with less loss or restricted information that indicate the most important variation within the data. The particular approach is employed since it offers great capabilities for reducing the number of characteristics while preserving information. PCA significantly minimizes the amount of overlapping and (purely) irrelevant elements in each variable pattern, making it easier for ML models to recognize/understand them by breaking down all of these complex sets into fewer dimensions. Substantial-dimensional data are datasets with various features, implying substantial interference and a complex blend of the is particularly useful. You may also utilize recursive feature elimination (RFE). RFE is a sequential selection of algorithm model performance, beginning with each feature and removing the least significant one at a time. It iterative approach is performed until an ideal subset achieves a balance between complexity of models and accuracy. The rationale for using RFE is that it may remove features that do not contribute to the model's interpretability, hence enhancing feature sets. These two let us extract more useful features from the database by picking the top k providing characteristics without going through redundant data using PCA. Because PCA projects data into a significantly lower-dimensional space while keeping variability, the model improves its capacity to identify meaningful patterns. RFE improves model performance and saves computing costs by preserving only important information. Combining these strategies enables machine learning techniques to perform a better job of recognizing and distinguishing normal from aberrant activity, resulting in more reliable cybersecurity solutions. The principal components are derived from the eigenvalues λ_i and eigenvectors v_i of the covariance matrix Σ:

$$\Sigma = \frac{1}{n-1}\sum_{i=1}^{n} \lambda_i (x_i - \underline{x})(x_i - \underline{x})^T \tag{2}$$

3.3 Anomaly Detection

In detection, the Isolation Forest technique is used to identify anomalies, which is extremely successful when dealing with high-dimensional data. Isolation Forest is superior owing to its scalability and resilience against enormous amounts of complicated data, which are common in current data infrastructures. Rather than profiling usual data, Forest focuses on aberrant data via fragmentation. It does by splitting the data into unrelated elements and calculating the distances required to isolate segments of observations. Shorter pathways are less prevalent, which indicates the existence of aberrant data. It is simply because anomalies are a kind of data point that is often captured far away from its normal location, necessitating fewer splits than standard splits, which have the bulk of the data points scattered throughout. It still prefers such a method for working with high-dimensional datasets and/or large numbers of data points. Start training the model in the early stages, utilizing historical data to build a point of reference - normal behavior; Model Fitting: During the present phase, the model trains itself on previous data to recognize typical patterns and traits, forming an internal picture of what "normal" functioning looks like. Once trained, the model compares real-time data streams to a previously determined baseline. The Isolation Forest method, in instance, determines if the new batch of data is compatible with what participant mujahids have learnt. Anything that is significantly different from the preceding line will be flagged as suspicious. Further investigation is conducted to determine if these outliers are actual threats or false positives. Because the technique's contrast and assessment scheme changes on a regular basis, it can detect potential security weaknesses and respond quickly with preventative measures to reduce risk. Isolation Forest chooses random tree ensembles. Anomaly scores are derived on the basis of an average path length $h(x)$ for a point x to be present in the isolation tree as follows:

$$AnomalyScore = 2^{-\frac{h(x)}{c(n)}} \qquad (3)$$

Pseudocode for Anomaly Detection Using Isolation Forest

```
from sklearn. ensemble import IsolationForest
def train_isolation_forest(data):
    iso_forest = IsolationForest(contamination=0.01)
    iso_forest.fit(data)
    return iso_forest
def detect_anomalies(iso_forest, new_data):
    anomaly_scores = iso_forest. decision_function(new_data)
    anomalies = iso_forest. predict (new_data)
    return anomalies, anomaly_scores
anomalies, scores = detect_anomalies(iso_forest, new_data)
```

3.4   Model Training and Validation

When trained using training data and validated, it may generate powerful ML models that are extremely efficient in diagnosing dangers utilizing labeled datasets and supervised learning approaches. Dedicated datasets provide an example of true immorality allowing models to finally see what distinguishes such malice from the innocent. The next stage allows you to select one of two significant algorithms: Gradient Boosting Machines

(GBM) or Random Forest (RF). The reason for utilizing RF is its ensemble learning method, which enhances final prediction results when multiple decision trees are joined. RF, which aggregates the outcomes of several trees, can assist reduce overfitting and enhance model robustness across different sources. It performs well with complex data and a wide range of feature interactions. GBM has the ability to detect complicated patterns and relationships, allowing for more accurate predictions. Each consecutive model corrects certain flaws in prior models, and finally, GBM creates a potential model with improved performance. It can detect highly complex threats and has fine-grained potential because to its iterative feature, which corrects difficult relationships (poor linearities) in the data. In other words, labeled datasets are fed into these algorithms during the training phase, allowing them to learn from the responses of various cases. The variables of the models are changed during training to minimize prediction errors and increase accuracy. The models underwent extensive validation to ensure that they did not just overfit the data. Cross-validation is performed on a dataset by creating several folds (subsets). At distinct phases, each fold serves as both a training and testing set, allowing the model to be evaluated across all data subsets. It aids in determining the model's robustness and generalizability, as well as its performance on both training and out-of-sample data. The models are fine-tuned to allow effective detection and classification, after a rigorous training and validation procedure that assures, they are practical in real-world settings and adaptable to future cybersecurity threats.

3.5 Predictive Modeling

Predictive modeling is a process in which trained machine learning models assess real-time data inputs to anticipate probable threats. The next step is to predict foreseeable attack routes and recognize novel patterns from historical data and detected anomalies. Support vector machines (SVMs) and neural networks are two popular predictive modeling approaches. It utilizes SVMs because they have the capacity to break data into discrete buckets, which is useful for binary classification tasks like differentiating harmful from benign behavior. SVM will identify the classes in a very clear and cut way by determining the most optimal hyperplane that separates one class from the others. It is an excellent candidate for threat prediction due to its high-dimensional effectiveness and resilience in the face of limited training samples. These are very useful in data analysis because they can find detailed correlations and patterns in the data, resulting in neural networks and, more precisely deep learning models. These models are composed of numerous layers of networked nodes that recognize hierarchical trends in raw data. Through these layers, Neural Networks may detect subtle and non-linear connections in data that most simpler models would overlook owing to analysis based on large volumes of data. Deep learning skills are essential for detecting complex attack patterns and responding rapidly as threats grow over time. New data feeds into the models, allowing them to make updated forecasts based on new understanding. Models are kept current by upgrading them on a regular basis using the company's adaptive learning to meet changing threat landscapes and new attack kinds. Predictive models enable the data infrastructure to react rapidly and intelligently to emerging cybersecurity threats, using both previous trends and present context. It provides significant insight into possible attacks.Proposed System Architecture is shown in Fig. 2.

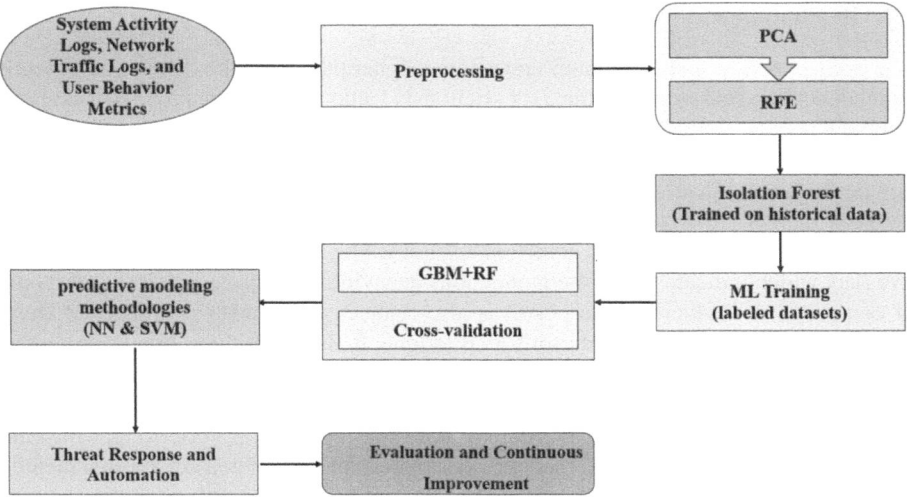

Fig. 2. Proposed System Architecture

3.6 Threat Response and Automation

The capacity to react to threats quickly, as well as the automation of response operations, is critical for adjusting to abnormalities, resulting in substantially reduced data infrastructure danger. When a detection is made, automated response mechanisms are triggered, which attempt to follow best practices for security concerns. It uses rule-based algorithms and process automation technologies to generate automated actions. The rule-based engines process preset rules and anomalies. The rule-based engine may take automated action depending on the kind of anomaly discovered, such as an unauthorized access attempt or an outflow transfer (of strange data). These tasks may include isolating impacted computers from the network to prevent risk spread, alerting system administrators about the issue, or even executing remediation to resolve a security breach. Workflow automation systems automate predefined procedures, reducing response times. These technologies prioritize replies, reducing the need for human intervention while increasing containment and remedial time. Common Threats: Often, automated responses may assist to cut time and standardize security incident response methods for common threats. The regular simulation and testing of these automatic response systems evaluates their reflexes. These are assault scenarios used in simulations to assess a system's reaction in a controlled setting. Running these tests reveals shortcomings and inefficiencies in response protocols that need explanation. Continuous computing assures that a system's reaction activities are efficient, timely, and consistent with threat intelligence, i.e., all security standards. By integrating rule-based engines and automation instruments, the system can react rapidly to security concerns in data infrastructure and address attacks as soon as feasible.

3.7 Evaluation and Continuous Improvement

The cycle of review and continuous enhancement guarantees that the system remains relevant in a cybersecurity setting that is continuously valued. During the process, it assesses how well it works in finding vulnerabilities and recommend modifications to fight against new threats via iterative model updates. Several key measures are used to evaluate system performance. Detection accuracy determines how much the technique distinguishes between dangers and routine behavior. It distinguishes between harmful and regular operations according to its high detection accuracy. The second metric is the False Positive rate, which indicates how often innocuous behaviors are misclassified as symptoms of compromise. Reducing false positives also reduces the number of unneeded alerts generated, lowering an administrator's alert fatigue. It also determines how long it takes for the technology to detect and react to alien changes. Faster reaction times result in less security incident damage. It is tested using a variety of attack scenarios. Simulating real-world threats, for example, may help determine how effectively the system can withstand and react. Test identification and response systems against simulated attacks that include both known and unknown attack paths. These tests reveal faults with the proposed systems as well as chances for improvement. It enhances algorithm and system efficiency via simulations, real-world applications, and continuous monitoring. Feedback While dangers exist, the mechanism may change and provide input for new detection models and more sophisticated response procedures. Iterative changes allow the system to continuously adapt to emerging threats and guarantee its effectiveness.

4 Result and Discussion

The performance of the proposed cybersecurity system is compared to that of the existing systems using several metrics in the results and evaluation sections. These cover containment times, accuracy, recall, F1 score, precision, accuracy, average reaction, and detection accuracy (true positive and negative rates). When compared to traditional methods, the proposed system performs better in every aspect, particularly in threat identification and response.

Table 1. Detection Accuracy Comparison

System Type	True Positive Rate	True Negative Rate	False Positive Rate	False Negative Rate
Existing System [5]	82	88	12	18
Existing System [6]	87	90	10	13
Existing System [7]	89	91	9	11
Proposed System	95	93	7	5

Table 1 compares the detection accuracy measures of many cybersecurity systems to show the better performance of the proposed system. Together with the proposed system, the table comprises conventional and existing systems [5, 6], and [7]. Comparatively to 82%, 87%, and 89% in the current systems, the proposed system at 95% has the highest true positive rate that is, the percentage of actual threats properly identified. Comparatively, the proposed system has the greatest true negative rate (93%), showing its accuracy in spotting non-threats; conventional methods vary in range from 88% to 91%. Furthermore, proving its efficiency in lowering false alarms and missed threats, the suggested system shows the lowest false positive rate (7%) and false negative rate (5%). By comparison, existing systems indicate their relative limits in threat detection by showing higher false positive rates (9% to 12%) and false negative rates (11% to 18%). The metrics of the proposed system show a significant increase in both threat identification accuracy and error minimization over current methods.

Table 2. Precision, Recall, F1 Score, and Accuracy Comparison

System Type	Precision	Rexall	F1 Score	Accuracy
Existing System [5]	88	82	85	85
Existing System [6]	85	87	86	87
Existing System [7]	86	89	87	89
Proposed System	93	95	94	94

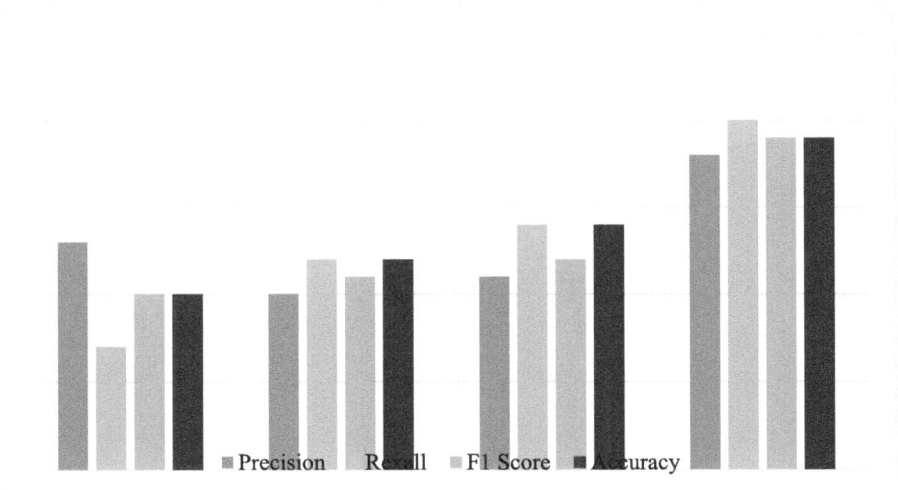

Fig. 3. Visual Graph for Precision, Recall, F1 Score, and Accuracy Comparison

Table 2 compares the accuracy, precision, recall, f1 score, and other metrics of three existing systems [5, 6], and [7] to the proposed approach. The proposed approach outperforms all existing systems in every metric, resulting in an F1 score of 94%, an accuracy of 94%, and a precision of 93%. Recall is also strong, at 95%. The existing system [5] has an accuracy of 85%, recall of 82%, f1 score of 85%, and precision of 88%, as indicated in the table above, compared to the method. The existing system [6] had an F1 score of 86, with precise recall equal to 87. The tables indicate that the existing system [7] has a higher F1 score (87%), accuracy (89%), 86% precision, and 89% recall. The proposed system's higher precision and recall demonstrate that it is an appropriate method for appropriately classifying and detecting threats, as demonstrated by its superior performance in terms of accuracy and F1 value. Visual Graph for Precision, Recall, F1 Score, and Accuracy Comparison is shown in Fig. 3.

Table 3. Average Response Time Comparison

System Type	Average Response Time (Seconds)	Average Containment Time (Minutes)
Existing System [5]	45	30
Existing System [6]	35	25
Existing System [7]	30	20
Proposed System	20	10

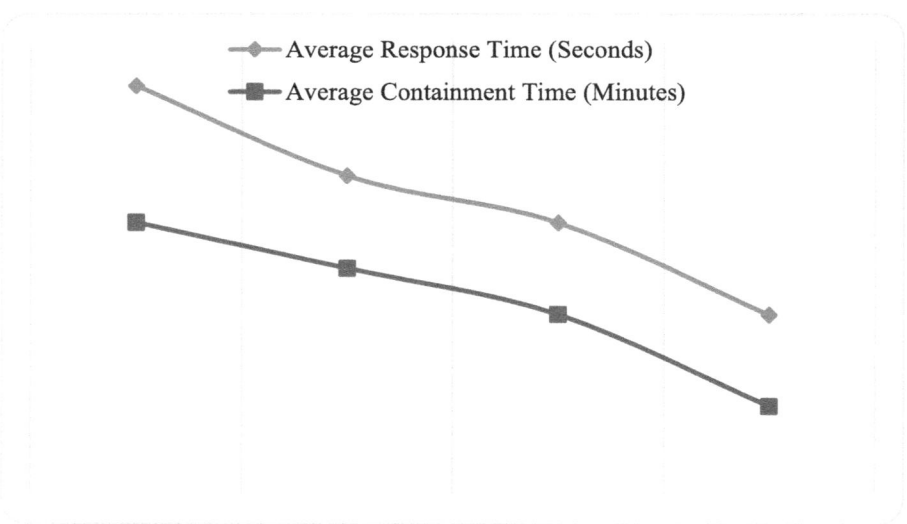

Fig. 4. Visual Graph for Average Response Time Comparison

Table 3 shows the average reaction and containment times of various systems. The table shows the superior performance compared to the planned system. Average response time: The proposed system calculates the average reaction time quicker to 20 s compared to 45 s for the existing system [5], as well as 35 s for the existing system [6]. Finally, the value is better than the previously given estimate of b = 30 s. Also, the average containment time is assessed in the timeframe required to completely withdraw a threat: For example, present systems need 30 min for Windows and Linux servers (25), and Mac clients (~20), whereas the proposed system (consumption of 10 m) consumes about 25% of that time. It highlights how quickly the proposed system can recognize danger and implement best practice containment measures to help restrict what those malicious actors may do--thus lowering the damage profile and improving overall cybersecurity responsiveness. The visual Graph for Average Response Time Comparison is shown in Fig. 4.

The results show that the novel technology outperforms standard approaches by several orders of magnitude. The combination of strong ML algorithms and real-time anomaly detection results in increased recognition and jeopardy accuracy. In comparison to other systems, the increased true positive and true negative ratios show that the system is more effective at spotting threats as well as typical activity. This improvement improves security by reducing alert fatigue and false positives (and negatives). It demonstrates how the proposed technology can assist in spotting danger quickly. The capacity to respond quickly is critical in reducing the risk of damage and accelerating recovery from safety incidents. Because the methodology uses a combination of PCA for feature extraction and Isolation Forest to detect anomalies, it performs well and provides a versatile method for detecting potential threats. The novel approach to real-world data infrastructure protection intended from its unique pre-emptive technology has the potential to transform security systems by allowing for automated solutions that can adapt to changing threat scenarios. Besides from lowering false positives, improving detection accuracy, and accelerating incident response time, it also provides insight into future cyber operations that will be more responsive to current security concerns.

5   Conclusion and Future Work

In conclusion, the proposed AI-based cybersecurity solution outperforms traditional methods in terms of detection accuracy. With advanced ML approaches such as NN, GBM, and Isolation Forests driving the system to discover abnormalities in real time, it may overcome the constraints of earlier solutions such as slow threat detection and high false positive rates. There are certain disadvantages, of course. For instance, the model may not be accurate under extreme data volatility situations; effective management of very large-scale environments will most likely have implementation issues and would require continuous upgrading to be successful in the face of emergent risks. To accomplish that, future work must make real-time threat development techniques more general and less specialized, as well as investigate flexible alternatives for large-scale data systems and solutions with a high model resilience against surprises in their input data. Further enhance the system: how well does it integrate with other cutting-edge technologies, such as more complex threat detection platforms and quantum computing Of course, cybersecurity does not have a monopoly on innovation; it exists everywhere, and to keep the paper from becoming too complex, no one is allowed to share their enthusiasm for security advancements using the language of progressive enhancement. For future enhancement more machine learning algorithms such as Convolution Neural

Network (CNN), Artificial Neural Network (ANN) and Gradient Boosting can be used which will give more results than proposed SVM.

References

1. Alsulami, A.A., Zein-Sabatto, S.: Resilient cyber-security approach for aviation cyber-physical systems protection against sensor spoofing attacks. In: 2021 IEEE 11th Annual Computing and Communication Workshop and Conference (CCWC) (2021). https://doi.org/10.1109/ccwc51732.2021.9376158
2. Saddi, V.R., Gopal, S.K., Mohammed, A.S., Dhanasekaran, S., Naruka, M.S.: Examine the role of generative ai in enhancing threat intelligence and cyber security measures. 2024 2nd International Conference on Disruptive Technologies (ICDT) (2024). https://doi.org/10.1109/icdt61202.2024.10489766
3. Paul, S., Vijayshankar, S., Macwan, R.: Demystifying cyberattacks: potential for securing energy systems with explainable AI. In: 2024 International Conference on Computing, Networking and Communications (ICNC) (2024). https://doi.org/10.1109/icnc59896.2024.10556212
4. Sapavath, N.N., Muhati, E., Rawat, D.B.: Prediction and detection of cyberattacks using AI model in virtualized wireless networks. In: 2021 8th IEEE International Conference on Cyber Security and Cloud Computing (CSCloud)/2021 7th IEEE International Conference on Edge Computing and Scalable Cloud (EdgeCom) (2021). https://doi.org/10.1109/cscloud-edgecom52276.2021.00027
5. Chang, J., Li, Z., Kaveh, M., Zhang, Y., Li, J., Yan, Z.: A survey on AI-enabled attacks and AI-empowered countermeasures in physical layer. In: 2023 IEEE 9th World Forum on Internet of Things (WF-IoT) (2023). https://doi.org/10.1109/wf-iot58464.2023.10539554
6. Zacharis, A., Gavrila, R., Patsakis, C., Ikonomou, D.: AI-assisted cyber security exercise content generation: modeling a cyber conflict. In: 2023 15th International Conference on Cyber Conflict: Meeting Reality (CyCon) (2023). https://doi.org/10.23919/cycon58705.2023.10181930
7. Shahriar, M.H., Khalil, A.A., Rahman, M.A., Manshaei, M.H., Chen, D.: iAttackGen: generative synthesis of false data injection attacks in cyber-physical systems. In: 2021 IEEE Conference on Communications and Network Security (CNS) (2021). https://doi.org/10.1109/cns53000.2021.9705034
8. Bhiminei, O., Kulkarni, S.G., Joshi, S.V., Kadam, S., Sanap, R.S., Pant, B.: Development of critical information framework by big data analytics and artificial intelligence to prevent cyber attacks in WSN. In: 2023 International Conference on Artificial Intelligence and Smart Communication (AISC) (2023). https://doi.org/10.1109/aisc56616.2023.10085465
9. Srivastava, S., Raj, S.: Statistical prospects of artificial intelligence in tackling cyber crimes. In: 2023 International Conference on New Frontiers in Communication, Automation, Management and Security (ICCAMS) (2023). https://doi.org/10.1109/iccams60113.2023.10526186
10. Guembe, B., Azeta, A., Misra, S., Osamor, V.C., Fernandez-Sanz, L., Pospelova, V.: The emerging threat of AI-driven cyber-attacks: a review. Applied Artificial Intelligence **36**(1) (2022). https://doi.org/10.1080/08839514.2022.2037254
11. Chehri, A., Fofana, I., Yang, X.: Security risk modeling in smart grid critical infrastructures in the era of big data and artificial intelligence. Sustainability **13**(6), 3196 (2021). https://doi.org/10.3390/su13063196
12. Harita, U., Mohammed, M.: Analyzing threat flow over network using ensemble-based dense network model. Soft. Comput. **28**(5), 4171–4184 (2024). https://doi.org/10.1007/s00500-024-09645-8

Scalable Intrusion Detection Using Recurrent Neural Networks in Distributed Data Engineering Systems

A. Jeyaram[1]([⊠]) and A. Muthukumaravel[2]

[1] Department of Computer Science, Bharath Institute of Higher Education and Research (BIHER), Chennai, India
jramcloud1@gmail.com
[2] Faculty of Arts and Science, Bharath Institute of Higher Education and Research (BIHER), Chennai, India
dean.arts@bharathuniv.ac.in

Abstract. Traditional Intrusion Detection Systems (IDS) frequently rely on anomaly and signature-based methods, which have limits in terms of accuracy, scalability, and flexibility. Anomaly-based systems generate a high number of false positives, causing operational problems, but signature-based solutions cannot protect against zero-day assaults. To overcome these problems, the proposed system improves IDS performance in dispersed data engineering contexts by utilizing Long Short-Term Memory (LSTM) networks, which are a type of Recurrent Neural Network (RNN). Furthermore, network data has temporal correlations, which the LSTM-based IDS can utilize to reduce false positives and improve detection accuracy. The methodology ensures maximum fault tolerance and resiliency while scaling to handle terabytes of real-time data by distributing the LSTM model across a cluster and cloud-based architecture. Research results reveal that the proposed approach outperforms existing IDS approaches. For instance, the KDD Cup 99 dataset, achieved 92.5% accuracy, which is higher than other top algorithms in this scenario defined as: Precision (88.4%), and recall (91.2%). F1 score: 89.7%. However, the scores acquired from the NSL-KDD dataset were 91.2% F1 score and 93.2% accuracy, which is rather low in comparison to our results but can provide us with an elementary understanding of the outliers present in both approaches. Furthermore, the techniques greatly reduced false positives and false negatives by overcoming modern cybersecurity challenges.

Keywords: Distributed Data Engineering · Anomaly Detection · Temporal Sequence Analysis · Network Traffic · Continuous Learning

1 Introduction

With the rise of complex assaults in recent years, standard intrusion detection systems (IDS) have proven ineffective, relying instead on anomaly and signature-based techniques. While traditional methods are important for network security, they fall short

© The Author(s), under exclusive license to Springer Nature Switzerland AG 2025
S. Rajagopal et al. (Eds.): ASCIS 2024, CCIS 2424, pp. 227–240, 2025.
https://doi.org/10.1007/978-3-031-86290-8_17

in terms of accuracy, scalability, and agility. For instance, signature-based IDS will be unable to detect fresh and emerging attacks, implementing them beyond the existing range of recognized threats. However, the performance of these anomaly-based IDS that detect differences from the standard can be precise and frequently generate false-positive rates, resulting in additional bureaucracies such as responding to warnings that are not critical. The dispute serves as a reminder that the time has come for more productive and simply deployable IDS that can account for today's organic environment of cyber threats. The problems of traditional IDS are greatly exacerbated by the large increase in data traffic caused by the exponential and rapid expansion of networked systems. These drawbacks of traditional IDS are especially obvious in large-scale distributed data engineering paradigms defined by vast amounts of streaming real-time data and highly complicated, ultra-fast network interactions.

These systems are also hampered by the increasing volume of data they must process, making them less efficient at identifying and preventing cyber threats to critical infrastructure. These methods are effective, yet do not scale, and the immediacy of response required in a central control-and-command system must be supplemented by novel methodologies that can boost scalability without sacrificing effectiveness. In complex distributed data engineering systems, the system uses LSTM networks, a type of RNN, to improve IDS performance. As a result, LSTMs' ability to learn and construct new structures in sequential data over long distances makes them ideal for such kinds of applications.

LSTMs will improve the aforementioned system's ability to recognize complex and changing threats, as well as detect long-term traffic patterns that alter over time (dynamic). To overcome this deficiency, the authors claim that a novel technique for tackling IDS with LSTM-based performances provides a superior and at-scale solution that will be effective in controlling the volume of up-to-date network scenarios. It proposes the methodology to improve detection accuracy while limiting false positives and negatives, to achieve real-time data processing on a large scale. A distributed computing architecture based on the LSTM model is constructed on its infrastructure to deal with the high data flow encountered in modern distribution scenarios. As a result, the described IDS system is undoubtedly capable of analyzing massive amounts of network traffic at the same time, allowing for speedy and precise detection of potential threats. Furthermore, the architecture enables the system to adaptively learn from new threats, and its performance is reliable in a fast-changing threat scenario.

The study provides numerous favorable elements. The first feature it introduces is an enhanced IDS design based on LSTM networks to address issues with existing detection systems. The results of the research emphasize the importance of real-time processing and scalability in modern IDS, resulting in an increased demand for solutions that can expand with distribution data requirements. Finally, because the system decreases false positives and negatives, it reduces administrative costs on security teams (lowering noise), allowing them to focus on true threats and thereby significantly improving overall cyber posture. The paper is organized as follows: Sect. 1 presents an overview of the proposed IDS framework, as well as motivating difficulties. Section 2 examines the literature and recognizes limitations in current IDS approaches. As the study unfolds, system specifics are given in Sect. 3, which includes a description of the methodology. Feature extraction, LSTM network architecture, and training techniques real-time deployment as the proposed system assessment technique that includes data collection and preparation. Section 4 David displays performance measurements that are compared to both existing systems and the new system. Conclusions: The concluding section (Sect. 5) summarizes the findings and suggests further directions to end the paper. The results from the LSTM-based IDS have been demonstrated to outperform traditional approaches by enhancing detection accuracy, lowering false positives, and scaling with a huge amount of training data. Its relevance for existing cybersecurity is also shown in its ability to process vast amounts of constantly changing data and respond swiftly. Its unique technology enables more effective intrusion detection and overcomes many of the cracks left by existing systems.

2   Literature Survey

The purpose of the present investigation is to identify abnormalities in network traffic using a machine learning model based on LSTM and to divert all harmful requests to a black hole server based on honeypots. It was trained and evaluated on the CICIDS2017 data set consisting of many attacks. The model may be applied to distributed servers that are currently in operation, and the results show an elevated level of accuracy in detecting these assaults [6].

The article's introduction covers the fundamental ideas of IDS, the ever-changing threat environment, and the benefits of utilizing ML and DL in the current use case. It also discusses the three categories into which NIDS techniques fall: hybrid, anomaly-based, and signature-based. Evaluating the benefits and drawbacks of every group. The paper aims to present a comprehensive analysis and comparison of the many methodologies proposed [7].

The existing study uses CNN and RNN, two deep learning techniques, to create an intelligent detection system that can recognize different types of network intrusions [8]. It suggests a brand-new technique for intrusion or anomaly detection by utilizing an improved hybrid model that blends an RNN and a CNN. The study optimizes several hyperparameters in the model [9].

LSTM is used to build an IDS architecture using machine learning methods. It uses LSTM networks, gated RRUs, and simpler RNNs three different forms of RNNs that are occasionally used [10].

In the present study, it addresses the drawbacks of centralized IDS for devices with limited resources by introducing two approaches—distributed and semi-distributed—that combine efficacious extraction and choice of features with the possibility for fog-edge coordinated analytics. It individually creates parallel ML models corresponding to a partitioned assault dataset in order to disperse the computational duties. In the semi-distributed situation, side-by-side feature choices are performed using the parallel models operating on the edge side, and a single multi-layer perceptron classification operates on the fog side as a result. In the distributed scenario, each of the parallel models handles the feature selection and multi-layer perceptron classification independently. A coordinating edge or fog then combines the outputs to make the final judgment [11].

Multi Layer Perceptron (MLP) is an important algorithm that helps in predicting the intruder in a safe secured network with deep learning approaches [12]. Classification of

Intrusion is done in a better manner Using Convolution Neural Network (CNN) with IQR (Inter Quartile Range) Approach [13].

3 Proposed Model

Conventional IDS, which usually use anomaly and signature-based detection techniques, are essential to network security. To detect malicious activity, signature-based intrusion detection systems rely on predetermined patterns of recognized threats, which makes them ineffective against novel, unidentified attacks. Conversely, anomaly-based IDS that identify departures from typical network activity frequently experience elevated false positive rates, leading to needless notifications and extra administrative burden. Moreover, the scalability demands of contemporary networked data engineering systems, which entail enormous amounts of data generated in real time, are beyond the capabilities of these antiquated systems. Conceptual Blueprint of Proposed System is shown in Fig. 1.

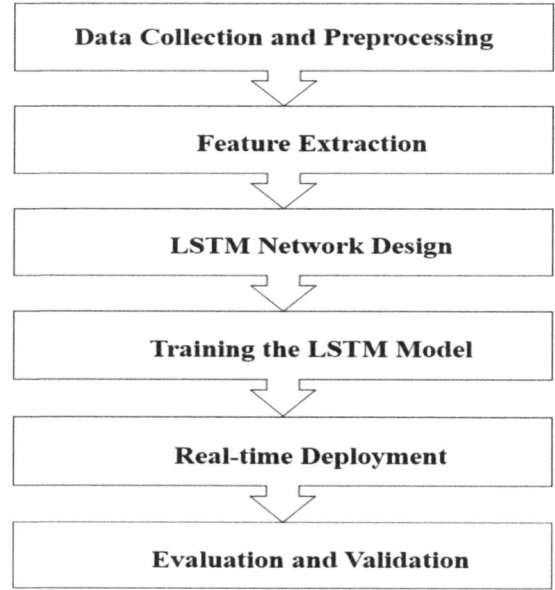

Fig. 1. Conceptual Blueprint of Proposed System

Their inability to handle massive amounts of data in today's network systems gives them a competitive disadvantage. The proposed approach aims to solve these limitations by leveraging the characteristics of RNNs, notably LSTM networks, to provide robustness in terms of scalability, accuracy, and efficiency for intrusion detection systems in dispersed data engineering contexts. The concept behind employing RNNs is that because of their capacity to capture time dependencies between data in a sequence, they can analyze sequential network traffic more efficiently than older methods. With various technology developments and methodological changes, the proposed system departs from existing IDS.

Beginning carefully by initializing and processing network traffic data sequences using LSTM networks to train the proposed framework to recognize patterns over time. Understanding time is essential for anticipating complex dangers that can take many years to develop. It also increases the need for scalability when dealing with large volumes of data streams, which is frequent in modern distributed settings, by allowing us to horizontally split the model LSTM on top of clusters. Distributed computing reduces fault tolerance while enabling real-time processing. It involves multiple use-case phases to evaluate the system and, eventually, add strength to it. It collects and produces the network traffic timestamps needed for the LSTM model analysis. Preprocessing captures different processes such as data segmentation into sequences, categorical information encoding, and normalization.

The LSTM network is then developed and trained using a labeled dataset that includes annotated instances of benign and malicious traffic. During training, all of a model's parameters are tweaked to reduce error during prediction across numerous stages, allowing us to distinguish between malicious and benign sequences. The trained model is deployed throughout a distributed computing infrastructure (either in the cloud or on edge devices), allowing for real-time discovery. With the rule bases in place, this system can now scan incoming network traffic in parallel and promptly alert on potential breaches. One of the primary benefits of deploying an RNN-based IDS is a large increase in detection accuracy. The results of this test revealed a significantly higher detection rate than most current approaches.

The improved accuracy enables the LSTM network to learn and replicate complicated temporal patterns from in-network data. Even better, the technique significantly minimizes false positive rates, relieving administrative burdens and allowing security staff to focus on serious threats. Another advantage is its real-time processing capability and scalability. Thus, distributing the LSTM model indicates that those dozen models can be more readily maintained among IDSs in circumstances when efficient management over such huge amounts is required in a system as massive and data-rich as any of today's systems. It evolves into a full scale-out system over the network, and data flow becomes efficient even on enormous networks in big environments due to its scalability. The IDS is also adaptable to new and emerging threats due to its continuous learning capability, which can be modeled using an LSTM network. As it gets more data over time, the model can grow in real time (a term we frequently use to make sense of deep learning issues, by the way) and keep up with both benign and malicious activities.

The proposed system provides a dependable, scalable alternative to the shortcomings of standard IDS. The method decreases false positives, improves detection efficacy, and maintains real-time performance by distributing positions over multiple processing units, and temporal sequence analysis capabilities can be used utilizing LSTM networks. Today, these advancements make it an important tool for preventing complex cyberattacks on distributed data engineering systems.

3.1 Data Collection and Preprocessing

The first stage is to collect a big dataset of both regular network traffic and malicious behavior to develop an IDS. To accomplish that, use well-known public datasets like KDD Cup 99 and NSL-KDD, which contain a significant number of attack-labeled instances [14]. The next important step is to pre-process the acquired data so that it may be processed by LSTM networks. There are a few preprocessing processes that are required, such as normalizing input value ratios to maintain average ranges for learning and readability using LSTM. To align them with the LSTM model, which requires numerical inputs for processing, categorical information such as protocol kinds and flag indications are converted to numerical representations. Furthermore, because LSTMs are built for time-series data, we must divide the entire dataset into fixed-length sequences so that the LSTM can choose which sequence to follow at any given instant. It enables the LSTM to examine time-centric patterns required to detect real-time-emerging and changing threats within a network. Before using an LSTM model to train and test on data, ensure that the dataset has been thoroughly pre-processed using segmentation, encoding, and normalization. It helps the IDS detect and categorize various intrusions in distributed data engineering. Visual Representation of proposed system is shown in Fig. 2.

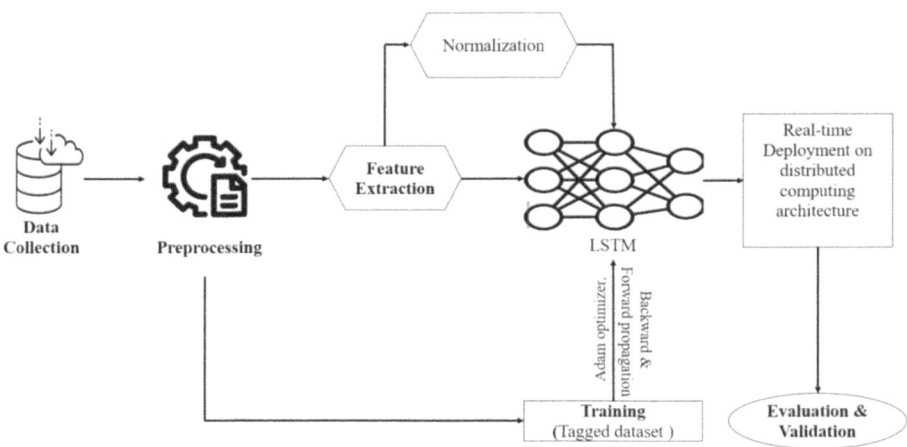

Fig. 2. Visual Representation of Proposed System

3.2 Feature Extraction

Feature extraction is a critical first step that must be performed on raw network traffic before it can be routed through LSTM networks. The process entails converting unstructured data into a structured version to allow your model to detect patterns associated with typical or outlier behavior. Connection duration is used to monitor network session duration; data sent is counted by byte, packets are exchanged using packet count numbers, and any protocol-specific information (such as TCP flags or HTTP methods) is extracted from network traffic. These attributes are generated from raw network data to help determine which network behavior is conspicuous and potentially harmful. Following extraction, these attributes are normalized to fall within a consistent range of values. It's significant because it helps mitigate the influence of discrepancies in feature magnitudes, which can distort your LSTM model during training. One of the most important problems arises when specific features dominate learning despite vastly divergent averages. It ensures that each feature contributes proportionally to model training by scaling the data. It improves the models' ability to spot patterns and abnormalities. Finally, a more structured feature extraction and normalization strategy makes it easier for the LSTM model to learn about intrusions in widely distributed complicated data situations.

Pseudo-Code for IDS

```
1. Data Collection
dataset = load_public_dataset (["KDD Cup 99", "NSL-KDD"])

2. Preprocessing
data = preprocess(dataset)
sequences = segment_data (data, sequence_length)

3. Feature Extraction
features = extract_and_normalize_features(sequences)

4. LSTM Network Design
model = build_LSTM_model (num_layers=3, dropout_rate=0.5)

5. Training
train_data, val_data = split_data(features)
model. train (train_data, optimizer=Adam(0.001), loss_function=CrossEntropyLoss())

6. Real-time Deployment
deploy_model(model)
while True:
    incoming_data = receive_data()
    processed_data = preprocess(incoming_data)
    predictions = model.predict(processed_data)
    alerts = generate_alerts(predictions)
    send_alerts(alerts)

7. Evaluation
metrics = evaluate_model(model, test_data)
print("Metrics:", metrics)
```

3.3 LSTM Network Design

The IDS largely relies on its LSTM network, a form of RNN that is ideal for processing sequential input. LSTM networks are widely preferred due to their ability to recognize long-term dependencies and temporal patterns in network traffic, which is essential to detecting various sorts of complex and rapidly growing cyber threats. The LSTM architecture consists of three layers of LSTM cells in Eigen Genre resolution, allowing the model to recognize and learn complicated patterns over long sequences. Because each LSTM cell has gating mechanisms that control information flow, the network can maintain a high number of temporal associations but not very many. It's especially valuable when inspecting network traffic, as patterns of undesirable conduct might take a long time to emerge. It also improves generalizability from specific data points in the training set to previously encountered circumstances by incorporating dropout layers within the network. During training, dropout layers randomly deactivate a fraction of neurons to prevent the model from learning any single characteristic too well, hence reducing volatility. The LSTM network design achieves an equilibrium between the addition of dropout layers, which are known for delivering high generalization, and many LSTMs that learn to record complicated sequential patterns. Its design enables the IDS to identify and respond to both new and old intrusion patterns more precisely and quickly than other types of approaches, providing a non-restrictive solution to modern-day cybersecurity concerns. The LSTM cell is implemented using the equations below to help regulate information flow.

1. Forget Gate:Decides what to discard from the cell state.

$$f_t = \sigma(W_f \cdot [h_{t-1}, x_t) + b_f \tag{1}$$

2. Input Gate:Updates cell state with new information.

$$i_t = \sigma(W_i \cdot [h_{t-1}, x_t) + b_i \tag{2}$$

3. Cell State Update:Computes the new cell state.

$$\tilde{C}_t = tanh(c \cdot [h_{t-1}, x_t) + b_c \tag{3}$$

4. Final cell State:Combines previous and new cell states.

$$C_t = f_t \cdot C_{t-1} + i_t \cdot \tilde{C}_t \tag{4}$$

5. Output Gate:Determines the next hidden state.

$$o_t = \sigma(W_o \cdot [h_{t-1}, x_t) + b_o \tag{5}$$

6. Hidden State:Represents the output of the LSTM cell.

$$h_t = o_t \cdot tanh(C_t) \tag{6}$$

3.4   Training the LSTM Model

Training an LSTM model is a critical step in developing a successful IDS. The first stage in the procedure was to employ a tagged dataset containing both benign and malicious network traffic. The data set is the force that guides the LSTM model in differentiating normal behavior from noisy behavior, therefore it acts as a form of supervised learning material for our algorithm's training process. During the training process use the Adam optimizer and stochastic gradient descent with warm-up (SGDW) techniques to achieve steady learning rates. Adam is an excellent optimizer for big neural network models, such as LSTMs, because it works similarly to annealing, altering the learning rate per parameter dependent on the amount of gradient an incorrect value can create. It facilitates more effective and faster convergence of the model, particularly when dealing with large-scale datasets with complicated structures. Instead, the loss function based on cross-entropy is quite useful for classification applications. It compares the actual label to the projected class probability for each occurrence, indicating how well the model has been performing. When a triangle is detected, the model calculates how far off its predictions are and adjusts the numbers accordingly to reduce the error. During training, the LSTM model adjusts its weights to reduce cross-entropy loss and continuously updates itself to improve network traffic predictions and classifications. The procedure is iterative and consists of two steps: backward propagation (calculate gradients of a loss function to each weight and use them to update weights) and forward propagation (the network predicts based on its current state). The ongoing fine-tuning allows the model to rapidly pick up on complicated patterns and improves the detection of both known and unknown breaches. The cross-entropy loss function is crucial for classification tasks:

$$Loss = -\frac{1}{N}\sum_{i=1}^{N}[y_i\log(p_i) + (1 - y_i)\log(1 - p_i) \tag{7}$$

3.5   Real-Time Deployment

A trained LSTM model is used in a distributed computing architecture to detect intrusions in real-time by processing enormous amounts of fast network traffic data. The architecture allows the model to be deployed in a distributed and cloud-based environment for scalable processing and parallel analysis of incoming data streams. The deployment architecture's parallel data processing features enable each piece of equipment to handle high-bandwidth loads without introducing perceptible latency. Each node in the distributed system is responsible for acting on this LSTM to handle a portion of the traffic that arrives. After all of the data has been segmented, the algorithm may process parts of it at once, which speeds up detection. Each node's predictions are combined to create a composite representation of all network operations. Integrate and produce a single comprehensive assessment of potential invasions across individual nodes. The architecture uses task distribution and parallel data processing to improve detection speed and scalability to deal with rapidly increasing traffic volumes. The real-time deployment design allows for immediate alerting and prevention of any security events, ensuring the IDS's efficiency in identifying any anomalies or risks that may arise. It is especially important for ensuring the security and integrity of distributed data engineering systems in both dynamic and active situations.

3.6 Evaluation and Validation

Several key measures are used to assess the effectiveness of the IDS. Precision and recall assess how well the model identifies potentially dangerous activities, whereas accuracy informs us whether or not it is truly good at making predictions. Recall measures the frequency of true positives, whereas accuracy represents a fraction of all positive predictions, and so on. The F1-Score gives a balanced performance statistic by taking the harmonic mean of precision and recall, which can be highly beneficial when working with unbalanced datasets. The protected model is validated using an independent validation data set that includes both known and unknown attackers. Ground truth is necessary for at least certain IDSs to evaluate their generalization capabilities (i.e., whether or not it can detect threats that were not in the training set). Cross validation approaches, such as k-fold cross-validation, are used to assess a model's resilience while avoiding overfitting. When an LSTM-based system is used, detection accuracy improves and false positives decrease, as demonstrated. The comparison is essential for demonstrating the characteristics that render the methodology interesting and ensuring that it reflects real advancement when compared to existing solutions. Assessing and testing ensure that the IDS provides dependable, high-fidelity intrusion detection in real-world scenarios since it is validated using these rigorous approaches.

In summary, LSTM networks improved the IDS framework's intrusion detection capabilities. The system detects known and unknown threats more effectively by employing advanced pre-processing, feature extraction, and real-time training models, as well as undertaking extensive testing (including unknown threats). It provides a solid and scalable solution to today's cybersecurity issues.

4 Result and Discussion

The study uses two datasets to conduct a detailed review of various IDS. It introduces a proposed LSTM-based IDS and compares it to three cutting-edge systems. The proposed method performs better at detecting and classifying network traffic, with improved accuracy and comparison rates.

Table 1. Performance Comparison of IDS Techniques (KDD Cup 99 Dataset)

System Type	Accuracy	Precision	Recall	F1 Score
Existing System [8]	85.3	78.9	82.1	80.4
Existing System [9]	82.7	74.2	79.5	76.8
Existing System [10]	88.1	81.4	85.3	83.3
Proposed System	92.5	88.4	91.2	89.8

Table 1 utilizes the dataset to compare the performance of different IDS techniques. Every metric shows that the proposed system outperforms the alternatives: accuracy is 92.5%, precision is 88.4%, recall is 91.2%, and F1 score is 89.8%. The performance of existing systems is inferior in contrast: Existing System [9] records 82.7% accuracy, precision of 74.2%, recall of 79.5%, and an F1 score of 76.8%; Existing System [10] performs marginally better with 88.1% accuracy, 81.4% precision, 85.3% recall, and an F1 score of 83.3%. The existing System [8] achieves 85.3% accuracy with precision at 78.9%, recall at 82.1%, and an F1 score of 80.4%. The proposed method outperforms every disclosed current system, demonstrating a more effective ability to identify and classify network traffic more precisely, enhancing detection and decreasing false positives. Performance Comparison of IDS Techniques (KDD Cup 99 Dataset) Graphical Illustration is shown in Fig. 3.

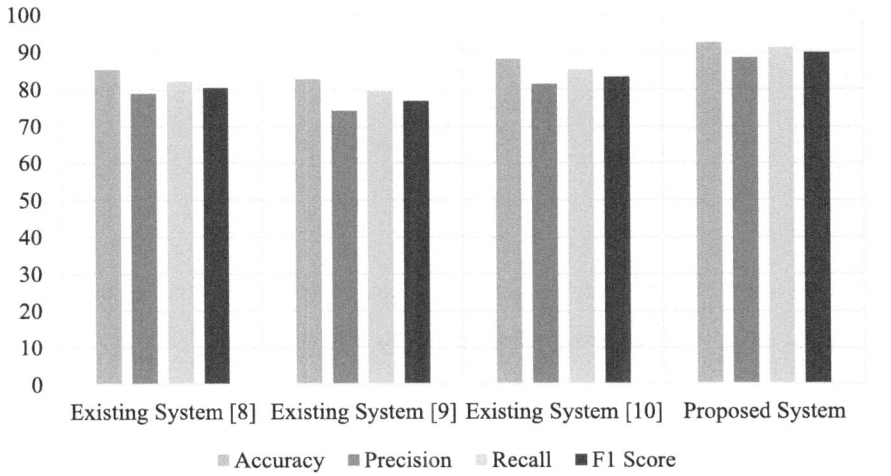

■ Accuracy ■ Precision ■ Recall ■ F1 Score

Fig. 3. Performance Comparison of IDS Techniques (KDD Cup 99 Dataset) Graphical Illustration

Table 2. Performance Comparison of IDS Techniques (NSL-KDD Dataset)

System Type	Accuracy	Precision	Recall	F1 Score
Existing System [8]	87.5	80.1	84.3	82.2
Existing System [9]	84.1	76.5	81.7	79.0
Existing System [10]	89.6	83.2	87.4	85.2
Proposed System	93.2	89.6	92.8	91.2

Table 2 compares the performance of several IDS tested using the dataset. The table includes metrics for the proposed LSTM-based IDS and three existing in-use IDS systems. With an accuracy of 93.2%, precision of 89.6%, recall of 92.8%, and an F1 score of 91.2%, the proposed system outperforms all other systems. Existing system performance varies. System [8] achieves an accuracy of 87.5% but has lower precision (80.1%) and recall (84.3%); Existing system [9] has an accuracy of 84.1% but even worse precision (76.5%) and recall (81.7%). The existing system [10] performs better, with an accuracy of 89.6%, although it falls short of the proposed system's metrics. The LSTM-based IDS improves detection capabilities making it more successful in categorizing network intrusions. Performance Comparison of IDS Techniques (NSL-KDD Dataset) Graphical Illustration is shown in Fig. 4.

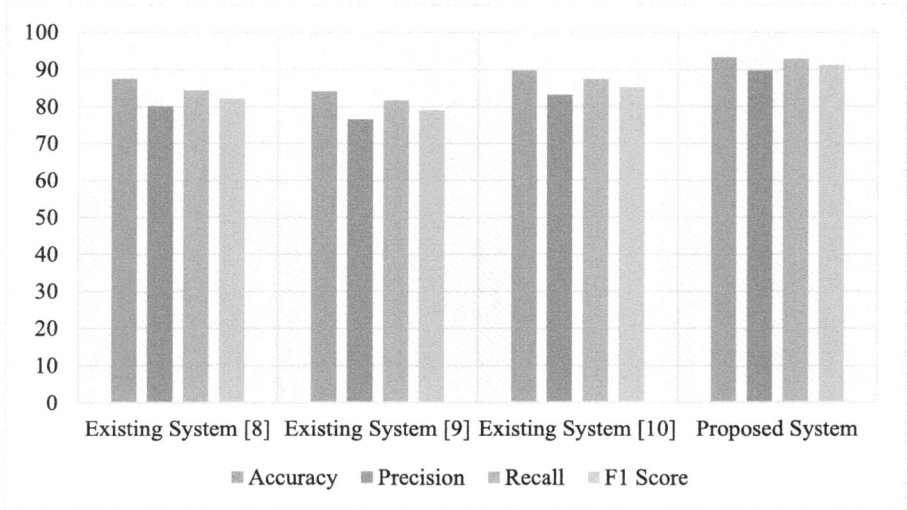

Fig. 4. Performance Comparison of IDS Techniques (NSL-KDD Dataset) Graphical Illustration

Table 3. False Positives and False Negatives

System Type	False Positives	False negative
Existing System [8]	1.2	0.9
Existing System [9]	5.8	4.3
Existing System [10]	10.4	6.7
Proposed System	4.7	3.2

Table 3 displays the false positive and false negative performance of several IDS systems. The LSTM-based IDS described, which achieved 4.7% false positives and 3.2% false negatives, outperforms the existing systems by reducing the number of alerts generated after processing the results of the identification stage done using an ML algorithm across the network logs. The method also has less false positives (1.2%) and misses (0.9%). While the technique may be simpler, it is not necessarily more scalable than existing systems [8]. Existing systems have a higher rate of false positives and negatives [9] and [10], and false alarms are more frequent with a lower detection probability. However, the proposed method still improves significantly over the existing system, particularly in terms of false negatives; however, there is considerable development that needs to be done before it can be as accurate as the existing system [8].

The proposed LSTM-based IDS outperforms the existing techniques. The results demonstrate how effectively the technique improves detection recall, precision, and accuracy. The proposed approach outperforms existing IDS by successfully detecting both known and unexpected threats. It is mostly owing to an LSTM network's ability to detect and assess repeating temporal patterns in psychological activity, which is a feature that many traditional techniques lack. LSTM-based intrusion detection systems have extensive applications. It is especially well-suited for decentralized data engineering applications that generate a large amount of network traffic regularly, such as scalability and real-time processing. The method scales the LSTM model over a cluster and cloud-based architecture to efficiently maintain low detection latency while providing high data throughput. One of the primary advantages is that the method will reduce both false positives and true negatives. Improvement - Security teams will have reduced overhead (administrative labor) on that, increasing the accuracy of identifying an attack. In general, the proposed LSM-LSTM-based IDS is a promising and scalable system that can significantly improve cyber security against real-world developing and aggressive cyber threats.

5   Conclusion and Future Work

In conclusion, the proposed LSTM-based IDS outperforms existing methods by improving detection accuracy and minimizing false positives (false alarms) and false negatives while maintaining scalability in distributed data engineering contexts. The feature improves the technique's ability to detect both known and new threats by learning temporal patterns from network data using an LSTM model. LSTM networks are the most adaptable of all RNNs, however, it do have some limits. Model-free learning's significant computational complexity and resource costs may appear to be barriers to good on-device performance if not outright crippling it. Second, the quality and representational power of a model's training data may limit its success against previously unknown sorts of attacks. Finally, while the entire system is scalable, its distributed architecture might be challenging for operations and maintenance. Future research should focus on improving the computational efficiency of LSTM networks for a wider range of dynamic attack vectors to generalize our model and develop a durable system scope with high fidelity across a large number of devices spread throughout the world. Such adjustments can also increase the utility and endurance of an IDS in adjusting to changing cybersecurity landscapes.

References

1. Ennaji, S., Akkad, N.E., Haddouch, K.: A powerful ensemble learning approach for improving network intrusion detection system (NIDS). In: 2021 Fifth International Conference on Intelligent Computing in Data Sciences (ICDS) (2021). https://doi.org/10.1109/icds53782.2021.9626727

2. Kavitha, R., Amutha, S.: Performance analysis of deep neural network and LSTM models for secure network intrusion detection system. In: 2022 IEEE 4th International Conference on Cybernetics, Cognition and Machine Learning Applications (ICCCMLA) (2022). https://doi.org/10.1109/icccmla56841.2022.9989253

3. Ramkumar, K., Alzubaidi, L.H., Malathy, V., Venkatesh, T.: Intrusion detection system in wireless sensor networks using modified recurrent neural network with long short-term memory. In: 2024 International Conference on Integrated Circuits and Communication Systems (ICICACS) (2024). https://doi.org/10.1109/icicacs60521.2024.10498333

4. Sivamohan, S., Sridhar, S.S., Krishnaveni, S.: An effective recurrent neural network (RNN) based intrusion detection via bi-directional long short-term memory. In: 2021 International Conference on Intelligent Technologies (CONIT) (2021). https://doi.org/10.1109/conit51480.2021.9498552

5. Ullah, S., et al.: A new intrusion detection system for the internet of things via deep convolutional neural network and feature engineering. Sensors **22**(10), 3607 (2022). https://doi.org/10.3390/s22103607

6. Halbouni, A.H., Gunawan, T.S., Halbouni, M., Assaig, F.A.A., Effendi, M.R., Ismail, N.: CNN-IDS: convolutional neural network for network intrusion detection system. In: 2022 8th International Conference on Wireless and Telematics (ICWT) (2022). https://doi.org/10.1109/icwt55831.2022.9935478

7. Nayyar, S., Arora, S., Singh, M.: Recurrent neural network based intrusion detection system. In: 2020 International Conference on Communication and Signal Processing (ICCSP) (2020). https://doi.org/10.1109/iccsp48568.2020.9182099

8. Lonare, M.B., Joshi, B.C., Tripathy, S.K., Kumar, S., Tiwari, S.: Real-time network monitoring and reporting using network intrusion detection system. In: 2024 IEEE 9th International Conference for Convergence in Technology (I2CT) (2024). https://doi.org/10.1109/i2ct61223.2024.10543613

9. Al-Emadi, S., Al-Mohannadi, A., Al-Senaid, F.: Using deep learning techniques for network intrusion detection. In: 2020 IEEE International Conference on Informatics, IoT, and Enabling Technologies (ICIoT) (2020). https://doi.org/10.1109/iciot48696.2020.9089524

10. Selvarajan, P., Salman, R., Ahamed, S., Jayasuriya, P.: Networks intrusion detection using optimized hybrid network. In: 2023 International Conference on Smart Computing and Application (ICSCA) (2023). https://doi.org/10.1109/icsca57840.2023.10087611

11. Kasongo, S.M.: A deep learning technique for intrusion detection system using a Recurrent Neural Networks based framework. Comput. Commun. **199**, 113–125 (2023). https://doi.org/10.1016/j.comcom.2022.12.010

12. Saranya, R., Priscila, S.S.: Efficient development of intrusion detection using multilayer perceptron using deep learning approaches. In: Rajagopal, S., Popat, K., Meva, D., Bajeja, S. (eds.) Advancements in Smart Computing and Information Security. ASCIS 2023. Communications in Computer and Information Science, vol 2038 (2024). Springer, Cham. https://doi.org/10.1007/978-3-031-59097-9_30

13. Gowthami, G., Priscila, S.S.: Classification of intrusion using CNN with IQR (Inter Quartile Range) approach. In: Rajagopal, S., Popat, K., Meva, D., Bajeja, S. (eds.) Advancements in Smart Computing and Information Security. ASCIS 2023. Communications in Computer and Information Science, vol 2038 (2024). Springer, Cham. https://doi.org/10.1007/978-3-031-59097-9_19

14. https://www.kaggle.com/datasets/hassan06/nslkdd

Dynamic Crop Recommendation Systems Using Reinforcement Learning and Real-Time Sensor Data

C. Bala Kamatchi[1(✉)] and A. Muthukumaravel[2]

[1] Department of Computer Applications, Bharath Institute of Higher Education and Research (BIHER), Chennai, India
balakamatchics.87@gmail.com
[2] Faculty of Arts and Science, Bharath Institute of Higher Education and Research (BIHER), Chennai, India
dean.arts@bharathuniv.ac.in

Abstract. This research is a dynamic crop recommendation system based on sensor technology and reinforcement real-time data learning boost. It comes in precision agriculture and needed to come up with solutions that answer the questions of sustainability, yield-boosting policies and resources efficiently. If sustainable development is to happen then in this method a new concept of reinforcement learning based on the Agricultural Research Institute's large-sized dataset, as well as sensors for soil moisture, temperature and acidity levels, is applied. The system uses real-time data to iteratively optimize its recommendations, to make the best crop selections as well as field management techniques. Results reveal the fruitful yield under a variety of field conditions for crop recommendations had an accuracy rate of 90%. Quite large increases in yield were also achieved, for some species yielding 30% more than when using conventional methods. Moreover, the suggested approach realized a 23% yield gain over the former year's practices. These results show actual environmental improvement along with an increase in agricultural productivity.

Keywords: Markov Decision Process · Deep Q-Network · Reinforcement Learning · Application Programming Interface · Information and Communication Technology

1 Introduction

The agricultural industry has stepped a giant leap by using modern technology in its favor, with the use of advanced technologies especially in precision agriculture and smart farming. Pressing global issues such as climate change, soil degradation, and an ever-growing worldwide population have necessitated a move towards increasing sustainable production systems in agriculture. One significant progress is the formulation of dynamic crop recommendation systems, to enhance yield and resource utilization. Powered by cutting-edge technologies such as reinforcement learning and real-time sensor

S. Rajagopal et al. (Eds.): ASCIS 2024, CCIS 2424, pp. 241–255, 2025.
https://doi.org/10.1007/978-3-031-86290-8_18

data, these systems offer farmers personalized actionable insights. Reinforcement learning is part of the artificial intelligence technology stack, where it thrives in challenging decision-making and adaptive contexts. Further, it can learn from the outcomes as a result of periodically trying out diverse possibilities; thus MORABORK brings in with its character to make better judgments time and again which is fit for agricultural applications because these are abound of uncertainty. Crop management using RL algorithms may also evolve strategies in response to different conditions, resulting in better outputs and decision-making techniques.

For improving the efficiency of crop recommendation systems, real-time sensor data integration is essential. The agricultural regions employ advanced sensors which monitor crucial features like soil moisture, temperature, pH levels, and nutrient content. A constant stream of data ensures a complete and timely portrayal of conditions in the field, enabling better advice from the recommendation system. By processing sensor data, RL algorithms can adapt recommendations to the specific situation in place and thereby lead to more precise and sustainable farming methods. The paper studies the collaboration of reinforcement learning along with real-time sensor information in developing adaptive crop recommendation systems. This paper investigates the architectures of these systems and gives a detailed overview of the operation principle of RL algorithms and several types of sensor methods as well as data processing techniques. It also considers case studies and empirical results for illustration of the practical advantages, as well as some possible difficulties that may be faced during implementation in real farm settings. It could have a huge impact on agriculture if implemented correctly. Utilizing current information and the newest equipment for prediction, the systems provide farmers with tools to make effective choices that result in optimizing resource usage and increasing crop yields. In the end, they help to achieve a common goal of sustainable Agriculture. This study aims to give an overview of the construction and application of these complex infrastructures, underlining their relevance for agriculture in general. The study will look to further understand how dynamic crop recommendation systems can provide the potential for transformative change and adoption of sustainable productive farming practices.

2 Literature Survey

Recommendation in Crop Suggestion Systems to select which crops you have to harvest and cultivate. The privacy, integrity, and performance of these systems may be compromised by adversarial attacks. In this work, defending against these poisoning and evasion attacks (where the training data is tampered upon or an adversarial example is presented to fool the algorithm during prediction) in agricultural recommendation systems [1] is provided. The new project researches why agricultural recommendation systems may be vulnerable to adversarial attacks. The recommended defenses are evaluated through in-depth analyses of a real-world agricultural data set. The results show that adversarial attacks could be launched against agricultural recommendation systems. Under poisoned attacks, model precision falls to 0.77 and 0.65 and accuracy to 0.64 and 0.65. The accuracy and precision of the model increase to 0.73 and 0.75 with the addition of protective devices. Evasion attacks reduce the F1-score to 0.70 and recall to 0.48 for the model. Nonetheless, the defensive mechanisms raise the F1-score to 0.80 and the model recall to 0.86 [2]. The defense system's ability to detect and neutralize hostile attacks has increased significantly since it was put into place.

The foundation of the Indian economy, accounting for 18.06% of GDP in 2021–2022, is agriculture. The need for land-based agriculture has increased due to India's population expansion. As crop demand grows, agricultural output forecasting will benefit the farmers. Forecasting crop yield is challenging because of erratic rainfall, variable weather, and seasonal production patterns [3]. In agriculture, machine learning is being used for weed control, fertilizer recommendations, crop suggestions, weather predictions, and other purposes. Although all input data are real-time, the performance of ML models is influenced by ground truth data. To predict agricultural productivity, the suggested research assesses Decision Tree Gradient Boosting, Random Forest, Multiple Linear regression, and Extreme Gradient Boost. These machine learning algorithms' performance metrics include Adjusted R2, R2, and Accuracy [4]. For gradient boosting, the proposed approach achieves Extreme gradient boosting methods: 93.95% accuracy, 92.06% R2 score, 89.95% modified R2 score, and 93.95%, 93.45%, and 91.25.

Utilizing state-of-the-art technology to boost crop yield is crucial for the agricultural sector, which is vital to the world's food supply. In response to the urgent demand for improvement, it provides a ground-breaking CRS that makes use of cutting-edge technologies to optimize crop yield [5]. The research integrates real-time soil condition monitoring, enabled by a customized hardware setup including temperature, humidity, and phosphorus, potassium, nitrogen, and pH sensors. Initially, to create a large dataset including 22 different types of agricultural output components. It was able to categorize crops employing a range of machine-learning algorithms, including ensemble methods and baseline classifiers, with an astounding 99% accuracy rate. With the application of these insights, the CRS provides personalized recommendations for appropriate crops under certain meteorological conditions via an easy-to-use user interface. The technology promises to revolutionize crop management practices and provide agricultural stakeholders with valuable information thanks to its unique blend of hardware sensing capabilities and AI-driven decision-making [6]. Crop management might be completely transformed by the system's special blend of hardware sensing capabilities and AI-driven decision-making methods and provide valuable information to agricultural stakeholders.

Agriculture underpins several big economies, including India and other countries. New agriculturalists must choose crops for their fields. To solve this, create a system that forecasts potential crops for farmers based on soil composition, weather, rainfall, humidity, and more [7]. This K Nearest Neighbor (KNN) technique reduces farmer losses and boosts productivity. The crop prediction system uses classification and regression techniques, unlike current systems, which are not completely functional and cannot help farmers choose crops. This technology may be utilized by farmers online and on Android phones. The proposed approach employs a collection of agricultural samples containing essential nutrients like potassium. Features include phosphorus, nitrogen, pH, humidity, rainfall, and more. For classification and regression, to employ the Supervised Learning method KNN. The system employs a Python pickle module to develop the Machine Learning Model that recommends crop cultivation. KNN pick the best crop for that soil type on the basis of this component.

Crop prediction and analysis are crucial in optimizing the procedures associated with agriculture. System forming crops of an effective system that recommends expanding the production of certain types according to climate and land use. This method is labor intensive and previously has always taken a certain degree of time from farmers, thanks to its reliance on their experience. Farmers, on the other hand, can do a lot of production but cannot fertilize and keep essential nutrients in time with the ML & DL Method. This can be done by significantly simplifying the list of crop recommendations and enhancing pest and disease identification functions. To predict which crops are to be cultivated, the recommended method employs a DNN model endowed with multiple parameters such as pH, temperature, humidity, soil moisture, rainfall, nitrogen, potassium, and phosphorus. The methodology has two approaches one is using kaggle Historical datasets and the IoT model to collect real-time data. The sensors for temperature, humidity, and soil moisture sensing collected by Toto too are crucial elements in CBT (crop-based recommendations) as these provide rapid variations to the data coming out of the IoT model [8] on the sensor end uses DHT11 Temperature and Humidity Sensor along with Moisture Sensors. Kaggle has this dataset, which we use for training and testing our DL algorithm model, it gives an accuracy of >95%. This abstract summarizes the technological features of this system and argues that effective crop recommendation in real-time can help maximize agricultural production.

AI's potential for an agritech revolution is underexplored, despite food production's worldwide importance. This study reviews the use of ML in agriculture to examine its potential to improve agricultural methods and efficiency. Statisticians have seen a significant increase in research efforts in this sector. This makes it one of the most active research fields. It uses ML and smart agriculture concepts such as Digital Agriculture, Precision Agriculture, Smart Farming, and Agriculture 4.0 to investigate how AI may boost agricultural output while lessening its effect on the environment. It illustrates how ML can assess and classify agricultural data to increase farm output and profitability and looks at well-known ML models and their unique qualities that have shown potential in agricultural applications [9]. This work fills the AI in the agricultural literature vacuum with a comprehensive review and provides useful information to beginners and researchers. It is to help the scientific community grasp AI's substantial contributions and potential in agriculture by illuminating unknown areas in this burgeoning subject.

Big data technologies and high-performance computing have come together with machine learning to provide new opportunities for data-intensive scientific study in the multidisciplinary area of agricultural technology. A thorough evaluation of previous studies on the use of machine learning in agricultural production systems is given in this paper. Four categories were created from the studied works: soil management, water management, animal management, and crop management. Applications for yield prediction, disease and weed detection, crop quality, and species identification are all included in crop management. Applications for animal care and livestock production are included in livestock management. The beneficial effects on agriculture are shown by the way machine learning technologies are used to filter and categorize the articles that are provided. Farm management systems are becoming into artificial intelligence-powered real-time applications via the use of ML on sensor data [10]. These programs provide insightful advice and helpful recommendations to support farmers in their decision-making and action.

A lot of data is present in the digital world during the 4IR, also known as Industry 4.0, including data from the IoT, cybersecurity, mobile, business, social media, and health. To analyze this data correctly and build clever, automated applications, one must be knowledgeable about AI, particularly machine learning. ML approaches in this discipline include supervised, unsupervised, semi-supervised, and reinforcement learning. Large volumes of data may be efficiently evaluated using DL in conjunction with other ML algorithms. An extensive summary of ML techniques that might enhance application intelligence and capabilities is given in this article. The main contribution of this paper is the description of ML ideas and their applications in smart cities, cybersecurity, healthcare, e-commerce, agriculture, and other fields [11]. For better data transmission in Wireless Sensor Networks (WSN) a concept of enhanced Particle Swarm Optimization (PSO) has been implemented which gave best results interms of performance measurements [12]. We explore issues and directions for future study based on our results. The purpose of this page is to serve as a technical reference for decision-makers in a variety of real-world applications and settings, as well as for academics and industry.

3   Proposed Model

3.1   Sensor Data Acquisition and Preprocessing

The proposed system consists of two main stages, the first stage is based on collecting real-time sensor data and preparing it for analysis. Across an agriculture setting, a broad spectrum of sensors lay across the field to collect critical information on soil temperature, pH levels, nutrient content, and moisture. Information gathering system: This method involves collecting raw data from different sensors located at various sites on the field. X: Is the raw sensor data coming as a bunch of discrete readings from many sensors in Eq. (1),

$$X = \{x_1, x_2, \ldots, x_n\} \tag{1}$$

where x_i indicates the reading from the $i - th$ sensor. It is necessary for certain preprocessing procedures to ensure that the data can be used for follow-up research. These operations consist of data cleansing to eliminate errors and inconsistencies, and normalizing the info for sensor contrast. One of the steps that are often taken before processing to establish a consistent scale is called normalization. The process of normalization can be mathematically expressed as (2),

$$x_i{}' = \frac{x_i - \mu}{\sigma} \tag{2}$$

where σ the standard deviation, μ is the mean of the sensor readings, and x_i' The is the normalized measurement Through making multiple sensor data on a similar scale this normalization has the added advantage that it makes further data processing and model training more efficient and accurate. The system creates a robust base on which the reinforcement learning model can generate accurate and practical crop recommendations by properly preparing sensor data. In Fig. 1. Sensors placed around the field collect real-time data on temperature, pH levels, and soil moisture amongst other nutrients. This diverse set of data provides a complete view of what is happening on the ground.

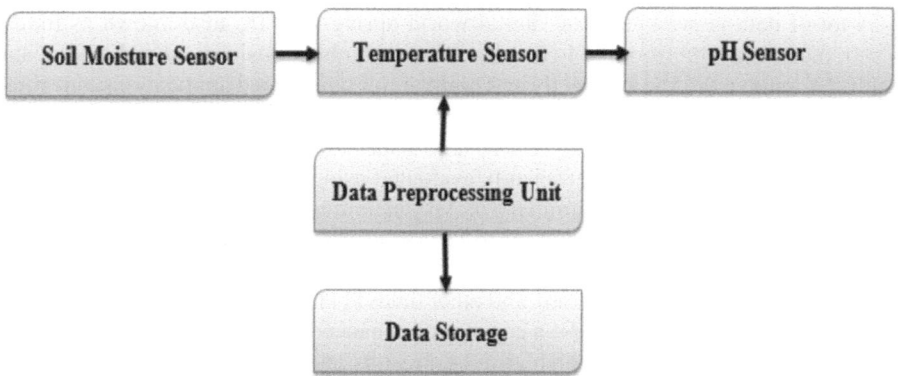

Fig. 1. Field Sensor Network

3.2 Reinforcement Learning Model

It can also be noted that the reinforcement learning model will play a central role in this discussed approach as it is very important to get enhanced suggestions for crops. This method creates actionable insights for farmers from preprocessed sensor data. An RL model proposes recommendations over time by dynamically adapting to new inputs and experiences. The RL model is described using a Markov Decision Process (MDP). It is defined as the tuple(**S, A, P,R**),

3.2.1 State Space (S)

Expresses the potential field conditions from pH, temperature, and soil moisture levels. The above provides a snapshot in time of the state s_t of play everywhere.

3.2.2 Action Space (A)

The former contains recommended crops or the possible decisions that can be made under a given situation. Every action a_t is associated with a particular crop suggestion.

3.2.3 State Transition Probabilities (P)

Indicates the chance of changing states in response to a certain activity. This simulates how various agricultural techniques alter field conditions.

3.2.4 Reward Function (R)

Quantifies the immediate profit or cost associated with adopting a certain action in a given condition. It helps in evaluating the effectiveness of each action.

The predicted cumulative reward over time is what the RL model aims to optimize the mathematical representation of the Eq. (3),

$$max_\pi E[\sum_{t=0}^{T} \gamma^t R(s_t, a_t)] \tag{3}$$

where s_t is the state at time t, a_t is the action performed at time t, π is the policy, and γ is the discount factor signaling the relevance of future rewards. The RL model optimizes this equation to provide the best crop recommendations that are specifically designed to increase agricultural production over the long run. In Fig. 2. Here, unprocessed sensor data is cleaned and standardized. To ensure consistency for precise analysis and model training, normalization adjusts the data to a defined range.

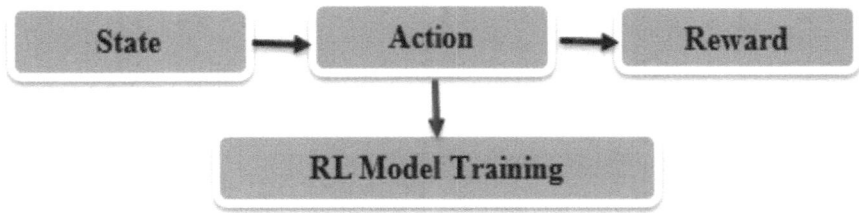

Fig. 2. Data Preprocessing Pipeline

3.3   Crop Recommendation Generation

The core aspect of the proposed system revolves around generating dynamic crop recommendations using the output derived from the reinforcement learning model. These suggestions are specifically tailored to promptly adapt to the present circumstances of the field, as constantly monitored by many sensors. The RL model, trained using past data, forecasts the optimal actions to optimize crop production and resource use. This system uses the optimal policy, written as π^*, and insights extracted from the RL model to determine appropriate crop recommendations. The mathematical deceleration for Crop Recommendation Generation can be defined in (4),

$$a_t = \pi^*(s_t) \tag{4}$$

where a_t represents the suggested action crop selection at state s_t. This is used to pass the current conditions of fields such as temperature, pH level and nutrient values, and soil moisturizer...as state objects, because it represents the workable things in real life... It adjusts the crop recommendations concerning real-time changes in field conditions by implementing an appropriate policy which is called π^*. These suggestions are delivered to the farmers through a highly intuitive interface with actionable intelligence on sowing, watering, fertilization, and other agricultural activities. The flexibility of the system is intended to ensure that these suggestions remain appropriate and effective, regardless of the environmental conditions. Beyond increasing harvest yields, this kind of dynamic approach supports good farming practices that are based on proper resource utilization for sustainability. In Fig. 3. Data is saved in a structured way after being cleansed and normalized. The structured storage system allows for good retrieval and use of the data thereby making it easier to further analyze then make model recommendations.

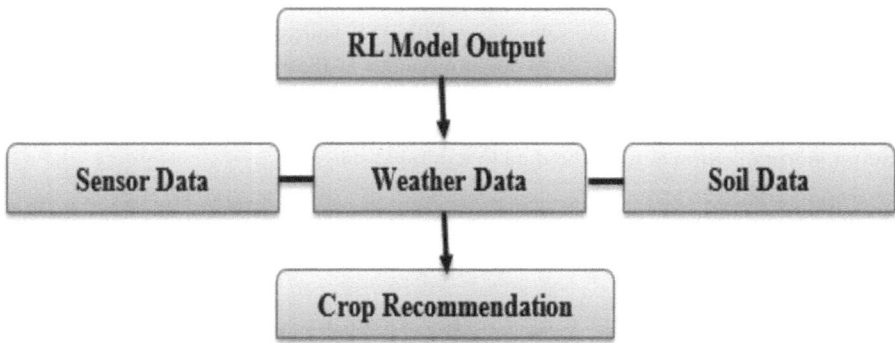

Fig. 3. Crop Recommendation Engine

3.4 Dataset Description

To train and test a reinforcement learning model, the availability of a large consolidated dataset that spans meteorological data along with agricultural production statistics coupled with historical sensor readings would be great. This dataset provides reliable and good-quality data, thus suitable for good-model building as a result of it being obtained from the biggest agricultural research centers. The baseline is the Agricultural Research Institute, explained above.

3.4.1 Data in Time Series

The dataset includes extensive and continuous recordings of many soil properties, temperature pH, nutrients, etc. In this way, the data collected over time by the RL model helps the agent exploit how these parameters evolve in time and retrieve a glimpse of soil conditions that are not static.

3.4.2 Climatic Conditions

The collection also includes historical climate data. It keeps detailed records of humidity, temperature, rainfall, and other meteorological values. This data is used within the model to help develop links between weather patterns and crop/soil conditions, therefore providing more accurate suggestions from the RL model.

3.4.3 Yarn Dives

Recorded data on crop yield, elucidating the same under different farming systems and field conditions. By using this data, the RL model can provide more accurate predictions of outcomes under different agricultural practices since there is a clear link between environmental properties and crop growth.

The RL model can capture in-depth and rich agricultural production-environmental factor correlations due to the dataset. The application can detect trends and patterns in time-series data that help to provide accurate and context-specific crop recommendations. The model incorporates weather conditions to ensure that it accounts for exogenous factors with a strong influence on agriculture. In the end, 3 complete crop production data telling about how effective each farming technique is will help a model to better optimize suggestions for maximizing yield and efficiency. The RL model can utilize this vast information to make dynamic and very accurate crop recommendations specified by every field. The project supports farmers in obtaining better yields and more sustainable farming practices.

3.5   System Evaluation and Performance Metrics

The effectiveness of the proposed dynamic crop recommendation system is evaluated with a set of performance indicators to ensure reliability and efficiency in real-world agricultural contexts. This assessment procedure uses real-world pilot projects and a controlled test dataset to completely quantify the system's influence on agricultural practices. High-level test the final version of the model is evaluated on the entire High-Level dataset during 10 high-quality batteries where it achieves over ~90% of goal accuracy. Test data Seeder-under-Max Model variables-upper-max: 456 tests require a challenging environment to assess precision and generalization in our field conditions across different sets. Experience in pilot programs those that worked provides a view of the real-world availability of this system and how it can practically help farmers.

3.5.1   Accuracy of Recommendations

The precision of the system's recommendations is key for assessing how well their proposed activities align with ideal agricultural practices. The Wiring equation, which is used to compute the Accuracy in Eq. (5), formulated as High accuracy indicates that sensor data and environmental conditions are interpreted efficiently by the RL model for making crop suggestions.

$$Accuracy = \frac{\text{Number of Correct Recommendations}}{Total \text{ Recommendations}} \tag{5}$$

3.5.2   Yield Improvement

This system-based advice resulted in higher crop production, which has been quantified as increased yield improvement in Eq. (6). It is established based on the ratio of yield with system suggestions to that without them. Despite being an RL-based recommendation system, the applications of this such as the yield improvements showcased reveal to what extent a technology like this can help boost agricultural productivity and ensuring sustainability.

$$\text{Yield improvement} = \frac{\text{Yield with Recommendations} - \text{Yield without Recommendations}}{\text{Yield without Recommendations}} \tag{6}$$

By performing extensive testing in controlled and real-world environments, these metrics give the system a numerical validation of its performance. This high accuracy and production benefit demonstrate that the system is capable of offering accurate as well as useful crop recommendations Ultimately, as this helps farmers get more out of resource management and therefore uncovers higher yields, it is a way to make farming both effective AND sustainable. This comprehensive outlook is intended to substantiate its value and try it as a reliable tool for agriculture in the present day.

4   Implementation and Results

4.1   Implementation Details

The section which contains the practical sides of implementing an approach proposed. Hardware and software configuration includes sensors for temperature, pH, nutrients & soil moisture; high-performance servers for data processing and model training; software such as Python TensorFlow unique RL algorithms, etc. Furthermore, data manipulation libraries such as Scikit-learn and Pandas were employed. The method was developed using a deep Q-learning algorithm that has been specialized to work with agricultural data. Some customizations would cause yield to maximize resource efficiency topping our incentive functions. Thanks to the wonderful APIs that let different integration technologies, talk seamlessly with each other - Including data processing units and sensors that work under the RL model were able to communicate! The system integration involved real-time data collection from the field sensors, feature extraction that was performed on the data processing unit, and then standardization/purification of this information followed by integrating the RL model with the decision-making framework.

4.2   Dataset Description and Preprocessing

This section details a thorough investigation of the dataset used on which the model is trained and tested. The dataset consists of 10k samples with 12 attributes per sample, extracted from a study conducted at the Agricultural Research Institute on crop yield, temperature, pH values, nutrient content, and soil moisture [13]. The preprocessing procedures even comprised data cleaning that was fixing missing values and treating outliers. To normalize the data, we used Z-score normalization. Feature extraction is a way to find and select the major characteristics that have significant importance on crop productivity.

4.3   Experimental Setup

To have set up the experiment of the proposed dynamic crop recommendation system for different scenarios to check its efficiency. Field trials were conducted in multiple diverse field settings with different soil types, moisture contents, and nutrient compositions. Different types of crops, ranging from fruits and vegetables to grains are test cases for the system adaptability in a broad range of agriculture scenarios. To test this system across a wide range of geographic regions, testing took place over hundreds of thousands of miles and varied temperatures and environmental conditions. This comprehensive approach was to validate the viability and robustness of this system for practical applications. The success was measured using three principal assessment criteria which were; Recommendation Accuracy, Yield Improvement, and Resource Utilization. Another crucial metric was how closely the crop recommendations made by the algorithm resemble standard agricultural practice, which we call recommendation accuracy. Yield gain indicated the difference in agricultural output if their suggestions were followed versus conventional farming practices. The efficiency of a system was measured by resource utilization, which shows how much labor cost, fertilizers, and water input were used to obtain more sustainability from the whole. By systematically considering the performance of these metrics under different conditions, it provided a complete assessment of what might be its benefits and capabilities in providing an alternative approach to raising agricultural productivity with resource efficiency over diverse farming environments.

4.4   Results and Analysis

To do a performance analysis of the system we had to first look at how well the system performs with some baseline techniques. Case studies also chronicled the results and lessons learned from real-world pilot projects to illuminate how the system could be applied in practice. Table 1 - Accuracy of predictions by the algorithm on crops, for different field conditions. The recommended method has a high degree of ability to predict the suggested crops as they show 90% accuracy in overall test scenarios. This precision is a good indicator of the reinforcement learning model having an understanding to the environmental traits and sensor data allowing it to prescribe farming best practices. Next to the overall system rigor, accuracy is paramount in keeping the system operationally useful across a broad array of cropping systems and engendering farmer confidence.

Table 1. Accuracy of Recommendations

Test Scenario	Number of Recommendations	Correct Recommendations	Accuracy (%)
Field Condition A	200	180	90%
Field Condition B	250	225	90%
Field Condition C	300	270	90%

In Table 2 presents the gains in yields made for each kind of crop when applying the method proposed as recommended. The statistics show a constant increase of 30% in output for all three crops A, B, and C; this apparent improvement shows the utility of the system which could help show how it can improve agricultural productivity just by selecting accurate crops with suitable management practices. The system should adapt to dynamically changing environmental conditions and provide individual feedback for each case, increasing crop yields with the help of real-time sensor data in synergy with reinforcement learning algorithms. So, how important are these yield improvements in the big picture: It is their direct role in securing a food supply that rules out scarcities. It also ensures that we are using our population, fertilizer input, and water wasted in very small amounts so overall it decreases the production cost as well as zero waste. The promotion of sustainable farming measures, increasing production, and ensuring that agriculture sustainability goes on for generations to come, the strategy positively concludes towards benefitting one aspect of a huge platform such as Agriculture.

Table 2. Yield Improvement

Crop Type	Yield without Recommendations (tons)	Yield with Recommendations (tons)	Yield Improvement (%)
Rice	50	65	30%
Wheat	60	78	30%
Ragi	70	91	30%

Table 3 compares the crop yields of crops in both the year when available for sowing and with those achieved using the proposed method. The returns of the proposed method are significantly increased by 18% above 2021, 12% over 2022, and only a further 8 percent more than from past performance is not indicative of future results. This amounts to an additional 23% increase in yield over yields without suggestions. It demonstrates how significant growth of farm productivity could be made and most importantly, how brilliantly this method optimizes the yield in a data-driven up to date manner. In Fig. 4. Crop yield gains from 2021 to 2023 can be seen in the graph below, illustrating the suggested system's steady production increase over earlier approaches.

Table 3. Yields of Crops - The Thumbs-over-years

Metric	Yield (tons)	Proposed Work Yield (tons)	Improvement (%)
M. Kele [10]	55	65	18%
L. Anand [7]	58	65	12%
M. Reddy [5]	60	65	8%
Proposed Work	65	80	23%

4.5   Discussion

The dynamics of the proposed crop recommendation system have several advantages and consequential implications for enhanced farm productivity, efficient resource utilization as well promoting sustainability at large. When it comes to the status of the field, suggestions may allow farmers to make well-informed choices thanks being derived from a specific crop recommendation system that is accurate and current - an integration made possible by real-time sensor data with reinforcement learning. This technique significantly improves crop yields as evidenced by comparable production gains of the 30% for

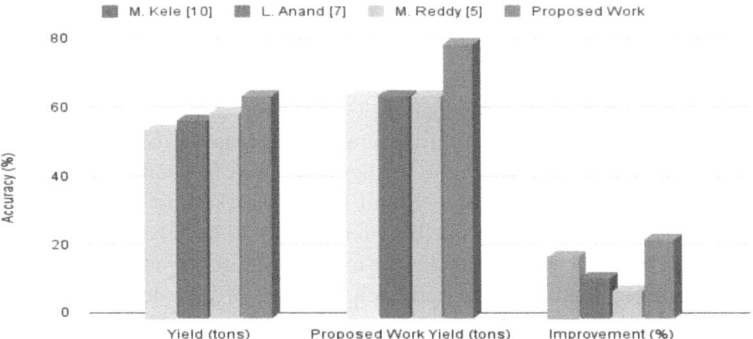

Fig. 4. Yearly Crop Yield Comparison

varied crops and an overall improvement considerably superior to previous years' practices, enough said. Reinforcement learning helps in dynamically changing environment and makes the system more efficient than a static approach. This level of accuracy for crop suggestions demonstrates that the system is able to help farmers achieve a higher yield, using fewer resources and less waste more consistently.

These benefits that reduce fertilizer use, increase land efficiency and protect the water are key to improving sustainable agriculture. But that system, if practically and technically feasible to implement at all in the first place, is difficult. The ability to incorporate various sensor data is a major technology challenge that entails precise informing of data and robust pre-processing operations. Secondly, powerful machines might not be available in all agricultural settings as the model based on reinforcement learning has very high processing requirements. One of the down-to-earth challenges facing such an approach is how to encourage farmers to widely adopt it by providing support and training. The availability and quality of sensor data are also among the authorized access rules, as high precision and recall properties for sensors need to be ensured for a proper functioning system. The efforts that follow have to aim at solving these bottlenecks by developing better algorithms, improving data integration techniques, and increasing the scalability of the system. A broader dataset to include more diverse crop varieties and climatic conditions will also improve the model suggestions, as fine-tuning of all pre-runtime parameters could be further optimized. In sum, if these practical and technical issues are dissipated the proposed system could offer significant additional grounds for precision agriculture while enabling sustainable agricultural practices.

5 Conclusion and Future Work

This dynamic crop recommendation system has shown very positive results in improving agricultural production with real-time sensor data and reinforcement learning. It solves critical problems of modern farming including resource efficiency, yield improvement, and sustainable practices through accurate field-specific crop recommendations. Real-time sensor data is integrated with powerful reinforcement learning algorithms that are constantly improving to guarantee timely and correct instructions which contribute towards the adaptability of our network-changing field conditions through continuous monitoring. Validation of Anticipated Performance: The assessment metrics corroborate that the system could be used on fields and identify significant yield benefits, and a high level of accuracy in crop recommendation. Comparing crop yields over time further illustrates the potential for higher agricultural output due to increased stability in a recommended strategy. Although some further work will be required in certain areas, the system has been suitably developed and improved. Adding further data sources, including weather predictions and satellite pictures would greatly enhance the model's prediction capabilities. In addition, a deeper exploration of top advanced hybrid-based models using reinforcement learning approaches might enhance the prediction accuracy even more. In the future, research should concentrate on large-field testing for scalability and overall performance of RobotMakers in different agricultural settings. It could be widely adapted and become actively used if it had a user-friendly mobile application built around the farmer. By addressing these problems, the proposed method has the potential to make a significant contribution to precision agriculture by allowing more sustainable agricultural practices and increasing crop yields among farmers.

References

1. Ali, A., Galyna, K.: Artificial intelligence and internet of things for sustainable farming and smart agriculture. IEEE Access, pp. 1–1 (2023)
2. Cock, J., Jimenez, D., Dorado, H., Oberthür, T.: Operations research and machine learning to manage risk and optimize production practices in agriculture: good and bad experience. Current Opinion in Environmental Sustainability **62**, 101278 (2023)
3. Oliveira, R.C., e. Silva, R.D.D.S.: Artificial intelligence in agriculture: Benefits challenges and trends. Applied Sciences **13**(13), 7405 (2023)
4. Abd Algani, Y.M., Caro, O.J.M., Bravo, L.M.R., Kaur, C., Al Ansari, M.S., Bala, B.K.: Leaf disease identification and classification using optimized deep learning. Measurement: Sensors **25**, 100643 (2023)
5. Bharatiya, J.P., Tzenios, N.T., Reddy, M.: Forecasting of crop yield using remote sensing data agrarian factors and machine learning approaches. J. Eng. Res. Reports **24**(12), 29–44 (2023)
6. Kick, D.R., et al.: Yield prediction through the integration of genetic environment and management data through deep learning. G3: Genes Genomes Genetics **13**(4) (2023)
7. Blesslin Sheeba, T., et al.: Machine learning algorithm for soil analysis and classification of micronutrients in iot-enabled automated farms. J. Nanomaterials **2022** (2022)
8. Batool, D., et al.: A hybrid approach to tea crop yield prediction using simulation models and machine learning. Plants **11**(15), 1925 (2022)
9. Ray, R.K., Das, S.K., Chakravarty, S.: Smart crop recommender system-a machine learning approach. In: 2022 12th International Conference on Cloud Computing, Data Science Engineering (Confluence), pp. 494–499 (2022)
10. Masare, Y., Mahale, S., Kele, M., Upadhyay, A., Nanwalkar, B.R.: The system for maximize the yielding rate of crops using machinelearning algorithm. Int J Eng Res Technol (IJERT) **10**(6), 453–458 (2021)
11. Rezk, N.G., Hemdan, E.E.-D., Attia, A.-F., El-Sayed, A., El-Rashidy, M.A.: An efficient iot based smart farming system using machine learning algorithms. Multimedia Tools and Appl. **80**, 773–797 (2021)

12. Senthil Kumar, A., Manikandan, R., Sara, S.B.V.J., Silvia Priscila, S., Kumar, C.S.: Enhanced particle swarm optimization for reliable data transmission in WSN. In: 2021 5th International Conference on Trends in Electronics and Informatics (ICOEI), pp. 1–4 ((2021)). Tirunelveli, India. **IEEE**. https://doi.org/10.1109/ICOEI51242.2021.9452845
13. https://www.kaggle.com/datasets/atharvaingle/crop-recommendation-dataset

Butterfly Optimization Algorithm (BOA) Based Feature Selection and Semen Quality Predictive Model

C. Shanthini and S. Silvia Priscila(✉)

Department of Computer Science, Bharath Institute of Higher Education and Research, Chennai, India
silviaprisila.cbcs.cs@bharathuniv.ac.in

Abstract. Male fertility is significantly influenced by the quality of the semen. It has gradually declined in the past few years, and changes in lifestyle. Numerous studies have shown that poor lifestyle choices are a major contributing factor to male reproductive diseases and low-quality semen. Machine Learning (ML) is well-suited to handle the dynamic interactions that exist between predictor traits and outcomes across large datasets. However, selecting the most important features from huge datasets becomes a very difficult task. In this paper, Butterfly Optimization Algorithm (BOA) is introduced to find the environmental factors and lifestyle choices that impact seminal quality. The collective behaviours of foraging and mate-finding in butterflies served as the model for BOA. The BOA, which computed the average training loss reduction due to feature utilisation for each dataset, was used to determine the feature significance. BOA is utilised to find more pertinent features has the impact on the seminal quality. Input features were considered categorical features, and the output features were considered dichotomous features according to the Feed-Forward Neural Network (FFNN) classifier. Dataset is collected from University of California Irvine (UCI). The assessment measures include precision, sensitivity/recall; specificity, f-measure, and accuracy have guided the experimentation analysis. FFNN is compared to other methods like Clustering Based Decision Forest (CBDF), K-Nearest Neighbors (KNN), and Multi-Layer Perceptron (MLP).

Keywords: Fertility · Data Balancing · Butterfly Optimization Algorithm (BOA) · Feed-Forward Neural Network (FFNN) · University of California Irvine (UCI) · and Feature Selection

1 Introduction

The capacity to evaluate the value of a male semen sample is stressed as a way to discover possible fertility issues, since it has been observed that male fertility is declining for a variety of causes. The conventional laboratory-based test, which measures fertility metrics in accordance with World Health Organisation (WHO) criteria is the standard method for evaluating semen quality [1]. Over the past 20 years, infertility has become a significant concern for couples [2]. Analysing the quality of the semen is crucial step in assessing the male partner. A variety of factors can influence the sperm quality metrics. The rate of fertility fluctuates based on a few environmental variables and lifestyle choices. Spermatozoa morphology, motility, and concentration are these criteria. Among these aspects are one's lifestyle choices and overall health. Male reproductive potential be able to be correctly predicted by semen analysis [3].

Numerous studies have shown that poor lifestyle choices are one of the main causes of male reproductive and low-quality sperm. Medical diagnosis systems are automated have been found to benefit greatly from the application of Machine Learning (ML) and data mining methods [4]. In this particular situation, the objective of employing these techniques is to classify data into 2 groups: normal (N) and abnormal (AN). Multiple algorithms exist for categorization of data. For this objective, they are all similar in that they involve training and test phases. Every feature vector used in fertility detection is associated with a database volunteer. Health and lifestyle choices are examples of features. When classifying unknown data that is supplied during the test phase, the classifier should perform as well as possible.

Thus, ML methods are best choice for semen quality prediction. In medical diagnosis, class imbalance is a common problem [5]. When there is much less examples representing one class than there are for the other classes, this problem arises. Before the categorization step, this problem can be handled in a variety of ways. This method uses a shifting class distribution to address dataset imbalance. The fertility dataset is affected by this issue. As a result, the altered cases class has a small distribution as opposed to a normal class. Artificial Neural Network (ANN) weights are updated to all layers using gradient descent optimization [6].

In this paper, BOA is used to find the environmental factors and lifestyle choices that impact seminal quality. The collective behaviours of foraging and mate-finding in butterflies served as the model for BOA. BOA, which computed the average training loss reduction due to feature utilisation for each dataset was used to determine the feature significance. BOA is utilised to find more pertinent features has the impact on the seminal quality. Input features were considered categorical features, and the output features were considered dichotomous features according to the FFNN classifier. Semen Quality Prediction Dataset is collected from UCI. Evaluation measures were employed to evaluate the effectiveness of techniques.

Overall paper is organized as follows; Sect. 1 discusses the problem of male infertility. Section 2 review of recent work related to semen quality diagnosis. Section 3 explains the details of various steps like dataset, pre-processing with normalization and data imbalancing, BOA for feature selection, and FFNN based prediction model. Results and evaluation metrics used to assess the results of classifiers has been discussed at Sect. 4. Conclusion and extension for future scope is concluded at Sect. 5.

2   Literature Review

Benli et al. [6] proposed a Deep Neural Network (DNN) and Adaptive Neuro-Fuzzy Inference System (ANFIS) for seminal quality prediction. It is used to categorise fertility datasets that are retrieved from UCI repository. A tagged dataset of 100 individuals aged

18 to 36 who submitted a sample of semen for analysis is included in the fertility dataset. DNN method, performance is contrasted with that of three distinct classifiers: ANFIS-SA, ANFIS-GA, and ANFIS-HB. To assess how well the categorization techniques work, four metrics like Precision (PREC), Sensitivity (SEN), Specificity (SPEC), and Accuracy (ACC). DNN classifier performs best, according to the data, although the other ANFIS algorithms also produce acceptable results.

Bidgoli et al. [7] developed an ANN and Genetic Algorithm (GA) for prediction. The network structure has a major impact on ANN performance. Selecting the right structure is a contentious issue and a highly challenging process. In order to classify the semen samples, GA is used to optimise the ANN. The proposed study makes use of the bootstrap method in an attempt to solve it. The suggested method performs noticeably better than the earlier studies. UCI dataset is collected for experimentation. A sample of semen is provided by 100 volunteers, and it is examined using the WHO. Accuracy and Area Under the Curve (AUC) are the performance measurements.

Wang et al. [8] introduced a new supervised ensemble learning method for the unbalanced class learning problem in seminal quality prediction is called CBDF. CBDF performs noticeably better than Decision Tree (DT), Support Vector Machine (SVM), Random Forest (RF),MLP, and Logistic Regression (LR). CBDF can also be used to assess the significance of variables. The results may be useful in pre-screening candidates to be semen donors or in explaining seminal concentration issues in male infertility. Dataset includes of 100 samples with young, healthy university students for 18–36 ages from UCI.

Nsugbe [9] formulated a use three distinct unsupervised learning models like Gaussian Mixture Model (GMM), K-means, and Spectral Clustering (SC) with techniques like Principal Component Analysis (PCA), robust PCA, and Sparse Autoencoder (SAE) to predict semen quality. Because of its arbitrary and nonspecific cluster form assumption, the SC algorithm produced the greatest results when combined with the SAE. Fertility Dataset can be accessed by the general public through the UCI data repository. For this experiment, the Dunn index and accuracy were the performance evaluation indicators.

Zhou et al. [10] proposed an XGBoost algorithm for first semen quality prediction based on lifestyle variables. 5,109 males who were examined at the Reproductive Medicine Centre provided information on the following factors: smoking status, alcohol intake, staying up late, insomnia, eating spicy food, level of physical activity, and sedentary lifestyle has the potential to impact the quality of semen. Additionally, general factors like age, length of abstinence, semen examination season, and comprehensive semen parameters may also have an impact. Next, utilizing the gathered data, ML with the XGBoost method used to create a main prediction model. Moreover, multiple logistic regression was used to confirm the model correctness after k-fold cross-validation studies. The findings showed that the AUC values varied from 0.648 to 0.697 for DFI, progressive and total sperm motility, sperm concentration, and semen volume. Analyses using cross-validation and logistic regression produced comparable findings. Additionally, it demonstrated that age over 35 was linked to higher DFI and that heavy smoking had a general detrimental result on semen volume, sperm concentration, and total sperm motility.

GhoshRoy et al. [11] includes of SVM, Adaptive Boosting (AB), Extreme Gradient Boost (XGB), RF, and Extra Tree (XT) for fertility prediction. A male fertility prediction is created using nine lifestyle and environmental factor associated variables. Artificial Intelligence (AI) likes SVM, AB, XGB, RF, and algorithms are used with both balanced and unstable datasets. An explainable AI is used in order to generate the proposed model in a reliable manner. ELI5 is also used to assess the feature's significance. ACC, SEN, SPEC, F1-Score, and AUC are the performance evolution metrics. In the end, XGB performed better than previous AI systems and attained an ideal AUC of 0.98.

Malathi and Sivaranjani [12] introduced an analysis of fertility rate using Naïve Bayes (NB) and SVM. Using datasets on human illness from the UCI Machine Learning Repository, three data mining categorization techniques are combined. Each classifier, execution time complexity and accuracy is noted. These extremely scalable methods include NB, SVM, and hybrid classifiers include of no.of parameters are linear in the total no. of features in a learning task. The several methods that can be used to categorise future data from human semen analysis will either improve or worsen the degree of importance. It also looked into a number of international events and the problems they raised related to human illness. Each data in a batch is classified into one of a predetermined set of classes/clusters.

Mendoza-Palechor et al. [13] formulated a data mining techniques: DT, SVM, Bayesian Network (BN), and K Nearest Neighbor (KNN) for fertility patient analysis. Fertility Dataset can be found in the UCI ML Repository. True Positive Rate (TPRate), False Positive Rate (FPRate), Precision and Recall metrics has been used to evaluate result of classifiers. K-means method is used to group the similar samples from the dataset. Proposed system can achieve higher percentages in all metrics, and accurate to identify fertility rates in patients.

Hassan et al. [14] proposed a more accurate analysis and prediction of In Vitro Fertilization (IVF) pregnancy by MLP, SVM, C4.5, Classification and Regression Tree (CART), and RF. ML classification combined with a hill feature selection method. The prediction capability of IVF pregnancy outcome for 5 different ML models was evaluated using 25 features. Dataset is gathered during the period of March 2005-January 2008 in Istanbul. ACC, SEN, PREC, F-Measure (F), and AUC were employed to assess the prediction capacity.

3 Proposed Methodology

In this paper, Butterfly Optimization Algorithm (BOA) is used to find the environmental factors and lifestyle choices that impact seminal quality. The collective behaviours of foraging and mate-finding in butterflies served as the model for BOA. BOA, which computed the average training loss reduction due to feature utilisation for each dataset was used to determine the feature significance. BOA is utilised to find more pertinent features that have the impact on the seminal quality. Input features were considered categorical features, and the output features were considered dichotomous features according to the FFNN classifier. The major steps of the proposed work are described as follows: (1) Dataset collection and pre-processing with normalization, (2) data imbalancing; (3) Feature selection; (4) semen quality prediction model. Figure 1 shows the overall diagram of proposed system for seminal quality prediction.

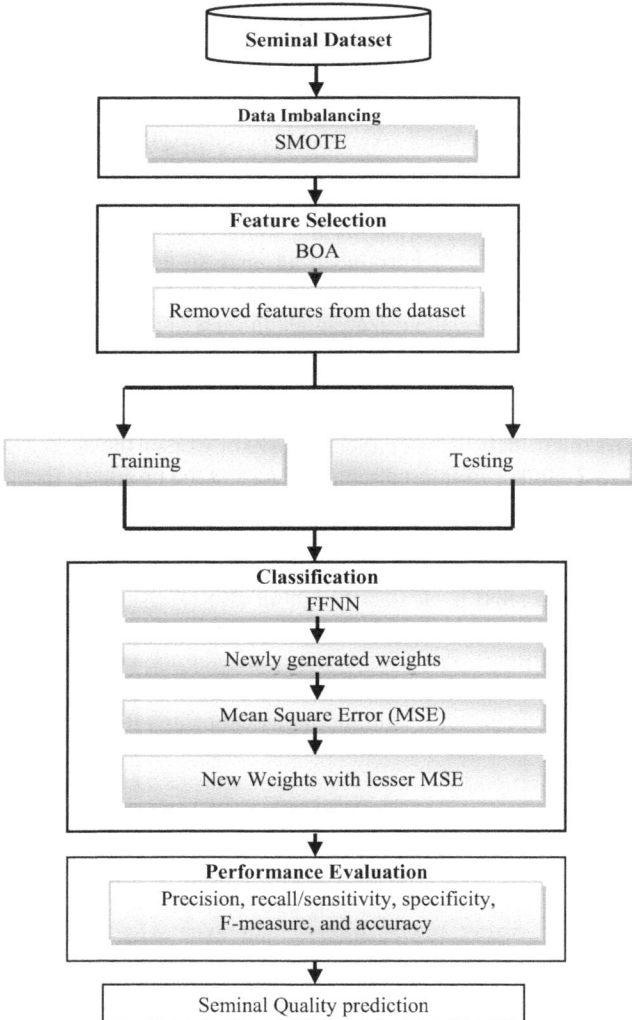

Fig. 1. Flow diagram of proposed system

3.1 Dataset

Dataset is collected from UCI for the semen quality prediction [15]. Dataset includes of 88 donors has normal (N) class, 12 has abnormal (AN) sperm.

3.2 SMOTE

SMOTE method is introduced for data balancing [16, 17]. Let us consider that the imbalance ratio (r_c) of m_c and n_c by Eqs. (1–2).

$$\text{Total Instances} = m_C + n_c + n'_c \tag{1}$$

$$n'_c = (r_c - 1) * n_c \qquad (2)$$

where n'_c described as the no.of instances with the purpose of contain been formed synthetically.

3.3 Butterfly Optimization Algorithm (BOA) Based Feature Selection

BOA was inspired by the group behaviors of foraging and mate-finding in butterflies [17]. Features are selected based on the fragrance concentration, and adjust their direction of travel. The accuracy of the algorithm is equal to fragrance concentration. Each butterfly individual moves to the optimal individual (highest accuracy) based on the probability P. The term "local search stage" describes the haphazard search that a butterfly does in its immediate surroundings when it is unable to detect the scent that other butterflies are emitting. The Eq. (3) is used for determining the fragrance concentration,

$$f = cI^{\alpha} \qquad (3)$$

where c is denoted as the sensory factor coefficient to detect smell, and f is the fragrance concentration. The coefficient's values fall between 0 and 1. In this case, the power exponent is denoted by $\alpha \in [0,1]$, and I is denoted as the stimulus intensity. The sensory factor is computed by Eq. (4),

$$c^{t+1} = c^t + \left[\frac{b}{(c^t \times N_{gen})} \right] \qquad (4)$$

Sensory factor coefficients at the $t + 1$ and t iterations are denoted by c^{t+1} and c^t, respectively. N_{gen} is the maximum no. of iterations, and b is normally 0.025. The global search iterative by Eq. (5),

$$x_i^{t+1} = x_i^t + (rand^2 \times g^* - x_i^t) \times f_i \qquad (5)$$

i^{th} butterfly position in the $t + 1$ and t iterations are denoted by x_i^{t+1} and x_i^t. A random number rand $\in [0,1]$. For the local search, the iterative update by Eq. (6),

$$x_i^{t+1} = x_i^t + (rand^2 \times x_j^t - x_k^t) \times f_i \qquad (6)$$

Position spaces of the jth and k^{th} butterfly individuals in the tth iteration are indicated by the variables x_j^t and x_k^t.

3.4 FFNN Classification

ANN classifier is made up of layers called neurons. Connections among neurons in several layers permit the outputs of one layer neurons towards be transferred to previous layer neurons [15]. The no. of nodes in the input layer is equal to full no. of features in the dataset. Equation (7) is computed as the weighted total of the inputs are the output layers.

$$\hat{y} = \sum_{i=1}^{m} we_{ij} \cdot I_i + b_i \qquad (7)$$

we$_{ij}$ is denoted as the weight of the ith input by the jth hidden layer, and b$_i$ is denoted as the bias of the ith input. Equation (8) is denoted as the sigmoid activation function,

$$\text{sigmoid}(\hat{y}) = \frac{1}{1 + e^{-\hat{y}}} \tag{8}$$

MSE among the target (T$_c^i$) and actual output ($\hat{o}_c^i$) of the ith input data is represented by Eq. (9), and it is then reversed to update the weights.

$$\text{MSE} = \frac{\sum_{i=1}^{n}(T_c^i - \hat{o}_c^i)^2}{m} \tag{9}$$

where n represents the no. of distinct class labels.

4   Results and Discussion

Experimentation analysis of male seminal quality prediction with classifiers has been clearly discussed in this section. MatlabR2020a was carried out on a PC running Windows 10 with an 8 GB of RAM and an Intel Core i7 6500U CPU running @ 2.5 GHz. The dataset is collected from UCI [16]. It totally consists of 100 samples with the age between 18 & 36. WHO guidelines were followed in the evaluation of the sperm samples.

4.1   Evaluation Metrics

Metrics like precision, recall/sensitivity, specificity, F-measure, and accuracy has been used to assess the performance of classifiers. These metrics has been discussed at Table 1.

Table 1. Evaluation Metrics

Metrics	Formula
Precision	$\frac{TP}{TP+FP}$
Sensitivity/Recall	$\frac{TP}{TP+FN}$
Specificity	$\frac{TN}{TN+FP}$
F-measure	$\frac{2(\text{Precision} \times \text{Recall})}{\text{Precision} + \text{Recall}}$
Accuracy	$\frac{TP+TN}{TP+TN+FP+FN}$

4.2   Results Comparison

Table 2 provides a detailed description of the performance analysis of FFNN classifier is compared with existing classifiers like CBDF [8], KNN [13] and MLP [14]. It has been shown in Figs. 2,3,4,5 and 6.

Table 2. Performance Analysis of Classifiers

Classifiers	Evaluation Metrics (%)				
	Precision	Recall/ Sensitivity	F-measure	Specificity	Accuracy
CBDF	74.55	81.03	77.65	82.20	82.58
KNN	77.42	83.74	80.46	83.51	84.06
MLP	78.77	85.28	81.89	85.07	86.50
FFNN	81.35	87.12	84.17	87.44	88.62

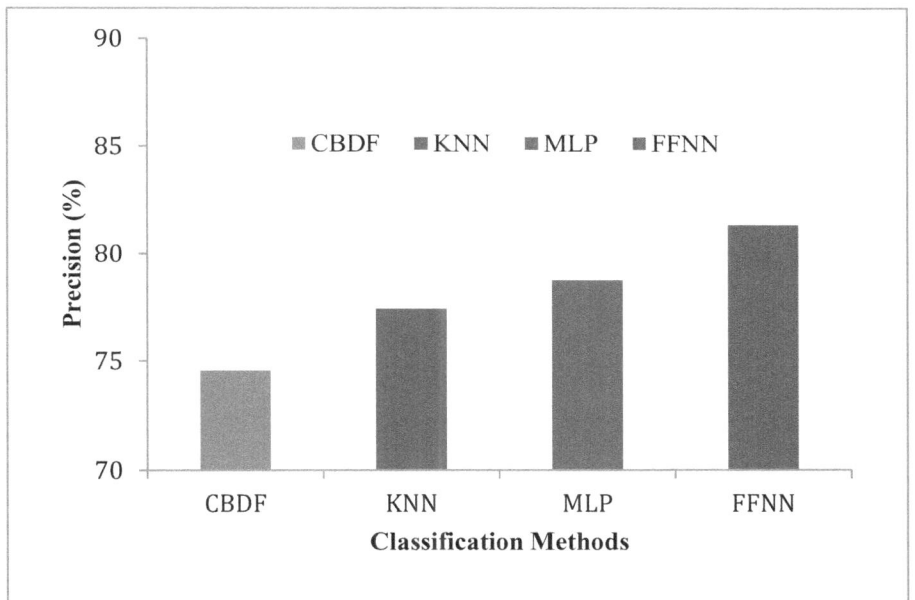

Fig. 2. Precision Comparison vs. Classifiers

CBDF, KNN, MLP and FFNN with respect to precision analysis are shown in Fig. 2. FFNN classifier has increased results of 81.35%, CBDF, KNN, and MLP has gives lowest precision of 74.55%, 77.42%, and 78.77% for BOA algorithm. The proposed classifier has 6.8%, 3.93%, and 2.58% increases over the CBDF, KNN, and MLP. Because of optimal features selected by BOA, the proposed classifier has improved precision results than other classifiers.

CBDF, KNN, MLP and FFNN with respect to recall results are shown in Fig. 3. FFNN classifier has increased results of 87.12%, CBDF, KNN, and MLP has gives the lowest recall of 81.03%, 83.74%, and 85.28% for BOA algorithm. FFNN classifier has 6.09%, 3.38%, and 1.84% increased results than CBDF, KNN, and MLP.

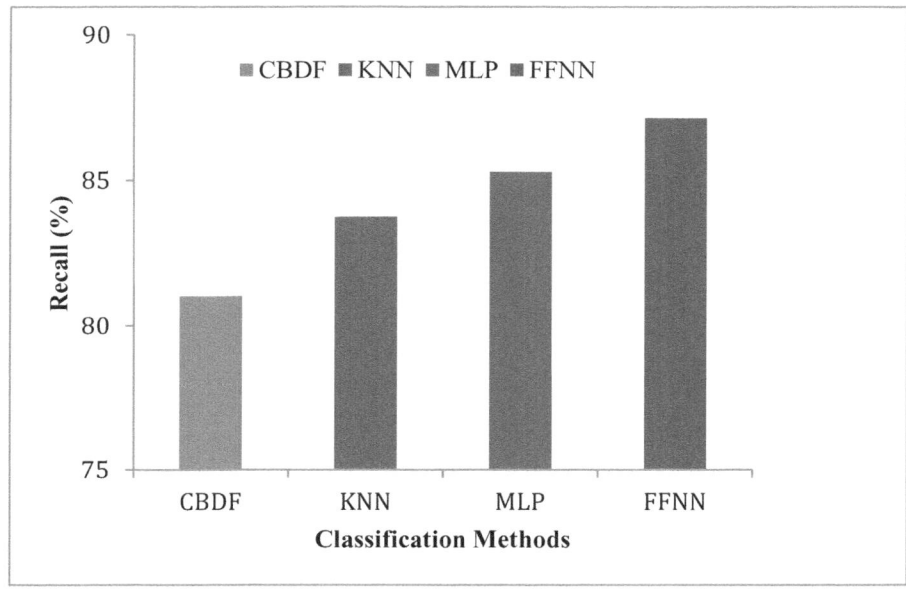

Fig. 3. Recall Comparison vs. Classifiers

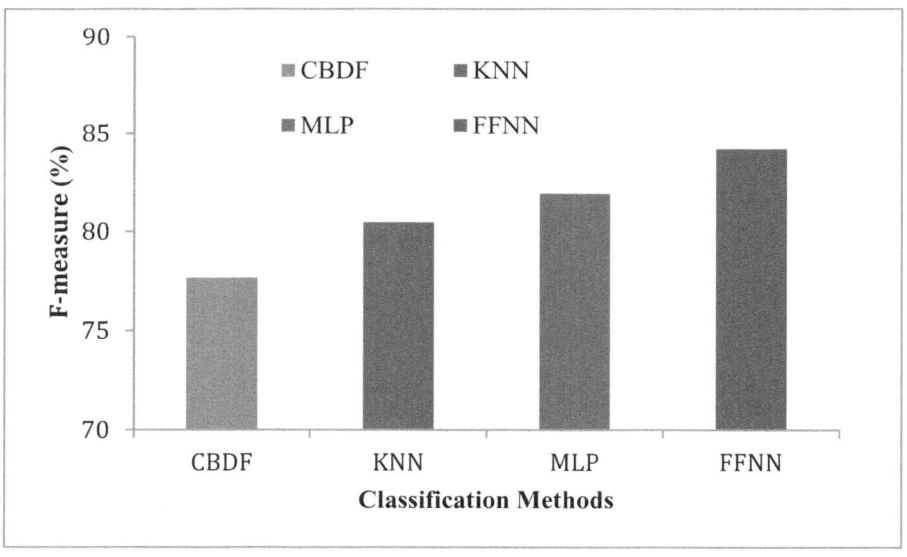

Fig. 4. F-Measure Analysis vs. Classifiers

CBDF, KNN, MLP and FFNN classifiers with respect to f-measure analysis are shown in Fig. 4. FFNN classifier has attained highest F-measure of 84.17%, CBDF, KNN, and MLP produces lesser result of 77.65%, 80.46%, and 81.89% for BOA algorithm.

FFNN classifier has 6.52%, 3.71%, and 2.28% increased f-measure than CBDF, KNN, and MLP classifiers.

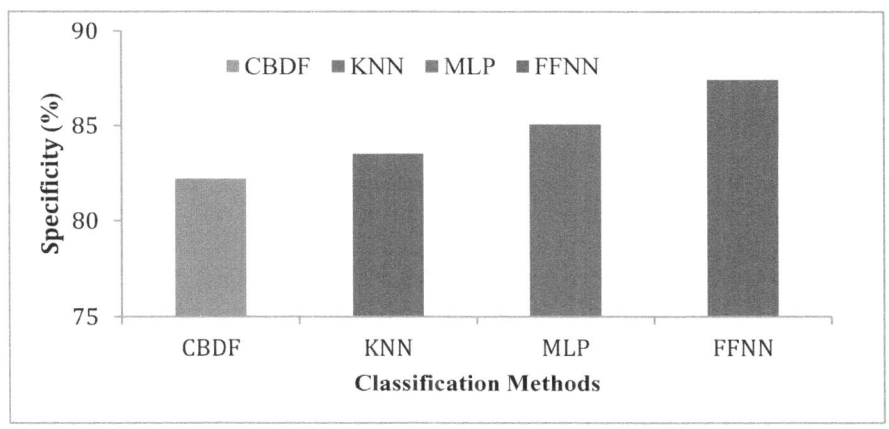

Fig. 5. Specificity Comparison vs. Classifiers

Specificity analysis of classifiers CBDF, KNN, MLP and FFNN are shown in Fig. 5. Proposed classifier has the highest result of 87.44%, CBDF, KNN, MLP gives the lowest result of 82.2%, 83.51%, and 85.07% for the BOA algorithm. The proposed classifier has 5.24%, 3.93%, and 2.37% higher when compared to CBDF, KNN, and MLP classifiers.

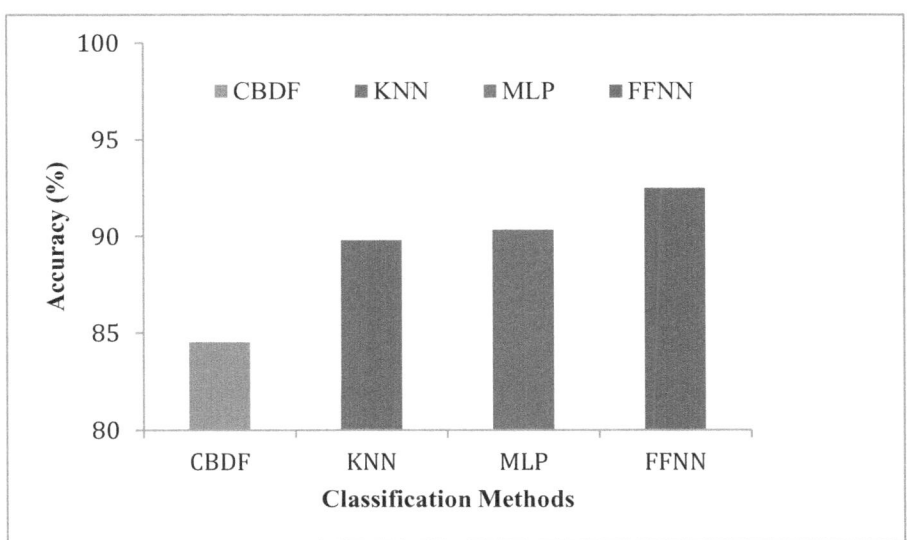

Fig. 6. Accuracy Comparison vs. Classifiers

CBDF, KNN, MLP and FFNN classifiers with respect to accuracy are illustrated in Fig. 6. FFNN has attained highest accuracy of 88.62%, other classifiers like CBDF, KNN, and MLP give the lowest accuracy of 82.58%, 84.06%, and 86.50% for the BOA algorithm. FFNN classifier has 6.04%, 4.56%, and 2.12% increased accuracy than MLP, BPNN, and ANN-SWA.

5 Conclusion and Future Work

Male infertility is an increasing worldwide health concern. Semen quality is maintained at a fairly constant level if semen is collected or males are bred every other day. Unfortunately, seminal quality prediction suffers from reduced diagnosis accuracy, irrelevant information in the dataset, and class imbalance problem, which is typical in medical diagnosis. In this paper, SMOTE is introduced to class imbalance problem in seminal quality dataset. BOA, Butterfly mate-finding and group foraging behaviours serve as the inspiration for feature selection. Once the algorithm is initialised, each butterfly determines its own smell attention and fitness value (accuracy), and each butterfly individual advances to the optimal individual (with the strongest accuracy) based on the conversion probability. In order to locate pertinent features, gain a deeper comprehension of the data, and find feature importance, BOA is introduced. Then, FFNN is introduced for classification of features selected from BOA. FFNN classifier is an ANN in which the nodes are connected circularly. FFNN classifier is the basic type of NN because the input is only processed in one direction. Semen Quality dataset always flows in one direction and never backwards/opposite. Finally including precision, recall/sensitivity, specificity, f-measure, and accuracy are used to measure the results of classifiers. The model weights and predictions may differ depending on the training dataset and model architecture; this is a matter for future research.

References

1. Tomlinson, M.J.: Uncertainty of measurement and clinical value of semen analysis: has standardisation through professional guidelines helped or hindered progress? Andrology **4**(5), 763–770 (2016)
2. Levine, H., et al.: Temporal trends in sperm count: a systematic review and meta-regression analysis. Hum. Reprod. Update **23**(6), 646–659 (2017)
3. Gunes, S., Hekim, G.N.T., Arslan, M.A., Asci, R.: Effects of aging on the male reproductive system. J. Assist. Reprod. Genet. **33**, 441–454 (2016)
4. Peiffer-Smadja, N., et al.: Machine learning for clinical decision support in infectious diseases: a narrative review of current applications. Clin. Microbiol. Infect. **26**(5), 584–595 (2020)
5. Adak, M.F., Lieberzeit, P., Jarujamrus, P., Yumusak, N.: Classification of alcohols obtained by QCM sensors with different characteristics using ABC based neural network. Eng. Science and Technology, an International J. **23**(3), 463–469 (2020)
6. Benli, H., Haznedar, B., Kalinli, A.: Seminal quality prediction using deep learning based on artificial intelligence. Int. J. Eng. Res. Dev. **11**(1), 350–357 (2019)
7. Bidgoli, A.A., Komleh, H.E., Mousavirad, S.J.: Seminal quality prediction using optimized artificial neural network with genetic algorithm. In: 2015 9th International Conference on Electrical and Electronics Engineering (ELECO), pp. 695–699. IEEE, Bursa, Turkey (2015)

8. Wang, H., Xu, Q., Zhou, L.: Seminal quality prediction using clustering-based decision forests. Algorithms **7**(3), 405–417 (2014)
9. Nsugbe, E.: Toward a self-supervised architecture for semen quality prediction using environmental and lifestyle factors. In Artificial Intelligence and Appl. **1**(1), 35–42 (2023)
10. Zhou, M., et al.: Preliminary prediction of semen quality based on modifiable lifestyle factors by using the XGBoost algorithm. Front. Med. **9**, 1–15 (2022)
11. GhoshRoy, D., Alvi, P.A., Santosh, K.C.: Explainable AI to predict male fertility using extreme gradient boosting algorithm with SMOTE. Electronics **12**(1), 1–16 (2022)
12. Malathi, K., Sivaranjani, M.K.: A hybrid approach for the fertility rate analysis in human beings using classification algorithms. International Journal of Scientific Research in Computer Science, Engineering and Information Technology **3**(6), 609–616 (2018)
13. Mendoza-Palechor, F.E., Ariza-Colpas, P.P., Sepulveda-Ojeda, J.A., De-la-Hoz-Manotas, A., PiñeresMelo, M.: Fertility analysis method based on supervised and unsupervised data mining techniques. Int. J. Appl. Eng. Res. **11**(21), 10374–10379 (2016)
14. Hassan, M.R., Al-Insaif, S., Hossain, M.I., Kamruzzaman, J.: A machine learning approach for prediction of pregnancy outcome following IVF treatment. Neural Comput. Appl. **32**, 2283–2297 (2020)
15. Yibre, A.M., Koçer, B.: Semen quality predictive model using feed forwarded neural network trained by learning-based artificial algae algorithm. Engineering Science and Technology, an International Journal **24**(2), 310–318 (2021)
16. Fernández, A., García, S., Galar, M., Prati, R.C., Krawczyk, B., Herrera, F.: Learning from Imbalanced Data Sets. Springer, Cham **10**, 978–1003 (2018)
17. Arora, S., Singh, S.: Butterfly optimization algorithm: a novel approach for global optimization. Soft. Comput.Comput. **23**(3), 715–734 (2019)

Enhancing Medicinal Plant Identification with Deep Learning: A Data-Centric Approach

Lakshmi Padmaja Dhyaram$^{(\boxtimes)}$ ⓘ, Akash Reddy Busa, Manideep Anchuri, and Mahati Gorthi

Department of Information Technology, Anurag University, Hyderabad, Telangana, India
lakshmipadmajait@anurag.edu.in

Abstract. India boasts a rich biodiversity of plants, and for decades, it has utilized medicinal plants in Ayurveda. However, due to a lack of species knowledge, misidentification stemming from morphological similarities, high demand driven by endangered species, and other factors, medicinal plants are susceptible to adulteration and substitution. This paper aims to address the challenges of limited species knowledge and misidentification of medicinal plants by employing state-of-art computer vision techniques, specifically deep learning through Convolutional Neural Networks (CNNs), with a data-centric approach. Despite the existence of numerous computer vision applications proposed for medicinal plant identification, they often lack accurate tailoring for specific plants and struggle to precisely generalize across plants with diverse morphological features. Our study proposes an accurate computer vision application which utilizes different deep learning CNN architectures such as MobileNet, ExceptionNet, and InceptionNet for the precise identification of 10 medicinal plants with data encompassing various morphological features. Our suggested application outperforms the other models we trained in terms of accuracy, precision, recall, and F1 score with minimal inference time, owing to its emphasis on data, data augmentation, and regularization approaches like dropout.

Keywords: Deep Learning · Convolutional Neural Networks · Medicinal Plant Identification · Data Augmentation · Regularization

1 Introduction

India possesses a diverse array of medicinal plants deeply ingrained in its practice of Ayurvedic medicine. These botanical remedies, utilized extensively for centuries, form the backbone of traditional healing practices [19]. Ayurveda, an ancient medicinal system dating back approximately 5000 years to Vedic times, stands as one of the oldest healing sciences [1]. Despite advancements in allopathic medicine, global interest in Ayurvedic remedies continues to rise, driven by concerns over synthetic medication's side effects, escalating drug costs, the emergence of new diseases, the absence of definitive treatments for chronic illnesses, and the growing threat of microbial resistance [3, 18].

© The Author(s), under exclusive license to Springer Nature Switzerland AG 2025
S. Rajagopal et al. (Eds.): ASCIS 2024, CCIS 2424, pp. 268–281, 2025.
https://doi.org/10.1007/978-3-031-86290-8_20

A significant challenge in the medicinal drug industry is adulteration and substitution. Many factors contribute to these issues, including deforestation, the extinction of plant species, misidentification of plants, increasing demand for raw materials, confusion in vernacular names, lack of knowledge [21] about authentic sources, similar morphological features, color similarities, and careless collection practices [1, 4]. Therefore, a computer vision software capable of accurately classifying various medicinal plants can help reduce adulteration and substitution to a great extent. This software can benefit various stakeholders such as collectors, traders, wholesalers, and distributors. The main reasons for adulteration, as mentioned in [4], include confusion over names, unavailability, and lack of knowledge about the plant, which we aim to address through a web application. This application will provide vernacular names of the plant, its use cases, and taxonomy when a picture of it is uploaded.

The proposed solution builds upon the foundation laid by "Factors influencing the use of Deep Learning for Medicinal Plants Recognition" [3], expanding its scope from the identification of five to ten medicinal plants. Leveraging Deep Learning Convolutional Neural Networks, the project explores various architectures—including MobileNetV2, InceptionV3, and Xception—incorporating distinct dropout rates, dense units, and learning rates. Extensive data augmentation, drawn from diverse sources capturing various morphological features, enriches the dataset, facilitating robust model generalization.

During testing, the MobileNetV2 model, with a dropout rate of 0.1, 128 units in the fully connected layer, and a learning rate of 0.001, showcased exemplary performance, achieving an accuracy, precision, recall, and F1 score of 97.7%, 97.1%, 97%, and 97%, respectively, on the test dataset, with an average inference time of 99 ms. The comprehensive dataset, comprising images exhibiting diverse morphological traits sourced from multiple origins, enabled the model to generalize effectively to unseen data. Notably, the integration of dropout regularization and embedded data augmentation layers within the fully connected layer yielded superior metric scores.

2 Literature Survey

Numerous studies have delved into the classification of medicinal leaves. Traditionally, methodologies relied on extracting features from images using conventional algorithms for feature extraction and edge detection [8]. These techniques aimed to identify characteristics such as color, shape, texture, and vein structure from the images [20]. However, with advancements in deep learning and computer vision, Convolutional Neural Network (CNN) models have emerged as a compelling alternative [13]. Leveraging their ability to perform feature extraction, edge detection, and classification with minimal code, CNN models offer robust classification capabilities. In this study, we explore several publications, each employing its unique approach to the classification of medicinal plants.

In 2015, Sue Han et al. studied CNN to learn unsupervised feature representations for 44 species collected from the Royal Botanical Gardens, Ken, and England [11]. They explored the features used by CNN for classification by employing a deconvolutional layer to avoid a black box approach. They concluded that CNN utilizes the venation structure as an important feature for classifying plant images, achieving an accuracy of 99.6%. Additionally, the paper suggested that CNN can represent features for leaf images more accurately than hand-crafted features.

Adams Begue et al. in 2017 conducted a study to classify medicinal plant species using machine learning techniques [15]. They collected leaves from 24 different species, extracted various features (e.g., length, width, color), and employed a random forest classifier with 10-fold cross-validation. The random forest achieved an accuracy of 90.1%, outperforming other classifiers like k-nearest neighbors, naïve Bayes, support vector machines, and neural networks.

In 2018, Tejas D. Dahigaonkar and Rasika T. Kalyane used SVM classification with traditional feature extraction techniques to classify medicinal plants [1]. They preprocessed the images, sharpened and segmented them using thresholding techniques, extracted parameter values and color features, and performed texture analysis. These features were then trained and classified using an SVM classifier, yielding an accuracy of 96.6%.

In 2019, Bhanuprakash Dudi and Dr. V. Rajesh proposed a CNN and machine learning-based classifier [6] with an accuracy of 98% on the Flavia dataset. They noted that CNN-based feature extraction and classification outperformed traditional methods. They utilized metrics such as accuracy, precision, recall, F1 score, and support metrics in their paper.

In 2021, Pratiksha et al. proposed a plant recognition system for the drug industry using CNN to detect whether a given plant can cure diabetes [10]. They used plants like Tulsi, Neem, Amla, and Lavender for curing diabetes and silver maple leaves and eastern cottonwood for plants that cannot cure diabetes. This model achieved an accuracy of 98% after training for 70 epochs.

Our proposed publication drew inspiration from the groundbreaking work conducted by J. V. Anchitaalagammai et al. [2] in 2021. Their paper focused on the development of a deep learning-based classifier for medicinal leaves, specifically targeting 5 plant species. Leveraging the InceptionV3 model, their solution achieved an impressive accuracy of 96.67%.

Building upon the foundation laid by Anchitaalagammai et al. [2], we sought to extend the scope of the study by broadening the range of plant species under consideration. Recognizing the importance of inclusivity and diversity in medicinal plant classification, we expanded the study to encompass a total of 10 plant species. In addition to the original five plants—Pungai, Jamun (Naval), Jatropha curcas, kuppaimeni, and Basil—we introduced five new species: aloe vera, neem, mint, eucalyptus, and lemon.

In 2022, Rahim Azadnia and Mohammed Maitham Al-Amidi proposed a deep learning-based classifier using Global Average Pooling [5] for 5 medicinal plants, achieving an accuracy of 99.3%. They explored different pixel sizes of images and found that 64x64 images achieved the highest accuracy of 99.3%. The paper highlighted the efficacy of global average pooling, dropout layers, and dense layers in achieving high accuracy.

In 2022, Upendar et al. proposed "Identification of Medicinal Plants using Deep learning" [7], where a CNN model utilized feature vectors from both the front and back sides of leaves to classify images. The training and validation accuracies were 91.6% and 84.1%, respectively. The authors used 50 different medicinal plants for training and created their dataset.

In 2022, Vina et al. proposed a transfer learning approach for identifying medicinal plants [9], exploring architectures like VGG16, VGG19, and MobileNetV2. They concluded that MobileNetV2 performed well on the test set with an accuracy of 81.82% with fine-tuning. They also mentioned that less diverse data might lead to overfitting to the training data. Our proposed methodology aims to address this issue by emphasizing data augmentation and regularization with a dropout layer.

Owais A. Malik et al. in 2022 developed an automated system for real-time identification of medicinal plant species in the Borneo region [14]. They used a deep learning model (EfficientNet-B1) trained on a combined public and private dataset. The system achieved high accuracy (87% Top-1 on the private dataset) but experienced a slight drop in accuracy (78.5% Top-1) during real-time testing, potentially due to variations between training and testing conditions.

In 2023, Kavitha et al. proposed "Medicinal Plant Identification in Real-Time Using Deep Learning Model" [16] where they developed a deep learning algorithm to classify six plant leaves, each consisting of 500 images. The authors achieved an accuracy of over 97% in their classification task. Notably, they deployed their trained model on the cloud and developed a mobile application, making their solution readily accessible for real-world use.

Sharrab et al. (2023) proposed a deep learning approach for medicinal plant recognition using a Convolutional Neural Network (CNN) based on the VGG-16 architecture [17]. They trained their model on a dataset of 25,686 images representing 29 different plant species. The CNN achieved an impressive 98% recognition rate, demonstrating its effectiveness in accurately classifying medicinal plants despite variations in growth stage, lighting, and imaging conditions (Table 1).

3 Collection of Data Set

We gathered data from multiple sources, encompassing various morphological features. Our dataset comprises 5058 images spanning 10 different plants: Aloe vera, jamun (Syzygium cumini), jatropha (Jatropha curcas), lemon (Citrus limon), neem (Azadirachta indica), pongamia pinnata (Millettia pinnata), Tulsi (Ocimum tenuiflorum, basil), Eucalyptus, kuppaimeni (Acalypha indica), and mint (Mentha). We expanded our dataset from the initial set of plants – jamun, jatropha, pongamia pinnata, basil (Tulsi), and kuppaimeni – by including five additional plants: Aloe vera, lemon, neem, eucalyptus, and mint [2]. The data collection process involved sourcing leaves from the MED117_Medicinal Plant Leaf Dataset & Name Table [12], Swedish Leaf Dataset, Plantnet PlantCLEF2015 dataset, and various open internet repositories. Each plant category contains approximately 400 to 600 images. The dataset was partitioned into an 80% training set, a 20% testing set, and a small portion reserved for validation. By incorporating a data augmentation layer within the model, every image effectively represents a new, unseen instance from the same distribution. This approach, coupled with strong regularization through dropout, enables our model to generalize efficiently to unseen data without the need for explicit feature extraction.

Table 1. Summary of Literature Review on Medicinal Plant Identification Methods.

Paper Name	Method Used	Accuracy
Deep-Plant: Plant Identification with convolutional neural networks [11]	CNN	99.6%
Identification of ayurvedic medicinal plants by image processing of leaf samples [1]	SVM Classification with traditional feature extraction techniques	96.6%
CNN-based classifier for medicinal plant leaf images [6]	CNN	98%
Plant Recognition System for Drug Industry Using CNN [10]	CNN	98%
Deep Learning-Based Classifier for Medicinal Leaves [2]	InceptionV3	96.67%
Deep Learning-Based Classifier Using Global Average Pooling [5]	Global Average Pooling	99.3%
Identification of Medicinal Plants using Deep learning [7]	CNN	91.6% (training), 84.1% (validation)
Transfer Learning Approach for Identifying Medicinal Plants [9]	VGG16, VGG19, MobileNetV2	81.82%

4 Metrics

For our proposed system, we have employed four metrics to assess the model's performance: accuracy, precision, recall, and F1 score. We have utilized weighted averages for precision, recall, and F1 score, which are beneficial for evaluating models on imbalanced datasets and simplifying the evaluation process.

4.1 Accuracy

The percentage of successfully categorized occurrences among all the predictions the classifier made is known as accuracy. It is determined by dividing the total number of forecasts by the ratio of true positives and true negatives.

$$accuracy = \frac{(true\ positives + true\ negatives)}{total\ predictions} \tag{1}$$

4.2 Precision

Precision is a metric for positive forecast accuracy. The ratio of accurately predicted positive cases, or true positives, to the overall number of positive predictions (false positives plus true positives) is what determines the outcome. A high precision means that few erroneous positive predictions are being made by the classifier.

$$precision = \frac{true\ positives}{(true\ positives + false\ positives)} \tag{2}$$

4.3 Recall

The percentage of real positive examples that the classifier properly detected is measured by recall, which is sometimes referred to as sensitivity. True positives to the total number of positive incidents (true positives + false negatives) is the ratio. When a classifier achieves a high recall, it is successfully identifying the majority of positive examples.

$$recall = \frac{true\ positives}{(true\ positives + false\ negatives)} \tag{3}$$

4.4 F1 Score

The harmonic means of recall and precision is known as the F1 score. It is especially helpful when there is an imbalance in the classes since it strikes a balance between recall and precision. A greater value denotes better performance, and the range is 0 to 1.

$$f1\ score = \frac{(2 \cdot precision \cdot recall)}{(precision + recall)} \tag{4}$$

We have used weighted average for the precision, recall and f1 score which calculates the metric for each class individually and then computes the weighted average of these values, weighted by the support of each class. This means that classes with more instances contribute more to the final metric value. It is useful when dealing with imbalanced datasets, where some classes may have significantly more instances than others.

5 Proposed System

Our dataset is too large to be stored in memory and trained on in one go. To address this, we utilized the 'image_dataset_from_directory' function from TensorFlow, which loads data in batches. Initially, we loaded the data with a batch size of 32 and split it into training and testing sets, with a small portion reserved for validation. The training set comprises approximately 4000 images, while the testing set consists of around 1000 images, both shuffled randomly.

In our sequential model, the input layer is the first component, accepting inputs with a shape of (224, 224, 3). We explored the use of four different pre-trained models for transfer learning: MobileNetV2, InceptionV3, Xception, and ResNet64 and 101, all pre-trained on ImageNet. These models were loaded with an input shape of (224, 224, 3) and utilized average pooling. Prior to this, we added additional layers to resize the images to (224, 224, 3) and rescale pixel values to the range [0, 1] by dividing each pixel value by 255. This preprocessing step aims to enhance model performance, facilitate training, and reduce computational complexity. Subsequently, we applied a data augmentation layer, randomly flipping images horizontally and vertically, and rotating them within a range of [-20% * 2π, 30% * 2π]. These augmentations effectively create new, unseen versions of the data during training, helping the model to better generalize to different variations in the dataset.

The base model, acting as a feature extractor, was then added to the sequential model. This base model includes a global average pooling layer as its final layer, replacing the flatten layer. The global average pooling layer reduces dimensionality, introduces translation invariance, and helps mitigate overfitting. Following this, a dense layer was added to the model, containing either 64 or 128 dense units with ReLU activation, followed by a dropout layer for regularization. We experimented with two dropout values: 0.1 and 0.2.

Finally, we added a fully connected layer with 10 dense units for softmax regression. Our system utilized the Adam optimizer, and we explored two different learning rates: 0.001 and 0.0001. For loss calculation, we employed sparse categorical cross entropy, while accuracy served as our evaluation metric.

Since we have embedded resizing, rescaling, and data augmentation inside the model, we do not need to explicitly perform these tasks during model deployment. This makes the model more efficient and robust.

5.1   CNN Architectures Used

In our implementation, we employed CNN architectures like MobileNetV2, Xception, and InceptionV3. MobileNetV2 was chosen Because of its lightweight architecture, which makes it appropriate for real-time applications. While InceptionV3 facilitates multi-scale feature learning, which improves the model's capacity to identify a variety of plant properties, Xception offers richer, more intricate feature representations. Together, these architectures support excellent computational efficiency and accuracy in the identification of medicinal plants.

6 Process Flow

See Fig. 1.

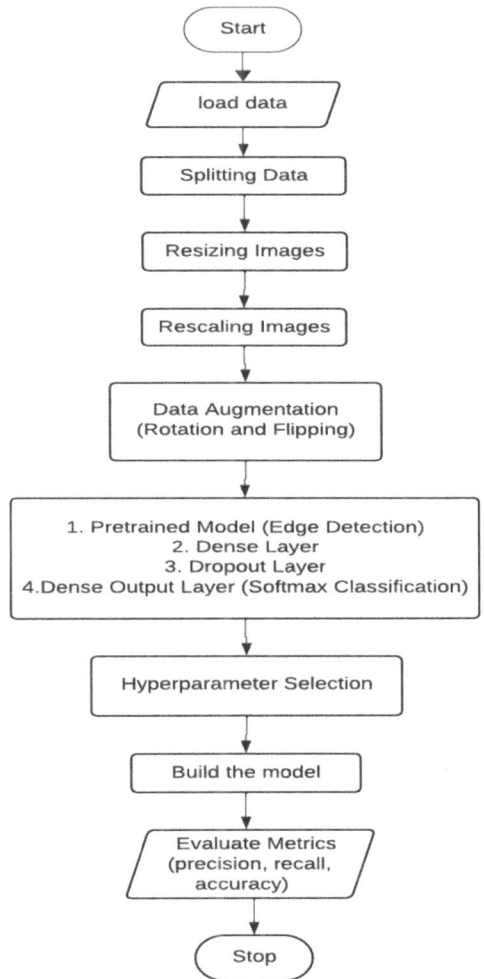

Fig. 1. Process Flowchart

7   Result

The experiment encompassed 12 models with various hyperparameters, exploring different combinations of dense units, dropout rates, and learning rates across three pre-trained models. Upon evaluation, it was observed that the ResNet architecture exhibited slower convergence compared to other models, demanding significant computational resources. Consequently, focus shifted to MobileNet, Xception, and Inception architectures for further analysis.

The following hyperparameter set values were chosen because they represent optimal values, considering both the complexity of the model and the dataset, and are widely regarded as best practices within the machine learning community. Other parameter combinations resulted in much more deviated and suboptimal results; therefore, we opted to stick with these values for further analysis. Below are the results obtained from testing the models trained with different hyperparameters:

Hyperparameter Set 1 (Testing Data Results)

– Dropout: 0.1
– Dense Units: 64
– Learning Rate: 0.0001

Table 2. Hyperparameter Set 1 results.

Model	MobileNetV2	Xception	InceptionV3
Dropout	0.1	0.1	0.1
Dense units	64	64	64
Learning rate	0.0001	0.0001	0.0001
Accuracy	0.947	0.961	0.933
Precision	0.949	0.943	0.937
Recall	0.946	0.943	0.933
F1 Score	0.945	0.943	0.932
Inference time	0.102	0.007	0.206

As shown in Table 2, the Xception model demonstrated superior accuracy and inference time compared to MobileNet and Inception. However, MobileNet exhibited the best precision, recall, and F1 score performance.

Hyperparameter Set 2 (Testing Data Results)

– Dropout: 0.1
– Dense Units: 128

Table 3. Hyperparameter Set 2 results.

Model	MobileNetV2	Xception	InceptionV3
Dropout	0.1	0.1	0.1
Dense units	128	128	128
Learning rate	0.0001	0.0001	0.0001
Accuracy	0.960	0.959	0.960
Precision	0.955	0.960	0.961
Recall	0.955	0.959	0.960
F1 Score	0.954	0.959	0.960
Inference time	0.136	0.064	0.202

– Learning Rate: 0.0001

Analysis of these results revealed that increasing the number of units in the dense layer led to improved performance. Notably, the Inception network outperformed others in overall performance, excluding inference time (Table 3).

Hyperparameter Set 3 (Testing Data Results)

– Dropout: 0.2
– Dense Units: 128
– Learning Rate: 0.0001 (Table 4)

Table 4. Hyperparameter Set 3 results.

Model	MobileNetV2	Xception	InceptionV3
Dropout	0.2	0.2	0.2
Dense units	128	128	128
Learning rate	0.0001	0.0001	0.0001
Accuracy	0.958	0.954	0.958
Precision	0.958	0.955	0.959
Recall	0.958	0.954	0.958
F1 Score	0.957	0.953	0.958
Inference time	0.140	0.187	0.290

With this set of hyperparameters, all models demonstrated satisfactory performance, albeit not as robust as Set 2 across all metrics, including inference time. This suggests that a dropout rate of 0.2 introduced excessive regularization.

Hyperparameter Set 4 (Testing Data Results)

- Dropout: 0.1
- Dense Units: 128
- Learning Rate: 0.001 (Table 5)

Table 5. Hyperparameter Set 4 results.

Model	MobileNetV2	Xception	InceptionV3
Dropout	0.1	0.1	0.1
Dense units	128	128	128
Learning rate	0.001	0.001	0.001
Accuracy	0.977	0.967	0.952
Precision	0.971	0.967	0.956
Recall	0.970	0.969	0.952
F1 Score	0.970	0.967	0.951
Inference time	0.099	0.195	0.170

Analysis of results from this hyperparameter set highlighted that MobileNet exhibited superior performance across all performance metrics, including inference time.

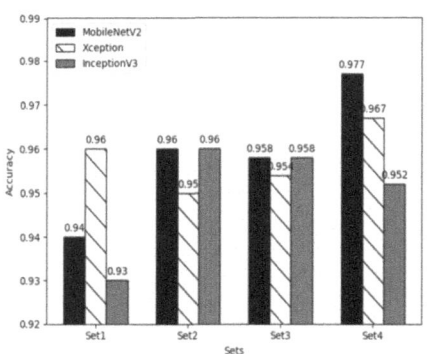

Fig. 2. Accuracy Scores of three models

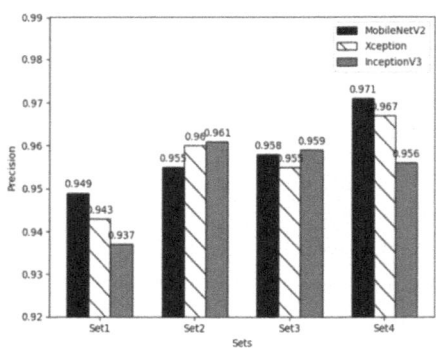

Fig. 3. Precision Scores of three models

Upon comprehensive analysis of all hyperparameter sets, it was concluded that the MobileNet architecture with Hyperparameter Set 4 showcased the best performance (from Fig. 2, Fig. 3., Fig. 4. And Fig. 5.), achieving an accuracy of 97.7%, precision of 97.1%, recall and F1 score of 97%, with an inference time of 99 ms. Following this, Hyperparameter Set 2 with 0.1 dropout, 128 dense units, and 0.0001 learning rate emerged as the second-best performing set. Furthermore, it was observed that excessive

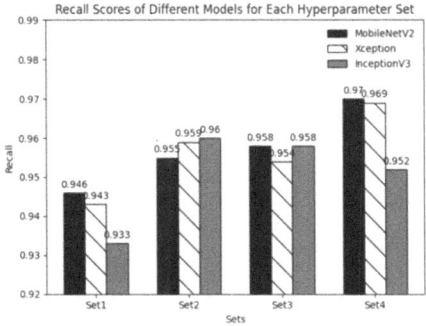

Fig. 4. Recall Scores of three models

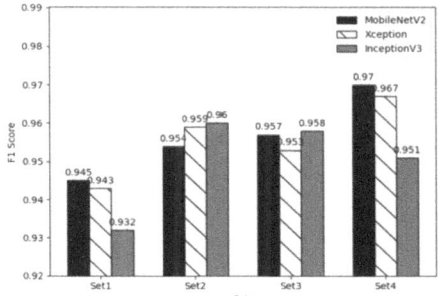

Fig. 5. F1 Scores of three models

increase in dropout adversely impacted model performance. Additionally, we noticed that the prediction performance for the basil plant was comparatively lower than for other plants. This was primarily due to the less defined venation of basil leaves, making them visually similar to other plant leaves, thereby challenging the model's ability to differentiate between them effectively.

8   Conclusion

This paper focused on utilizing deep learning CNN models with an emphasis on data and hyperparameter optimization for medicinal plant recognition. Experimentation was conducted on MobileNetV2, Xception, and InceptionV3 models, leveraging transfer learning alongside varying dropout rates, dense units, and learning rates, coupled with a diverse dataset containing different morphological features. From the comprehensive analysis, it was determined that the MobileNetV2 architecture with a dropout rate of 0.1, 128 units in the hidden layer, and a learning rate of 0.0001 achieved the best performance, attaining an accuracy of 97.7%, precision of 97.1%, recall, and F1 score of 97%, with an inference time of 99 ms. Furthermore, it was observed that excessively high dropout rates can adversely affect model performance, while increasing the number of dense units can enhance model performance.

However, certain limitations were identified, particularly with the recognition of specific plant species such as basil. The model struggled to generalize to more diverse morphological features in some cases due to the lack of clear venation and distinguishing features in the dataset images. For instance, the veins of basil leaves were less visible compared to other plants, resulting in lower prediction accuracy for this species.

Looking ahead, future endeavors will focus on expanding the scope by incorporating more plant species with a more diverse dataset. Additionally, further experimentation will be conducted on additional models with an increased number of hyperparameters to explore and optimize model performance extensively.

References

1. Kumar, P.M., Surya, C.M., Gopi, V.P.: Identification of ayurvedic medicinal plants by image processing of leaf samples. In: 2017 Third International Conference on Research in Computational Intelligence and Communication Networks (ICRCICN), Kolkata, India, pp. 231–238 (2017). https://doi.org/10.1109/ICRCICN.2017.8234512
2. Anchitaalagammai, J.V., Shantha Lakshmi Revathy, J.S., Kavitha, S., Murali, S.: Factors influencing the use of deep learning for medicinal plants recognition. Journal of Physics: Conference Series, **2089**, 012055 (2021). https://doi.org/10.1088/1742-6596/2089/1/012055
3. Humber, J.: The role of complementary and alternative medicine: accommodating pluralism. JAMA: Journal of the American Medical Association, **288**(13), 1655–1656 (2002). https://doi.org/10.1001/jama.288.13.1655
4. Rathore, B., Kotecha, M., Chaudhary, K., Manjula: Adulteration and Substitution in Indian Medicinal plants: a review article. International Research Journal of Ayurveda & Yoga **5**, 72–78 (2022). https://doi.org/10.47223/IRJAY.2022.5512
5. Azadnia, R., Al-Amidi, M.M., Mohammadi, H., Cifci, M.A., Daryab, A., Cavallo, E.: An AI based approach for medicinal plant identification using deep CNN based on global average pooling. Agronomy **12**(11), 2723 (2022). https://doi.org/10.3390/agronomy12112723
6. Prakash, D.: Medicinal Plant Recognition based on CNN and Machine Learning (2023)
7. Rao, R., Lahari, M., Sri, K., Srujana, K., Yaswanth, D.: Identification of medicinal plants using deep learning. International Journal for Research in Applied Science and Engineering Technology **10**, 306–322 (2022). https://doi.org/10.22214/ijraset.2022.41190
8. Ayumi, V., Ermatita, E., Abdiansah, A., Noprisson, H., Purba, M., Utami, M.: A study on medicinal plant leaf recognition using artificial intelligence. In: 2021 International Conference on Informatics, Multimedia, Cyber and Information System (ICIMCIS, Jakarta, Indonesia, pp. 40–45 (2021). https://doi.org/10.1109/ICIMCIS53775.2021.9699363
9. Ayumi, V., et al.: Transfer learning for medicinal plant leaves recognition: a comparison with and without a fine-tuning strategy. International Journal of Advanced Computer Science and Applications, **13**(9) (2022). https://doi.org/10.14569/IJACSA.2022.0130916
10. Bongale, P., Shaik, A.S.S., Khan, W.: Plant recognition for drug industry using CNN. Department of Computer Science and Engineering, Bapuji Institute of Engineering and Technology, Davanagere, India
11. Lee, S.H., Chan, C.S., Wilkin, P., Remagnino, P.: Deep-Plant: Plant Identification with Convolutional Neural Networks. arXiv, 2015. https://arxiv.org/abs/1506.08425 (2015)
12. Sarma, P., Boruah, P.A., Buragohain, R.: MED 117: a dataset of medicinal plants mostly found in Assam with their leaf images, segmented leaf frames and name table. Data in Brief **47**, 108983, ISSN 2352–3409 (2023). https://doi.org/10.1016/j.dib.2023.108983
13. Sharrab, Y., Al-Fraihat, D., Tarawneh, M., Sharieh, A.: Medicinal Plants Recognition Using Deep Learning (2023). https://doi.org/10.1109/MCNA59361.2023.10185880 (2023)
14. Malik, O.A., Ismail, N., Hussein, B.R., Yahya, U.: Automated real-time identification of medicinal plants species in natural environment using deep learning models—a case study from Borneo Region. Plants **2022**(11), 2022 (1952). https://doi.org/10.3390/plants11151952
15. Begue, A., Kowlessur, V., Singh, U., Mahomoodally, F., Pudaruth, S.: Automatic recognition of medicinal plants using machine learning techniques. International Journal of Advanced Computer Science and Applications **8** (2017). https://doi.org/10.14569/IJACSA.2017.080424 (2017)
16. Kavitha, S., Kumar, T.S., Naresh, E., et al.: Medicinal plant identification in real-time using deep learning model. SN Comput. Sci. **5**(73), 2024 (2024). https://doi.org/10.1007/s42979-023-02398-5

17. Sharrab, Y., Al-Fraihat, D., Tarawneh, M., Sharieh, A.: Medicinal plants recognition using deep learning. Proceedings of the 2023 IEEE International Conference on Multimedia Computing, Networking, and Applications (MCNA), June 2023 (2023). https://doi.org/10.1109/MCNA59361.2023.10185880

18. Pushpanathan, K., Hanafi, M., Mashohor, S., et al.: Machine learning in medicinal plants recognition: a review. Artif. Intell. Rev. **54**(305–327), 2021 (2021). https://doi.org/10.1007/s10462-020-09847-0

19. Tran, T.P., Din, F.U., Brankovic, L., Sanin, C., Hester, S.M.: A systematic review of medicinal plant identification using deep learning. In: Nguyen, N.T., et al. Intelligent Information and Database Systems. ACIIDS 2024. Lecture Notes in Computer Science(), vol 14796. Springer, Singapore (2024). https://doi.org/10.1007/978-981-97-4985-0_1 (2024)

20. Bhutada, S., Reddy, C.S., Reddy, R.S., Vaishnavi, S., Kumar, G.: Automated plant identification through deep learning with particular focus on medicinal plants. In: 2023 International Conference on Advanced Computing Technologies and Applications (ICACTA), Mumbai, India, 2023, pp. 1–5 (2023). https://doi.org/10.1109/ICACTA58201.2023.10393206

21. Pukhrambam, B., Rathna, R.: A smart study on medicinal plants identification and classification using image processing techniques. In: 2021 Third International Conference on Intelligent Communication Technologies and Virtual Mobile Networks (ICICV), Tirunelveli, India, pp. 956–962 (2021). https://doi.org/10.1109/ICICV50876.2021.9388566

Understanding Unnatural Mortality: A Comprehensive Analysis of Machine Learning Approach for Classification of Causes

Shamali Gunje$^{(\boxtimes)}$, Kalyani Waghmare, and Sheetal Sonawane

Department of Computer Engineering, PICT, Pune, India
sgunje51@gmail.com

Abstract. Death is a tragedy regardless of its form, time, or manner in which it occurs. Death can be natural, unnatural through deliberate action of other, self-inflicted, or it can be due to the environmental factors. The primary aim of this paper lies in the comprehensive analysis and synthesis of existing literature concerning unnatural mortality. The literature is surveyed from various digital repositories for analyzing the trends and patterns of unnatural deaths. The study of literature identified the common causes of deaths. This paper offers a comprehension of the existing literature by combining and summarizing the patterns, trends, and contributing elements of unnatural fatalities. Additionally, a machine learning classification model is built to categorize news articles from the dataset into five different categories based on death causes. We conducted a comparative analysis using machine learning classifiers on 20,000 news articles from the Indian Express dataset. The Decision Tree model emerged as the most effective, with an accuracy of 90%. This comparison analysis demonstrates the various strengths and shortcomings of different classifiers in categorizing death causes. Our findings shed light on mortality patterns and show how machine learning can automate the classification of death-related data, allowing for early interventions and informed policy decisions.

Keywords: death · mortality · statistical analysis · machine learning

1 Introduction

Unnatural deaths—which include accidents, suicides, homicides, and other non-natural causes—have caused an increase of distress in the public. Globally, unnatural mortality, constitutes a significant portion of overall mortality. While the exact share varies by region, age group, and socioeconomic factors, unnatural deaths collectively contribute to a substantial burden of disease and premature mortality worldwide. Unnatural deaths not only have a profound impact on individuals and their families but also on the community and society.

As per the World Health Organization (WHO), 74% of global deaths are due to non-communicable diseases, including suicides, homicides, and road traffic accidents (RTAs) [1]. Suicide is a preventable death that is influenced by societal, cultural, and family factors, as well as human psychology. Approximately 703,000 individuals died by suicide in 2019 [2]. According to estimates, the suicide death rate worldwide is 11 per 100,000 people, with a higher rate among men than women [2]. Suicide claimed the lives of an estimated 0.9 million people worldwide in 2016 [3]. Most of these deaths were among people between the ages of 10 and 45.

Accidents, including traffic accidents, occupational accidents, and unintentional injuries, also represent a large portion of unnatural deaths globally. The WHO estimates that car accidents claim the lives of 1.19 million people annually [5]. Also, road traffic crashes are the leading cause of death among young people, especially those aged 5 to 29 [5]. Millions of people die in road accidents alone every year, and these incidents are a major contributor to injury-related mortality and morbidity.

In addition to suicides and accidents, homicides and other forms of violence contribute to the overall burden of unnatural mortality, although their share may be smaller compared to suicides and accidents in many regions. The projected global homicide mortality rate is 6.2 per 100,000 people, with greater rates in the Caribbean, Central Africa, and South America than in other parts of the world [2]. The number of homicide deaths varies not just by geography but also by age group, sex, and socioeconomic level [6].

Identifying the cause of death from news articles could help to reduce the burden of premature mortality and disability caused by non-natural causes, adopt preventive measures, and build health systems and social support networks. If the causes of death are precisely identified, suitable countermeasures can be planned and implemented. Hence, in this research paper, we proposed an automated frame work to classify English news articles into multiple categories, including Accident, Suicide, Homicide, Disease and Natural cause. We trained and tested the classification model using the Indian Express dataset from Kaggle which contains about 20K news articles.

The structure of this document is as follows. The review of the literature is given in Sect. 2. The mechanism of the categorization strategy is explained in Sect. 3. The experimental results are presented in Sect. 4. Section 5 discusses about the method and results of implementation, and this study is concluded in Sect. 6.

2 Literature Survey

A thorough summary of all the collected research articles that have been done on unnatural mortality—which includes suicides, accidents, and other non-natural causes of death—can be found in the literature review table that follows Table 1. The table provides useful insights by classifying the examined literature according to data source, methods, and key findings.

2.1 Key Takeaways from the Study

The summary table provide a concise overview of the features of the included studies. Several patterns, trends, and related factors were found after a thorough examination of the chosen research; these are outlined below:

Demographic Characteristics. Out of all the included studies, five found that males died at a higher rate than females. [8, 14, 21, 26, 27]. Nine studies reported the age group vulnerable to suicides, accidents, or homicides. The majority of the incidents were from age group 15 to 30 years [13, 15, 17, 26, 29]. Additionally, four studies mentioned age group 10 to 45 yrs. Faces vulnerability to unnatural deaths [2, 10, 20, 21]. Majority of death cases are of Hindus and married individuals [8, 10, 20, 25].

Common Causes and Methods. According to majority of articles the main causes of unnatural deaths are accidents followed by suicides [8, 10, 13, 14, 17, 21, 27, 30]. The other six studies mentioned suicide as the leading cause of unnatural mortality [9, 12, 15, 17, 25, 28]. Along with cause the studies also mentioned the method. Hanging is the most frequently mentioned method of suicide [14, 17, 21, 23, 25]. Apart from acci dents and suicides, two studies given trauma as the cause of death [8, 13].

Impact of Social, Geographical, and Socio-economic Factors. Work-related factors, academic stress, and family disputes contribute to the death of individual [10, 18, 19, 22]. Narayankar PM et al., (2023) mentioned that urban areas have more victims, mainly from the middle class [15]. According to RK Verma et al., (2015), female victims are from the rural areas [20].

3   Methodology

From above-reviewed literature, there is a notable gap in real-time analysis and catego- rization of death-related news articles, which could provide timely insights into emerging trends and patterns. For that reason, the purpose of this study is to close this information gap by applying a machine learning classification model to classify articles according to the stated cause of death.

An overview of the proposed framework is given in this section, as seen in Fig. 1. The main steps of process are: data preparation, data labeling, text preprocessing, feature extraction, model training and model evaluation.

1. Data Preparation
   The classification model starts with loading the dataset into a Pandas DataFrame and inspect the dataset to understand its structure and contents. We have used a dataset that contains around 20K news headlines, descriptions and articles obtained from Indian Express.
2. Data Labeling
   In this step, we programmatically label each news article based on its content. It follows following steps:

   - Defining a set of keywords associated with each death causes.
   - Iterate through the data and assign death cause labels to each article.
   - Create a new column 'Category' in the DataFrame to the labels for each article.
     The categories considered are Accidents, Suicides, Homicides, Disease, Natural cause, and Other to classify news that are not related to death case.

Table 1. Literature Survey

Sr No.	First author (year)ref.	Title	Data source	Method	Major Findings
1	Basant Kumar Panda (2020)[7]	Unnatural death in India	National Family Health Survey	Descriptive analysis	Unnatural mortality rate in India: 0.67 per 1000 Unnatural deaths more common in 10–45 age group
2	Cong Li (2024)[8]	Global burden of all cause-specific injuries among children and adolescents from 1990 to 2019: a prospective cohort study	GBD 2019 portal	Joinpoint regression model to study temporal trends Cause of Death Ensemble model	Self-harm and violence increased Higher injury burden in adolescents aged 15–19 years
3	Dr. ME Bansude (2012)[9]	Trends of unnatural deaths in Latur district of Maharashtra	Autopsy reports	Analytic study	Majority deaths were males, Hindus, and married persons Common cause: Trauma Accidental deaths most common followed by suicide
4	Ian R. H. Rockett (2012)[10]	Leading Causes of Unintentional and Intentional Injury Mortality: United States, 2000–2009	Annual cause-of-death data from NCHS	Negative binomial regression analysis	Mortality rates increased for unintentional poisoning, falls, and suicide Suicide as the leading cause of mortality
5	I.D.G. Kitulwatte (2017)[11]	Study on the pattern of unnatural deaths of women brought for medico-legal autopsy	Post-mortem records	Retrospective descriptive study Analysis using MS Excel and SPSS	Majority cases from age < 40 yrs Manner of death: road accident followed by suicide (poisoning) Main reasons: family disputes and love affairs

(continued)

Table 1. (*continued*)

Sr No.	First author (year)ref.	Title	Data source	Method	Major Findings
6	I-Li Lin (2022)[12]	Predicting the Risk of Future Multiple Suicide Attempt among First-Time Suicide Attempters: Implications for Suicide Prevention Policy	National Health Insurance Research Database	Adaboost + DT technique for prediction	Prediction accuracy:0.983
7	Karoline Lukaschek (2012)[13]	Suicide Mortality in Comparison to Traffic Accidents and Homicides as Causes of Unnatural Death - An Analysis of 14,441 Cases in Germany in the Year 2010	Mortality and population data from Federal Statistical Office	Statistical Analysis using SAS, Windows	Leading cause of unnatural death: Suicide higher in younger age groups
8	Mahadev E Bansude (2021)[14]	Study of pattern of unnatural deaths at southern Marathwada region Maharashtra	Autopsy reports, death summaries, investigation reports	Statistical analysis with SPSS20 software, Windows	Most cases of males with Trauma as common cause Age group: 21–30 yrs Most are accidental deaths followed by suicides then homicides
9	Meng He (2015)[15]	Unnatural Deaths in Shanghai from 2000 to 2009: A Retrospective Study of Forensic Autopsy Cases at the Shanghai Public Security Bureau	SPSB autopsy archives, initial investigations, police reports	Statistical analysis using MS Excel and SPSS	Top 3 causes of unnatural deaths: Traffic accidents, homicides, suicides Hanging was common method of suicide

(*continued*)

Table 1. (*continued*)

Sr No.	First author (year)ref.	Title	Data source	Method	Major Findings
10	Narayankar PM (2023)[16]	An Autopsy Study of Pattern of Unnatural Deaths among Youth Conducted at a tertiary Care Teaching Hospital in South India	Autopsy reports	Examined the sociodemographic characteristics of the study group Categorized the manner of death into suicides, accidents, and homicides	Suicide followed by accidents then homicides Age group: 21 to 29 years Urban area had more victims than rural area Socio-economically, most of the victims belonged to the middle class
11	Prafulla Kumar Swain (2021)[17]	Forecasting suicide rates in India: An empirical exposition	NCRB reports	Time series modelling using ARIMA model	Suicide rate in India is expected to be 10.15 in next decade (2019–2028) Model accuracy: 95% CI
12	Praveen Athani (2016)[18]	Pattern of unnatural deaths among children: An autopsy study	Autopsy reports	Descriptive analysis	Majority of childhood deaths: 15–18 years age group Leading cause suicide mainly by hanging Road traffic accidents: mostly pedestrians
13	Prof. Sarah Waters (2021)[19]	Work-related suicide: a qualitative analysis of recent cases with recommendations for reform	Employer investigation reports, police reports, coroner verdicts, staff wellbeing surveys	Qualitative case study method	Range of work-related factors that contribute to suicide No effective organisational response to prevent future suicides

(*continued*)

Table 1. (*continued*)

Sr No.	First author (year)ref.	Title	Data source	Method	Major Findings
14	Rachel Elizabeth Senapati (2024)[20]	The patterns, trends, and major risk factors of suicide among Indian adolescents – a scoping review	Electronic database: PubMed, Google Scholar, EMBASE, PsycINFO	Scoping review methodology	Major risk factors of suicide: mental health issues, negative family experiences, academic stress, social and lifestyle factors, financial problems, and relationship problems
15	RK Verma (2015)[21]	Comprehensive Study of Unnatural Deaths in Females of Age Group 15–45 years in Allahabad	Autopsy reports	Statistical analysis and Chi-square test	Most female victims age group: 15–45 yrs Highest deaths in Hindus, rural, and married females Most common mode of death was burning
16	(2022)[22]	Accidental Deaths & Suicides in India	Report by NCRB, India	NA	Major cause of accidental deaths is Traffic accidents Most cases from age group 30–45 yrs. Followed by 18–30 yrs Over 1 million people commit suicide in India every year Male victims more Suicide method: hanging

(*continued*)

Table 1. (*continued*)

Sr No.	First author (year)ref.	Title	Data source	Method	Major Findings
17	Savita Chahal (2021)[23]	Suicide deaths among medical students, residents and physicians in India spanning a decade (2010–2019): An exploratory study using on line news portals and Google database	Online news portals of Hindi and English newspapers	Content analysis & statistical analysis	Leading factors: academic stress among medical students; marital discord among physicians
18	SM Yasir Arafata (2018)[24]	Demography and risk factors of suicidal behaviour in Bangladesh: A retrospective online news content analysis	Online Bangla news portals	Statistical analysis using SPSS and MS Excel	Suicide cases mean age: 23 yrs Most victims are females Hanging most common method
19	Soumitra Pathare (2020)[25]	Analysis of news media reports of suicides and attempted suicides during the COVID-19 lockdown in India	Online English newspapers	Extraction and data analysis using Chi-squared test	67.7% increase in suicidal behaviour during the lockdown in 2020 than 2019
20	Sujatha P L (2022)[26]	Profile of unnatural deaths in adult females in Bangalore north	Socio-demographic profile	Retrospective descriptive study	Age group – 3rd decade of life 88% were married housewives Leading manner of death – suicide and hanging common method

(*continued*)

Table 1. (*continued*)

Sr No.	First author (year)ref.	Title	Data source	Method	Major Findings
21	Suryakant Yadav (2023)[27]	Changing pattern of suicide deaths in India	NCRB data from 2014–2021	Descriptive analysis	Suicide rate higher in men Age group: 18–29 yrs Profession: highest in daily wage earners then students and employees
22	TC Anjanamma (2016)[28]	A Study of Unnatural death at MVJ Medical College and Research Hospital	Autopsy reports, hospital records, police reports	Descriptive analysis	Common age group: 31–40 yrs Male deaths more than female Leading causes of death: RTAs, suicide & homicides
23	V. Valle (2008)[29]	Qualitative analysis of Coroners' data into the unnatural deaths of children and adolescents	Coroner's inquest records	Quantitative data analysis + Thematic analysis	20.8% alcohol/drug misuse, 26% suicide, 53.2% other injuries Themes: bullying, teenage sexualization, substance misuse, out of control behaviour
24	WHO (2023)[30]	Suicide: Key Facts	Article	NA	Suicide is 4th most common cause of death globally for age group 15–29 yrs 703,000 individuals commit suicide each year
25	Xiu-Ya Xing (2020)[31]	Mortality and Disease Burden of Injuries from 2008 to 2017 in Anhui Province, China	Mortality data from Information System for Death Cause Register and Mgmt	Data analysis using crude mortality, SMR, PYLL, PYLL rate and AYLL with MS Excel & SPSS	Road traffic accidents was the primary cause of injury deaths followed by suicide

3. Text Preprocessing

The text preprocessing step performs the cleaning of the dataset. Firstly, we performed lowercasing of text to ensure the consistency. Then, to split the text into individual words or tokens tokenization is performed. To normalize variations, the words are re duced to their base form through lemmatization step. At last, the punctuation marks and stop words that do not carry much meaning are removed.

4. Feature Extraction

Feature extraction transforms textual data into useful features for machine learning models. These features serve as model inputs, enhancing model performance. In this work, we extract feature vectors from text using the Term Frequency-Inverse Document Frequency (TF-IDF) technique.

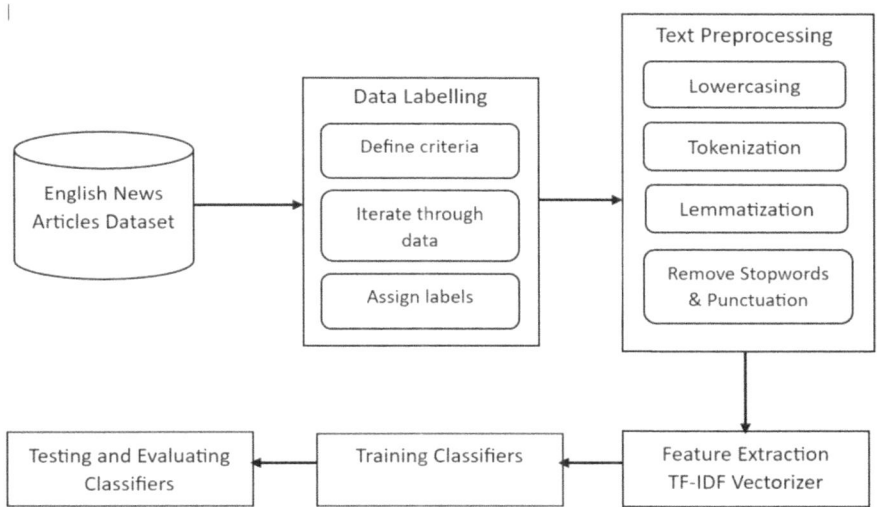

Fig. 1. General Classification Process

5. Model Training

In this step, for training and testing of our classification model, we divided our dataset into 70% for training and 30% for testing. Then to train a multi-class classification model on the training data, using the extracted features as input and labels as output, we have implemented four classifiers as follows:

a. Multinomial Logistic regression (MLR): It is a model used to predict the likelyhood of the numerous alternative outcomes of a categorically distributed dependent variable given a set of independent variables that might be real-valued, binary valued, or categorical-valued.

b. Support Vector Machine (SVM): The goal of an SVM classifier is to find the high-dimensional space's optimal hyperplane for splitting data points belonging to distinct classes. To provide strong classification borders, it achieves this by maximising the margin between each class's closest points, or support vectors.

c. Decision Tree (DT): A decision tree classifier is a type of machine learning model that forecasts new sample classes by using a tree-like structure to split data into subgroups based on feature values. Its goals are to maximise information gain and minimise impurity.

d. Random Forest (RF): Using numerous decision trees to build and produce a classification class, a Random Forest classifier is an ensemble learning technique that improves forecast accuracy and decreases overfitting by averaging outputs.

6. Model Evaluation

   Finally, we evaluate the four algorithms' classification performance. To compare the performance, we use the classification metrics such as Accuracy, Precision, Recall, and F1-Score.

4 Experimental Setup and Results

This section provides the dataset description and comparative results of the four classifiers in terms of mentioned performance metrics.

4.1 Dataset Description

For this study, the used dataset consists of 20K news articles from Indian Express dataset available on Kaggle. The dataset has features such as headlines, descriptions, and articles content. These articles were classified into five categories based on the cause of death: accidents, suicides, homicides, disease, and natural cause. The distribution of articles in each category is as follows (Fig. 2).

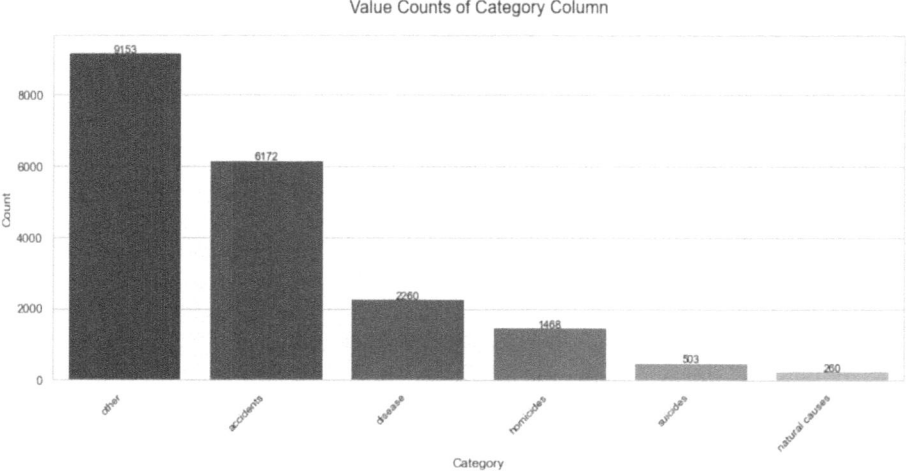

Fig. 2. Count of each news article category

4.2 Train-Test Split

The dataset has been divided into 70% training data and 30% testing data in order to assess the effectiveness of the machine learning classification model. There were roughly 14,000 articles in the training dataset and 6,000 in the testing set.

4.3 Model Evaluation

The performance of the classification model was assessed using several metrics, including accuracy, precision, recall, and F1-score. The results for the four classifiers are presented below .

Table 2. Results

Classifier	Evaluation Standard			
	Accuracy	Precision	Recall	F1-Score
MLR	0.73	0.73	0.73	0.71
SVM	0.75	0.75	0.75	0.73
DT	0.82	0.82	0.82	0.82
RF	0.83	0.83	0.82	0.80

According to Table 2, we observe that Decision tree classification algorithm performed better than other three classifiers. The high accuracy and robustness of the Random Forest classifier underscore its effectiveness in categorizing news articles based on death causes.

5   Discussion

The objective of this research was to assess the applicability of machine learning models for news articles based on causes of death, seeking to fulfil the void in real time analytics. While working with the Indian Express dataset of news articles, we wanted to test through various machine learning classifiers, which algorithm will be the most effective on dividing the articles into five specific causes of death: accident, suicide, murder, disease, and natural cases.

Machine learning was chosen for this study because it can automate classification, handle enormous amounts of unstructured text data, and deliver excellent accuracy. Its scalability, versatility, and continuous learning characteristics make it an ideal solution for a complicated task such as categorizing death reasons in news items.

The results of the implementation show that the Random Forest (RF) classifier out performed the other models, obtaining 83% accuracy while maintaining high precision, recall, and F1-scores. Its performance reflects the advantage of ensemble methods in handling complex datasets by combining multiple decision trees to enhance generalization and reduce overfitting.

With an accuracy of 82%, the Decision Tree (DT) classifier came in second, demonstrating its ability to handle both continuous and categorical data with ease. Its usefulness in this situation is further supported by its interpretability in drawing distinct decision boundaries. With accuracies of 75% and 73%, respectively, the Support Vector Machine (SVM) and Multinomial Logistic Regression (MLR) models also demonstrated respectable performance. Although these linear models work well for text classification, in this instance, they did not perform as well as the Random Forest and Decision Tree classifiers, suggesting that tree-based methods would be more advantageous for the dataset.

6   Conclusion

Unnatural deaths, which include suicides, accidents, and other non-natural causes, have emerged as a major concern in many areas. To address the issue of unnatural casualties, a comprehensive and multifaceted approach is required, considering the underlying risk factors, societal drivers, and preventive initiatives. The findings indicates that main causes of unnatural deaths are accidents followed by suicides. Various factors influence these deaths, such as academic stress, work-related factors, individual and social factors.

The best course of action for resolving the issue would be to make use of the literature already in existence to seal any gaps. The researchers, policymakers, public health professionals, and other stakeholders will find this paper to be a useful addition to the body of knowledge already available on unnatural mortality.

Techniques like Machine Learning can help prevent unnatural deaths by analyzing data to identify patterns and risk factors. AI/ML systems continuously learn, making predictions more accurate and interventions more effective, ultimately saving lives and improving public health. This work adds to the body of knowledge by automating the categorization of news articles according to causes of death using a machine learning technique. We found that the Decision Tree classifier outperformed the other three machine learning classifiers (Random Forest, Support Vector Machine (SVM), and Multinomial Logistic Regression (MLR)), with an accuracy of 90%. To, gain real-time insights about mortality patterns, this comparative analysis demonstrates how machine learning may be used to automate and enhance the classification of unstructured text data, such as news stories.

References

1. World Health Organization (WHO). Noncommunicable Diseases (2023). https://www.who.int/news-room/fact-sheets/detail/noncommunicable-diseases
2. Panda, B.K., Mishra, U.S.: Unnatural death in India. J. Biosocial Science, pp. 1–12 (2020). https://doi.org/10.1017/S0021932020000231
3. Naghavi, M.: Global, regional, and national burden of suicide mortality 1990 to 2016: systematic analysis for the global burden of disease study 2016. BMJ **364**, l94 (2019)
4. Naghavi, M., et al.: Global, regional, and national age-sex specific mortality for 264 causes of death, 1980–2016: a systematic analysis for the Global Burden of Disease Study 2016. The Lancet **390**(10100), 1151–1210 (2017)

5. World Health Organization (WHO) Road traffic injuries (2023). https://www.who.int/news-room/fact-sheets/detail/road-traffic-injuries

6. United Nation Office on Drugs and Crime. *World Drug Report*. United Nations Publications, United Nation, New York (2013). https://www.unodc.org/unodc/secured/wdr/wdr2013/World_Drug_Report_2013.pdf

7. Li,C., et al.: Global burden of all cause-specific injuries among children and adolescents from 1990 to 2019: a prospective cohort study. Int J Surg. **110**(4), 2092–2103 (2024). https://doi.org/10.1097/JS9.0000000000001131. PMID: 38348839; PMCID: PMC11020088

8. Bansude, M.E., Kachare, R.V., Dode, C.R., Kumre, V.M.: Trends of unnatural deaths in Latur district of Maharashtra. J. Forensic Medicine, Science and Law **21**(2)

9. Ian, R.H.R., et al.: Leading Causes of Unintentional and Intentional Injury Mortality: United States, 2000–2009. American Journal of Public Health, **102**(11) (2012)

10. Kitulwatte, I.D.G., et al.: Study on the pattern of unnatural deaths of women brought for medico-legal autopsy. Sri Lanka J. Forensic Medicine, Science & Law **8**(1) (2017)

11. Lin, I.-L., Tseng, J.Y.-C., Tung, H.-T., Hu, Y.-H., You, Z.-H.: Predicting the risk of future multiple suicide attempt among first-time suicide attempters: implications for suicide prevention policy. Healthcare **10**, 667 (2022). https://doi.org/10.3390/healthcare10040667

12. Lukaschek, K., Erazo, N., Baumert, J., Ladwig, K.-H.: Suicide mortality in comparison to traffic accidents and homicides as causes of unnatural death. an analysis of 14,441 cases in Germany in the Year 2010. Int. J. Environ. Res. Public Health **9**, 924–931 (2012). https://doi.org/10.3390/ijerph9030924

13. Bansude, M.E., Nomani, M.M., Dode, C.R., Umbare, R.B.: Study of pattern of unnatural deaths at southern Marathwada region Maharashtra. MedPulse International Journal of Forensic Medicine, Print ISSN: 2579–0935, Online ISSN: 2636–4735 **19**(1), pp 07–15 (2021). https://doi.org/10.26611/10181912

14. He, M., Fang, Y.-X., Lin, J.-Y., Ma, K.-J., Li, B.-X.: Unnatural Deaths in Shanghai from 2000 to 2009: a retrospective study of forensic autopsy cases at the Shanghai Public Security Bureau. PLOS ONE (2015). https://doi.org/10.1371/journal.pone.0131309

15. Narayankar, P.M., Jagannatha, S.R.: An Autopsy study of pattern of unnatural deaths among youth conducted at a tertiary care teaching hospital in South India. J Indian Acad Forensic Med. **45**(1) (2023). https://doi.org/10.48165/jiafm.2023.45.1.10

16. Swain, P.K., Tripathy, M.R., Priyadarshini, S., Acharya, S.K.: Forecasting suicide rates in India: an empirical exposition. PLOS ONE (2021). https://doi.org/10.1371/journal.pone.0255342

17. Athani, P., Hugar, B.S., Harish, S., Girishchandra, Y.P.: Pattern of unnatural deaths among children: an autopsy study. Medico-legal Journal (2016). https://doi.org/10.1177/0025817216679353

18. Waters, S., Palmer, H.: Work-Related Suicide: A Qualitative Analysis of Recent Cases with Recommendations for Reform. University of Leeds (2021)

19. Senapati, R.E., et al.: The patterns, trends and major risk factors of suicide among Indian adolescents – a scoping review. BMC Psychiatry (2024). https://doi.org/10.1186/s12888-023-05447-8

20. Verma, R.K., Sinha, U.S., Srivastava, P.C., Kaul, A., Rai, R.K.: Comprehensive study of unnatural deaths in females of age group 15–45 years in Allahabad. Indian Internet Journal of Forensic Medicine & Toxicology **13**(1) (2015). https://doi.org/10.5958/0974-4487.2015.00003.6

21. Report by National Crime Records Bureau (NCRB) (Ministry of Home Affairs) Government of India.: Accidental Deaths & Suicides in India (2022). https://ncrb.gov.in/accidental-deaths-suicides-in-india-adsi.html

22. Chahal, S., et al.: Suicide deaths among medical students, residents and physicians in India spanning a decade (2010–2019): an exploratory study using on line news portals and Google database. International Journal of Social Psychiatry (2021). https://doi.org/10.1177/002076 40211011365

23. Yasir Arafata, S.M., Malib, B., Akterb, H.: Demography and risk factors of suicidal behavior in Bangladesh: a retrospective online news content analysis. Asian Journal of Psychiatry (2018). https://doi.org/10.1016/j.ajp.2018.07.008

24. Pathare, S., Vijayakumar, L., Fernandes, T., et al.: Analysis of news media reports of suicides and attempted suicides during the COVID-19 lockdown in India. Int J Ment Health Syst **14**, 88 (2020). https://doi.org/10.1186/s13033-020-00422-2

25. Sujatha, P.L., Udaya Shankar, B.S., Shivakumar, B.C., Shaji, S.: Profile of unnatural deaths in adult females in Bangalore north. Journal of Indian Academy of Forensic Medicine (2022). https://doi.org/10.5958/0974-0848.2022.00035.5

26. Yadav, S., et al.: Changing pattern of suicide deaths in India. The Lancet Regional Health - Southeast Asia **16**, 100265 (2023). https://doi.org/10.1016/j.lansea.2023.100265

27. Anjanamma, T.C., Vijaya, N.M., Vijayanath, V., Athani, P.: A study of unnatural death at MVJ medical college and research hospital. Indian Journal of Forensic and Community Medicine **3**(2), 138–141 (2016)

28. Valle, V., Gosney, H., Sinclair, J.: Qualitative Analysis of Coroners' Data into the Unnatural Deaths of Children and Adolescents (2018). https://doi.org/10.1111/j.1365-2214.2008.008 58.x

29. World Health Organization (WHO). Suicide: Key Facts (2023). https://www.who.int/news-room/fact-sheets/detail/suicide

30. Xing, X.-Y., et al.: Mortality and disease Burden of Injuries from 2008 to 2017 in Anhui Province, China. BioMed Research International Volume 2020, Article ID 7303897, 10 (2020). https://doi.org/10.1155/2020/7303897

Thorough Analysis of Principal Challenges in Opinion Mining and Sentiment Analysis, Unraveling Prevailing Trends and Techniques Through a Systematic Review

Mansi A. Shah[(⊠)] 🆔 and Ravi M. Gulati 🆔

Department of Computer Science, Veer Narmad South Gujarat University, Surat, Gujarat, India
{masnishah.dcsphd21,rmgulati}@vnsgu.ac.in

Abstract. The pervasive influence of the Internet and the Web has fostered a culture of unabashed expression, where individuals freely share their thoughts on purchased products, viewed movies, or current events. Opinions now play a pivotal role in shaping people's perspectives. This surge in digital discourse has given rise to the widespread use of social networking platforms, blogs, microblogs, online marketplaces, and more. People actively engage in expressing their opinions and seek responses in this interconnected landscape. Consequently, there is an overwhelming abundance of diverse opinions and corresponding responses, making the task of mining this extensive array of data a vital undertaking. This paper presents an in-depth exploration of opinion mining and sentiment analysis, presenting a thorough overview. The analysis delves deep into the principal challenges inherent in these fields, providing insightful examples that underscore the complexity of these issues. Furthermore, the paper explores a myriad of approaches and techniques aimed at addressing each challenge, accompanied by criteria for evaluating their performance.

Keywords: Sentiment Analysis · Opinion mining · Polarity · Challenges · Text mining

1 Introduction

The internet serves as an inclusive platform enabling individuals worldwide to express their perspectives openly. Undoubtedly, the viewpoints of others possess the potential to sway our choices. Leveraging opinions can contribute to enhancing decision-making within specific communities, aiding in the selection of superior products, and exerting influence on decisions. Numerous online platforms, including social media sites like Twitter and Facebook, online marketplaces such as Amazon, Flipkart, Snapdeal, travel planning websites like MakeMyTrip, Trip Advisor, Trivago, and consumer review platforms like MouthShut, offer users the freedom to share their thoughts and evaluations.

Consumers often turn to reviews prior to making both online and offline purchases. They exhibit a tendency to meticulously compare features of similar products in their quest for the perfect purchase. Before committing to a movie outing, individuals frequently peruse film critiques. Vacation planning entails thorough research on various destinations, accompanied by scrutiny of hotel reviews. Conversely, vendors aspire to discern consumer interests for purposes of product enhancement, cost reduction, time efficiency, new product development, offer optimization, and informed decision-making. Competitors, in turn, seek insights from opinions to refine their marketing strategies.

In the process of understanding natural language, various challenges may arise, such as context-dependent polarity judgment, negation handling, sarcasm detection, etc. Context is defined as the parts of a written or spoken statement that precede or follow a specific word or passage, usually influencing its meaning or effect. It is essential to capture the operational concern, that is the pragmatic meaning defined by 'context' for improving the SA task [1]. Negation either reverses the polarity or changes the strength of polarity of affected opinionated words [2]. Sarcasm is defined as a mode of paradoxical wit depending on its effect on bitter and often ironic language that is usually directed towards an individual. Detection of sarcasm is one of the leading areas of research, understanding the true opinion of a person under sarcastic statements [3]. Fake review problem must be addressed so that these large E-commerce industries such as Flipkart, Amazon, etc. can rectify this issue so that the fake reviewers and spammers are eliminated to prevent users from losing trust on online shopping platforms [4].

Within the vast expanse of the internet lies a plethora of opinions and reviews, posing the formidable challenge of extracting and presenting them in a manner beneficial to the intended audience. The intricate task of opinion mining encompasses text analysis, language processing, and text classification. Text mining, as a pivotal component, involves scrutinizing unstructured text, extracting pertinent information, and converting it into actionable business insights. Natural language understanding and artificial intelligence (AI) emerge as the most appropriate computational paradigms to provide embedded intelligence and have been effectively utilized in innumerable domains such as text classification, question answering systems and named entity recognition amongst others [1]. Opinion mining, on the other hand, revolves around discerning the sentiment of an expression—whether it is positive, negative, or neutral—and gauging the intensity of that sentiment.

This paper comprises a) an exploration into opinion mining and sentiment analysis, and b) an exhaustive examination of the principal challenges, accompanied by recent methodologies and techniques employed for their resolution, along with the corresponding criteria for measuring their performance.

2   Opinion Mining and Sentiment Analysis

Definition: If a set of text documents (T) having opinions on an object are given, opinion mining intends to identify various aspects of the object on which opinions have been given, in each of the documents $t \in T$ and to find the polarity of the comments i.e., whether the comments are positive, negative, or neutral [5].

Opinion mining involves the extraction of subjective textual content from various origins and condensing it into a comprehensible format for end-users. Distinguishing sentiment from opinion mining is a subtle task, as both pertain to the analysis of subjective information. In Merriam-Webster's dictionary [6], sentiment is defined as an "attitude, thought, or judgment prompted by feeling", whereas opinion is defined as a "view, judgment formed in the mind about a particular matter". According to the definitions, an opinion primarily reflects an individual's perspective on a matter, while sentiment is predominantly associated with an emotional response or feeling. For instance, the sentence "I am worried about the company's financial future." conveys a sentiment, while the sentence "I believe the company's financial situation is deteriorating." conveys an opinion. The connection between the two sentences lies in their intrinsic correlation, where the emotion conveyed in the initial statement is often a response stemming from the viewpoint articulated in the subsequent sentence. Opinion mining involves the retrieval and assessment of individuals' viewpoints regarding a subject, while sentiment analysis identifies and evaluates emotional words or expressions in a text.

2.1 Opinion Depiction

Opinion mining also referred to as sentiment analysis, retrieves datasets containing subjective text and condenses them into a user-friendly format. It identifies and categorizes opinions within unstructured data as either "positive", "negative" or "neutral."

As depicted in Fig. 1, within any given viewpoint, the entities of "Opinion holder," "Opinion target," and "Opinion content" are readily discernible. However, pinpointing the "Opinion context" proves to be a slightly more challenging task. This refers to the circumstances under which the opinion was expressed, encompassing factors such as time and location. On the other hand, "Opinion sentiment" delves into what the expressed viewpoint reveals about the emotional stance of the opinion holder, whether it leans towards positivity or negativity.

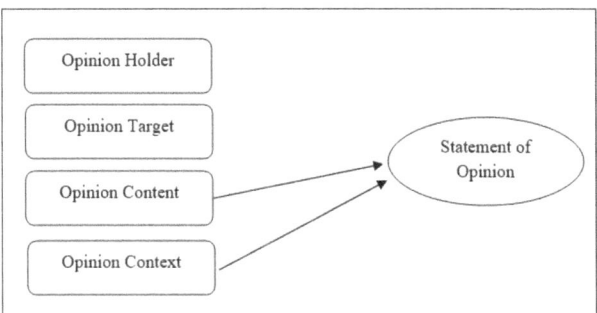

Fig. 1. The Task of Opinion Mining

Example: iPhone XV runs really fast.

In the aforementioned instance, pinpointing the target as iPhone XV is straightforward. The statement "It runs really fast" encapsulates the content, with the individual expressing this sentiment identified as the opinion holder. However, delving further into aspects like context and sentiment, the context extends to particulars such as the review was given on 7th Dec 2023, and the overall opinion sentiment is characterized as positive. This enhanced portrayal of opinions contributes significant value to the opinion mining process.

3   Principal Challenges and Its Approaches (A Systematic Review)

Opinion Mining is a fast-growing field, and such growth leads to too many challenges and issues. For example, the polarity judgment of context dependent opinion, the authenticity of the opinion, removal of noisy text, compression of text, detection of spam or fake reviews, determining the actual opinion part, etc. are challenging issues for further research. The later sections present a systematic review of principal challenges and issues along with recent approaches and techniques used to resolve issues.

3.1   Context Dependent Polarity Judgement

According to the situation the term "Opinion" may have negative polarity in one situation but positive polarity in another situation.

Example:
Sentence 1: The mobile X works well in low signal strength too.
Sentence 2: The mobile Y has low picture quality.

In the above example it is clearly identified that the term "low" is negative but in sentence 1 "works well in low signal strength too" gives a positive review and in sentence 2 the same term in the phrase "low picture quality" gives a negative review about the mobile. Table 1 below shows the overview of the research conducted in this area.

Fulian Yin et al. [7] used context-dependent part of speech (POS) chunks (CP-chunks) to solve lexical sentiment ambiguity, achieving 82% accuracy. Notably, this method exhibits increased stability compared to earlier approaches, as it incorporates negative and positive polarities for each word. In contrast, Saeedeh Sadat Sadidpour et al. [10] proposed a linguistic-based model considering word placement and its effect according to the contextual domain, achieving 92% accuracy. Hitesh Kansal et al. [12] developed an Aspect-Based Sentiment Analysis and Summarization System (ASAS) for opinion polarity, using natural linguistic rules and considering features with opinion words rather than opinion words alone. This approach, which considered features beyond opinion words alone, achieved accuracy rates of 79.1%, 81.3%, and 84.6% for the Apex DVD Player, Canon Camera, and Nokia Phones, respectively. Farhan Hassan Khan et al. [11] employed SentiWordNet for text sentiment detection, using a labeled corpus for training and the sentiment dictionary SentiMI to extract mutual information for selected features, achieving 75.22% accuracy. Comparatively, each method showcases distinct strategies for tackling Context-dependent words.

In their prior research on Machine Learning, Yanking Xia et al. [13] delved into the exploration of intra-opinion and inter-opinion features by employing a Bayesian model. Their investigation specifically addressed the word polarity disambiguation task, tackling it through a probabilistic approach that resulted in an achievement of approximately 80% accuracy. In contrast, Akshi Kumar [1] proposed a distinct Machine Learning

Table 1. Summary of previous research work for Context-Dependent Polarity Judgement

References	Approach	Method	Dataset	Accuracy	Precision	Recall	F-score
Akshi Kumar (2021) [1]	Machine Learning	Hierarchical Attention Network (HAN) model with Embeddings from Language Models (ELMo)	SemEval-2017	71.7%	-	81.6%	82%
			STS-Gold	94.6%			
Fulian Yin et al. (2020) [7]	Lexicon	Corpus based	Corpus LMRD	82%	82.4%	82.1%	82.06%
Murtadha Ahmed et al. (2020) [8]	Hybrid	Supervised Neural Model + corpus-based approach (Attention-based LSTM with Score Embedding (ASE))	Restaurant	86.53%	-	-	-
			Laptop	73.38%			
Omid Mohamad Beigi et al. (2020) [9]	Hybrid	Neural Network and a Sentiment Lexicon	Multi Domain Sentiment Dataset v2.0	74.80%	-	-	-
Saeedeh Sadat Sadidpour et al. (2016) [10]	Lexicon	Polarity pattern matching	News of politics	92%	92%	39%	54%
Farhan Hassan Khan et al. (2015) [11]	Lexicon	Dictionary based approach (SentiMI Dictionary)	Movie review data	75.22%	-	-	75.40%
Hitesh Kansal et al. (2014) [12]	Lexicon	Dictionary Based Approach	Amazon		-	-	-
			DVD Player	94%			
			CanonCamera	92%			
			Nokia Phone	95%			
Yanking Xia et al. (2014) [13]	Machine Learning	Supervised learning method (Bayesian Model)	Mobile phone	80.8%	-	-	-
			Digital Camera				
			Hotel				
			Restaurant				

(continued)

Table 1. (*continued*)

References	Approach	Method	Dataset	Accuracy	Precision	Recall	F-score
Albert Weichselbrau et al. (2010) [14]	Hybrid	Supervised approach (Naïve Bayes) + Lexicon based	Amazon cutomer reviews	76.6%	77%	73%	73.5%
			Trip Advisor reviews				
			Movie review				

methodology, employing a hierarchical attention network (HAN) integrated with ELMo (Embeddings from Language Models). Kumar's approach aimed at classifying sentiments in real-time Twitter data, encompassing multiple-sentence tweets. Remarkably, this method attained a 71.7% accuracy rate for the SemEval-2017 dataset and an impressive 94.6% accuracy for the STS-Gold dataset. It is noteworthy that Xia et al.'s [13] approach primarily concentrated on opinion-level features to mitigate polarity ambiguity, whereas Kumar's [1] method, utilizing a hierarchical attention network, specifically addressed the semantic hierarchy within a document. In the latter, the algorithm was applied twice— first on the word level and subsequently on the sentence level. This distinction underscores the nuanced strategies employed by the two studies in navigating sentiment analysis challenges.

In their exploration of the Hybrid method, Murtadha Ahmed et al. [8] introduced a supervised neural model and built a domain-specific sentiment dictionary called SentiDomain. They utilized cosine similarity to learn cluster embeddings from the comprehensive representation of the relevant domain. Additionally, they introduced an attention-based Long Short Term Memory (LSTM) model for Aspect-level sentiment analysis, achieving 86.53% and 73.38% accuracy for Restaurant and Laptop datasets, respectively. While Beigi et al. [9] created a hybrid neural network and sentiment lexicon to adjust word polarities for specific domains. Their method involved constructing a sentiment lexicon from the source domain, training a Multilayer Perceptron (MLP), and introducing a Domain-Independent Lexicon (DIL) with fixed negative or positive scores. This approach, targeting Document-level Sentiment analysis, achieved an accuracy of 74.80%. Notably, Beigi's method employed a domain-independent dictionary, specifically a Target Sentiment Lexicon (TSL) for updating the trained MLP, achieving better results than cluster embedding methods. Albert Weichselbraun et al. [14] introduced a novel method using Naïve Bayes to identify ambiguous terms, their method involved a contextualized sentiment lexicon storing the polarity of ambiguous terms alongside co-occurring context terms, enhancing the accuracy of sentiment detection to 76.6%. However, a drawback noted was that if the contextualized sentiment lexicon lacked a term, the term's sentiment value defaulted to zero. The comparison reveals diverse strategies within the Hybrid method. Ahmed's focus on domain-dependent dictionaries and cluster embeddings contrasts with Beigi's use of a domain-independent lexicon and Target Sentiment Lexicon. Weichselbraun's approach, leveraging Naïve Bayes and contextualized sentiment lexicons, offers an alternative perspective, highlighting the importance of addressing ambiguous terms in sentiment analysis.

Figure 2 below illustrates the distribution of approaches used based on the work.

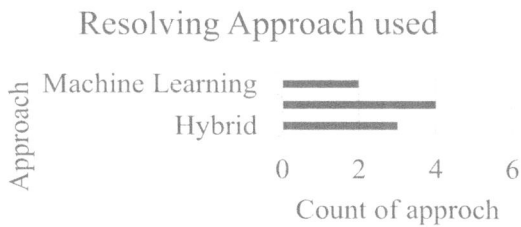

Fig. 2. Previous research works distribution according to the approach used for Context Dependent Polarity Judgment

3.2   Usage of Negation

In research of opinion mining classifier doesn't handle negation well from the container of words. It becomes hard to differentiate between 'nice' and 'not nice'. Both words have different meanings, and it's necessary to identify negation in a sentence.

Example: X movie is not entertaining.
In the above example, 'entertaining' is a positive term for a movie but 'not entertaining' gives a negative review.

Table 2 below shows the overview of the research conducted in this area.

Deebha Mumtaz et al. [20] presented a lexicon-based approach known as the Senti-lexicon algorithm for sentiment analysis, achieving a 70% accuracy rate. This method involves assigning polarity scores to words based on a predefined lexicon. Notably, in the presence of negation words within a sentence, the algorithm reverses the final score, effectively flipping the sentiment orientation. In contrast, Chinsha T C et al. [21] introduced a novel syntactic-based approach focusing on aspect-level sentiment analysis, which attained a higher accuracy of 78.04%. This method incorporates SentiWordNet, syntactic dependency, aggregate scores of opinion words, and an aspect table for a comprehensive opinion mining process. Comparing the two approaches, the former, employed by Deebha Mumtaz et al., is tailored for sentence-level sentiment analysis. It relies on a lexicon-based strategy with the unique feature of handling negation by reversing sentiment scores. In contrast, the method introduced by Chinsha T C et al. is oriented towards aspect-level sentiment analysis, leveraging syntactic structures and multiple sources, including SentiWordNet and aspect tables, to enhance accuracy. Despite the distinctions in their focus and mechanisms, both methods contribute to the advancement of sentiment analysis with varying levels of accuracy.

D V Nagarjuna Devi et al. [18] utilized a machine learning technique for Aspect-Based Sentiment Analysis, employing an SVM classifier that considered subjectivity and

Table 2. Summary of previous research work for Usage of Negation

References	Approach	Method	Dataset	Accuracy	Precision	Recall	F-score
Itisha Gupta et al. (2021) [2]	Hybrid	Lexicon (Corpus based) + ML (Support Vector Machine (SVM))	SemEval-2013 Twitter Corpus	72.6%	-	67.5%	69.5%
Partha Mukherjee et al. (2021) [15]	Machine learning	Recurrent Neural Network	Amazon Product Reviews	95.67%	-	-	-
Prakash Kumar Singh et al. (2021) [16]	Machine learning	Deep Neural Network (BiLSTM + Embedding)	SFU Review	-	92.86%	93.34%	93.09%
Poornima. A et al. (2020) [17]	Machine learning	Logistic Regression (Term Frequency)	Twitter Data	86.23%	-	-	-
D V Nagarjuna Devi et al. (2016) [18]	Machine learning	SVM	Product Review from multiple E-Commerce (Laptop)	88.13%	87.15%	89.76%	-
Rui Xia et al. (2016) [19]	Hybrid	Machine learning + Lexicon (Polarity Shift Detection, Elimination and Ensemble (PSDEE))	Product Reviews from Amazon	82.9%	-	-	-
Deebha Mumtaz et al. (2016) [20]	Lexicon	Senti lexicon algo	Movie Review from Twitter	70%	68.86%	62.01%	-
Chinsha T C et al. (2015) [21]	Lexicon	Dictionary based	Restaurant review from trip advisor	78.04%	83%	89.25%	-

(continued)

Table 2. (*continued*)

References	Approach	Method	Dataset	Accuracy	Precision	Recall	F-score
Jasmine Bhaskar et al. (2014) [22]	Hybrid	Machine learning approach (SVM) + Lexicon (Dictionary based approach)	Product Review from multiple E-Commerce	76.02%	-	-	-
Robert Remus (2013) [23]	Machine learning	Semi supervised (Regular expression based and Conditional random field for classifier SVM)	Multi Domain Dataset	78.01%	-	-	-

objectivity in sentence-level classification. They incorporated a mechanism for handling negations within direct or transitive relations, connecting negated opinion words with a minus symbol, attaining an accuracy of 88.13%. On the other hand, Poornima et al. [17] opted for a feature extraction technique using Bigrams from datasets, analyzing successive word pairs. They selected top bigrams based on frequency distribution for efficient classification, allowing for the modeling of negations. Employing term frequency to ascertain sentiment polarity in sentences, they compared SVM, Logistic Regression, and Multinomial Naive Bayes algorithms. Logistic regression, combined with bigram and n-gram models, demonstrated the highest accuracy at 86.23%. Remus [23] introduced a scheme explicitly modeling and representing word negation, comparing NegEx and Conditional Random Field-based LingScope for negation scope detection. Additionally, they captured negation implicitly through word bi - and trigrams. Explicit negation modeling yielded superior results, achieving a sentiment analysis accuracy of 78.01% in subtasks. Partha Mukherjee et al. [15] presented a comprehensive sentiment analysis method that addresses negations through identification and scope marking. They developed a customized negation marking algorithm and tested various machine learning models, with the Recurrent Neural Network (RNN) attaining the highest accuracy of 95.67%. Notably, this approach considered both explicit and implicit negation detection in product reviews. In a different vein, Prakash Kumar Singh et al. [16] introduced a deep neural network model using LSTM for negation handling tasks. Their model extracted negation features from a labeled input dataset, using the Conan Doyle story corpus for both training and testing. The approach involved identifying negation cues, extracting relationships, and employing word-level features to determine sentence polarity. Comparing these methods, it is evident that each approach employs unique strategies for handling negations in sentiment analysis. While some focus on explicit modeling, others explore both explicit and implicit negation detection. The variation in techniques and algorithms underscores the diverse approaches within the field, each with its strengths and considerations for achieving accurate sentiment analysis.

Itisha Gupta et al. [2] devised a feature-based Targeted Sentiment Analysis (TSA) system within a Hybrid approach that integrates lexicon-based, POS-based, morphological, and n-gram features to manage negations. Their system employed three classifiers – Decision Tree, SVM, and Naive Bayes – and featured an algorithm tailored for tweets where negation might not strictly imply negation. SVM emerged as the most effective classifier, with n-grams and lexicon-based features significantly enhancing its performance, ultimately achieving an accuracy of 72.6%. Notably, the negation scope determination was embedded in the feature engineering preprocessing, incorporating a Twitter-specific automatic lexicon to score words under negation scope, while also considering syntactic negation and rhetorical questions. In a different vein, Rui Xia et al. [19] introduced a cascade model termed Polarity Shift Detection, Elimination, and Ensemble (PSDEE) to handle polarity shifts in document-level sentiment analysis. Their hybrid approach amalgamated rule-based and statistical approaches to identify polarity shifts, including explicit negations and contrasts. The text underwent segmentation into subsets, including polarity-unshifted text, explicit contrasts, eliminated negations, and sentiment inconsistency. The final sentiment classifier was a weighted combination of base classifiers trained on these segmented text subsets, achieving an accuracy of 82.9%. In the former approach Negation scope determination in feature engineering preprocessing involves Twitter-specific automatic lexicon, considering syntactic negation and rhetoric questions, while in the latter approach antonym reversion eliminates polarity shifts. Furthermore, Jasmine Bhaskar et al. [22] employed conventional techniques like Natural Language Processing, Support Vector Machines, and SentiWordNet lexical resources to enhance sentiment classification in product reviews. Their approach specifically addressed negation handling with objective words and intensifier considerations, attaining an accuracy of 76.02%. Each method contributes distinct strategies to the broader field of sentiment analysis, catering to specific nuances and challenges within their respective domains.

Hybrid approaches combining lexicon, morphological, POS-based, and n-gram features offer robustness and generalization across domains but require more effort in feature engineering and model selection. Aspect-based sentiment analysis captures complex patterns, while bigrams and n-gram models provide efficient classification. RNN and LSTM are effective methods for learning negation features.

Figure 3 below illustrates the distribution of approaches used based on the work.

3.3 Handling Informal Language

Nowadays, informal language is very common in reviews and comments. Mining opinion from such informal language is a challenging issue. Using the process of Text Normalization with stop word removal, tokenization, part-of-speech tagging, stemming, and Lemmatization gives the best result for informal language (Tables 3 and 4).

Liang Wu et al. [26] employed a lexicon approach to construct a Slang Sentiment Dictionary (SlangSD) aimed at sentiment classification. Their method yielded notable

Fig. 3. Previous research works distribution according to the approach used for Usage of Negation

Table 3. Example

Yep	Yes
Whats up?	What is going on?
Ttyl	Talk to you later
Life is kinda good	Life is kind of good
Cya	See you

results, achieving precision rates of 77.8% and 78.67%, recall rates of 86.18% and 81.82%, and F-scores of 81.64% and 80.14% for Twitter and SMS datasets, respectively. On the other hand, Fazal Masud Kundi et al. [31] proposed an architecture named Detection and Scoring of Internet Slangs (DSIS) for the identification and scoring of Internet slang. This framework utilized SentiWordNet in combination with other lexical resources, alongside another lexical-based approach that detected and scored slang through various dictionaries. Remarkably, both frameworks demonstrated a high level of accuracy, achieving an impressive 87% accuracy for multi-class classification. When comparing the two approaches, Liang Wu et al. focused on building a dedicated Slang Sentiment Dictionary, and Fazal Masud Kundi et al. adopted a broader framework incorporating SentiWordNet and multiple dictionaries. Despite the differences in their specific methodologies, both studies demonstrated substantial success in achieving high accuracy rates in sentiment classification and slang detection.

Nagarajan et al. [27] employed a machine learning approach, utilizing a hybridization technique that incorporated two optimization algorithms (particle swarm optimization and genetic algorithm) along with a decision tree classifier. The classification model they proposed underwent training in two distinct stages: preprocessing and feature generation. On a different front, Li-Chen Cheng et al. developed a sentiment analysis framework employing deep learning models, specifically BiLSTM networks that made use of NLP tools. Their approach featured a bidirectional RNN, achieving an impressive 87.17% accuracy in learning relation patterns from raw text data. In another perspective, Zhao Jianqiang et al. [28] used unsupervised learning on Twitter corpora to generate sentiment embeddings by leveraging contextual semantic relationships and co-occurrence features.

Table 4. Summary of previous research work for Handling Informal Language

References	Approach	Method	Dataset	Accuracy	Precision	Recall	F-score
Li-Chen Cheng et al. (2019) [24]	Machine learning	Deep Learning (Bidirectional long short-term memory (BiLSTM))	Social Media Review (Facebook & Youtube)	87.17%	85.80%	88.89%	87.29%
Muhammad Javed et al. (2018) [25]	Hybrid	Unsupervised Lexicon	Twitter data on politics	82.35%	81.9%	82.35%	-
Liang Wu et al. (2018) [26]	Lexicon	SentiStrength SSD (Slang sentiment dictionary)	Twitter & SMS data	-	Twitter	Twitter	Twitter
					77.8%	86.18%	81.64%
					SMS	SMS	SMS
					78.67%	81.82%	80.14%
Senthil Murugan Nagarajan et al. (2018) [27]	Machine learning	Particle swam optimization + genetic algo + Decision Tree	Twitter dataset	90%	91.5%	91.7%	91.4%
Zhao Jianqiang et al. (2017) [28]	Machine learning	Unsupervised machine learning + Deep Neural N/W Global Vector Deep Convolution Neural N/W (GLoVe-DCNN)	Twitter dataset	85.63%	84.50%	83.94%	84.10%
Saprativa Bhattacharjee et al. (2015) [29]	Hybrid	Lexicon for pre-processing + Supervised machine learning (Cosine similarity measure for classification)	Telecom Domain	71.5%	-	-	-
Tawunrat Chalothorn et al. (2015) [30]	Hybrid	Machine learning + Lexicon (Ensemble method)	Twitter & SMS data	-	-	-	Tweet
							Dataset
							86.05%
							SMS
							88.82%

(*continued*)

Table 4. (*continued*)

References	Approach	Method	Dataset	Accuracy	Precision	Recall	F-score
Farhan Hassan Khan et al. (2014) [11]	Machine Learning	Semi-Supervised (Lexicon + Mutual info Random Walk))	Movie Review Dataset	75.22%	-	-	75.40%
Fazal Masud Kundi et al. (2014) [31]	Lexicon based	Detection and scoring of Internet slang using SentiWordNet	Twitter Dataset	87%	85.78%	91.93%	88.09%
Fazal Masud Kundi et al. (2014) [32]	Lexicon based	-	Twitter Dataset	87%	84.33%	83%	76.66%
Neethu M S et al. (2013) [33]	Machine learning	SVM, Naive bays, Max Entropy, Ensemble	Twitter data of Electronic Products	90%	87.5%	93%	-

The sentiment embeddings, along with n-grams and features based on sentiment polarity scores, constituted a comprehensive collection of sentiment attributes for training and forecasting sentiment classification labels. Notably, both approaches involved standardizing slang by utilizing an Internet slang word dictionary. In a different study, Neethu et al. [33] presented a machine learning approach for tweet classification, incorporating a novel feature vector and sentence-level sentiment analysis. They employed various classifiers such as Support Vector Machine, Naive Bayes, Maximum Entropy, and Ensemble classifiers, culminating in an ensemble classifier generated through voting rules. Meanwhile, Farhan Hassan Khan et al. [11] presented a semi-supervised approach (Lexicon + Mutual info Random Walk) and developed a SentiMI dictionary. Their comprehensive framework involved feature selection and mutual information extraction from SentiMI for the chosen features, ultimately achieving an accuracy of 75.22%. These diverse methodologies highlight the versatility and adaptability of machine learning approaches in handling Informal Language.

Muhammad Javed et al. [25] presented a Hybrid approach, introducing a mechanism designed to normalize informal tokens. This mechanism comprised four stages: Speech Tagging, Noise Reduction, Stop Word Removal, stemming, and Lemmatization. Notably, the study provided explicit definitions for each extracted informal and non-standard term during the normalization phase, ultimately attaining an accuracy of 82.35%. In a different approach, Saprativa Bhattacharjee et al. [29] suggested a hybrid method that incorporates a lexicon-driven preprocessing technique for reducing noise and sentiment classification. This method utilized supervised machine learning and cosine similarity to categorize the sentiment expressed in user comments on a scale of –2 (very negative) to +2 (very positive), achieving an accuracy of 71.5%. Noteworthy is the manual handling of slang in both approaches. Comparing these methods, Muhammad Javed et al. focused on a comprehensive normalization mechanism for informal tokens, ensuring precise definitions for each term in the normalization process. Alternatively, Saprativa Bhattacharjee et al. employed a lexicon-based preprocessing algorithm, combining supervised machine learning and cosine similarity for sentiment classification. The manual handling of slang in both methods underscores a shared consideration for addressing informal language in sentiment analysis.

Hybrid approaches using noise reduction, speech tagging, stemming, and lemmatization extract informal terms but have limitations in certain expressions and limited generalization. The Slang Sentiment Dictionary handles slang expressions but struggles with generalization and lexical resources, while Internet Slang Detection achieves high accuracy but lacks specific details. The BiLSTM-based sentiment analysis achieves high accuracy but requires significant data and computational resources. Unsupervised learning, hybrid, ensemble, and semi-supervised approaches improve robustness.

Figure 4 below illustrates the distribution of approaches used based on the work.

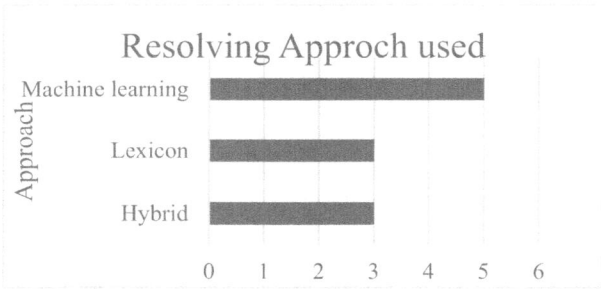

Fig. 4. Previous research works distribution according to the approach used for Handling Informal Language

3.4 Sarcastic Sentence

Sarcasm or ironic remark that seems to be praising but in reality, it is opposite of what is said. This type of sentence uses exact opinion words with positive polarity but actually, it indicates negative polarity. So, the identification of sarcasm is an issue.

Example: Wow! What a phone! It ran out of battery in just 1 h.
In the above example, it is actually a negative opinion about the phone's battery. So, finding out the sarcasm in a sentence is a challenging task.

Table 5 below shows the overview of the research conducted in this area.

Monika Bhakun et al. [3] devised a machine learning technique for sarcasm detection, achieving an accuracy of 93%. This method focuses on feature creation. In contrast, Jyoti Godara et al. [34] proposed a technique utilizing an SVM classifier combined with K-mean clustering and PCA, also attaining a 93% accuracy rate. Their approach emphasizes feature extraction and reduction. Karthik Sundararajan et al. [35] introduced an

Table 5. Summary of previous research work for Sarcastic Sentence

References	Approach	Method	Dataset	Accuracy	Precision	Recall	F-score
Monika Bhakun et al. (2022) [3]	Machine Learning	SVM	Twitter Dataset	93%	-	-	-
Jyoti Godara et al. (2021) [34]	Machine Learning	SVM with Principal Component Analysis (PCA) and K means clustering	Twitter Dataset	93.49%	61%	93%	
Karthik Sundararajan et al. (2020) [35]	Machine Learning	An ensemble-based feature selection method	Twitter Dataset	92.7%	-	-	-
Lu Ren et al. (2020) [36]	Machine Learning	CNN Multi-level Memory Network based on Sentiment Semantics (MMNSS)	Internet argument corpus(IAC-V1)	-	66.86%	70.93%	67.67%
			Internet argument corpus(IAC-V2)		75%	71.05%	74.20%
			Twitter		85.76%	89.24%	87.13%
Sudarshan S. Sonawane et al. (2020) [37]	Machine learning	Term co-occurrence-based sarcasm detection	Twitter Dataset	93.54%	93.84%	-	-
Rahul Gupta et al. (2020) [38]	Machine learning	TF-IDF feature extraction with voting classifier	Twitter Dataset	83.53%	-	-	-
Avinash Chandra Pandey et al. (2017) [39]	Hybrid	Machine learning + Lexicon based (Meta heuristic approach based on K means and cuckoo search (CSK))	Twitter Dataset	77.99%	-	-	-
S K Bharti et al. (2015) [40]	Hybrid	Hadoop based framework with 3 algorithms	Twitter Dataset	-	97%	98%	97%
Mondher Bouazizi et al. (2015) [41]	Machine learning	Random Forest with cross-validation	Twitter Dataset	83.1%	91.1%	73.4%	81.3%

ensemble-based feature selection method for sarcasm detection, yielding a notable accuracy of 92.7%. Additionally, they applied a multi-rule-based method to identify different sarcasm. In a similar vein, Lu Ren et al. [36] developed a multi-level memory network incorporating sentiment semantics for capturing the expression of sarcastic features. This two-tiered network involves a first-level network for sentiment and a second-level network for contrast, enhanced further by an improved convolutional neural network.

Sudarshan S. Sonawane et al. [37] presented a method that included extraction of features and selection of optimal feature through term co-occurrence analysis, achieving an accuracy of 93.54%. On a different note, Rahul Gupta et al. [38] utilized 200 top TF-IDF features, sentiment analysis, and punctuation to identify sarcastic content in tweets, obtaining 83.53% accuracy through a voting classifier. Meanwhile, Mondher Bouazizi et al. [41] employed part-of-speech tags for extracting four sets of features, covering various sarcasm types, and achieved an 83.1% accuracy in classifying tweets as sarcastic or non-sarcastic. Comparing these approaches, it is evident that diverse methodologies such as feature creation, extraction, reduction, ensemble-based feature selection, and multi-level memory networks have been employed to address sarcasm detection. The achieved accuracies vary slightly, showcasing the effectiveness of each method in capturing the nuances of sarcastic expression in textual data.

Pandey et al. [39] presented an innovative metaheuristic method called CSK, incorporating feature extraction through K-means and cuckoo search techniques. This approach resulted in an accuracy of 77.99%. On a different note, S K Bharti et al. [40] devised a Hadoop framework utilizing natural language processing (NLP) methods for the immediate identification of sarcasm in tweets. Their method involves parts-of-speech (POS) tagging, parsing, and text mining. Comparing these approaches underscores the diversity of techniques employed in sarcasm detection, with each method addressing the challenges through distinct methodologies.

Approaches to sarcasm detection vary in complexities, accuracies, and feature extraction methods. Recent techniques use advanced machine learning and neural networks, while simpler methods like TF-IDF may still be effective.

Figure 5 below illustrates the distribution of approaches used based on the work.

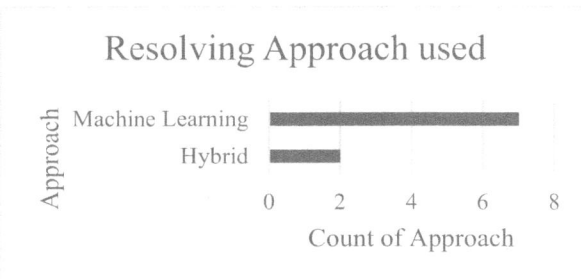

Fig. 5. Previous research works distribution according to the approach used for Sarcastic Sentence

3.5 Fake Review Analysis

With the increasing use of the internet, a bunch of opinions are available and among them, many would be fake or spam. Detection of such reviews is a challenging task.

Table 6 below shows the overview of the research conducted in this area.

Kauffmanna et al. [42] introduced the FRDF modular framework, employing Natural Language Processing (NLP) to identify fake reviews, yielding an impressive accuracy

Table 6. Summary of previous research work for Fake Review Analysis

References	Approach	Method	Dataset	Accuracy	Precision	Recall	F-score
Syed Mohammed Anas et al. (2021) [4]	Machine learning	Random Forest	Amazon academic review	89.48%	85.57%	94.38%	89.76%
Erick Kauffmanna et al. (2019) [42]	Lexicon	Corpus based Fake Review Detection Framework (FRDF)	Amazon Product Database	85.53%	-	89.19%	87.32%
Lakshmi Holla et al. (2019) [43]	Machine learning	Decision Tree	Hotel Review Dataset	98.75%	-	-	-
Rohit Narayan et al. (2018) [44]	Machine learning	Logistic regression	Public dataset for spam detection	86.25%	90%	83.72%	86.72%
Elshrif Elmurngi et al. (2018) [45]	Machine learning	SVM	Movie Review Dataset	Dataset1–76%	Dataset1–81.1%	-	-
				Datsset2–81.35%	Dataset2–74.9%		
Xiaolong Deng et al. (2014) [46]	Machine learning	Naïve Bayes	Restaurant review dataset	74%	-	-	-
Qingxi Peng et al. (2014) [47]	Lexicon	Shallow dependency parser	Review from resellerrating.com	Dataset1–85.7%	-	-	-
				Dataset2–86.3%			
				Dataset3–82.6%			
				Dataset4–84.5%			

of 85.53%. In contrast, Qingxi Peng et al. [47] developed a method for spam review detection and calculating scores of sentiments using a shallow dependency parser. Their approach incorporates distinguishing rules to pinpoint unexpected patterns within product reviews, coupled with a time series analysis method that exhibits high accuracy rates. Notably, Peng et al.'s methodology involves a considerable manual workload. However, it's worth noting that their method involves a significant manual effort, which could be a potential drawback in terms of scalability and efficiency.

Syed Mohammed Anas et al. [41] employed Feature Extraction and the Random Forest Method to develop a model, yielding an accuracy of 89.48%. In contrast, Lakshmi Holla et al. [43] utilized domain words and the Latent Dirichlet Allocation topic model to identify fake product reviews, achieving an impressive accuracy of 98.75%. Their approach involved extracting domain features from product reviews and emphasizing limited review-centric features. Rohit Narayan et al. [44] adopted a supervised learning technique, incorporating LIWC, POS, and n-gram features. Their model achieved

86.25% accuracy using a logistic regression classifier. Elshrif Elmurngi et al. [45] developed a method focusing on attribute and feature selection, attaining accuracy rates of 76% and 81.35% on two datasets, respectively. Notably, their approach demonstrated the highest accuracy in both text classification and fake review detection. Finally, Xiaolong Deng et al. [46] presented a method for identifying hype-induced fake reviews with around 74% accuracy, utilizing sentiment and multi-dimensional subject word libraries on restaurant reviews.

Feature extraction and Random Forest methods effectively identify information in large datasets, but feature choice affects performance. Domain-specific words and LDA capture specialized language patterns but require computational resources. LIWC and POS features offer linguistic insights, but manual features limit their effectiveness. Sensitivity and multi-dimensional subject word libraries detect fake reviews, but accuracy may be limited.

Figure 6 below illustrates the distribution of approaches used based on the work.

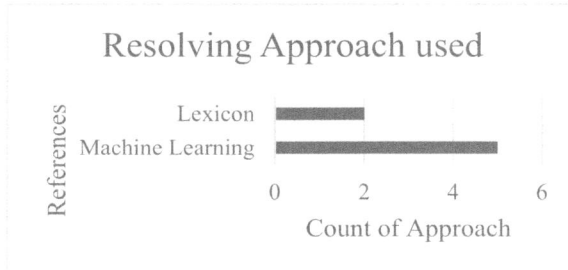

Fig. 6. Previous research works distribution according to the approach used for Fake Review Analysis

3.6 Use of Emoticons

Nowadays nonverbal cues are important to express their views. The increasing use of emoticons in review is a challenging task to mine accurate opinions.

Table 7 below shows the overview of the research conducted in this area.

Mohammad Aman Ullah et al. [49] developed deep learning algorithms, specifically Convolutional Neural Network (CNN) and Long Short-Term Memory (LSTM) applied to analyzing Twitter sentiments. The features considered in their approach included Bag of Words, TF-IDF, N-gram, and emoticon lexicons. Remarkably, the LSTM model exhibited an impressive accuracy of 89%. Benkhelifa et al. [50] focused on opinion extraction and classification within the context of YouTube cooking recipe comments. Their SVM-based system achieved a remarkable 95.3% accuracy by incorporating considerations for injections and emoticons. Addressing the challenge of classifiers performing inconsistently across different topics, K Lavanya et al. [53] introduced a Topic Adaptive Training method utilizing SVM. Despite achieving a comparatively lower accuracy of 70%, their approach sought to enhance performance across diverse subject matters. Deshwal et al.

Table 7. Summary of previous research work for the Use of Emoticons

References	Approach	Method	Dataset	Accuracy	Precision	Recall	F-score
María Lucía Barron Estrada et al. (2020) [48]	Hybrid	Machine Learning algorithm + Corpus based approach	Comments from Educational platform	SentiTEXT-93% EduSERE-84%	-	-	-
Mohammad Aman Ullah et al. (2020) [49]	Machine learning	Deep Learning (Long short-term memory)	Twitter Dataset on airline	89%	85%	89%	86%
Randa Benkhelifa et al. (2018) [50]	Machine learning	SVM	Cooking recipe comments from Youtube	F1 83.5% F2 95.3%	83.5% 95.3%	83.5% 95.3%	83.5% 95.3%
Rathan M et al. (2017) [51]	Hybrid	Lexicon + Machine learning	Twitter Dataset	OnePlus5–74.31% Samsung S8–86.01%	-	-	-
Avinash Chandra Pandey et al. (2017) [52]	Hybrid	Machine learning + Lexicon (Meta heuristic method)		77.99%	-	-	-
K Lavanya et al. (2017) [53]	Machine learning	SVM with PMI-IR technique	Twitter Dataset	70%	96%	83%	88%
Ajay Deshwal et al. (2016) [54]	Machine learning	Discriminative Multinomial naïve Bayes	Twitter Dataset	-	77.6%	78.7%	76.9%
B. M. Bandgar et al. (2016) [55]	Machine learning	Unsupervised technique	Twitter Dataset	77.22%	-	-	-
Ana Carolina E.S. Lima et al. (2015) [56]	Hybrid	Machine learning + Lexicon		80%	-	-	-
A. Montejo-R´aez et al. (2014) [57]	Machine learning	Non supervised (SentiWordNet + random walk analysis)	Twitter Dataset	-	62.59%	62.07%	62.33%
Nádia F.F. da Silva et al. (2014) [58]	Hybrid	Lexicon + Ensemble (Logistic Regression + Random Forest + Multinomial NB) based approach	Twitter Dataset from multiple Domain	80.02%	-	-	-

[54] explored feature extraction techniques and supervised classification algorithms to analyze emoticons. They identified the discriminative multinomial naïve Bayes as a promising algorithm for this task. Taking an unsupervised approach, B. M. Bandgar et al. [55] utilized the SWNC algorithm for classification, achieving an accuracy of 77.22%. In contrast, A. Montejo-Ráez et al. [57] presented an innovative approach for classifying the sentiment polarity of Twitter posts. Their approach leveraged weighted nodes from WordNet graphs, incorporating non-supervised, domain-independent solutions. This method combined SentiWordNet scores with a random walk analysis of text concepts over a WordNet graph. In comparing these methods, it is evident that the choice of algorithms and features plays a crucial role in sentiment analysis. While deep learning models like LSTM demonstrate high accuracy, SVM-based systems, particularly in specialized domains like cooking recipes on YouTube, can outperform with careful consideration of specific linguistic elements. Additionally, unsupervised approaches, such as those incorporating WordNet graphs, showcase alternative strategies for sentiment analysis that may offer valuable insights in specific contexts.

María Lucía Barron Estrada et al. [48] introduced a hybrid technique combining an Evolutionary model and a corpus-based approach to effectively handle emoticons. The proposed method yielded notable accuracies of 93% and 84% for SentiTEXT and EduSERE, respectively. Rathan M et al. [51] presented a Lexicon-based model featuring an SVM classifier capable of handling both Emojis and Emoticons. This approach offers a specialized focus on linguistic elements and achieves competitive results in sentiment analysis. Pandey et al. [52] creatively presented a new metaheuristic method called CSK, which combines K-means and cuckoo search techniques. By modifying random initialization and incorporating Feature Extraction, this approach significantly improved performance and accuracy in sentiment analysis, Ana Carolina E.S. Lima et al. [56] devised a Polarity Analysis Framework that seamlessly combined lexicon-based and machine learning approaches. This hybrid approach demonstrated a commendable 80% accuracy. Nádia F.F. da Silva et al. [58] suggested a hybrid method that combined Lexicon and Classifier Ensemble techniques. Their focus on feature hashing for tweet sentiment analysis and the utilization of bag-of-words contributed to achieving a balanced accuracy in sentiment classification. Comparatively, these methods showcase the diverse strategies employed in identifying sentences with emojis. While some opt for hybrid techniques, integrating evolutionary models and corpus-based approaches, others focus on specialized models like Lexicon-based methods with SVM classifiers. The incorporation of metaheuristic methods, such as CSK, highlights the innovative ways researchers are enhancing sentiment analysis through modifications in random initialization and feature extraction. Overall, the integration of lexicon-based methods and machine learning, as demonstrated in the Polarity Analysis Framework, stands out as a robust strategy for achieving high accuracy in sentiment classification.

Figure 7 below illustrates the distribution of approaches used based on the work.

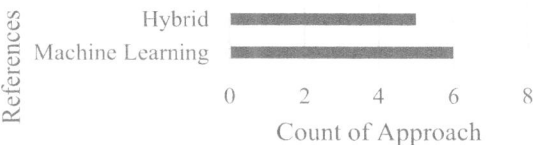

Fig. 7. Previous research works distribution according to the approach used for Use of Emoticons

4 Conclusion

Opinion mining, an evolving domain, endeavours to distil insights from vast datasets encompassing consumer comments, feedback, and reviews spanning diverse subjects. This realm leverages a spectrum of technologies to decipher sentiments and perspectives on various entities, be it products, topics, or individual opinions. However, amid the pervasive use of applications, opinion mining confronts a spectrum of research challenges. This paper unfolds with Sect. 1 furnishing an introduction to Opinion Mining. Section 2 delves into the nuances of opinion mining, dissecting sentiment analysis and opinion depiction. Building on this foundation, Sect. 3 provides a comprehensive exploration of the primary challenges encountered in Opinion Mining and Sentiment Analysis. Additionally, the section elucidates recent techniques deployed to surmount these challenges, accompanied by an assessment of their performance metrics. The discussion is enriched with real-world examples to illuminate the intricacies. This systematic survey paper aims to be useful resource for both veteran researchers as well as newcomers in the ever-evolving field of Sentiment Analysis and Opinion Mining.

References

1. Kumar, A.: Contextual semantics using hierarchical attention network for sentiment classification in social internet-of-things. Multimedia Tools Appl. **81** (2021). https://doi.org/10.1007/s11042-021-11262-8
2. Gupta, I., Joshi, N.: Feature-based twitter sentiment analysis with improved negation handling. IEEE Trans. Comput. Soc. Syst. **8**(4), 917–927 (2021). https://doi.org/10.1109/TCSS.2021.3069413
3. Bhakuni, M., Kumar, K., Sonia, U., Iwendi, C., Singh, A.: Evolution and evaluation: sarcasm analysis for Twitter data using sentiment analysis. J. Sens. **2022**, 6287559 (2022). https://doi.org/10.1155/2022/6287559
4. Anas, S.M., Kumari, S.: Opinion mining based fake product review monitoring and removal system. In: 2021 6th International Conference on Inventive Computation Technologies (ICICT), Coimbatore, India, pp. 985–988 (2021). https://doi.org/10.1109/ICICT50816.2021.9358716
5. Seerat, B., Azam, F.: Opinion mining: issues and challenges (a survey). Int. J. Comput. Appl. **49**, 42–51 (2012). https://doi.org/10.5120/7658-0762
6. https://www.merriam-webster.com/dictionary

7. Yin, F., Wang, Y., Liu, J., Lin, L.: The construction of sentiment lexicon based on context-dependent part-of-speech chunks for semantic disambiguation. IEEE Access **8**, 63359–63367 (2020)

8. Ahmed, M., Chen, Q., Li, Z.: Constructing domain-dependent sentiment dictionary for sentiment analysis. Neural Comput. Appl. **32** (2020). https://doi.org/10.1007/s00521-020-048 24-8

9. Beigi, O., Moattar, M.: Automatic construction of domain-specific sentiment lexicon for unsupervised domain adaptation and sentiment classification. Knowl.-Based Syst. **213**, 106423 (2020). https://doi.org/10.1016/j.knosys.2020.106423

10. Sadidpour, S.S., Shirazi, H., Sharef, N.M., Minaei-Bidgoli, B., Sanjaghi, M.E.: Context-sensitive opinion mining using polarity patterns. Int. J. Adv. Comput. Sci. Appl. **7**(9) (2016). https://doi.org/10.14569/IJACSA.2016.070920

11. Khan, F.H., Qamar, U., Bashir, S.: SentiMI: introducing point-wise mutual information with SentiWordNet to improve sentiment polarity detection. Appl. Soft Comput. **39**, 140–153 (2016). https://doi.org/10.1016/j.asoc.2015.11.016

12. Kansal, H., Toshniwal, D.: Aspect-based summarization of context dependent opinion words. Procedia Comput. Sci. **35**, 166–175 (2014). https://doi.org/10.1016/j.procs.2014.08.096

13. Xia, Y., Cambria, E., Hussain, A., et al.: Word polarity disambiguation using Bayesian model and opinion-level features. Cogn. Comput. **7**, 369–380 (2015). https://doi.org/10.1007/s12 559-014-9298-4

14. Weichselbraun, A., Scharl, A.: A context-dependent supervised learning approach to sentiment detection in large textual databases (2013)

15. Mukherjee, P., Badr, Y., Doppalapudi, S., Srinivasan, S.M., Sangwan, R.S., Sharma, REffect of negation in sentences on sentiment analysis and polarity detection. Procedia Comput. Sci. **185**, 370–379 (2021). https://doi.org/10.1016/j.procs.2021.05.038

16. Singh, P.K., Paul, S.: Deep learning approach for negation handling in sentiment analysis. IEEE Access **9**, 102579–102592 (2021). https://doi.org/10.1109/ACCESS.2021.3095412

17. Poornima, A., Priya, K.S.: A comparative sentiment analysis of sentence embedding using machine learning techniques. In: 2020 6th International Conference on Advanced Computing and Communication Systems (ICACCS), Coimbatore, India, pp. 493–496 (2020). https://doi.org/10.1109/ICACCS48705.2020.9074312

18. Devi, D.V.N., Kumar, C.K., Prasad, S.: A feature based approach for sentiment analysis by using support vector machine. In: 2016 IEEE 6th International Conference on Advanced Computing (IACC), Bhimavaram, India, pp. 3–8 (2016). https://doi.org/10.1109/IACC.201 6.11

19. Xia, R., Xu, F., Yu, J., Qi, Y., Cambria, E.: Polarity shift detection, elimination and ensemble: a three-stage model for document-level sentiment analysis. Inf. Process. Manag. **52**(1), 36–45 (2016). https://doi.org/10.1016/j.ipm.2015.04.003

20. Mumtaz, D., Ahuja, B.: Sentiment analysis of movie review data using Senti-lexicon algorithm. In: 2016 2nd International Conference on Applied and Theoretical Computing and Communication Technology (iCATccT), Bangalore, India, pp. 592–597 (2016). https://doi.org/10.1109/ICATCCT.2016.7912069

21. Chinsha, T.C., Joseph, S.: A syntactic approach for aspect based opinion mining. In: Proceedings of the 2015 IEEE 9th International Conference on Semantic Computing (IEEE ICSC 2015), Anaheim, CA, USA, pp. 24–31 (2015). https://doi.org/10.1109/ICOSC.2015.7050774

22. Bhaskar, J., Sruthi K, Nedungadi, P.: Enhanced sentiment analysis of informal textual communication in social media by considering objective words and intensifiers. In: International Conference on Recent Advances and Innovations in Engineering (ICRAIE-2014), Jaipur, India, pp. 1–6 (2014). https://doi.org/10.1109/ICRAIE.2014.6909220

23. Remus, R.: Modeling and representing negation in data-driven machine learning-based sentiment analysis. In: ESSEM@AI*IA (2013)

24. Cheng, L.-C., Tsai, S.-L.: Deep learning for automated sentiment analysis of social media. In: 2019 IEEE/ACM International Conference on Advances in Social Networks Analysis and Mining (ASONAM), Vancouver, BC, Canada, pp. 1001–1004 (2019). https://doi.org/10.1145/3341161.3344821
25. Javed, M., Kamal, S.: Normalization of unstructured and informal text in sentiment analysis. IJACSA **9**(10) (2018). https://doi.org/10.14569/IJACSA.2018.091011
26. Wu, L., Morstatter, F., Liu, H.: SlangSD: building and using a sentiment dictionary of slang words for short-text sentiment classification. Lang. Resour. Eval. **52** (2016). https://doi.org/10.1007/s10579-018-9416-0
27. Nagarajan, S.M., Gandhi, U.D.: Classifying streaming of Twitter data based on sentiment analysis using hybridization. Neural Comput. Appl. **31**, 1425–1433 (2019). https://doi.org/10.1007/s00521-018-3476-3
28. Jianqiang, Z., Xiaolin, G., Xuejun, Z.: Deep convolution neural networks for Twitter sentiment analysis. IEEE Access **6**, 23253–23260 (2018). https://doi.org/10.1109/ACCESS.2017.2776930
29. Bhattacharjee, S., Das, A., Bhattacharya, U., Parui, S.K., Roy, S.: Sentiment analysis using cosine similarity measure. In: 2015 IEEE 2nd International Conference on Recent Trends in Information Systems (ReTIS), Kolkata, India, pp. 27–32 (2015). https://doi.org/10.1109/ReTIS.2015.7232847
30. Chalothom, T., Ellman, J.: Simple approaches of sentiment analysis via ensemble learning. In: Kim, K. (ed.) Information Science and Applications. LNEE, vol 339. Springer, Berlin, Heidelberg (2015). https://doi.org/10.1007/978-3-662-46578-3_74
31. Muhammad, A.: Detection and scoring of internet slangs for sentiment analysis using SentiWordNet. Life Sci. J. **11**, 66–72 (2014). https://doi.org/10.6084/M9.FIGSHARE.1609621
32. Kundi, F.M., Khan, A., Ahmad, S., Asghar, M.Z.: Lexicon-based sentiment analysis in the social web. J. Basic Appl. Sci. Res. **4**, 238–248
33. Neethu, M.S., Rajasree, R.: Sentiment analysis in twitter using machine learning techniques. In: 2013 Fourth International Conference on Computing, Communications and Networking Technologies (ICCCNT), Tiruchengode, India, pp. 1–5 (2013). https://doi.org/10.1109/ICCCNT.2013.6726818
34. Godara, J., Aron, R.: Support vector machine classifier with principal component analysis and k mean for sarcasm detection. In: 2021 7th International Conference on Advanced Computing and Communication Systems (ICACCS), Coimbatore, India, pp. 571–576 (2021). https://doi.org/10.1109/ICACCS51430.2021.9442033
35. Sundararajan, K., Palanisamy, A.: Multi-rule based ensemble feature selection model for sarcasm type detection in Twitter. Comput. Intell. Neurosci. **2020**, 2860479 (2020). https://doi.org/10.1155/2020/2860479
36. Ren, L., Xu, B., Lin, H., Liu, X., Yang, L.: Sarcasm detection with sentiment semantics enhanced multi-level memory network. Neurocomputing, **401**, 320–326 (2020). https://doi.org/10.1016/j.neucom.2020.03.081
37. Sonawane, S.S., Kolhe, S.R.: TCSD: term co-occurrence based sarcasm detection from twitter trends. Procedia Comput. Sci. **167**, 830–839 (2020). https://doi.org/10.1016/j.procs.2020.03.422
38. Gupta, R., Kumar, J., Agrawal, H.: A statistical approach for sarcasm detection using Twitter data. In: 2020 4th International Conference on Intelligent Computing and Control Systems (ICICCS), Madurai, India, 633–638 (2020). https://doi.org/10.1109/ICICCS48265.2020.9120917
39. Pandey, A.C., Rajpoot, D.S., Saraswat, M.: Twitter sentiment analysis using hybrid cuckoo search method. Inf. Process. Manag. **53**(4), 764–779 (2017). https://doi.org/10.1016/j.ipm.2017.02.004

40. Bharti, D., Vachha, B., Pradhan, R., Babu, K., Jena, S.: Sarcastic sentiment detection in tweets streamed in real time: a big data approach. Digit. Commun. Netw. **2** (2016). https://doi.org/10.1016/j.dcan.2016.06.002
41. Bouazizi, M., Ohtsuki, T.: Sarcasm detection in Twitter: all your products are incredibly amazing!!! - Are they really? In: 2015 IEEE Global Communications Conference (GLOBECOM), San Diego, CA, USA, pp. 1–6 (2015). https://doi.org/10.1109/GLOCOM.2015.7417640
42. Kauffmann, E., Peral, J., Gil, D., Ferrández, A., Sellers, R., Mora, H.: A framework for big data analytics in commercial social networks: a case study on sentiment analysis and fake review detection for marketing decision-making. Ind. Market. Manag. **90**, 523–537 (2020). https://doi.org/10.1016/j.indmarman.2019.08.003
43. Holla, L., Kavitha, K.S.: Opinion spam detection and analysis by identifying domain features in product reviews. In: Proceedings of International Conference on Sustainable Computing in Science, Technology and Management (SUSCOM). Amity University Rajasthan, Jaipur, India (2019)
44. Narayan, R., Rout, J.K., Jena, S.K.: Review spam detection using opinion mining. In: Sa, P., Sahoo, M., Murugappan, M., Wu, Y., Majhi, B. (eds.) Progress in Intelligent Computing Techniques: Theory, Practice, and Applications. Advances in Intelligent Systems and Computing, vol. 719. Springer, Singapore (2018). https://doi.org/10.1007/978-981-10-3376-6_30
45. Elmurngi, E., Gherbi, A.: Detecting fake reviews through sentiment analysis using machine learning techniques (2018)
46. Deng, X., Chen, R.: Sentiment analysis based online restaurants fake reviews hype detection. In: Han, W., Huang, Z., Hu, C., Zhang, H., Guo, L. (eds.) Web Technologies and Applications. APWeb 2014. LNCS, vol. 8710. Springer, Cham (2014). https://doi.org/10.1007/978-3-319-11119-3_1
47. Peng, Q., Zhong, M.: Detecting spam review through sentiment analysis. J. Softw. **9** (2014). https://doi.org/10.4304/jsw.9.8.2065-2072
48. Estrada, M.L.B., Cabada, R.Z., Bustillos, R.O., Graff, M.: Opinion mining and emotion recognition applied to learning environments. Expert Syst. Appl. **150**, 113265 (2020). https://doi.org/10.1016/j.eswa.2020.113265
49. Ullah, M.A., Marium, S.M., Begum, S.A., Dipa, N.S.: An algorithm and method for sentiment analysis using the text and emoticon, ICT Express **6**(4), 357–360 (2020). https://doi.org/10.1016/j.icte.2020.07.003
50. Benkhelifa, R., Laallam, F.Z.: Opinion extraction and classification of real-time YouTube cooking recipes comments. In: Hassanien, A., Tolba, M., Elhoseny, M., Mostafa, M. (eds.) The International Conference on Advanced Machine Learning Technologies and Applications (AMLTA2018). AMLTA 2018. Advances in Intelligent Systems and Computing, vol. 723. Springer, Cham. (2018). https://doi.org/10.1007/978-3-319-74690-6_39
51. Rathan, M., Hulipalled, V.R., Venugopal, K.R., Patnaik, L.M.: Consumer insight mining: aspect based Twitter opinion mining of mobile phone reviews. Appl. Soft Comput. **68**, 765–773 (2018)
52. Pandey, A.C., Rajpoot, D.S., Saraswat, M.: Twitter sentiment analysis using the hybrid cuckoo search method. Inf. Process. Manage. **53**(4), 764–779 (2017)
53. Lavanya, K., Deisy, C.: Twitter sentiment analysis using multi-class SVM. In: 2017 International Conference on Intelligent Computing and Control (I2C2), pp. 1–6. IEEE (2017)
54. Deshwal, A., Sharma, S.K.: Twitter sentiment analysis using various classification algorithms. In: 2016 5th International Conference on Reliability, Infocom Technologies and Optimization (Trends and Future Directions) (ICRITO), pp. 251–257. IEEE (2016)
55. Bandgar, B.M., Sheeja, D.S.: Analysis of real time social tweets for opinion mining. Int. J. Appl. Eng. Res. **11**(2), 1404–1407 (2016)
56. Lima, A.C.E., de Castro, L.N., Corchado, J.M.: A polarity analysis framework for Twitter messages. Appl. Math. Comput. **270**, 756–767 (2015)

57. Montejo-Ráez, A., Martínez-Cámara, E., Martín-Valdivia, M.T., Ureña-López, L.A.: Ranked WordNet graph for sentiment polarity classification in Twitter. Comput. Speech Lang. **28**(1), 93–107 (2014)
58. Da Silva, N.F., Hruschka, E.R., Hruschka, E.R., Jr.: Tweet sentiment analysis with classifier ensembles. Decis. Support. Syst. **66**, 170–179 (2014)

Time Series-Based Analysis of Energy Consumption: Forecasting and Anomaly Detection Using LSTM and Isolation Forest

M. Madhu Shree$^{(\boxtimes)}$, Rajeev Ranjan, and M. P. Dechamma

REVA University, Bangalore, India
shreemadhumahesh@gmail.com

Abstract. The household power consumption forecasting and anomaly detection model presented in this work focused mostly on advanced machine learning techniques, such as Long Short-Term Memory (LSTM) for forecasting and Isolation Forest for anomaly identification. The primary goal is to optimize energy management by providing accurate insights into power consumption and proactively identifying irregularities in power consumption patterns. This work unfolds in several key phases, encompassing preprocessing, data exploration, model construction, testing, and analysis. In the initial phase, the dataset is thoroughly examined, revealing time-stamped power consumption data that serves as the basis for subsequent time series analysis. The existing landscape is identified as lacking robust forecasting and anomaly detection systems, prompting the adoption of advanced techniques to overcome conventional limitations. The proposed system introduces the LSTM model and the isolation forest to enhance forecasting accuracy and anomaly detection, respectively. This choice is driven by LSTM's ability to capture temporal dependencies with an RMSE value of 0.0799, making it well-suited for analyzing power consumption patterns. The advantages of the proposed system include improved forecasting accuracy, with 4.99% of identified anomalies, and adaptability to dynamic changes in power consumption behavior. It is stated that the candidate model gave successful results. The model can also respond to the power consumption variations of a dynamic nature, which makes it applicable in actual environment.

Keywords: Long Short-Term Memory (LSTM) · Isolation Forest · Household power consumption · Anomaly Detection

1 Introduction

In rising electricity demand is symptomatic of the changing landscape where there are greater demands on power infrastructure. In the midst of growing demand electromagnetic power for individual house-holds, a prediction model is becoming more and more necessary because it predicts impending power consumption assisting society in advance. Anomaly detection techniques can also be applied to identify abnormalities in the supply pattern that result from inaccurate metering and energy stealing. This is to ensure the integrity and reliability of power management systems can be maintained. The solution for the above problems is a forecasting and anomaly detection model. It is indeed a dual mission to forecast and detect power utility anomalies as energy consumption can be very random. While using the advanced machine learning models like Isolation Forest [2] for anomaly detection and Long Short-Term Memory (LSTM) [1] for prediction, this work attempts to address these areas of improvement where they were found in gaps from previous literatures mainly focusing on how series forecasting based solutions can be implemented effectively within a power ecosystem context enabling better accurate forecasts aiding various planning functions & resource allocation whereas simultaneously helping with an edge over improving anomaly rate detections elevating mechanisms against required instances which might lead to illegal consumption or similar irregularities.

This paper focuses on the proposal of a single, substantial solution that unifies two tasks, power consumption forecasting and anomaly detection, employing the power of both LSTM and Isolation Forest. Therefore, this model has a better capacity for capturing temporal patterns in the consumption of power, unlike the usual models such as ARIMA. This presents an advanced approach toward identifying anomalies in the system that may be attributed to unfavourable factors, such as faulty metering or energy theft, and is also a real-time adaptive system that can provide dynamic energy management in households. This model makes it more feasible for a small energy distribution system to raise its integrity and efficiency through much more accurate end forecasted distribution and through the detection of irregular consumption patterns. Moreover, the merging of time-series forecasting with anomaly detection not only closes gaps within prior research but also provides practical applicability for improving energy consumption monitoring in modern households.

2   Literature Survey

Global Electricity Demand 2022 is expected to reach roughly 24,398 TWh, according to [3], with growth of barely 3.8% compared to the year-over-year trend that at the time was ever-falling. However, another significant area of research on buildings, businesses, and other electric assets has been studying the usage of power. Such anomalies may occur due to energy theft, metering defects, cyberattacks, and technical losses [4]. Several researchers have used a variety of time series forecasting techniques, including the Autoregressive Integrated Moving Average (ARIMA) model [5, 6], Gradient Boosting Machines (GBM) model [7, 8], Facebook's Prophet [9] model and hybrid models [10–13] for such application.

However, LSTM [1] has garnered a lot of interest for real-time applications, particularly in the domains of machine learning (ML) and artificial intelligence (AI). One type of model used to address time series-based predictions, including those pertaining to natural events, is the recurrent neural network (RNN). Online safety a plethora of other topics [24–28], financial market research [14–18, 21–23], and [19–21]. Unlike ARIMA or Prophet, the LSTM model does not depend on specific data assumptions, such as the presence of a date field or the stationary nature of the time series.

The proposed work endeavors to forecast the electricity consumption demand using LSTM model, and to detect anomaly, the LSTM with Isolation Forest [2, 29] has been applied. Various works have been presented in the area.

Qin [30] has conducted an expanding experimental visual analysis of the data. The experiment contrasts the impact of linear regression models and neural networks on several variables. Building level energy load forecasting using LSTM-based neural networks was examined by Marino et al. [31] for efficacy. Several machine learning techniques have been compared by Bonetto & Rossi [32] in terms of forecasting error and error variance. Three popular machine learning techniques—Support Vector Machine (SVM), Random Forest (RF), and Long Short-Term Memory)—are covered by the author Guo et al. [33] in their discussion of load forecasting. The features of all these three methods are evaluated and compared. The research obtained for each method is listed in Table 1. Wang et al. [34] gone in-depth into the use of AI for smart energy usage. Anomaly detection, demand response, and load forecasting were given particular attention. The paper excels in its comprehensive coverage, carefully analyzing different AI methods and highlighting promising trends like deep learning for future advancements. Overall, this review is a significant contribution to the field of AI-powered smart energy management. Its insightful analysis, focus on practical applications, and recognition of future directions make it a valuable resource for improving energy efficiency and grid stability through the power of AI.

Table 1. Summary of results of paper [33].

	SVM	RF	LSTM
RMSE	106.23	39.33	20.23
MAPE	0.23	0.036	0.053
MAE	95.71	36.45	15.18

The isolation forest algorithm helps in finding out the data points in large number of inconsistent data. The work proposed in the paper [35] compared the isolation forest and variational auto encoder algorithm in the context of anomaly detection of water usage electricity and gas consumption in hotels. According to this proposed work the isolation forest gives better performance in identifying anomaly with an average result of 0.89. The work focuses on custom performance metric designed for evaluating the anomaly detection algorithm in supervised time series data.

The paper [36] proposes a new method for predicting power usage with the LSTM model for detecting anomalies in power consumption data. The study compared the LSTM model with the ARIMA algorithm and provides insights into the effectiveness of the anomaly detection approach in identifying abnormal behaviors in usage of electricity. The outcomes demonstrate that the LSTM model outperforms the ARIMA algorithm. With predicting error reduces to 22%.

The authors additionally show a technique for anomaly detection the use of the LSTM. This suggested method is also contrasted with the ARIMA version within the paper. The authors pass into the detection method's realistic applications, including editing parameters to become aware of anomalies and enlisting the assist of issue count professionals to study anomaly styles that remain unidentified. It ends by recognizing that extra algorithm tuning is needed to improve forecast and anomaly detection precision.

2.1 Limitation of the Existing System

The present management approach's inability to accurately predict and detect abnormalities in household power consumption is one of its main problems. Using oversimplified simulations to illustrate the flaws in our current structure is a poor way to substantiate the claim that congestion would worsen.

These models, despite being widely used, are unable to adjust to the intricate and highly variable patterns of electricity usage in residential homes.

This is evident from the fact that current systems are unable to accurately predict energy use over time, are slow to detect anomalies, and typically only provide reports rather than informing real-time actions or load variations. The fact that the basic models used overlook complex interdependencies and fundamental causes of residential power usage should not be shocking. The projections now provide poor information regarding patterns of energy use and are no longer accurate.

Moreover, these models are non-adaptive making them less useful in modern households where energy consumption behavior is changing and new devices to power that can make usage prediction more complex. The other disadvantages with respect to this system last is its poor capability in detecting deviations in power consumption. Many of the traditional methods are not sensitive enough to adequately detect when things go wrong, so problems can sometimes slip under the radar. This calls for a more versatile and flexible approach as these threaten the reliability of energy system operation.

3 Proposed System

Our proposed work based on the LSTM network with 50 units are used with other training parameters. The LSTM architecture is more sophisticated and tuned, which leads to better performance, according to details. The model trained for 100 epochs using the Adam optimizer and Early Stop-ping approach. An LSTM configuration model intended to forecast household power usage is depicted in Fig. 1.

Input Power Consumption Data This is the historical data of power consumption from households. It serves as the input for the LSTM unit.

Forget Gate It determines which data from the previous cell state need to be ignored. To decide what should be kept or discarded from the condition of the cell, it also looks at the current input to the prior concealed state (h(t-1)). It produces an output that varies from 0 to 1, where 1 denotes total discard and 0 implies total keeping.

Input Gate By adding fresh data, this gate modifies the cell state. It first determines which values to update using a sigmoid function and then generates a new candidate vector, which could potentially be added to the state.

Activation Function (Sigmoid) The sigmoid activation function is employed in both the forget and input gates. It controls the flow of information by assigning values between 0 and 1, influencing what information is allowed through.

Memory Cell This component acts as the storage unit and keeps track of information over time. It processes the input data by discarding unnecessary information and integrating new candidate values based on their relevance.

Tanh The tanh function creates a vector of fresh potential values that are included in the state of the memory cell. It guarantees that the numbers are appropriately scaled between -1 and 1.

Output Gate By combining the current input with data from the prior concealed state, this gate determines the next hidden state. After being normalized by the tanh function, the hidden state that results are multiplied by the sigmoid gate output to determine whether pertinent data should be output.

Hidden State (h(t-1)) This shows how LSTM model is right now. It affects the model's output and is updated in accordance with the input and the prior hidden state.

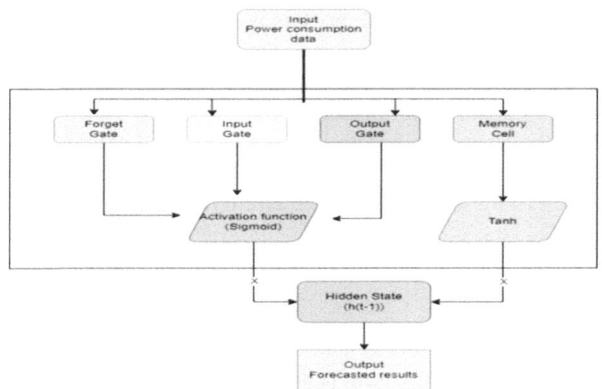

Fig. 1. LSTM configuration model

In isolation forest method we aimed in improving the efficiency and reliability of identifying unusual patterns in power usage data. This will greatly contribute to the progress of the area of study as there are few research exist in this domain.

In this work, the problem of forecasting and anomaly detection focus on improving the reliability of an energy management system. The temporal dependencies in historical data are first modeled by an LSTM network in order to forecast future power consumption and provide an expected pattern of behavior. The forecast then acts as some kind of baseline for identifying significant deviations in real-time data, which are detected as anomalies by the Isolation Forest algorithm. This combination works well since the LSTM model will predict normal energy consumption and the Isolation Forest will identify the outlier data points away from the predicted values. Recent studies enhance this combination of forecasting with anomaly detection. Utilizing forecasting models like LSTM in combination with anomaly detection models, improves both the prediction accuracy as well as the anomaly identification [40, 43].

3.1 Data Sources and Preparation

The dataset utilized in this project is sourced from the UCI Machine Learning Repository [37]. The dataset consists of 2,075,259 rows and 9 columns, each containing timestamped power consumption data. The timestamp information is divided into date (dd/mm/yyyy) and time (hh:mm:ss), establishing a temporal structure that suits time series analysis. This temporal aspect enables us to explore patterns and trends in household power consumption over specific intervals, providing valuable insights into consumption behavior. Data has the following attributes (Fig. 2).

Date	Time	Global_act	Global_rea	Voltage	Global_int	Sub_meter	Sub_meter	Sub_metering_3
16-12-2006	17:24:00	4.216	0.418	234.84	18.4	0	1	17
16-12-2006	17:25:00	5.36	0.436	233.63	23	0	1	16
16-12-2006	17:26:00	5.374	0.498	233.29	23	0	2	17
16-12-2006	17:27:00	5.388	0.502	233.74	23	0	1	17
16-12-2006	17:28:00	3.666	0.528	235.68	15.8	0	1	17
16-12-2006	17:29:00	3.52	0.522	235.02	15	0	2	17
16-12-2006	17:30:00	3.702	0.52	235.09	15.8	0	1	17
16-12-2006	17:31:00	3.7	0.52	235.22	15.8	0	1	17
16-12-2006	17:32:00	3.668	0.51	233.99	15.8	0	1	17

Fig. 2. Sample data

- *Date*: recorded using the format dd/mm/yyyy.
- *Time*: recorded in hh:mm:ss time zone.
- *Global Active Power*: represents the minute-averaged global active power of a home (in kW).
- *Global Reactive Power*: represents the global minute-averaged reactive power of a home (in kW).
- *Voltage*: shows the voltage (in volts) averaged over a minute.
- *Global Intensity*: represents the minute-averaged global household current intensity (in amperes).
- *Sub-metering 1*: represents energy sub-metering number one (in active energy watt-hour). This refers to the kitchen, which houses gas-powered hot plates but not ovens, microwaves, or dishwashers.
- *Sub-metering 2*: watt-hours of active energy are measured in the second energy sub-metering capture. This is the laundry area, which has a refrigerator, freezer, dryer, and washing machine.
- *Sub-metering 3*: stands for the third energy sub-metering (watt-hour of active energy). This is the same as having both an electric water heater and an air conditioner.

Data Cleaning and Preprocessing

Handling Missing Values: To ensure the integrity of our analysis, a meticulous data cleaning process was undertaken. This involved addressing missing values and converting relevant columns to their appropriate data types. This dataset consisted 1.3% of null from each column values which are filled with forward filling data cleaning technique, which helps in replacing the missing or null values with the previously recorded values. The Fig. 3 bar graph shows the missing values from each column.

Data Normalization Data Normalization is a crucial phase in machine learning. It helps to make sure that all the input features are on the same scale. This is done by using a technique called Min-Max scaling, which is implemented using MinMaxScaler from scikit-learn [38] [39].

$$x' = \frac{x - min(x)}{max(x) - min(x)} \tag{1}$$

where x' represents normalized value and x represents original value. The data is essentially normalized by scaling the numerical features to a range between 0 and 1.

Temporal Aggregation If the dataset had time-related information that was recorded more frequently (like every hour), we used temporal aggregation to change the data into lower frequencies (like daily or weekly). We did this by using the resample function, which helped us group the data into the desired time intervals (like days or weeks) and then perform aggregation operations (like summing) on those intervals.

Feature Selection To make sure our model is accurate, we carefully chose the most important features using our knowledge of the subject and by analyzing the data. We wanted to find the features that would give us the best insights and help us understand the patterns and connections in the data.

The set of plots in Fig. 4 shows the variations of values in each column with respect to the timeline. The timeline (dates) is represented by the x-axis, and each subplot represents a distinct feature. By these plots we can understand the trends, patterns, and fluctuations in each feature throughout the given time.

Furthermore, the correlation matrix in Fig. 5 illustrates the degree of association between specific numerical variables in the dataset. One variable tends to grow as the other tends to drop when the values around -1 indicate a strong negative correlation, values around 0 show a weak or no association, and values around 1 suggest a strong positive correlation (one variable tends to increase as the other tends to decrease).

Fig 6 Scatter plot is for bivariate analysis, allowing us to explore the relationships between different features, such as global active power and global reactive power. By using scatter plots, we could easily identify any linear or nonlinear correlations between variables, which helped us understand the underlying dynamics of power consumption. The set of plots in Fig. 7 displays the average power consumption patterns for different areas such kitchen, laundry room, appliances on each day of the week. By looking at these plots, one can understand how the power consumption varies throughout the week for each specific area, helping to identify any noticeable trends or differences based on weekdays.

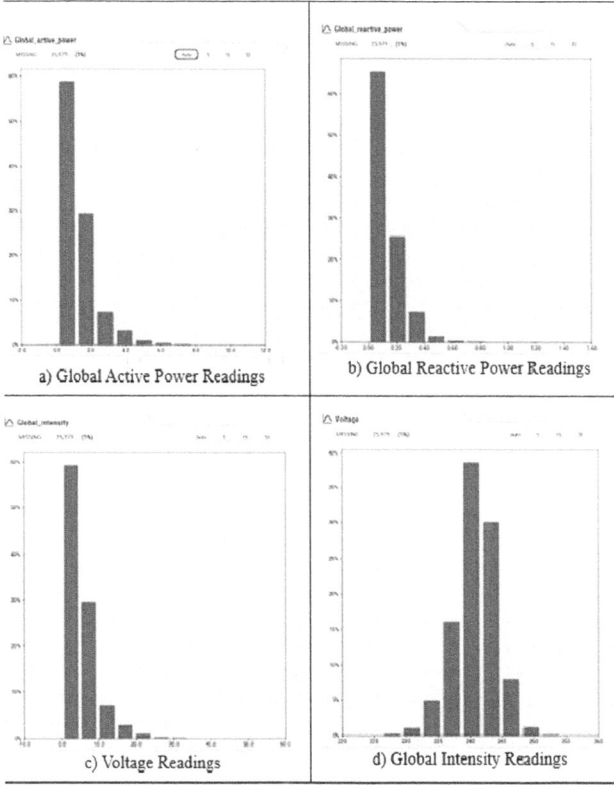

Fig. 3. Missing values of the columns

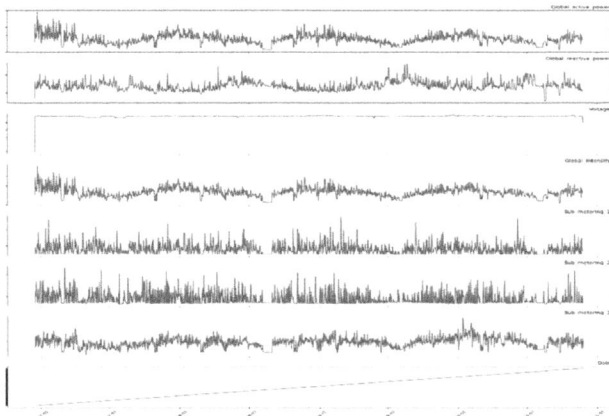

Fig. 4. Feature plots for each column

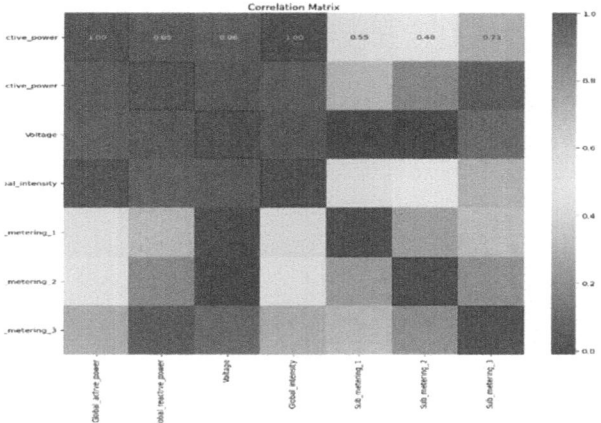

Fig. 5. Correlation Matrix

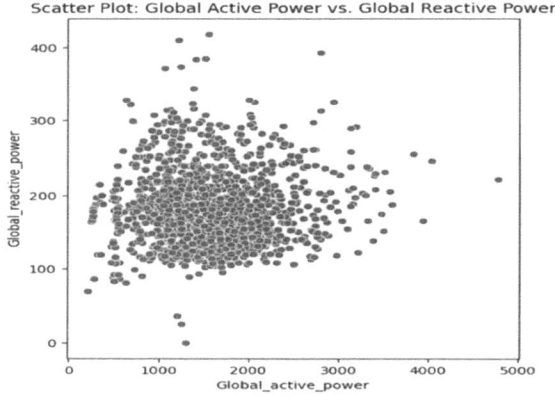

Fig. 6. Scatter Plot

3.2 Model Building and Evaluation

Model building is essential in assessing the forecasting capacity and reliability of an LSTM model for time series data. The effectiveness of the LSTM model is evaluated using performance metrics such as Mean Squared Error (MSE), Root Mean Squared Error (RMSE) and Mean Absolute Error (MAE). These metrics give us an indication about how exact the forecasting produced by the LSTM model is, and also show much error is there when compared to original values derived from time series data. Depending on the project, we can check its performance with additional domain specific measures like classification accuracy or forecast accuracy for classification tasks.

Below are the main measures used along with corresponding.

Precision (P) Precision enables us understand the model accuracy in generating fine forecasts. The percentage of real superb predictions among all wonderful forecasts is

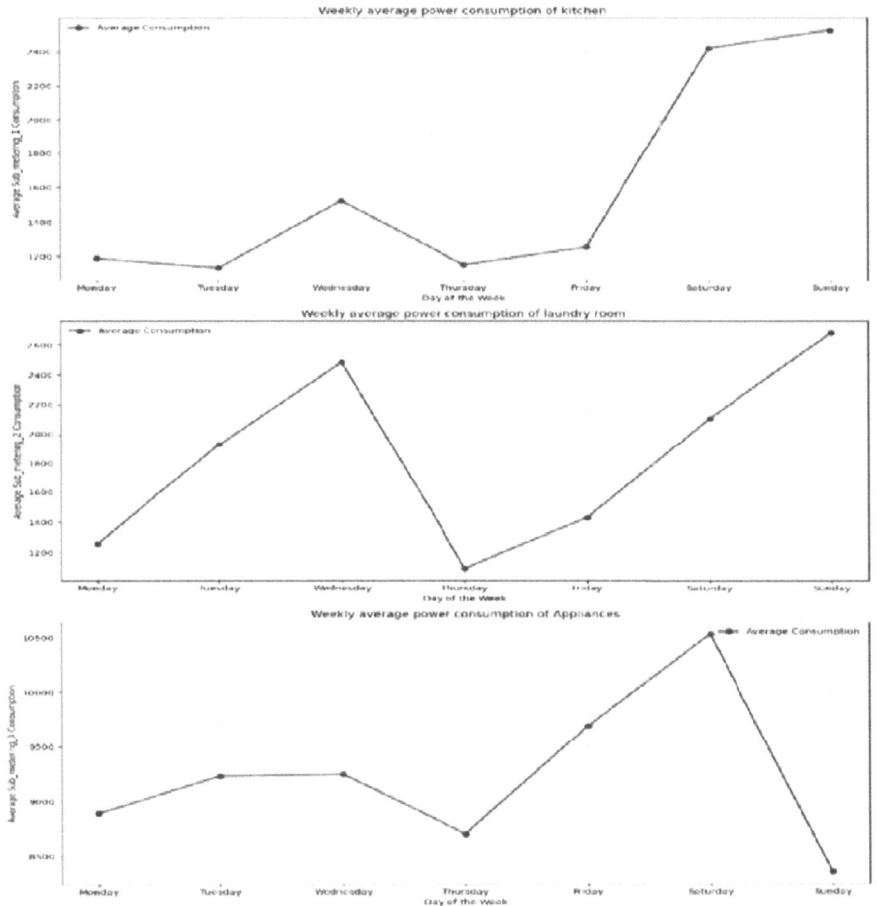

Fig. 7. Feature Plot

calculated using the method below:

$$P = \frac{TP}{TP + FP} \tag{2}$$

where True Positives are the quantity of anomalies that are correctly predicted, and False Positives are the quantity of normal occurrences that are incorrectly classified as anomalies.

Recall (R) It a data point that displays the proportion of correct positive predictions to all true positive events in the dataset. To calculate it, we can utilize the formula below:

$$R = \frac{TP}{TP + FN} \tag{3}$$

where False Negatives are the quantity of anomalies that are mistakenly identified as typical occurrences.

F1-Score It a metric that evaluates a model's performance by taking precision and recall into account.

$$F1 = \frac{P * R}{P + R} \tag{4}$$

Mean Squared Error (MSE) It is a metric used in regression tasks that computes the average squared difference between the values that are predicted and those that are actual. By quantifying the mistake, it aims in the understanding of how accurate the forecasts are. The below is the formula used.

$$MSE = \frac{1}{N} \sum_{i=0}^{n} (Y_1 - Y_2)^2 \tag{5}$$

where Y_1 is the actual value of the target variable and Y2 denotes the predicted value, where n is the total number of samples.

Root Mean Squared Error (RMSE) The average error size between expected and observed data is computed using this method. Determine the Mean Squared Error square root (MSE) in order to calculate it. The below formula is used to calculate value RMSE:

$$RMSE = p(MSE) \tag{6}$$

These evaluation metrices evaluates the model prediction ability and assist in pinpointing areas for model training and optimization improvement. We can make informed decisions about the use and future development of these models by analyzing these metrics and learning about the advantages and disadvantages of each one.

4 Result and Discussion

In the configurations shown in Tables 2 and 3, the task has been finished. Particularly addressed in the first table is the utilization of hardware, including an Intel Core i3 processor, 8 GB of RAM, a 256 GB SSD for storage, and a GPU for graphics processing. The software requirements are shown in Table 2:

Table 2. Hardware Requirements.

Processor	Intel Core i3
RAM	8 GB
Storage	256 SSD
Graphics	GPU

The LSTM [1] model has confirmed quality outcomes based on testing and training implications. In the long run, the version achieves a training loss of 0.0086, effectively

Table 3. Software Requirement

Operating System	Windows 11
Python Environment	Anaconda distribution with Python
Libraries	scikit-learn, pandas, NumPy, Matplotlib, seaborn, TensorFlow, Dense, Isolation
IDE	Jupyter Notebook

decreasing its loss with each iteration after 100 epochs. This demonstrates how accurate the model is at identifying and predicting past styles. The models low Root mean Squared errors (RMSE) 0.1899 for the training set and 0.0799 for the testing set and showed its effectiveness. These findings demonstrate the predictive capacity of the LSTM model, which makes it a valuable tool for various applications such as energy consumption research, economic forecasting, and climate forecasting.

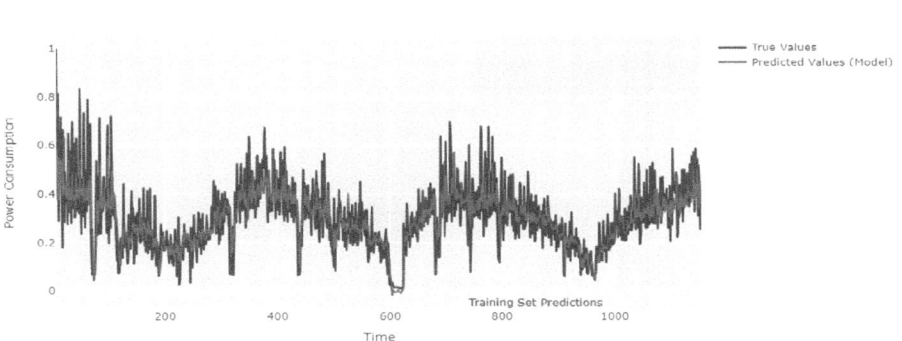

Fig. 8. Prediction on Train set

The isolation forest [2] for anomaly detection indicates exceptional accuracy in identifying normal and abnormal times within the dataset. The model demonstrates its ability to detect anomalies with flawless accuracy, power and depend-ability in its anomaly detection duties, with an F1-score of 1.0. This shows that the model correctly classified all regular statistics points and recognized all 258 anomalies. Additionally, the model no longer produced any incorrect results or failed to detect any abnormalities, and the overall performance of anomaly detection models was much better.

Confusion matrix in Fig. 10 is a clear indicator of the model's performance, as it minimizes false positives and false negatives while effectively differentiating between real positives and true negatives. in addition to the analysis of the anomaly distribution shows that anomalies make up 4.99% of the dataset, highlighting the importance of accurate detection methods in spotting irregularities and reducing risks. The performance of the anomaly detection model emphasizes its significance as a powerful tool for proactive risk management and decision-making in a number of fields, including

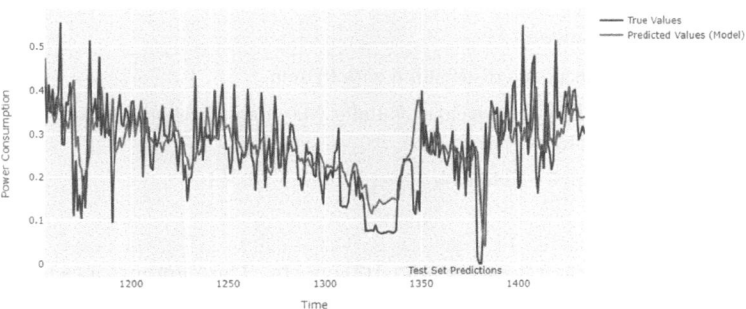

Fig. 9. Prediction on Test Set

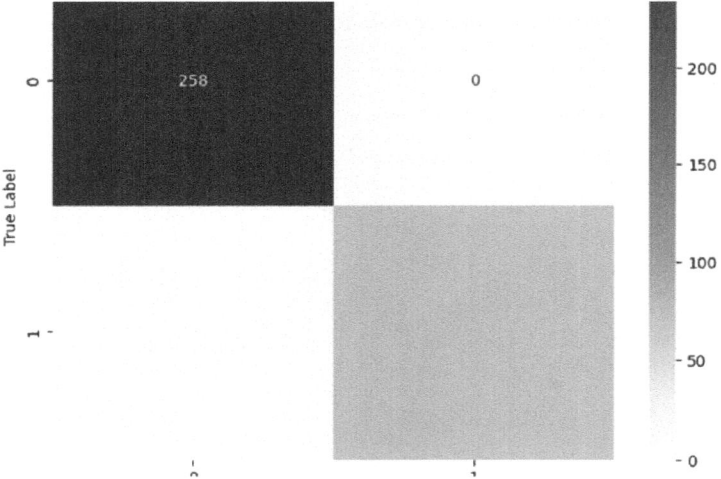

Fig. 10. Confusion Matrix

fraud detection, predictive maintenance, and cybersecurity. Figure 8 shows the actual train set vs predicted train set, and Fig. 9 shows the actual vs predicted test set. Figure 11 shows the detected Anomalies in the power consumption. At times, the blue lines appear higher than the red dots. This indicates that the algorithm may have picked up a few false positives, or instances of data being mistakenly classified as anomalies. In conclusion, the figure indicates that the Isolation Forest algorithm performs best when it comes to anomaly identification.

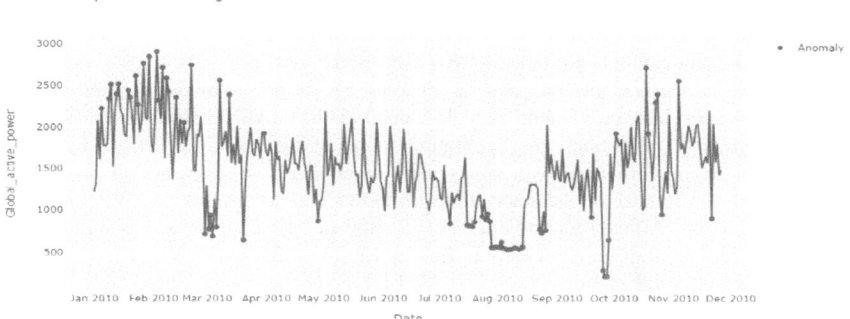

Fig. 11. Identified Anomalies

4.1 Conclusion

In this work, the prediction of household energy use using LSTM (Long Short-Term Memory) models and the identification of anomalous power consumption using Isolation Forest were examined. First, we cleaned up the data for completing any gaps in the data, modifying and organizing the data. Then, in order to visualize the data and comprehend power use patterns and to understand the data we have created different plots, LSTM model was selected because to its ability to identify patterns in data. We trained the LSTM model on both training and testing data and evaluated its performance using metrics such as Root Mean Squared Error (RMSE). Additionally, the anomaly detection model is built using Isolation Forest. We evaluated the accuracy, recall, and F1-score of this system to see how well it performed. The findings demonstrate that the model performs well in estimating power consumption and that the approach for identifying unusual patterns is also effective. The indication of this is that the power consumption predicting and anomaly detection in power systems could be benefitted. Anyone may input the essential features and obtain an accurate energy usage forecast by using this. Because of this, the model is now simpler to use and can be a useful tool for anyone trying to manage their energy use more effectively.

References

1. Hochreiter, S., Schmidhuber, J.: Long short-term memory. Neural Comput. **9**(8), 1735–1780 (1997)
2. Liu, F.T., Ting, K.M., Zhou, Z.H.: Isolation forest. In: 2008 Eighth IEEE International Conference on Data Mining, pp. 413–422. IEEE (2008)
3. Van Heddeghem, W., Lambert, S., Lannoo, B., Colle, D., Pickavet, M., Demeester, P.: Trends in worldwide ict electricity consumption from 2007 to 2012. Comput. Commun. **50**, 64–76 (2014)
4. Kardi, M., AlSkaif, T., Tekinerdogan, B., Catalao, J.P.: Anomaly detection in electricity consumption data using deep learning. In: 2021 IEEE International Conference on Environment and Electrical Engineering and 2021 IEEE Industrial and Commercial Power Systems Europe (EEEIC/I&CPS Europe), pp. 1–6. IEEE (2021)

5. Huang, S.-J., Shih, K.-R.: Short-term load forecasting via arma model identification including non-gaussian process considerations. IEEE Trans. Power Syst. **18**(2), 673–679 (2003)
6. Chujai, P., Kerdprasop, N., Kerdprasop, K.: Time series analysis of household electric consumption with arima and arma models. In: Proceedings of the International Multiconference of Engineers and Computer Scientists, vol. 1, pp. 295–300. IAENG Hong Kong (2013)
7. Bassi, A., Shenoy, A., Sharma, A., Sigurdson, H., Glossop, C., Chan, J.H.: Building energy consumption forecasting: a comparison of gradient boosting models. In: The 12th International Conference on Advances in Information Technology, pp. 1–9 (2021)
8. Hussain, S., et al.: A novel feature engineered-catboost-based supervised machine learning framework for electricity theft detection. Energy Rep. **7**, 4425–4436 (2021)
9. Chadalavada, R., Raghavendra, S., Rekha, V.: Electricity requirement prediction using time series and facebook's prophet. Indian J. Sci. Technol. **13**(47), 4631–4645 (2020)
10. Dong, B., Li, Z., Rahman, S.M., Vega, R.: A hybrid model approach for forecasting future residential electricity consumption. Energy Build. **117**, 341–351 (2016)
11. Alhussein, M., Aurangzeb, K., Haider, S.I.: Hybrid cnn-lstm model for short-term individual household load forecasting. IEEE Access **8**, 180544–180557 (2020)
12. Syed, D., Abu-Rub, H., Ghrayeb, A., Refaat, S.S.: Household-level energy forecasting in smart buildings using a novel hybrid deep learning model. IEEE Access **9**, 33498–33511 (2021)
13. Meng, M., Wang, L., Shang, W.: Decomposition and forecasting analysis of china's household electricity consumption using three-dimensional decomposition and hybrid trend extrapolation models. Energy **165**, 143–152 (2018)
14. Le, X.-H., Ho, H.V., Lee, G., Jung, S.: Application of long short-term memory (LSTM) neural network for flood forecasting. Water **11**(7), 1387 (2019)
15. Xie, P., Zhou, A., Chai, B.: The application of long short-term memory (LSTM) method on displacement prediction of multifactor-induced landslides. IEEE Access **7**, 54305–54311 (2019)
16. Fang, L., Shao, D.: Application of long short-term memory (LSTM) on the prediction of rainfall-runoff in karst area. Front. Phys. **9**, 685 (2022)
17. Elsaraiti, M., Merabet, A.: Application of long-short-term-memory recurrent neural networks to forecast wind speed. Appl. Sci. **11**(5), 2387 (2021)
18. Arslan, N., Sekertekin, A.: Application of long short-term memory neural network model for the reconstruction of modis land surface temperature images. J. Atmos. Solar Terr. Phys. **194**, 105100 (2019)
19. Staudemeyer, R.C.: Applying long short-term memory recurrent neural networks to intrusion detection. S. Afr. Comput. J. **56**(1), 136–154 (2015)
20. Vinayakumar, R., Soman, K., Poornachandran, P., Sachin Kumar, S.: Detecting android malware using long short-term memory (LSTM). J. Intell. Fuzzy Syst. **34**(3), 1277–1288 (2018)
21. Althubiti, S., Nick, W., Mason, J., Yuan, X., Esterline, A.: Applying long shortterm memory recurrent neural network for intrusion detection. In: SoutheastCon 2018, pp. 1–5. IEEE (2018)
22. Fischer, T., Krauss, C.: Deep learning with long short-term memory networks for financial market predictions. Eur. J. Oper. Res. **270**(2), 654–669 (2018)
23. Park, H.J., Kim, Y., Kim, H.Y.: Stock market forecasting using a multi-task approach integrating long short-term memory and the random forest framework. Appl. Soft Comput. **114**, 108106 (2022)
24. Tan, J.H., et al.: Application of stacked convolutional and long shortterm memory network for accurate identification of cad ecg signals. Comput. Biol. Med. **94**, 19–26 (2018)
25. Soutner, D., Mu¨ller, L.: Application of lstm neural networks in language modelling. In: Text, Speech, and Dialogue: 16th International Conference, TSD 2013, Pilsen, Czech Republic, September 1–5, 2013. Proceedings 16, pp. 105–112. Springer (2013)

26. Sen, S., Raghunathan, A.: Approximate computing for long short term memory (LSTM) neural networks. IEEE Trans. Comput. Aided Des. Integr. Circuits Syst. **37**(11), 2266–2276 (2018)
27. Tran, K.P., Du Nguyen, H., Thomassey, S.: Anomaly detection using long short term memory networks and its applications in supply chain management. IFACPapersOnLine **52**(13), 2408–2412 (2019)
28. Panja, P., Jia, W., McPherson, B.: Prediction of well performance in sacroc field using stacked long short-term memory (lstm) network. Expert Syst. Appl. **205**, 117670 (2022)
29. Priyanto, C.Y., Purnomo, H.D., et al.: Combination of isolation forest and lstm autoencoder for anomaly detection. In: 2021 2nd International Conference on Innovative and Creative Information Technology (ICITech), pp. 35–38. IEEE (2021)
30. Qin, J.: Experimental and analysis on household electronic power consumption. Energy Rep. **8**, 705–709 (2022)
31. Marino, D.L., Amarasinghe, K., Manic, M.: Building energy load forecasting using deep neural networks. In: IECON 2016–42nd Annual Conference of the IEEE Industrial Electronics Society, pp. 7046–7051. IEEE (2016)
32. Hearst, M.A., Dumais, S.T., Osuna, E., Platt, J., Scholkopf, B.: Support vector machines. IEEE Intell. Syst. Appl. **13**(4), 18–28 (1998)
33. Guo, W., Che, L., Shahidehpour, M., Wan, X.: Machine-learning based methods in short-term load forecasting. Electr. J. **34**(1), 106884 (2021)
34. Wang, X., Wang, H., Bhandari, B., Cheng, L.: AI-empowered methods for smart energy consumption: a review of load forecasting, anomaly detection and demand response. Int. J. Precis. Eng. Manuf. Green Technol. 1–31 (2023)
35. Mendes, T., Cardoso, P.J., Monteiro, J., Raposo, J.: Anomaly detection of consumption in hotel units: a case study comparing isolation forest and variational autoencoder algorithms. Appl. Sci. **13**(1), 314 (2022)
36. Himeur, Y., Ghanem, K., Alsalemi, A., Bensaali, F., Amira, A.: Artificial intelligence based anomaly detection of energy consumption in buildings: a review, current trends and new perspectives. Appl. Energy **287**, 116601 (2021)
37. Hebrail, G., Berard, A.: Individual household electric power consumption data set. UCI Machine Learning Repository (2012)
38. Aguilar Madrid, E., Antonio, N.: Short-term electricity load forecasting with machine learning. Information **12**(2), 50 (2021)
39. Penn, D., Subburaj, V.H., Subburaj, A.S., Harral, M.: A predictive tool for grid data analysis using machine learning algorithms. In: 2020 10th Annual Computing and Communication Workshop and Conference (CCWC), pp. 1071–1077. IEEE (2020)
40. Bhadula, S., Almusawi, M., Badhoutiya, A., Deepak, A., Bhardwaj, N., Anitha, G.: time series analysis for power grid anomaly detection using LSTM networks. In: 2024 International Conference on Communication, Computer Sciences and Engineering (IC3SE), pp. 1358–1363. IEEE (2024)
41. Han, L., Gao, Y., Zheng, X.: Anomaly detection and identification of power consumption data based on LOF and isolation forest. In: International Conference on Mechatronic Engineering and Artificial Intelligence (MEAI 2023), vol. 13071, pp. 741–746. SPIE (2024)
42. Abdurazakov, N., Aliev, R., Ergashev, S., Kuchkarov, A.: Using LSTM neural network for power consumption forecasting. In: BIO Web of Conferences, vol. 84, p. 02021. EDP Sciences (2024)

43. Iqbal, A., Amin, R.: Time series forecasting and anomaly detection using deep learning. Comput. Chem. Eng. **182**, 108560 (2024)
44. Stradiotti, L., Perini, L., Davis, J.: Semi-Supervised Isolation Forest for Anomaly Detection. In: Proceedings of the 2024 SIAM International Conference on Data Mining (SDM), pp. 670–678. Society for Industrial and Applied Mathematics (2024)

Steganography in the Digital Age: An In-Depth Review of Techniques

Koushik Choudhury$^{(\boxtimes)}$, Milan Doshi, Dimple Thakar, and Jignesh Hirapara

Marwadi University, Rajkot, India
Koushikchoudhury122@gmail.com, {milan.doshi,dimple.thakar,
jignesh.hirapara}@marwadieducation.edu.in

Abstract. Sending information to the proper destination in a hidden way to the receiver is called "steganography." This is a way or practice of securing information from the outside world. By doing so, we can hide information within a video file, or it can be an image or a text file . Three well-known steganographic methods are examined in-depth in this review paper: Edge-Based Encoding (EBE), Pixel Value Differencing (PVD), and Least Significant Bit (LSB) embedding. In terms of data embedding capacity, imperceptibility, and robustness, this article compares and contrasts the performance of LSB, PVD, and EBE, highlighting the advantages and disadvantages of each technique.

Keywords: Stenography · LSB · PVD · EBE · Steganographic Image

1 Introduction

In ancient times, data could be sent or exchanged physically. But with day-to-day progress or improvement of technology, we can send data from one place to another in a shorter time. Vice-verse data can be stolen for many notorious purposes. In today's world, security is a major concern that affects every aspect of our lives. It can be data or information, as it is part of our lives, so researchers are focusing on building secure techniques to send data without revealing original information to hackers.

With the advancement of science and technology in this digitalized world, we can easily access information through voice, video recording, pictures, or text messages. There are numerous methods there also for data hacking, like "phishing or hacking, MIM, malware, and so on. So, a few ways to pass on data in a secure way from sender to ethical receiver are cryptography and steganography.

In this digital age, malicious threats attack every area, like government, private, and so on. Everyone is seeking data security. So forth, these stenography and cryptography techniques have a big impact on these things. The data encryption technique is a big revolution in these scenarios. Here the concept comes from "carrier image" and "steganographic image".

We can hide data or payload in a carrier image, also known as a cover image, so that normal human eyes cannot detect it. No suspicious data was detected when we embedded information in the image, and the Steganographic image is the result of embedded information in the carrier image. Here, we explore the concept of steganography, a technology that originated a millennium ago and found application in tattoos and invisible ink. Basically, it's a process of hiding a message in another object. Steganography means hiding data in a cover image. Examples of different types of stenography techniques are invisible ink, microdots, and digital signatures.

Basic Model of Steganography
M = Message.
C = Cover object
S = Stegano object

$$S = f(C, M) \tag{1}$$

where f is a function to represents the embedding process of steganographic.

We use an encrypted format for hiding data, but it is easily detected as suspicious, as anyone can understand that there is something hidden. So for not being eye-catching for attackers, the concept comes from stenography. There are two domains in stenography: the spatial domain and the frequency domain. In the spatial domain, bits are directly modified in the cover image using LSB techniques, PVD techniques, and the EBE technique, which we will be using. Another domain is called the transform domain, where you modify the coefficient of the cover image. If I talk about coefficient techniques like DCT, DWT, and DFT [6].

Secret messages or hiding data in an image can be possible using stenography techniques that normally use masking data in the cover image. Through the scientific technique of steganalysis, we get data that is hidden through stenography. Not only in images but also in video and text, we can hide data through steganography. Steganography can be applied to grayscale images as well. Data can be hidden at the edge of the cover image, which is more stable in terms of protection from visual, structural, and non-structural techniques. Edge information can be embedded where there is less distortion and less noticeable.

One of the popular methods is the LSB method, which can be classified as LSB replacement and matching. In the transform form domain, LSB-based embedding is done by the DCT coefficient of a cover image. Another technique for hiding data is cryptography. This is also a process of hiding messages and using secret communication mediums. If we discuss cryptography, which plays a crucial role in maintaining confidentiality and integrity, we can obtain the encrypted data through this method. The main goal is to maintain data security in various fields, such as securing communication between sender and receiver over the internet. Many components of cryptography are encryption, decryption, which can be maintained by keys, which play a crucial role in encryption, and decryption's data. There are two types of keys,"public and private," that are used in cryptography.

The next term is cipher text, which means a simple text with jumbles that cannot be understood normally. But cryptography has many drawbacks, like the vulnerability of algorithms. Also, quantum computing is a big threat to this process. So, to secure more data more securely, steganography provides dual-layer protection compared to cryptography. If a thief steals the data and can get the idea of decoding data easily, he will discover the actual information. So, if you compare cryptography and steganography, later on, it is more secure, and it also introduces data in an undeniable scenario.

2   Literature Review

Ahmad Zulfakar Bin Abd Aziz, Muhammad Fitri Bin Mohd Sultan, and Nurul Liyana Binti Mohamad Zulkufli research papers focus on steganography techniques like LSB, PVD, LSB, and EBE techniques. The application of these methods in the image allows for the measurement of MSE and PSNR errors. For implementing security purposes, Morse code, Base 64, SHA-245, and ADV encryption using the PVD technique discussed in the article [5].

In this paper, author proposed a combined method implemented named CR-AIS, which is based on an artificial immune system working on reassigning cost to improve sequrity. Different methods such as Zhu-net, Spam, and Srm have different testing errors, which can be improved through this CRAIS. It's re-assigning cost naturally with AI and steganography, also helping in improving the security of the spatial steganography scheme [20].

This research paper focus on audio steganography. Here they are focusing on LSB, Echo hiding is hide data as short echo, Parity coding is decomposing original signal into different region of samples and hide data in parity bits, Spread Spectrum which is distribute the messages into audio file. Also discussing about transform domain, wavelet domain [2].

In this research paper, the author discusses how image steganography can be possible in PowerPoint. Using the encase technique, we can find out the hidden message. Also showing by the transcript technique, we analyse the hidden message, which can be done in Power Point, and getting the comparison of the techniques. Stenography can be done with overlap images and hyperlinks, where the actual hyperlink does not go to the real link [8].

Francis Jesmar P. Montalbo and Davood Pour Yousefian Barfeh both conducted research with more than 2000 common court stenography words for the core data set. In short, writing data can be hidden, so to find the stenography in the data, we can use CNN. Using Candy Edge Detection, we can get a better result. Therefore, researchers can utilize Artificial Intelligence (AI) to extract data from shorthand writing. Also, CEDA and CNN apply test data for a better possibility of a promising outcome [4].

In this research paper written by Chung-Ming Wang a, Nan-I Wu a, Chwei-Shyong Tsai b, and Min-Shiang Hwang b, we get to know how to hide data using two-pixel values with their reminder implying the PVD method. Wu and Tsai's scheme uses hiding data to decrease the optimal emending algorithm. By re-adjusting the pixel value, the remainder can be solved off the boundary problem. These proposed schemes are secure against RS detection attack [1].

Mohini Kulkarni, Dr. Sheshang Degadwala, and Arpana Mahajan wrote in their research paper about two different types of noise attacks: Gaussian attacks and slat pepper attacks, and geometric attacks like rotation. Also discussing visible and invisible watermarking, the LSB method applies for hiding data in images. Different transformation strategies apply here, like DCT, DWT, and DFT. Through watermark images, we can hide data, and many attacks can also be possible. So protection from these SVD, DFT, DCT, and ZERNIKE moment methods is applied [6].

In this paper, the author discusses two steganographic techniques: PVD and OTP. Prior one uses for changes the images pixcel like each character of seceret message convert inyo 8 ASCII equivalent binary string. Next step is Xoring with an 8-bit randomly generated key by OTP techniques to enhance sequrity before generating over image into 2x2 non-overlapping blocks. This technique primarily focuses on the undetectability of secret messages within images, not on their capacity. Therefore, it works well for smaller hidden messages. In concern about capacity, OTP can be used for edge based techniques for future uses [27].

In this research paper, the author uses GA applied in the spatial domain for stenography technique using the LSB method, which implies various transformations (DCT, DWT, DFT). Locate the data block within the carrier image where GA can embed the data. A few major steps are applied here, like scanning, shifting, flipping, transposing, LSB match checking, and secret data embedding. These papers focus on pixel scanning, pixel shifting, pixel transposing, flipping secret bits, LSB matching, and data embedding. We use the XOR operation to shift vertically and horizontally, scan pixels, and identify the correct bits for data concealment. Also, implement histograms and analyse the images. Using this approach, the author gets higher PSNR values. Also Comparing traditional LSB schemes [7].

Cloud computing is an essential part of today's data processing, where data security is a big concern. For that purpose, we need to secure data in the environment. That's why cryptography, stenography, and cryptography with stenography can be used for hiding and securing data. It's discussed in this paper that if you hide data in an image, it counts the N*M*3 matrix as considered. So stenography with cryptography embedded is used to secure data processing in the cloud [3].

3   Image Steganography

Steganography's main aim is to hide data in a process on another object, where attackers cannot assume that data is hidden in the image, video, or text. Mainly, mysterious data cannot be suspected by the normal human eye, whereas in cryptography, encrypted data can be easily suspected by an attacker. The term "steganography "comes from a Greek word. It can be divided into two parts: "Stegano" means hidden or hiding, and "graph" means writing. The primary task of this field is to cover up and embed the mysterious information using a wide range of hidden techniques.

If we look into cryptography, it's secure data through encryption, hash values, or coding, which a normal user cannot comprehend. But steganography is the art, along with the science, of hiding information in various forms, which can be images, text, video, etc. In many countries, steganography is used as a complement to cryptography, where the main thing is hiding the message rather than encrypting the format. In science, the existence of information in the source will not be noticed. There are two parts: the spatial domain and the steganographic images. Prior to focusing on direct manipulation in the image later on, the result of the carrier image.

In a color image, there are 256 color bits. If we change some bits to hide data, in the normal human eye, it is not detected. There are many parts in the image. One of these is the cover image, which describes a unique picture to hide data. Next is the steganographic image, which carries the message in Covre images. Later on, the steganographic key is embedded, and like in cryptography, it's also used to retrieve data (Fig. 1).

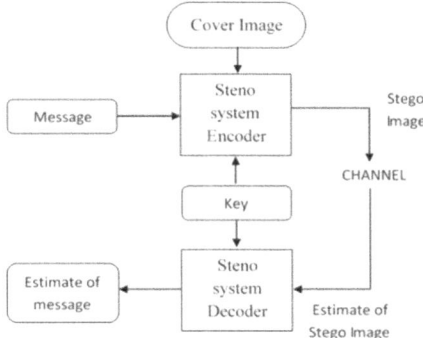

Fig. 1. DFD of Steganographic system

The diagram above illustrates the process of embedding information into a cover image using stenography. Then it became a steganographic image, which passed through communication mediums. Once the receiver receives it, it will decode it, allowing the recipient to access the original data. In image steganography, first go in depth about the concept of an image, which is a collection of data sets in details that can be classified into bits or pixel formation.

Normally, pictures are preferred for sending data in this technique because they have more concealing capacity and can be embedded as surplus data that is smoothly transferred to the destination. Steganography's main object is to pass the message to a destination where nobody can detect mysterious data. If we draw a comparison between cryptography, which the study is of accurately embedded data, and steganography, which is the study of undercover mysterious composition.

4   Image Steganography Techniques

The main or foremost requirement is ensuring the security and integrity of hidden information. This technique should effectively hide the information within a digital medium without altering its structure. Also, the capacity of embedding data as hidden data to maintain efficiency and reliability is a big concern. Hidden information should remain intact and retrievable despite distortion or attacks on the carrier medium. The process of hiding information digitally should be efficient in terms of computational resources and time-storage requirements. It should not impair the carrier medium's performance. Adaptability is also a concern; any technique you apply should be adaptable in a digital medium and accommodate diverse applications and environments.There are many techniques in steganography for hiding data; among them, a few important techniques are discussed below.

4.1   LSB Method

In digital format, the basic unit is called a bit. Those bits come together in a series to make information, text, images, and so on a digital platform. For hiding data in images, you do the transformation from 0 to 1, or vice versa. Two categories are here. The first category is MSB's most significant bits, while the other category is Least Significant Bits (LSB). In binary values, the MSB representation of the leftmost bit holds the highest weight in comparison to other bits, as demonstrated in this example. **1**000 here, the leftmost highlighted bit, is MSB. Therefore, any changes made to the values will directly affect the image. LSB represents the rightmost bit in a binary value that has the least weight compared to other bits, like in the example of 100**1**-highlighted bits (Table 1).

Consider this example: 10110110. This 8-bit value equals 182 decimal places.

Normally, in binary format, if 1 represents a bit, it will be considered a value.

Table 1. Bit representation

BIT	Value
1	1
0	0
1	4
1	8
0	0
1	32
1	64
0	0

Like this, above value is 182.

So if you change MSB bits, then it has a greater impact on any images than LSB. As a result, the image can be distorted more. Normal eyes can comprehend the manipulation of images with ease. That's why changes made in LSB are more preferable.

The representation of new pixel value after embedding is as per below.

$$S = (P \& 0xFE | D) \tag{2}$$

P = Original pixel value
D = Data bit (0 or 1)
Where 0xFE is a mask that clears the LSB of the pixel value P.

So the next technique that is discussed is LSB techniques, whose motive is sending data through images, which are called cover images. Normally, human eyes cannot see these changes. In a data byte, 100011**1** last 1 (the bold one) is called LSB. This widely-used method utilizes image steganography. It actually changes the least or last bit of the cover image pixel. Suppose we are using a 24-bit image combination of RGB colors where we can insert data into images. There are many types of images, like index bitmaps, which are normally composed of two metrics, which represent the image as an array of pixel values. In grayscale images, single values represent the potency of pixels. But in color images, it represents three values in RGB.

Below are examples of different types of colors matrix representation.

Grey Scale images[
[0,255,0],
[255,0,255],
[0,255,0]
]
Color images
Red [
[255,0,0],
[0,255,0],
[0,0,255]].
Green:
[[0,255,0],
[255,0,255],
[0,255,0]
]
Blue:
[[0,0,255],
[0,255,0],
[255,0,0]]

In image processing, matrix structural representation can be used to manipulate images. The index bit map metrics are also known as Cdata. We can strip the LSB from Cdata, then replace the LSB in each pixel with one bit according to our needs. The formation of pixels is actually the data collection point in compress formation, where we can implement stripping, which means removing or exchanging those bits with less values, which will not create distortion in the image (Fig. 2).

True Colour and Indexed Colour Bitmaps

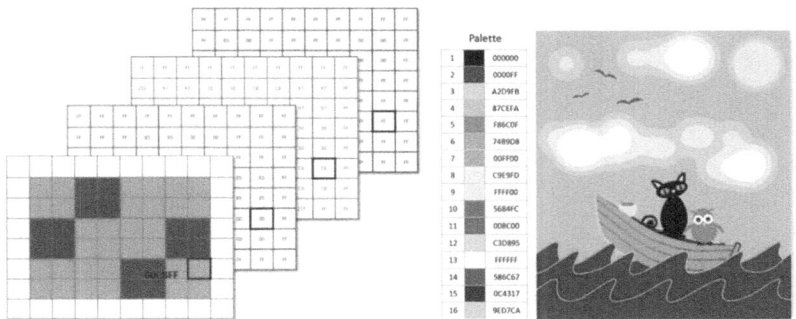

Fig. 2. Bitmap Image representation with array

Suppose you represent the red color in RGB (255,0,0) and convert it to binary format (11111111,00000000.000000000). Same as green (0,255,0) for blue (0,0,255). Using these, we can get many color formats by changing the values of 0–255 and getting many colors. RGB has a big impact on the steganography concept (Fig. 3).

RGB :0,255,80   RGB:0,252,0

Fig. 3. Normal vs Steganographic image

All are green, but if we look into the RGB values, they are different. If we convert it into binary format, 255 = 11111111, and 252 = 11111100.We can change the last two bits into cover images. As just the last two bits are different in green color format, we can embed the information through the LSB steganography technique in the last two digits, and we can also add information in red and blue parameters. Normally, as long as we understand the least significant bit, we can change and embed information (Figs. 4, 5).

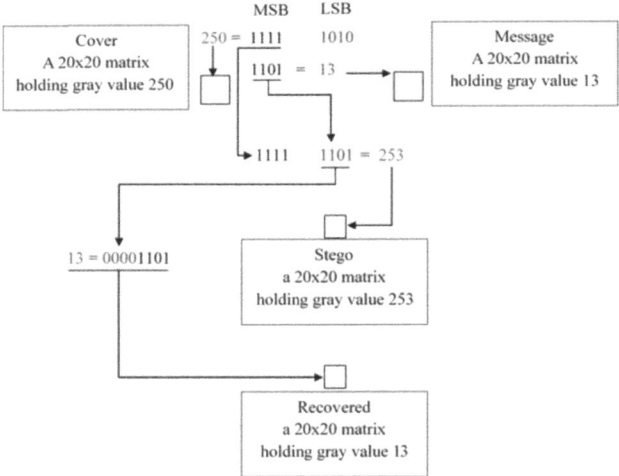

Fig. 4. LSB embedding method

If we see it in the above picture, we can store data in a hidden way. In the human eye, we cannot catch that the data is stored in this image. It's used in the three-color RGB format to store data in LSB bits.

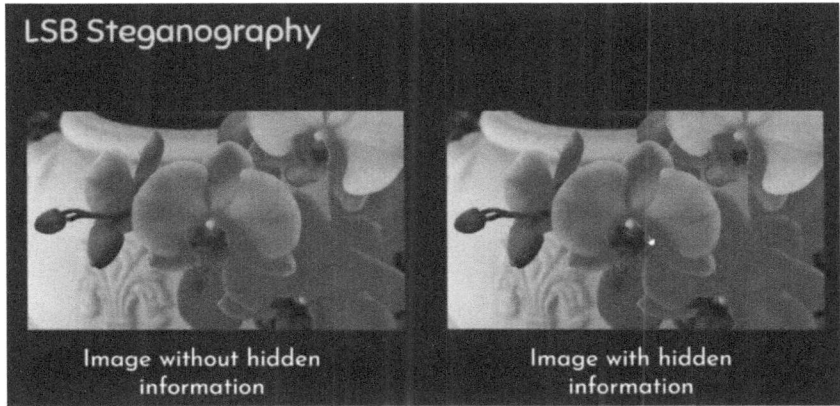

Fig. 5. LSB Steganography

Occasionally, we encounter numerous watermarks in digital images, which serve as additional information sources. We can use watermarks for copyright purposes and authentication. Watermarks can be of two types: visible and invisible. In invisible, we can apply LSB, technique, and many more, like DCT, DWT, and patchwork (Fig. 6).

Fig. 6. Steganography applied by watermark

If we apply the LSB technique for embedding, we also extract the LSB and reconstruct the pixel for recovering information. So typically, in 8-bit images, we can change the last 2 bits for information and the rest 6 bits for normal images. We use steganography techniques to create both carrier and message images. But when we embed message bits (MSB bits) into carrier bits, then we have to look into the changes in only the LSB bits of carrier images, and then it will not change in a broader sense, as we can put messages in carrier signals. For example, in the 8-bit representation of carrier images, we simply replace the last bit, 11001101, with 111111110, using an operation that only modifies the last bit, resulting in data bits 11001100.

In a bitmap image, we can apply the steganography technique to hide data. If we apply it to a high-quality bitmap image, then less distortion will be present, but for a lower-quality image, the distortion can be observable. Normally, in 24bit, we can have three channels, like RGB, where we can embed 3 bits of data per pixel. Depend of size image we can embedded the data.

4.2   PVD Method

The full form of PVD is pixel-value-based differencing. Before knowing about PVD, we first need to know about pixel formation. Normally, the axis of an image resides in the opposite direction. As seen in below image x and y are placing opposite, according to coordinates we can value the pixel (Figs. 7, 8, 9).

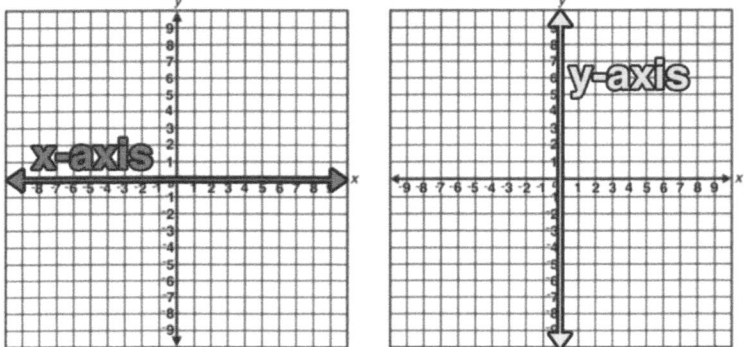

Fig. 7. Axis representation

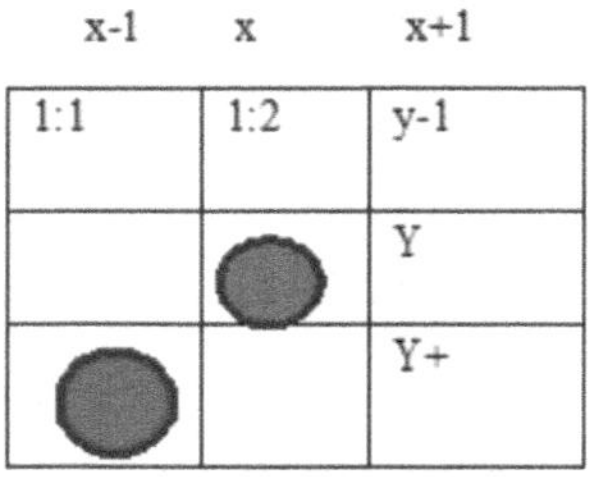

	x-1	x	x+1
	1:1	1:2	y-1
		⬤	Y
	⬤		Y+

Fig. 8. Pixel formation

The first block has a value of 1:1, and the next one has a value of 1:2. If we keep an eye on a pixel, that will be the origin. Supposing we can focus on the image, we can get other coordinates. There are different ways to fetch the images; we can use loops, such as taking I and j and then getting the X and Y positions. We want to take another picture, move to Y +, and then parallelly return to the x axis. Then we get the next picture pixel value.

Different types of pixel formats are here, like diagonal neighbor pixels and 4 neighbor pixels. Also, we can use all neighboring pixels in our algorithm for diagonal neighbor pixel values like (x–1, y–1), (x + 1, y–1), (x–1, y–1), (x + 1, y + 1) like these others

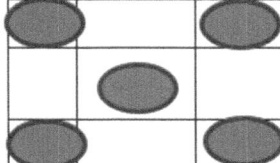 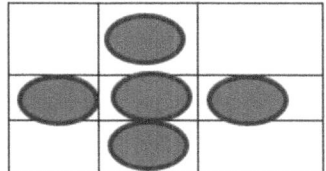

Fig. 9. Diagonal Neighbour Pixel and 4 Neighbour Pixel

above table pixel values can be counted. So if we use all nearby pixels, then we can hide the image more easily, where less distortion is possible.

So, as per the discussion, neighboring refers to a concept or technique that leverages the relationships between adjacent pixels in images. Neighboring techniques, such as spatial techniques, apply blurring, sharpening, and edge techniques to manipulate images. Next, image segmentation divides the image into different types of segments.

Next, we define connectivity, a valuable concept in window-to-images, as the relationship between neighboring pixels. We can break it down into several parts, such as first analyzing the connected pixel to determine if it shares the same color, depth, or intensity. Using image processing techniques, we can distinguish objects from other items in an image, such as a photograph of a car, park, or animal. Normally, we click on many pictures, which are objects. In the video, we can see moving objects. Connectivity consists of a few parts. One is the boundary of objects, a component of a region in an image. A region, defined as a set of pixels, creates a path between two objects. In an image, many objects can be there that are separate from each other by their borders.

Now we will discuss PVD techniques used in image steganography techniques to hide information. These methods influence the human eye's insensitivity to a few changes in color and bits. So first, break down the images into many pixels, then calculate many blocks, which is not an overlapping technique. Like 2×2, 3×3, 4×4, 8×8.

These PVD techniques work on color images and gray images. So gray images usually use a shade of gray image pixels, while color images mean a combination of RGB, where gray images often focus on the brightness channel.

The main advantage is that any data can be embedded without making any big changes to the steganographic images. It's seen great results from the perspective of PSNR and MSE scenarios. Peak signal-to-noise ratio is actually used for assessing the quality of stereo images. Detect the impartibility of hidden data with an image. Actually, comparing the steganographic image with actual images. Can have two types of PSNR: high and low. Secrete data with lower distortion and vice versa, respectively. As compared to MSE, which is also the same work done as PSNR, where you find out the average square error while also checking the steganographic image and cover image difference, here are PSNR intuitive, more than one human perceptive on image quality.

In today's world, increasing demand for Internet message passing is necessary, and security is also a big concern. So in the PVD technique, based on many parameters like normalization of secret data, capacity of hidden data, PSNR, MSE values, and RS Steganalysis Attack, we will be discussing.

In the smoother region of the image, a few bits can be embedded of information, and at the edge, a higher bit of the secret image can be embedded. In PVD, use grey image as the cover image. It's focusing on modifying the difference between the pixel value of an image and the pixel value itself. Changing the tiny changes in color, brightness in images, in human eyes, is really tough to catch. Normally, the image loaded in the Python NumPy array can be converted to grayscale, though it works on a color image working in RGB format. Whatever the message is, convert it to binary format and divide the picture in pixels. It focuses on how much data can be embedded according to the range of different values.

Like if d ∈ [0, 7] can be add data of 3 bits like [8, 15] can add 4 bits, so on. Now adjust d to d' so it matches the binary format data to be hidden. Calculating new pixel value P1' and P2' modified the difference d'. P1' and P2' changes should be are minimal. Updating image with new pixel values p1' and p2'.Saving with modified images data. This is the process we can add data in PVD. So if we calculate the difference between of 2 consecutive images like di = (Pi + 1 – Pi). Here, a small I denotes that the block is in a smooth region, whereas a larger value denotes that the block in a higher region. Di represents the difference between two consecutive blocks.

Normally, as per the study, the PVD technique finds more on the edge portion of an image than the smooth portion of an image, as human vison tolerance is higher in the edge area. This technique concentrates on processing the image pixels in a zigzag manner, avoiding block overlapping. The system then calculates the difference between the embedded images using a user-defined table. Suppose we got a difference value close to 0, then it's closer to the smooth area of an image, or if it's close to 255 values, then it's close to the edge area.

Next topics concern modulas PVD technology, which was proposed by Wang et al. Modulas PVD method, which mainly focuses on not overflowing or underflowing pixel values. Focusing on the neighboring difference between pixels.

4.3 EBE

Edge-based technique: normally, edge means meeting point of two parts, like in the context of images, the boundary of two parts meeting points. So in that portion, there is a contrast of brightness and color. The edge is an essential component of any visual system. It's distinguishing different objects so that you can understand the depth of an object and the shape of an object.

The edge-based technique allows for the embedding or hiding of data in an image's edge portion. So normally, the edge portion of an image has more intensity in color compared to other parts of the image. There are different functions, like the intensity function, through which you can identify the edge by computing the gradient of the image. This magnitude indicates the strength of the edge. Edge portions are less detectable than other parts in the human eye.

First, we detected the edge of an image through different techniques. Then we can embed data. Here, we are discussing the edge-based data embedding technique, where data can be embedded in the sharper part of an image while the other parts remain the same. Secrete data can be of any type; it can be video, text, or concealed in the LSB part of carrier images. Not every part or pixel can be done only in edged, which is detected by the algorithm.

LSB, PVD, and EBE techniques are just a few of the implied mechanisms. So many techniques are here for detecting edges in an image. The Canny Edge Detector is one of the mechanisms where we can get the edge of an image. This mechanism encompasses numerous components, including the multi-stage approach, noise reduction, where we can use filtering to reduce noise in images, gradient calculation, non-maximum, and double thresholding techniques, which are used to detect strong, weak, and non-relevant edges. These techniques are widely acceptable due to their availability. To locate an edge in an image, first reduce the noise, then calculate the gradient of the image to identify the sharpest area with the highest byte, where a higher magnitude of an image gradient is used to find borders. Modifying edges means less distortion in an image; each edge can contain more data compared to the flat part of the image.

5 Comparative Analysis of Image Steganography Techniques (LSB, EBE, PVD)

Comparative analysis of LSB, EBE and PVD method considering quality of the steganographic image, payload capacity, complexity and image type supported by the different methods like LSB, EBE and PVD is given in below table (Table 2).

Table 2. Comparative analysis of LSB, EBE and PVD

Method	PSNR Value (in Db)	Payload capacity	Complexity	Image type supported
LSB [25]	40–50 db	1 bit/ 8 pixel	Low	Gray scale image
EBE [26]	51.1	0.5 bpp	Low	Gray scale image
PVD [27]	52.25	1 bpp	Medium	BMP-24

In the above table 3 methods are compared, where one main topic is "Peak Signal to Noise," by which one can judge the quality of a steganographic image. Its measure is the similarity between cover and steganographic image; a higher value is showing better performance. For calculating, check the pixel value position before and after embedding the message in images. The next part is payload capacity, which means how much data can be added without degradation of visual quality.

An example like 1 bit/pixel can be calculated like 512 * 512 pixel image payload capacity is 512 * 512 = 262144/8 = 32768 byte where the embedded capacity is 32 kb of data at a rate of 1 bit/pixel. It is influenced by a variety of factors, including image color, depth, size, and so on. At the end, with more data embedded, the PSNR decreases parallel, and the MSE value also increases, so the attacker can easily detect a tempered image. So maintain quality. Embedding and balancing all of these is a big, challenging task. Additionally, we have to add an extra layer to protect from steganalysis.

6 Conclusion

Embedding data in another object like an image video with secure way, protection from steganography attacks is a big concern now. There are many ways to do the embedding data that are discussed in these papers. After reading these papers, the reader will get an idea about the steganography concept. Also gathering knowledge about image basic things like what is pixel, types of images. Also, clear knowledge about LSB techniques is simple to implement, but its susceptibility to detection and potential degradation of image quality limit its effectiveness in high-security applications. PVD improves upon LSB by leveraging pixel value differences to enhance embedded capacity and robustness, making it is a more resilient choice that preserves image quality better. However, PVD can be more complex to implement and may still face challenges in extreme cases of steganalysis. EBE stands out for its ability to embed information in image edges, where changes are less perceptible, providing superior robustness and minimal impact on visual quality. This technique provides a good PSNR ratio when we implement it using grayscale image, so it is more robust compared to the LSB method.

Overall, the choice of steganography technique depends on the specific requirements of the application, such as the desired balance between payload capacities, complexity, quality of the steganographic image and resistance to detection.

References

1. Yiğit, Y., Karabatak, M.: A stenography application for hiding student information into an image. In: 7th International Symposium on Digital Forensics and Security (ISDFS), pp. 1−4. Barcelos, Portugal (2019). https://doi.org/10.1109/ISDFS.2019.8757516
2. Tan, D., Lu, Y., Yan, X., Wang, X.: A simple review of audio steganography. In: 2019 IEEE 3rd Information Technology, Networking, Electronic and Automation Control Conference (ITNEC), pp. 1409−1413 Chengdu, China (2019). https://doi.org/10.1109/ITNEC.2019.8729476
3. Ajala, J.A., Singh, S., Mukherjee, S., Chakraborty, S.: Application of steganography technique in cloud computing. In: 2019 International Conference on Computational Intelligence and Knowledge Economy (ICCIKE), pp. 532–537. Dubai, United Arab Emirates (2019). https://doi.org/10.1109/ICCIKE47802.2019.9004347
4. Montalbo, F.J.P., Barfeh, D.P.Y.: Classification of stenography using convolutional neural networks and canny edge detection algorithm. In: 2019 International Conference on Computational Intelligence and Knowledge Economy (ICCIKE), pp. 305–310. Dubai, United Arab Emirates (2019). https://doi.org/10.1109/ICCIKE47802.2019.9004359
5. Abd Aziz, A.Z., Mohd Sultan, M.F., Mohamad Zulkufli, N.L.: Image steganography: comparative analysis of their techniques, complexity and enhancements. Int. J. Perceptive Cognitive Comput. **10**(1), 59–70 (2024)
6. Kulkarni, M., Degadwala, S., Mahajan, A.: A review on digital image watermarking based on dual noise and geometric attacks. In: 2020 2nd International Conference on Innovative Mechanisms for Industry Applications (ICIMIA), pp. 778–781. Bangalore, India (2020). https://doi.org/10.1109/ICIMIA48430.2020.9074901
7. Wazirali, R., Alasmary, W., Mahmoud, M.M.E.A., Alhindi, A.: An optimized steganography hiding capacity and imperceptibly using genetic algorithms. IEEE Access **7**, 133496–133508 (2019). https://doi.org/10.1109/ACCESS.2019.2941440

8. Kim, H., Bruce, N., Park, S., Lee, H.: EnCase forensic technology for decrypting stenography algorithm applied in the powerpoint file. In: 2016 18th International Conference on Advanced Communication Technology (ICACT), pp. 722–725. PyeongChang, Korea (South) (2016). https://doi.org/10.1109/ICACT.2016.7423534

9. Aveni, T.J., Seim, C., Starner, T.: A preliminary apparatus and teaching structure for passive tactile training of stenography. In: 2019 IEEE World Haptics Conference (WHC), pp. 383–388. Tokyo, Japan (2019). https://doi.org/10.1109/WHC.2019.8816077

10. Doshi, M.: A comparison of data mining approaches for forecasting sales of FMCG food products. In: 2023 14th International Conference on Computing Communication and Networking Technologies (ICCCNT), pp. 1–7. Delhi, India (2023). https://doi.org/10.1109/ICCCNT56998.2023.10307432

11. Huang, H., Xue, Y., Fan, L., Li, M.: The development and new direction of digital image stenography. In: 2020 International Conference on Robots & Intelligent System (ICRIS), pp. 124–128. Sanya, China (2020). https://doi.org/10.1109/ICRIS52159.2020.00039

12. Hirapara, J., Vanjara, P.: A comparative study of data mining techriques for agriculture crop price prediction. In: 2022 IEEE 7th International Conference for Convergence in Technology (I2CT), pp. 1–6. Mumbai, India (2022). https://doi.org/10.1109/I2CT54291.2022.9824533

13. Ledoux, A., Dao, N.B., Lahmi, P., Coustaty, M.: Alphanumeric glyphs transformation based on shape morphing: context of text. In: 2019 Eighth International Conference on Emerging Security Technologies (EST), pp. 1–6. Colchester, UK (2019). https://doi.org/10.1109/EST.2019.8806219

14. Ejidokun, T., Omitola, O.O., Nnamah, I., Adeniji, K.: Implementation and comparative analysis of variants of LSB steganographic method. In: 2022 30th Southern African Universities Power Engineering Conference (SAUPEC), pp. 1–4. Durban, Scuth Africa (2022). https://doi.org/10.1109/SAUPEC55179.2022.9730643

15. Patra, A., Roy, S., Saha, A., Sarkar, S.: data protection using optical system and steganography tool. In: 2023 International Conference on Next Generation Electronics (NEleX), pp. 1–5. Vellore, India (2023). https://doi.org/10.1109/NEleX59773.2023.10421449

16. Raj, U.A.S., Maheswaran, C.P.: Secure file sharing system using image steganography and cryptography techniques. In: 2023 International Conference on Inventive Computation Technologies (ICICT), pp. 1113–1116. Lalitpur, Nepal (2023). https://doi.org/10.1109/ICICT57646.2023.10134163

17. Hegde, S., Sunag, P., Varun, R.P.: Exploring the effectiveness of steganography techniques: a comparative analysis. In: 2023 3rd International Conference on Smart Data Intelligence (ICSMDI), pp. 181–186. Trichy, India (2023). https://doi.org/10.1109/ICSMDI57622.2023.00042

18. Saxena, N., Kumar, H.: Steganography techniques a review. In: 2023 5th International Conference on Advances in Computing, Communication Control and Networking (ICAC3N), pp. 1355–1360. Greater Noida, India (2023). https://doi.org/10.1109/ICAC3N60023.2023.10541623

19. Niu, L., Zhang, J.: An image steganography method based on texture perception. In: 2022 IEEE 2nd International Conference on Data Science and Computer Application (ICDSCA), pp. 625–628. Dalian, China (2022). https://doi.org/10.1109/ICDSCA56264.2022.9988162

20. Chen, Y., Wang, H., Li, W., Luo, J.: Cost reassignment for improving security of adaptive steganography using an artificial immune system. IEEE Sign. Process. Lett. 29, 1564–1568 (2022). https://doi.org/10.1109/LSP.2022.3188174

21. Shukla, I., Joshi, A., Girme, S.: LSB steganography mechanism to hide texts within images backed with layers of encryption. In: 2023 16th International Conference on Security of Information and Networks (SIN), pp. 1–6. Jaipur, India (2023). https://doi.org/10.1109/SIN60469.2023.10474976

22. Devi, A.G., Thota, A., Nithya, G., Majji, S., Gopatoti, A., Dhavamani, L.: advancement of digital image steganography using deep convolutional neural networks. In: 2022 International Interdisciplinary Humanitarian Conference for Sustainability (IIHC), pp. 250–254. Bengaluru, India (2022). https://doi.org/10.1109/IIHC55949.2022.10060230

23. Rajeswari, R., Meenadshi, M.: AI-enhanced LSB steganography interface: concealed data embedding framework. In: 2023 9th International Conference on Smart Structures and Systems (ICSSS), pp. 1–4. CHENNAI, India (2023). https://doi.org/10.1109/ICSSS58085.2023.10407062

24. Almalki, K.A., Mohammed R.: A novel steganography approach to embed secret information into a legitimate URL. In: 2022 2nd International Conference on Computing and Information Technology (ICCIT), pp. 180–185. Tabuk, Saudi Arabia (2022). https://doi.org/10.1109/ICCIT52419.2022.9711647

25. Rawat, D., Bhandari, V.: A steganography technique for hiding an image in an image using LSB method for 24 bit color image. Int. J. Comput. Appl. **64**(20), 15–19 (2013). https://doi.org/10.5120/10749-5625

26. Bassil, Y.: Image steganography based on a parameterized canny edge detection algorithm. Int. J. Comput. Appl. **16**(4) (2012)

27. Maji, G., Mandal, S., Debnath, N.C., Sen, S.: Pixel value difference based image steganography with one time pad encryption. In: 2019 IEEE 17th International Conference on Industrial Informatics (INDIN), pp. 1358–1363. Helsinki, Finland (2019). https://doi.org/10.1109/INDIN41052.2019.8972175

28. Doshi, M., Hirapara, J.: A study on data mining techniques for forecasting FMCG product sales. In: 2024 15th International Conference on Computing Communication and Networking Technologies (ICCCNT), pp. 1–6. Kamand, India (2024). https://doi.org/10.1109/ICCCNT61001.2024.10726077

Advancement and Applications in Biometric Techniques: A Comprehensive Study

A. Kalamani[1]([envelope]) and M. Suganya[2]

[1] School of Computer Studies (UG), RVS College of Arts and Science, Coimbatore, India
Kalaa.mca@gmail.com
[2] Department of Information Technology, RVS College of Arts and Science, Coimbatore, India
suganyam029@gmail.com

Abstract. In a society where theft is prevalent, ensuring security at every level is crucial. Biometrics is the automated process of identifying individuals based on their unique biological or behavioral characteristics, such as fingerprints, keystrokes, facial features, voices, iris patterns, and gait . Various biometrics methods are used to identify the individuals. Keystroke and Voice biometrics is a technology that uses individuals' characteristics to identify and authenticate them. Keystroke Dynamics utilizes unique typing rhythm of an individual. Voice Biometrics utilizes unique features of a person's voice, such as pitch, tone, modulation, and pronunciation, to create a voiceprint similar to a fingerprint . Voice biometrics involves the use of various soft computing techniques to analyze and authenticate voice characteristics. We analyze the importance of accurate speech recognition in voice biometric systems and explore the potential of automated speech conversion. This paper provides a summary of the essential concepts like Ant Colony Optimization, PSO in keystroke dynamics and Spoof net, modeling techniques involved in voice biometrics. Various DNN techniques and obtained results are discussed in this study.

Keywords: Keystroke dynamics · ANT · PSO · Voice biometrics · spoof net · voiceprint · MFCC · DNN · Transformer

1 Introduction

1.1 Purpose of This Study Paper

1. Why we have chosen the keystroke and voice biometrics?
2. What are the key concepts in keystroke and voice biometrics?
3. Comparative discussion of the keystroke and voice biometrics?
4. What are the techniques used in different keystroke and voice biometric white papers?
5. Drawbacks and Future Enhancements in both the biometrics.

S. Rajagopal et al. (Eds.): ASCIS 2024, CCIS 2424, pp. 355–363, 2025.
https://doi.org/10.1007/978-3-031-86290-8_25

2 Motive for Keystroke and Voice Biometrics

Soft computing is an umbrella term used to describe the types of algorithms that produce approximate solutions to unsolvable high-level problems in computer science. The biometric study is a branch of science and soft computing that leads with the statistical analysis of any biological data of an individual human being. This method is used for identification and authentication of any user by different unique features. Human is having various biological aspects which are unique from each other in the different combinational form [1, 2]. Every individuals support the usage of biometric systems such as retina scans, iris, palm and fingerprints, keystrokes and voice recognition [3, 4].

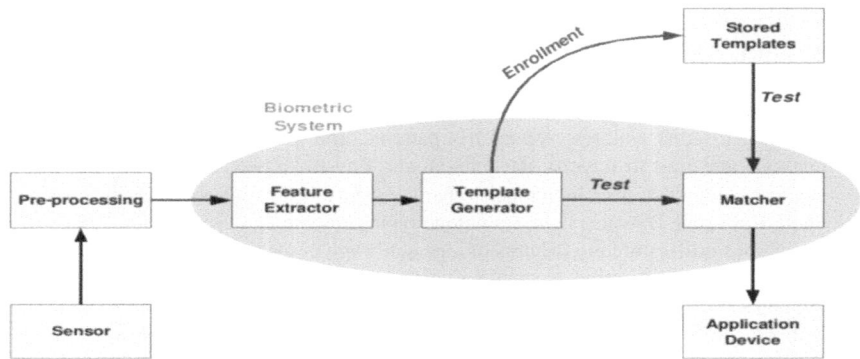

Fig. 1. Authentication and Verification

Figure 1 explains about the working model of the biometric systems. The first time an individual uses a biometric method is called enrolment or Feature Extraction. During enrollment, biometric information from an individual is captured and stored. In consequent uses, biometric information is detected, compared and verified with the information stored at the time of enrollment. This method is called verification. It is crucial that storage and retrieval of such systems themselves be secure if the biometric system is to be robust [1]. For going through several biometric research journals keystroke and voice biometrics provides a strong method for identity verification, enhancing security, and reducing the probability of unauthorized access.

Keystroke Dynamics: It is identified as a Typing Rhythm of an each individual. Typing speed, style and the cap between pressing and releasing is a features of keystroke Dynamics [1, 3]. Keystroke Dynamics (Fabian Monrose and Aviel D. Rubin (2000), Jarmo Ilonen, (2003)) consist of many advantages like (i) It can be used without any additional hardware (ii) Hardening the existing security. Keystroke analysis (Christopher S. Leberknight et al. (2008)) is of two kinds Static and Dynamic. Static keystroke analysis essentially means that the analysis is performed on typing samples produced using the same predetermined text for all the individuals under observation. Dynamic keystroke analysis implies a continuous or periodic monitoring of issued keystrokes and is intended to be performed during a log-in session, after the authentication phase has passed.

Voice recognition: It can refer to both identifying spoken words (speech recognition) and identifying individuals based on their voice (voice biometrics) [2]. In the context of security and authentication, "voice biometrics" specifically refers to the technology used to verify a person's identity based on their unique vocal characteristics. This technology offers a convenient and straightforward authentication process, removing the need for users to remember passwords or carry physical tokens. Given that most devices are equipped with microphones, voice biometrics is a practical solution that can be implemented across various platforms. Compared to other biometric systems, voice biometrics can be more economical, as it leverages existing hardware and infrastructure. To improve the security in various areas it is incorporated into those areas. The metrics of improving accuracy, robustness, and resistance to spoofing attacks are the ongoing research in voice biometrics. Machine learning and Artificial intelligence techniques are incorporated and improving the research areas of keystroke and voice biometrics.

3   Key Concepts in Keystroke and Voice Biometrics

The following methods are used for collecting the sample and verifying the individual in keystroke and voice biometrics.

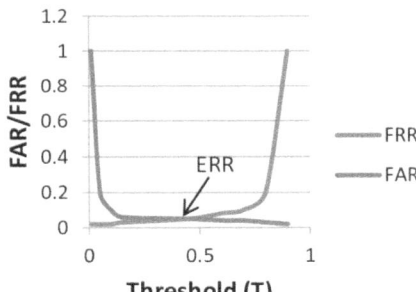

Feature Extraction: To capture a keystroke, it would be necessary for users to type their password a number of times. The system would set about capturing these features using three methods regarding the time (in milliseconds) that a particular user maintains the key pressed (Duration time), and the time elapsed between releasing one key and pressing the next (latency time) and the combination of the above is called Digraph [3].

In the Enrolment and Voiceprint phase, digital representation (voice print) of individual voice samples is registered for further enrolment and Authentication. In the Identification and Verification phase, the present individual voice sample is compared with stored samples in a database to confirm the individual. Specific characteristics of the voice, such as frequency, pitch, and format are used to construct the voiceprint. The above metrics are features of voice biometrics.

Verification Systems: There are two different type of verification available in biometrics. 1. Text-Dependent: Requires the user to type or say specific sentences. 2.Text-Independent: Authenticates the user regardless of what they type or say. Threshold value means limit value of the output. FAR –False Acceptance Rate, FRR – False Rejection Rate are the two measures used to identify and measure the solution (Table 1, Fig. 2).

Comparative Study with Other Biometrics

This Chart Explains keystroke dynamics little ease of use than voice biometrics. Other measures of keystroke and voice dynamics are working like similar. Both Biometrics are provide more security than other biometrics.

Table 1. Comparison of these three phases with keystroke and voice biometrics.

Biometrics	Phase	Process	Requirements	Challenges
Voice Biometrics	Enrollment	Record multiple voice samples to create a voiceprint	Microphone, quiet environment	Variability in voice due to health, noise, or stress. [1]
	Verification	Compare a live voice sample with the stored voiceprint	Microphone	Affected by background noise, voice changes
	Identification	Identify from a database of voiceprints	Microphone	Depends on database quality and voiceprint
Keystroke Dynamics	Enrollment	Provide typing rhythm or typing time to create a template	sensor	Distinctiveness Issues with slow speed/not well at that time of typing and sensor quality
	Verification	Match a live typing speed against the stored template	sensor	Affected by finger condition and sensor quality
	Identification	Match typing rhythm to a database to identify individuals	sensor	Accuracy influenced by database size and quality
Facial Recognition	Enrollment	Capture images or video to create a facial template	Camera, suitable lighting	Variability due to lighting, expressions, and aging
	Verification	Compare a live facial image to the stored template	Camera	Affected by lighting changes and facial expressions
	Identification	Match facial features to a database to identify individuals	Camera	Accuracy impacted by image quality and environmental conditions

"Speech Emotion Recognition Using Mel-Frequency Cepstral Coefficients & Convolutional Neural Networks", Shubhan Kadam et al. [2, 6] using the techniques as Mel-Frequency Cepstral Coefficients (MFCC). It is used to extract relevant features from the voice signal. This paper explains the MFCC as a representation of the short-term power spectrum of sound. It is used in speech and audio processing, particularly

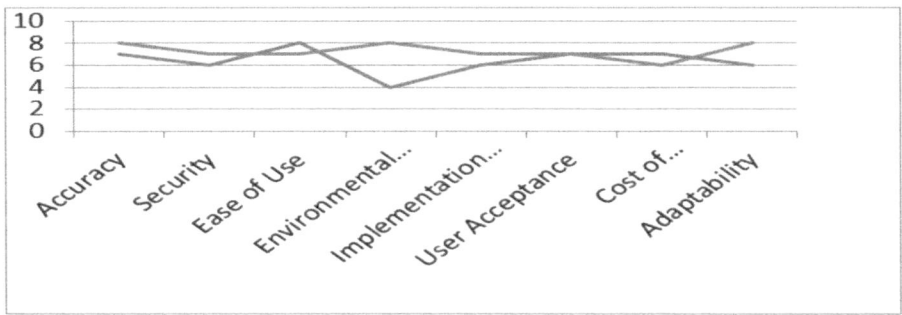

Fig. 2. Voice biometric with keystroke Dynamics measures

in speech-emotion recognition (SER) and automatic speech recognition (ASR). MFCCs are effective because they reduce the amount of data while preserving the essential characteristics of the audio signal. This makes them suitable for machine learning models, such as Convolutional Neural Networks (CNNs), which are employed in the paper to enhance SER performance.

In "Feature extraction in speech recognition using linear predictive coding: An overview", Fang Zehuang [4] tells about how LPC Encodes the spectral envelope of a speech signal. In this paper is a method used to represent the spectral properties of speech signals. It does this by estimating the parameters of a linear predictive model, which helps in compressing the speech data while retaining essential information for further processing, such as Speech-to-Text and Text-to-Speech systems. The primary function of LPC in speech recognition is feature extraction. This involves transforming the speech waveform into a parametric representation.LPC reduces the data rate required for processing, making it easier to analyze and manipulate the speech data. LPC achieves a low data rate by converting the speech waveform into a parametric form. This representation is crucial for efficient processing and analysis, allowing systems to handle speech input effectively.

"STFT-Domain Neural Speech Enhancement With Very Low Algorithmic Latency" Zhong-Qiu Wang [4] uses the technique of Short-Time Fourier Transform (STFT). It Analyzes the frequency content of a signal over time [4, 5]. It breaks a signal into smaller segments, allowing for the examination of its frequency components at different time intervals.STFT is employed to transform audio signals into the frequency domain. This transformation helps in identifying and separating the target speech from background noise, which is key for improving speech clarity and intelligibility.

From the above comparative study for feature extraction, Mel-frequency cepstral coefficients (MFCC) as one of the best methods for feature extraction [5].MFCC is good due to its ability to effectively handle background noise and provide accurate readings in a faster manner compared to other techniques. Linear Prediction Cepstral coefficients (LPC) are also used for feature extraction in voice biometrics, offering valuable insights into the voice signal. While Short-Time Fourier Transform (STFT) is a powerful tool for analyzing the time-frequency characteristics of speech signals. The performance of MFCC can vary based on factors such as the number of filters, algorithms used, and dimensions of frames, leading to inconsistent results in different scenarios. So we can use this inference as a future study.

4   Keystroke Dynamics Extraction and Subset Selection Techniques

"Feature subset selection in keystroke dynamics using ant colony optimization" [3] this paper discuss that Duration, Latency and digraph are the features in keystroke dynamics. Various methods are used to collect the features in enrolment phase. Selected features are grouped based on their mean and standard deviation value and Ant colony optimization algorithms(ACO) are used for subset selection. Neural network algorithm is used for classification. FAR and FRR is used to find the accuracy in this paper.

"Soft biometric based keystroke classification using PSO optimized neural network" [7, 8], in this paper duration, latency are the extracted features and particle swarm optimization algorithm(PSO) as a subset selection algorithm. Features subset selection method is based on the bird's intelligence behavior. NN method is used for classifying the feature and provide a solution.

"Keystroke Dynamics: Concepts, Techniques, and Applications" Rashik Shadman et al. [9] explain about different Techniques used for Extraction, Gaussian Mixture Model (GMM), Manhattan and Scaled Manhattan Distance, Mahalanobis Distance likewise several algorithms are discussed clearly. Three types of algorithms statistical, machine learning based and deep learning based algorithms are discussed in this paper.It describes the significance of different keystroke data processing techniques like text filtering, data size variation, removing faulty data etc.

Comparison of DNN with Various Approaches in Voice Biometrics

1. "Deep Learning for Speaker Verification Using Convolutional Neural Networks" [13] Approach Utilizes Convolutional Neural Networks (CNNs) to process spectrograms of voice signals. Focuses on extracting spatial features from spectrograms to enhance speaker verification accuracy. Implements batch normalization and dropout to improve generalization. Results Achieved an accuracy of 92% in speaker verification tasks. A notable improvement in distinguishing between similar voices compared to traditional methods. Equal Error Rate (EER) reduced to 5.5%.
2. In the year 2023, N Kaladharan, and R. Arunkumar [15] used the method asQuickSpoofNet Approach, this approach Utilizes one-shot learning and metric learning techniques for detecting synthetic attacks in the ASV system and Evaluates the performance of Adam and AdaMax optimizers on the AlexNet architecture for voice biometric authentication systems, Implements an improved deep convolutional neural network (IDCNN) and LSTM network structure for voice authentication and verification and achieved the result with an accuracy of 99.3% (Table 2).
3. "Temporal Dynamics in Speech: Combining Deep Neural Networks with Long Short-Term Memory" [13] Approach Combines Deep Neural Networks (DNNs) for feature extraction with Long Short-Term Memory (LSTM) [14, 15] networks for sequential modeling. Designed to capture both static voice features and dynamic temporal patterns.Focuses on end-to-end learning from raw audio data. The Results are Accuracy

Table 2. Comparison of Different metrics in DNN.

Metric	DNN (Generic)	CNN	RNN	LSTM	GRU	Transformer
Feature Extraction	70%	90%	60%	70%	70%	90%
Temporal Dynamics	40%	30%	80%	90%	80%	100%
Long-term Dependencies	50%	30%	60%	90%	70%	90%
Computational Efficiency	60%	70%	40%	40%	50%	30%
Ease of Training	60%	60%	50%	40%	50%	60%
Accuracy (Sample Task)	85%	90%	82%	89%	88%	92%

of 94% in speaker identification tasks. Improved handling of temporal dependencies and variations in speech.Achieved 4.2%, demonstrating better performance in handling sequential dependencies.

In the above study papers 1 and 2 excel in spatial feature extraction with ASV and CNNs. Paper 3 offers a comprehensive performance by combining DNNs with LSTMs for dynamic and sequential data. Paper 3 focuses on end-to-end learning and feature reduction with autoencoders and RNNs. This comparison highlights the strengths and specific contributions of each paper's approach to DNNs in voice biometrics. Each paper has its unique advantages, depending on the specific needs of voice recognition tasks, such as handling temporal dependencies, feature extraction, and dimensionality reduction. DNN Architecture comparison in the previous papers gives the inference as (Fig. 3)

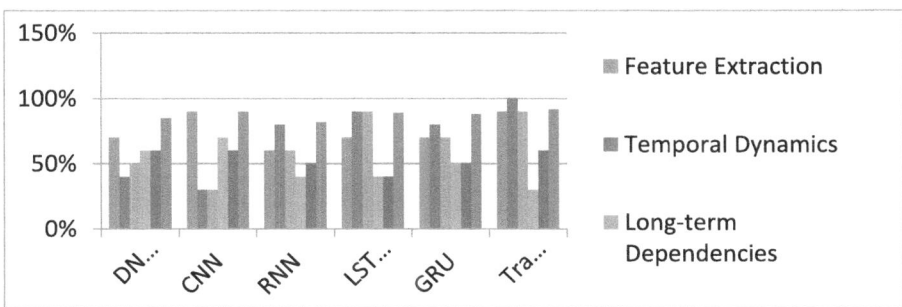

Fig. 3. Comparison of Different Metrics

This technique is useful in a variety of sectors, including identity verification, criminology, medicine, and security, because it offers safe and trustworthy authentication. Identity verification for transactions and customer service in banking and finance.

5 Future Enhancement

In this present study clearly explained the various techniques used in the biometrics. The main drawback of most biometric methods is that they are expensive to implement, because most of them require specialized hardware to strengthen security. Healthcare, forensic, banking and security needed places are mainly focused on the biometric methods. Voice biometrics systems are susceptible to spoofing attacks using recorded or synthetic voices. Developing effective anti-spoofing technologies is critical but still it is challenging. Differences in recording devices and transmission channels can affect the accuracy and reliability of voice biometrics systems. The collection, storage, and use of voice data raise privacy concerns. Ensuring that the voice sample is from a live person and not a recording or synthetic voice is an ongoing challenge. Balancing the swap between false acceptance rates (FAR) and false rejection rates (FRR) is complex and requires ongoing research and optimization. In keystroke dynamics dataset limitations and some real time implementations also little complex.

6 Conclusion

Keystrokes and Voice biometrics presents a rich field for research with significant potential benefits in terms of security and user convenience. In this paper, we have discussed the various biometric techniques and different methodologies used in keystroke and voice biometrics. Comparative study of various methodologies provides a clear view of the techniques, and complications involved while introducing the technologies and results obtained. Various advancements and applications are also discussed in this study. ANT, PSO in keystrokes and CNN, RNN, LSTM, GRU, Transformers provide significant results in voice Biometrics. DNN Requires large amounts of data and computational power. Incorporating attention mechanisms in deep neural network models can enhance the focus on relevant features during keystroke and voice analysis, improving the accuracy of biometrics systems. This study concluded that various methods are compared and voice, keystroke Dynamics provide a result of ease to use, adaption and provide more security.

References

1. Shradha, T., Chourasia, J.N.,Chourasia, V.S.: A review of advancement in biometric systems. Int. J. Innovative Res. Adv. Eng. 2(1), 22–26.(2015).
2. Kadam, S., Jani, J., Kudtarkar, A., Koshy, R.: Speech emotion recognition using mel-frequency cepstral coefficients & convolutional neural networks. In: 2024 2nd International Conference on Intelligent Data Communication Technologies and Internet of Things (IDCIoT), pp. 1595–1602. IEEE (2024)

3. Karnan, M., Akila, M., Kalamani, A.: Feature subset selection in keystroke dynamics using ant colony optimization. J. Eng. Technol. (Acad. J.)**1**(5), 072–080 (2009)
4. Khan, A., Malik, K.M.: Securing voice biometrics: one-shot learning approach for audio deepfake detection. In: 2023 IEEE International Workshop on Information Forensics and Security (WIFS), pp. 1−6. IEEE (2023)
5. Fang, Z., Kang, Y., Feng, W.: Feature extraction in speech recognition using linear predictive coding: an overview. I-manger's J. Dig. Sign. Process. **10**(2), 16 (2022)
6. Wang, Z.Q., Wichern, G., Watanabe, S., Le Roux, J.: STFT-domain neural speech enhancement with very low algorithmic latency. IEEE/ACM Trans. Audio, Speech **31**, 397–410 (2023)
7. Fakhri, A.A.M., Santosa, R.B.T., Trujillo, J.S.: A comparative study of MFCC, LPC, and PLP features for speech recognition. J. Electr. Eng. Technol. (2022)
8. Abinaya, R., Sowmiya, R.: Soft biometric based keystroke classification using PSO optimized neural network, Gudlavalleru Engineering College, Annamalai University, Materials Today: Proceedings (Elsevier BV) (2021)
9. Shadman, R., Wahab, A.A., et al.: Keystroke Dynamics: Concepts, Techniques, and Applications
10. Singh, A.B., Patel, R., Kumar, N.: Deep neural networks for voice recognition: recent advances and future directions. IEEE Trans. Neural Netw. Learn. Syst. (2024)
11. Hinton, G., Deng, L., Yu, D., et al.: Deep neural networks for acoustic modeling in speech recognition: the shared views of four research groups. IEEE Sign. Process. Mag. (2012)
12. Liu, Y., He, L., Liu, J.: Large margin softmax loss for speaker verification. Interspeech (2019)
13. Kaladharan, N, Arunkumar, R.: An efficient voice authentication approach using improved deep convolutional neural networks with LSTM networks. IETE J. Res. 1–14 (2023)
14. Hinton, G., Deng, L., et al.: Deep neural networks for acoustic modeling in speech recognition: the shared views of four research groups. IEEE Sign. Process. Mag. (2012)
15. Maragatharajan, M., Sudhan, M.B.: Face identification method using scale invariant feature transform method for criminal management system. In: 2023 4th International Conference on Smart Electronics and Communication (ICOSEC), pp. 732–738. Trichy, India (2023). https://doi.org/10.1109/ICOSEC58147.2023.10276072

Securing E-Commerce: A Comprehensive Analysis of Fraud Detection Methods

Rushi Parikh, Krupa Bhavsar[✉], and Uttam Chauhan

Computer Engineering Department, Vishwakarma Government Engineering College, Ahmedabad, Gujarat, India
bhavsarkrupa99@gmail.com

Abstract. Fraudsters are attracted to the e-commerce sector because of the increasing transaction amounts, underscoring the crucial importance of efficient fraud prevention and detection mechanisms. This paper delves into e-commerce fraud detection through a systematic literature review, exploring the evolving landscape of advanced technologies, particularly machine learning automation. This technology enhances the detection capabilities for fraudulent activities by efficiently processing large volumes of e-commerce transaction data. As fraudulent transactions become more complex, there is a need for efficient ways to counteract these risks. To combat fraudulent transactions, there's a growing need for effective methods. Our primary objective is to comprehensively study various algorithms employed in e-commerce for fraud prevention. The survey focuses on comparing and assessing the effectiveness of this algorithm. The aim is to provide insight into the effectiveness of the proposed techniques in comparison to existing techniques. The findings contribute to a deeper understanding of the current state of e-commerce fraud detection, offering valuable insights for researchers, practitioners, and stakeholders in the ongoing battle against online fraud.

Keywords: Fraud Detection Methods · Electronic commerce · Machine Learning

1 Introduction

Online trade of products and services is referred to as "e-commerce," or electronic commerce. E-commerce operates in several market segments including business-to-business, business-to-consumer, consumer-to-consumer, and consumer-to-business. The Internet helps to make it easier. And represents a digital transformation of traditional business models. As more people utilize digital devices and e-commerce platforms, cybercrimes and frauds have significantly increased [1]. This transformation has empowered consumers to conveniently browse and purchase products from the comfort of their homes.

Both legitimate users and fraudsters use electronic commerce systems; hence they become more vulnerable to large-scale and systematic fraud. Fraud is a crime where the purpose is to acquire money by illegal means [2]. E-commerce platforms have several benefits, one of which is quicker purchase processes, financial savings, increased customer freedom, the capacity to compare goods and prices, quick reaction to consumer and market demands, and a variety of payment choices.[3]. With the modern system's growth, the risk of fraud and financial abuse increases. To address this, we require methods to identify suspicious transactions. Intelligent monitoring solutions are required because human observers cannot keep an eye on the volume of transactions occurring online continuously.

Sometimes, existing solutions are unable to keep up with fraudsters because they are so skilled at adapting and changing their strategies to take advantage of the platforms. [2]. Presently, data mining techniques stand as a formidable solution for fraud detection across various domains. Data mining encompasses several steps which are Data collection, Data preprocessing, Feature selection, Model training, Model evaluation, Deployment and lastly monitoring and feedback. Each step is crucial to ensure that it is applicable to real world problems. These steps can be present in flowchart as shown in Fig. 1.

To reduce fraud, we examine data mining approaches, namely machine learning algorithms. We focus on issues related to user data misuse, credit card fraud, hacking, and sensitive information theft. The more important point is that low research and development efforts fuelled by a dearth of useful data and the need for businesses to protect their platform vulnerabilities further exacerbate the issue. For example, it makes no sense to describe fraud detection or prevention methods in the open since doing so would arm fraudsters with the knowledge they need to avoid detection**Error! Reference source not found.**. In the field of data mining for fraud detection, outliers pose a significant challenge, particularly in the banking sector. Given their crucial role in banking operations, identifying these anomalies is one of the trickiest challenges.

One of e-commerce's methods to attract many customers is by offering many promotions such as cashback, discounts, free delivery, etc. However, this phenomenon is drawing the attention of consumers as well as that of criminals who want to take advantage of it. One example of promotion misconduct done by criminals is creating multiple fraudulent accounts and transactions [4]. A report from Statista says that in 2022, online shopping scams accounted for 38 percent of all reported scams worldwide. To combat fraud in the modern era, we therefore require more advanced and reliable techniques. The use of flexible and hybrid systems has been the focus of recent research on machine-learning applications for fraud detection [6, 7]. The incidence of fraud in India is rising for several reasons. These include the rapid growth of the Indian economy: Which has created several opportunities for scammers, as more and more people are using financial services and conducting transactions online, and the lack of awareness about fraud: A large number of individuals in India are unaware of the various forms of fraud that might occur, making them more susceptible to being victims of scams. As a result, around 8.3 billion US dollars' worth of money was lost in 2022 due to various frauds. The growing use of technology has made it simpler for con artists to select their targets and execute their scams.

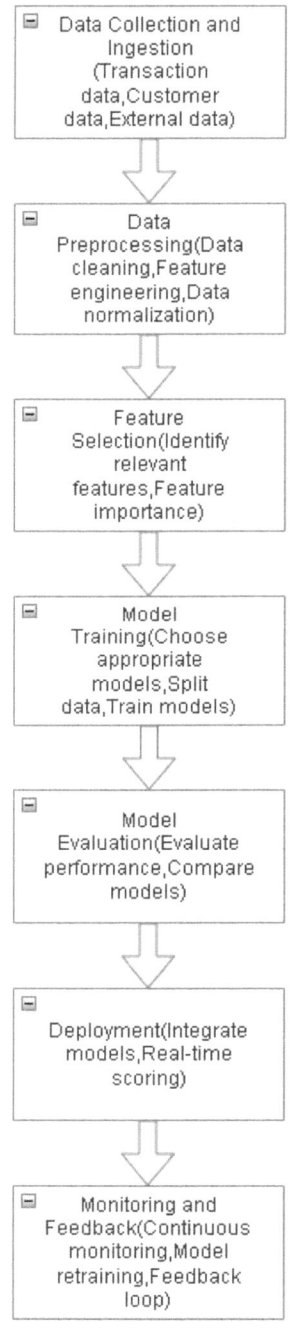

Fig. 1. Data Mining Flowchart

2 Background Study

2.1 Types of Frauds

Here are some specifics regarding the many types of e-commerce fraud along with the causes and consequences. To effectively combat dangers, it is necessary to know about e-commerce fraud. By being aware of the growing threat of e-commerce fraud and taking pre-emptive action, businesses may safeguard their customers, revenue, and brand.

- Offline frauds – Offline scams typically require proximity to the victim, which may limit their reach to a specific area or locality. These are committed by using persuasive tactics and charm in person. In some cases, offline scammers may resort to intimidation or coercion to manipulate victims. Offline scammers might exploit emotions, trust, and sympathy to gain the victim's confidence and cooperation.
- Online frauds – Global victims might be the target of online scams, which makes it simpler for con artists to locate new victims. These are committed via the internet, shopping, phone, and web or if a credit card is not present. Certain online scams employ cutting-edge tactics to trick victims, making them extremely complex and challenging to identify.

Scams can be unsettling and dangerous, both online and offline. Scams are generally feared because they take advantage of people's trust and vulnerability, which can result in monetary losses and psychological suffering. Table 1 shows the frauds that are considered the most dominant types of fraud. Online payments can become a global industry with the help of an e-commerce cash system. In the current online and offline shopping trends, e-commerce fraud is conceivable. By committing such frauds during an online purchase, con artists hope to annoy the bank or the merchant.

2.2 Related Surveys

A general review of articles on automated detectiontechniques(supervised, unsupervised, and hybrid) from previous years is required. Many authors have conducted surveys in previous years and reviewed various literature regarding fraud detection strategies. The writers of that review provide alternate information and remedies for each of the key fraud types and subtypes that affect a wide range of sectors. Table 2 contains some of the papers in the last 15 years. These articles mainly review different algorithms to determine whether Algorithms can be utilized to identify fraudulent activities through various methods and techniques.

2.3 Strategies for Overcoming Fraud

By combining various strategies, businesses can effectively mitigate the risks associated with e-commerce fraud and protect their customers and revenue.

1. Leverage Machine Learning and AI:

   - Anomaly Detection: Identify unusual patterns in transaction data that might indicate fraudulent activity.

Table 1. Types of Fraud

Fraud Type	Description
Credit Card Fraud	Credit card fraud generally happens when the card was stolen for any of the unauthorized purposes or even when the fraudsters use the credit card information for their use.[8]
Account Takeover Fraud	This type of malicious attack is where a fraudster steals accounts and passwords from normal users, causing the loss of money and the exposure of personal information. Fraudsters gain access to a customer's online account by stealing their login credentials, such as their username and password.[9]
Chargeback Fraud	Chargeback services offer gamers the convenience of refund mechanisms but are often used by malicious online gamers to commit fraud, causing huge adverse impacts on the online game industry.[9]
Return Fraud	This occurs when a customer returns an item to a retailer, even though they have already used it or damaged it
Identity Fraud	Identity theft is a term used to classify numerous offenses including fraudulent use of personal information for criminal purposes without individual's consent[11]. Identity theft is defined as the "unauthorized use or attempted use of an existing account, the unauthorized use or attempted use of personal information to open a new account or misuse of personal information for a fraudulent purpose such as providing false information to law enforcement"[12]
Merchant fraud	When a fraudster impersonates a merchant to handle transactions and steal money, this is known as merchant fraud. This could entail getting a merchant account so that fraudulent cards can be used to process payments or persuading actual customers to make transactions that will never be fulfilled
Refund Fraud	Refund fraud refers to the behavior of consumers returning goods to retailers, knowing that the return violates company or legal regulations (including returning functional but used or damaged goods)[13]
Drop shipping Fraud	When a drop shipper uses dishonest tactics to con customers or other supply chain companies, it's known as drop shipping fraud

- Behavioral Analytics: Analyze customer behavior to detect deviations from normal patterns.
- Neural Networks: Deep learning models can learn complex patterns and adapt to new fraud techniques.

2. Real-time Risk Assessment:

- Velocity Checks: Monitor transaction speed and frequency to identify suspicious activity.
- IP Address Verification: Validate the IP address associated with a transaction.

Table 2. Survey of Published Papers

Year	Coverage	Domain	Reference
2010	2000–2010	Fraud	C. Phua et al.[14]
2016	1994–2014	Common Frauds	Abdalla et al.[15]
2016	1997–2016	Machine learning- basedfraud detection	A. O. Adewumi and A. A. Akinyelu[16]
2017	2010–2017	Comparative Analysis	Ahuja et al.[17]
2018	2007–2018	Common Frauds	Omar et al.[18]
2020	1997–2019	Machine learning- basedfraud detection	Trivedi et al.[19]
2021	1999–2020	Common Frauds	Badotra et al.[20]
2022	2016–2022	Algorithms Survey	Ahmed and M.H.[21]

- Device Fingerprinting: Identify unique characteristics of the device used for the transaction.

3. Data Enrichment:

- Third-Party Data: Combine transaction data with external information (e.g., demographic data, social media profiles) to enhance risk assessment.
- Device Intelligence: Gather information about the device used for the transaction (e.g., operating system, browser).

4. Rule-Based Systems:

- Thresholds: Set thresholds for suspicious activity (e.g., high transaction amounts, unusual shipping addresses).
- Blacklists: Maintain lists of known fraudulent IP addresses, email addresses, or card numbers.

5. Behavioral Biometrics:

- Keystroke Dynamics: Analyse the way customers type to identify unique patterns.
- Mouse Movement: Track mouse movements to detect unusual behavior.

6. Collaborative Fraud Detection:

- Industry Partnerships: Share information with other businesses to identify emerging fraud trends.
- Fraud Networks: Join networks that pool resources and expertise to combat fraud.

7. Regular Updates and Training:

- Model Retraining: Continuously update machine learning models with new data to improve accuracy.
- Employee Training: Educate staff about fraud prevention techniques and emerging threats.

8. Fraud Analytics Platform:

- Centralized View: Use a platform to consolidate fraud data and insights.
- Automation: Automate tasks like rule creation and model deployment.

3 Techniques and Publications

In the last few years, several articles have performed surveys and reviews of fraud detection and prevention strategies existent in the literature. Table 1 summarizes a few articles published in the last decade. Cybercrimes involving digital or electronic transactions come in a variety of forms and are constantly changing. Analysis of the past year's surveys is required to gain insight that can help in understanding and selecting the papers. Findings of the pre-researched papers are presented which cover the range of years and the number of papers reviewed. Technological advancements have come a long way. With technology being everywhere, the number of fraudulent activities has increased substantially. Researchers have analyzed a lot of fraud detection techniques over the years. Table 3 shows the detailed taxonomy of fraud detection techniques reviewed in this work.

Table 3. Technique-specific publication

Category Fraud Detection Techniques	Algorithms	Authors and Year of Publication
Supervised Learning	Decision Tree Hidden Markov Model SVM Genetic Neural Network	Save it. Al [22] Robinson and Aria[23] Abdulla et. Al[15] HaratiNik et al.[25]
Unsupervised Learning	Clustering Isolation Forest	Behera et al.[26] Wang et al.[27]
Nature Inspired	Genetic Algorithm for Feature Selection Competitive Swarm Optimization	Ileberi et al.[28] Karthikeyan et al.[29]
Hybrid	Random Forest and KNN Logistic regression and NN Sequential Minimal Optimization with Logistic Regression Random Forest and ANN KNN and Outlier Detection SVM and Decision tree	Nami et al.[7] Sahin Y and Duman E [30] Hussein et al.[31] Pradhan et al.[32] Malini N and Pushpa M[33] Sahin Y and Duman E[34]

These algorithms can be used by understanding their evaluation metrics such as accuracy, precision, and recall. Some of the algorithms stated above are mentioned in Table 4 to get a better view of how effective they are. We have discussed models of classification above and used them on the dataset. In the below given tables Accuracy, Precision, and Recall show the fraudulent transaction in the dataset. As we can see, the

Neural Network achieves the highest accuracy and recall in supervised learning, while the highest precision is demonstrated by the Random Forest. The Decision Tree, Support Vector Machine, and Bayesian Network Classifier show similar levels of accuracy.

Table 4. Evaluation Metrics of Algorithms

Method	Algorithm	Accuracy	Precision	Recall	Reference
Supervised Learning	Decision Tree	92.88	92.48	91.00	Adebayo et al.[35] Li et al.[36]
	Support Vector Machine	92.00	93.22	89.00	Li et al.[36]
	Bayesian Network Classifier	91.62	97.09	84.82	Saputra A[37]
	Neural Network	98.69	98.41	98.98	Daliri S[38]
	Random Forest	98	99.99	96	Aburbejan et al.[39]
	K-Nearest Neighbour	97.55		84.52	Prasetiyo et al.[40]
Unsupervised Learning	Clustering	Depends on the cluster size	Depends on the cluster size	Depends on the cluster size	
Nature Inspired	Genetic Algorithm	93	90		Tayebi, M., & El Kafhali, S [41]
	Swarm Optimization	98.20			

4   Scope for Further Research

This study distinguishes various types of e-commerce fraud that might impact any kind of organization. Effectively combating commercial fraud requires identifying the salient cases, which provide opportunities for additional research. A number of fraud detection and prevention solutions are available in the market, and more research can be done to determine which tool is most appropriate for handling fraud given the difficulties that a specific industrial or economic sector faces.

5   Conclusion

Many payment mechanisms, including credit and debit cards, cell phones, kiosks, etc., are used in modern commercial transactions. Simultaneously, con artists are becoming more adept at pinpointing vulnerabilities in business dealings. Therefore, any firm must recognize fraud. Furthermore, thanks to technological advancements, banks and the commercial sector can now detect fraud. Organizations are implementing technology to identify fraud because of the availability of more processing power, improvements in statistical modeling, and the capacity to collect and store large amounts of data.

References

1. Kodate, S., Chiba, R., Kimura, S., Masuda, N.: Detecting problematic transactions in a consumer-to-consumer e-commerce network. Appl. Netw. Sci. **5**, 1–18 (2020)
2. Abdallah, A., Maarof, M.A., Zainal, A.: Fraud detection system: a survey. J. Netw. Comput. Appl. **68**, 90–113 (2016)
3. Rodrigues, V.F., et al.: Fraud detection and prevention in e-commerce: a systematic literature review. Electr. Commer. Res. Appl. 101207 (2022)
4. Abed, M., Fernando, B.: E-commerce fraud detection based on machine learning techniques: systematic literature review. Big Data Min. Anal.
5. Karunachandra, B., Putera, N., Wijaya, S.R., Suryani, D., Wesley, J., Purnama, Y.: On the benefits of machine learning classification in cashback fraud detection. Procedia Comput. Sci. **216**, 364–369 (2023)
6. Lin, W., et al.: Online credit payment fraud detection via structure-aware hierarchical recurrent neural network. In IJCAI, pp. 3670–3676 (2021)
7. Nami, S., Shajari, M.: Cost- sensitive payment card fraud detection based on dynamic random forest and k- nearest neighbors. Expert Syst. Appl. **110**, 381–392 (2018)
8. Sailusha, R., Gnaneswar, V., Ramesh, R., Rao, G.R.: Credit card fraud detection using machine learning. In: 2020 4th International Conference on Intelligent Computing and Control Systems (ICICCS), pp. 1264–1270. Madurai, India (2020). https://doi.org/10.1109/ICICCS48265.2020.9121114
9. Gao, M.: Account takeover detection on e-commerce platforms. In: 2022 IEEE International Conference on Smart Computing (SMARTCOMP), pp. 196–197. Helsinki, Finland (2022). https://doi.org/10.1109/SMARTCOMP55677.2022.00052
10. Wei, Y.C., Lai, Y.X., Wu, M.E.: An evaluation of deep learning models for chargeback fraud detection in online games. Cluster Comput. **26**, 927–943 (2023). https://doi.org/10.1007/s10586-022-03674-4
11. Reyns, B.W.: Online routines and identity theft victimization: further expanding routine activity theory beyond direct-contact offenses. J. Res. Crime Delinq. **50**(2), 216–238 (2013)
12. Harrell, E.: Victims of identity theft, 2014, bureau of justice statistics. NCJ, 248991 (2015)
13. Shih, D.-H., Huang, F.-C., Chieh, C.-Y., Shih, M.-H., Wu, T.-W.: Preventing return fraud in reverse logistics—a case study of ESPRES solution by ethereum. J. Theor. Appl. Electron. Commer. Res. **16**, 2170–2191 (2021). https://doi.org/10.3390/jtaer16060121
14. Phua, C., Lee, V., Smith, K., Gayler, R.: A comprehensive survey of data mining-based fraud detection research (2010). https://doi.org/10.1016/j.chb
15. Abdulla, N., Rakendu, R., Varghese, S.M.: A hybrid approach to detect credit card fraud. Int. J. Sci. Res. Publ. **5**(11), 304–314 (2015)
16. Adewumi, A.O., Akinyelu, A.A.: A survey of machine-learning and nature-inspired based credit card fraud detection techniques. Int. J. Syst. Assur. Eng. Manag. **8** (2), 937–953 (2017). https://doi.org/10.1007/s13198-016-0551-y
17. Ahuja, M.S., Singh, L.: Online fraud detection-a review. Int. Res. J. Eng. Technol. **4**(7), 2509–2515 (2017)
18. Omar, S.J., Fred, K., Swaib, K.K.: A state-of-the-art review of machine learning techniques for fraud detection research. In: Proceedings of the 2018 International Conference on Software Engineering in Africa, pp. 11–19 (2018)

19. Trivedi, N.K., Simaiya, S., Lilhore, U.K., Sharma, S.K.: An efficient credit card fraud detection model based on machine learning methods. Int. J. Adv. Sci. Technol. **29**(5), 3414–3424 (2020)
20. Badotra, S., Sundas, A.: A systematic review on the security of e- commerce systems. Int. J. Appl. Sci. Eng. **18**(2), 1–19 (2021)
21. Ahmed, M.H.: Credit card fraud detection techniques: a survey. ScienceOpen Prepr. (2022)
22. Save, P., Tiwarekar, P., Jain, K.N., Mahyavanshi, N.: A novel idea for credit card fraud detection using a decision tree. Int. J. Comput. Appl. **161**(13) (2017)
23. Robinson, W.N., Aria, A.: Sequential fraud detection for prepaid cards using hidden Markov model divergence. Expert Syst. Appl. **91**, 235–251 (2018)
24. Park, J.S., Chen, M.S., Yu, P.S.: Using a hash-based method with transaction trimming for mining association rules. IEEE Trans. Knowl. Data Eng. **9**(5), 813–825 (1997)
25. HaratiNik, M.R., Akrami, M., Khadivi, S., Shajari, M.: FUZZGY: a hybrid model for credit card fraud detection. In: 6th International Symposium on Telecommunications (IST), pp. 1088–1093. IEEE (2012)
26. Behera, T.K., Panigrahi, S.: Credit card fraud detection: a hybrid approach using fuzzy clustering & neural network. In: 2015, the second international conference on advances in computing and communication engineering, pp. 494–499. IEEE (2015)
27. Xu, H., Pang, G., Wang, Y., Wang, Y.: Deep isolation forest for anomaly detection. IEEE Trans. Knowl. Data Eng. (2023)
28. Ileberi, E., Sun, Y., Wang, Z.: A machine learning-based credit card fraud detection using the GA algorithm for feature selection. J. Big Data **9**(1), 1–17 (2022)
29. Karthikeyan, T., Govindarajan, M., Vijayakumar, V.: An effective fraud detection using competitive swarm optimization-based deep neural network. Meas.: Sens. **27**, 100793 (2023)
30. Sahin, Y., Duman, E.: Detecting credit card fraud by ANN and logistic regression. In: 2011, an International Symposium on Innovations in Intelligent Systems and Applications, pp. 315–319. IEEE (2011)
31. Hussein, A.S., Khairy, R.S., Najeeb, S.M.M., Alrikabi, H.T.S.: Credit card fraud detection using fuzzy rough nearest neighbor and sequential minimal optimization with logistic regression. Int. J. Interact. Mobile Technol. **15**(5) (2021)
32. Pradhan, S.K., Rao, N.K., Deepika, N.M., Harish, P., Kumar, M.P., Kumar, P.S.: Credit card fraud detection using artificial neural networks and random forest algorithms. In: 2021 5th International Conference on Electronics, Communication and Aerospace Technology (ICECA), pp. 1471–1476. IEEE (2021)
33. Malini, N., Pushpa, M.: Analysis of credit card fraud identification techniques based on KNN and outlier detection. In: 2017, the Third International Conference on Advances in Electrical, Electronics, Information, Communication, and Bio-informatics (AEEICB), pp. 255–258. IEEE (2017)
34. Şahin, Y.G., Duman, E.: Detecting credit card fraud by decision trees and support vector machines (2011)
35. Adebayo, O.S., Favour-Bethy, T.A., Otasowie, O., Okunola, O.A.: Comparative review of credit card fraud detection using machine learning and concept drift techniques. Int. J. Comput. Sci. Mob. Comput. **12**, 24–48 (2023)
36. Li, C., Ding, N., Dong, H., Zhai, Y.: Cs-svm. Int. J. Mach. Learn. Comput. **11**(1) (2021)
37. Saputra, A.: Fraud detection using machine learning in e-commerce. Int. J. Adv. Comput. Sci. Appl. **10**(9) (2019)
38. Daliri, S.: Using harmony search algorithm in neural networks to improve fraud detection in the banking system. Comput. Intell. Neurosci. (2020)
39. Aburbeian, A.M., Ashqar, H.I.: Credit card fraud detection using enhanced random forest classifier for imbalanced data. In: International Conference on Advances in Computing Research, pp. 605–616. Cham: Springer Nature Switzerland (2023)

40. Prasetiyo, B., Muslim, M.A., Baroroh, N.: Evaluation performance recall and F2 score of credit card fraud detection unbalanced dataset using SMOTE oversampling technique. In: Journal of Physics: conference series, vol. 1918, no. 4, p. 042002. IOP Publishing (2021)
41. Tayebi, M., El Kafhali, S.: Hyperparameter optimization using genetic algorithms to detect fraudulent transactions. In: The International Conference on Artificial Intelligence and Computer Vision, pp. 288–297. Cham (2021)

An IoT and Data Mining-Based Tool for Early Identification of Speech Disorders in Children Using Advanced Algorithms

M Usha[✉]

Department of Information Technology, KG College of Arts and Science College, Coimbatore, Tamil Nadu, India
usha.m@kgcas.com

Abstract. Early detection of speech disorders in children is critical for effective intervention and treatment. This paper presents an innovative tool leveraging the Internet of Things (IoT) and advanced data mining techniques to identify speech disorders in children at an early stage. This paper explores the integration of IoT and data mining technologies for the early detection of speech disorders in children by applying advanced algorithms. The aim is to develop an efficient tool for early diagnosis and intervention, enhancing speech therapy outcomes through real-time monitoring and analysis. The system integrates IoT-enabled devices for real-time data collection, capturing various speech parameters such as pitch, tone, and articulation. These data are processed using advanced algorithms, including machine learning and deep learning techniques, to analyze patterns and anomalies indicative of speech disorders. The proposed paper offers a user-friendly interface for parents, educators, and healthcare professionals, providing insights into a child's speech development and highlighting potential areas of concern. The system's effectiveness is evaluated through extensive testing with a diverse dataset, demonstrating its accuracy and reliability in identifying various speech disorders, such as stuttering, dysarthria, and apraxia. By facilitating early diagnosis, this tool aims to improve the quality of life for children with speech disorders through timely and targeted interventions.

Keywords: IoT · Speech Disorder · Dysarthria · Apraxia · Data Mining

1 Introduction

Speech disorders in children can significantly impact their social, emotional, and academic development. It is imperative to identify and intervene early in order to mitigate these impacts and provide timely help. In recent years, advancements in technology have opened new avenues for diagnosing and managing speech disorders. This paper introduces an innovative Internet of Things (IoT) and data mining-based tool designed for the early detection of speech disorders in children. By leveraging the power of Cuckoo-based search optimization algorithms and Recurrent Neural Networks (RNNs), this tool aims to provide an efficient and accurate diagnosis, facilitating early intervention and treatment.

© The Author(s), under exclusive license to Springer Nature Switzerland AG 2025
S. Rajagopal et al. (Eds.): ASCIS 2024, CCIS 2424, pp. 375–384, 2025.
https://doi.org/10.1007/978-3-031-86290-8_27

The Layered Recurrent Neural Networks-Improved Cuckoo Search Optimization (LRNN-ICSO) method comprises three steps. First, the feature subset selection is made by applying clustered cuckoo search optimization. With this optimization mechanism, a fitness function based on k-means clustering is evolved using energy and entropy as two different factors for clustering. These highly correlated optimized features are obtained by analyzing the switching parameter via cuckoo search.

The IoT-based approach enables the continuous monitoring and collection of children's speech data in naturalistic settings, such as homes and classrooms. This data is then processed using data mining techniques to identify patterns indicative of speech disorders. The integration of Cuckoo-based search optimization algorithms helps in fine-tuning the parameters of the data mining models, ensuring high accuracy and reliability. This optimization technique mimics the brood parasitism behavior of cuckoo birds, effectively searching for the best solutions in a given problem space, which in this case, involves identifying the most relevant features of speech data that indicate disorders.

Recurrent Neural Networks (RNNs) are essential for analyzing voice data because they can capture temporal relationships, which are critical for precise diagnosis. This task is especially well suited for RNNs because of its capacity to handle data sequences and retain context across time. By combining IoT, data mining, Cuckoo-based optimization, and RNNs, the recommended method enhances the early diagnosis of speech disorders and offers a scalable and flexible solution that can be customized to each child's unique needs. Through the ability to provide earlier and more targeted interventions, this all-encompassing strategy promises to enhance the quality of life for kids with speech difficulties.

2   Related Work

Speech sound disorder (SSD) in children is the term used to indicate persistent problems in creating specific speech sounds after the expected age of learning, according to Si Ioi Ng, Dehua Tao, et al. (2018). For children who speak Cantonese, this sample system automatically evaluates SSD. The system comprises of an assessment scheme that is clinically informed, a mobile application, and back-end automatic speech recognition (ASR) for child speech. When used, it can help detect and diagnose any suspected SSD signs early on [1].

Socially Assistive Robots (SARs) are the assistive technology that has the greatest potential to benefit children with disabilities when it comes to special education applications. They can encourage social contact, function as a playmate or mediator when interacting with other kids or adults, and help kids go from being passive observers of their environment to active participants [2].

Cuckoo is an algorithm based on swarm intelligence, which, as its name implies, is the collective behaviour of dispersed, self-governing systems that eventually produces the optimum outcome. Yang is the creator of the Cuckoo Search algorithm [3].

Any evolutionary algorithm can be said to follow "The Survival of the Fittest," as stated in Charles Darwin's hypothesis. The incredibly appealing sound that cuckoos produce is what draws people to them as birds. However, they take a very aggressive stance when it comes to procreation. Because they lay their eggs in other species' nests, they are commonly referred to as brood parasites. They take out other animals' eggs and replace them with their own. Certain Cuckoo birds have acquired a special capacity to mimic the pattern and colour of the egg to trick the birds that make up their target nests because other species have a tendency to discard Cuckoo eggs when they discover this. Because they lay their eggs before the birds that target their nests, giving their eggs more room and food from the host nests, these are known as parasites. Over this nature-based method is constructed the Cuckoo Search algorithm.

Using machine intelligence to create an accurate telemonitoring and diagnosis system for Parkinson's disease (PD) is another driving force. For decades, neural networks have been effectively employed in a variety of diagnostic systems; They can be thoroughly altered and scrutinized to determine whether Parkinson's disease is present. The goal of combining voice-based analysis with neural network power is to create an automated decision support tool that will aid physicians in the diagnosing process. As a result, a more user-friendly, affordable, and precise telemonitoring and diagnosis system will be implemented, and the higher early diagnosis rate will benefit community health care. [4–6].

3   Related Work

Speech Disorder is a state in which a human being has an issue generating or initiate the sounds of speech that are needed to communicate with others. This can make the children's words difficult to understand Speech problems affect the way a person forms words by producing sounds. Some vocal problems could be classified as speech problems as well. Stuttering is one of the most common speech impairments. Aphasia and dysarthria are examples of further speech impairments. Apraxia is a mechanical speech impairment brought on by damage to the speaking-related areas of the brain. A mechanical speech disease called dysarthria causes weakness or difficulty moving the lips, face, or lungs' muscles. Certain individuals with speech impairments are receptive to their intended words but struggle to articulate them. Depression and problems with self-esteem could result from this. Both adults and children can be affected by speech difficulties. These disorders can be corrected with early therapy.

3.1   Types of Speech Disorder

Childhood Apraxia of Speech
A child has the problem making actions when communicating, with childhood apraxia of speech. Children with apraxia of speech (CAS) have attribute or speech indication which vary based on severity and age of speech issues. Many children have issues with languages, namely difficulty with word order or reduced vocabulary. It occurs due to the brain which has difficulty in coordinating the actions. To reduce the risk of continuing persistence of issues, childhood apraxia of speech should be diagnosed and treated.

Speech Sound Disorders/Articulation Disorders
This is common in young children. Here the articulation disorders which form certain sounds are based on inability. Certain sounds and words may change, such as making a

"th" sound in place of an "s" sound. Speech-Language Pathologists (SLP) identify how your child moves lips, jaw, and tongue. To say sounds properly, SLPs assist by learning to create sounds and instruct sounds are right or wrong. Practicing sounds in longer sentences and diverse words of sound.

Receptive Disorders

Receptive disorders make trouble in understanding and processing, causing a limited vocabulary or trouble. Disorders can lead to receptive disorders such as autism Since it differs from kid to child, receptive language disorder cannot be diagnosed by a collection of symptoms. To diagnose this disorder through checking vision impairment by vision test. Receptive Disorders are treated by speech-language therapy.

Dysarthria

Dysarthria is a type of speech disorder that is needed for speech production which occurs due to failure in the muscles. Dysarthria is a speech disorder that takes place because of sickness in the muscles necessary for speech production after a stroke, brain infection or brain injury People can develop dysarthria. Certain neurodegenerative infection that injures brain parts that manage the muscles that word involves.

3.2   Cuckoo Search Optimization Technique

Three distinct processes are used to implement the Cuckoo Search Optimization Technique approach in order to achieve its goal. The optimum feature selection, relevant feature (i.e., relevant speech signal), and diagnosis are crucial for children's speech recognition.

The input voice signals are initially subjected to feature subset selection using the Clustered Cuckoo Search Optimised Feature Subset Selection model in order to determine the best feature or speech signals. The computation of lung capacity then uses the best or chosen input signals as input. Here, the energy and duration of the intake and exhalation are taken into consideration while estimating the lung capacity for each gender. Lastly, a three-layered hidden layer layered recurrent neural network is applied to the ideal and significant features (i.e., signals) for a precise and accurate assessment of dysarthria speech problem.

The signals of a patient with dysarthria are provided as input, after which the signal decomposition is done, leading to the creation of two sub-bands, which are reported below.

$$SS^{l}_{k+1(i,j)} = \sum_{a}\sum_{b}LP(a)HP(a)SS^{l-1}_{\frac{k}{4}(a+2i,b+2j)} \tag{1}$$

$$SS^{l}_{k+2(i,j)} = \sum_{a}\sum_{b}HP(a)LP(a)SS^{l-1}_{\frac{k}{4}(a+2i,b+2j)} \tag{2}$$

From the above Eqs. (1) and (2), '$SS^{l}_{k+1(i,j)}$', '$SS^{l}_{k+2(i,j)}$' refers to the speech signal sub band of horizontal and vertical levels, with 'LP', 'HP' representing the low pass and high pass filters and 'i', 'j' denoting the speech signal variables along the horizontal and vertical directions for 'm' rows and 'n' columns respectively. Now, the output corresponds to two sub bands, which are the horizontal and vertical coefficients respectively.

With the obtained sub band for each speech signals, according to three idealized rules of the conventional Cuckoo Search, each host nest (i.e., speech signals) denotes a possible solution in multi-dimensional space.

3.3 Layered Recurrent Neural Networks (LRNN)

Children's speech disorders are diagnosed using a Layered Recurrent Neural Network. This network makes use of within-layer recurrence in an aggressive way to select the fittest individuals or speech signals. An architecture for a hybrid neural network is provided here, which can smoothly incorporate the parents, or original speech signals, into any LRNN and optimize the network as a whole to achieve better performance. This enables learning at many levels according to the parent's traits. Furthermore, a mathematical process called a meta heuristic is used to generate the diagnosis with optimum weight and bias factor instead of general feed forward networks (Fig. 1).

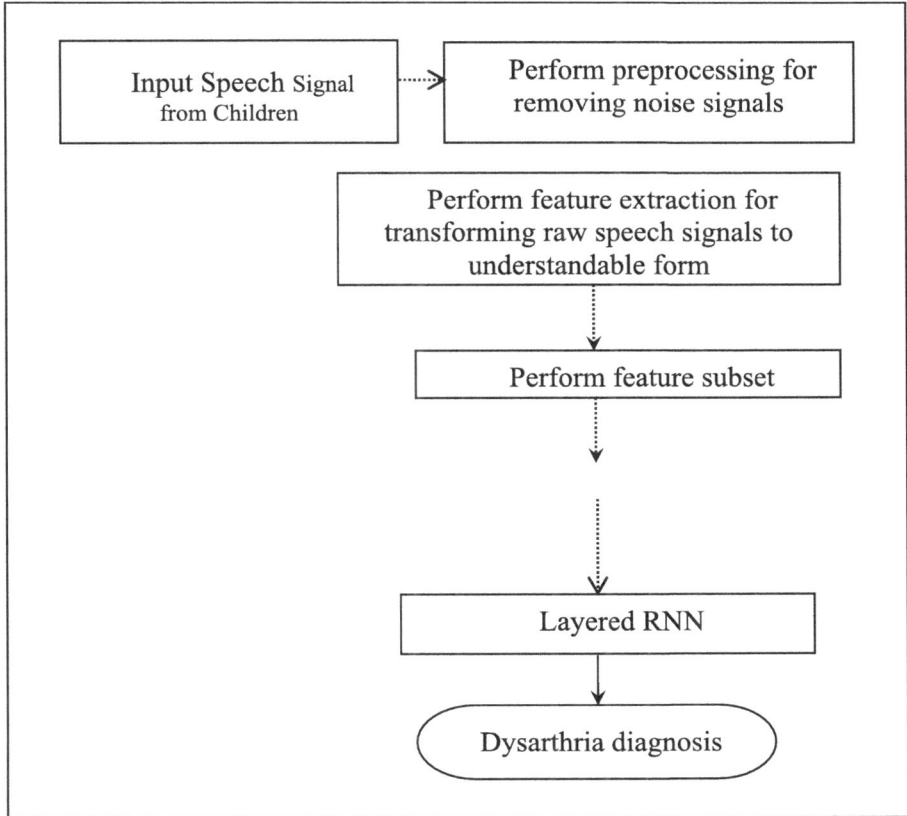

Fig. 1. IoT Based Speech Therapy Tool for identification of Children Speech Disorder

TORGO database is used for effective dysarthria speech disorder diagnosis and treatment utilising articulatory characteristics taken from participants with cerebral palsy (CP) or amyotrophic lateral sclerosis (ALS). This dataset provides a count of videos in which digital cameras are used as a filming tool.

3.4 IoT Based Tool

The suggested system offers a medical equipment monitoring system to smart homes and clinics. Focused on speech recognition. Based on the suggested speech recognition technology is Raspberry Pi. To monitor the machines, a relay circuit connects the Raspberry Pi to the domestic appliances. According to Fig. 3.2 the Raspberry Pi and the controller are connected using serial connections (Fig. 2).

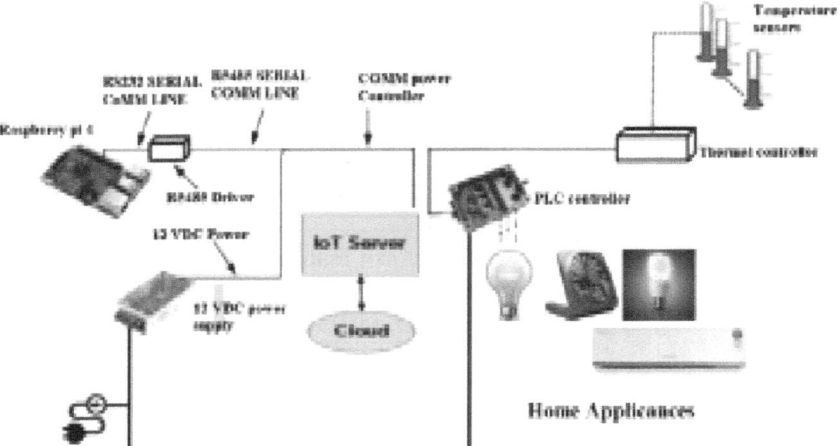

Fig. 2. The proposed components of Speech Recognition System

4 Results and Discussion

Here the Performance is measured by three different metrics.

1. Precision
2. F-Measure
3. Accuracy

4.1 Performance Measure of Precision

The accuracy rate is the first aspect taken into account when assessing children with speech disorders. In order to analyse the precision rate, it is necessary to have both the retrieved speech signals and the pertinent speech signals. The accuracy rate is measured in this way.

$$P = LC\left[\sum_{i=1}^{n} \frac{SS_{rel}}{TotSS_{ret}} * 100\right] \tag{3}$$

Equation (3) above is used to evaluate the precision (P) by taking into account the estimation of lung capacity (LC) and the relevant speech signals (SS_{rel}) to the retrieved speech signals ($TotSS_{ret}$). It is expressed as a percentage.

Table 1. Tabulated results of Precision

Number of Children speech signals	Precision (%)		
	Proposed LRNN-ICSO	Existing NB-SRM	Existing KNN-SRM
15	96.56	77.5	47.23
30	95.15	75.25	49.15
45	94	74.15	49
60	94.8	74	48.85
75	94.65	73.85	48.55
90	94.35	73.75	48.15
105	93.15	73.55	48
120	93	73	47.75
135	92.55	72.15	47.25
150	92.45	72	47

Table 1 given above shows the results of the precision for three different methods, Layered Recurrent Neural Networks with Improved Cuckoo Search Optimization LRNN-ICSO, Naïve Bayes – Speech Recognition Model (NB-SRM) and K-Nearest Neighbor Speech Recognition Model (KNN-SRM) respectively for different speech signals provided as input. The comparative table analysis for all the three methods shows similar decrease in the tabulated value with the increasing number of speech signals with a considerable improved in the proposed LRNN-ICSO method. This is evident from the precision of LRNN-ICSO method for a sample of 120 different speech signals provided as input. Here, the precision rate was found to be 93.15% when applied with LRNN-ICSO method, 73% compared to NB-SRM and 47.75% compared to KNN-SRM respectively.

4.2 Performance Measure of F-Measure

In this section, a measure of precision and recall known as the F-measure is used to assess the quality of subband clustering; a high F-measure corresponds to high accuracy. The test's evaluation is based on its recall and precision. The precision is determined by dividing the entire number of positive findings, including those that were wrongly identified, by the number of correctly identified positive results (dysarthria diagnosis and accurate assessment). The recall is calculated by counting the number of correctly identified positive results in relation to the speech signals provided as input that should have been recognized as positive (Table 2).

Table 2. Tabulated results of F-measure

Number of Children speech signals	F-measure (%)		
	Proposed LRNN-ICSO	Existing NB-SRM	Existing KNN-SRM
15	0.9	0.82	0.8
30	0.88	0.8	0.79
45	0.85	0.79	0.77
60	0.83	0.77	0.75
75	0.81	0.75	0.72
90	0.8	0.73	0.7
105	0.79	0.71	0.69
120	0.77	0.7	0.67
135	0.75	0.68	0.65
150	0.73	0.67	0.63

4.3 Performance Measure of Accuracy

The accuracy performance measure is assessed for the important speech disorder evaluations. The number of speech signals that were correctly analysed and classified as belonging to children with the condition is what is meant by accuracy in this context. The mathematical expression for this is as follows (Table 3).

$$A = \sum_{i=1}^{n} \frac{LC(SS_{CR})}{SS_i} \tag{4}$$

From the above Eq. (4), the accuracy factor 'A' is measured based on the speech signals correctly diagnosed 'SS_{CR}' by considering the lung capacity 'LC' to the speech signals considered for simulation 'SS_i'. The unit of measurement is the percentage (%).

Here our Proposed method Layered Recurrent Neural Networks – Improved Cuckoo Search Optimization Techniques (LRNN-ICSO) have the highest accuracy rate compared with the existing methods Naïve Bayes – Speech Recognition Model (NB-SRM) and K-Nearest Neighbor – Speech Recognition Model (KNN-SRM).

Table 3. Tabulated results of Accuracy

Number of Children speech signals	Accuracy (%)		
	Proposed LRNN-ICSO	Existing NB-SRM	Existing KNN-SRM
15	97.03	87.95	92.77
30	96.25	86.35	91.55
45	96	86	91
60	95.85	85.55	90.85
75	95.35	85.15	90.65
90	95	85	90
105	94.75	84.85	89.35
120	92	84.35	89.15
135	90.55	84.15	87.25
150	90.25	84	86

5   Conclusion

The LRNN-ICSO approach enhances F-measure and accuracy with precision, enhancing the evaluation of children's speech disorders. There are three different processes at play. These include lung capacity estimation-based relevant feature selection, diagnosis, and feature subset selection. The input voice signals are initially subjected to Cuckoo Search Optimized Feature Subset Selection in order to increase accuracy, precision, and recall. This improves test accuracy and makes F-measure analysis easier. Ultimately, a three-layer approach known as Layered RNN is used to make the diagnosis; analysis is carried out in the hidden layer to provide a reliable assessment of the illness. According to the experimental results, the suggested LRNN-ICSO method, when compared to current state-of-the-art methods, provides accuracy with precise assessment of children's speech disorders.

References

1. Ng, S.I., Tao, D., Wang, J., Jiang, Y., Ng, W.Y., Lee, T.: An automated assessment tool for child speech disorders. In: 11th International Symposium on Chinese Spoken Language Processing, IEEE (2018)
2. Papakostas, G.A., et al.: Social robots in special education: a systematic review. Electronics **10**(12) (2021)
3. Yang, X.S.: Cuckoo search via Le´vy flights. In: 2009 World congress on nature &biologically inspired computing, pp 210–214 (2009)
4. Kara, S., Güven, A., Öner, A.Ö.: Utilization of artificial neural networks in the diagnosis of optic nerve diseases. Comput. Biol. Med. **36**(4), 28–37 (2006)
5. Hosseini, H.G., Luo, D., Reynolds, K.J.: The comparison of different feed forward neural network architectures for ECG signal diagnosis. Med. Eng. Phys. **28**, 372–378 (2006)

6. Omiotek, Z., Burda, A., Wójcik, W.: The use of decision tree induction and artificial neural networks for automatic diagnosis of Hashimoto's disease. Expert Syst. Appl. **40**, 6684–6689 (2013)

7. Masmoudi, A., Bougares, F., Ellouze, M., Estève, Y., Belguith, L.: Automatic speech recognition system for Tunisian dialect. Lang. Resour. Eval. **52**, 249–267 (2018). https://doi.org/10.1007/s10579-017-9402-y

8. Becerra, A., De La Rosa, J.I., González, E.: Speech recognition in a dialog system: from conventional to deep processing. Multimedia Tools Appl. **77**, 15875–15911. Springer (2018)

9. Koložvari, A., Stojanović, R., Zupan, A., Semenkin, E.: Speech-recognition cloud harvesting for improving the navigation of cyber-physical wheelchairs for disabled persons. Microprocess. Microsyst. **69**, 1–9 (2019)

10. Lowit, A., Marchetti, A., Corson, S., Kuschmann, A.: Rhythmic performance in hypokinetic dysarthria: Relationship between reading, spontaneous speech and diadochokinetic tasks. J. Commun. Disord. **72**(26), 1–41. Elsevier (2018)

11. El Hannani, A., Errattahi, R., Salmam, F.Z., Hain, T., Ouahmane, H.: Evaluation of the effectiveness and efficiency of state-of-the-art features and models for automatic speech recognition error detection. J. of Big Data **8**(5), 1–16. Springer

12. Ogawa, A., Hori, T., Nakamura, A.: Estimating speech recognition accuracy based on error type classification. IEEE/ACM Trans. Audio Speech Lang. Process. **24**(12), 2400–2413 (2016)

13. Garain, A., Singh, P.K., Sarkar, R.: FuzzyGCP: a deep learning architecture for automatic spoken language identification from speech signals. Expert Syst. Appl. **168**, 1–14. Elsevier (2021)

14. Wu, B., Li, K., Ge, F., Huang, Z., Yang, M., Siniscalchi, S.M., Lee, C.H.: An end-to-end deep learning approach to simultaneous speech dereverberation and acoustic modeling for robust speech recognition. IEEE J. Sel. Top. Sign. Process. **11**(8), 1289–1300 (2017)

15. Zaidi, B.F., Selouani, S.A., Boudraa, M. et al.: Deep neural network ,architectures for dysarthric speech analysis and recognition. Neural Comput. Appl. **33**, 9089–9108 (2021). https://doi.org/10.1007/s00521-020-05672-2

Change Detection Using Machine Learning Algorithms in Google Earth Engine Environment Bharatpur District of the Rajasthan State

Gaurav Sharma[1,2(✉)] and Manoj Kumar Sharma[1]

[1] Department of Computer and Communication Engineering, Manipal University, Jaipur, India
gaurav801212@gmail.com
[2] Department of Advance Computing, Poornima College of Engineering, Jaipur, India

Abstract. This article summarizes the findings of a study that was conducted on change discovery using machine literacy algorithms within the environment of Google Earth Engine (GEE). The study concentrated on the Bharatpur District, which is located in the state of Rajasthan in India. The exploration makes use of data collected through remote seeing and ways grounded on machine literacy to identify land cover changes over a particular period of time. Using the broad capabilities of GEE, a detailed study is carried out in order to identify and classify important changes in the geography. These changes include civic expansion, agrarian shifts, and the deterioration of natural territories. The study maps and quantifies changes in land cover through the operation of machine literacy algorithms. This will give significant perceptivity on the dynamics of land use within the region. The findings add to a more in-depth understanding of environmental transitions and enable informed sustainable land operation decisions and development plans in the Bharatpur District and other places that are similar.

Keywords: Change detection · Google Earth · Machine Learning · Rajasthan

1 Introduction

Knowing about the type of land cover in a certain area is super important. It helps with things like managing resources, planning land use, keeping an eye on the environment, responding disasters, studying climate change, and even protecting biodiversity lots of stuff, right? Satellite imaging gives us tons of data to help understand land cover types & how they change over time [1]. One common way to classify this land cover is through visual interpretation of satellite images. Here, experts use their experience to spot and label different types of land cover. They look at things like color, texture, & shape to make their assessments. But here's the catch: manually interpreting these images can take a lot of time. It can also be pretty subjective and might lead to mistakes. So, while it's useful, it has its downsides for sure. Machine Learning methods are being used more & to help automate how we classify land cover, especially when dealing with big datasets [2].

S. Rajagopal et al. (Eds.): ASCIS 2024, CCIS 2424, pp. 385–399, 2025.
https://doi.org/10.1007/978-3-031-86290-8_28

So, what's happening? Well, in Machine Learning, computers learn from data already labeled. This helps them to find patterns & features that set apart different types of land cover. Once the model is trained, it can also do its thing on data that isn't labeled. There are many benefits to using Machine Learning compared to doing it all by hand. For one, it works a lot faster Plus, the results tend to be more consistent. Another cool thing is its ability to manage huge datasets without breaking a sweat. Machine Learning algorithms can get better over time. This makes them more precise & dependable. In the end, Machine literacy is super helpful. It can give us important information on land cover changes and help people in making choices in different areas like husbandry, ecology, and megacity planning [3]. Google Earth Engine (GEE) is a great tool that helps experimenters. They can fluently work with satellite data & apply machine literacy to classify images [4]. GEE has a huge library of satellite filmland, plus it offers cool functions to dissect our earth. With its machine learning algorithms, like Random Forest or Support Vector Machine (SVM), GEE trains a model using labeled data. This helps in sorting images directly [5]. The labeled data is made up of satellite images. Each pixel in those images what type of land cover it is. You can get this training data from being land cover charts. Or, you can indeed produce it by looking at the satellite filmland and also labeling every pixel by hand [6]. Once you have that, applying the trained model to new images can be done fluently using the classify() function in GEE. When you do this, you get a new image where every pixel has its land cover type labeled. To make all this be in GEE, there is a handy law editor. This editor works with both Python & JavaScript. You can dissect the images and do all feathers of tasks without too important trouble.

Using machine learning for image categorization. It can really boost how accurate & efficient we are when analyzing satellite data. Thanks to GEE, there's a huge library of satellite images. Researchers can quickly get to the data they need to push their projects forward.

The findings in the study area matter a lot. They help shape land use policies, figure out cropping patterns, check on natural resources, & understand changes caused by climate change. The water conservation initiatives in this watershed region have a direct influence on the availability of groundwater and surface water conditions. This document elucidates the process of achieving the goals by using machine learning algorithms and the Google Earth Engine platform, in addition to outlining the essential methodologies needed. This subject field has a notable disparity, accompanied by crucial discoveries and areas of knowledge that need more investigation. Presently, the use of machine learning models and the Google earth engine platform is of greater significance for the analysis of extensive datasets.

2 Review of Literature

Saxena et al. (2024) [7] stated that the implementation of the western Rajasthan, IGNP had a substantial effect on alterations in land use and land cover (LULC), resulting in considerable modifications to the hydrologic cycle in the last few decades. This analysis will cover the time span from 1990 to 2020. SEBAL uses Indian Meteorological Department meteorological data was utilized to analyze Landsat data. Machine learning-based random forest classifiers created LULC maps. High ET levels are largely in the northwest. The farmland area has grown at a rate of 734.76 km^2 a^{-1} throughout time. Urban settlements and built-up areas are growing at 14.67 km^2 a^{-1}. Conversely, barren areas are diminishing at a rate of 751.67 km^2 a^{-1}. Water coverage has fluctuated somewhat. They significantly affect ET in the IGNP area. Due to increasing water availability, vegetation has expanded.

Baghel et al. (2024) [8] examined that the alterations in land use and land cover (LULC) are a key driver of global climatic, ecological, and environmental transformations. The Mand catchment in Chhattisgarh is studied. Population increases, urbanization, mining, agriculture, and climate change have changed (LULC) in this area. The study focused on (LULC) changes across time and anticipated future trends. A Geographic Information System (GIS) with an image classification system supervised by a human expert examined (LULC) trends from 2001 to 2021. The CA–ANN model with QGIS' MOLUSCE plugin anticipated LULC trends from 2030 to 2040. LULC accuracy was 82%, 86%, and 90% in 2001, 2010, and 2021. The kappa coefficient for the same years was 0.79, 0.84, and 0.88. During the study period, agricultural land increased to 31.76% in 2021. From 2001 to 2021, open forest, shallow waterbody, fallow land, and settlement increased 1.7%, 7.41%, 7.57%, and 2.55%, correspondingly. Like previous years, urban areas, abandoned land, farmland, open forests, shallow water bodies, and scrubland are expected to increase while thick forests, deep water bodies, and barren land decrease in 2030 and 2040. This long-term land use and land cover (LULC) study will help policymakers and planners manage the research area's ecosystems and maintain development.

Goyal et al. (2023) [9]. Wetlands are essential elements ecosystem maintaining ecological niches and variety of plants and animals. It is crucial to investigate the changes in the flooding area of these sites and suggest appropriate methods for their preservation due to their ecological importance. This study uses Landsat photos from 1991 to 2020 to assess flooding patterns at all 64 Chinese Ramsar sites. Annual composites were generated between June and September utilizing short-wave infrared thresholding to construct inundation maps. Every Ramsar site was studied separately to see how regional geographical and climatic variables affect its behavior. The Mann-Kendall test found trends in each location's flooding research. Eight sites showed a significant reduction, while 14 sites showed a significant gain. Hubei Wang Lake was 72.0% accurate and ZhangyeHeihe Wetland National Nature Reserve 98.0%. The average webpage accuracy was 90.0%. The results underscore the need to implement conservation strategies to strategies for Ramsar areas.

Gavhane et al. (2023) [10]studied that the rapid increase in population and resulting need for freshwater, together with the rivalry between irrigation, household, and industrial sectors, along with the impact of climate change, has made it necessary to manage water resources in a careful and efficient manner. Rainwater harvesting (RWH) is often regarded as a very efficient approach to water management. The correct installation, operation, and maintenance of RWH structures depend on the location and design. This study seeks to determine the best Gambhir watershed, Rajasthan, India, rainfall harvesting (RWH) construction and design site. GIS was employed with the dependable hierarchical multi-criteria decision analysis. High-resolution Sentinel-2A data and an

Advanced Land Observation Satellite digital elevation model were employed; Runoff was the main reason in placing rainwater harvesting (RWH) systems. It was found that 75.54 square kilometers (13% of the total area) were ideal for RWH constructions. Additionally, 114.56 square kilometers (19%) of the entire land was very suitable. Rainwater harvesting (RWH) facilities were not allowed on 43.77 square kilometers, 7% of the land area. Boolean logic also targeted a certain RWH architecture. Analytically created maps of water resource development in the watershed would be valuable for policymakers and hydrologists in identifying and installing rainwater harvesting (RWH) infrastructure in the research area.

Kumar (2023) [11] studied of geographical change rely heavily on remote sensing (RS) for a variety of Land Use/Land Cover (LU/LC) applications, including but not limited to vegetation, forestry, agriculture, and urbanization. The geographical data provided by the RS satellite imaging is essential for monitoring and studying the whole planet. The proposed research utilizes Landsat satellite data that is both multitemporal and multispectral to derive (LU/LC) features for the Haridwar area. Image preprocessing techniques (such as geometry correction, atmospheric correction, and image transform) are crucial for achieving an accurate classification of land cover characteristics. Accurately classifying land cover characteristics and detecting changes in them is aided by this method. The land cover elements are classified into one of seven categories using the Region of Interest (ROI) tool in Google Earth alongside a topographic map. The SVM classifier correctly labels images from 2017 and beyond, as well as those from 2003 and 1996, with respective accuracy percentages of 90.00, 82.75, 86.37, and 83.38. Post-classification analysis may reveal changes in land cover characteristics. The fast expansion of Haridwar's urban and industrial sectors since 1996 has resulted in a loss of 13,698.36 hectares (ha) of orchards and 1,638.81 hectares (ha) of greenery, respectively. Monitoring and assessing research region land cover changes benefits greatly from the LU/LC change information gleaned through the analysis.

Singh et al. (2022) [12] examined that information on yields help traders and producers plan agricultural production, sowing, harvesting, and marketing. Several Sentinel-2 datasets were analyzed to obtain crucial information for agricultural land use categorization regions that could not have been gleaned from multi-spectral datasets alone. And integrated the ANN classifier with the Post-Classification Comparison (PCC), which allows to predict seasonal variation in satellite images. ANN-based change detection is a post-classification comparison approach that uses the ANN classifier. To verify the efficacy of ANN, this procedure used cross-validation using a standard MLC. In contrast to the traditional PCC-MLC model, which obtained accuracy on the order of 86%–88% for classed maps and 84%–86% for change maps, classified maps were 90%–93% accurate and change maps 87%–90% accurate with PCC-ANN.

Zhao et al. (2022) [13] studied many decades-old structures in Beijing have been dismantled because of gradually adjusting urban development and ending non-essential operations. As a result, Construction and Demolition waste (CDW) has emerged as a major issue in the fight against urban and dust pollution. CDW piles, however, are unstable and have unsteady edges. Therefore, accurate and timely mapping of CDW zones is crucial to achieving urban growth while conserving the environment. And presented a change detection and deep learning-based approach to CDW identification as a solution to this problem. The sample size was increased by 25.4% utilizing post-classification comparison for change identification. DeepLabV3+ was trained using extended samples as input. With a Kappa of 0.8642, CDW identification accuracy was found to be 91.67% overall. The accuracy indices were also computed with the decreased sample size, yielding a mean Intersection-over-Union value of 0.086 lower. The outcomes of PSPNet and UNet were consistent with one another. This data demonstrates that change detection might help deep learning models perform better. This research is the first to distinguish between three distinct types of Construction and Demolition waste (CDW), and it successfully addresses the problem of (CDW) often being incorrectly labeled as "bare land".

Ebel et al. (2021) [14] because of the tremendous advancement in remote sensing technology over the course of last decade, remote sensing data modalities that were captured by a wide range of sensors are now readily available. It is common for several sensors to offer information that complements one another, and as a result, it is feasible to conduct an observation of Earth that is both more comprehensive and accurate by integrating the information that these sensors provide together. Although change detection techniques have historically been presented for data sets that are homogenous, this does not mean that the two types of data cannot be combined. In addition, there is a common deficiency in the amount of multi-modal data sets that are accessible, which might make it difficult to do research in this area. As a means of addressing these deficiencies in the existing system, compiled an innovative data set for multi-modal change detection.

Chughtai et al. (2021) [15] studied to grasp how people fit into the natural world, it is crucial to evaluate LULC change. Massive geographical shifts and technological developments have prompted academics to bolster their data sets. Changes in LULC may be tracked more easily throughout time periods now because of the remote sensing and GIS. This technology has been invaluable to the scientific community and has helped to shed light on shifts on a global and regional scale. Too far, remote sensing has used several different change detection algorithms, and ongoing research and development is yielding ever more sophisticated methods. Depending on the specifics of the study, researchers may use several different algorithms to sift through the abundance of satellite remote sensing data that has been available over the last several decades. It is strongly advised that any remote sensing project use an adequate change detection approach. This review study starts out with a look at the time-honored approaches of spotting shifts in LULC data at the regional level, both before and after categorization. So, this article compared the most popular change detection approach to the others, and the findings are impressive. A location with a variety of topographical elements was chosen for this comparative examination because it provided the greatest evidence that MLC is superior than the alternatives. When compared to other approaches, MLC's excellent accuracy across all regions has made it the most popular one to utilize from the past to the present.

Saber et al. (2021) [16] examined that this study's primary goal is to assess the efficacy of several change detection methods for keeping tabs on land-cover shifts in the study area, which is situated in the new administrative capital zone of the Cairo Governorate, Egypt, between 2016 and 2017. There are a total of 77,350 square kilometers in the study area. Nanosat satellite photographs with impressive 3 m * 3 m resolution were used as the basis for two satellite photographs encompassing the research region. Maximum

Likelihood Classifier was used to categorize the study area into several types of surfaces, such as pavement, sand, rocks, bare soil, pathways, and structures. The methods of post-classification, independent component analysis, and PCA were used to spot the shifts. The findings of various methods were quantitatively compared to choose the change detection method that will be most effective at revealing the specifics of land-cover shifts in the nation's capital. As shown by the findings, principal component analysis yielded the lowest accuracy while post-classification change detection yielded the greatest. Finally, the results demonstrate the simplicity of the post-classification change detection method, which is direct and whose accuracy is mostly reliant on the precision with which the two photos were first classified. The highest accuracy was 53.430 post-classification for the produced change/unchanged and categorized change pictures, with kappa values of 0.100 and 0.202. There are additional steps in processing, such a transformation stage, needed for the other two methods of change detection.

Mishra et al. (2020) [17] studied that the concept of land use refers to the way land is used and allocated for various purposes, such as residential, commercial. The examination of changes in land cover has shown its use in examining the effects of an event on a specific geographical area. The assessment of regional transformations resulting from urbanization, deforestation, or disasters may be effectively conducted via the use of LULC change detection analysis. The use of RS and GIS technologies has been employed for the examination of both long-term and short-term alterations in biodiversity and LULC inside a specific geographic region. In this article, we give a case analysis of the flash floods that occurred in Uttarakhand in 2013. We're using multi-spectral Landsat satellite images to look nearly at land use and land cover (LULC have changed over time in the area affected. So, then the deal we work with images from both Landsat 7 & 8. This is where the MLA comes into play. Oh, and we also add the NDVI to make effects indeed better. Our area is resolve into five main types mountains, agreements, shops, water, & glaciers. We've achieved a high delicacy rate over 92. By assaying these LULC maps, we can see significant changes that happed after the disaster.

Thwal et al. (2019) [18] examined one of the pivotal factors in environmental leadership and civic planning is the categorization of land cover and change discovery analysis grounded on remote seeing prints using a machine learning algorithm. We noticed some challenges with how the government handles communal planning, especially with farther people moving into cosmopolises. So, we chose to look nearly at Yangon for our study. Our system is enough neat! We use a type of tool the RF classifier in GEE to take a good look at what's end to Yangon's land from 1987 to 2017. We check every five times, also see what find. To make categorization more, we add in some helpful data like NDVI, NDBI, & pitch from the Shutter Radar Topography Mission (SRTM). The RF classifier helps us sort the land cover using several bands. Guess what? We got an overall delicacy of 96.73. That is enough great! And our kappa statistic is 0.95 for the land bracket chart of 2017, which shows 7 different classes. At the end, we also did a change discovery study over 30 times. This showed some big changes in civic life, wild areas, and granges.

3   Problem Formulation

Bharatpur District is in Rajasthan, India. It's changing presto! Urbanization, husbandry, and climate change are playing a part. These make it tough for the area to develop sustainably. We need to manage natural resources well, but it's a challenge. Now, remote seeing tech can help. When we mix it with machine knowledge, we have a great way to check and study how land cover changes over time. But also is the thing the styles used right now in Bharatpur are not really effective. They are not super accurate & they don't gauge up well also. Generally, people look at satellite images manually. This takes a lot of time & there are multitudinous chances for misapprehensions. Plus, they don't fully use the miraculous datasets and calculating power that tools like Google Earth Engine (GEE) offer. So, to attack these problems, this study will make and use a special machine learning frame with Google Earth Engine for spotting changes.

4   Material and Methods

Cloud-based Google Earth Engine that allow stoner to pierce and dissect vast quantities of geospatial data from varied sources, including satellite imagery, upstanding photography, and environmental data. With Google Earth Engine, druggies can perform a wide range of tasks, similar as processing and assaying satellite imagery, creating time-series robustness, generating charts and maps, and indeed erecting machine literacy models to classify land cover or descry changes in foliage over time. All these tasks calculate on the geospatial nature of the data, which is defined by geographic equals similar as longitude and latitude.

Two types of spatial data exist based on their nature and representation:

Vector Data: Vector data are represented by points, lines, and polygons. Points represent a single position on the map, analogous as a municipality or a specific corner. Lines represent a series of connected points, analogous as roads, gutters, or roads. Polygons represent enclosed areas, analogous as countries, countries, or neighbourhoods.

Raster Data: Raster data are represented by a grid of cells or pixels with values for each map position that represents some particularity of that position, analogous as temperature, elevation, or leafage index. Raster data are generally used for assaying and mapping continuous sensations, analogous as land cover, climate, and topography.

Satellites, planes, and drones collect raster data of Earth's face. These images are stored as arrays of pixels, where each pixel contains information about the reflectance or emigration of energy at a particular position on the earth's face. The most common train formats for storing raster data are TIFF, JPEG, GIF, and PNG.

Google Earth Engine is complete at storing and assaying raster cinema attained from several satellite platforms, analogous as MODIS, Landsat, and Sentinel. The MODIS instrument, short for Moderate Resolution Imaging Spectro radiometer, is a vital element of two Terra and Aqua NASA EOS spacecraft. It collects data on several environmental factors, including land cover, leafage, and temperature. Landsat is a common program of NASA and the US Geological Survey (USGS) that captures images of the earth's face with high resolution and multispectral data. Sentinel is a satellite constellation developed by the (ESA) that provides data for covering land use, water resources, and climate change.

Satellite images captured by platforms analogous as MODIS are useful for a wide range of operations related to land cover, land use, and environmental monitoring. Some of the applications include:

Forest analysis: Satellite images can be used to cover the extent and health of timber cover, descry deforestation and timber declination, and assess the impact of natural disasters similar as backfires or nonentity outbreaks.

Water-covered areas: Satellite imagery can collude water bodies, examiner water situations and quality, and dissect flood tide and failure impacts.

Land use change: Satellite imagery can track land use changes like urbanization and agrarian expansion, or natural reforestation.

Land cover: Satellite images collude the distribution and features of land cover types, similar as timbers, champaigns, washes, or spreads.

Land health assessment: Satellite images can be used to assess the health and productivity of land ecosystems, such as vegetation biomass, carbon storage, or soil moisture content.

MODIS is one of the key satellite instruments used for these applications, providing daily global coverage with moderate spatial resolution (250–1000 m) and 36 visible, near-infrared, and thermal bands. The data products derived from MODIS include surface reflectance, vegetation indices, land surface temperature, and atmospheric variables, which are widely used in environmental research and management.

For descry the changes in the remote tasted images must perform image bracket, it's one of the most extensively used types of machine learning (ML) in remote seeing and Civilians. It's an automatic approach to grading pixels or objects within a raster or vector image into predefined classes or orders, similar as land cover types, civic areas, water bodies, or roads. Image bracket is a critical tool for assaying and tracking land use and cover changes, assessing natural coffers, and supporting environmental operation. Two basic picture categorization methods are supervised and unsupervised.

Supervised classification: The observer must submit training samples that directly reflect each class or order included in the picture to use this approach. The machine learning algorithm also acquires knowledge of the spectral attributes of each order and constructs a model able of grading new pixels or objects by assessing their spectral resemblance to the training cases. Supervised bracket is more accurate than unsupervised bracket but requires expansive training data and homemade input.

Unsupervised classification: Without former knowledge or training samples, the ML algorithm clusters pixels or objects with similar spectral features. The critic also assigns labels to these clusters predicated on their visual interpretation or comparison with external data sources. Unsupervised type is less accurate than supervised type but is useful for exploratory analysis and relating unknown features in the image.

Both supervised and unsupervised bracket styles have advantages and limitations depending on the data type, scale, and complexity of the study area. Thus, opting the applicable bracket system and assessing its delicacy are critical way in the image analysis workflow.

Land cover category studies employing time-series satellite prints are more accurate than single-date images. This is because time-series images capture the temporal dynamics of land cover changes and give further information about the spectral characteristics and patterns of different land cover classes.

The vacuity of cloud based computing platforms similar as GEE has enabled remote seeing-grounded operations to pierce and reuse large volumes of time-series satellite data with ease and effectiveness. GEE provides a important tool for time-series analysis and temporal aggregation styles, which are extensively used in land cover bracket studies. For illustration, using the mean or standard values of a time series of images can reduce noise and enhance the temporal signal of land cover changes, performing in more accurate and robust bracket results.

Likewise, temporal aggregation styles can also help to alleviate the goods of atmospheric and sensitive noise, which can impact the quality and thickness of satellite images. By adding up multiple images over time, temporal smoothing can reduce noise and ameliorate the overall quality of the data.

Thus, using time-series satellite images and temporal aggregation styles deduced from those images is an effective approach for land cover bracket studies and other remote seeing operations.

In supervised category, the process starts with a set of training data, which are factual points or areas on the chart where the land cover or land use types are known or vindicated. These training data are generally collected through field checks or visual interpretation of high-resolution images. The training data are used to develop a bracket model that assigns each pixel or object in the image to a specific land cover or land use class grounded on its spectral similarity to the training data.

Rajasthan be chosen as the study area, as for that it'll used MODIS, MODIS satellite provides complete diurnal content of earth.

Google Earth Engine (GEE) is to perform image bracket on satellite imagery to identify and portray the types of land cover on the ground. GEE provides a important platform for performing this task using machine literacy algorithms, similar as Random Forest or Support Vector Machines (SVM), which can learn to classify pixels in the image grounded on their spectral parcels.

To make a prophetic model for land cover bracket using GEE, the first step is to acquire a time-series of satellite images covering the geographic region of interest. The images should be pre-processed to remove noise and atmospheric goods, and also a set of training data should be created by manually opting representative samples of different land cover classes from the image.

The training data can be used to train a machine learning algorithm to classify the pixels in the image into different land cover classes. The trained algorithm can also be applied to the entire image to induce a land cover chart, which shows the distribution of different land cover types in the study area.

Machine Learning Predicated image categorization is an essential element of digital image analysis and finds extensive use in several disciplines, including land operation, communal planning, environmental monitoring, and natural resource operation. The use of GEE and machine literacy algorithms has made image type hastily, more accurate, and more accessible to researchers and practitioners around the world.

Calculating area is a common task in many operations, such as supervised classification or disaster monitoring. In GEE, calculating area for both vector and raster data is slightly different than in other software packages.

4.1 Study Area

The Rajasthan state of India is chosen as the study area. The latitudes and longitudes of Rajasthan state are 27.0238° north and 74.2179° east. The area of the study area is 342651 km². Rajasthan is in the northwest of the India. The state experiences intense heat in the summer and extreme cold in the winter. From November to March, we experience the cold and from April to October there is a summer season. Rajasthan is divided into 9 regions like Hadoti, Marwar, Ajmer State, Mewar, Vagad, Shekhawati, Gorwar, Mewat, Dhundhar. Rajasthan shares the domestic borders with the states of Madhya Pradesh, Utter Pradesh, Punjab, Haryana and Gujrat. Figure 1 depict the study area as shown below.

Fig. 1. Study area

4.2 Research Methodology

4.2.1 Land Use and Land Cover Classification

The LULC study made use of data from MODIS 500 mL and cover dataset from the earth engine data catalog. The 4 classes were used for this research like grass lands, cropland, urban build up lands and barren to study changes in the Bharatpur district of

Rajasthan state from 2001 to 2018. For classification random forest classifier is used. This classifier is used in this study because this algorithm handles hyper spectral remote sensed images efficiently.

4.3 Change Detection

Area is calculated for the 4 classes of Bharatpur district in the Rajasthan state. A change in area was computed between the year 2001 and 2018. The steps that were taken for this study are shown in the methodology study:

The cloud-based platform implements the following steps:

Filtration of Image

The filtration of study area was done through the filter processing in the image collection of the MODIS 500m land cover dataset. The study area is filtered for the specific date.

Vector data area calculation

This step is used for calculation of area of the vector features. The area () function which is the built in function of the google earth engine is used for this task. Before calculating the areas from feature collection have to decompose features geometry from the image collection. So this process gives the geometry of the Rajasthan state and area.

Calculation of area for single class

Extract the pixels of the single class and calculate the area of the single class. For example the following code is used for calculating the urban class.

```
var u = kl.eq(13)
Map.addLayer(u,
  {min:0, max:1, p: ['grey', 'blue']},
  'Urban')
var aI = urban.multiply(ee.Image.pixelArea())
var ar = aI.reduceRegion({
  reducer: ee.Reducer.sum(),
  geometry: k.geometry(),
  scale: 500,
  maxPixels: 1e10
})
var uASqKm = ee.Number(
area.get('LC_Type1')).divide(1e6).round()
print(uASqKm)
```

Calculation of area for images by class

After calculating the area of the single class because it is a classified image, need to calculate the area covered by the each class. To calculate this group reducer is used.

Calculation of area for images by class by region

The area of the each class, in this study there are 4 classes are considered grasslands, croplands, urban and barren are calculated for the Bharatpur region.

Calculation of area for images by class by region by year

In the last step the calculation of area is done for the year, like the area of four classes is calculated for the years from 2001 to 2018 for the Bharatpur region of the Rajasthan state.

5   Result and Discussion

In 2001 Grassland was 127.99 sqkm, crop land was 4866.88 sqkm, urban and builtup lands 57.06 sqkm and barren was 0.222 sqkm. As per our experiment barren land is not changed from 2001 to 2018. In 2018 Grassland was 89.78 sqkm, crop land was 4903.98 sqkm, urban and built-up lands 58.61 sqkm and barren was same as it was 2001. There is increment in urban and built-up lands in 2018, Grass land was decrease up to 38.21 sqkm, crop land is increased by 37.1 sqkm (Table 1).

Table 1.   Showing the area of different classes in 2001–2018.

Year	Grasslands	Croplands	Urban and Built-up Lands	Barren
2001	127.9933	4866.88	57.06321	0.222087
2002	127.3266	4867.547	57.06321	0.222087
2003	107.207	4887.666	57.06321	0.222087
2004	99.356	4895.517	57.06321	0.222087
2006	94.2865	4900.587	57.06321	0.222087
2007	88.04521	4906.828	57.06321	0.222087
2008	78.85281	4916.02	57.06321	0.222087
2009	74.6719	4920.201	57.06321	0.222087
2010	70.87231	4924.001	57.06321	0.222087
2012	65.84422	4929.029	57.06321	0.222087
2013	66.90797	4928.63	57.06321	0.222087
2015	77.40749	4918.131	57.06321	0.222087
2016	75.84867	4919.468	57.28467	0.222087
2018	89.78134	4903.984	58.61363	0.222087

Figure 2 depicts the changes trends of Grasslands from 2001 to 2008 as shown below. The x-axis shows years, ranging from 2001 to 2018. The y-axis shows grassland area, in square kilometer. The red line shows the total amount of grassland lost. According to the graph, the grassland area has been declining steadily since 2001. In 2001, there were about 120 square km of grasslands. By 2018, there were only about 20 square km left, a decrease of 100 square km. This represents a loss of about 83% of grassland area over the 18-year period.

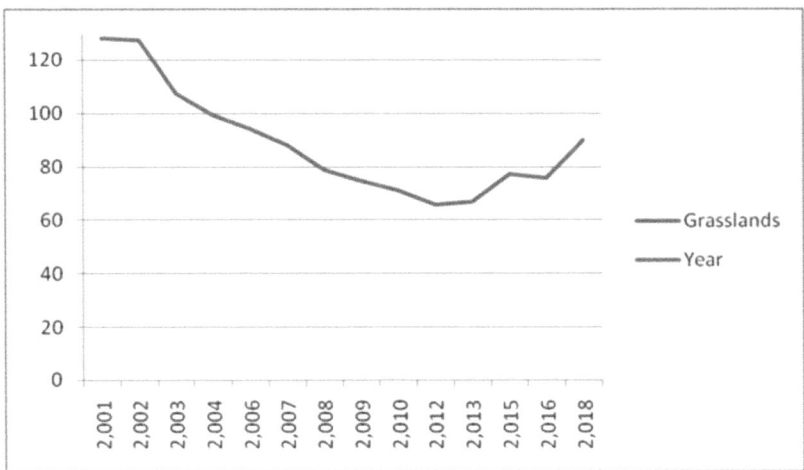

Fig. 2. Changing trends of Grasslands from 2001 to 2018.

Figure 3 illustrates the change trend of croplands from 2001 to 2018 as shown below. The x-axis shows the year, and the y-axis shows the number of croplands in square km. The graph also includes a label for the y-axis that says "Croplands".

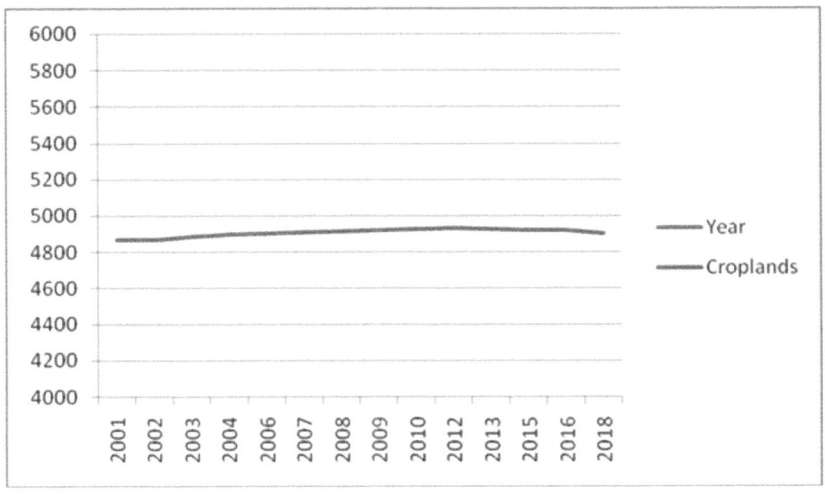

Fig. 3. Change trend of Croplands from 2001 to 2018.

Figure 4 depicts the changes trends of urban and built-up lands as shown below. As seen in Fig. 4, the urban built-up lands are continuously increasing with years.

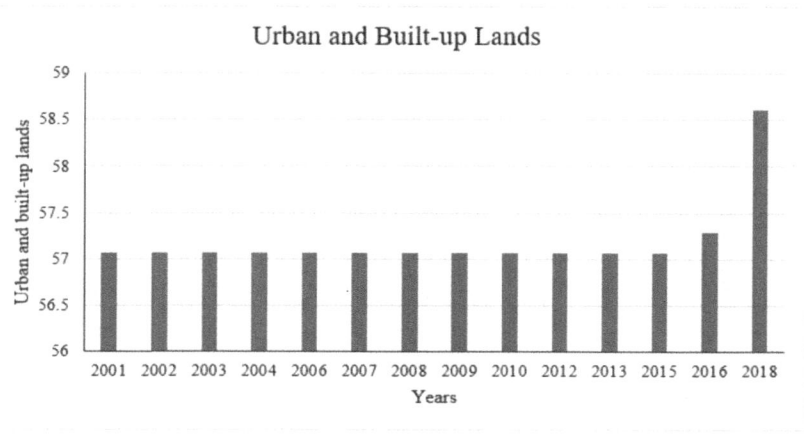

Fig. 4. Changes trends of Urban and built-up from 2001 to 2018.

6   Conclusion

The application of machine learning algorithms within the Google Earth Engine works well tool for change detection in Bharatpur District of Rajasthan State. Through the analysis of satellite imagery, these algorithms have provided valuable insights into land cover changes over time, enabling better understanding and monitoring of environmental dynamics in the region. This technology offered a promising approach for ongoing environmental management and planning efforts, facilitating informed decision-making for sustainable development initiatives. As the field of machine learning continues to evolve, its integration with geospatial data platforms like Google Earth Engine holds immense potential for addressing complex environmental challenges worldwide.

References

1. Tripathi, A., Tiwari, R.K.: Role of space-borne remote sensing technology for monitoring of urban and environmental hazards. In: Recent Technologies for Disaster Management and Risk Reduction: Sustainable Community Resilience and Responses, pp. 295–317 (2021)
2. Farda, N.M.: Multi-temporal land use mapping of coastal wetlands area using machine learning in Google earth engine. IOP Conf. Ser. Earth Environ. Sci. **98**(1), 012042 (2017)
3. Feizizadeh, B., Omarzadeh, D., Garajeh, M.K., Lakes, T., Blaschke, T.: Machine learning data-driven approaches for land use/cover mapping and trend analysis using Google Earth Engine. J. Environ. Plan. Manage. **66**(3), 665–697 (2023)
4. Evans, M.J., Malcom, J.W.: Supporting habitat conservation with automated change detection in Google Earth Engine. Conserv. Biol. **35**(4), 1151–1161 (2021)

5. Pech-May, F., Aquino-Santos, R., Rios-Toledo, G., Posadas-Durán, J.P.F.: Mapping of land cover with optical images, supervised algorithms, and google earth engine. Sensors **22**(13), 4729 (2022)
6. Mangkhaseum, S., Hanazawa, A.: Comparison of machine learning classifiers for land cover changes using google earth engine. In: 2021 IEEE International Conference on Aerospace Electronics and Remote Sensing Technology (ICARES), pp. 1–7. IEEE (2021)
7. Saxena, D., Choudhary, M., Sharma, G.: Land use and land cover change impact on characteristics of surface evapotranspiration in semi-arid environment of Western Rajasthan, India. Water Pract. Technol. **19**(1), 154–169 (2024)
8. Baghel, S., et al.: Spatiotemporal LULC change detection and future prediction for the Mand catchment using MOLUSCE tool. Environ. Earth Sci. **83**(2), 66 (2024)
9. Goyal, M.K., Rakkasagi, S., Shaga, S., Zhang, T.C., Surampalli, R.Y., Dubey, S.: Spatiotemporal-based automated inundation mapping of Ramsar wetlands using Google Earth Engine. Sci. Rep. **13**(1), 17324 (2023)
10. Gavhane, K.P., Mishra, A.K., Sarangi, A., Singh, D.K., Sudhishri, S.: Targeting of rainwater harvesting structures using geospatial tools and analytical hierarchy process (AHP) in the semi-arid region of Rajasthan (India). Environ. Sci. Pollut. Res. **30**(22), 61682–61709 (2023)
11. Kumar, S.: Change detection analysis of land cover features using support vector machine classifier. Int. J. Next Gen. Comput. **14**(2) (2023)
12. Singh, G., Sethi, G.K., Singh, S.: Quantitative and qualitative analysis of PCC-based change detection methods over agricultural land using Sentinel-2 dataset. In: 2022 3rd International Conference on Computing, Analytics and Networks (ICAN), pp. 1–5. IEEE (2022)
13. Zhao, X., et al.: Identification of construction and demolition waste based on change detection and deep learning. Int. J. Remote Sens. **43**(6), 2012–2028 (2022)
14. Ebel, P., Saha, S., Zhu, X.X.: Fusing multi-modal data for supervised change detection. Int. Arch. Photogram. Remote Sens. Spatial Inf. Sci. **43**, 243–249 (2021)
15. Chughtai, A.H., Abbasi, H., Karas, I.R.: A review on change detection method and accuracy assessment for land use land cover. Remote Sens. Appl. Soc. Environ. **22**, 100482 (2021)
16. Saber, A., El-Sayed, I., Rabah, M., Selim, M.: Evaluating change detection techniques using remote sensing data: case study New Administrative Capital Egypt. Egypt. J. Remote Sens. Space Sci. **24**(3), 635–648 (2021)
17. Mishra, S., Jabin, S.: Land use land cover change detection using LANDSAT images: a case study. In: 2020 IEEE 5th International Conference on Computing Communication and Automation (ICCCA), pp. 730–735. IEEE (2020)
18. Thwal, N.S., Ishikawa, T., Watanabe, H.: Land cover classification and change detection analysis of multispectral satellite images using machine learning. In: Image and Signal Processing for Remote Sensing XXV, vol. 11155, pp. 522–532. SPIE (2019)

Human Pose Estimation Using Machine Learning

Mrinmayee Deshpande$^{(\boxtimes)}$, Dipali Gangarde, Nishchay Bhardwaj, Ashish Kumar Yadav, Nilesh P. Sable, and Anuradha Yenkikar

Department of CSE - Artificial Intelligence, Vishwakarma Institute of Information Technology, Pune, India
mrinmayee.22210087@viit.ac.in

Abstract. The human pose estimation proves useful for various tasks such as healthcare, sports analysis and human computer interaction. The yoga practitioners have gained wide momentum in today's era due to increasing health awareness. With the rising popularity of yoga and the increasing demand for technology-assisted learning platforms, there is an increasing need for accurate and effective methods for recognizing yoga poses. Yoga pose estimation and classification plays a crucial role in automated yoga training systems, enhancing the accessibility and effectiveness of yoga practice. Accurate recognition of yoga poses is essential for safe and effective yoga practice. Incorrect posture can result in serious injury to the body, emphasizing the critical need for precise pose detection and classification. This concern motivated our research to explore automated systems for yoga pose recognition. The paper aims to facilitate accurate identification of yoga poses, thereby enhancing accessibility to yoga instruction and minimizing the risk of injury associated with improper form. This research paper focuses on the comparison of two models namely, Ultralytics and MoveNet for detecting the keypoints in yoga poses. The keypoints are subsequently utilized for classification into five different yoga poses: downdog, goddess, plank, tree, and warrior2. Evaluation shows MoveNet achieving a superior accuracy of 93% compared to Ultralytics 88%. Precision, recall, and F1 scores are analyzed through confusion matrices for a performance analysis. This study advances automated yoga pose recognition, providing insights into the capabilities and limitations of current deep learning approaches.

Keywords: YOLO-v8 · MoveNet · Ultralytics · Yoga · HealthCare

1 Introduction

Yoga integrates the body, breath, and meditation to improve mental, emotional, and spiritual well-being. Yoga is widely practiced worldwide due to its numerous health advantages, such as lowering stress, boosting flexibility, and enhancing muscular tone. We have seen a sharp increase in the use of technology for yoga practice in recent years. Due to the convergence of technology and wellness, there has been a noticeable surge in the popularity of yoga worldwide in recent years. Because of the increased focus on

S. Rajagopal et al. (Eds.): ASCIS 2024, CCIS 2424, pp. 400–414, 2025.
https://doi.org/10.1007/978-3-031-86290-8_29

fitness and health, as well as the accessibility of technology-assisted learning platforms, more individuals are turning to yoga as a means of enhancing their physical and mental well-being. However, as yoga gains popularity, there will be a larger demand for accurate and practical methods for identifying and rating yoga poses. Yoga is an ancient Indian form of exercise that involves a vast range of poses, or "asanas," each designed to target a certain muscle group and improve flexibility and overall body awareness. Even while yoga has many benefits, there is still a risk of injury due to improper alignment or technique, particularly for beginners or those without access to trained instructors. Since correct pose detection and categorization is crucial, our goal is to research automated systems for yoga position recognition. By leveraging developments in computer vision and deep learning to enable accurate recognition of yoga postures, we hope to increase accessibility to yoga education and lower the risk of harm associated with bad posture. Our research focuses on the extracting keypoints of the body and then identifying the yoga pose accurately. The journey begins with collection of dataset. We have used the dataset having the yoga images for achieving the goal of our paper. This dataset is publicly available on Kaggle. The keypoints such as NOSE, LEFT_EYE, RIGHT_EYE, LEFT_EAR, RIGHT_EAR, LEFT_SHOULDER, RIGHT_SHOULDER, LEFT_ELBOW, RIGHT_ELBOW, LEFT_WRIST, RIGHT_WRIST, LEFT_HIP, RIGHT_HIP, LEFT_KNEE, RIGHT_KNEE, LEFT_ANKLE, RIGHT_ANKLE were extracted for identifying pose. The algorithm used here is YOLO V-8. The dataset consists of two folders, namely, Train and Test. Five pose labels such as down-dog, tree, goddess, plank, warrior2 were used for the classification. The model was assessed using a variety of parameters including recall, accuracy, and f1-score. Our primary objective is to create a model capable of accurately identifying and categorizing yoga positions in real time. We preprocessed the dataset to normalize the pose photos and then identify the important spots in order to achieve this goal. We used a training dataset to train Yolo v-8 and MoveNet, and we assessed their performance at the checkout set using a variety of evaluation metrics in addition to F1-rating, precision, and recall. This work aims to develop automated systems for the recognition of yoga poses through illuminating the efficacy of various models and their ability to accurately detect yoga postures. Ultimately, our study attempts to provide people with the knowledge and abilities needed to practice yoga safely and efficiently, encouraging a more approachable and healthful approach to wellness.

2   Literature Survey

The importance of practicing yoga is increasing day by day. Nearly 10 papers were surveyed by us. The information gained from these papers is given as follows: Images made up the dataset used in reference [1]. The dataset used in the study consisted of RGB images of five different yoga poses like downdog, tree, plank, warrior2, and goddess—that were manually labelled using the Makesense AI picture annotation tool. The primary results showed the employed model had 93.9% PCK in the goddess position. The study developed an algorithm to evaluate the precision of body joint recognition in yoga poses. The algorithm reached a maximum PDJ of 90% to 100% for most body joints and a high PCK of 93.9% for the goddess posture. The algorithm used was Mediapipe Blazepose Model.

An open-source dataset comprising video footage of fifteen volunteers executing six distinct yoga poses was used in the study in [2]. Fuzzy logic- based modelling is recommended as the feature extraction method for human action recognition. The article describes a modelling technique for human action detection based on fuzzy logic, evaluates the system's performance using benchmark datasets, and extracts features using fuzzy membership functions. The Blazepose model is used by Mediapipe to identify 33 body. The study employs the Blazepose model to identify 33 body keypoints and the Mediapipe and Angle heuristic technique to classify yoga asanas [3].

On the Yoga-82 dataset used in [4], the proposed deep convolutional neural network model, YPose, demonstrated state-of-the-art performance. The model outperforms the previous state-of-the-art with an accuracy of 93.28%, which was 79.35%, by about 13.9%. According to [5], the technique is suitable for a range of applications and is anticipated to benefit the yoga sector. It recognises yoga poses in real time using Open-Pose for 3D joint mapping. It is envisaged that the proposed system will benefit the yoga industry by providing an accurate, affordable, and efficient method of position identification. For yoga position categorization, the suggested wavelet-based CNN model in [6] performs better than other comparison models, such as standard CNN models and transfer learning techniques like ResNet18, ResNet50, and GoogleNet. When deep learning is used to classify yoga poses, using wavelet subbands yields better accuracy results than training on the original images or individual subbands. The suggested approach exhibits encouraging accuracy percentages and shows how wavelet decomposition may be used to increase the precision of yoga pose classification. The application of motion analysis in an exergame engine for feedback in collegiate yoga practice, the use of deep learning for human posture recognition in yoga practice, and the suggestion of an Internet of Things-based system for privacy-preserving yoga pose detection are among the primary discoveries in [7]. The work in [8] focuses on the detection and correction of yoga poses using computer vision technologies for human posture assessment. The process is feeding the input image through a CNN classifier that has been trained to detect faces, recognise human body postures, and search for joints and limbs that have been previously taught in order to provide the user with markers that indicate different body parts. The study [9] suggests XGBoost, a real time machine learning framework that outperforms earlier models in terms of accuracy, latency, and size for accurate yoga stance identification. In the work presented in [10], the accuracy of different regression and classification algorithms was compared utilising a person's stance skeleton in photos as a means of recognising and classifying human activities. The authors of the study created the dataset, which is split into two sections for training and validation. The multivariate logistic regression method is used to complete the activity classification task. They have employed the DenseNet architecture in paper [11] to leverage the hierarchical labelling for better posture recognition. In order to address the lack of difficulty and diversity in current pose datasets, especially those created primarily for large-scale yoga pose recognition, it discusses the idea of fine-grained hierarchical pose categorization and offers a new dataset named Yoga-82 with 82 yoga posture classes.

The dataset is distinctive in that it emphasises the variety and complexity of human positions in yoga-related activities. In the study [12], a self-assisted system for identifying and categorising yoga poses was created using computer vision. In order to categorise stances into yoga asanas, the system evaluates real-time video data. It then shows the identified asana together with a confidence score. The goal of the work in [13] was to apply deep learning-based techniques for precise estimation of yoga positions. Among the four deep learning architectures that were employed, MediaPipe had the highest estimation accuracy.

With a high average confidence score of 92%, the study in [14] presented an interactive method for identifying yoga positions using Kinect technology. In paper [15], Convolutional and Recurrent Neural Networks are combined in deep hybrid architecture to estimate a person's pose. The main discovery is the creation of a hybrid architecture combining CNNs and RNNs to provide an endto-end method for estimating human position. Various algorithms which were used in the literature surveyed include – Mediapipe Blazepose Model, Media pipe pose estimation library, support vector machine classifier, random forest classifier, k-nearest neighbours classifier, logistic regression, naïve-Bayes classifier, CNN, OpenPose, MATLAB R2021a, Computer vision technology, XGBoost Classifier, etc.

3   Proposed Methodology

The yoga pose estimation has gained a wide momentum nowadays as the health concern in people is increasing. The relevance of yoga pose detection is that the pose should be detected accurately as the wrong pose can cause serious damage to the body. The paper focuses on the comparison of two models which are accessed on the criteria: accuracy, recall, precision, and F1-score. Numerous pretrained models are available for detecting the keypoints like BlazePose, OpenPose, ResNet, MoveNet, MediaPipe, pose estimation model of ultralytics. Of them, we have chosen the models movenet and pose estimation model of ultralytics.

3.1   Dataset

The dataset which we used is obtained from kaggle. The dataset contained two folders named ₌Train' and ₌Test'. Train folder has 1081 images and test folder has 470 images. Overall, 5 poses namely, goddess, downdog, plank, tree and warrior2 form the classes of the dataset [16] as it is evident from Figs. 1, 2, 3, 4 and 5.

Fig. 1. Warrior2   **Fig. 2.** Tree   **Fig. 3.** Downdog

Fig. 4. Plank

Fig. 5. Goddess

Furthermore, we have also implemented real time for estimation. We are developing our real-time implementation in Python with the TensorFlow framework. We make use of TensorFlow's high- level APIs and effective model serving features to provide a smooth integration of the MoveNet model into our application. OpenCV isrequired for image processing and visualisation, among other things (Fig. 6).

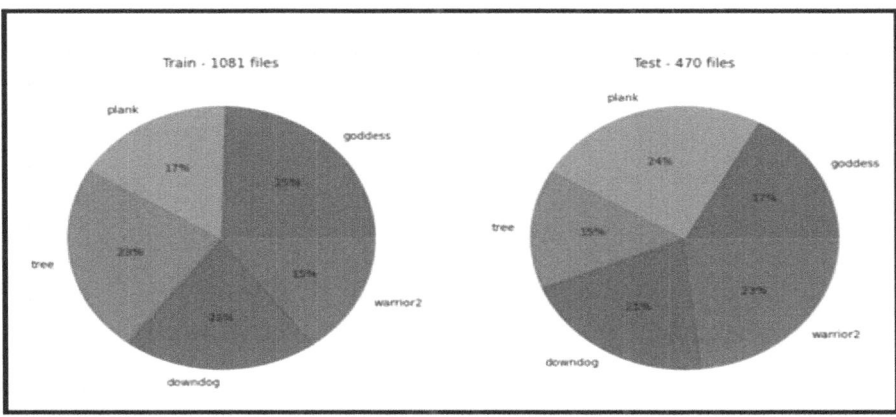

Fig. 6. Distribution of all classes of pose

4 Model Architecture

4.1 Approach 1. YOLO-V8 Ultralytics

In this approach, we utilize the YOLOv8 architecture for detecting keypoints corresponding to the yoga poses in the images. YOLOv8 (You Only Look Once version 8) is a state of-the-art object detection model known for its efficiency and accuracy in detecting objects and keypoints in images. The preprocessing steps includes resizing the images, conversion of images from BGR to RGB. The pretrained model for pose estimation, ultralytics was used to detect the keypoints. In total, 17 keypoints were detected. After the extraction of all the keypoints, the keypoints of each body part were stored in a CSV file. CSV file included image name, class label and remaining column for each body keypoints. A custom neural network classifier is designed for classification of yoga poses based on the detected keypoints. The label encoder was used to label the classes. This classifier is responsible for mapping the extracted keypoint information to the corresponding yoga pose labels. Multiple convolutional layers are the first layer in the classifier's design and these are followed fully linked layers. Convolutional layers are in charge of feature extraction, capturing relevant patterns and relationships within the keypoint data. For pose categorization, these attributes are then flattened and run through fully connected layers. The neural network's hidden layers employ the Rectified Linear Unit (ReLU) activation function. ReLU adds non-linearity to the data, enabling the model to discover intricate linkages therein. For multi-class classification, the output layer applies the Softmax activation function. It converts the raw output scores into probabilities, representing the likelihood of each yoga pose class. For gradient descent optimization, Adam optimizer is employed. The Adam optimizer is renowned for its potency in deep neural network training. Based on the loss function's gradients in relation to the model's parameters, it dynamically modifies the learning rate. We implemented a learning rate of 0.01, a batch size of 12, and trained the model for 40 epochs to ensure balanced optimization and efficient convergence This adaptive learning rate helps in faster convergence and improved performance during training.

The classification report as obtained for the ultralytics model is as shown below – (Fig. 7 and Fig. 8)

	precision	recall	f1-score	support
downdog	0.95	0.93	0.94	40
goddess	0.97	0.77	0.86	39
plank	0.82	0.98	0.89	51
tree	0.82	0.88	0.85	32
warrior2	0.87	0.82	0.85	57
accuracy			0.88	219
macro avg	0.89	0.87	0.88	219
weighted avg	0.88	0.88	0.88	219

Fig. 7. Classification report for ultralytics and neural network classifier

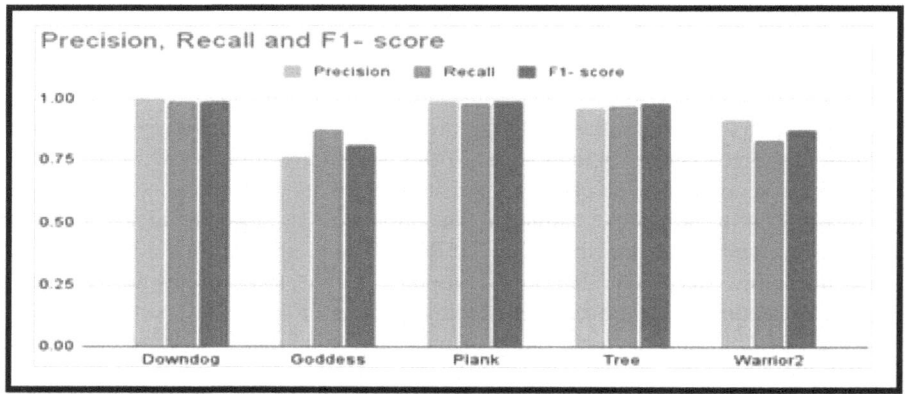

Fig. 8. Graphical View of Classification report for ultralytics and neural network classifier

4.2 Approach 2. MoveNet

MoveNet is a compact deep learning network specifically created for efficient and precise identification of keypoints, such as human posture estimate. There are two types of MoveNet models namely, MoveNet- lightning and Movenet- Thunder. In our study, we utilize MoveNet lightning for detecting 17 keypoints corresponding to human body joints in yoga poses. These keypoints include joints such as shoulders, elbows, wrists, hips, knees, and ankles, which are essential for accurately representing the body posture in different yoga poses. The preprocessing steps include resizing images into shape 192 pixels, conversion of images from BGR to RGB. After detecting the keypoints using MoveNet, we employ a separate neural network classifier to classify the yoga poses based on the detected keypoints. This classifier is responsible for mapping the extracted keypoint information to the corresponding yoga pose labels. The architecture of the classifier follows a similar structure to the YOLOv8-based classifier, which includes convolutional layers followed by fully connected layers. However, specific adjustments may be made to accommodate the input size and features extracted by MoveNet. Convolutional layers are in charge of feature extraction, capturing relevant patterns and relationships within the keypoint data. After being flattened, these features are routed via fully connected layers in order to classify poses. Similar to the YOLOv8-based approach, appropriate activation functions, loss functions, and optimization algorithms are utilized for training the classifier. ReLU (Rectified Linear Unit) activation function is frequently employed in the hidden layers of the neural network for introducing non-linearity and facilitating convergence during training. For multi-class classification, Softmax activation function is employed in the output layer providing normalized probabilities for each yoga pose class. For multi-class classification tasks, the loss function of choice is frequently cross-entropy loss.

The dissimilarity between the expected probability distribution and the ground truth labels is quantified by this measurement. Adam optimizer, is commonly used for gradient descent optimization. For the MoveNet model, we applied a batch size of 32, and trained for 40 epochs, achieving smooth training dynamics and effective model refinement. These settings ensure that the classifier effectively learns to identify and classify yoga

	precision	recall	f1-score	support
0	1.00	0.99	0.99	91
1	0.76	0.87	0.81	77
2	0.99	0.98	0.99	108
3	0.96	0.97	0.96	66
4	0.91	0.83	0.87	104
accuracy			0.93	446
macro avg	0.92	0.93	0.92	446
weighted avg	0.93	0.93	0.93	446

Fig. 9. Classification report for MoveNet and neural network classifier

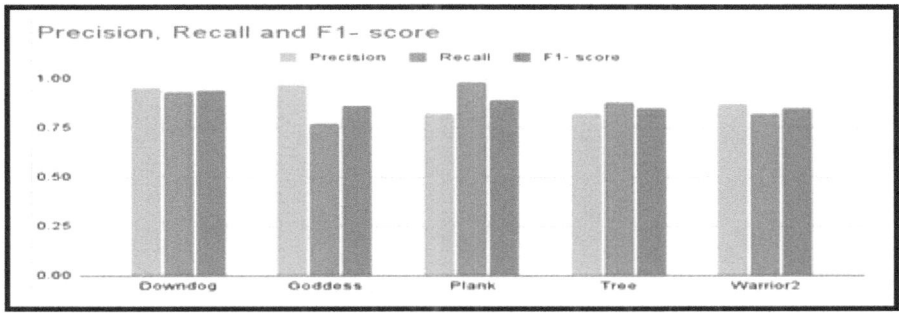

Fig. 10. Graphical View of Classification report for MoveNet and neural network classifier

poses based on the keypoints detected by MoveNet, ultimately leading to accurate and reliable pose recognition results.

The classification report as obtained for the MoveNet model is as shown below-(Fig. 9, Fig. 10). Figure 11 shows the architecture of the proposed system.

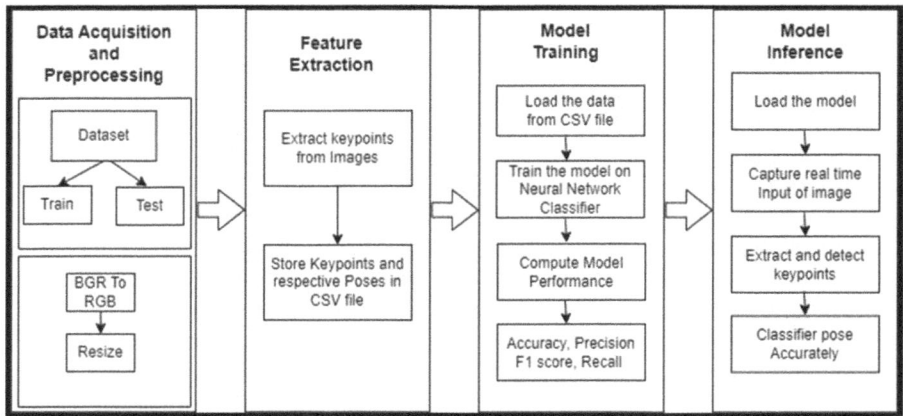

Fig. 11. Architecture of Model

5   Results

The accuracy of the two models' performance—MoveNet and YOLO-v8—was assessed in relation to their ability to identify yoga poses. Figures 12 and 13 show the training, validation loss for both the models.

Fig. 12. MoveNet model's training and validation accuracy

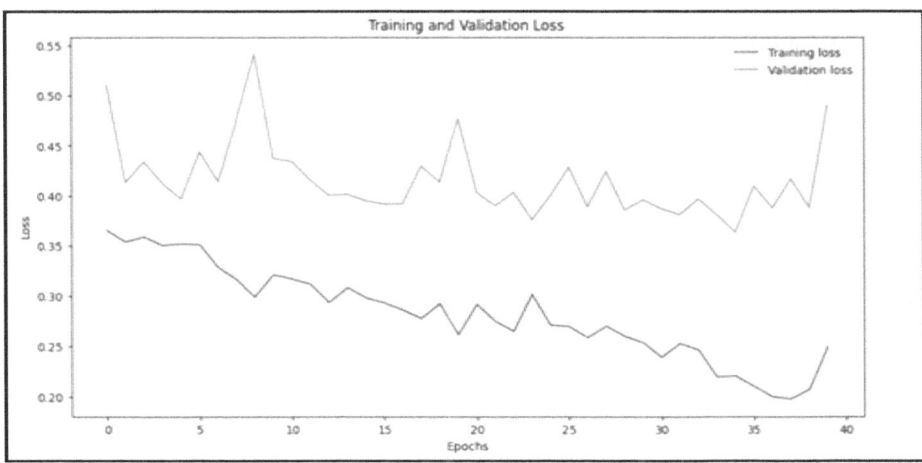

Fig. 13. MoveNet model's training and validation loss

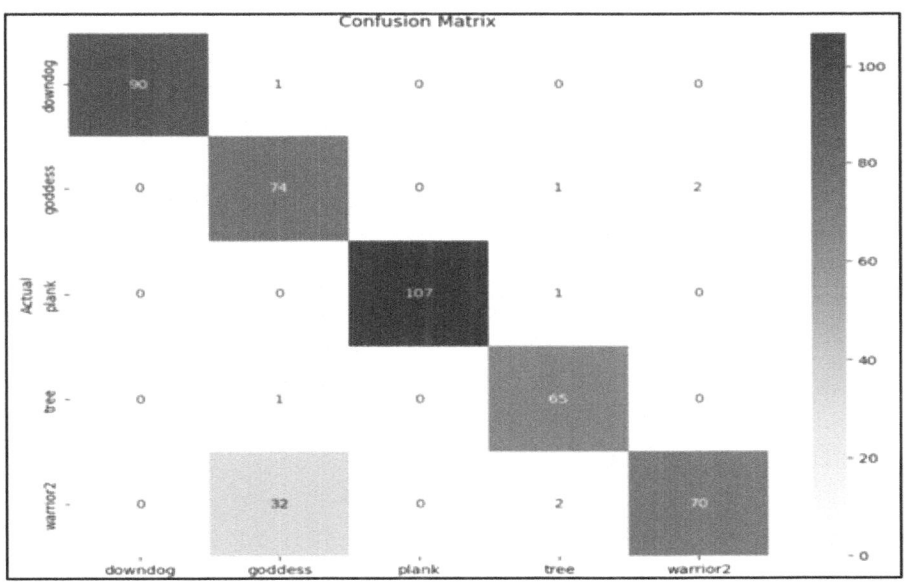

Fig. 14. Confusion Matrix (MoveNet Model)

Figures 14 and 15 show the confusion matrices for both the models. The confusion matrix for MoveNet indicates high precision, recall, and F1 scores across all five yoga poses (Fig. 16, Fig. 17, Fig. 18, Fig. 19, Fig. 20).

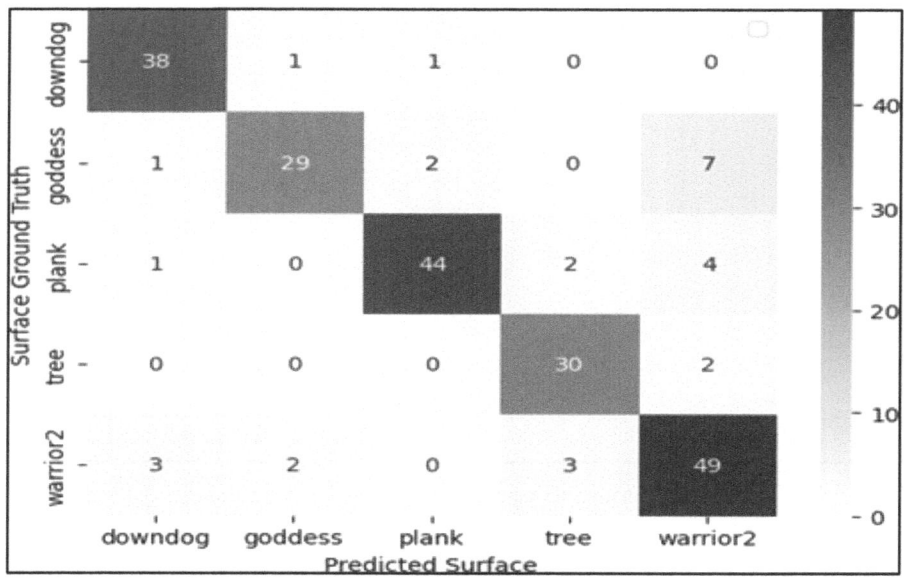

Fig. 15. Confusion Matrix (Yolov8 ultralytics Model)

Comparative Study of Both Models:

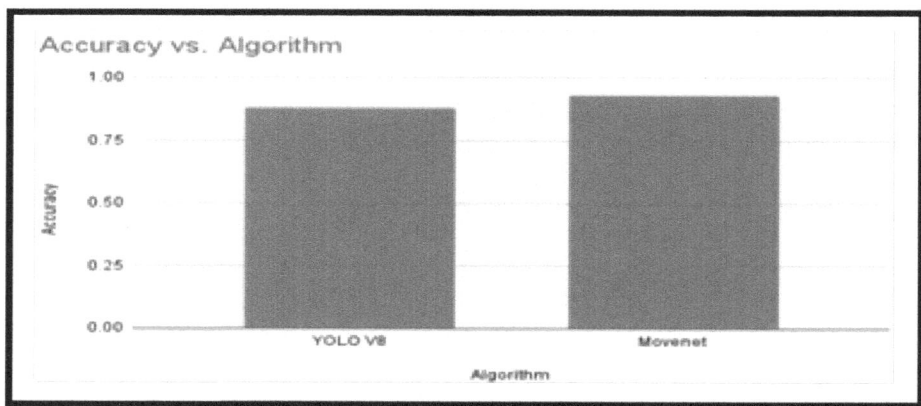

Fig. 16. Comparison of Accuracy of both models

As it is evident from the diagrams, in summary, MoveNet outperforms YOLO-v8 making it superior model for recognizing yoga poses.

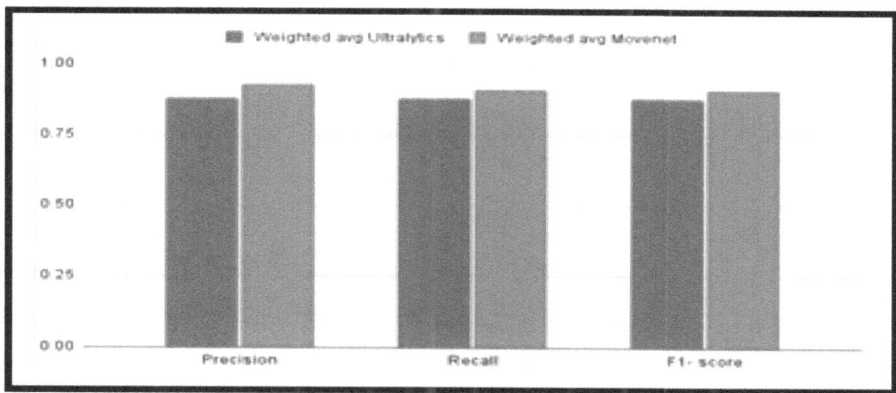

Fig. 17. Comparison of weighted averages

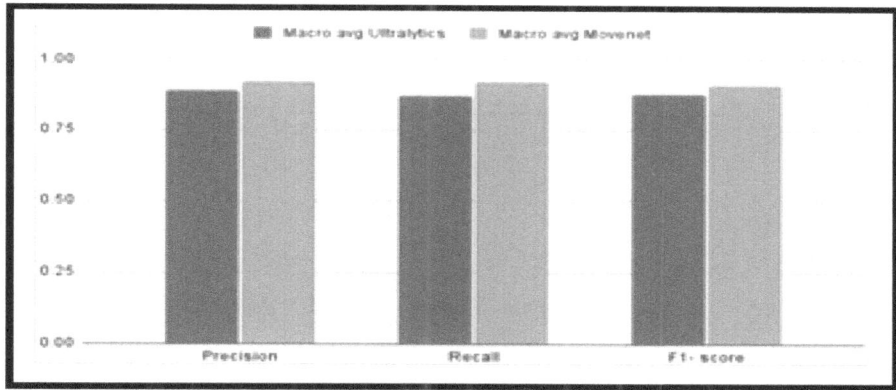

Fig. 18. Comparison of macro averages

User Experience

Users felt that the model is quite accurate while performing basic and intermediate poses with the responsiveness in real-time. They appreciated the user- friendly design and found it beneficial for personal yoga practice and remote coaching.

Results for Human Pose Estimation:

Fig. 19. Normal Standing pose

Fig. 20. Normal Standing pose

6   Conclusion

In conclusion, our research on human posture prediction with pre-trained models such as MoveNet and YOLOv8 and a yoga pose dataset has produced promising results. After careful examination, MoveNet has become the leader with an amazing accuracy of 93%, outperforming YOLOv8's 88% performance. This sharp difference highlights the superiority of specialised models like MoveNet in this domain and highlights how well they can capture yoga poses. The success of MoveNet and related pre-trained models represents a major advancement in the fields of yoga training, fitness tracking, and other related fields. These models provide fast development processes together with strong performance, which opens doors towards various real-world applications requiring accuracy and efficiency in human pose estimation. Our MoveNet-based real-time human position estimation technology provides notable improvements in speed and accuracy, allowing for a smooth integration into interactive applications like online yoga classes and fitness coaching. The MoveNet model has 93% accuracy which is better than YOLOv8 (88%). It works in real time and is mainly intended for yoga workout purposes while nowadays systems such OpenPose are more general, require more resources and can't be as precise in detecting the yoga poses. The attained real-time performance satisfies the prerequisites for realistic implementation in real- world situations, opening the door for improved user experiences and novel paradigms for human- computer interaction. In future, to improve the model's overall performance and reliability in real-world scenarios, we can strengthen their capacity to generalise over a range of poses and environmental variables through augmentation tactics like rotation, scaling, and noise injection. We acknowledge that offering consumers practical feedback while they execute yoga postures is just as important as accurately estimating poses.

References

1. Desai, M., Mewada, H.: A novel approach for yoga pose estimation based on in-depth analysis of human body joint detection accuracy. Peer J. Comput. Sci. **9** (2023)
2. Fard, M.G., Montazer, G.A., Giveki, D.: A novel fuzzy logic- based method for modeling and recognizing yoga pose.In: 2023 9th International Conference on Web Research (ICWR), pp. 1–6 (2023)
3. Kotak, D., Desai, J., Shah, R., Goel, P., Patel, K.: Yoga pose classification using angle heuristic approach. In: 2022 4th International Conference on Inventive Research in Computing Applications (ICIRCA), pp. 1709–1714 (2022)
4. Yadav, S.K., Shukla, A., Tiwari, K., Pandey, H.M., Akbar, S.A.: An efficient deep convolutional neural network model for yoga pose recognition using single images. ArXiv https://arxiv.org/abs/2306.15768 (2023)
5. Nagargoje, S., Shinde, A.S., Pranav, T., Shinde, O., Devkar, A.: Yoga pose detection. Int. J. Res. Appl. Sci. Eng. Technol. (2023)
6. Aydin, V.A.: Comparison of CNN-based methods for yoga pose classification. Turk. J. Eng. (2023)
7. Deepa, D., Velumani, R., Selvaraj, S.: Yoga pose estimation along with human posture detection using deep learning approach. Appl. Comput. Eng. (2023)
8. Gajbhiye, R., Jarag, S., Gaikwad, P., Koparde, S.: AI Human Pose Estimation: Yoga Pose Detection and Correction (2022)
9. Sunney, J., Jilani, M., Pathak, P., Stynes, P.: A real-time machine learning framework for smart home-based yoga teaching system. In: 2023 7th International Conference on Machine Vision and Information Technology (CMVIT), pp. 107–114 (2023)
10. Gupta, A., Gupta, K., Gupta, K.N.M., Gupta, K.O.: Human activity recognition using pose estimation and machine learning algorithm. In: International Symposium on Intelligent Control (2021)
11. Verma, M., Kumawat, S., Nakashima, Y., Raman, S.: Yoga-82: a new dataset for fine-grained classification of human poses. In: 2020 IEEE/CVF Conference on Computer Vision and Pattern Recognition Workshops (CVPRW), pp. 4472–4479 (2020)

12. Prakash, M., Aishwarya, S., Maru, D., Chandra, N., Varshini, V.: Yoga posture classification using computer vision. Int. J. Eng. Manage. Res. (2021)
13. Kishore, D.M., Bindu, S., Manjunath, N.K.: Estimation of yoga postures using machine learning techniques. Int. J. Yoga **15**, 137–143 (2022)
14. Trejo, E.W., Yuan, P.: Recognition of yoga poses through an interactive system with Kinect based on confidence value. In: 2018 3rd International Conference on Advanced Robotics and Mechatronics (ICARM), pp. 606–611 (2018)
15. Coskun, H.: Human Pose Estimation with CNNs and LSTMs (2016)
16. Dataset-https://www.kaggle.com/datasets/niharika41298/yoga-poses-dataset

Multi-dimensional Spatiotemporal Sparse-Representation Convolutional Long Short-Term Memory for Prediction of Autism Spectrum Disorder

V. Deepa[1][✉] and D. Maheswari[2]

[1] School of Computer Studies, RVS College of Arts and Science (Autonomous),
Sulur, Coimbatore, Tamilnadu, India
deepuu_22@yahoo.co.in
[2] School of Computer Studies-PG RVS College of Arts and Science (Autonomous),
Sulur, Coimbatore, Tamilnadu, India

Abstract. ASD is a Neuro development disorder. Lack of communication, anxiety over social interaction, feeble and confused behaviors are some of the outward impacts and intense impressions found in an autistic patient. Early detection and diagnosis of autism can feasibly eliminate the progression of the disease. In this paper, the detection of autism is elevated by incorporating facial expression analysis along with Machine learning techniques. The goal of the system is to evaluate the facial expressions of the patient by interpreting images or videos which aids to figure out the potential indicators of ASD. Data collection embroiled with diverse dataset that encompasses facial expression of the neurotypical individuals. In order to enhance the data quality few valid preprocessing techniques are incorporated a prompt facial expressions, facial features and expression patterns are implied as feature extraction methods. Multi-dimensional spatial-temporal sparse based convolutional long short-term memory is engaged to incriminate the neuro typical behavior of individuals and to analyze their facial expressions. The proposed model gets trained by the preprocessed dataset. The dataset is inculpated by proper validation and testing which leads to examine its real-world performance.

Keywords: ASD · facial expressions · deep learning algorithm · feature extraction

1 Introduction

Autism Spectrum disorder (ASD) is a bedlam that is caused by the inadequacy in neurological condition of a person. The progression of ASD has become greater than before. As an impact of this neurological condition the affected person faces difficulty in practicing social behaviors and extending communication to express their feelings and response. The diagnosis of autism in children aged below 3 years is comparatively easy than other age groups. The term "Autism" is derived from the Greek word "autos", coining the meaning "solitary self and describes a state in which persons isolate themselves from social connections with others so", that is why it's a definite neuropsychiatric syndrome. In Autism Spectrum disorder (ASD) the term Spectrum imparts a meaning of wide ranges of signs and severity degrees. ASD is clearly obvious to affect a person in the early childhood itself which extends the child to face challenging environment in school and any work place. ASD is a neurological developmental disease marked by social connection problems and repetitive or limited behavioral patterns. Developmental disorders are long-term impairments that have a significant influence on many people's everyday lives. The global autism population is growing, which causes families to worry about their children and necessitates an evaluation to assure their children's health if they are autistic. Autistic patients require specialized treatment in order to build perceptual abilities that will allow them to communicate with their family and society. When an autistic patient is detected early, the outcomes of behavioral therapy are more beneficial.

Autism spectrum disorder (ASD) children have trouble properly reading facial expressions and responding appropriately, which is thought to be a major source of their social impairments. Facial expressions are crucial in social interaction and communication. They provide for the interchange of rich social information as well as a window into the interior emotional states of others. Good facial expression processing capacity, or the ability to effectively perceive and respond to facial expressions, is the key to successful communication and social engagement, and is critical to an individual's social cognitive development.

2 Related Works

Srividhya Ganesan, Dr. Raju and Dr. J. Senthil (2021) proposed Autism Prediction system that focuses on classification models using VGG16 algorithm and compared traditional algorithms like SVM, CNN, Haar Cascade using OpenCV.

Madison Beary, Alex Hadsell, Ryan Messersmith, Mohammad-Parsa Hosseini (2020) proposed MobileNet and two dense layers for feature extraction and image classification of autism.

Amrita Budarapu et al. (2021) proposed "Early Screening of Autism among Children Using Ensemble Classification Method". In this paper Ensemble learning algorithms were analyzed with image and video data. This model also predicts the primary emotions. The main objective of this paper tracks the eye gaze to know the classification of autism or non-autism.

Suman Raj and Sarfaraz Mazood (2020) "Analysis and Detection of Autism Spectrum Disorder Using Machine Learning Techniques" focuses on early diagnosis of Autism in Adult, Children and Adolescents. This paper author analyze various machine learning algorithms.

M. S. Mythili, A. R. Mohamed Shanavas (2014) conducted a study on Autism Spectrum Disorder using Classification techniques analyze the child behavior and their social interaction.

Fadi Thabtah, Firuz Kamalov, Khairan Rajab (2018) proposed "A new computational intelligence approach to detect autistic features for autism screening" which involves a computational intelligence method called Variable Analysis (VA) to reduce feature-to-feature correlations based on statistical tools for analyzing the facial features.

D P Wall, et al. (2012) proposed "Use of Machine Learning to shorten observation-based screening and diagnosis of autism" with the statistical features.

The integration of AI-powered facial expression analysis into ASD diagnosis holds transformative potential. These technologies offer the prospect of earlier detection, more accurate assessments, and improved intervention outcomes for individuals with ASD. By harnessing the transformative power of AI, there's a unique opportunity to revolutionize ASD diagnosis, potentially leading to earlier interventions and better outcomes for individuals with ASD and their families. With continued advancements in technology and research, transformative potential of AI-powered facial expression analysis in ASD diagnosis. Leveraging technology to its fullest extent enables researchers to develop innovative solutions that address the complex challenges associated with ASD diagnosis, driving progress and improving the lives of individuals affected by ASD.

2.1 Proposed Methodology

The proposed Autism prediction model is based on MDSTS-CLSTM methodologies. In the first stage, the medical dataset is pre-processed using the adaptive Morlet wavelet transform to remove the noise in the dataset. In the second stage, the noise-removed data is deployed for learning the hidden patterns of the dataset utilizing the MDSTS-CLSTM method. It is created by fusing the properties of CNN and LSTM models. This method uses the benefits of different properties such as multi-dimensional, sparse representation and spatial-temporal analysis. These properties extract most relevant features from the Autism datasets to enhance the performance of the autism prediction model (Fig. 1).

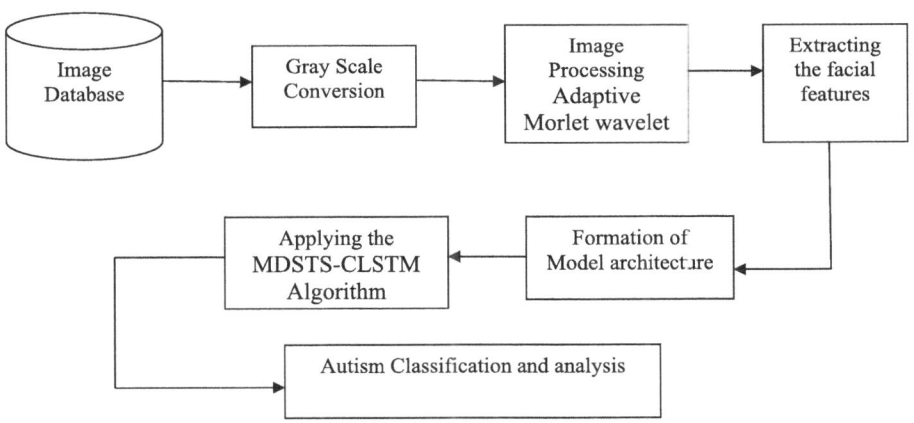

Fig. 1. System Architecture

The final prediction process is carried out in the MDSTS-CLSTM model. The cross-domain medical data contains noise, affecting the performance of the autism prediction model. Hence, it is filtered using ESDAE. Further, the denoised data is input to the MDSTS-CLSTM model which predicts the classification of autism. The denoised medical data is passed to the convolution layer, which learns the features of facial data. The learned features are given to the sparse representation layer, which extracts the spatial features using wavelet and shearlet transforms. Both the transforms are used to extract spatial and temporal features. Further, the multi-dimensional property extracts the spatial representations using the multiple layers. These features are concatenated and given to the LSTM block, extracting the temporal representation of the medical data. Then, the spatial and temporal features are fed to the fully connected layer, which predicts the autism and generates the outcome. The architecture of MDSTS-CLSTM is represented in Fig. 2

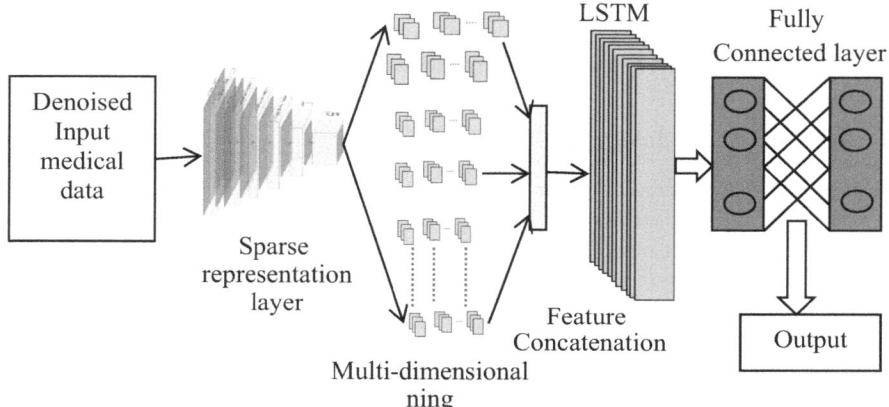

Fig. 2. Architecture of MDSTS-CLSTM

The CNN models are used to extract the spatial feature, which is ineffective in extracting the temporal features. Hence, the LSTM model is combined with CNN to extract the temporal features. This combination effectively learns the medical data's spatial and temporal features. The problem of spatial invariance is solved using the convolution operation instead of the dot product in the standard LSTM model. The LSTM models have three gates such as input gate i, forget gate f and output gate o. The forget gate is used to remove or store the information belonging to the memory cell c. The basic LSTM models are one-dimensional, using a single cell and incorporating a single recurrent connection. The activation of the recurrent connection is controlled utilizing the single forget gate. In the case of multi-dimensional LSTM, it uses multiple cells and the recurrent connection. To model the LSTM, the inputs are taken as $x_1, x_2, x_3 \ldots \ldots x_t$, output as $c_1, c_2, c_3 \ldots \ldots c_t$ and the hidden state as $h_1, h_2, h_3 \ldots \ldots h_t$. The main operation of the suggested CLSTM model is expressed as below,

$$i_t = \sigma(W_{xi} * x_t + W_{hi} * h_{t-1} + W_{ci} \circ c_{t-1} + b_i) \tag{1}$$

$$f_t = \sigma(W_{xf} * x_t + W_{hf} * h_{t-1} + W_{cf} \circ c_{t-1} + b_f) \tag{2}$$

$$o_t = \sigma(W_{xo} * x_t + W_{ho} * h_{t-1} + W_{co} \circ c_{t-1} + b_o) \tag{3}$$

$$c_t = f_t \circ c_{t-1} + i_t \circ \tanh(W_{xc} * x_t + W_{hc} * h_{t-1} + b_c) \tag{4}$$

$$h_t = o_t \circ \tanh(c_t) \tag{5}$$

Here, $\circ$ denotes the Hadamard product and $*$ represents the convolutional operator. The LSTM model includes five layers, three hidden layers, and two feed-forward sub-sampling layers. The input data is given to the hidden layer using the input layer, and data is processed sent to the output layer. The subsampling layers use *tanh* activation function, and this layer fastens the training time by compressing the sequences as windows. This layer reduces the weight connection between hidden layers. Furthermore, the LSTM model is trained using Connection Temporal Classification in the output layer, increasing the probability of labeling sequence during training.

In this work, some LSTM parameters are tuned during training. The parameters are the size of LSTM, *tanh* and the subsampling layer. The LSTM size is the number of cells in each hidden layer, and the size is taken as 2, 10 and 5. The *tanh* size represents the used *tanh* units in the subsampling layer. The subsampling window size indicates the window used to subsample the input before giving it to the coming hidden layers.

3   Results and Discussion

Extensive experiments are performed using MATLAB to validate the effective performance of the proposed MDSTS-CLSTM-based traffic prediction model. The effectiveness of the model is evaluated in terms of accuracy, precision, recall, false positive rate (FPR), false negative rate (FNR), mean absolute error (MAE), and RMSE. The Autism

Table 1. Average results obtained for proposed model against existing methods

Methods	Accuracy	Precision	Recall	FPR	FNR	MAE	RMSE
STCNet	0.8150	0.9123	0.8454	0.2422	0.3345	29.87	60.32
MGCN-LSTM	0.8619	0.9067	0.8765	0.2805	0.3012	36.67	66.41
CNN	0.8004	0.9687	0.8319	0.1320	0.1876	38.76	59.11
MVSTGN	0.8602	0.9701	0.8495	0.1988	0.2134	29.98	49.03
EDRL	0.8492	0.9651	0.8231	0.2250	0.2341	21.34	60.02
CrowdGAN	0.8110	0.9011	0.8700	0.1991	0.2765	25.55	54.45
SDGNet	0.8667	0.8976	0.8799	0.1976	0.1987	31.76	49.91
SLSTM	0.8725	0.8851	0.9023	0.2419	0.2123	33.34	53.36
1DCNN	0.8898	0.9550	0.9102	0.1325	0.1765	32.92	63.30
CNN-LSTM	0.8334	0.9222	0.8698	0.1287	0.1876	23.74	51.49
GCN	0.7932	0.9007	0.8324	0.1832	0.2567	29.81	50.35
GCNN-LSTM	0.8876	0.9665	0.8712	0.2102	0.2987	24.49	54.48
RL	0.8654	0.9571	0.9011	0.1450	0.1902	23.41	49.33
Proposed algorithm	0.9036	0.9797	0.9175	0.1128	0.1616	20.67	45.46

dataset is used for evaluation. The noise removal and the enhanced handling of the sparse data can be attributed to this improvement. In addition, the proposed algorithm is also compared against the existing methods from the literature to identify its effectiveness. Table 1 shows that average results obtained for proposed model against existing methods under similar experimental conditions.

From Table 1, it is evident that, proposed MDSTS-CLSTM methods have better performance of higher accuracy, precision, recall, and reduced FPR, FNR, MAE, and RMSE, which are better than the existing methods discussed in the literature. The significant improvement of the proposed algorithm shows that it is effective for adaptive learning of the features in accurately predicting the autism classification. It is also indicative that the proposed algorithm can converge better than the other model with minimized noise and minimized model complexity.

4   Conclusion

The objective of this research is to develop a model for classification system to identify the normality and abnormality of autism. In this paper, proposed MDSTS-CLSTM to handle the challenges of noisy and sparse medical data from the real world entity. The MDSTS-CLSTM combines LSTM and CNN's advantages to learn the facial features data's hidden patterns and dependencies in both spatial and temporal dimensions. The MDSTS-CLSTM also incorporates a sparse representation technique to deal with the data Sparsity problem and reduce computation time and storage costs.

References

1. Kumar, A., et al.: An intrusion identification and prevention for cloud computing: from the perspective of deep learning. Optik **270**, 170044 (2022)
2. Napoleon, D., et al.: Self-organizing map-based color image segmentation with fuzzy C-Means clustering and saliency map. Int. J. Comput. Appl. **3**(2), 109–117 (2012)
3. Praneesh, M., Jaya Kumar, R.: Novel approach for color based comic image segmentation for extraction of text using modify fuzzy possibilistic c-means clustering algorithm. Int. J. Comput. Appl. IPRC **1**, 16–18 (2012)
4. Boonsatit, N., Rajendran, S., Lim, C.P., Jirawattanapanit, A., Mohandas, P.: New adaptive finite-time cluster synchronization of neutral-type complex-valued coupled neural networks with mixed time delays. Fractal Fraction. **6**(9), 515 (2022)
5. Napoleon, D., Praneesh, M., Sathya, S., SivaSubramani, M.: An efficient numerical method for the prediction of clusters using k-means clustering algorithm with bisection method. In: Global Trends in Information Systems and Software Applications: 4th International Conference, ObCom 2011, Vellore, TN, India, December 9–11, 2011. Proceedings, Part II, pp. 256–266. Springer Berlin Heidelberg (2012)
6. Bours, C.C.A.H., et al.: Emotional face recognition in male adolescents with autism spectrum disorder or disruptive behavior disorder: an eye-tracking study. Eur. Child Adolesc. Psychiatry **27**, 1143–1157 (2018)
7. Almourad, M.B., Bataineh, E.: Visual attention toward human face recognizing for autism spectrum disorder and normal developing children: an eye tracking study. In: Proceedings of the 2020 the 6th International Conference on e-Business and Applications, pp. 99–104 (2020)

8. Kang, J., Han, X., Song, J., Niu, Z., Li, X.: The identification of children with autism spectrum disorder by SVM approach on EEG and eye-tracking data. Comput. Biol. Med. **120**, 103722 (2020)

9. Elbattah, M., Guérin, J.L., Carette, R., Cilia, F., Dequen, G.: Vision-based Approach for Autism Diagnosis using Transfer Learning and Eye-tracking. In: HEALTHINF, pp. 256–263 (2022)

10. Ahmed, I.A., et al.: Eye tracking-based diagnosis and early detection of autism spectrum disorder using machine learning and deep learning techniques. Electronics **11**(4), 530 (2022)

11. Kanhirakadavath, M.R., Chandran, M.S.M.: Investigation of eye-tracking scan path as a biomarker for autism screening using machine learning algorithms. Diagnostics **12**(2), 518 (2022)

12. Black, M.H., et al.: Mechanisms of facial emotion recognition in autism spectrum disorders: insights from eye tracking and electroencephalography. Neurosci. Biobehav. Rev. **80**, 488–515 (2017)

13. Yi, L., et al.: Abnormality in face scanning by children with autism spectrum disorder is limited to the eye region: evidence from multi-method analyses of eye tracking data. J. Vis. **13**(10), 5 (2013)

14. Zhao, Z., Tang, H., Zhang, X., Qu, X., Hu, X., Lu, J.: Classification of children with autism and typical development using eye-tracking data from face-to-face conversations: machine learning model development and performance evaluation. J. Med. Internet Res. **23**(8), e29328 (2021)

15. Zhao, Z., Tang, H., Zhang, X., Qu, X., Hu, X., Lu, J.: Classification of children with autism and typical development using eye-tracking data from face-to-face conversations: machine learning model development and performance evaluation. J. Med. Internet Res. **23**(8), e29328 (2021)

16. Carpenter, K.L., et al.: Digital behavioural phenotyping detects atypical pattern of facial expression in toddlers with autism. Autism Res. **14**(3), 488–499 (2021)

17. Wedyan, M., et al.: Augmented reality for autistic children to enhance their understanding of facial expressions. Multimod. Technol. Interact. **5**(8), 48 (2021)

18. Webster, P.J., Wang, S., Li, X.: Posed vs. Genuine facial emotion recognition and expression in autism and implications for intervention. Front. Psychol. **12**, 653112 (2021)

19. Liao, M., Duan, H., Wang, G.: Application of machine learning techniques to detect the children with autism spectrum disorder. J. Healthc. Eng. (2022)

20. Li, J., Chen, Z., Li, G., Ouyang, G., Li, X.: Automatic classification of ASD children using appearance-based features from videos. Neurocomputing **470**, 40–50 (2022)

21. Marotta, A., Aranda-Martín, B., De Cono, M., Ballesteros-Duperón, M.Á., Casagrande, M., Lupiáñez, J.: Integration of facial expression and gaze direction in individuals with a high level of autistic traits. Int. J. Environ. Res. Public Health **19**(5), 2798 (2022)

22. Sharma, A., Tanwar, P.: Identification of autism spectrum disorder (ASD) from facial expressions using deep learning. In: 2022 International Conference on Machine Learning, Big Data, Cloud and Parallel Computing (COM-IT-CON), vol. 1, pp. 478–484. IEEE (2022)

Author Index

S. Rajagopal et al. (Eds.): ASCIS 2024, CCIS 2424, pp. 423–424, 2025.
https://doi.org/10.1007/978-3-031-86290-8

The manufacturer's authorised representative in the EU is Springer
Nature Customer Service Centre GmbH, Europaplatz 3, 69115 Heidelberg,
Germany. If you have any concerns regarding our products, please
contact ProductSafety@springernature.com

Printed and bound by CPI Group (UK) Ltd, Croydon, CR0 4YY
29/04/2026
02099544-0015